OVERWRITING CHAOS
Aleksandr Solzhenitsyn's Fictive Worlds

Cultural Revolutions: Russia in the Twentieth and Twenty-First Centuries

Series Editor
Boris Wolfson (Amherst College)

Editorial Board
Anthony Anemone (The New School, New York)
Robert Bird (The University of Chicago, Chicago)
Eliot Borenstein (New York University, New York)
Angela Brintlinger (The Ohio State University, Columbus)
Karen Evans-Romaine (Ohio University, Athens)
Jochen Hellbeck (Rutgers University, New Brunswick, New Jersey)
Lilya Kaganovsky (University of Illinois, Urbana-Champaign)
Christina Kiaer (Northwestern University, Evanston, Illinois)
Alaina Lemon (University of Michigan, Ann Arbor)
Simon Morrison (Princeton University, Princeton)
Eric Naiman (University of California, Berkeley)
Joan Neuberger (University of Texas, Austin)
Lyudmila Parts (McGill University, Montreal)
Ethan Pollock (Brown University, Providence)
Cathy Popkin (Columbia University, New York)
Stephanie Sandler (Harvard University, Cambridge)

OVERWRITING CHAOS
Aleksandr Solzhenitsyn's Fictive Worlds

RICHARD TEMPEST

BOSTON
2019

Library of Congress Cataloging-in-Publication Data

Names: Tempest, Richard, 1956- author.
Title: Overwriting chaos : Aleksandr Solzhenitsyn's fictive worlds / Richard Tempest.
Other titles: Aleksandr Solzhenitsyn's fictive worlds
Description: Boston : Academic Studies Press, 2019. | Series: Cultural revolutions: Russia in the twentieth and twenty-first centuries | Includes bibliographical references and index.
Identifiers: LCCN 2019037153 (print) | LCCN 2019037154 (ebook) | ISBN 9781644690123 (hardback) | ISBN 9781644690130 (adobe pdf)
Subjects: LCSH: Solzhenitsyn, Aleksandr Isaevich, 1918-2008--Criticism and interpretation. | Solzhenitsyn, Aleksandr Isaevich, 1918-2008--Political and social views. | Solzhenitsyn, Aleksandr Isaevich, 1918-2008--Interviews. | Russia in literature.
Classification: LCC PG3488.O4 Z88867 2019 (print) | LCC PG3488.O4 (ebook) | DDC 891.73/4--dc23
LC record available at https://lccn.loc.gov/2019037153
LC ebook record available at https://lccn.loc.gov/2019037154

Copyright © 2019 Academic Studies Press
All rights reserved.

ISBN 978-1-64469-460-2
ISBN 978-1-64469-013-0 (adobe pdf)

Book design by PHi Business Solutions Limited.
Cover design by Ivan Grave.

The cover photograph shows Solzhenitsyn on board the Lev Tolstoy steamship in 1956 during a cruise along the Volga and Oka rivers, as well as a facsimile of a written interview he gave the author in 2007.

Published by Academic Studies Press.
1577 Beacon Street
Brookline, MA 02446, USA

press@academicstudiespress.com
www.academicstudiespress.com

Table of Contents

Acknowledgments	vii
A Note on Translations and Transliterations	xi
Preface	xiii
Timeline of Solzhenitsyn's Life and Works	xxi

PART ONE
The Writer In Situ — 1

1. The Quilted Jerkin: Solzhenitsyn's Life and Art	3
2. Ice, Squared: "One Day in the Life of Ivan Denisovich"	69
3. "Turgenev Never Knew": The Shorter Fictions of the 1950s and 1960s	106
4. Meteor Man: *Love the Revolution*	161
5. Helots and Heroes: *In the First Circle*	181
6. Rebel versus Rabble: *Cancer Ward*	259

PART TWO
The Writer Ex Situ — 337

7. Twilight of All the Russias: *The Red Wheel*	339
8. Return: The Shorter Fictions of the 1990s	468
9. Modernist?	530
Appendix. Three Interviews with Aleksandr Solzhenitsyn (2003–7)	574
Notes	591
Selected Bibliography	697
Index	701

Acknowledgments

First of all, I should like to thank Natalia Solzhenitsyna. A remarkable woman of numerous and varied gifts, she is a former mathematician who once rowed for the USSR national youth team and later gave up a promising academic career to join Moscow's dissident underground. Mrs. Solzhenitsyna was the editor of all of her husband's works (beginning with *August 1914*), his closest collaborator and best advisor, and is now the passionately dedicated custodian of his legacy. As Aleksandr Solzhenitsyn's wife, helpmeet, and the mother of his children, she gave him, for the first time in his life, true and abiding happiness after decades of mortal peril and personal tragedy. Wherever the Solzhenitsyn family happened to find itself—the Soviet Union, Switzerland, the United States, or post-communist Russia—she built a complete domestic world, a Russian world, where the author was able to work, ponder, and engage with the issues of the day surrounded by the people he loved.

Mrs. Solzhenitsyna, whom I first met in 2003, spoke to me at length and in detail about the books her husband wrote and the books that he read, the people he knew, the places he visited, and the environments he inhabited. She was my chief informant on the private processes that shaped his literary productions, and shared with me hundreds of photographs from the family archive. I importuned Natalia Dmitrievna with questions in person, by phone, and electronically, and she was always ready to respond. Not all of our conversations were directly related to the themes in this book. Mrs. Solzhenitsyna shared with me bits of family lore, including the fact that when they were growing up in leafy Vermont, her sons became fans of the rock band Metallica to which they would listen while their father toiled away, at a safe distance, in a cabin next door to the main house. The austere-minded author may have regarded rock music as an abomination, but he was broadminded enough to allow his kids their high decibel fun.

Some of our meetings took place in Mrs. Solzhenitsyna's study at the Russian Social Fund, which she chairs. Founded by the Solzhenitsyns in 1974, and sustained with royalties from *The Gulag Archipelago*, the Fund assists communist-era political prisoners and preserves the memory of those who suffered and died in the Soviet carceral system. Until the end of 2018, the offices of the RSF were located in the former family apartment next to Tverskaya Street, Moscow's central thoroughfare. Aleksandr and Natalia Solzhenitsyn and their children lived here during the final stages of the writer's epic confrontation with the Soviet state in the early 1970s, although his domicile in the flat was illegal, since the authorities had refused to issue the required residence permit. Many were the times that I came out of the Chekhovskaya Metro station and after walking for a few minutes along the Tverskaya turned left into Kozitsky Lane, crossed this cozy side street, skirted a striped red and white barrier, and entered the courtyard of an elegant apartment house which faces several high-end retail stores, one of them a business selling imported eyeglasses. Where flat-footed KGB agents once skulked under the Solzhenitsyns' windows, stylishly dressed Muscovites now squeeze past late-model limos and SUVs that are parked, or double-parked, along the length of the building (hence that barrier). On Tuesdays, when Mrs. Solzhenitsyna keeps office hours, one may see a cluster of invited and uninvited visitors milling at the door to entrance No. 12—ex-prisoners and Soviet-era dissidents, lavishly bearded priests, petitioners of various kinds, as well as fans of her husband's books, or merely the curious.

On one memorable occasion, Natalia Dmitrievna described the writer's arrest on February 12, 1974, acting out the parts of her husband, herself, her mother, their friend Igor Shafarevich, and the arresting officers as she demonstrated where each participant in this drama stood and what he or she was doing. And when I tried to track down volume nine of *The Red Wheel*, which for some mysterious bibliographical reason was nowhere to be found in Moscow, she presented me with a copy that contained her own editorial markings, executed in red pencil. I still have it in my possession. Mrs. Solzhenitsyna also made available to me the new English translation of *The First Circle* months before it was published and helped me obtain a number of other books and articles I needed for my research. Finally, Natalia Dmitrievna arranged the interviews I conducted with her husband in 2003–7.

Although this book is not a biography, it contains new factual material about Solzhenitsyn's life and work, most of it provided by Mrs. Solzhenitsyna and their sons Ignat, an internationally renowned pianist and conductor based in New York, and Stephan, who works for the Moscow branch of a major management consulting firm. Like their mother, the two younger Solzhenitsyns shared with me memories of family life in America and Russia and were always there when I needed my questions answered.

I am grateful to Nadezhda Levitskaya, a veteran of the gulag and a co-author of the standard bibliography of Russian sources on Solzhenitsyn, who until her retirement in 2012 acted as the keeper of the RSF archives. In the 1960s and 1970s Ms. Levitskaya was one of Solzhenitsyn's "invisible allies," the courageous men and women who made it possible for him to continue writing and speaking out even as the powers that be tried their utmost to reduce him to silence, or worse. During my visits to Moscow she would spend hours tracking down difficult-to-find print sources at my request. Another "invisible ally," the Swedish TV journalist Stig Fredrikson, who once smuggled some of the writer's manuscripts out the Soviet Union, related to me his impressions of Solzhenitsyn as he knew him in Moscow and Vermont.

Dr. Pavel Spivakovsky of the Department of Twentieth-Century Russian Literature at Moscow State University was my most important academic interlocutor. Many of the ideas and approaches I developed for this study grew out of the discussions we had in a succession of Moscow cafés and, later, American campus offices when he was a visiting professor at the University of Illinois in 2012–13. Professor Aleksandr Urmanov, head of the Department of Russian literature at Blagoveshchensk State Pedagogical University, was equally helpful in stimulating my engagement with the writer's texts. Professor Alexis Klimoff (Vassar College) and Professor Michael Finke (University of Illinois) read sections of the manuscript and gave me valuable feedback. Lyudmila Saraskina, the author of the official Solzhenitsyn biography, shared her insights into the writer's life and works, which she had collected over a decade or more of research. Aleksandr Markevich, a rock lyricist and all-round free spirit who is one of my oldest Moscow friends, operated a dedicated electronic newsfeed, supplying me with hundreds of Russian media items pertaining to Solzhenitsyn and his reception at home and abroad. Thanks are also due to my other friends and colleagues in the United States, the United Kingdom, France, and Russia: Edward J. Ericson; Daniel Mahoney; Anne Lounsbery; Michael Nicholson; Catriona Kelly; Nikita Struve; Ilya Kukulin; Andrei Nemzer; Vladimir Kantor; and Evgenia Ivanova. The staff at the Aleksandr Solzhenitsyn House of Russia Abroad in Moscow, which regularly hosts conferences and round tables on the writer, were always supportive and welcoming. Natalya Pushkareva of the Russian National Library in St. Petersburg kindly sent me a selection of materials pertaining to Solzhenitsyn's visit there in 1996. The students in the

Acknowledgments

Solzhenitsyn seminars I taught in 2006, 2008, 2012, and 2015 constituted the first audience for the analyses and interpretations contained in this study. They listened to me patiently even when my pedagogical enthusiasms outran the bell, and gave me valuable feedback during and after class. My analyses of *The First Circle* and *Cancer Ward* benefited from the scientific knowledge and sensitivity to literary nuance of one of my seminarians, Katerina Polychronopoulos, a psychology and computer science undergraduate who is now a West Coast lawyer. She once told me that she had learned to love Solzhenitsyn after reading "Matryona's Home," whose heroine reminded her of a great aunt who lived on the Greek island of Kefalonia—a confirmation, if one is needed, that this writer continues to speak to audiences far removed in time and place from Russia and its difficult history. I am grateful to my former PhD student, Anna Arkatova, who worked as my formal and informal research assistant during the concluding stages of this project. I wish to express my appreciation to the University of Illinois for granting me academic leave in spring 2014 and for providing the research support without which it would not have seen the light of day.

Finally, my heartfelt gratitude goes to my wife, Anne Tempest, who was my first and last reader and edited (and reedited) every page I wrote, thereby giving this book its final polish and form.

Richard Tempest
Urbana, Illinois

A Note on Translations and Transliterations

All quotations from Russian and other foreign language sources are in English. When transcribing Russian words and titles, I used a simplified version of the American Library Association-Library of Congress system, which omits the diacritic and tie marks, the single and double apostrophe for the soft and hard sign, and renders *io* as *ë*. The bibliographical references in the endnotes follow the same rules, but retain the transliterative apostrophes. Occasionally, when discussing the nuances of meaning in a translated passage, I quote the original Russian using this modified ALA-LC transcription, again, with apostrophes. In the main text, the established English spelling of Russian names, titles, and toponyms such as Tolstoy, *Novy Mir*, or Ryazan has been retained. The names of Solzhenitsyn's characters are spelled as they appear in the published English translation, for example, Georgi Vorotyntsev. All English and Russian quotations retain the original spelling, punctuation, and type style. In the quotations, italics are always the author's; my own italicizations are marked *RT*.

Preface

The sudden, astounding appearance of the Hero, who bursts out of the narrative void to embark on his Quest, is an indispensable topos of literature and myth. Aleksandr Solzhenitsyn erupted into the world's consciousness in 1962, when his camp tale "One Day in the Life of Ivan Denisovich" was published to almost universal acclaim. Ever since, the writer has been the focus of prolific commentary: one not-so-recent bibliography lists 8559 books and articles just in Russian,[1] and there are many thousands more in other languages. Taken together, these explicative and biographical evaluations cover a broad spectrum of approaches, from the panegyrical to the conspiratological, from the psychoanalytical to the post-structuralist, while the fact and extent of their existence points to the author's continuing centrality in contemporary culture.

Yet, it is only in the last twenty years or so that Solzhenitsyn studies, or to use the Russian term, *solzhenitsynovedenie*, has become an established discipline, with an accompanying paraphernalia of learned monographs and articles, international conferences, and dedicated university courses. Though celebrated (and denounced) in his own lifetime and since, Solzhenitsyn still awaits a definitive assessment. To quote Friedrich Nietzsche, "Some [men] are born posthumously."[2] In the meantime, the oeuvre is being codified and assembled with a thoroughness characteristic of the Russian academic tradition. (As the creator of densely scripted literary productions which are extant in multiple print versions, Solzhenitsyn has been a boon to that honorable cohort of literary scholars, the textologists). These dedicated souls have brought to the study of his writings the diligence and attention to detail of an earlier generation of *pushkinisty*, or Pushkin specialists. They have their work cut out. When completed, the author's *Collected Works*, the publication of which began in 2006, will comprise thirty volumes of extensively annotated novels, stories, plays, poems, journals, articles, essays, interviews, book and film reviews, and memoirs, as well as historical and lexicographical writings.

The English-speaking audience has not been forgotten either. A century ago Virginia Woolf lamented that when rendered into English, Tolstoy, Dostoevsky, and Chekhov were "like men deprived by an earthquake or a railway accident not only of all their clothes, but also of something subtler and more important— their manners, the idiosyncrasies of their characters."[3] This is emphatically not the case with recent translations of Solzhenitsyn. They include Edward E. Ericson and Daniel J. Mahoney's *Solzhenitsyn Reader* (2006), and a new translation of the definitive "atomic" version of *The First Circle*, magnificently executed by the late Harry Willetts, which came out in 2009. *Apricot Jam*, a collection of the shorter fictions of the 1990s, appeared two years later. *August 1914* and *November 1916*, the first two "Knots" or novels in the *Red Wheel* cycle, were made available in 1989 and 2000 respectively, and the publication of Knots III and IV is now underway. Also soon to appear are *Two Hundred Years Together*, Solzhenitsyn's controversial history of Russian-Jewish relations, and *Between Two Millstones*, a memoir of his life in Switzerland and the United States.

However, in spite of such formal and informal signs of a continuing and growing interest in the writer's life and art, no full-length study of his fictional works exists, either in Russian or in any other language, an omission I have tried to correct in this book. In doing so, I aimed to accomplish three objectives.

First, to provide informed commentary on Solzhenitsyn's prose by investigating its cosmologies, architectonics, stylistics, and genre poetics, and tracing his connection to other writers, Russian and foreign, classical, and modern. To that end, I bring to bear on his novels and stories a set of analytical instrumentalities developed by Mikhail Bakhtin, Erich Auerbach, Georges Bataille, Tzvetan Todorov, Carlo Ginzburg, Gérard Genette, Jacques Lacan, Roland Barthes, Michel Foucault, Umberto Eco, Susan Sontag, Julia Kristeva, Judith Butler, and Brian McHale. I suggest that his vast literary output may be read as a monumental attempt to reverse the Modernists' reconfiguration of the text and its epistemological function, with the writer asserting the healing and redemptive function of imaginative literature as he relates his characters, and the spaces they construct, inhabit or destroy, to stable moral, cultural, and historical meanings. I also look at Solzhenitsyn's ethics of artistic creativity (his "hypermorality," to use Bataille's term) in the twentieth-century terror state; his pursuit of fictive consilience—in other words, the melding of the literary and the scientific in both a thematic and an expressive sense; his practice of encoding into his texts scenes and passages from earlier authors—for example, Dostoevsky and Tolstoy, as a parodic, pastichistic, or exegetic device; his self-description as a polyphonic writer; his surprising predilection for literary puzzles and games à la Nabokov or even Borges; and his dismantling of the significant myths of Lenin, Stalin, and the Russian Revolution by means of satire and counter-semiosis. In doing so, I acknowledge that this is a severely autobiographical writer who populates his worlds with direct self-representations and authorial emanations that coexist and interact with the invented characters.

Second, to trace Solzhenitsyn's evolution as a literary artist, from the unconventional realism of his early autobiographical novel *Love the Revolution*, through his middle period, exemplified by such mimetically verisimilar works as "One Day in the Life of Ivan Denisovich," *Cancer Ward*, and *The First Circle*, to the experimental style of *The Red Wheel* and the later stories. This line of investigation focuses on his *positive* engagement with Modernism, which began as he was completing the final version of *The First Circle*. It is my contention that during his later years the writer, despite his indignant rejection of the aesthetics and ideology of Modernism, to a considerable extent and in ways that were highly idiosyncratic, came to adopt the former, though not the latter, as he pursued his goal of national redemption and remembrance.

Third, to share my readerly preferences—biases—where Solzhenitsyn's writings are concerned and to explain why some of them fill me with enthusiasm and joy while others do not move me as deeply. I try to show how his heroes and heroines possess a fictive presence so textured that it makes *this* reader readily imagine them as figures of flesh and blood and thought and feeling, as perceptually palpable as "real" men and women in "real" life. For such is the magic of the literary act, as practiced by Solzhenitsyn's predecessors Tolstoy, Dostoevsky, and Dickens, those inventors of imaginary worlds and people.[4] The sublime deceptions of literature!

At the same time, owing to their special thaumaturgic power Solzhenitsyn's novels and stories—and even *The Gulag Archipelago*, his magisterial history of the Soviet penal system—exercised a positive, normalizing effect, particularly on Russian readers. Inside his literary spaces they encountered human beings who had retained their humanity while living under conditions far more traumatic than those that prevailed during the last three decades of communist rule or in the chaotic years of the post-communist transition. For even as he recorded the horrors of tyranny, Solzhenitsyn gave hope and proposed strategies for resistance or, failing that, honorable survival which remain valid today, when the Soviet Union is no more and the political doctrine that sustained it is but a dusty husk.

Of course, the terms "imaginary world" or "fictive world," which I employ throughout this study, are a kind of shorthand. To quote Tzvetan Todorov, "The novel does not imitate reality, it creates reality."[5] Yes, but for that created reality to be accessed, there must be someone *there*. In addition to its model reader, that notional figure lurking in its notional nook of reception, the text brings into being real-life, real-time readers, and Solzhenitsyn has millions of them. It is they who now do the imagining. I have known quite a few of them.

A few years ago I taught a seminar on Solzhenitsyn at the University of Illinois. When we came to *Cancer Ward*, my students, enthralled by the created universe they had encountered, expressed anxiety about the fate of its hero, the courageous Oleg Kostoglotov. The novel ends on a poignant note, with the protagonist, who has seemingly recovered his health, lying prone on a bunk in the railway car that is taking him away from the woman the loves: "The train went on and Kostoglotov's boots dangled toes down over the corridor like a dead man's."[6] Despite my confident avowals that this was no more than a somber simile, the students' disquiet persisted. So much so that, for their sake, I decided to break my skepticism about authorial intent, and in a subsequent conversation with Mrs. Solzhenitsyna sought her confirmation, which she was pleased to give, that the hero exits the novel very much alive. I conveyed her assurance to my worried seminarians, much to their relief.

As for Solzhenitsyn's dramatic, poetic, historical, journalistic, and autobiographical works, these are discussed with reference to their thematic and structural connections to his prose. In other words, I approach them as author-generated *sources* and *contexts*, a procedure which in no way implies that these productions are in some formal or intellectual sense inferior to the novels and stories.

Solzhenitsyn is an exciting subject to write about, for there is so much to discover and explore. After all, this is a writer who, in the words of one commentator, had known "five lives, five destinies, each one of which might have filled a single person's entire existence."[7] In my analyses, I proceed from the textual to the extra-textual, that is, the political, social, and cultural environments in which the fictions were written or which they were meant to represent. I parse and interpret the texts using a variety of theoretical platforms and analytical methodologies, my goal always being to demonstrate the often underappreciated subtleties of this author's style, the multilayeredness of his narratives, and the way that they locate and script the model, moral reader as well as other, less righteous categories of receptors. When discussing public events or figures, I do so narrowly, with a view to showing their relation to the meanings of the work in question. This procedure informs my treatment of Nikita Khrushchev, the Soviet leader who allowed

"Ivan Denisovich" into print, thereby making Solzhenitsyn the published writer possible. I look at Khrushchev as one of his first empirical readers but also as a larger-than-life political personality whom the author found intriguing and even sympathetic; and whose historical role he subjected to thoughtful evaluation.

I also seek to identify new meanings in Solzhenitsyn's fictions by matching them against certain non-Russian contexts. Throughout his life this artist, who was so rooted in the literature and history of his country, pondered and questioned the intellectual tradition of the West, that 2000-year-long agglomeration of texts bookended by Plato's dialogues and Nietzsche's aphorisms and diatribes.[8] Plato, who defined the main lines of philosophical inquiry for all subsequent thinkers, and inaugurated the utopian (and thereby also the anti-utopian) strand in the realms of literature and the social imagination, casts his shadow across the entirety of Solzhenitsyn's oeuvre. At times this Platonic penumbra acquires a concrete, citational presence, as in the figure of the mystic Pavel Varsonofiev, whose eyes are like caves (*The Red Circle*). The connection to the German philosopher is just as important, although it was unacknowledged, perhaps even unrecognized, by the writer himself. Nonetheless, he identified in Nietzsche "the physical counter-stance against suffering. It is almost like a training, almost like a sparring."[9] The differences between Solzhenitsyn and Nietzsche are profound, particularly in their attitudes to Christianity and its ethical systems, yet both men were psychologists of culture who subjected the consensuses of the age to radical and even incendiary criticism. If Nietzsche "was fond of expressing himself paradoxically and with a view to shocking contemporary readers,"[10] then so was Solzhenitsyn. The German thinker's esteem for Gogol and Dostoevsky, as well as the value he placed on "'Russian fatalism,'" by which he meant the practice of "accepting oneself as if fated,"[11] is another link. Thus, the occasional adductions of Plato and Nietzsche as referents for the literary works I examine.

So, in some ways this is a very personal project, one that reflects my own readerly agenda, though I have tried to give my take on each individual text in a manner which, I trust, opens up avenues of discussion rather than forecloses them.

During the first decade of his public prominence Solzhenitsyn's writings tended to be viewed through the prism of current events. Later, the academic treatment of his literary works began to change, with important and positive results:

> The primitive, politicized reading of his works now seems hopelessly archaic and inadequate, whereas their intellectual, religious, and ethical content, which went unnoticed or was misapprehended during those heated political debates, is acquiring ever greater significance.[12]

I would go further. It is my belief that Solzhenitsyn is yet to be fully understood and appreciated as a literary artist per se, a teller of tales, an inspired inventor of alternative realities, even a purveyor of pleasure for all those who love a good story. During a visit to a Moscow high school in 2008, I discussed his books with a class of fifteen-year-olds, one of whom told me that he had enjoyed reading *The Gulag Archipelago* because of its exciting stories of adventure and escape (a comment that met with Mrs. Solzhenitsyna's approval). I hope I was able to show how this writer casts his spell and allows us to get carried away by the exercise of his creative imagination, or by his manner of telling a tale.

The study is intended for the academic reader as well as a broader audience, especially those who either love Solzhenitsyn's writings or find them puzzling, exasperating, or of a narrowly contingent value; that is, receptors who have truly engaged with the texts. This category also includes readers who are selective, privileging for instance the works written in the Soviet Union over *The Red Wheel* and the later bipartite tales. Then there are those who simply refuse to read his stories and novels, or read them antagonistically. Perhaps my book will persuade a few such skeptics to suspend their disbelief and step into Solzhenitsyn's fictive universe with a view to closer inspection.

I have divided my study into two parts, entitled "The Writer In Situ" and "The Writer Ex Situ," which cover the defining periods in Solzhenitsyn's long, amazingly varied, and exceedingly productive life.

The first period, 1918–74, was one of *belonging*, when the author was physically present in Russia or the Soviet Union, with the exception of the few months that he spent as a frontline officer in Poland and East Prussia in 1944–5. Even in the years of his imprisonment and the near-mortal illness that followed, or during his perilous struggle with the authorities in the 1960s and early 1970s, he was surrounded by the people, sights, and sounds of his native land. He was at home, within his culture: he was in place. Or as my personal favorite among his heroes, rebellious Kostoglotov, says: "This is my country. Why should I be ashamed?"[13] Solzhenitsyn's best-known, best-loved works, the literary and polemical texts that won him worldwide fame, were written during this stage in his life. Thus, part one is devoted to his Soviet-era fictions, excluding *August 1914*, the first novel in *The Red Wheel* cycle, which was begun in

1969 and published in 1971, but expanded following his banishment from the Soviet Union three years later.

The second period, 1974–2008, was one of *displacement*. After the Soviet government forcibly extruded the author from his native cultural space, he set up home in Switzerland before moving to the United States, where he spent eighteen years living in austere writerly isolation on his wooded estate near Cavendish, Vermont (pop. 1,355).[14] For the first time ever, he could devote himself unreservedly to the business of writing, with no political or lifestyle distractions to interrupt his work: from now on Solzhenitsyn's modus operandi was that of a professional man of letters. Nevertheless, while in body he may have resided in New England, or the United States, or the West, spiritually and intellectually he remained in Russia. Indeed, he went back in (Russian) time, for his two American decades were dedicated to the *The Red Wheel*, his epic of World War I and the February Revolution of 1917. Solzhenitsyn completed its latter volumes, which depict the fall of the Russian Empire, as the centrifugal and entropic processes unleashed by Gorbachev's perestroika overwhelmed the Soviet Union and led to its collapse.

On May 25, 1994, twenty years after he was bundled onto an Aeroflot flight at Moscow's Sheremyetevo airport and deported to Frankfurt-on-the-Main, the writer resumed his physical movement across the globe, but this time in the direction of home. "He returned, arriving in his native country, like the sun, from the east."[15] Accompanied by a BBC film crew, Solzhenitsyn flew to Alaska, Magadan, and Vladivostok, and thence traveled by discrete stages along the Transsiberian Railway to Moscow, where he arrived on July 21. After all, "trains have played an almost mystical role in Russian history and literature."[16] The country he encountered was a national project in the making or unmaking, a strange and alien land, and all the more foreign for being in so many ways familiar. It was not only the brutish realities of robber capitalism that had fragmented the national landscape. The textures of the culture had altered as well, with literature losing its privileged place in the spectrum of artistic practices, which were now suffused with a postmodern sense of irony that all too often devolved into existential cynicism or the nihilism of despair. Inevitably, the novelist found these changes galling, even as he continued to insist that literature still mattered, more than most things and certainly more than the tawdriness of political life in post-communist Russia. Hence, part two deals with the post-1974 works: the four novels of *The Red Wheel* saga as well as the tales that he composed upon his return.

This study comprises nine chapters, with the first and last one offering a conceptual framework for an evaluation of Solzhenitsyn's life, work, and cultural impact, while the others are each devoted to one of the longer works or sets of stories. An appendix contains my three interviews with the author (2003–7), in which he discussed his writings as well as a broad range of literary and historical topics. I am happy I was able to act as an agent of transmission for these often revealing comments.

Timeline of Solzhenitsyn's Life and Works

December 11, 1918

Born in Kislovodsk, Russian Soviet Republic, to Taissia Solzhenitsyna, née Shcherbak, the daughter of a wealthy Ukrainian-Russian family dispossessed by the Soviets, and Isaaki Solzhenitsyn, a peasant's son and ex-officer who died in a hunting accident six months earlier.

1927

Starts school in Rostov-on-the-Don.

1931

Joins the Young Pioneers (communist children's organization).

1932

Solzhenitsyn's grandfather Zakhar Shcherbak walks into the Rostov secret police headquarters and is never seen again.

1935

Joins the Komsomol (communist youth organization).

1936

Leaves school with top grades in every subject. Enters the Physics and Mechanics Department, University of Rostov. Meets Natalya Reshetovskaya (b. 1919), a fellow student. Conceives idea for a large-scale work about the Russian Revolution, which will eventually be realized as *The Red Wheel* (*Krasnoe Koleso*).

1939

Enrolls as an extramural student at the Institute for Philosophy, Literature, and the Arts in Moscow.

1940

Awarded Stalin Stipend for academic excellence. Solzhenitsyn and Reshetovskaya marry.

1941

Graduates from the University of Rostov with a "gold certificate." Nazi Germany invades the Soviet Union. Teaches at a school in Morozovsk, Rostov Province. Conscripted into the Red Army.

1942

Attends an artillery officers' training course in Kostroma. Promoted to lieutenant. Appointed commander of a sound reconnaissance battery.

1943

Posted to the front. Promoted to first lieutenant and awarded Order of the Patriotic War, Second Class.

1944

Promoted to captain. Awarded Order of the Red Star. Taissia Solzhenitsyna dies.

1945

Arrested while on active service for criticizing Stalin in his correspondence with Nikolai Vitkevich. Transported to Moscow's Lubyanka prison. Convicted of anti-Soviet activities and sentenced to eight years. Forced labor on a Moscow building site.

1946

Transferred to a *sharashka* (science prison) in Rybinsk.

1947

Transferred to a sharashka at Zagorsk and then at Marfino. Begins the narrative poem *The Road* (*Dorozhen'ka*)—published 1999.

1948

Begins the novel *Love the Revolution* (*Liubi revoliutsiiu*)—published 1999. Reshetovskaya divorces Solzhenitsyn in absentia.

1950

Transferred to the Ekibastuz Special Camp, Kazakhstan, where he completes *The Road* (1952) and composes the plays *Victory Celebrations* (*Pir pobeditelei*) —written 1951–3, published 1981, and *Prisoners* (*Plenniki*)—written 1952–3, published 1981.

1952

Diagnosed with cancer of the groin. Undergoes operation in the camp hospital.

1953

Released into perpetual exile at Kok-Terek, Kazakhstan. Stalin dies. Teaches physics, math, and astronomy at the local school. Cancer returns. Doctors give him three weeks to live.

1954

Admitted to the Tashkent Oncological Clinic for treatment. Cancer in full remission. Writes play *Republic of Labor* (*Respublika truda*) published 1981, known in its abridged version as *The Love-Girl and the Innocent* (*Olen' i shalashovka*)—written 1962. Full text published under the same title in the Moscow *Collected Works* (2018).

1956

Khrushchev's Secret Speech. Solzhenitsyn is released from exile and leaves for Russia. Teaches at the Mezinovsky Secondary School, Vladimir Province while renting a room from Matryona Zakharova in the village of Miltsevo.

1957

Sozhenitsyn and Reshetovskaya remarry. Formally rehabilitated by the Military Collegium of the USSR Supreme Court. Moves to Ryazan, where he teaches at Secondary School No. 2 (1957–62).

1958

Completes *Love the Revolution* and the "atomic" version of *In the First Circle* (*V kruge pervom*). Starts work on *The Gulag Archipelago* (*Arkhipelag GULAG*)—completed 1967). Begins first cycle of "Miniatures" ("Krokhotki")—completed 1960 and published 1964 in the émigré journal *Grani*. Soviet government forces Boris Pasternak to renounce Nobel Prize in Literature.

1959

Writes "One Day in the Life of Ivan Denisovich" ("Odin den' Ivana Denisovicha"), "Matryona's Home" ("Matrënin dvor"), and the film script *Tanks Know the Truth!* (*Zhaiut istinu tanki*)—published 1981.

1960

Writes "The Right Hand" ("Pravaia kist")—published 1968, and the play *Candle in the Wind* ("Svet, kotoryi v tebe/Svecha na vetru")—published 1981.

1961

Submits "Ivan Denisovich" to *Novy Mir*.

1962

"Ivan Denisovich" published.

1963

"Matryona's Home," "Incident at Kochetovka Station," and "For the Good of the Cause" ("Dlia pol'zy dela") published. Writes "Prayer" ("Molitva"). Begins *Cancer Ward* (*Rakovyi korpus*). "Ivan Denisovich" is nominated for the Lenin Prize in Literature.

1964

Completes abridged "medical" version of *The First Circle*. The "Miniatures" start circulating in samizdat. Leonid Brezhnev replaces Khrushchev as Party leader.

1965

Completes "What a Pity" ("Kak zhal'")—published 1978.

1966

"Zakhar-the-Pouch" ("Zakhar-Kalita") published; thereafter Solzhenitsyn is banned from print in the Soviet Union. Writes "The Easter Procession" ("Paskhal'nyi krestnyi khod")—published 1969.

1967

Cancer Ward completed. "Letter to the Congress of Soviet Writers" ("Pis'mo IV Vsesoiuznomu s"ezdu Soiuza sovetskikh pisatelei").

1968

Restored and revised "atomic" version of *The First Circle* completed. Meets Natalia Svetlova (b. 1939). The "medical" version of *The First Circle* and *Cancer Ward* published.

1969

Begins work on *The Red Wheel*. Expelled from the Union of Soviet Writers.

1970

Awarded the Nobel Prize in Literature. Yermolai Solzhenitsyn is born.

1971

First version of *August 1914* (*Avgust Chetyrnadtsatogo*), the opening novel of the *Red Wheel* cycle, published. KGB makes an attempt on Solzhenitsyn's life.

1972

Nominates Vladimir Nabokov for the Nobel Prize in Literature. Nobel Lecture published. Ignat Solzhenitsyn is born.

1973

Divorce from Reshetovskaya is finalized. Solzhenitsyn and Svetlova marry. Nominates Andrei Sakharov for the Nobel Peace Prize (awarded 1975). Sends "Letter to Soviet Leaders" ("Pis'mo vozhdiam Sovetskogo Soiuza"—published 1974) to Brezhnev and co. Volume one of *The Gulag Archipelago* published (volumes two and three published 1974 and 1975). Stephan Solzhenitsyn is born.

1974

Arrested on a charge of treason, stripped of his Soviet citizenship, and expelled to West Germany. "Live Not By Lies!" ("Zhit' ne po lzhi!") released. Moves to Zurich, Switzerland. The Solzhenitsyns establish the Russian Social Fund (Russkii obshchestvennyi fond pomoshchi presleduemym i ikh sem'iam). Accepts Nobel Prize in Stockholm.

1975

The memoir *The Oak and the Calf* (*Bodalsia telënok s dubom*) and the novel *Lenin in Zurich* (*Lenin v Tsiurikhe*) published.

1976

Moves to the United States and settles near Cavendish, Vermont.

1978

Harvard Address. Publication of a twenty-volume *Collected Works* commences (Paris, 1978–91); volumes one and two contain the "atomic" version of *The First Circle*.

1983

August 1914 (expanded version) published. Solzhenitsyn awarded the Templeton Prize. Templeton Lecture.

1984

November 1916 (*Oktiabr' Shestnadtsatogo*) published.

1985

Mikhail Gorbachev becomes Soviet leader.

1986

Books one and two of *March 1917* (*Mart Semnadtsatogo*) published.

1987

Book three of *March 1917* published.

1988

Book four of *March 1917* published. "Live Not By Lies!" appears in the newspaper *Rabochee slovo* (Kiev). Soviet authorities allow Solzhenitsyn's writings into print.

1989

Novy Mir publishes selections from *The Gulag Archipelago*. *The Journal of "R-17"* (*Dnevnik "R-17"*) completed (unpublished as of 2018).

1990

"Rebuilding Russia?" ("Kak nam obustroit' Rossiiu?") and *The Russian Dictionary for the Expansion of the Language* (*Russkii slovar' iazykovogo rasshireniia*) published. Serialization of *The Red Wheel* in multiple "thick journals" commences (1990–93). Solzhenitsyn's Soviet citizenship is restored. Awarded State Prize in Literature for *The Gulag Archipelago* (declined).

1991

April 1917 (*Aprel' Semnadtsatogo*) published. *The Love-Girl and the Innocent* premieres at the Moscow Art Theater. Boris Yeltsin elected president of Russia. Communist hardliners attempt coup. Solzhenitsyn is cleared of the charge of treason. Gorbachev resigns. Soviet Union is dissolved.

1993

"The Relentless Cult of Novelty" ("Igra na strunakh pustoty") published. Yeltsin disbands the Supreme Soviet.

1994

Dmitry Tyurin, Natalia Solzhenitsyna's son by her first husband, dies. Solzhenitsyn returns to Russia and is received by President Yeltsin.

1995

Victory Celebrations premieres at the Maly Theater, Moscow. *Meetings with Solzhenitsyn* (*Vstrechi s Solzhenitsynym*) program airs on Russian TV but is subsequently canceled. Solzhenitsyn moves to Troitse-Lykovo near Moscow. "Ego," "Times of Crisis" ("Na kraiakh"), "The New Generation" ("Molodnyak"), "Nastenka," "Apricot Jam" ("Abrikosovoe varen'e"), "No Matter What" ("Vsë ravno"), and *"The Russian Question" at the End of the Twentieth Century* ("*Russkii vopros*" *k kontsu XX veka*) published.

1996

Advises boycott of the Russian presidential election. Yeltsin reelected. "Fracture Points" ("Na izlomakh") and corrected and expanded second edition of *The Oak and the Calf* published.

1997

Elected to the Russian Academy of Sciences. First annual Solzhenitsyn Prize (Literaturnaia premiia Aleksandra Solzhenitsyna) awarded, to philologist Vladimir Toporov. Part of the second cycle of "Miniatures" published (remaining "Miniatures" published 1999). Serialization of essays from the *Literary Collection* (*Literaturnaia kollektsiia*) commences—published 1997–2005 (additional essays published posthumously).

1998

Russia in Collapse (*Rossiia v obvale*) published. Serialization of a second book of memoirs, *Between Two Millstones* (*Ugodilo zërnyshko promezh dvukh zhernovov*), commences (1998–2003). Awarded the Order of St. Aleksandr Nevsky (declined).

1999

"Zhelyabuga Village" ("Zheliabuzhskie vyselki") and "Adlig Schwenkitten" published.

2000

Yeltsin resigns. Vladimir Putin elected president. Visits Solzhenitsyn at Troitse-Lykovo.

2001

Volume one of *Two Hundred Years Together* (*Dvesti let vmeste*) published. Volume two appears the following year.

2003

Natalya Reshetovskaya dies.

2005

Completes redaction of *The Red Wheel*—published 2006–9 in the second *Collected Works*.

2006

The First Circle, a miniseries, airs on Russian TV. Annotated and corrected text of *The First Circle* released. Publication of a thirty-volume *Collected Works* commences (ongoing).

2007

Awarded State Prize "for humanitarian endeavors." Second visit by President Putin. Announces future publication of *A Different Time, A Different Burden* (*Inoe vremia, inoe bremia*), his third book of memoirs.

August 3, 2008

Solzhenitsyn dies at Troitse-Lykovo of acute heart failure. He is laid to rest in the grounds of the Donskoi Monastery in Moscow.

All I have is a voice
To undo the folded lie.

—W. H. Auden, "1 September 1939"

Part One

THE WRITER IN SITU

CHAPTER ONE

The Quilted Jerkin: Solzhenitsyn's Life and Art

One must pay dearly for immortality: one has to die several times while still alive.
—Friedrich Nietzsche, Ecce Homo

I believe that truth has only one face: that of violent contradiction.
—Georges Bataille, "The Dead Man"

God made everything out of nothing, but the nothingness shows through.
—Paul Valéry, Mauvaise pensées et autres

The entire course of the world has known but one truth, the truth of God.
—Aleksandr Solzhenitsyn, "Our Pluralists"

1

His life was long, varied, hard, heroic, and each of its successive stages provided the factual ingredients for his literary creations: posthumous son of a World War I veteran who had married the daughter of a wealthy farmer soon to be dispossessed by the revolution; fatherless orphan brought up by his ailing mother in extreme poverty; ardent Komsomol; brilliant math student; decorated frontline officer; political prisoner; cancer survivor; provincial schoolmaster; world-renowned author; outspoken dissident; reclusive exile in Vermont; anxious analyst of the chaotic Russia of the 1990s; and in his last years, the country's literary patriarch-in-residence. If, in Nabokov's fanciful phrase, novels are "fairy tales ... loosely fitted by their authors into certain historical frames,"[1] then those that Aleksandr Solzhenitsyn selected for his canvases were of a brutal, hellish kind, for such were the realities that shaped the world in which he lived. He felt he was called to depict them and, through the mimetic act of literary representation, to interpret and situate them in a larger national context.

Solzhenitsyn held the view that the duty of an artist is not to his art, but to his people, and not to the here and now, but to history. In the Nobel Lecture he proclaimed his vision of the writer as "a humble apprentice under God's heaven"[2] who creates beauty from a moral imperative to present the truth "in concentrated and vibrant form."[3] In other words, he was a believer in the special mission of the Russian writer and the record shows that this belief proved justified, because his texts produced empirical outcomes that changed minds, lives and, arguably, political systems. But always, it was the sheer artistic power of Solzhenitsyn's productions that secured their effect on his readers. He recognized that truth alone, however wrenching and terrible, is not enough and so he condensed it and made it resonate through his fictional men and women, and their fictional lives, joys, and sorrows. He also believed that

> the struggle against chaos is the historical struggle of humanity, on a planetary scale and on the scale of a single human life. Chaos is death, entropy, the leveling of all potentialities. The artist should confront it, destroy entropy, and construct a variety of potentialities.[4]

This *positive* stance against the loss of lives and meanings wrought by a universal evil was equally central to his literary project.

"One Day in the Life of Ivan Denisovich," *The First Circle, Cancer Ward,* and *The Red Wheel* are now part of the canon, while their creator is customarily identified as the last in a sequence of literary giants such as Fyodor Dostoevsky, Leo Tolstoy, and Boris Pasternak, artificers of vast, densely plotted novels of private life describing a search for individual or collective identity against a backcloth of historical upheaval. And then there are the three volumes of *The Gulag Archipelago,* an impassioned, grandiloquent yet factually precise denunciation of tyranny and murder, which is both a monument in words to the victims of the Russian twentieth century and an extraordinarily frank account of Solzhenitsyn's own prison experiences. Harold Bloom's comment about Tolstoy, that he "remains both an epic figure and a creator of epic,"[5] is equally applicable to Solzhenitsyn. He was a supremely stylish artist who textualized history, textualized himself in history, and by so doing, made history.

Even in Solzhenitsyn's lifetime his books already featured on high school syllabi in Russia, the United States, and other countries, while phrases and idioms he had crafted were anthologized in numerous books of quotations:

"For a country to have a great writer is like having a second government."

"The line separating good and evil passes not through states, nor between classes, nor between political parties either—but right through every human heart."

"Live not by lies."

"The Gulag."

These and other Solzhenitsynian locutions frequently drop from the lips of politicians and public figures, including some who have never read a single line written by their author.

As the winner of the 1970 Nobel Prize in literature and a passionate opponent of the Soviet government, Solzhenitsyn is often included in the select company of famous figures who in that stock journalistic phrase "brought down the Berlin Wall" and so destroyed one of the great despotisms of the twentieth century. Even the sardonic Joseph Brodsky, another great Russian artist and Nobel laureate, saw things this way, despite his many artistic disagreements with the author. One of Brodsky's last interviews, which he gave to the Polish ex-dissident Adam Michnik, includes this lapidary exchange:

Brodsky: Solzhenitsyn would never have achieved anything if it hadn't been for the Poles.

Michnik: The Poles would never have succeeded if it hadn't been for Solzhenitsyn.[6]

Still, for Solzhenitsyn, arguments like these were beside the point, for all his life he saw himself as first and foremost a writer: "Of course, I have an innate passion for politics. Yet for me it comes *after* literature, it is of a secondary, lower importance."[7] Ever since he rose to prominence he always denied he had a political agenda, while acknowledging that his moral engagements not only determined the content of his fictions but were designed for maximum public impact. After the fall of the Soviet Union he kept his distance from the centers of power, though in the early years of the post-communist transition many observers felt that had he so wished, he might have attained high office, perhaps even the presidency of Russia.

Instead, Solzhenitsyn continued to do what he had been doing for decades before: make literature. He was "the man who kept on writing."[8] Through the exercise of his creative imagination he strove to bridge the chasms and ruptures that defined Russia's national experience in the modern age. "Solzhenitsyn's strength—his majestic strength—lies in his capacity to recover the past."[9] He celebrates the human worth of those who suffered while depicting their tormentors as soiled souls who inflict pain on men and women who are better, wiser, nobler than they are. At the same time, he portrays these minions of terror as recognizably human, if sometimes grotesquely so. The fictions feature relatively few out-and-out evildoers. Rather, Solzhenitsyn shows how ordinary people are forced to do evil by the fierce pressure of history, how a system of government can be designed to privilege mediocre spirits and low minds, and how a single politician or general—or assassin—may determine the course of world events, for good or ill. He explores the minutiae of daily life under a dictatorship, that gray normality where people, even though they may be chattels of the Big Lie, fall in and out of love, raise families, pursue careers, enjoy works of art, and dream of a better tomorrow. Yet elsewhere, behind concrete walls and barbed wire, millions of huddled prisoners endure the unendurable and long to rejoin the world of the free, who, of course, are never truly free.

As his Nobel Lecture shows, Solzhenitsyn was quite aware that like every other kind of imaginative writing, his literature of truth employed pleasing forms to depict human suffering. In one of the "Miniatures" or prose poems, "The City on the Neva" ("Gorod na Neve"), the authorial persona ponders the architectural glories of Leningrad/St. Petersburg, a city erected by Peter the Great on the bones of thousands of peasants in Russia's first national construction project.

> It is awesome to contemplate: our own ungainly and wretched lives, our explosive disagreements, the groans of the executed and the tears of their

wives—will all this, too, be clean forgotten? Will from this, too, come such perfect and undying beauty?[10]

Indeed, not all of the horrors depicted by Solzhenitsyn occur in the interrogation rooms and prison camps of the gulag. In *The First Circle*, Klara Makarygina, an ethically aware and empathetic young woman, learns about the human cost of the fighting on the Eastern Front when she visits a flea market in Tashkent, the Central Asian city to which she has been evacuated.

> The most frightening of the war cripples was the "Samovar," as they called him: He had lost both arms and both legs; his boozy wife carried him on her back in a basket; people tossed money into it. When they had collected enough, they bought vodka and drank it, loudly abusing everybody and everything.[11]

Solzhenitsyn's novels and stories, though they deal with uniquely twentieth-century barbarities, show many points of contact with nineteenth-century literature. A Victorian reader would have no trouble relating to the form of "Ivan Denisovich" or *Cancer Ward*, if not to their terrifying content. These and other works are oriented toward that very ideal of a "perfect and undying beauty" which Solzhenitsyn's more artistic characters, such as Gleb Nerzhin (*The First Circle*) or Vera Gangart (*Cancer Ward*), like to invoke explicitly. And herein lies an old conundrum. Through its mimetic function, imaginative literature programmatically aestheticizes the ugly or the cruel. The text selects, copies, and reproduces, generating its simulacra of people, sensations, and situations. It prompts the receptor to sympathetic or antipathetic acts of *recognition* and *complicity*: hence the pleasure. On some private level, he will almost always derive enjoyment from the readerly contemplation of that which, when unmediated fictively, is simply, starkly evil. This is a problem with serious ethical implications and it has preoccupied artists and thinkers for two thousand years. The classical commentator Longinus drew a distinction between beauty and sublimity, which despite its association with "the terrifying"[12] "carries one up to where one is close to the majestic mind of God."[13] The same binary was given psychological meaning—beauty relates to pleasure, sublimity to pain, and danger, and death—by Edmund Burke in *A Philosophical Inquiry into the Origin of Our Ideas of the Sublime and Beautiful* (1757). In the twentieth century, which "has proved to be crueler than its predecessors,"[14] our culture(s) were forced to confront the relation of art to morality with special urgency. Theodor Adorno famously observed that "to write poetry after Auschwitz is barbaric,"[15] though his dictum begs the question, what does it mean to write poetry *in* Auschwitz? For this is the very thing Solzhenitsyn accomplished as a prisoner of the gulag, in the most direct meaning of the word. During but especially following his incarceration, the writer dedicated himself to composing redemptive narratives that depict an unprecedented historical and social catastrophe and to showing its terrible effects on both the nation and the individual. These works employ a system of *beautifully* designed, evolving fictive techniques that undergird a "[discourse] of the unrepresentable, of the event or object that destabilizes language and demands a vocabulary and syntax in some sense incommensurable with what went before."[16] The formulation I quoted comes from a book review of recent academic studies of historical trauma, but it is entirely applicable to Solzhenitsyn's own discourse of suffering.

In the end, the practice of creating and consuming literary texts entails two separate ethical negotiations, by the author and the receptor, as Georges Bataille understood:

> Literature is either the essential or nothing. I believe that the Evil—an acute form of Evil—which it expresses, has a sovereign value for us. But this concept does not exclude morality: on the contrary, it demands a "hypermorality."
>
> Literature is *communication*. Communication requires loyalty. A rigorous morality results from complicity in the knowledge of Evil, which is the basis of intense communication.
>
> Literature is not innocent. It is guilty and should admit itself so.[17]

This is Bataille's ethical corrective to Nietzsche's "proposition" in *Beyond Good and Evil*: "Almost everything we call 'higher culture' is based on the spiritualization of *cruelty*, on its becoming more profound."[18] Yet in *Cancer Ward*, Elizaveta Anatolievna, who was once comfortably middle-class but now cleans floors for a living, finds that the French novels she reads are "a blessing,"[19] for they give her warm comfort as she grieves over the death of her exiled daughter and the probable death of her imprisoned husband.

Brodsky understood the complexities in question. Although his literary sensibilities were entirely different from Solzhenitsyn's, he saw the terrifying beauty in his art and knew how to relate it to the sublime (and the immoral):

> It is possible that two thousand years from now a lecture of *The Gulag* will provide the same pleasure as a lecture of the *Iliad* does today. But if we do

not read *The Gulag* today it may so happen that much sooner than two thousand years hence there will be no one left to read either book.[20]

And on a scholarly note, Leona Toker, one of this author's most subtle academic readers, observes that literary narratives were uniquely appropriate for the depiction of extreme suffering in the gulag:

> History books or archival materials are of little help here—one needs more effective aids to imagination and thought. Quality writing about atrocities is ethically significant not only because it captures potentially reluctant audiences, but also because it stages and mediates a closer engagement with its material.[21]

Solzhenitsyn's own view of the ethical dimension of literature was almost poetic. In the Nobel Lecture he declared that art is generated by the creative fusion of Truth, Goodness, and Beauty. Yet, if the first two of these elements are crushed or thwarted because of the operation of some malignant external force, "then perhaps the whimsical, unpredictable, and ever surprising shoots of Beauty will force their way through ... thereby fulfilling the task of all three."[22] And thereby expand the reader's moral imagination.

2

So what about this writer's style? To begin with, a passage by Solzhenitsyn, whether fictional or nonfictional, is instantly recognizable, in the same way that Tolstoy's, Nabokov's, or Joyce's authorial signatures seem diagonally emblazoned across the lines of print.

> Solzhenitsyn was able to infuse the Russian language, which by the second half of the twentieth century had somewhat wilted, with a new vigor, a new elastic terseness and power. Solzhenitsyn's speech thrills and captivates, even when one disagrees with him about the issue at hand. His language, so vivid, imaginative and yet extraordinarily precise, is bewitching.[23]

Beyond this distinctive authorial diction (which the translations will, inevitably, sometimes muffle), there is the matter of Solzhenitsyn's mimetic stance. He was a pragmatic artist who chose the textual tools that would best serve his extra-textual purposes, which fell into two broad categories: the search for historical truth and the affirmation of moral values in an immoral society. Though celebrated as a prison writer, he was also among the first in his unhappy country to address other forbidden themes: the Soviet Union's catastrophic environmental record, its pervasive exploitation of women, the poverty and grind of everyday existence for millions of people in the countryside, the drabness of working-class life. At the same time, his works assert the autonomy and dignity of the imaginative writer against the philistine doctrine of Socialist Realism, which "demanded the reality of the wedding photograph or holiday brochure."[24] Instead, this writer combines elements of Tolstoy's narrative method and his gift for characterization with a focus on the nature of evil and the human response to extreme suffering which recalls Dostoevsky, while displaying a sometimes radical predilection for formal experimentation. "The strongest influence on me has been *War and Peace* [although] the spiritual values of Dostoevsky are closer to me than Tolstoy's."[25] If one were to sum up (and simplify) the writer's connection to his two great predecessors, his "teachers," as he called them,[26] one might say that he shows us Tolstoyan characters who find themselves in Dostoevskian predicaments within twentieth-century settings that are meticulously and unsparingly depicted from firsthand knowledge. As for SocRealism, in Solzhenitsyn's book it is as dull as dishwater.

In a celebrated essay, *Dostoevsky and the Legend of the Grand Inquisitor* (*Legenda o Velikom inkvizitore F. M. Dostoevskogo*; 1891), the philosopher Vasily Rozanov observed that for all of that writer's genius, the axiological content of his productions manifests a quality of one-sidedness or incompleteness that becomes especially evident in his last novel, *The Brothers Karamazov* (*Brat'ia Karamazovy*; 1880):

> With this understanding of darkness, chaos, and destruction, there was undoubtedly connected in the soul of the artist himself a certain absence of harmony, order, and consistency. As a matter of fact, *The Brothers Karamazov* shows only how the old dies; the regeneration is, of course, outlined, but only briefly, and from without. But just *how* this regeneration comes about—that is a secret Dostoevsky took with him to the grave. To judge from the last page of *Crime and Punishment*, it was his life-long intention to depict this, and it was finally to appear in the subsequent volumes of *The Brothers Karamazov*; but, because of the author's death, that was not to be. Dostoevsky had outlined the most important task of his life but had failed to complete it.[27]

In this regard there is, one finds, a complementarity between Dostoevsky's artistic practices and those of Solzhenitsyn. His best heroes and heroines act, sometimes unbeknownst to themselves, as agents of *harmony, order,* and *consistency*, even though the worlds they inhabit are far more morally and materially diseased, and far more chaotic, than those imagined by his nineteenth-century predecessor. Each novel and story admits the possibility, and usually presents the reality, of the ethical and spiritual reconstitution of the individual or national self, under a variety of traumatic historical circumstances. This is true even of Solzhenitsyn's most tragically themed works such as *The Red Wheel*, which shows the fall of old Russia and its civilization, and *The Gulag Archipelago*, which describes the systems of evil that were born of that collapse. Both epic productions depict, to use Rozanov's language, the "truly satanic features"[28] of history but also "the incomprehensible strength and beauty of life."[29] A few of the shorter fictions such as "Apricot Jam" and "Nastenka" show that beauty comprehensively defeated, but they are the exception; and even here, on some level of representation or implication, there is still hope.

A rationalist by inclination, a mathematician by education, Solzhenitsyn possessed the chip of ice in the heart that according to Graham Greene every writer must carry. Behind the novels and stories, which display a strict internal logic that is almost Cartesian, there is a disciplined, organizing intelligence. In the manner of nineteenth-century novelists such as Tolstoy and Dickens, this author is the demiurge of his created universe. Its fictive worlds or planets are many-layered constructs with their own population, history, geography, meteorology, and flora and fauna. "Imagination, producing new metaphors or revivifying old, is not the cause of truth, but its condition" (C. S. Lewis),[30] and Solzhenitsyn's imaginaries of truth are wonderfully metaphorical. Some of the shorter works and all of the novels rely on a defining referential matrix, one that may be borrowed or bespoke, which informs the treatment of the characters' moral identities and life situations. In *The First Circle*, for instance, this overarching system of meanings derives from the *Divine Comedy*, with the narrative periodically invoking Dante's poem, sometimes explicitly, on multiple textual levels. The fictions may also include elaborate subsets of tropes that are secondary to the organizing structure, such as the astronomical citations in *Love the Revolution* and *Cancer Ward*, which invite us to navigate the text by the stars, as it were.

Solzhenitsyn once told an American journalist, "From a Christian point of view, history is the result of the interaction of the Will of God and free human wills [and] is irrational, we can never truly understand it."[31] The language may be emphatically anti-secular, but the underlying notion is not necessarily so. The writer implied that the past is best apprehended intuitively or imaginatively, that is, through the practices of art rather than by analytical reasoning; or existentially, rather than conceptually: shades of Schelling, perhaps. For Solzhenitsyn, history is a subject of literature. So, he fills the culture's semantic voids with text, densely structured and innovatively formatted. His authorial motivation is both a patriotic and a pragmatic one: "If we don't know our own history, we will simply have to endure all the same mistakes, sacrifices and absurdities all over again."[32]

The representation of landscapes, public events, social customs, psychologies, gender realities, and institutions owes a great deal to Tolstoy. So does the use of elaborately crafted set pieces—meals, celebrations, church services, battle scenes—which signpost important plot developments and show the characters assembling and interacting in accordance with, or in violation of, a fixed cultural code. In the way of Dostoevsky and Dickens (and sometimes Tolstoy), *nomen est omen*, so that character names come bearing a message as aptronyms or jobonyms: nominative determinism is a favorite Solzhenitsynian device. In *The Red Wheel*, the surname of the epic's fictional extremist-in-chief, Sasha Lenartovich, points at his future vassalage to Lenin. We find this onomastic trope operating even in the case of real-life figures, as when we are told that prime minister Stolypin "lived up to his name, the pillar [*stolp*][33] of the Russian state"[34] (*August 1914*). On the other hand, the writer was careful not to be too extravagant when naming his imagined men and women, criticizing Mikhail Bulgakov for excessive flamboyance on that score.[35] Some Christian names mediate a lexically or imaginatively valorized connection between a hagiographic source and a character's personal traits, as in the case of the patriotic soldier *Georgi* Vorotyntsev, who is associated with the story of St. George and the dragon: in Solzhenitsyn, dragons symbolize the revolution and the terror state it brought into being.[36] The author also employs those Tolstoyan tropes of free indirect discourse, when the third-person narrative is colored by the personality and perceptions of a given dramatis persona; defamiliarization, whether figurative or periphrastic, whereby a commonplace object or situation is perceptually "refreshed" and acquires an uncommonly vivid or alien aspect; and emotional eavesdropping, that is, the technique of describing a sensation which, though instantly recognizable to the reader, is one that he may never have verbalized or even named. Take, for instance, the reference to "the shame you always feel when you step around a woman washing a floor" (*The First Circle*).[37] Passages like this have a quality of immediacy that make us start in surprise. As is true of all great novelists, Solzhenitsyn's sentences stay in one's mind long after one has closed the book.

Another connection to Tolstoy is this writer's preference for character types that are distributed along the median of the human condition. When Vorotyntsev, the main fictional presence in *The Red Wheel*, tells his wife Alina during a marital argument, "You should have the humility to recognize you are one of those ordinary persons that comprise the human race...,"[38] he gives angry voice to a Tolstoyan truth, even if the harshness of the reproach stems from the hero's realization that the collapse of his marriage is as nothing compared with the collapse of Russia that is now in train. And although most of this writer's characters tend to be "ordinary," everyday men and women, this is far from true of the things they must endure, which are often harrowing in the extreme. As for Tolstoy and Solzhenitsyn's respective historiosophical positions, they could not be more different. Anyone who has read *War and Peace* (*Voina i mir*; 1865–69) will recall its anti-intellectual interpretation of the events of the past, which were, or so that novel tells us, determined by "an incalculable number of causes"[39] and not by the actions of any individual or institution, however seemingly powerful. Tolstoy would never have treated Nicholas II and Lenin (*The Red Wheel*), or Stalin (*The First Circle*) as emblematic, let alone defining, historical figures. Solzhenitsyn, however, is firm: "There is no fatalism in history.... It all depends on the individual, the mob, the parties."[40]

He also differs from Tolstoy on another point. Where the latter delights in mocking, even lampooning generously credentialed experts, this writer treats his educated professionals with marked sympathy. He also admires adventurous spirits who set themselves a high purpose and make things happen:

> I find it strange that Russian literature, partly owing to the influence of Gogol, whose merciless eye discerned every vice ... ignored the praxis of creation in our history. What about the people who built this state, who extended it to Siberia, the Pacific Ocean, Alaska?! ... But with us it's always ... either an Oblomov, or some "superfluous man," or a Pechorin, an Onegin, it's always the same so called "superfluous men." Where are the tycoons, the builders, the creators, I ask? This is where Russian literature fell short.[41]

Solzhenitsyn's novels and stories feature dozens of able and dedicated military officers, industrial managers, entrepreneurs, farmers, artisans, physicians, scientists, engineers and even professors who clearly know what they are doing, and do a great deal of good. They exemplify Ortega y Gasset's ideal of "the select man, the excellent man [who] is urged, by interior necessity, to appeal from himself to some standard beyond himself, superior to himself, whose service he freely accepts."[42] The hardworking doctors and nurses in *Cancer Ward* are a case in point, controverting Tolstoy's disdain for the medical profession as recorded in *Anna Karenina* (1875–7) and *The Death of Ivan Ilyich* (*Smert' Ivana Il'icha*; 1886).[43] Here the camp quack Stepan Grigorich ("Ivan Denisovich") is a rare exception. Solzhenitsyn even has time for the odd mystic or two, provided they talk some sort of sense. Thus the bookish seer Pavel Varsonofiev (*The Red Wheel*), a Swedenborgian figure with mesmerizing eyes who straddles the realms of history and the unearthly.

The writer employs the term *uzel* ("knot" or "node"—the point at which a curved line or three-dimensional curved surface self-intersects) to describe those critical moments in the historical process when, as it were, it curls inward, contracts like a spring, and then unfurls in a new direction: the Battle of Tannenberg, the February Revolution, the Russian civil war, Stalin's collectivization of agriculture, Hitler's attack on the Soviet Union, Khrushchev's de-Stalinization campaign, the fall of the USSR. This nodal premise shapes the treatment of historical figures across the fictions, and in the case of *The Red Wheel*, determines its formal division into four Knots or novels, which cover the "episodes where ... the course of events was being decided."[44] Moreover, for Solzhenitsyn human agency is the deciding factor not only in times of war, revolution, or national collapse, but even for established, stable societies, whatever their political systems. In *The First Circle*, the fortunes of the Soviet regime at the midpoint of its existence are determined not by the dynamics of economic development or the interplay and inter-killing of the elites, but by the will of one man, Joseph Stalin.

The same principle is at work in *The Red Wheel*, an epopee[45] (Solzhenitsyn's preferred designation) that is ten times the length of the very lengthy *First Circle*. The saga's titular image, which metaphorizes the Russian Revolution as a steamroller or juggernaut, may ultimately derive from Dostoevsky's novel *Devils* (*Besy*; 1871) and its "red rubber ball,"[46] the "Man-God" Kirillov's ineffably sinister accessory. In *The Red Wheel*, historical actors are categorized by their degree of informed activism (prime minister Stolypin), defeatist listlessness (General Samsonov), intellectual inadequacy (Nicholas II), meretricious play-acting (Kerensky), or destructive drive (Lenin). At the same time, Tolstoy is a constant target: a hint, perhaps, of a Bloomian anxiety of influence or, more probably, a non-Bloomian will to polemicize. On one occasion, the author of *War and Peace* appears in person, when a youthful Sanya Lazhenitsyn, a fictionalization of Solzhenitsyn's father, visits the famous writer on his estate of Yasnaya Polyana in the opening pages of *August 1914*, the first novel in the series, but as a rule Tolstoy's presence is textually or even visually citational, as when his portrait with plough gladdens the eye of the sybaritic Roman Tomchak, Sanya's future brother-in-law. Later in the novel we meet a Russian corps commander, General Blagoveshchensky, a self-proclaimed military Tolstoyan (now, there's a contradiction in terms!) who employs *War and Peace* as a field manual and refuses to march to the sound of guns without the spontaneous reactive impulse of the soldierly masses he notionally commands. More often, however, Solzhenitsyn prefers to conduct his dialogue with Tolstoy on the plane of fictive implication and intertextual allusion. His in-text engagement with Dostoevsky follows similar lines but lacks that polemical edge: Alyosha the Baptist ("Ivan Denisovich") is an updated, gulag version of Alyosha Karamazov, while the character of Father Severyan (*The Red Wheel*), an enlightened cleric with ecumenical leanings, is accompanied by discursive and artifactal markers that refer us to Father Zosima, again from *The Brothers Karamazov*.

The idea that Solzhenitsyn wished to put across in *The Red Wheel* was that in the early years of the last century Russia's urban and rural population and the country's elites separately took a succession of wrong turns that led directly to the tragedy of 1917. Although both sets of actors bore heavy guilt for the national catastrophe, that of the politicians and generals and artists was greater than that of the people: the exercise of power, whether material or cultural, bestows on those who wield it a national duty of care towards the state and its subjects. There is a connection here to the analysis of twentieth-century mass politics advanced by Ortega y Gasset, who distinguished between the artists and intellectuals, who build and sustain civilization, and "mass-man," who takes it for granted, if he notices it at all. Solzhenitsyn's views on this subject may be qualified, to coin a phrase, as democratic or common-sense elitism.

3

As a trained mathematician Solzhenitsyn understood and appreciated the scientific mindset and like C. P. Snow, another scientist-turned-novelist, was concerned by the ever-widening gulf in modern culture between those who study the physical world, and humanists, artists and, of course, writers. He depicts the benign and malign consequences of scientific progress, from advanced cancer treatments to advanced industrial warfare. *The First Circle* is, among other things, a novel about real science and pseudo-science as well as the relationship between the exact disciplines and the arts, and shows how both may be abused by the terror state. The play *Candle in the Wind* (1960), set in an "unknown country at an unspecified period,"[47] shares the cerebral, polemical themes of contemporary Western science dramas such as Max Frisch's *The Chinese Wall* (*Die Chinesische Mauer*; 1946; 1955) and Friedrich Dürrenmatt's *The Physicists* (*Die Physiker*; 1961) while anticipating the get-rich realities of Russia in the 1990s.

Solzhenitsyn has a marked fondness for mathematical allusions and symbols. This element in his literary works was noted by none other than the writer himself: "Approached by art, every individual phenomenon becomes a 'bundle of intersecting planes,' to use a mathematical analogy: several planes of reality are unexpectedly seen to intersect at the chosen point."[48] The remark I quoted dates from 1966, but it applies to all of Solzhenitsyn's poetry, drama, and prose, whose character is programmatically conciliatory, harmonizing the methodologies of art and science. In terms of form and imagery, his productions are pronouncedly "computational," "geometrical." And once in a while, those "intersecting planes" become fictively materialized. An example is a scene in *March 1917* where Colonel Kutepov, a monarchist officer on the run from the new revolutionary authorities, narrowly escapes arrest. He is hiding in the corner of a drawing room, which is connected to two enfilades that stand at a right angle to each other.

Opposite each door was a large mirror, so that a person walking toward it could see his reflection from a distance.

In each mirror he saw a worker with a revolver in hand running down each suite of rooms and drawing closer. The workers were so much alike, of similar height and appearance, with the same black clothes and the same red rosette on the left side of the chest, that at first he imagined they were a reflection of each other; but then he realized this was impossible.

Then he realized that if he could see them from his corner, they would be able to see him as well.

But as it turned out, they didn't see him. Probably they were enthralled by their own terrifying appearance, for it was unlikely they were used to such large mirrors. Also, bright sunlight was streaming in through the windows. And so it happened that they reached the doors at the very same instant, and barely turning their heads they saw each other with their drawn revolvers, both tired from running all the way to this empty room.

Without further ado, they turned round, also in unison, and hurriedly retraced their steps, and now the mirrors showed their backs which were also alike, but without the patch of red.[49]

The episode is a thing of vectors and vertices. The shape and disposition of the walls and doors and mirrors all have geometrical value, as do the routes followed by the twin custodians of revolutionary justice, so that the passage *directs* the reader to search it for encoded meanings along these *lines*. There is so much structure here: the clone-like similitude of appearance and motion and even self-perception of the two armed workers; the concordances between objects and their reflections; the color symbolism of the black-hued clothes and red boutonnieres; the proleptic intimations of the episode that would end Kutepov's life, his kidnapping by Soviet agents in Paris thirteen years later, in the course of which he died, either violently or of a heart attack.

A brief aside. Solzhenitsyn's oft-voiced opposition to the territorial settlements agreed to by post-Soviet Russia and its neighbors, which preserved "Lenin's false borders,"[50] was geometrically scripted. Rightly or wrongly, the writer felt that if these boundaries were to be re-drawn in keeping with the demographic facts, millions of people would have a chance to live better lives. The de facto states and statelets dotting the peripheries of the former Soviet space confirm his point. But what are borders if not lines on a map, cartographic abstractions that are a fixed expression of power relations and function as mensurable signifiers of the historical realities, and injustices, on the ground?

Next, let us look at the other quantifiable components of Solzhenitsyn's prose.

He is a binary writer, first of all in a topographical sense. Spatial antinomies and dichotomies serve as an organizing element in his fictive worlds, which are shaped by the chronotopic opposition, historiographically, culturologically or ethically defined, between a densely scripted, three-dimensional enclosed space and a wider, open-sided, open-ended space that surrounds it: the Russian trenches and dugouts versus the autumnal Polish countryside (*The Red Wheel*); the science prison at Marfino versus the Ozymandian capital of Moscow (*The First Circle*); the Special Camp versus the snow-covered Kazakh steppe ("Ivan Denisovich"); the oncological clinic versus the colorful, sprawling city of Tashkent (*Cancer Ward*); a peasant hut versus the rolling expanse of central Russia ("Matryona's Home"). The characters think, emote, suffer, move, work, kill, die and, of course, speak inside these cubic, parallelepipedal, prismatic, cylindrical, tubular, spherical—but always symmetrical—interiors.

Occasionally Solzhenitsyn's fictional bodies are contorted, even tormented by the narrowness of their physical environments, particularly when they find themselves stuck in the interstices of the terror state. As Innokenty Volodin (*The First Circle*) calls the US embassy in an *ethical* act of high treason, he awkwardly holds on to the door of the callbox as he dials the fateful number, "the phone booth floor … burning under Innokenty's feet, and the black receiver … melting in his hand."[51] This is a moment of spatial/corporeal foreshadowing: upon his arrest three days later, the hero will be taken to the Lubyanka and placed in a "box," a "high but narrow three cubic meters of space"[52] where "even sitting comfortably was impossible":[53] the smallest inhabited space in the whole of Solzhenitsyn. True, *Love the Revolution* contains a reference, presented in the form of one of those frightening rumors that do the rounds under a dictatorship, to "rooms the size of a man where the door is used to crush the prisoner against the wall."[54]

The fabulatory structure of Solzhenitsyn's fictions is often binary as well. *The First Circle* has two parallel plots, centered respectively on Volodin, the high-ranking diplomat who makes that fateful phone call, and Nerzhin, the aspiring writer imprisoned at Marfino. Both men are in their early thirties; both are orphans; both have problematic marriages; both insist on owning themselves in the Nietzschean sense, as proudly autonomous personalities who reject the behavioral codes of their spiritual inferiors. *Cancer Ward* is shaped by a confrontation between raging, super-masculine Kostoglotov, a veteran of the gulag, and flaccid Rusanov, a Party apparatchik. The 6000-plus pages of *The Red*

Wheel contain multiple character dyads: the cosmopolitan nihilist Lenin and the rooted state-builder Stolypin; preening General François and devout General Samsonov; vain Lenartovich and earnest Lazhenitsyn; wifely Alina and sexy, cerebral Olda. Interestingly, these paired personalities never meet, kept apart as they are by one or more degrees of fictive separation. Character oppositions may also be collective, as in the story "The Easter Procession" where the celebrants with their "unworldly gaze"[55] come face-to-face with a mob of bug-eyed blasphemers; or internal, as in the case of Colonel Vorotyntsev, who is both a guardian of order and a lifelong maverick. And then there are the two-part tales of the 1990s, whose paired sections are linked thematically even when they do not share a common plot.

The manner in which this writer encodes his characters' physical and moral selves is binary as well. Their bodies are refracted or marked through second-order signification, that is, onomastically, symbolically, metaphorically, metonymically. *The Red Wheel* shows Lenin imaginatively diagnosing his developing arteriosclerosis as a "mold" growing on the "apparatus" of his brain:[56] a figurative fungus attacking an imaginary machine. Each semiotic alteration informs, shapes, or misshapes a character's identity, or his or her worth or unworth; and is dual to a second imaginative sign that often remains untextualized. In *The First Circle*, the copies of the communist party newspaper *Pravda* (Truth) that Volodin's Uncle Avenir obsessively collects constitute a chronicle of the mutable *untruths* of the Soviet regime. Avenir's other hobby is gardening and he has turned the plot next to his house into a verdant orchard. Later in the novel we learn that the cretinous party secretary at the Marfino prison, Stepanov, raises porkers in his suburban Moscow home: the ignoble pig farmer standing in intratextual contrast to the noble gardener. Another instance of counter-coding occurs in *The Red Wheel*, where the arms of an economics professor pontificating about the political situation assume the appearance of "gigantic pliers" or "wrenches"[57]: a salon academic whose flabby limbs become incongruously proletarianized. Clearly, these mechanized mitts are not the tools of his trade. Hundreds of chapters later (the epopee is prodigiously long), the professor makes a second appearance and once again holds forth, but this time it is his elbows that are successively transformed into "tongs"[58] and "gears."[59] What we have here is a descriptive *déformation non professionelle* suggestive of a steam-punk automaton assembled from iron and steel parts. The two passages positively invite an imaginative reader-response: polysemy not on the macro- but micro-textual level, as so often happens in this writer's prose.

4

Of course, great writers always look for new ways of enchanting or educating their readers, and Solzhenitsyn more so than most. In this regard, the "certain classification of narratives"[60] devised by Roland Barthes may be usefully applied to the manner in which the author's storytelling techniques evolved over the decades:

> Some narratives are heavily functional (such as folk tales), while others on the contrary are heavily indicial (such as "psychological" novels); between these two poles lies a whole series of intermediary forms, dependent on history, society, genre.[61]

In such a Barthian sense, the earlier fictions tend to be functional (informational about the characters' "doing") rather than indicial (informational about the characters' "being"), with the sum of the works, however, manifesting a steady movement across the genres from functionality to indiciality; and from the representational and narratological formats of Solzhenitsyn's nineteenth-century predecessors to a laconic, lexically innovative, and metaphor-rich authorial diction that interrogates these classic literary models as much as it does the conventions of official Soviet literature. This shift becomes very apparent in *The Red Wheel* and some of the bipartite tales, which explore themes of catastrophic national and individual entropy and are overtly, even flamboyantly experimental in ways that the earlier prose is not.

Solzhenitsyn once remarked, "It is very easy for me to write about things I have experienced, but I cannot *invent*."[62] Of course, this was laying it on with a trowel: his novels and stories are replete with characters, situations, and locales that are wholly invented and wholly convincing. Many of Solzhenitsyn's heroes and heroines possess the verisimilitudinal attribute of tangibility and believability that was first identified by Samuel Coleridge: "With the same illusion as we read any tale known to be fictitious, as a novel, we go on with [the] characters as real persons, who had been nicknamed by their neighbours."[63] Dignified, intensely practical Ivan Denisovich in the eponymous tale, idealistic Innokenty Volodin in *The First Circle*, defiant Oleg Kostoglotov, flabby Pavel Rusanov, shady Maksim Chaly, and sexy Zoya in *Cancer Ward* are all products of Solzhenitsyn's writerly imagination, rather than writerly recollection. What holds true for all his characters, including those that inhabit the later, maximal narrator texts, is that they are metonymically representative, of a generation, a profession, or a historical experience.

Solzhenitsyn's heroes and heroines, whether autobiographical or imagined, tend to be purposeful, self-contained personalities, though they are also high-functioning members of their particular social group, however small or vulnerable or spatially isolated. They may be individualists but they are not individual. They are also densely historicized. Solzhenitsyn's publisher Nikita Struve observes of Solzhenitsyn's novels that

> the characters depend not so much on the development of their own spiritual forces, as on external events and impacts. They are part of a social and historical whole, and experience conflict with each other, or even within themselves, owing to external circumstances.⁶⁴

Actually, this point applies to most of this writer's characters across most of his fictions. True, in "Ivan Denisovich" the hero's personality remains largely unaffected by his experience of war and prison, even as his body bears brutal evidence of those realities, but then, like the peasant widow Matryona and the jack-of-all-trades Spiridon (*The First Circle*), Ivan Denisovich resides in the realm of prehistory, stubbornly holding onto an identity and a way of seeing the world that is tribal and magical rather than national and secular. Moreover, Solzhenitsyn's narratives lack that all-encompassing focus on the inner man or woman which we encounter in Dostoevsky or, say, Knut Hamsun and Thomas Mann. Like Dickens, this writer prefers to reveal his heroes and heroines' private selves through their social interactions and the manner of their response to patterns of often wrenching historical change.

As mentioned earlier, Solzhenitsyn writes whereof he *knows*. He cribs the events of his life for his fictions, which are also a record of the books he read and the conversations he had. Much of his prosaic and dramatic oeuvre, and all of his poetry, forms a grand autobiographical sequence, a literary account of his journey through the twentieth century.

The author's fictional self-iterations number a dozen or more. His most celebrated alter ego is Gleb/Sergei Nerzhin, whose destiny is shaped by war and prison, with the latter constituting his most "decisive" life experience.⁶⁵ We first meet this character as a starry-eyed student and raw Red Army conscript in the unfinished novel *Love the Revolution* and the narrative poem *The Road*, which describes his service as an artillery officer in World War II and his arrest three months before the fall of Berlin. The comedy *Victory Celebrations* shows the hero *enjoying* his last days of freedom, while the drama *The Republic of Labor*, better known as *The Love-Girl and the Innocent*, describes Nerzhin's first months in a brutal work camp.⁶⁶ In *The First Circle*, the most famous work in the series, he is a captive researcher at a secret science prison who is painfully constructing a new worldview while facing difficult life choices. This multigeneric quintology constitutes a composite autobiographical *Bildungseppopee*, a quasi-Dickensian account of a young man's progress from orphaned innocence to worldly-wise maturity via the stages of love, war, and prison. The scientist Alex, the enigmatic protagonist of the futuristic drama *Candle in the Wind*, is another self-portrait in time, the empirical Solzhenitsyn self-projected and self-extrapolated into a dystopian neverwhen.

Like the Nerzhin narratives, many of the shorter fictions describe events from Solzhenitsyn's life. He disguises himself as newly commissioned Lieutenant Pozushan in the binary tale "No Matter What," a recovering cancer patient in "The Right Hand," a weary ex-prisoner, Ignatich, in "Matryona's Home," and a history-loving cyclist touring the sights of central Russia in "Zakhar-the-Pouch." Another two-part tale, "Zhelyabuga Village," splices a fictionalized wartime experience that occurred at the eponymous hamlet in 1943 with a diaristic account of the author's return visit half a century later. His last published prose work, the war novella "Adlig Schwenkitten," is based on an episode from January 1945 when Captain Solzhenitsyn's artillery brigade found itself behind enemy lines and had to fight its way out of encirclement.

Finally, large sections of *The Red Wheel*, Solzhenitsyn's epic of World War I and the Russian Revolution, extends this autobiographical sequence to the decade before he was born. The cast of characters includes his parents and grandparents as well as other family members. Sanya Lazhenitsyn is a figure based on Solzhenitsyn's father, Isaaki, but he is also reminiscent of the young Solzhenitsyn (who was known to his friends as Sanya), down to his habit of tilting his head and thick sandy hair. And if Sanya is something of a portrait of the author in his twenties, the sage of Yasnaya Polyana as depicted in *August 1914* cues us to another literary patriarch, the Solzhenitsyn of the 1970s and thereafter, who wrote the novel where Tolstoy makes his brief appearance. Lazhenitsyn's conversation with the creator of *War and Peace* becomes an instance of mediated authorial self-commentary, perhaps even self-referential irony. Most of *August 1914*, however, is devoted to the catastrophic defeat suffered by the imperial Russian army at Tannenberg. Here the novelist brings into play his memories of doing battle in the flatlands and forests of East Prussia in the last months of World War II. Sanya is a prominent presence in subsequent volumes, where he is shown fighting, enduring, and intellectually maturing in the trenches of eastern Poland. These episodes are part-fictionalizations of Solzhenitsyn' wartime experiences as well. Finally, in *April 1917* we find Sanya courting Ksenia Tomchak, an intelligent and sensitive young woman who is a biographically accurate representation of the author's mother. Sanya and Ksenia make plans for a future life together and talk about having a son: they are certain it will be a boy.

Such self-referential doublings or triplings can also be oblique, when the writer smuggles himself into his narratives in coded, pseudonymous or anonymous ways. Thus the cameo appearance by a pale poet in a lieutenant's uniform, a Solzhenitsyn lookalike who recites some Leninist doggerel penned by the author in his youth ("Incident at Kochetovka Station"); or the way Solzhenitsyn's own eyes gaze at a beautiful, sad young woman from a photograph on her wall (*Cancer Ward*). One of the prisoners in *The First Circle* composes secret tales of the gulag in Solzhenitsyn's own handwriting. In each instance, the artist's *sub rosa* intrusions into his text are *arresting*, for they prompt the careful reader to pause and ponder, so that the narrative self-opens, as it were, and reveals its authorial-mythic dimension.

These autobiographical complexities extend to some of the non-autobiographical heroes. Shukhov and Kostoglotov are entirely invented characters, but Solzhenitsyn gave the former his impressions and sense perceptions in the Special Camp where he was incarcerated in the early 1950s, while the latter reads the same books, meets the same people, suffers from the same disease, and undergoes the same medical treatments as did the author himself at the Tashkent Oncological Clinic in 1954. Georgi Vorotyntsev, the stalwart hero of *The Red Wheel* to whom the author gifted some of his marital and military experiences, is also a character in *Prisoners*, where as a sixty-nine-year-old zek[67] he meets Andrei Kholudenev, best friend to Gleb/Sergei Nerzhin in *Love the Revolution* and *The Road*: Kholudenev is modeled on Nikolai Vitkevich, Solzhenitsyn's soul mate in high school and college, but in *Prisoners* he becomes an autobiographical stand-in for the author himself. Also present in the play are Lev Rubin (briefly glimpsed in *The Road*) and Valentin Prianchikov, that is, Solzhenitsyn's fellow zeks Lev Kopelev and Valentin Martynov, who reappear in *The First Circle*, the novel in which Nerzhin is a principal presence. An aspiring writer, he is working on a book about "the New Time of Troubles," the 1917 revolution,[68] a project that sounds very much like *The Red Wheel*. Consider also Vladimir Lenin as portrayed in that saga. D. M. Thomas offers the evocative formula, Shukhov is "Sanya without education" and Lenin is "Sanya without conscience,"[69] though there is much more to Solzhenitsyn's depiction of the Bolshevik leader than just a quasi-self-portrait.

Natalia Solzhenitsyna describes *The Red Wheel* as "the first steps of a descent into the netherworld of the *Gulag*, hence the darkness, whereas the *Gulag* is a catharsis, the beginning of the ascent, hence the light."[70] In this interpretation, the ten-volume epic becomes a colossal prologue to *The Gulag Archipelago*, with Solzhenitsyn's fictional magnum opus and his greatest work of nonfiction linked into an informal duology, a magisterial *Übertext* composed over a span of decades that narrates the foundational tragedies of modern Russian history.

After settling in Cavendish, Vermont following his banishment from the Soviet Union, Solzhenitsyn for the first time in years had the opportunity for systematic, uninterrupted reading. So with typical thoroughness, he went through those volumes of Dostoevsky's *Collected Works* that he had missed when he was living in Russia.[71] He also read Andrei Bely's *Petersburg* (*Peterburg*; 1913),[72] the most important Modernist novel in Russian literature ("an unbridled and morbidly unbalanced talent").[73] He kept up with a few contemporary literary figures, notably Brodsky, whose poetry he did not really like, yet valued for the sweep of its ambition. While he was poring over writers of the past and present he jotted notes, which he brought together in his *Literary Collection*, serialized after his return to Russia and slated for inclusion in a forthcoming volume of the *Collected Works*. The *Collection* includes a harsh review of Brodsky's verse as well as essays on Anton Chekhov, Yevgeny Zamyatin, Mikhail Bulgakov and many others, and amounts to another act of self-exegesis, in a roundabout kind of way: by commenting on his favorite and not-so-favorite books, Solzhenitsyn reveals, wittingly or otherwise, his own literary priorities and agendas. The journal version of the *Collection* contains barely half of these critical (dis)appreciations, so we can look forward to reading a great many more in the not-too-distant future.[74] Here I should mention that despite his interest in the Western cultural tradition, Solzhenitsyn made it a point of almost always limiting his literary and historical researches to Russian sources, in keeping with a lifelong determination to find a *national* answer to "'The Russian Question' at the End of the Twentieth Century," to quote the title of one of his essays. This stance was due not to some lack of intellectual curiosity, but rather, his adherence to a principle that was so memorably formulated by Nietzsche: "I want, once and for all, *not* to know many things. Wisdom sets limits to knowledge too."[75]

There are also the three books of memoirs, *The Oak and the Calf*, *Between Two Millstones*, and the as yet unpublished *Another Time, Another Burden*. We await the appearance of *The Journal of "R-17"*, the diary Solzhenitsyn kept as he toiled away on *The Red Wheel* in the Soviet Union, Switzerland, and

Vermont. These works are companion pieces to the fictions and fill in the factual gaps in the author's amalgamated automythobiographical record. Leona Toker calls *The Oak and the Calf* "a literary life-sequel to the camp-life memoirs of *The Gulag Archipelago*"[76] and *Invisible Allies* (*Nevidimki*), the Fifth Supplement to *The Oak and the Calf*, "a sequel to a sequel to *The Gulag Archipelago*."[77] And so the textual chain lengthens and its structure grows ever more intricate.

5

Erich Auerbach observes that Russian realism "came into its own only during the nineteenth century and indeed only during the second half of it [and] it is fundamentally related rather to Old-Christian than to modern occidental realism,"[78] a comment that surely would have resonated with Solzhenitsyn. In any evaluation of his art, the centrality of the writer's Christian faith to his literary project must be acknowledged. This contrarian critic of the post-Renaissance and post-Enlightenment processes of secularization and the manner in which they shaped our world would also have agreed with Czeslaw Milosz's judgment that for the creative artist,

> There is only one theme: an era is coming to an end which lasted nearly two thousand years, when religion had primacy of place in relation to philosophy, science and art; no doubt this simply meant that people believed in Heaven and Hell. These disappeared from imagination and no poet or painter would be able populate them again, though the models of Hell exist here on earth.[79]

Solzhenitsyn's gulag narratives show one of these infernal models in operation while confirming that in a twentieth-century literary text, traditional depictions of Hell such as those created by Dante or Milton may be present only as symbols, allegories, or cultural citations.[80] In the public debate about the extent to which the Russian people are God-fearingly, God-bearingly religious, begun in 1847 by the pietistically inclined writer Nikolai Gogol and the radical critic Vissarion Belinsky, he sides with the former, posing the question, "In what other country was the practice of repentance, public repentance, as widespread?"[81] Still, contumacious Kostoglotov, perhaps this author's most memorable creation, is an unapologetic atheist, while some of the most important peasant characters, such as Ivan Denisovich, Spiridon and Matryona, are very far from being conventional people of faith. Arguably, they are Eastern

Orthodox Christians in name only. Matryona is as free from sin as a member of the Church may aspire to be, but she is also a "heathen"[82] whose core beliefs are essentially animistic, whereas for Spiridon religion, like socialism or Russia itself, means simply "family."[83] In fact, clerics like the cerebral Father Severyan (*The Red Wheel*) or lay Christians like the folksy Aunt Styofa (*Cancer Ward*) and ethereal Agnia (*The First Circle*) are not that uncommon in the fictions, but most of the time religious values and notions are presented implicitly, even counteractively. In *March 1917*, two middle-aged terrorist harpies, Agnessa and Adalia, wander the streets of revolutionary Petrograd, thrilling and shrilling at the sight of *The Antichrist* going on sale in Nevsky Prospect, that central avenue in Russian literature.[84] Point made!

Yet as *The Red Wheel* also shows, Russia's de-Christianization began in the years and decades before the revolution, owing to some of the same social and cultural factors that were contemporaneously operating in the secularizing societies of Western Europe. After its seizure of power, the Bolshevik party transformed this pre-existing estrangement from religious belief into a nationwide deicidal project, with systematic persecutions and exterminations that changed the character of the country and its people, perhaps irrevocably (see "Nastenka"), though Solzhenitsyn remained hopeful that in the fullness of time his nation would recover its religious soul.

As a rule, this Christian sensibility is a muted presence in the novels and stories, though it is overt in the "Miniatures" and conspicuous in the polemical works. Sometimes it becomes fictively concretized, as when the stern brigadier, Tyurin, warns his fellow prisoners that the Lord punishes those that are unjust in merciless ways ("Ivan Denisovich"); Nerzhin's professor at the University of Rostov, Goryainov-Shakhovskoy, mathematically proves the existence of God[85] (*The First Circle*); or Joseph Stalin, the chieftain of a godless state, makes "a vow to God" that if "he survived in his post" after the Nazi invasion, he would restore the Church, and keeps that promise.[86] Beyond such religiously inflected passages, Solzhenitsyn's prose is suffused with an authorial awareness of a divine *design* that extends through time and space, for all space and time, and beyond. His God, like Alexander Pope's, is a Celestial Architect and a Natural Philosopher.

> If plagues or earthquakes break not Heav'n's design,
> Why then a Borgia, or a Catiline?
> Who knows but he, whose hand the light'ning forms,
> Who heaves old Ocean, and who wings the storms?[87]

To repeat, on some level of authorial perception or faith, the numen is present in *all* of Solzhenitsyn's stories and novels, with the exception, perhaps, of "For the Good of the Cause." It presides over the historical proceedings in *The Red Wheel* and *The Oak and the Calf*, in which the author's providential reading of his literary and supra-literary mission proved to be one of that memoir's most controversial components. I should add that through her investigations into the folkloric and Christological elements in Solzhenitsyn's works, Svetlana Sheshunova has identified a dyad of opposing, faith-based figurative tropes, the Cross and the Wheel, which control the metaphorical register in *The Red Wheel*, but also across the corpus of the literary and non-literary texts.[88]

Nonetheless, Solzhenitsyn ought not to be defined as a Christian writer per se.[89] In fact, he was a passionate anti-dogmatist who ventured to interrogate some of the most important teachings of his church. As a public thinker, he argued that while changing human beings in order to bring them closer to God is an urgent and noble task, so is the need to improve the political and social environments in which they live. These two strands in the writer's thinking found a definitive expression in *The Red Wheel*. Pyotr Stolypin, Solzhenitsyn's favorite statesman of all time, grasps the all-important "paradox" that the historical actor ought to seek a balance between a concern for the common good and considerations of a transcendent kind: "Freedom of action and prosperity are necessary if a man is to stand up to his full height on this earth, but spiritual greatness dwells in eternal subordination, in awareness of oneself as an insignificant particle."[90] Herein lies Solzhenitsyn's fundamental disagreement with the man who wrote *Dead Souls*, for the latter wished to reform the individual reader rather than the reader's world. *The Red Wheel* concludes with Gogol's famous troika, his symbol of Russia's manifest destiny, upended in a world-historical carriage crash. This is no accident.

6

The lives of Solzhenitsyn's characters are conditioned by space. Their physical selves loom textually large *because* they are encased and constricted, sometimes on pain of death, by walls, corridors, landings, stairwells, fences, trenches. The cramped surroundings geometrically adumbrate the characters' ethical and existential dilemmas, reflecting the author's own life experience: "The confined setting is … a result of my own biography. I have spent the greater part of my life in closed premises."⁹¹ These autobiographically themed hermetic loci, which are a function of such constants of the human condition as tyranny, war, poverty and disease, include the frozen world of the labor camp in "Ivan Denisovich" and the dungeons of the Lubyanka in *The First Circle*, where Volodin undergoes the terrifying carceral processing of his body. Soviet prisons were predicated on the notion that humanity is just a situational state of being. Here a diehard communist could be transformed into an "enemy of the people" or a man into a woman, as nearly happens to the tragic Ektov in the story "Ego."⁹² After all, as the cynical hack Golovanov observes, human beings are nothing more than "material involved in a historical event" (*The First Circle*).⁹³ Nonetheless, Solzhenitsyn's heroes and heroines resist this ideological notion of human contingency and strive to retain their personhood even under the most traumatic circumstances, and none more so than Ivan Denisovich Shukhov, the humble, semiliterate peasant depicted in the eponymous tale.

Shukhov's only protection against the forty-degree cold of the Kazakh winter is the clothes on his back: a fibrous shield against the elements. The knowledgeable reader perceives in these scraps of cotton and fabric connections to the writer's own life. When we first meet him, Shukhov is huddled on his bunk, his feet squeezed into the sleeve of his quilted jerkin, which he wears every waking hour, in or out of doors. There is a story behind that prison coat, and it is an extra-textual one. The jerkin is a personal loan from the author to his hero. It can be seen in the famous photograph of Solzhenitsyn scowling at the camera in his prison uniform, a picture he took himself in the spring of 1953 upon his release from the Special Camp at Ekibastuz: one of the most serious selfies in history. The same worn-out jacket makes an appearance in "Matryona's Home" where Ignatich, the author's alter ego, merely *covers* his legs with it: "That jerkin held memories for me: It had kept me warm in the bad years";⁹⁴ in it, we learn from *The Oak and the Calf*, the writer would chop wood when he lived in Ryazan. A journalist who visited him there in December 1962 gives this description of Solzhenitsyn in the first weeks of fame: "He wore a quilted jerkin and a hat with ear flaps. Dumbfounded, I thought of Ivan Shukhov."⁹⁵ The cross-textual story of the jerkin continues into 1969, the year when the cellist Mstislav Rostropovich and his wife, the soprano Galina Vishnevskaya, gave Solzhenitsyn refuge at their villa near Moscow. On the day the writer moved in she noticed a dark object lying on his bed—

Solzhenitsyn's Life and Art | **29**

an old, black quilted jacket like those issued in labor camps, so worn out it had holes. It was wrapped around a thick pillow in a patched pillowcase. One could see that the patches in both jacket and pillowcase had been sewn by a man—they were pieced together with big, awkward stitches. All was neatly tied with a cord from which hung a dull aluminum teakettle. It was as if a man had just returned from a concentration camp and was getting ready to go back.[96]

Vishnevskaya's womanly eye was quick to register the severely masculine appearance of this odd-looking bundle. Of course, the padded jacket as worn by Solzhenitsyn in his domestic environments was not a mythopoetic prop but a supremely casual piece of clothing owned a man who cared nothing for sartorial style or fashion. Yet little by little it became autobiographically textualized as a marker of the writer's former zek identity, with a presence in his fictions ("Ivan Denisovich," "Matryona's Home") as well as witness accounts such as Vishnevskaya's. The jerkin has been exhibited in Geneva (2011),[97] Moscow (2013–14),[98] and St. Petersburg (2014),[99] and is a showpiece in the new Solzhenitsyn museum in Moscow. Thanks to this writer, the *telogreika* or *vatnik* has acquired a totemic literary value second only to that of Akakii Akakievich's *overcoat* in Gogol's eponymous story ("Shinel'"; 1842). It is therefore unfortunate that Russia's liberal opposition, an enthusiastic co-participant in the ongoing coarsening of the country's public discourse, chose this humble piece of clothing, which had kept warm generations of Soviet workers and prisoners, to designate Putin's lower-class supporters as Jerkins (*vatniki*) or Cotton Balls (*vata*).

There are some brilliant minds portrayed, particularly in *The First Circle*, with its population of captive world-class scientists, and *The Red Wheel*, where Professor Olda Andozerskaya shines with a bright academic light that dazzles her lover, the rugged Vorotyntsev; while the prodigal beauty Zinaida Altanskaya, who teaches herself philosophy and literature, is the work's most unusual intellectual presence. On an eerier note, the necromancer Pavel Varsonofiev, the Merlin of the epic, glides along the mystical axes of Russia's past, present and future, his whispers and nightmares a source of apocalyptic warnings about the approaching End. Elsewhere in the epopee we encounter a gallery of notable historical figures, among them prime minister Stolypin, who is identified as Russia's savior-that-might-have-been, and the Bolshevik leader Vladimir Lenin, an ideological fanatic determined to bring down not just the Russian Empire, but Russia itself. A monomaniac of destruction, he is a mixture of the cerebral, the obsessive, and the mundane, and one of those rare Solzhenitsyn characters that is a thoroughly Dostoevskian personality.

Plato famously defined people as featherless bipeds, and the biological realities of the human condition loom large in the fictions. Where bodies are concerned, this author displays a Tolstoyan interest in their health or unhealth, their beauty or their flaws, most prominently, of course, in *Cancer Ward*. Often there is a strong correlation between the characters' physiologies and physiognomies, and their intellectual and moral worth, almost along the lines of Giambattista della Porta, Lavater, and Lombroso. In Solzhenitsyn's narratives, whether you are good or bad, it *shows*, though the exceptionally good-looking Sasha Lenartovich, a budding Bolshevik zealot, is an exception to this rule. Heroes and villains are assigned appropriately sympathetic or grotesque corporeal markers and referents. The author is hard on his evildoers. These unethical uglies are often shown as a body part with a personality attached, in a manner that recalls the words of Nietzsche's Zarathustra: "I walk among men as among the fragments and limbs of men."[100] In *The Red Wheel*, the physical Lenin is a gigantic head that rolls across the spaces of geography and history. Other antiheroes boast faces and torsos that are variously bovine, porcine, saurian, batrachian, piscine, vermicular and even vegetative. The range of nomenclatures and qualifiers, of metaphors and similes is Darwinian: every stage on the evolutionary scale is present on some descriptive or imaginative level. Solzhenitsyn's therianthropes include Stalin's hulking secret police chief, Abakumov, a (sub-apocalyptic?) "red beast" (*krasnyi zver'*)[101] (*The First Circle*), and the partocrat Rusanov, who oozes and glistens like a garden slug (*Cancer Ward*). The narrow-shouldered, dark-haired terrorist Bogrov is a slithering black serpent and the obese revolutionist Parvus is an "elephant" crossed with a "hippopotamus,"[102] a colossal undulating sack of flesh squirting toxic body fluids into arid Lenin as the two conspirators conceive their plots upon a fantastically levitating camp bed (*The Red Wheel*).[103]

Most of the principal characters are male, which is to be expected in this emphatically autobiographical writer who sets so many of his fictions in carceral or military environments. As a rule, Solzhenitsyn's women are fabulated through their relationships with the men in their life: husbands, fathers, lovers, or (Party) bosses, though in *Cancer Ward* nurse Zoya and Dr. Gangart, that novel's two heroines, are fictively co-equal with its central character, Oleg Kostoglotov, to whom they are romantically connected. In *The Red Wheel*, Olda Andozerskaya, the alluring bluestocking who has an affair with Vorotyntsev (not the other way round!), is entirely self-sufficient on her own intellectual and psychological terms, as is freethinking and free-loving Zinaida or the liberal school principal Aglaida Kharitonova. Sometimes the female characters are conclusively confined to the domestic sphere, for instance villagers like the elderly widow Matryona and the young wife Katyona (*The Red Wheel*). Yet always, the cold hand of history intrudes into the heroines' rustic or private spaces and turns them into its witnesses, subjects, or objects. *The Red Wheel* features a range of female personae, several of whom, like the poetic Likonya, passionate Zinaida, and academic Olda, stake out cultural or ideological positions that support the epic's conceptual treatment of revolutionary violence as a homicidal form of national self-indulgence. In general, Solzhenitsyn excels in his depiction of older women, especially women who are past the age of childbearing. Matryona may be a symbolic embodiment of Mother Russia, but she is also a sixty-year-old retiree on a meager pension, untidy and sometimes testy, who has odd little habits and a shy, fleeting smile; and Polya, Georgi and Vera Vorotyntsev's cantankerous old nurse, is the presiding matriarchal figure in *The Red Wheel*, even though her total presence in the epic amounts to a mere dozen pages. And while this writer's plots are consistently patrilineal and the male personalities outnumber and sometimes out-function their female counterparts, the authorial diction is almost never paternalistic.

In fact, the female presences are bearers of important feminine truths that they articulate as full and equal participants in the multivocality of the text, as when they "[express], sometimes implicitly or obliquely, a particular, individualized interpretation of the tragic events of war and revolution."[104] The fictions show the patterns of female resistance, especially a woman's refusal, whether conscious or not, to submit to the defined social and sexual roles that she is assigned by a male-dominated Party and state, or before 1917, by a patriarchal, quasi-feudal society. Some heroines rise above the squalor of everyday Soviet existence by pursuing a romantic ideal that they both assimilate and transcend (Nadya and Simochka in *The First Circle*); or find professional fulfillment in an institutional setting (Vera and Zoya in *Cancer Ward*, Lydia Georgievna in "For the Good of the Cause"); or hold onto an old-world gentility that can be surprisingly effective in thwarting male authority (Anna Modestovna in "What a Pity"). With her insistence on structuring her professional and private life contrary to the epoch's androcentric societal norms, the monarchist Olda Andozerskaya is no less an exponent of early feminism than her political antipode, the Bolshevist Alexandra Kollontai (*The Red Wheel*).

Perhaps because of his biographical distance from the female experience, the author defamiliarizes it in a variety of inventive ways. Often the personality and body of a young woman are narratively filtered through the longing perceptions of a would-be lover: the male gaze lingers, appraises, and records, for the reader's benefit, while revealing its own contingent and range-bound quality. A vivid instance is to be found in *Cancer Ward* where saucy Zoya and cultivated Vera draw the eye of the hyper-masculine but ailing and vulnerable Kostoglotov. *November 1916* features a neatly gendered role-reversal when Olda, just before she is introduced to Vorotyntsev, surreptitiously scans the colonel's brawny figure and weathered features from the corner of a crowded drawing room. Such secret glances between the sexes are not limited to romantic encounters. In "Matryona's Home," Ignatich watches the old woman who has given him shelter with the unspoken, untextualized yearning of a parentless, friendless middle-aged man for maternal affection. Finally and most intriguingly, here and there we encounter a few epicene personalities, notably Lieutenant Nadelashin, a sympathetic prison warden, who sashays rather than struts and harbors a secret passion for sewing dresses (*The First Circle*).

There are few children in Solzhenitsyn. Their absence in his worlds is usually a direct consequence of war or tyranny:

> Nerzhin ... suddenly saw clearly that Stalin had robbed him and Nadya of their children. Even if he was released after serving his sentence and they were together again, his wife would be thirty-six or perhaps forty years old. Too late to have a child.[105]

And if a child is born into one of Solzhenitsyn's worlds, it will often live for just a few weeks or days: Matryona's six sons and daughters all perish in infancy, as do the children of the scientist Gerasimovich (*The First Circle*) and Zinaida's baby boy (*November 1916*). In *The Red Wheel*, the terrible fate of Tsar Nicholas's children hangs like a black promise over the imperial family chapters. One scholar finds that the tsar and tsarina as well as the other parental figures that are present in the saga display "a multitude of nuances in their attitude toward children ... which may reflect an evolution in the author's view of the child."[106] At the same time, when boys and girls and their environments are depicted, the textual treatment can sometimes be sketchy. In "For the Good of the Cause," a story set in a junior technical college, the students are mere silhouettes, raucous units of closely recorded youth slang, while the dramatic proceedings are dominated by the teachers and Party administrators. The boarding school where Ksenia Tomchak (*The Red Wheel*) spends her formative years is never shown in any detail, or even shown at all, although the pedagogical philosophy of its headmistress, the stern but fair Mrs. Kharitonova, is described at some considerable length. Instead, the narrative focuses on Ksenia's extramural connection to the Kharitonov family, with whom she rooms while attending the educational establishment in question. Only in *Love the Revolution* and "Nastenka" do we encounter (brief) descriptions of the classroom and its dynamics of teaching, learning, or slacking off: a surprising omission for a writer who used to be a schoolmaster, and by all accounts a very good one.

Several adolescent characters stand out. Sixteen-year-old Asya in *Cancer Ward* is a nicely drawn portrait of a Soviet bobbysoxer circa 1955 and studious Dyoma, fifteen, who falls hopelessly in love with her, is full of teenage angst, a Russian version of Holden Caulfield. Both suffer from malignant tumors and go under the knife. Fourteen-year-old Kolya Bruyakin (*The Red Wheel*), the village of Kamenka's juvenile delinquent-in-residence, is destined for bigger and badder things in the years of nationwide violence that loom ahead. Such a conclusion is supported by the episodes in *March 1917* that show a succession of gloating "street youths"[107] who enthusiastically participate in the murders and pogroms sweeping revolutionary Petrograd. Finally, there is Kolya's coeval Yurik Kharitonov, the youngest son of the formidable Mrs. Kharitonova, who has two chapters in *April 1917* all to himself. A hormonally charged half-boy, half-man, he inhabits a world of make-believe, pretending that his school satchel is a soldier's knapsack while longing to exchange "ardent kisses" with "one, two, five, or seven" girls of his acquaintance.[108]

Indeed, the human sexual drive, that biological prerequisite of parenthood, is depicted with a fair degree of frequency. Notable in this regard is *Cancer Ward*, with its intensely moving love scenes that mark the stages in Kostoglotov and Zoya's affair. More often, however, Solzhenitsyn's narratives dwell on the emotional preliminaries rather than the subsequent conjoining of bodies. He is particularly good at showing male desire, thwarted or deferred: in "The Right Hand," a cancer patient hungrily eyes the women who cross the verdant park where he is taking the sun, even as he remains wrenchingly aware of his cadaverous appearance. Dotnara Volodina (*The First Circle*) is a sexy Stalinist beauty whose voluptuous appeal intoxicates Stalinist and anti-Stalinist men alike, and the depiction of languid Likonya as the personification of enticing bohemian femininity makes this one of the most memorable portraits in *The Red Wheel*. There are other erotic moments in that saga such as the illicit affairs between Vorotyntsev and Olda, and Kovynev and Zinaida. The latter, who walks about her parents' house naked for her lover's pleasure, possesses a seductive presence that is reminiscent of the bewitching Margarita in Mikhail Bulgakov's novel *The Master and Margarita* (*Master i Margarita*—written 1928–40; published 1966–7). Also in *The Red Wheel*, we meet a predatory wanton, Marusya, whose crimson lips promise, and deliver, a range of forbidden delights to the men of Kamenka, the epic's most important locus of peasant life. This kind of adult writing often entails an elaborately metaphorical adumbration of the sexual act itself, though the scene in which one of Marusya's neighbors, Katyona Blagodareva, goads her husband into lovingly flagellating her with birch twigs inside a bathhouse, is unambiguously revealing of the carnal side in their happy marriage.

At the same time, Solzhenitsyn is keenly aware of the dynamics of revolutionary sexuality, "that volatile ambivalence, that mixture of aversion and attraction" which so often defined relations between hostile classes and races in "The Age of Hatred."[109] Conflicted Volodin (*The First Circle*) is the product of one such loveless union. His Red sailor father took to wife a fragile girl of noble birth and enjoyed every conjugal moment of her submission: "They loved smacking their lips over delicately nurtured young ladies from good homes. That was the most mouthwatering prize the Revolution had to offer them."[110] In "Fracture Points," a working-class Stalinist marries a former landowner's daughter out of the same politico-sexual calculus. Of course, even in times of revolutionary upheaval not every marital or extra-marital situation is an instance of horizontal class warfare. The eponymous heroine in part one of "Nastenka," a Komsomol in good standing, endures a succession of defilements and rapes at the hands of her Bolshevik bosses, followed by a term of service in a secret police brothel, all of which makes this late story the most explicit treatment of sexual abuse in any work by Solzhenitsyn.

An intriguing feature of the fictions is the manner in which they treat young married love. Its depiction is always narratively compressed: once again, a reflection of the author's own biographical experience. Nadya Nerzhina remembers the time when she and Gleb were newlyweds as "a commonplace student marriage,"[111] and nothing more. In "Fracture Points," Part One, a Soviet industrial manager (the son of that blue-blooded daughter) "married one of his classmates, but they had no honeymoon,"[112] and in part two, a post-Soviet banker must buy a flat "so he could get married (to Tanya, who was in her final year in the Faculty of Literature)."[113] Eros is notably absent from both relationships. Even Arseni and Katyona Blagodarev, Solzhenitsyn's exemplars of erotically charged love, enter true marital bliss only after the birth of their second child, and after that bathhouse power exchange. On the other hand, this writer is adept at limning families and their internal dynamics, especially generational tensions and conflicts, which are invariably problematized in the context of history. Impassioned Sonya, the revolution-loving daughter of the patriotic engineer Ilya Arkhangorodsky, berates him for serving an oppressive autocracy as the family sit at their well-appointed dinner table (*The Red Wheel*), and Klara Makarygina, whose brutal father stands high in the Party's favor, deprecates his proletarian credentials to his well-fed face, reducing dastardly Dad to a Stalinist stutter (*The First Circle*). In the epopee, the chapters that describe the lives and times of the Tomchaks, that is, Shcherbaks, and the courtship of Sanya Lazhenitsyn and Ksenia Tomchak, that is, Isaaki Solzhenitsyn and Taissia Shcherbak, amount to a fictionalized history of the writer's family on both sides and show a Tolstoyan spectrum of happy, unhappy, and fair-to-middling relationships and life situations.

The longer works as well as some of the stories such as "Matryona's Home" and "Zakhar-the-Pouch" display a stylistic and fabulatory orientation toward the epic; and all the fictions are encyclopedic in the sense that they offer a comprehensive, factological description of a given social or political milieu or practice. *The Red Wheel* is a historical saga on the grandest of scales that includes hundreds of pages of nonfictional text segregated into dozens of intermittent chapters or sections dealing with a range of political and military topics. Yet even *The First Circle* and *Cancer Ward*, where most of the action takes place inside a single building, describe epochal events, comprehend broad swaths of Russia and the world, and include characters that are larger-than-life, symbolic, or archetypal. Arguably, some of these ensembles are overpopulated. Numbers of prisoners and guards in *The First Circle* lack that extra fictive texture and are therefore not very memorable, even though every one of them was reconstructed by Solzhenitsyn from memory. Many of the historical and invented personalities in *The Red Wheel* do duty as dramatized archival references rather than fully-fledged novelistic personalities. Still, the tetralogy is constructed according to experimental, trans-fictive and post-realist specifications that generate their own formal rules, as I show in chapters seven and nine.

The Red Wheel was conceived and written as a *War and Peace* for the twentieth century, and the status of Tolstoy's fictions as referents for those of Solzhenitsyn is a reminder that Russian literature happens to be peculiarly rich in instances of creative borrowing. A passage or character from a preexisting production acquires a readable presence in a work by another author, where it is reconfigured through some type of stylistic mimicry or imitative recasting. Many a Russian novel is, among many other things, a hypertext, that is, to quote Gérard Genette's definition, a "text derived from a previous text [hypotext] through simple transformation ... or through indirect transformation."[114] This meta-trope shaped the formation of the national canon: "References to external texts or situations inherent in parody, satire and intertextuality have figured prominently in the evolution and fluctuation of literary genres and schools." One sequence of such hypertextual transfers extends from Ivan Turgenev's novel *Home of the Gentry* (*Dvorianskoe gnezdo*; 1859) to *November 1916*, by way of *War and Peace* and *The Kreutzer Sonata* (*Kreitserova sonata*; 1889).[115]

In *Home of the Gentry*, the protagonist, rooted Fyodor Lavretsky, is married to Varvara, a darkly pretty wanton who may be the first *femme fatale* in Russian literature. He reacts to his wife's adultery with an oleaginous Frenchman by falling into a jealous rage, but chooses flight over fight: "Lavretsky began trembling all over and flung himself out of the room; he felt that at that instant he was in a condition to tear her apart, beat her half to death, in peasant fashion strangle her with his own hands."[116]

At a similar moment of marital crisis Pierre Bezukhov, one of the main heroes of *War and Peace*, who is described as being of a peasant-like appearance, behaves toward his flamboyantly promiscuous wife in a manner that is just as agricultural, but a good deal less tremulous:

> "I'll kill you!" he shouted, and seizing the marble top of a table with a strength he had never before felt, he made a step toward her brandishing the slab.
>
> Hélène's face became terrible, she shrieked and sprang aside.... He felt the fascination and delight of frenzy. He flung down the slab, broke it, and swooping down on her with outstretched hands shouted, "Get out!" in such a terrible voice that the whole house heard it with horror.[117]

One can almost hear Tolstoy's authorial voice whispering into Turgenev's authorial ear: this is how it's done!

The next scene in this chain of connubial confrontations occurs in *The Kreutzer Sonata*. Finding himself in the same predicament as Pierre, the brooding Vasily Pozdnyshev throws a paper weight in the direction of Mrs. Pozdnyshev, though not actually *at* her: he is constitutionally incapable of Bezukhov's strong-arm tactics. The token nature of this act of husbandly violence, with a small item of office decor substituting for the massive marble slab, makes the scene intertextually parodic, an unusual example of self-referential burlesque within the Tolstoy oeuvre. At the same time, the antihero's gesture is proleptically sinister, for it anticipates Pozdnyshev's eventual murder of his wife by means of a dagger thrust through her corset and into her abdomen, an episode which echoes Raskolnikov's murder of the moneylender in *Crime and Punishment* (*Prestuplenie i nakazanie*; 1866) and, in fact, competes with it on the level of graphic descriptiveness.

Finally, we come to the episode in *November 1916* where the Vorotyntsev couple, their marriage under strain because of Georgi's affair with Olda, arrive at a country hotel to celebrate Mrs. Vorotyntseva's birthday. Here in a "little square room,"[118] one of those constricting spaces that are so central to Solzhenitsyn's axiological purposes, the colonel confesses he has been unfaithful, though he forbears to reveal his lover's name.

> His sword hung like a threat on the naked wall behind them ...[119]
>
> He ... directed his full gaze on his wife (he could still see his sword on the wall out of the corner of his eye).[120]

The officer's curved blade (*shashka*) so menacingly suspended at eye level serves as a counter-allusion to the fateful dagger that hangs over the sofa in the Pozdnyshev home, yet when Alina thinks to herself that her husband had "wounded her mortally,"[121] this is merely a marital metaphor. As we learn in the course of the saga, there is a distinct tinge of melodrama to this heroine's interactions with her stolid spouse. On the same plane of figurative representation, the blade's crescent shape corresponds to the halting, *elliptic* way in which the colonel gives Alina the bad news: "His tongue could not utter it, he could not find words."[122]

Earlier I referred to this writer's Tolstoyan proclivities. In fact, the novels and stories feature several ontological meetings between Solzhenitsyn and his great predecessor. The most remarkable of these textual encounters occurs in chapter two of *August 1914*. The teenage Sanya Lazhenitsyn visits Tolstoy on his estate of Yasnaya Polyana to question—challenge—him on the details of his teachings:

> "But are you sure, Lev Nikolayevich, that you don't exaggerate the power of human love? Or at any rate of what is left of it in modern man? What if love is not so strong, not necessarily present in all men, what if love cannot prevail ... wouldn't that mean that your teaching lacks ...?"—he couldn't finish the phrase—"is extremely premature?"[123]

Here Solzhenitsyn allows Sanya to borrow one of his most controversial ideas. In a 1983 TV interview with the French journalist Bernard Pivot, the writer seemed to be addressing the shade of Tolstoy as much as his audience of Gallic viewers:

> Christianity cannot give up its maxim, Christianity rightfully [*pravomerno*] calls on us to love. ... But when we descend into the sphere of ordinary life, to call for love at present, today, in everyday conversations, everyday decisions, means to be ineffective. We may call for love, but before we do so we ought to at least call for justice. At least try not to go against your conscience, if you find it impossible to love then don't, but don't violate your conscience. That is the first step.[124]

The notion that the Christian imperative of love is "ineffective" has an almost Nietzschean ring, viz., "My brothers, love of the neighbor I do not recommend to you: I recommend to you love of the farthest."[125] Like Nietzsche and Tolstoy, Solzhenitsyn had the courage to pose supremely uncomfortable questions to the society and culture of which he was a part. One should add that while the author, in his own words, had "great sympathy for simple and defenseless people like Matryona or Ivan Denisovich," he felt "an even greater sympathy for those who fight for universal justice," because "ordinary decency is not a sufficient response to world evil."[126]

Gore Vidal called Solzhenitsyn a "noble engineer" who is "good at describing how things work,"[127] again, just like Tolstoy. "Ivan Denisovich" and *The First Circle* are anthropological guidebooks to the gulag, *Cancer Ward* shows us the medical practices of a mid-twentieth-century hospital, "For the Good of the Cause" explains the conventions of provincial governance in the Khrushchev era, and "Fracture Points" dissects the structure of the Soviet military-industrial complex. Occasionally, the stories and novels become overtly didactic: take for instance the concluding section of "Matryona's Home," with its message that without righteous people Russia shall perish, or the way that *Cancer Ward* cites Tolstoy's moral tale "What Men Live By" ("Chem liudi zhivy"; 1885) and then updates it for the age of Stalin and Hitler. *The Red Wheel* saw Solzhenitsyn develop a new set of formal techniques adequate to his purpose of narrating the fall of the Russian Empire and with it, an entire national way of life. Just compare the treatment of Joseph Stalin in *The First Circle* and Vladimir Lenin in the epic. Solzhenitsyn's Draculean Stalin is a lampoon, a nocturnal grotesque who is as pathetic as he is evil, whereas the passionately pedestrian Lenin of *The Red Wheel* is a cool study in twentieth-century cultural psychology.

7

Moscow is far from being the fulcrum of Solzhenitsyn's universe, as it was for so many other writers and poets. It is small-town and rural Russia that looms large in the writer's heart and his fictions. Anne Lounsbery explains that

> Russian letters' awareness (or invention) of a "provincial problem" dates back to the eighteenth century ... but it was the work of Nikolai Gogol that transformed the provincial backwater into one of Russian literature's governing tropes ... [a] trope of the wretched and anonymous provincial place.[128]

The author replaces this hoary image with his own fictive geography. For him, the provinces are historically differentiated loci of national authenticity, sites of collective memory. In "Zakhar-the-Pouch," Kulikovo Field, where a Muscovite army once defeated a Mongol host, is reconstructed as a cultural teaching space, but one which is populated by Soviet peasants with their own dialect and way of life; "Ego" and "Times of Crisis" correlate the forested landscapes of the central Russian province of Tambov with the events of the civil war period; and in "No Matter What" the Angara, one of the great Siberian rivers, is transfigured into a sacral watercourse consecrated to that land beyond the Urals. What this writer values in cities and towns is rootedness, of the demographic and architectural kind, which is why authentically Russian Kostoglotov is so charmed by authentically Asian Tashkent with its tea taverns, souks, and adobe houses (*Cancer Ward*).

As for Moscow, in its monumental Stalinist iteration it is a cold, pharaonic metropolis where "the sky ... is low. And people walk about in a herd."[129] (When he was offered a Moscow apartment during the period of his official fame, Solzhenitsyn turned it down out of a dislike for these pastures of concrete and stone.) Things were different before Soviet planners set about turning the ancient capital into a Stalinist *Welthauptstadt*. Vorotyntsev, who was born and grew up in the provinces, sees the city as an urban idyll:

> ... Boulevard after boulevard, building after building ... the great houses ... the spacious grounds behind them. And then, in a lane hard by, the sort of tavern you would find in a run-down country town, a cheap bathhouse, life going on as it had two centuries ago, people drinking tea from samovars in weedy yards.[130]

The writer admires St. Petersburg/Petrograd/Leningrad/St. Petersburg as an aesthetic locale, but its abstract perfection of form lacks spiritual resonance for this believer in organic, communal development. In *The Red Wheel*, major sections of which are set in the imperial capital, its streets, squares, and buildings acquire the aspect of stage spaces where the demonstrations and riots that bring down the tsar unfold in the manner of a public performance or even a "play,"[131] though this revolution would not be televised.

The national collapse of 1917 set in train a series of events that caused Petrograd to lose its status as Russia's pre-eminent city within a year, yet in Solzhenitsyn's reading, this outcome was implicit in the capital's problematic status as an artificial creation of Peter the Great:

> So concluded the two-hundred-year-long historical process whereby the whole of Russia found its expression in this city, which was forcibly erected by Peter's knobstick and Italian architects in the fenlands of the north, ON A MARSH WHERE THEY DON'T THRESH GRAIN, BUT

THE BREAD THEY EAT IS WHITER THAN OURS. Now the city itself was being given expression not by the thinkers whose books lined the shelves of its somber Public Library, nor the loquacious deputies in the State Duma, but by the street bullies who went about smashing shop windows because the mountainous consignment of bread the marsh had been expecting was not delivered in time.[132]

Solzhenitsyn is the sorrowful recorder of the degradation of the Russian countryside during the seven decades of communist rule. In "Matryona's Home" and *The First Circle*, urban outsiders visit farming settlements that are dying a collectivized, polluted death. To quote an American commentator, these are "not villages so much as population clusters."[133] Many consider "Matryona's Home" the foundational text of the Village Prose movement whose representatives such as Valentin Rasputin and Viktor Astafiev showed the wounds inflicted on the peasantry and its way of life by the practices of Soviet modernity. In his post-exilic binary tales, Solzhenitsyn goes back in time to record the brutal beginnings of this transformation in the 1920s ("Nastenka"; "Apricot Jam") as well as its wretched aftermath during the post-communist transition ("No Matter What"; "Zhelyabuga Village").

The writer always looked to Russia's rural population as the keeper of the nation's authentic values and portrayed it accordingly. Nonetheless, he retained a clear-eyed view of the parochialism and small-mindedness of country life, as we can see from his depictions of peasant communities as they existed before the revolution. Sanya Lazhenitsyn's native village of Sablinskaya is a place where educated speech is considered "strange and ridiculous,"[134] "'to get a letter' … was pretentious, ostentatious,"[135] and any divergence from traditional norms of behavior or belief invites "disgust and derision,"[136] while in the semi-idyllic Kamenka (the home of the Blagodarev couple), "the nickname your village inflicts on you … is meant to rankle. Those who invent it have suffered in their time and want to see you squirm":[137] an unexpected parallel with twenty-first-century American high schools.

Although Solzhenitsyn had a "hatred for cities, asphalt, tall buildings,"[138] he was fond of Ryazan,[139] the central Russian town where he lived before and during the dawn of his fame.[140] Dearest of all to the author is nature, which he loves in the manner of a town dweller for whom such sylvan spaces possess the charm of remoteness. These attitudes inform the very popular "Miniatures," prose poems that eulogize the landscapes of his homeland while deploring their devastation by an industrializing and collectivizing state. The "Miniatures" contain descriptions of animals and birds, which are unapologetically anthropomorphized, as are trees and even insects. Nonetheless, Solzhenitsyn is not a nature writer per se. In his prose, mountains, forests, fields, rivers, and lakes are metaphorical locations of the national spirit, but ultimately evoke the biblical account of the Creation, whether they remain pristine or, as so often is the case, are deformed by the hand and machines of man. In either case, the textual representation of these sites is usually scripted as a direct projection of, or an implied-authorial counterpoint to, a given character's ethical stance or situation. Even Solzhenitsyn's unsympathetic characters such as Lenin (*The Red Wheel*) and Marshal Zhukov ("Times of Crisis") are alive to the beauties of nature, though they respond to them in ways that are expressive of their corrupted inner selves. On the day that news of the February Revolution reaches him in faraway Switzerland, the Bolshevik leader climbs one of the hills that overlook the city of Zurich, out of the pragmatic notion that "in the mountains you can stretch your legs and organize your thoughts."[141]

> He could see a large stretch of the lake with its serene, metallic waters. Beyond it the whole of Zurich lay at the bottom of an airy basin [*pod kotlovinoi vozdukha*] that had never been blasted by exploding shells or shaken by the shouts of the revolutionary crowd. The sun was setting, not down there but almost at eye level, behind the shallow slope of the Uetlichberg.[142]

The antihero's nihilistic imagination transmutes this picture postcard view into a scene of violent class conflict complete with artillery barrage. But there are additional Leninist meanings encoded here. In *August 1914*, the Leader's bare brow, his most distinctive physical feature, was likened to an "upended cauldron" (*perevërnutyi kotël*),[143] so that now this Lenin-inflected description of the valley acquires, via the intratextual cognate pairing *kotël—kotlovina*, the quality of a cranial self-projection. Truly, it's all inside Lenin's head.

Love the Revolution depicts in sometimes humorous detail city boy Nerzhin's struggles to learn his way around horses as a Red Army conscript in a transport unit, though eventually he teaches himself to care for them and even to commune with them. Matryona's cabin is a Noah's ark of domestic fauna, including a wonderfully drawn lame cat, the most vivid animal presence in the oeuvre. Mostly, however, the different orders of the zoological kingdom are present as a source of emblems, symbols, and metaphors, with *The First Circle* containing a highly developed system of reptilian and ruminant images that do textual duty as satirical markers for the Stalinists and the system they serve. Such figurative language can also be arboreal: in *Cancer Ward* Vera and Oleg separately search the city of Tashkent for the fantastical *uriuk* or Asian apricot tree, their secret token of love and life, and in one of the "Miniatures," "The Larch" ("Listvennitsa"), the eponymous conifer serves as an allegory of courage and fortitude. I should add that this writer's worlds are landlocked: other than the scenes of mutiny on the ships of the Imperial Russian Navy (*March 1917*), the sea as such lacks any presence in his prose, except in the metaphorical register ("Matryona's Home"; *The Gulag Archipelago*).

Although Solzhenitsyn is a highly imaginative artist, he is seldom whimsical in an exuberant, Gogolian sense. In one of his essays he notes that Gogol and Bulgakov are distinguished by the "glitter of humor [*blesk iumora*], which is so rare in Russian literature," and in a revealing comment, concedes that

> no author in Russian literature has given me less than Gogol, for, simply put, I borrowed *nothing* from him. He is more foreign to me than any other writer. Whereas with Bulgakov, on the whole, it is the opposite: although I did not borrow anything from him either, and the features of our writing are completely different, and I was unable entirely to accept his most important novel [*The Master and Margarita*], I retain a warm, familial feeling for him, truly seeing him as an elder brother, although I am quite unable to explain the nature of this affinity.[144]

Still, both *The First Circle* and *The Red Wheel* contain some Gogolian resonances, with the latter work featuring a gallery of eccentrically shaped noses. And on the same note of literary non-appropriation, Solzhenitsyn admitted to Alexander Schmemann that he had a "dislike of Turgenev" (*neliubov' k Turgenevu*).[145] In *The First Circle*, ethereal Agnia, who likes "to wander in the forest for days on end … studying the secrets of the forest," finds Turgenev's famous nature scenes "superficial."[146]

The closest this writer comes to a magical sleight of pen à la Gogol or Bulgakov is in "Matryona's Home" and chapter forty-four of *The First Circle*, which show distant villages populated by dark omens and attended by sinister foreshadowings; and in places, *The Red Wheel*, with its mystic symbols mystically imprinted on the bodies and fates of its characters. Yet other than the extraordinary Lenin-Parvus sequence in that epic, there is no integrative scripting of the real and the magical, and text and extra-text, into a single ontological continuum, as happens in Gogol's tales or *The Master and Margarita*. The diviner

Varsonofiev, who makes occasional appearances in successive Knots of the epopee, is the only occult character in the whole of Solzhenitsyn. His terrifying visions of a grotesque service in a boarded-up church and the Christ Child carrying a bomb into the Petersburg stock exchange extend the epic's "discrete stretches of time" to the astral sphere. Yet even here, there is an autobiographical element at work, for Varsonofiev's phantasmagorias are actually dreams dreamt by the author. Always the careful recorder of his own thoughts, he kept a notebook at his bedside where he would jot down his nighttime reveries,[147] a habit Varsonofiev is allowed to share.[148] *The Red Wheel* acquired its dreamscape, a necessary element in any epic, straight from the writer's own nightmares.

As this private detail shows, Solzhenitsyn was eminently grounded, even when deploying his subconscious for a literary purpose. Natalia Solzhenitsyna, who knew him better than anyone else, explains: "He has this uncanny ability to see certain things that I do not and most people do not. It is not mystical. There is just a certain level of profundity that sets him apart."[149] Indeed, despite the undeniably vatic accents in many of the polemical writings, Solzhenitsyn is best described not as an ideological prophet but a cultural rebel. He possessed the same "heretical impulse" that Bloom discerns in Dickens,[150] one of Solzhenitsyn's favorite novelists,[151] and always enjoyed pricking the bubble of the self-important and self-satisfied, both in his books and his public statements.

Another parallel with Dickens is Solzhenitsyn's skill at integrating inhabited spaces and personal artifacts within the narrated world and endowing them with a peculiar life, even personhood, of their own. Matryona's cabin is as vivid a domestic structure as the Dombey house in *Dombey and Son*, while the scuffed table across which prisoner Gerasimovich and his wife meet at the Lefortovo prison (*The First Circle*) may be the most memorable piece of furniture in all of twentieth-century Russian literature. Solzhenitsyn also shares with the author of *Oliver Twist* an ear for the vernacular. This one-time playwright reproduced, explored, or subverted established patterns of speech with theatrical flair. His characters' voices are beautifully individualized, their vocabulary and tone almost always spot-on. The fictions abound in sociolects that are descriptive of every segment of Soviet society during its seventy years of existence, while *The Red Wheel* extends this range of recorded speech patterns back to the late imperial period. Solzhenitsyn's heroes are excellent talkers, even if some of them, like cautious Nerzhin or flinty Vorotyntsev, occasionally require an external prompt to let loose rhetorically. The novels and stories contain pages of dynamic dialogue that holds the reader's attention even when it pertains to specialized topics such as electrical engineering (*The First Circle*) or industrial pollution on Siberia's Angara River ("No Matter What"). Some characters are assigned a memorably crafted idiolect that defines the fictional personality in question, as in the case of Dashkin, an embittered Red Army soldier (*Love the Revolution*) who likes to boast of the murders he committed in his Bolshevik youth, or Natasha Anichkova, a bubbly nurse who is amazingly fond of telling tall tales (*March 1917*) that are one part Gogol and two parts Tynianov. Dialogue is often employed as a tool for putting across key ideas or concepts: talking points, rhetorically formatted. One example is the lengthy, two-chapter argument about the dialectic between the communist Rubin and the elitist Sologdin (*The First Circle*), in the course of which Marxism-Leninism is deconstructed down to its dusty foundations, but there are many others. And even in the theatrical works, which critical opinion deemed not very stageable—though in recent years they have been playing to full houses in Russia—what the characters say and how they say it can be very interesting, sometimes more so than the characters themselves. Like George Bernard Shaw's plays, these productions are not so much dramas of action as dramas of ideas.

To use Auerbach's description of late Roman pagan and Christian writing, the representation of public events occasionally hinges on the "invasion of a glaringly pictorial realism into the elevated style" ("The Easter Procession," *The Red Wheel*).[152] On a related note, Solzhenitsyn's fictions abound in instances of the grotesque, for the discontinuities of Russian and Soviet history provided him with plenty of material in this regard. In *March 1917*, the devolving fortunes of the imperial regime approach their nadir when the tsar's preantepenultimate prime minister, the doddering Ivan Goremykin, is succeeded by the tottering Boris Stürmer: "Goremykin's two widely separated prongs of beard were replaced by a single long, limp mop which looked as if it was glued on like Santa Claus's whiskers."[153] *Love the Revolution* presents for our inspection a local secret police chief, a tall hunchback with the look of a communist Quasimodo and "the confident walk of one who rules over the land."[154] There is a connection here to one of Solzhenitsyn's favorite writers: "The incongruous distortion which characterizes the grotesque becomes an essential element of Dickens's faithful depiction of reality."[155]

Solzhenitsyn has an astringent sense of humor, though it is one that normally operates on the plane of sarcasm or pastiche. He takes a wicked delight in mocking political jargon, as in the portrait of Rakhmankul Shamsetdinov, an ill-educated bore who travels up and down the country giving soporific lectures on Marxist-Leninist philosophy (*The First Circle*). But it is when he goes to the source that Solzhenitsyn strikes literary gold. His fictional Lenin

(*The Red Wheel*) is a concatenation of cleverly ironized internal monologues and external rants, many of them verbatim quotations from the Leader's writings. This rhetorical chowder of cod ideology, spiced with four- and forty-letter words reviling the bourgeois enemy and his "opportunist" collaborators, continuously boils inside the "cauldron" of Lenin's head from whence it pours out in an incontinent stream of (class) consciousness: "We carry out a socialist revolution in Switzerland—the only way to deliver the Swiss masses from rising prices and hunger!"[156] Such fictive fun, however, must always serve a purpose: "You have to experience our crude Soviet propaganda to realize that there is no way of responding other than through satire; it takes the sharp thrust of satire to shift this ton of lies."[157]

As the example of Lenin's abortive Swiss revolution shows, Solzhenitsyn has a knack for picking out and turning to his writerly advantage the quirks of history. In *March 1917*, there is a scene that takes place inside the offices of Aleksandr Balk, the mayor of Petrograd, during the early days of the revolution:

> A Frenchwoman accompanied by a maid managed to make her way inside. She was unhappy and persistent: she had been unable to find any white bread anywhere, but rye bread made her ill. Balk gave the order, and the woman was served a French roll [*frantsuzskaia bulka*] on a tray. The visitor was in raptures and departed lavishing thanks.[158]

The author had learned of this incident from a memoir by Balk kept in the Hoover Institution Archive at Stanford (it has since been published).[159] In the epic, the episode is reconfigured as a satirical allusion to Marie Antoinette and her cakes. Earlier we learn that a likeness of the French queen decorates Empress Alexandra's bedroom[160] and chapters later witness the latter conjure up an image of Marie Antoinette inspecting her Swiss Guards.[161] This sequence of clues complements, and corrects, the enthusiastic references to the French revolution made by a number of historically minded historical actors, chief among them Aleksandr Kerensky, the future head of the Provisional Government. His conceits—he likes to imagine himself as a reincarnation of Danton or even Napoleon—call to mind a passage in Jean-Paul Sartre's *Nausea* (*La Nausée* [1938]): "They explain the new by the old—and the old they explain by the older still, like those historians who turn a Lenin into a Russian Robespierre, and a Robespierre into a French Cromwell: when all is said and done, they have never understood anything at all."[162] Solzhenitsyn had his differences with Sartre, but the author of *The Red Wheel* would have nodded yes to the line I just quoted.

Finally, music is a frequent presence, whether as the subject of cultural commentary, as when the schoolteacher Ignatich and the peasant widow Matryona discuss the merits of Chaliapin's singing and Glinka's romances ("Matryona's Home"), or as a referent for a particular character, for instance, the physician Vera Gangart, for whom Tchaikovsky's ballet *Sleeping Beauty* is the soundtrack of her solitude, and her love for the ex-prisoner Kostoglotov (*Cancer Ward*).

In fact, for long stretches Solzhenitsyn's life was lived to the accompaniment of music. His first wife, Natalya Reshetovskaya, was a semi-professional musician, the cellist Mstislav Rostropovich was one of his closest friends, and his middle son, Ignat, began a successful career as a pianist and conductor during the Solzhenitsyn family's domicile in the United States. While living in Vermont, the writer would review the local public radio station's music programming schedule in order to select the week's listening in advance.[163] He adhered to the same routine after he returned to Russia, where his station of choice was *Orfei*.[164] According to Mrs. Solzhenitsyna, "he liked music that showed interior restraint," but whose "emotional content should expand the rigid form."[165] The author's preferences ran to the German and Russian Romantics: "In music, I like Tchaikovsky above all the others. If I were told that there was only one piece [of music] to be left in the world, I would choose his Sixth Symphony, even though it might seem that I am closer to Beethoven."[166] However, to the culturologist Solomon Volkov he confided that when he was writing, "he first of all hear[d] the music of Beethoven."[167] In *Cancer Ward*, a recovering Kostoglotov recalls the "restless strained beginning" of Tchaikovsky's Fourth Symphony[168] and hears "Beethoven's four muffled chords of fate" as he notices the first signs of the de-Stalinization campaign.[169] The writer was also fond of Bach and Brahms,[170] and among twentieth-century composers, Sibelius[171] as well as Shostakovich,[172] who he hoped might one day write the music for *Tanks Know the Truth!*,[173] Solzhenitsyn's film script about the Kengir camp uprising. His favorite genres were symphonies and piano pieces. Mrs. Solzhenitsyna reports that in later years her husband developed an interest in Wagner, respecting the creator of the *Ring* as one of those artists who "pursued large-scale goals."[174] That said, Ignat Solzhenitsyn insists—and he should know—that his father was above all a Schubert man.[175]

8

Like many bookish children, Solzhenitsyn started composing stories almost as soon as he learned to read: "From the age of nine, I knew I was going to be a writer, although I didn't know what I was going to write about."[176] Lyudmila Saraskina's biography contains hitherto unknown details about his juvenilia, which predictably fall under the heading of adventure or science fiction and bear titles such as "Land of the Pyramids" and "The Rays."[177] Solzhenitsyn did not think his *Kindernovellen* worthy of study or publication and it took some persuasion on the biographer's part to get him to share these childhood opuscules. In truth, the interest they present is purely biographical, as early pointers to a literary future. Yet if we go forward a few years, the picture changes.

On November 18, 1936,[178] as he was walking down a tree-lined boulevard in Rostov-on-the-Don, the city of his youth, the seventeen-year-old Sanya Solzhenitsyn, then a Leninist of a romantic bent, conceived the idea for a large-scale fictional work about the Russian Revolution, after "a reading of *War and Peace* had fired his imagination."[179] The novel he thought up during that youthful writerly promenade would become *The Red Wheel*, but even then the project's structure, minus its distinctive multiple time frames, was already taking shape in his mind. All in all, it took the author fifty-five years to bring his masterwork to completion, for World War II, prison, exile, cancer, and his literary commitments of the 1950s and 1960s intervened: history preventing the writing of history. Solzhenitsyn later explained:

> Camp existence ... seemed to be leading me away from the central theme I wanted to work on—the history of our revolution. On the other hand, it turned out to be God's wish, as they say, for the camp experience was the ideal preparation for that other theme, which really *was* the main one.[180]

So in a private authorial sense, the writer's best-known productions, the novels and stories that won him the Nobel Prize and fixed his presence in the public imagination, were but a vast detour on the road to *The Red Wheel*. A paradox? Well, perhaps.

Solzhenitsyn's wartime works were lost in the bowels of the Lubyanka, though to judge by the unfinished novel *Love the Revolution*, which dates from the time when he was a prisoner at the Marfino sharashka, these were probably realist but not really socialist. Together with his other papers, the manuscript was preserved and later returned to the author by a young female MGB[181] officer who became the inspiration for Simochka, Nerzhin's prison girlfriend in *The First Circle*. The poems and plays Solzhenitsyn wrote in the camp, thousands of lines composed entirely in his head in an amazing,

Homeric feat of mnemonic prowess,[182] anticipate the themes of the prose works that would eventually bring him fame. As we saw, these prison writings feature several characters that would later appear in *The First Circle*, or in the case of Vorotyntsev, *The Red Wheel*. Yet even after his release into *perpetual exile*, or subsequently as a schoolteacher in the Russian provinces, when he was at last able to put down his texts on paper and work at a table, however small and rickety, the author continued to function in a clandestine mode, always on guard against spies and snitches.

If in the late 1950s one of those busybodies had peered through the window of Solzhenitsyn's wooden house in the central Russian city of Ryazan, he would have glimpsed a curious scene. A middle-aged schoolteacher[183] living a life of "modest comfort and degrading conformity"[184] spends his entire free time composing novels, stories, and plays. He writes day in, day out, calmly, steadily, doggedly, filling thousands upon thousands of sheets of cheap foolscap with tiny, neatly executed script. All his productions are autobiographical, and many of them are prodigiously long. He shows his writings only to his wife and a few trusted friends. He avoids people, lest they learn of his private literary activities. He secretes his manuscripts in cunningly designed hiding places. He refuses to read published authors, for he considers them hacks, liars, or sellouts. He never knows "creative crises, fits of despair and impotence."[185] Surely, our hypothetical snoop would have concluded, the schoolteacher is a graphomaniac, that peculiar, tragic Russian type. Yet it so happened that among the thousands of compulsive writers to be found across the length and breadth of the Soviet Union, the schoolmaster from Ryazan was the one real thing, an artist destined for greatness.

Many at the time considered the publication of "Ivan Denisovich" a miracle. This was a view shared by the author: "The appearance of my tale in the Soviet Union of 1962 could ... be compared to a phenomenon that defies physical laws, a situation where objects would rise instead of falling, or cold stones would grow hot of their own accord."[186] A striking simile by this writer with a scientific mind!

Just before "Ivan Denisovich" came out, the poet Anna Akhmatova warned its creator, "You do realize that a month from now you will be the most famous person on the planet?"[187] The appearance of the tale caused a sense of excitement and shock that rivaled the impact of Khrushchev's Secret Speech six years earlier. Thousands of readers felt that the author had changed not just the country but their own lives: the beginning of the intense relationship between Solzhenitsyn's texts and their receptors that would endure until

his expulsion from the USSR, and beyond. As Rozanov observed of a writer whom Solzhenitsyn admired,

> The *miracle* of Dostoevsky's creations lies in their erasure of the distance between the subject (the reader) and the object (the author), by virtue of which the latter becomes *the most cherished* [*rodnoi*] of all the writers that have ever lived and even, perhaps, of all future writers, or all possible writers.[188]

In the weeks that followed the publication of "Ivan Denisovich" its author made a point of "resisting the temptations of fame"[189] by conducting himself in a reserved and cautious manner. In fact, he was exhilarated. Upon receiving an advance copy of *Novy Mir* containing his tale, he told his wife, "My star has risen!"[190] Hubris? No, just another metaphorical statement of the truth.

As for hubris, Cyril Connolly once warned, "Whom the gods wish to destroy they first call promising."[191] Solzhenitsyn's early reviewers certainly called him that and much more, even a second Tolstoy. The stories that subsequently appeared in *Novy Mir*, such as "Matryona's Home" and "Zakhar-the-Pouch," gave further proof of his talent. Yet, this newly acquired reputation could only be sustained if Solzhenitsyn were to produce a work of appropriately Tolstoyan scope, length, and power. Fortunately, he delivered. It was after the publication of *The First Circle* and *Cancer Ward* that the author received critical endorsement as a living classic, in Russia clandestinely, outside it openly, and the success of the two novels led directly to the Nobel Prize.

During his brief period of official acceptance Solzhenitsyn operated more or less in plain view as a practicing member of the Union of Writers and a candidate for the Lenin literature prize. The installation of Brezhnev's neo-Stalinist regime in 1964 and mounting official harassment thereafter once again constrained the logistics of his creative enterprise, but now he had dozens of helpers and thousands of *samizdat* readers to provide him with feedback and moral support. Soon after he fell out of favor with the authorities his domestic circumstances also changed. His marriage to Natalya Reshetovskaya, portrayed as Nadya Nerzhina in *Love the Revolution* and *The First Circle*, had been in trouble for some years when in 1968 he met beautiful, clever Natalia Svetlova, a young mathematician who was an active member of Moscow's dissident community. She became the love of his life, the mother of his children, and his literary assistant and public spokesman. They married in 1973, after his divorce from Reshetovskaya finally came through. If Solzhenitsyn "never had an inner censor, was pure before himself and the sheet of white paper lying in front of him,"[192] then by the same token he had lacked an editor, that stern, indispensable co-participant in the creative process whose job is to appraise, delete, improve. True, for a brief time this function was ably performed by Aleksandr Tvardovsky, the head of *Novy Mir*, but Solzhenitsyn's relationship with the larger-than-life poet and Party grandee was too emotionally charged for the arrangement to endure.[193] After meeting Svetlova the author finally acquired *his* editor, yet one who was never afraid to examine his manuscripts with a critical eye. Recalling the time when he was working on *April 1917*, the concluding novel of *The Red Wheel*, Solzhenitsyn writes:

> Alya copied each chapter into an IBM machine, using the wide margins of the printout to jot down points of disagreement, offer advice, and suggest

transpositions, contractions, and occasionally excisions. Her comments were a form of quality control that at times irritated me and at other times filled me with admiration.[194]

Mrs. Solzhenitsyn is just as frank about the dynamics of the editorial process. "Sometimes we have real fights over this or that page or line," she told me in Moscow when her husband was still alive. While fully sharing his worldview and public commitments, this gifted woman brought to their joint trans-literary project her own complementary perspectives, which included an informed knowledge of life in the United States and the textures of its culture.

Александр и Наталия Солженицыны. Вильямсбург (Вирджиния), 4 июля 1975

Once he had set up home in Vermont, the author could revisit his published texts and tinker with them at his leisure, as he did in the case of *The First Circle* but also "Ivan Denisovich," "Incident at Kochetovka Station," and of course *August 1914*. Although already in print, that novel was now substantially expanded. For the first time ever, Solzhenitsyn was living the life of a professional novelist. The house at Cavendish, where he spent eighteen prodigiously productive years, has been described as a family-operated literary "factory,"[195] with husband, wife, mother-in-law and, as they grew up, the children all involved in the collective enterprise, workers in a "cosmic cottage industry."[196] Solzhenitsyn needed all the help he could get, for he was consumed by the gigantic task of completing *The Red Wheel*. On his own admission, during his years in America the writer "never picked up the phone,"[197] though in 1992 he took a call from President Boris Yeltsin when the latter was visiting the United States. Occasionally he interrupted his labors to jot off a topical article or deliver a public speech such as the celebrated Harvard Address, but his magnum opus always remained his chief priority. Closeted in his literary keep, Solzhenitsyn was now known among his Russian readers as "the sage of Vermont" or "the Vermont recluse." Meanwhile echoes of the writer's enigmatic presence penetrated into the farthest reaches of the American cultural consciousness, where they sometimes became strangely refracted. In Stephen King's horror novel *Firestarter* (1980), a group of cantankerous Mainers sit in a rural general store chewing the cud about the Green Mountain State next door, with its income tax, "snooty bottle law," as well as a certain "Russian laid up in his house like a Czar, writing books no one could understand."[198]

As Solzhenitsyn toiled away on his epic in the quiet of a New England forest, the Soviet Union began to implode and disintegrate, in ways that reminded the author of the patterns of Russian imperial collapse he was concurrently depicting. He grew anxious about the danger of "Februarism," a repetition of the historical blunders that turned the democratic revolution of February 1917 into a prelude to tyranny.[199] Nonetheless, he recused himself from publicly commenting on the events that were unfolding in his homeland. For much of the perestroika period he kept his own counsel, seeming to abandon his former vatic mode of self-presentation for a Delphic one. The truth was simpler:

> I wanted to warn Gorbachev, "Don't pull the thread if you're not a tailor." But when you are not in a position to criticize and find it hard to give praise, what is left? Only silence. So I kept silent. (Yet with all that euphoria and elation about, I could not even give my reasons.)[200]

And so he waited and worried and hoped, until 1990 and the publication of his essay "Rebuilding Russia," a current-affairs addendum to *The Red Wheel*, in which he proposed the establishment of a confederation of the Slavic nations and lands of the still extant USSR to replace that doomed Leviathan.

Solzhenitsyn was first offered the opportunity to return home just before the essay appeared, when he received an oddly worded invitation from Prime Minister Ivan Silaev of the Russian Federation to visit him in Moscow as a "personal guest."[201] The invitation was politely declined. Nor did he go back in 1991, after the abortive anti-Gorbachev putsch of August; nor in 1992, when Russia was re-constituted as a sovereign state and President Yeltsin embarked on his experiment in capitalist deconstruction; nor in 1993, when Yeltsin sent tanks against the Supreme Soviet and secured a new political settlement. Many were baffled, even upset by the writer's reluctance to leave his Vermont "manor,"[202] for in those early years of the post-communist transition he was regarded by large sections of public opinion as a sort of national paragon, perhaps even a savior-in-waiting. In fact, Solzhenitsyn's reasons for deferring his departure were professional—literary: he was determined to complete *The Red Wheel* before re-immersing himself in his native cultural space. And complete it he did. A few days after landing on Russian soil in May 1994, Solzhenitsyn announced: "I have already written all of my books and fulfilled my literary task."[203] There have been few writers who could say the same thing.

The author's journey home lasted several weeks and was widely covered in the national media. By taking the route that he did—from Cavendish to Moscow via Alaska, the Far East, and Siberia—Solzhenitsyn completed the circumnavigation of the planet he had unwillingly begun twenty years earlier when he was deported from Sheremetevo airport to Frankfurt-on-the-Main. His return was an elaborate production involving a succession of public visits and speeches, all of them filmed by the BBC, as in, "Tolstoy with Eisenstein."[204] He never left Russia again: his life's itinerary was complete.

С женой и сыновьями, 1998

9

A dedicated contrarian, this author insisted on writing against the cultural grain. He did so with passion and panache. Nietzsche's comment on Heinrich Heine, "He possessed that divine malice without which I cannot imagine perfection,"[205] rings just as true for Solzhenitsyn. Occasionally he can be severe, as in his comments about the Party theorist Nikolai Bukharin, many a Western historian's favorite Bolshevik. Bukharin's widow, Anna Larina, who spent eighteen years in the camps, heroically preserved her husband's death cell testament, with its desperate invocations of "the victory of socialism ... the achievement of October ... the proletarian revolution,"[206] and published it after her release. Solzhenitsyn dismisses this document in one cold line: "However, it did not shake the world to its foundations."[207] Such merciless mockery makes some readers uncomfortable, others angry. Nevertheless, he felt he had earned the right to pass harsh judgments, having paid in heavy coin for the knowledge that a belief system that demands total obedience deserves total rejection.

A man of vigorous, combative, and austere temperament, Solzhenitsyn was very much an Old-Christian personality in the Auerbachian sense. As an artist, he was driven by a compelling desire to inform and to teach. The same urge shaped his public, extra-literary statements. He was far from being a political or moral authoritarian, but his pronouncements on the big issues were occasionally categorical and invariably expressed in vivid, emphatic language: "... Though Solzhenitsyn is often accused of preaching, his works are actually always parts of a conversation, of polemics in which one sometimes overstates one's points."[208] The author's son, conductor Ignat Solzhenitsyn, concurs, though his phrasing is a good deal earthier: "There is this notion that Solzhenitsyn was so intolerant, that everything was black and white for him and, well—bollocks! ... His strident political tone was not compatible with typical western discourse."[209] In fact, the writer had a keen understanding of the stylistics of that discourse and his own cultural incompatibility with it:

> When I fought the dragon of communist power, I fought it at the highest pitch of expression. The people in the West were not accustomed to this tone of voice. In the West, one must have a balanced, calm, soft voice; one ought to make sure to doubt oneself, to suggest one may, of course, be completely wrong. But I didn't have the time to busy myself with this.[210]

And lest my more skeptical readers accuse me of special pleading, let me share another quotation, one that seems remarkably appropriate when judging Solzhenitsyn's rhetorical excesses, if excesses they were: "Our spiritualization of *hostility* ... consists in a profound appreciation of the value of having enemies: in short, it means acting and thinking in the opposite way from that which has been the rule."[211] Thus Nietzsche. Thus Solzhenitsyn.

Indeed, this writer had a deep-rooted dislike of thoughtless conformism and blind obedience to authority that extended to matters of religious faith, and he could be as critical of the Russian Orthodox Church to which he belonged as of any other institution or doctrine he felt had strayed from the truth. Despite years spent in prison and exile and ferocious government persecution in the 1960s and 1970s that culminated in an attempt on his life in 1971,[212] despite his denunciation of Soviet communism for treating millions of men and women as "experimental sculpting material convenient for molding into ... forms,"[213] Solzhenitsyn was an advocate of peaceful resistance to despotic rule: "Anyone who has once proclaimed violence as his *method* must inexorably choose the lie as his *principle*."[214] Yet he honored the practice of anti-totalitarian insurrection when the oppressed are goaded by their oppressors beyond the power of human endurance, as happened at the Kengir labor camp in 1954 or in Budapest in 1956.[215] "The real dilemma is the choice between peace and evil," observes Father Severyan,[216] an important intellectual presence in *The Red Wheel*. Even *The Gulag Archipelago*, in some readings, is less a call to national repentance than to national rebellion. For as Solzhenitsyn observed of the minions of evil in the essay "Live Not By Lies!" his most Nietzschean statement of the nobility of revolt, a self-aware, self-loathing slave is still a slave:

> And as for him who lacks the courage to defend even his own soul: Let him not brag of his progressive views, boast of his status as an academician or a recognized artist, a distinguished citizen or general. Let him say to himself plainly: I am cattle, I am a coward, I seek only warmth and to eat my fill.[217]

Certainly, some of his best-drawn characters, like Kostoglotov in *Cancer Ward* or Nerzhin, Volodin, and Klara Makarygina in *The First Circle*, are rebels who refuse to bow to tyrants and dogmatists and insist on the right to make their own decisions and even their own mistakes; and are prepared to stake their lives to that end. They are free men and women in a non-Russian, non-Western, even non-Christian sense. Such figures resemble Nietzsche's "emancipated individual"[218] who is "the possessor of a protracted and unbreakable will" and has contempt for liars and "feeble windbags":

> The proud awareness of the extraordinary privilege of *responsibility*, the consciousness of this rare freedom, this power over oneself and over fate, has in his case penetrated to the profoundest depths and become instinct, the dominating instinct. What will he call this dominating instinct, supposing he feels the need to give it a name? The answer is beyond doubt: this sovereign man calls it his *conscience*.[219]

Solzhenitsyn's Life and Art | 57

That said, in his prose productions Solzhenitsyn favors balance and restraint. He recalls that when he emerged from the literary underground and began "lightening" his works for publication, he discovered that "a piece only gained, that its effect was heightened, as the harsher tones were softened."[220] Thereafter meiosis (rhetorical understatement) became a much-employed device, often used to generate irony. As a rule, authorial antipathies (or sympathies) are seldom stated in plain text. When given an explicit narrative presence they tend to be articulated through the words of a character that has a good reason to hate the modern systems of evil. The prisoners in "Ivan Denisovich" and *The First Circle*, and the ex-prisoner Kostoglotov in *Cancer Ward* have some choice things to say about Stalin and his cohorts, but do so with proper fictive justification, rather than as mouthpieces for an opinionated author. The most terrible words uttered by any character in Solzhenitsyn may belong to the peasant, soldier, and convict Spiridon, who cries out to his friend Nerzhin:

> "Gleb, if somebody told me right now there's a plane on the way with an atom bomb on board—d'you want it to bury you like a dog here under the stairs, wipe out your family and a million other people, only old Daddy Whiskers and their whole setup will be pulled up by the roots so that our people won't have to suffer anymore in prison camps and collective farms and logging teams"—Spiridon braced himself, pressing his tensed shoulders against the stairs as though they threatened to collapse on him, with the roof itself and all Moscow to follow—"believe me, Gleb, I'd say, 'I can't take it anymore, I've run out of patience,' and I'd say"—he looked up at the imaginary bomber—"I'd say, 'Come on then! Get on with it! Drop the thing!'"[221]

In his moment of rage and despair Spiridon is transformed into a *titanic* figure, an Atlas or Samson, whose "tensed shoulders" no longer wish to carry the weight of the world, or the Marfino prison, which before it was taken over by the secret police was a *religious* seminary. Soviet-thinking critics, however, are blind to such subtleties, whether biblical or more broadly intertextual and intercultural. Instead, they have adduced this passage, as well as another one in *The Gulag Archipelago* that describes how Solzhenitsyn and his fellow zeks defiantly screamed at the guards, "Just wait, you vermin! Truman will see you off! They'll drop the atom bomb on your heads!,"[222] as evidence of the writer's warmongering bent. A representative comment on this score belongs to Deacon Vladimir Vasilik, who is also a Balkan Studies professor. After dismissing *The First Circle* as a "mediocre enough novel," this post-communist cleric adduces the Spiridon-as-Samson passage as evidence that the author, "whether he wanted to or not, informationally supported a possible nuclear attack on the USSR."[223] *Diaconus dixit.*

Vasilik aside, Solzhenitsyn has been described as "undoubtedly, a great man" (Mikhail Gorbachev), "an exemplar unrivalled since Voltaire and Tolstoy" (George Steiner) and "the dominant writer of the twentieth century" (David Remnick), though others have accused him of "Christian authoritarianism" (Arthur Schlesinger Jr.) and "reactionary intolerance" (Günter Grass). Enoch Powell, a particularly acerbic voice, even remarked, "No Englishman needs to take lessons in freedom from a Russian."[224] Still, most of the critical comments, as well as the harshest, have come from his compatriots. In Russia there has always been a body of opinion that finds Solzhenitsyn peculiarly grating, and I don't mean just unrepentant communists or knuckle-dragging Stalin-worshippers. One commentator refers to "a dislike . . . which, especially within the Russian émigré community, reaches the intensity of a religious ecstasy."[225] Even less ecstatic readers could not forgive the writer for "The Smatterers," a 1974 essay in which he described the mass of Soviet intellectuals as a caste of snobbish, hypocritical colluders with the communist government, though the word itself, *obrazovantsy*, took root and is now part of the language.

Another term that entered the public discourse thanks to Solzhenitsyn is *skrepy* ("trusses" or "props" or "ties"), that is, the ethical principles that hold, or are intended to hold, or fail to hold, the nation together. It occurs once in the Nobel Lecture ("the national tongue . . . that main tie which holds a nation together")[226] and on multiple occasions in *The Red Wheel*,[227] but was popularized by none other than Vladimir Putin, who in the thirteenth year of his tenure borrowed it to identify a "deficit of spiritual values" (*defitsit skrep*) in the country.[228]

Solzhenitsyn was an enthusiastic collector and coiner of words, as evidenced by his *Dictionary for the Expansion of the Russian Language* and his later, stylistically experimental prose. The writer hoped that his people and its cultural spokesmen would recover the full richness of their native tongue, which had been eroded by Soviet newspeak, though he was careful to make the point that these were merely suggestions, not the dictates of a grammar guru. Yet like so many of his "tentative proposals" (*posil'nye soobrazheniia*),[229] these lexicographical ideas were ignored or attacked by a category of commentators who were unreflectively hostile to everything he wrote or said.

Occasionally the desire to denounce would lead his opponents into interpretations that can only be described as surreal. In 1971 Nikolai Ulyanov, an émigré historian who taught at Yale, penned an emotionally charged article denying that the author of "Ivan Denisovich" had ever existed.[230] The figure known as Aleksandr Solzhenitsyn, Ulyanov ululated, was a cleverly designed composite, a team of literary professionals employed by the KGB for a nefarious purpose. The ivy-covered conspirologist based his hypothesis on the alleged impossibility for one man to have written such a large number of works with such a variety of characters and plots. The empirical novelist is ontologically nixed and hypothetically fragmented: a speculative procedure far more radical than the intermittent postulations by Russian scholars and cultural commentators, among them Solzhenitsyn himself, that Mikhail Sholokhov was not the real author of *The Quiet Don* (*Tikhii Don*; 1928–40). Forty years have passed since this accidental ironist, this postmodernist *malgré soi* put forward his surmise.[231] What would he have said today, when the size of the published oeuvre has tripled, if not quadrupled!

Indeed, over the five decades he spent in the public eye Solzhenitsyn wrote and said plenty of things that were controversial, to use that anodyne word. If Tolstoy was magnificently territorial, railing against artists and heroes who were commensurate to himself on the scale of genius (Dante, Shakespeare, Wagner, Napoleon), Solzhenitsyn, that dedicated asker of questions, was critical or dismissive about many of the values privileged by the consensual discourses of our age. Consequently, the more his views became known, the more they were disputed, even while his novels and stories continued to be widely read east of west, and west of east. A summary of these points of disagreement is illuminating. Where Solzhenitsyn's general principles are concerned, one might mention his oft-stated opinion that without religious faith, whether Christian or other, "all attempts to find a way out of the plight of today's world are fruitless,"[232] and the corollary of that position, his skepticism, even hostility toward the post-Renaissance and post-Enlightenment secular dispensation. As for the particularities, there was his criticism of the United States and its allies as culturally decadent and historically craven in their confrontation with communism; mistrust of political systems that privilege the rule of law over moral righteousness; denial that parties are indispensable institutions in the democratic process; refusal to recognize the "Soviet-German war" of 1941–5 as a true patriotic war; effort to rehabilitate General Andrei Vlasov and his followers who, willingly or otherwise, made common cause with the Third Reich; transposition of the political realities of the Russian Revolution to the fratricidal conflicts in the Vendée in the 1790s or Spain in the 1930s; endorsement of middlebrow ideologues of the past (Ivan Ilyin) or present (Igor Shafarevich); advocacy of the economic and demographic reorientation of Russia toward its insalubrious northeast;

comparison of NATO's intervention in the wars of the Yugoslav succession to Nazi aggression; anti-globalization stance; and in the last years of his life, support for President Vladimir Putin. And the list goes on: these are just some of the opinions that a (notional) Burkian conservative or bien-pensant liberal or democratic socialist might singly or collectively find objectionable. Or even a Russian nationalist: Solzhenitsyn may have denounced the Yeltsin government's acceptance of the Soviet-era borders with Estonia and Ukraine, which he believed left historically Russian lands under foreign rule, but he advocated the return of the Kurile Islands to Japan and (briefly) the granting of independence to insurgent Chechnya. Always, however, he advanced strong and beautifully phrased arguments in support of his positions, which by no means defined or circumscribed the literary works that are the subject of this book. In fact, this determination to question political or historical beliefs considered by so many to be self-evidently true makes Solzhenitsyn *more* interesting as an artist, not least because his novels and stories retain the ability to reach and enthrall readers of all nationalities and all persuasions.

Solzhenitsyn was a firm proponent of the idea that each nation and tribe possesses an ethical personhood of its own. His programmatic thesis on this subject reads: "The profoundest similarity between the individual and the nation lies in the mystical nature of their 'givenness.' And human logic can show no cause why, if we permit value judgments on the one mutable entity, we should forbid them in the case of the other."[233] And: "The nation is mystically welded together in a community of guilt, and its inescapable destiny is common repentance."[234] These attitudes inform the author's literary and non-literary treatments of the historical interactions among the peoples of the Eurasian landmass. In his polemical writings, he keeps careful score of the wrongs inflicted upon the Russians by the Germans, Poles, Lithuanians, Estonians, Latvians, Hungarians, and Jews, and vice versa: perhaps an impossible task. Still, it's the thought that counts. But then there are the Tatars. "The memory of the Tartar yoke in Russia must always dull our possible sense of guilt toward the remnants of the Golden Horde."[235] Elsewhere, he explains: "The idea was simple: we were not the first to intrude upon them. I was referring to events that took place during the six hundred years after the defeat of the Horde, including the [Russian] conquest of Kazan and Astrakhan."[236] This writer had a long memory. For Solzhenitsyn, the Mongol-Tatar invasion of 1237–40 was a catastrophe second only to the Russian Revolution. Yet the representation of non-Russian identities in the fictions tends to be much more subtle and empathetic than these comments might suggest. Apropos *Cancer Ward*, the author notes: "You may remember the tenderness with which I described the dying Sibgatov, who will never be able to return to the Crimea?"[237] This exiled Tatar suffers from an incurable tumor but is "the gentlest and most courteous patient in the whole clinic."[238] The novel comes very close to showing him as a Muslim exponent of that most Christian of spiritual practices, *philia*. Solzhenitsyn was famously disdainful of smiles, especially the plastic rictus of American political discourse. Sibgatov, however, is always smiling, though his smile is one of suffering. "Often he would smile very weakly, as if to ask pardon for the trouble he had been causing for so long."[239] And finally, despite his enduring stress on the importance of national rootedness and patriotic belonging, the writer valued cosmopolitanism when it "unites and absorbs all national cultures" while eschewing "European chauvinism."[240]

We should also recognize that Solzhenitsyn was not afraid to adjust some of his cherished convictions in the light of new empirical or intellectual evidence. In a 1998 interview, he revisited his notion that Russia and the West are two distinct and separate civilizations, which he had formulated in the Harvard Address.

> Today, when we say the West we are already referring both to the West and to Russia. We could use the word "modernity" if we exclude Africa, and the Islamic world, and partially China. With the exception of those areas we should not use the word "the West" but the word "modernity." The modern world.[241]

And in another interview he gave late in his life, he made this comment: "I see no gulf of principle between Russian literature and other world literatures."[242]

There is, however, general agreement that Solzhenitsyn is an emblematic figure whose importance transcends the purely literary and extends into the broader public realm. Dmitry Bykov, a Russian literary critic, points out that "this author has a remarkable instinct for identifying the major issues."[243] In fact, as always happens with important writers who pronounce on matters of current interest, Solzhenitsyn's literary works are considerably more subtle, multivalent, and open to interpretation than his *Tendenzenschriften*. Take the treatment of the Vlasovites in the epic poem *The Road*,[244] where they are shown as victims of a fateful national predilection for extreme, either/or solutions:

> what blinded you into mistaking
> that spidered symbol for Russia's star?
> When will life teach us Russians
> not to fight evil with evil?[245]

Or what about the talented researcher Aleksandr Bobynin (*The First Circle*), a tough, gravel-voiced personality whose powerful mind is his moral curse? The twists of twentieth-century history placed him in an impossible situation not once but twice. During the war he was captured by the Germans, who put him to work in a weapons design bureau. Now he is confined in a Soviet science prison where he must toil for a different set of masters. Bobynin hates the Stalinists as much as he did the Nazis. Yet he applies himself, in spite of himself, in the service of evil men: "Then again, it can be interesting, damn it. Right now it is interesting. ... I despise myself, of course, for feeling that way."[246]

Finally, where Solzhenitsyn's oft-stated insistence on the importance of religious faith is concerned, his portrait of the deeply devout but terminally mediocre Tsar Nicholas II (*The Red Wheel*) suggests that, after all, a sincere belief in God is neither a necessary, nor a sufficient requirement for a statesman or even a family man.

In fact, where Russian history is concerned this writer was a dedicated mythoclast. He always endeavored to strip the Lie of its storybook sheen. In 1976, referring to *The Red Wheel*, he declared, "My sole task is to create the living Lenin, just as he was, ignoring all the official haloes and official legends."[247] He consistently attacks such state-sponsored narratives in his fictions, showing a sharp understanding of their semiotic content, which he dissects and subverts with gusto and rigor as well as palpable writerly enjoyment.

Solzhenitsyn acknowledged that he found Vladimir Lenin hateful. The Bolshevik leader was a sly, Janus-faced fanatic, "the greatest villain in Russian and world history,"[248] "merciless and consistent to the end,"[249] but also a "genius of the revolution,"[250] and is portrayed as such in *The Red Wheel*, where he is the most vividly drawn historical figure. Joseph Stalin, the presiding malevolent presence in *The First Circle*, was Lenin's equal in cruelty, though not in intellect, a "butcher"[251] with "tigerish"[252] yellow eyes.[253] Solzhenitsyn hardly ever deigns to mention Leonid Brezhnev by name, dismissing him as a cipher, the "continuator of that which preceded him."[254] Nor did the writer have much time for Gorbachev, whom he deprecated as a "narrow politician, adroit in what are known as the corridors of power,"[255] though upon finally meeting the former Soviet leader, at a Swedish embassy reception for Russia's Nobel Prize laureates, he warmed to him personally.[256] In a 2007 interview, he granted that history's last general secretary "gave freedom of speech and movement to the citizens of our country."[257]

Of the seven Soviet caesars, only Nikita Khrushchev is treated in Solzhenitsyn's writings with a measure of sympathy, and even warmth. A look at his evaluation of the maverick Soviet leader can tell us a good deal about the author's historiosophical stance and his technique for scripting political actors and events, which he most notably employed in *The First Circle* and *The Red Wheel*.

To begin with, Solzhenitsyn discerns in Khrushchev signs of a complex, contradictory humanity. The former First Secretary, he writes, was "a paradoxical figure," who "because of some psychological peculiarity within him would on occasion free himself from the oppression of Marxist dogma, which is when he took certain liberating steps, of which the greatest was the mass freeing from Stalin's camps."[258] Unlike "the fanatics in Lenin's Politburo, or the sheep in Stalin's,"[259] he had begun to realize that the regime's ideological premises were false. The Soviet premier was genuinely committed to the cause of peace: "When in 1964 he perhaps conceived a serious intention to begin disarmament, he was removed within a few months."[260] True, Solzhenitsyn also refers to Khrushchev as a "petty tyrant"[261] (*samodur*)[262] and "madcap"[263] (*sumasbrodnyi*)[264] and denounces him for undertaking "the cruelest persecution of religion since the time of Lenin."[265] This judgment chimes with the one offered by the Yugoslav dissident Milovan Djilas, who described Khrushchev as "an autodidact ... constantly improving himself" through reading and also through his "lively and many-sided activities. It is impossible to determine the quantity and quality of that knowledge, for equally astonishing is his knowledge of some rare fact and his ignorance of some elementary truth."[266] In a broader sense, what Djilas and Solzhenitsyn valued in Khrushchev was this ability to surprise, to do the unconventional and sometimes noble thing, even while they remained fully cognizant of his direct complicity in some of Stalin's worst crimes.

Together with a sense of historical gratitude to Khrushchev the Liberator, Solzhenitsyn felt a private obligation to Khrushchev the man, as the person who allowed him into print and thereby enabled the writer to bear public witness on behalf of the countless victims of the gulag:

> Khrushchev's departure released me from a debt of honor. I, who had been raised up by Khrushchev, would never have enjoyed real freedom of action while he was there: I would have had to go on showing my gratitude to him ... that ordinary human gratitude which no self-righteous political orthodoxy can abolish. Released from patronage ... I was also excused from gratitude.[267]

As for the premier's place in history, Solzhenitsyn repeatedly remarks upon the unfulfilled promise of Khrushchev the statesman. This assessment of his political role relies on several implied (and sometimes openly stated) counterfactuals. The First Secretary could have effected a decisive, irreversible change in the nature of the Soviet state. He could have gone much further in reforming its stultifying ideological structures and made its policies and institutions conform more closely to the needs of its subjects. Khrushchev failed to realize fully his historical potential because of his personal limitations. This, says Solzhenitsyn, was the Soviet leader's tragedy, as it was Russia's: "Khrushchev never carried anything through to completion, and the deposition of Stalin was no exception. He had only to go a little further, and no one would ever again have unclenched his teeth to bay about the murderer's 'great services.'"[268]

Alas, the current state of affairs in Russia casts doubt on the particulars of this statement. The historical record is now freely accessible, the truth about the Soviet terror state available to all who can read, thanks in no small part to Solzhenitsyn himself. Yet, plenty of politicians, proletarians, and peasants—and sometimes priests—happily bay Stalin's praises, even if these Jurassic diehards represent the "unenlightened, socially backward half of Russia."[269]

But to return to Solzhenitsyn's reading of Khrushchev, so wistfully scripted in the historiographical subjunctive. The writer's attitude toward this unusual political personality contains pronounced mythic overtones. In a passage at the beginning of his memoir *The Oak and the Calf*, Solzhenitsyn identifies a hidden religious element in the First Secretary's way of seeing the world: "Khrushchev always became solemn and subdued when he spoke of our common mortality and of man's limited span. This note could be heard in his public speeches too. It was a Christian trait in him, of which he was unconscious." The author continues: "Nikita was a tsar who completely failed to understand his own true nature and his historical mission ... who had never had and never felt the need to seek a wise counselor."[270] The Good Tsar and the Wise Counselor are archetypes in Russian folklore, whereas the term "historical mission" comes from historicist, post-Hegelian discourse. I wrote, Russian folklore. Yet, Russia has known instances of famous writers acting as the Ruler's private advisors, his enlightened guides through the labyrinths of power and history: thus the relationship between Nikolai Karamzin and Tsar Alexander I, or Pushkin's one-time hopes of playing a similar role vis-à-vis Alexander's successor, Nicholas I. Solzhenitsyn's cautiously supportive stance toward President Putin, who visited the author at his home on two much-publicized occasions in 2000 and 2007, should be viewed in this light.

As for President Yeltsin and his role in Russia's transition from communism, Solzhenitsyn's verdict was succinct: "He's very Russian. Too

Russian."²⁷¹ He considered the late Russian leader a brutal adventurer, though one with a larger-than-life personality and considerable ability.²⁷² He was scathing about the Yeltsin government's application of Western forms to economic and political life, particularly its privatization policy which created a class of flamboyant oligarchs but caused the immiseration of the young, the old, and the newly unemployed. In his tracts "Rebuilding Russia" and *Russia in Collapse*, he argued that Russia ought to reconstitute itself as a multi-ethnic, mixed economy state that combines a respect for the law characteristic of Western Europe and the United States with traditional social and religious practices. His history of Russian-Jewish relations *Two Centuries Together*, enjoyed a *succès de scandale*. All three works were denounced by much of the country's intellectual elite as anti-modern and anti-Western, with *Two Centuries Together* attracting accusations of cultural insensitivity or worse. A TV version of *The First Circle*, which was based on a script by Solzhenitsyn, who also provided the voiceover, aired in 2006 and was a big hit, though for some viewers the series' Stalin-era discursive and artifactal elements fitted into a red-tinted, retro-utopian view of the Soviet past, a development of which the elderly and still hopeful writer fortunately remained unaware.

The congruence of Vladimir Putin's political priorities with the national agenda enunciated by Solzhenitsyn is worth noting. Alexander Rahr, a leading German specialist on Russia, suggests that "if the West wants to understand Putin better, it should consider the ideas of ... Aleksandr Solzhenitsyn. ... His idea was the transformation of the communist Soviet Union into a strong Russian national state."²⁷³ Indeed, the author regarded the broad thrust of the Putin internal and foreign policy as being in the country's interest and supported it accordingly. When in 2007 he was awarded the State Prize for "notable achievements in the field of humanitarian endeavor,"²⁷⁴ the Russian president acknowledged that "some of the steps we have undertaken to a considerable extent conform to Solzhenitsyn's ideas as expressed in his writings."²⁷⁵ That same year the government launched a national debate on Solzhenitsyn's essay "Reflections on the February Revolution" ("Razmyshleniia nad Fevral'skoi revoliutsiei"; 1995), which the official media presented as a "manual of counterrevolutionary strategy," that is, a very good thing.²⁷⁶ Robert Horvath explains:

> First, Solzhenitsyn had been one of the most ferocious critics of the oligarchic system that emerged under Boris Yeltsin. ... Second, hostility to revolution was one of the lodestars of Solzhenitsyn's public life. ... His hostility to political parties and his emphasis on grass-roots democracy diminished

the room for conflict over the Kremlin's suppression of political competition and the imposition of an authoritarian "vertical of power."[277]

Solzhenitsyn approved of the president's efforts to forge a new national narrative for post-communist Russia, even though as part of that endeavor the authorities routinely encouraged the propagation of Soviet and Russian imperial nostalgia, especially among the lower socio-economic orders, discomfited and disoriented as they were by the trauma of robber capitalism. At the same time, the author freely expressed disagreement with certain government actions, whether symbolic or material, such as the restoration of the Soviet national anthem[278] or the abolition of single-member parliamentary constituencies.[279] He regretted the absence of a "constructive, clear and large-scale opposition" under Putin.[280] He continued to advocate a system of limited representative government, with universal suffrage but "non-partisan elections":[281] the author's honest dislike of political parties is reminiscent of George Washington, who famously warned against "the ill-conceived and incongruous projects of faction."[282] Wisely, Solzhenitsyn insisted on keeping a distance between himself and the country's rulers, whatever his points of agreement with certain aspects of government policy. As for Russia's second and fourth president, his stated attitude to the writer and his works was invariably positive, even encomiastic, for example, "Millions of people around the world see a connection between Aleksandr Solzhenitsyn's name and his works and the destiny of Russia."[283]

Solzhenitsyn's obsequies in August 2008 were a state occasion which was attended by both Putin, who held the premiership at the time, and President Dmitry Medvedev, even if popular reaction to the writer's death remained strangely muted, a consequence, perhaps, of the continuing lack of a national consensus about the meaning of his life and art; or a symptom of the declining importance of imaginative literature in twenty-first-century Russian culture. In a symbolic move, Moscow's Great Communism Street (*Bol'shaia kommunisticheskaia ulitsa*) became Solzhenitsyn Street, predictably giving rise to protests by Soviet nostalgists. The author had already received celestial recognition, when an asteroid was named after him following the demise of the Soviet Union.[284] Under a government mandate, a monument to Solzhenitsyn was erected in the capital in December 2018 and the former family apartment on the Tverskaya became a museum. Putin continues to quote Solzhenitsyn in his public statements and has gone on record to say that he is a paragon for our times like Gandhi and Nelson Mandela.[285] More important, it was thanks to the Russian leader's personal initiative[286] that in 2010 a one-volume version of

The Gulag Archipelago, abridged by Natalia Solzhenitsyna with her husband's reluctant consent, was included in the high school syllabus,[287] which already featured "Matryona's Home" and "Ivan Denisovich." Mrs. Solzhenitsyna has commented on this development in characteristically measured terms: "When the deeds of our political figures are weighed on the scales of history, this decision will matter a great deal."[288]

The author's status as a Russian classic may now carry an official imprimatur inside and outside the classroom, but Mrs. Solzhenitsyna is determined that his writings and name should not be coopted by the powers-that-be or some faction thereof. To that end, she confines her actions and statements in the public realm to those that in her judgment would have met with Solzhenitsyn's approval; and even so, she speaks on matters of current interest only occasionally, and sparingly. The recent shift in the reception of Brodsky, who in the wake of the Russia-Ukraine conflict was unexpectedly reconfigured as a poet of empire and a source of neo-colonial quotes, demonstrates that in this febrile atmosphere even a renowned artist's standing is vulnerable to a narrow, topically inspired posthumous reinterpretation by self-appointed, or appointed, nationalist voices. Mrs. Solzhenitsyna's endeavor to protect Solzhenitsyn's legacy calls for political sensitivity and cultural nous, qualities that she possesses in abundance. In a December 2014 TV interview, she stated: "Patriotism must possess a keenness of vision [*dolzhen byt' zriachim*], it must be like a sea voyager's chart: if it doesn't show us the sites where we suffered defeats and great losses, our immediate future will come under threat."[289] In any case, Natalia Dmitrievna prefers to take a long view, for her purpose is the same as her late husband's, that is, to teach modern audiences about the nation's tragic history and to encourage them to honor the memory of its victims. These are lessons that a large portion of society and the elites are still reluctant to assimilate.

If there is a consensus about Solzhenitsyn's status across ideological boundaries and theoretical platforms, it may have been best expressed by one of his foreign biographers: "He is ... the last writer of an extraordinary period in Russian literature in which the writer knew it was his duty to embody truth."[290] Another commentator takes the same notion further by giving it a provocative twist: "Solzhenitsyn is the last classical writer of the Russian land, and he may have become the founder of our new literature, polemical journalism [*publitsistika*] formatted as imaginative literature."[291]

Solzhenitsyn's place in the canon may be secure, but his posthumous reputation will rest, rise, or fall on the reception of his writings, and particularly his prose, by twenty-first-century readers. The thirty-volume *Collected Works* are far from being, or from being presented as being, an *opera omnia*, for they omit the correspondence, private diaries, drafts and other productions that the author's literary executors deemed unsuitable for placement in the public domain at this time. "I'm afraid that I will not be able to finish everything and after death I think I will still have enough unpublished material for several volumes," the writer confided to an American scholar in 1998,[292] contradicting his statement of half a decade earlier that he had written all the books he had intended to write. Still, one should never hold an author to that kind of promise. It is certain that future years will witness the appearance of new Solzhenitsyn texts whose very existence at present is unsuspected, just as Tolstoy's death was followed by the publication of works that are now considered classics such as the story "The Devil" ("D'iavol"; 1889; 1909), the novel *Hadji Murad* (*Hadzhi-Murat*; 1904), or the play *The Living Corpse* (*Zhivoi trup*; 1900).

Solzhenitsyn always kept his faith in the power of the written and spoken word. In the end, he much preferred to be judged as an artist rather than a public intellectual, however prominent or influential. So perhaps we should do the same, whether we agree or disagree with the details, central or peripheral, of his religious, political, and cultural doctrines. Those mysterious and wonderful "shoots of Beauty" that he seeded are still forcing their way through, and I suspect that they will continue to grow and blossom for many years to come.

CHAPTER TWO

Ice, Squared: "One Day in the Life of Ivan Denisovich"

> *A state, is called the coldest of all cold monsters.*
> —Friedrich Nietzsche, *Thus Spoke Zarathustra*

> *I dream of yellow lights, choking in my sleep.*
> —Vladimir Vysotsky, "Gypsy Song"

1

Aleksandr Solzhenitsyn entered the public ken in 1962, his "annus mirabilis,"[1] through a concatenation of "exceptional personalities" and "extraordinary circumstances."[2] Just imagine. In the wake of the Twenty-Second Party Congress, that last, euphoric stage of Khrushchev's de-Stalinization campaign, a manuscript of curious appearance is delivered to the editorial offices of *Novy Mir*, the country's leading literary journal. It is the text, typed on both sides of the sheet without spaces or margins, of a novella describing twenty-four hours in the life of a Russian peasant held in one of Stalin's work camps. The author of this tale, which bears the Orwellian title *Shch-854*, is a middle-aged schoolteacher from Ryazan, a city some 400 miles south of Moscow. The manuscript might have landed in the office waste paper basket but for a discerning copy editor. She arranges for it to be re-typed and induces the editor-in-chief to take a look. After reading just three or four pages, he *knows*. A lengthy sequence of political moves and literary intrigues ensues until the tale, now retitled "One Day in the Life of Ivan Denisovich," is brought to the attention of the country's ruler. He authorizes its publication, in part because he likes the main character. Soon the schoolmaster is reading press reviews in which he is hailed as a second Tolstoy. Three decades and four general secretaries later, the processes of systemic decline to which the appearance of the tale contributed in some considerable measure would lead to the fall, first, of the Soviet Empire, next, of the Communist Party, and lastly, of the Soviet Union itself.

Those early reviewers had a point. "Ivan Denisovich" exhibits a number of elements that qualify as Tolstoyan, among them the hero's emblematic averageness and the representative nature of his diurnal experiences, which is *pre-confirmed* by the title: this day in the life is no better and no worse than the thousands of other days he has already spent in the gulag. The narration's continually defamiliarizing function is also reminiscent of Tolstoy, whereas the carceral environment in which Ivan Shukhov lives and labors, and the array of prison personalities and voices that surround him, link the tale to Dostoevsky's prison novel *The House of the Dead* (*Zapiski iz mërtvogo doma*; 1862).

Like the majority of Solzhenitsyn's fictions, "Ivan Denisovich" is a third-person narrative, a format that presupposes a degree of authorial distance from the characters and their situations. Large stretches of the text take the form of free indirect speech, with Shukhov's idiolect as its controlling function, a beautifully realized mixture of folksy language, camp slang, as well as a few politically tinged locutions that he has picked up over the years. At the same time, the diction is clipped, even "ascetic."[3] This laconic, idiolectal style forms a contrast to the tale's meta-referent, *The House of the Dead*, and its wordy, discursive flow. Yet the "fulcrum and neutral background" for the hero's distinctive speech patterns is standard literary Russian: "A work composed entirely in the form of jargon or dialect cannot become part of the nation's artistic patrimony."[4]

The mass of cultural, historical, political, sociological, and economic information presented is sifted through the hero's matter-of-fact, here-and-now perceptions and thoughts. Occasionally there are instances where this "making it strange," Shukhov-inflected diegesis generates descriptions that are memorably blunt in that classic Tolstoyan manner, as when the hero observes the filmmaker Tsezar talking to another intellectual: "These Muscovites could scent each other a long way off, like dogs. And when they got together they had their own way of sniffing each other all over."[5]

As for the narrator per se, he is a fictive personality in his own right, with an intellectual awareness that is much broader than the hero's factual and literal view of things. Yet, the narrator's voice retains the essential homeliness of Shukhov's speech patterns even when it explains, elucidates, and (very occasionally) pronounces judgment; and then, the protagonist and his perceptual stance once again take over. Such diegetic shifts may occur within a single paragraph or even sentence. Here is a scene, set in the building site mess hut, where we successively encounter several different angles of vision or understanding, which intersect across their respective planes of narration:

[1] Fetyukov hadn't the nerve to swipe anything for himself but he was a champion scrounger.
[2] Buynovsky was a sitting a little way along the table.
[3] He had finished his gruel some time ago, didn't know that [Gang] 104 had extra portions, and hadn't looked to see how many the deputy foreman had left.
[4] He had grown sluggish as he warmed up, and hadn't the strength to rise and go out into the cold air or to the chilly "warming shed" that warmed nobody.
[5] Now he was behaving like those he had tried to drive away with his metallic voice five minutes ago—taking up space to which he was not entitled and getting in the way of the gangs just arriving.
[6] He was new to camp life and to general duties.
[7] Moments like this, though he didn't know it, were very important to him: they were turning the loud and domineering naval officer into a slow-moving and circumspect zek: only this economy of effort would enable him to endure the twenty-five years of imprisonment doled out to him.[6]

Sentences one to two give us Shukhov's take on the work gang's resident lowlife, Fetyukov, and the camp newbie, ex-Captain Buynovsky of the Red Navy; sentence three conveys the extradiegetic/authorial narrator's all-knowing perspective; sentence four, Buynovsky's sense of self, at the same moment in time; in sentences five to seven the omniscient narrator resumes his role as the custodian of diegesis while expanding the purport of the scene into the future—Buynovsky's future, if he has one. The operative register is Shukhov-centered, Shukhov-colored, Shukhov-filtered, but at the end of the passage those homely tones elide into the narrator's literary accents, as in, "a slow-moving and circumspect zek" (*malopodvizhnyi osmotritel'nyi zek*).[7]

Among Solzhenitsyn's fictive worlds, this one is the most geometrically structured. The events described occur within or along the perimeters of several square, rectangular, cubic, or parallelepipedal loci: the camp, the construction site, and the lesser spaces they contain—barracks, sick bay, canteen, mess hut, guard house, auto-repair shop, punishment block. Only when the column of zeks, Ivan Denisovich Shukhov among them, troops to and from the building site does the narration divagate into an open, unbordered area, the snow-covered Kazakh steppe: an endless white plain/plane.

The novella's chronological frame is defined in the title. Although we are occasionally given the hour of the day (or night), as a rule the passage of time is marked by reference to the routine of camp life: reveille, slop-out, breakfast, work parade, march to forced labor, dinner break, march back, evening count, supper, evening roll-call, lights out. Shukhov possesses an instinct, a "clock in his guts,"[8] set to these immutable prison rhythms.

The tale begins with a passage that fixes the action within a first set of spatial and temporal coordinates (there will be several others):

> The hammer banged reveille on the rail outside camp HQ at five o'clock as always. Time to get up. The ragged noise was muffled by ice two fingers thick on the windows and soon died away. … Outside, it was … pitch-black, except for three yellow lights visible from the window, two in the perimeter, one inside the camp.[9]

In Solzhenitsyn, the sounding of the rail is a fixed aural image of camp life: a gulag topos. The narrative poem *The Road* (composed in the Special Camp at Ekibastuz) and the play *The Love-Girl and the Innocent* open in exactly the same way.

To reach Shukhov's ears, the harsh sound must travel across yards of open space between the HQ hut and the barrack; penetrate the layer of ice on the barrack window; then go through the pane itself. Hence it is ice and glass—not distance—that muffles the metallic clangs. An authorial awareness of the manner in which sound waves or light beams radiate, reflect, refract is present across Solzhenitsyn's prose. The reference to ice on the panes evidences the freezing temperature, the chief environmental threat to the inmates' health and indeed their lives.

Only three of the perimeter lights can be seen from Shukhov's vantage point at the barrack window. We now realize the narrowness of the field of vision afforded by that window and acquire a sense of the barrack's location inside the compound.

In this opening paragraph, the connections between space, time, temperature, and color—the four physical values that loom large in the narrative—are out*lined*. As the hero goes about his daily business, space will become concretized, time measured, colors enumerated and depicted, and the effect of cold and warmth on the prisoners' bodies explored, in telling detail.

When Shukhov leaves the barrack we get a broader view of the camp: "Two big searchlights from watchtowers in opposite corners crossed beams as they swept the compound. Lights were burning around the periphery, and inside the camp, dotted around in such numbers that they made the stars look dim."[10]

For an instant, the pair of electrical beams become xanthic diagonals dissecting the square or rectangular territory of this penal colony: another, visually materialized set of coordinates. Thus far, the empirical perspectives are the diegetic narrator's, whose angle of perception is the same as the hero's, including the reference to the stars overhead, when the down-to-earth protagonist implicitly cranes his neck to examine the still darkened sky.

Shukhov is always in motion, always on the go. In the morning and evening he hustles about the camp compound, entering and exiting buildings and interacting with a variety of other characters, never without reason or purpose. At the work site he lays bricks in the open air, warms himself in the auto-repair shop, eats in the mess hut. The trajectory of his movements adumbrates the area inside and outside the camp fence, so that as we track them we acquire a mental grid that encompasses this prison space and its environs. Fences, posts, walls, windows, doors, tables, bunks are the grid's vertices.

Nine colors are referenced in the text: black, yellow, white, blue, green, red, brown, pink, and gray. The camp's nighttime color scheme comprises the blackness of the night, the whiteness of the snow, and the yellow brilliance of the lights dotting the compound. These are stark contrasts. In daytime, however, the paints and pigments tend to be lackluster. The tobacco Shukhov smokes is "reddish-brown"[11] (*burovaten'kii*);[12] the glass top on the desk in the sick bay is "greenish"[13] (*zelenovatoe*);[14] warden Tartar's blue collar tabs[15] are "grubby"[16] (*zamuslennye*);[17] the red sun is "dim"[18] (*krasnoe, mglistoe*.)[19]

The fictive cosmography includes odors and specimens of animal and plant life. Degrees of smell are related to degrees of temperature: cold air is a poor conductor of odorants. Only when at the end of the day Shukhov is back inside the relative warmth of the barrack does he have one or two olfactory experiences: "a quick glance and a sniff"[20] tell him what victuals are contained in another prisoner's food parcel, while the dishwater-like liquid in the tea bucket reeks of "moldy wood pulp."[21] No reference is made to the reek from the latrine bucket: the human nose can get used to any ambient stench.

The fauna in this desolate place consists of specimens from two zoological classes, Mammalia and Insecta: the guard dogs, the hospital cat, and the bedbugs that infest Shukhov's barrack. As for things that grow from seeds, "wheat sprouts only in the bread-cutting room, oats put out ears only in the food store":[22] a botanical negative. A century ago Wladimir Köppen, one of the founders of modern climatology, posited that climate zones are defined by native vegetation. Solzhenitsyn's tale makes the same point, in carceral terms. When winter comes to these parts, plant life is possible only in protected, man-made environments, so while the enclosed space of the camp has its own sparse flora, the open space without has none. "Not so much as a sapling to be seen out on the steppe, nothing but bare white snow to the left and right."[23] Fence posts, not trees, stand tall in the white expanse. We also learn about soil quality: "The ground was stone even in summer."[24] There are no virgin lands here.

The camp is located in the barren steppe of central Kazakhstan, part of the vast ecoregion of grasslands that stretches from Mongolia to Ukraine. In *The House of the Dead*, this cross-continental prairie is associated with freedom: "The sun shone on the endless white sheet of the snow; if only one could have flown away somewhere into those steppes."[25] Here the reverse is true, for the steppe is one more environmental reality that has a carceral value.

The chief feature of the landscape is its flatness, a quality that seems to carry over into the prisoners' posture. They cringe and huddle in the bitter cold, trudging to the work site "hands behind backs, heads lowered."[26] On some ghostly, gelid plane these shivering zeks join a procession of other ragged figures from other Russian texts dragging themselves through the ice and snow like furtive Akakii Akakievich in Gogol's "The Overcoat" or the terrified former bourgeois in Zamyatin's "Cave" ("Peshchera"; 1920). In *this* fictive world, however, the prisoners follow a geometrically ordained route (it runs in a *straight* line) to which they must cleave, on pain of death, as specified in the "daily 'prayer'"[27] recited by the escort commander. "One step to the right or left will be considered an attempt to escape and the guards will open fire without warning!" he bellows before the inmates, Shukhov among them, set off to perform the day's quota of hard labor.[28]

Many, and probably most, of the zeks slogging across the steppe must be superior in intellect or spirit to that stentorian figure. A Red Army sergeant, in the tale's moral scheme of things he is nothing but a bully, one of those twentieth-century bearers of Nietzsche's herd principle. But then, the guards treat the zeks exactly as if they were a herd: "'Halt!' roared the sentry. 'Like a flock of sheep! Sort yourselves out in fives!'"[29] Still, the inhuman tendencies of the individual turnkeys and guards are, mostly, only hinted at, with the exception of the warders Tartar, a martinet with a weirdly hairless head, and Volkovoy, a pedantic sadist who "never forgot or forgave."[30] Their repulsive natures are visibly *embodied*. Normally, however, the author's watchwords are narrative restraint and descriptive reserve. He will offer an expansive, metaphorically coded typology of Stalin's henchmen and honchos in *The First Circle* and situate these types ethically and sociologically in *The Gulag Archipelago*.

Once the prisoners pass through the camp gates they emerge into the open steppe, "walking into the wind and the reddening sunrise" (we now know the direction in which they are going and get a sense of the hour).³¹ By the time the column reaches its destination, it is dawn (another temporal indicator), and we are given a panoramic view of the place: "Looking through the wire gate, across the building site and out through the wire fence on the far side, you could see the sun rising, big and red, as though through a fog."³² A sanguine solar disk horizontally intersected by strands of barbed wire is an almost heraldic image. *Voilà le soleil du goulag!* These visuals are all the more effective because the text leaves it to the reader to complete the picture.

2

The ideas for his literary projects would sometimes come to Solzhenitsyn in a flash, while the author was in a state of physical motion, as per Nietzsche's dictum, "The sedentary life is the very sin against the Holy Spirit. Only thoughts reached by walking have value."³³ We may recall that the writer thought up *The Red Wheel* while wandering the streets of Rostov as a first-year student, and *Cancer Ward* was conceived in the same peripatetic fashion, as he was making his way to the commandant's office in Tashkent in 1955.³⁴ In the case of "Ivan Denisovich," the moment of artistic ideation occurred in circumstances that were much less promising. The year was 1952 and Solzhenitsyn was nearing the end of his sentence at Ekibastuz:

> It was just another day in the camps, the work was hard—I was teamed with another fellow, hauling hand-barrows—and it occurred to me that the best way to describe the whole camp world would be through a single day ... everything that happened in one day ... as experienced by an average, quite unremarkable man, from morning through to evening.³⁵

"The whole camp world," "a single day," "everything that happened." Place, time, action: the three classical unities were present at the inception, even though the text itself was not only as yet unwritten, but also largely unimagined.

In addition to the geometrical values of length, width, and height which frame the characters and their movements inside and outside the barbed wire fence, the relationships among the denizens of the Special Camp, both prisoner and free, constitute a kind of fourth dimension. I use this term advisedly, for there is a unity of style, imagery, and aesthetic content between the sustained emphasis on the topography of the camp and the descriptions of camp society. The fictional personalities in "Ivan Denisovich" inhabit not just a given prison space but also a peculiar kind of social space; and must constantly negotiate and renegotiate their standing within both sets of parameters.

The tale is comprehensively, consistently factological; informative; educational. After all, this writer is an explicator who wills his readers to learn. In *The Gulag Archipelago*, Solzhenitsyn describes the Soviet penal system as "an almost invisible, almost imperceptible country inhabited by the zek people."[36] Like his three-volume "literary investigation," "Ivan Denisovich" was designed to make the invisible visible, the imperceptible perceptible, and the prisoners, grayly anonymous in their huddled multitudes, individually identifiable as living and suffering human beings. If the Soviet Union, in the words of a famous patriotic song of 1935, was a secular paradise where "man never breathed so freely," then "Ivan Denisovich" shows a representative section of it, a place where every breath may be one's last.

As for Solzhenitsyn's original notion of organizing the narrative around a multiplicity of "fragments," traces of it are present in the scenes where the hero acts or interacts or is acted upon in a succession of camp loci. "Ivan Denisovich" offers up a mosaic of individual life stories, fictive dossiers of the major and minor characters, which are situated within the tragic contexts of twentieth-century Russian history. These biographical chronicles are always centered round the political sins of commission or omission, of thought or deed, of parentage or association that led to the incarceration of the prisoner in question. Information about a zek's background is presented discontinuously, in snippets of fact scattered here and there in the text, which are sometimes delivered in the character's own distinct accents, as happens with the former naval officer, Buynovsky: "Well, it's like this, I spent nearly a month on a British cruiser, had my own cabin. I was liaison officer with one of their convoys."[37] However, the former peasant, Tyurin, is the only personality accorded the textual privilege of articulating his life story uninterruptedly and at length, though even he is unable to do so from beginning to end, so that we never learn the details of his actual arrest.

Together, these mini-biographies and the main narrative that encases them contain the nine topoi of gulag literature identified by Leona Toker: The Arrest; Dignity ("the Socratic realization that true dignity ... consists in deserving rather than in being given credit");[38] Stages (transportation and relocation within the prison system); Escape (actual jailbreaks but also a flight into "dreams, imagination, memories, or poetry");[39] Moments of Reprieve ("the more pleasant moments in camp life");[40] Room 101 ("some special type of depravity, suffering, or horror");[41] Chance ("survival was a matter of luck no less than of moral or physical strength");[42] The Zone and the Larger Zone ("the camp is but a *more condensed* expression of the tendencies at work in the country as a whole");[43] End-of-Term Fatigue. Tyurin relates the story of his descent from a so-called kulak's son to social pariah in classic story-telling fashion, to a rapt audience gathered around a flickering fire. The coda to his tale is an unvarnished account of how an unforgiving Deity meted out death to the good Soviets who persecuted him, which constitutes the work's moment of "catharsis"[44] or, perhaps, its earnest of retribution.

This oral affirmation of divine justice occurs inside a carceral environment from which its human analogue is conspicuously absent. The Special Camps, established in 1949, held prisoners convicted for political offences under Article 58 of the Criminal Code (ex-Captain Solzhenitsyn was one of them). We encounter victims of successive waves of arrests and persecutions, human entries in a catalogue of Stalinist repression. Other than Shukhov himself, a living example of the regime's maltreatment of its soldiers during World War II, the important characters are the tough Tyurin, the foreman of Gang 104, who was sent to the camps as a member of the kulak class; stouthearted Pavlo, an anti-Soviet partisan from Western Ukraine, a region occupied by the Red Army in 1939; mild-mannered Kildigs, a Latvian whose country was annexed to the Soviet Union a year later; hot-tempered Buynovsky, a naval officer guilty of receiving a courtesy gift from a British admiral; lanky, hard-of-hearing Klevshin, a former prisoner at Buchenwald now serving ten years for allowing himself to be captured by the Germans;[45] and urbane Tsezar Markovich, a film director from Moscow who run afoul of the postwar "anti-cosmopolitan" campaign. Self-effacing Alyosha, a devout Baptist whose kenotic gentleness of spirit calls to mind Dostoevsky's Alyosha Karamazov, could have been arrested at any time during the Soviet period. Another referent for this figure is the childlike, cheerful, Gospel-reading Tartar Aley in *The House of the Dead*, for "the two young men resemble each other not only in name but psychologically and physically."[46]

Alyosha is the first in a line of heterodox figures of faith featured in Solzhenitsyn's fictions. It is interesting that the tale's resident Christian believer is a Baptist. In the Soviet Union members of this denomination were treated as "sectarians" (*sektanty*), at best religious exotics, at worst traitorous adherents of a foreign cult. Church members were known for being uncompromising in their faith, a point the text makes explicit: "They'd been lumbered with twenty-five years apiece just for being Baptists. Fancy thinking that would cure them!"[47]

Also mentioned should be the aged zek Yu-81, admiringly observed by the hero at supper in the camp canteen. Yu-81 is a dignified, stern-visaged veteran of the gulag now in his fourth decade of incarceration: "This old man had been in prison time out of mind—in fact, as long as the Soviet state had existed."[48] A survivor from the earliest, Leninist stage of repression, he may be a White Guard officer or a member of the pre-revolutionary nobility or "perhaps just an elderly intellectual."[49]

Tinker, tailor, soldier, sailor, rich man, poor man, beggar man, thief. The entire gallery of social types listed in the nursery rhyme is to be found inside this patch of steppe cordoned off by barbed wire. Camp society is brutally hierarchical. It is, to use a term from anthropology, *ranked*. At the bottom are the scavengers like Fetyukov, who are reduced to licking the bowls in the camp canteen. They are the camp's marginals, and their fate is death. Then come the prisoners assigned to "general duties," like Shukhov and his friends in Gang 104, who do hard labor on sites outside the compound. These men form the majority of the camp population. Above them are the deputy foremen and foremen, and then the trusties, inmates who perform chores within the penal facility in conditions of relative comfort: cooks, hairdressers, medical personnel, even artists. Next, we have the stooges and stoolies like the wicked Der or the barrack orderly, a professional criminal who "isn't afraid of anybody, because he's got the camp brass behind him."[50] Finally come the warders and guards. At the apex of this prison pyramid stands the camp commandant, a remote and sinister figure whose name we never learn.[51]

The Special Camp is an icy parody of the ideal state, Kallipolis, described by Plato in the *Republic*. The Greek philosopher divided the population of his utopia into three hereditary classes: the guardians, who rule; the auxiliary class, who police and fight on their behalf; and the laborers, who are the most numerous and least privileged group. These Platonic parallels may be extended. What art exists in the Special Camp has, like art in Kallipolis, been harnessed to the service of the state: it is *useful*. The murals decorating the free workers' recreation center, painted by three captive artists, are, we surmise, examples of Soc-Realist kitsch. One can just imagine these bastardized versions of Diego Rivera's wall works in fresco, garish images exhorting the toiling masses to greater heights of labor productivity. Or if we find them hard to imagine, we can turn to the stage directions in *The Love Girl and the Innocent*: "A poster-like industrial landscape, depicting cheerful, apple-cheeked, muscular men and women working away quite effortlessly. In one corner … a joyful procession is in progress complete with flowers, children and a portrait of Stalin."[52]

On a more symbolic note, that painterly threesome is employed to draw the prisoners' identity numbers: another *useful* job. The artists must catalogue suffering human beings graphically, numerically: objectification with the flick of a paintbrush. Working on the side, the painters also execute commissions for the camp bosses, presumably flattering portraits or prettified landscapes to soothe the totalitarian gaze. One of the artists, an elderly man with a goatee, renews Shukhov's prisoner number on his jerkin: "The way his brush moved as he painted a number on a cap made you think of a priest anointing a man's forehead with holy oil."[53] This is the hero's naively defamiliarizing impression as he watches the old painter at work. Here notions of art and religion intersect with despotic authority in a three-in-one schema that shows Solzhenitsyn at his imaginative best.

The numbers the prisoners wear, on the cap, chest, and left knee, must be legible, under pain of confinement to the punishment block. Another regulation requires the inmates to "take off their caps when they see a warder five paces away, and keep them off till they are two paces past him,"[54] just as in the Nazi camps, from which the practice was borrowed. But Soviet guards are not as pedantically cruel as their counterparts in the SS-*Totenkopfverbände*: "Some warders wandered by blindly, but others made a meal of it."[55] Or what about evening roll call, when Shukhov takes his place—characteristically, in the second row—"with a cig in his mouth"?[56] His every furtive puff represents a tiny victory over the camp's dehumanizing disciplinary code.

There are no women here: this is a completely male universe.[57] Shukhov, malnourished and wholly preoccupied with the business of physical survival, knows no sexual longings. When a warder jibes, "Did you never see your old woman clean a floor? . . .," Prisoner Shch-854 answers back in his homely way, "They parted my old woman and me in '41, citizen officer. I don't even remember what she looks like."[58]

That "citizen officer," slovenly in his soiled uniform, is no warrior, no bearer of the soldierly virtues. Quite a contrast to Shukhov himself, who was drafted into the Red Army when Hitler invaded Russia and was wounded at the front a year later; and who made his way back across enemy lines after his unit was encircled, only to be arrested, beaten, and sentenced as a spy. But the hero rarely thinks about such things. The city, the countryside, his native village, even the war are to him but a faded memory, one that has the quality of a dream. He lives in the present, suspended between an almost imaginary past and an unimagined future.

The chances of survival for the individual prisoner depend on the type of space in which he works. The ordinary zeks toil *outside*, in the open steppe, where they not only do physically exhausting work but must cope with the extreme weather. Shukhov's day in the life occurs in January 1951.⁵⁹ The climate in this part of the Eurasian landmass is harshly continental: "The wind whistles over the bare steppe—hot and dry in summer, freezing in winter," the narrator informs us in spare, stark tones.⁶⁰ The trusties are assigned to light duties which they perform *inside* buildings that are heated and relatively comfortable, like the parcel room or the mess hut. In the camp, protection from the elements is a life-saving privilege.

In addition to the all-important hierarchy of camp status or caste, there are other hierarchies in this little community, which are based on the individual differences among the inmates: of prison experience, age, character, nationality, profession, religion, education, class, political belief, wealth, health. When crafting his characters, the author never forgets to include such markers of the human condition, in the manner of his literary paragons Dickens and Tolstoy.

3

Few writers are able to invent a character that becomes proverbial, a symbol of some national truth or trait. Tvardovsky accomplished this feat with his narrative poem *Vasily Tyorkin* (1942–5), whose earthy, cheerful hero came to be seen as the archetypal Russian peasant at war. In "Ivan Denisovich," Solzhenitsyn did the same for the peasant in the gulag. "[The] hero, Ivan Denisovich Shukhov, was a striking new kind of Everyman, a Russian Sancho Panza or Good Soldier Schweik or a 'shrewd Jack-of-all-trades' whose sly resourcefulness embodied the plight of the Russian people under Communist rule."⁶¹ The author loved Tvardovsky's poem, which he had read as a frontline officer. "Ivan Denisovich" shares several topoi with *Vasily Tyorkin*: both heroes suffer wartime wounds, survive encirclement by the Germans, derive the keenest of pleasures from the simplest of foods, and fall soundly asleep in the most uncomfortable of places. On a homelier note, both keep a spoon hidden inside their boot in the traditional way of the muzhik.

Solzhenitsyn's works feature many characters that were modeled on people he had known, but Shukhov is an entirely invented personality, even if the author borrowed the name itself from an "elderly" soldier who served in his battery during the war.⁶² Vladimir Dahl's *Dictionary of the Great Russian Language* (*Tolkovyi slovar' zhivogo velikorusskogo iazuka*; 1863–6), which Solzhenitsyn carried with him during his eight years in the gulag, lists *shukhobotit'* as a north Russian dialect word that means "to tinker" or "to sew."⁶³ "Shukhov" is a fitting jobonym for this protagonist who, as we learn, tinkers and tacks when he is not doing hard labor.

In *The Gulag Archipelago*, the prisoners of the terror state are described as a "powerful tribe of *zeks*, unique on the face of the earth."[64] Like Professor Chelnov in *The First Circle*, who "lists [his] nationality as 'zek,'"[65] the hero of the tale is one of those tribesmen. Levelheaded, inventive, and supremely knowledgeable about his environment, Shukhov is above all a survivor: perhaps the most beautifully drawn survivor in modern literature.

"The nomad is constantly on the move, eats and drinks when he can, braves all weathers, is grateful for small mercies. Everything he possesses can be bundled up at a moment's notice and his food moves with him . . ."[66] Now, the camp inmates are fixed in space. They are not nomads, though they dwell in the steppe, the nomads' traditional roaming ground. Instead, they are wanderers in place, living on intimate terms with the physical world, always ready for the unexpected, always prepared to endure the violence of nature or man. When Shukhov sets off for the building site, he carries with him the sum total of his belongings: every item of clothing he owns, a supply of food (a bread crust saved from breakfast), his tools (a needle and thread hidden in his hat, that spoon inside his felt boot), and all the money he has in the world (secreted inside the padding of his jerkin).

The prisoners are excused from general duties when the temperature falls below minus-forty degrees, a value which is identical on the Centigrade and Fahrenheit scale. Three thermometers are mentioned in the text. Two of them record the air temperature: one is on a post in the middle of the camp, the other inside the auto repair shop at the work site. When Shukhov visits the sick bay, the medical orderly takes his temperature with a clinical thermometer. So even though there is nothing scientific about the way the main character sees things, on this day he is in a position to mensurate not just the coldness of the air but the warmth of his body: "The air temperature was twenty-seven below and Shukhov's temperature was thirty-seven above. No holds barred!"[67] Generally, however, the hero tracks the cold by its mediated or unmediated effect on discrete parts of his physical self: his hands, which are inadequately protected by thin mittens, his ears when they are left uncovered by the earflaps on his cap, or the toes of his left foot, the boot on which is cracked.

Shukhov's clothes are his carapace. Just as an anthropologist might describe the dress of a native from a distant, unfamiliar land, the narrator explains in precise detail the design and function of the layers of clothing that protect the hero's body and head. The text carefully records the sensory and physical effects of the cold, the snow, and the ice on living human flesh, or the way it responds to the sudden change in ambient temperature when a character enters or leaves one of the heated camp buildings. These meticulous depictions are directly informed by Solzhenitsyn's experience of prison life but they may also owe something to Jack London's stories of the Great Quiet of the North that he used to read as a boy.

In Solzhenitsyn, as in all good writers, it is the little details that make a fictional personality come alive. For example, the hero's ravaged body is a kind of calendar. He notes the passage of days by the growth of his facial hair: "With his free hand he felt his face—his beard had come on fast in the last ten days.... It would be bath day again in three days' time."[68] We thus learn that the prisoners are allowed to wash twice a month: an instance of narrative economy that is typical of this writer. The years of hard living have left their mark: Shukhov's jaw was shattered on the river Lopat when he was fighting the Germans; he lost some teeth from scurvy in 1943 at the terrible Ust-Izhma camp; the skin on his fingers is so rough, he can hold a glowing cigarette tip without burning himself; his face is "case-hardened."[69] This is hypesthesia (tactile insensitivity) as an attribute of heroic biography—and carceral geography.

Shukhov's skin functions as a gauge of heat or cold, but he is not the only character whose physical frame is mimetically configured as a living indicator of the harsh weather conditions. As Tsezar waits to be marched back from the work site with the rest of Gang 104, a dusting of rime forms on his luxuriant mustache and by the time he is back in the camp it is white at the bottom.[70] Need we be told more about how cold it is that evening?

No one has ever been released from this place, so although the hero is nearing the end of his sentence, with two more years left to serve, he has little hope he will regain his freedom: "When your ten years were up, they could say goodbye, have another ten."[71] Time in the world outside may be measured in Five Year Plans and Stalin jubilees, but inside it is circular and tribal: "Prisoners are not allowed clocks. The big boys tell the time for them."[72] Still, Shukhov is not too bothered. Like a Bedouin or a Plains Indian, he can tell the hour of the day from the position of the sun.[73] And he has his intestinal chronometer as a backup.

Tribal or linear, time for the zeks is something precious. Like food, it is the currency of camp life. Shukhov employs the ninety minutes between reveille and work parade to do chores for others so he can "earn a bit on the side."[74] Timewasting by another inmate is theft. A tardy prisoner holds up the column of zeks returning to the camp: "It was no joke—he'd robbed five hundred men of more than half an hour of their time."[75] If we multiply those thirty minutes by

500, the number of prisoners in the group, we arrive at the figure of 250 hours: the hapless inmate is guilty of stealing a total of ten days from his comrades.

If, to quote Auerbach, the great Russian writers of the nineteenth century posited "the creatural dignity of every human individual regardless of social rank and position,"[76] then Solzhenitsyn not only reasserts this principle for the edification of a modern audience but develops it further by imbuing it with a concrete, and ennobling, physiological content. The bodies of his zeks, weather-battered, maimed, sometimes diseased, carry ethical meaning.

Sozhenitsyn's unassuming peasant exemplifies the value of dignified endurance under extreme conditions. There is a strange poetry in the descriptions of how Prisoner Shch-854 uses his meager rations and threadbare clothes to defend against the elements. On several occasions, Shukhov experiences a kind of rapture while ingesting a bowl of skilly, or chewing on a piece of black bread, or sucking on a piece of sausage. He is not the only one. Proud Captain Buynovsky who had "sailed all around Europe and across the Great Northern Sea Route ... bowed his head happily over less than a ladleful of thin gruel with no fat in it at all, just oats and water."[77] Book nine of the *Republic* identifies the processes whereby man is restored to a natural condition: eating when hungry, sleeping when tired, regaining his health when ill. Such sensuous pleasures, Plato explains, "are mere shadows and pictures of the true," which is "wisdom and virtue."[78] Unbeknownst to himself, Shukhov has disproved the ancient philosopher as well as the numberless eremites and ascetics throughout the centuries since, who willingly starved themselves for the love of God: this peasant prisoner has learned to invest the simple act of eating (or recovering from a chill, or toiling as a slave) with "wisdom and virtue." And he loves his smokes, even though the cigarettes he rolls are filled with the coarsest kind of homegrown.

Dignity is manners. In every culture, the consumption of food is governed by social or religious rules. Shukhov never eats wearing his hat (nor does Tyurin). Like his fellow zeks, he makes a point of not spitting the fish bones in the skilly on the floor, which is considered impolite. By the same token, the hero has retained the very human, very private habit of fastidiousness: he cannot bring himself to eat the fish eyes floating in this Stalinist slop, though he does not mind them when they are still attached to the head. Human beings can be quirky, even in a concentration camp. At any rate, he has his standards and he sticks to them.

The hero is also thoughtful about the comfort of others, in his usual undemonstrative way. As he lies smoking at the end of the day, Shukhov is careful to drop his ash into the space between the bunk and the window, lest he burn the absent Buynovsky's belongings on the bunk below.

Shukhov's bunk is his home space, his little den or nest, which he has made as comfortable and cozy as his modest resources will allow. I am reminded of that other peasant, soldier and captive, Platon Karatayev in *War and Peace*, so "Russian, kindly, and round,"[79] so adept at making himself at home on a bed of straw in the prisoner-of-war barrack. Karatayev "baked, cooked, sewed, planed, and mended boots. He was always busy."[80] A Karatayev for the twentieth century, Shukhov is utterly unselfconscious, in a pre-modern, tribal way, as Akhmatova noted: "A Russian man. Above all, completely natural. He never strikes a pose. Not only is he not theatrical, he actually cannot understand how one can adopt some guise, imagine oneself to be someone else."[81]

If Shukhov is a zek tribesman, Gang 104 is his clan, and the foreman, Tyurin, his stern tribal chief:

> Your foreman matters more than anything else in a prison camp: a good one gives you a new lease of life, a bad one can land you six feet under. … Shukhov had no dealings with the camp commandant, the Production Planning Section, the site managers, or the engineers: his foreman was always in there standing up for him … But if he twitched an eyebrow or lifted a finger—you ran and did whatever he wanted. Cheat anybody you liked as long as you didn't cheat Tyurin, and you'd get by.[82]

The members of the gang share a sense of solidarity that subsumes the differences in their individual views and life experiences, which are vast. Tyurin hates the Stalin regime with a steady, cold hatred; his deputy, Pavlo, is a former Ukrainian nationalist guerrilla and therefore not just anti-Soviet but anti-Russian; Buynovsky is an ardent Soviet patriot; Alyosha is a pacifist Christian. But all work together, all look out for each other: they are "like a big family."[83] Outside the camp, they would have been strangers to each other, and perhaps even enemies; but in this frozen world, such disparities and distinctions are cryonically suspended.

Relationships inside 104 are governed by a set of unspoken agreements between the foreman and his men, and among the men themselves. These compacts, entered into by twenty-two zeks, not freely but through force of circumstance, ensure their collective survival. Actually, there are twenty-four souls in the gang, but one of them, Panteleyev, is a stool pigeon and the other, cringing Fetyukov, feels no bond of loyalty or friendship to any of his fellow prisoners. Both are outside that circle of trust, whatever their respective status (Panteleyev's privileged, Fetyukov's liminal) in the camp's social hierarchy.

Tyurin, an epic figure with "a chest of steel"[84] and skin "like the bark of an oak,"[85] is the unquestioned, autocratic leader. He commands the complete loyalty of his men. "Like a father to us, the foreman is," Shukhov thinks to himself,[86] words that reconfirm the work-gang-as-family simile and turn it into a textual leitmotif. The rugged foreman has many responsibilities. He negotiates with the camp bosses over work assignments and speaks up for individual prisoners if they get in trouble. When at the end of Shukhov's day a warder comes to the barrack to take the captain to the punishment block, Tyurin does his best to shield him by pretending he is nowhere to be found, until the naïve Buynovsky voluntarily identifies himself. The foreman relies on Shukhov and Kildigs, his two best workers, to perform important tasks on the construction site, such as building the brick wall at the Power Station. "Rich" prisoners like Kildigs and Tsezar, who receive food parcels from home, give a portion of their victuals to the foreman, which he trades for favors on the gang's behalf while keeping some for himself. Another perk to which he is entitled is double rations. In fact, Gang 104 is just as ranked as the camp population at large: "You'd never get Buynovsky to sit watching a bowl, and there were jobs Shukhov left to those beneath him."[87]

Meanwhile, the hero has his own economic transactions to perform. He runs errands on Tsezar's behalf, for which the latter remunerates him with food, rents out a folding knife he has fashioned out of bits of industrial waste, and makes slippers for sale to other prisoners, some outside the gang. Thus, the political economy of the camp. There is even a system of taxation in place. The guards collect a portion of the firewood pilfered by the prisoners from the work site, but only a portion: "They had to leave some wood for the warders, and some for the zeks themselves, otherwise nothing at all would be brought in."[88] Still, not every relationship in 104 is defined by self-interest or group-interest. Gopchik, a sixteen-year-old serving a twenty-five-year sentence, is the gang mascot, a "calf,"[89] "rabbit"[90] or "goat,"[91] loved by the men for his jaunty attitude. Shukhov, whose own son died in infancy, perhaps when his village was collectivized, is especially fond of the cheerful teenager. Tyurin gives his extra ration of gruel to his deputy, Pavlo, who in turn passes a bowl of skilly that Shukhov had swiped to Buynovsky: "Shukhov ... thought it only right that the captain should get the spare portion. He might learn to look after himself someday, but so far, he had no idea."[92] When the captain is led away to the punishment cell Tsezar slips him a couple of cigarettes and a few minutes later Shukhov shares a precious biscuit with Alyosha, whose meek nature is as big a disadvantage in the brutal business of camp survival as Buynovsky's lingering attachment to the ways of the quarterdeck.

4

The clanging of the hammer on the iron bar at reveille, a gulag tocsin; the sentry herding the zeks like a "flock"; the "daily prayer" warning them that they will be shot on sight should they break ranks; the column of prisoners making its way across the snow "as if to a funeral";[93] the artist retouching the number on Shukhov's hat like a priest anointing a congregant. These tropes are suggestive of a diabolical distortion of Christian rituals and norms, institutionalized in a man-made version of hell on earth.

Now, Hell has been a frequent image, metaphor, and theme in Western and Russian culture: "Hell hath no limits ... where we are is Hell" (Marlowe); "Myself am Hell" (Milton); "Hell is a city much like London" (Shelley); "Hell is oneself" (T. S. Eliot); "Hell is other people" (Sartre).[94] Wuthering Heights in Emily Brontë's eponymous novel is a Satanic household: the referent for this work was Milton's *Paradise Lost* (1667). In Nikolai Gogol's novel *Dead Souls* (*Mërtvye dushi*; 1842), the land of Russia is transformed into a gray inferno where worm-like Pavel Chichikov, "a traveling salesman from Hades,"[95] barters titles of ownership to the souls of dead peasants with a succession of bestial and even demonic landowners.

In fact, Russian literature is full of novels and poems in which petty—sometimes grand—demons ascend from Gehenna to torment, trick, or tempt the good and the un-good. Dostoevsky's *Devils* and *The Brothers Karamazov* are a case in point. The normally anti-mystical Tolstoy also tried his hand at the fictional representation of chthonic places and persons. His satirical "legend," "The Destruction of Hell and the Restoration Thereof" ("Razrushenie ada i vosstanovlenie ego"; 1902), features a collection of demons, from a hairy-legged Beelzebub to a potbellied devil in a "short pelerine"[96] who "invented the Church"[97] and thereby recreated Hell, which had been destroyed when Christ died on the cross. Even Tvardovsky explored these Tartarean themes. In *Tyorkin in the Other World* (*Tërkin na tom svete*; 1963), a burlesque sequel to his folksy ballad of World War II, the soldier hero tours a very Stalinist, ornately decorated, and ineptly run infernal pit that looks a lot like the Moscow metro.

As we have seen, of the many torments the prisoners in the Special Camp must suffer, the chief one is trial by wintertide. "For prisoners and exiles the greatest of hardships is severe cold," *The Gulag Archipelago* confirms.[98] Although Hell is commonly associated with the proverbial fire and brimstone, ice and snow are an important element in traditional descriptions of the infernal regions. *The Apocalypse of Paul*, a text dating from the fourth century, shows the damned suffering not only in pits of fire but also in pits of snow. In *The Vision of Tundale* (1149), the eponymous hero, an Irish knight who visits Hell, sees "a mountain with fire on one side, ice and snow on the other, and hailstorms in between."[99] Another medieval work, the *Elucidarium* (c. 1098), lists nine kinds of tortures inflicted on the damned, one of which is torture by unbearable cold. Works such as these formed the tradition that shaped Dante's depictions of Hell, which are the most famous and enduring in Western literature, but which also inspired Gogol's and later Bulgakov's para-chthonic fictionalizations of Russia. In the *Inferno*, every successive circle of suffering is colder than the one before and Satan dwells at its center, half-submerged inside Lake Cocytus, which is a single colossal block of ice.

Popular Russian representations of Hell also referred to terrible cold. The "spiritual verses" (*dukhovnye stikhi*), a quasi-folkloric genre that appeared in pre-Petrine Muscovy but attained particular popularity in the eighteenth century, show it as a place where "they that are without pity shall know a mighty fierce freeze [*mraz zelo liut budet nemilostivym*]."[100] In one of these spiritual poems, "The Day of Judgment" ("Strashnyi sud"),

> The Lord spoke to the sinners,
> "Sinful and accursed slaves!
> Go ye into the pits of the earth!
> "There ye shall know worms that never sleep,
> and a winter without warmth,
> scalding pitch boils there!"
>
> [*Gospod' greshnym proglagole:*
> "*Raby vy greshny, okaiannye!*
> "*Izydite vy v propasti zemlianyia!*
> "*Tam vam chervi neusypaemye,*
> "*Zima vam nesogremaia,*
> "*Smoly kipiat liutoimyia!*"][101]

As a metaphorically transmuted presence, in Solzhenitsyn's fictions Hell tends to have distinctly medieval European, Dantean features, although recent scholarship has shown that notions and images of the demonic in *The Red Wheel* reflect popular Russian, or more broadly, East European Slavic, eschatological beliefs.[102] The *Inferno* is a frequent referent, most obviously in *The First Circle*, but when I read "Ivan Denisovich," I think of another poet. The Special Camp in the icy steppes of Kazakhstan calls to mind the outer reaches of Milton's Hell, described in book two of *Paradise Lost*. Beyond the four infernal rivers of Styx, Acheron, Cocytus, and Phlegeton, on the far side of Lethe, the river of oblivion,

> A frozen Continent
> Lies dark and wilde, beat with perpetual storms
> Of Whirlwind and dire Hail, which on firm land
> Thaws not, but gathers heap, and ruin seems
> Of ancient pile; all else deep snow and ice.[103]

Here the damned undergo torture alternatively by flames and ice, and "cold performs th'effect of Fire."[104] On a more Modern(ist) note, Zamyatin's stories "The Dragon" and "The Cave" are set in an infernally cold Petrograd, a city of hummocks and glaciers, during the first winter after the Bolshevik takeover. And on a satirical one, Tvardovsky's *Tyorkin in the Other World* shows the work camps of Siberia magically moved to the jurisdiction of Hell by bureaucratic fiat, permafrost and all.

The most terrible place in the Special Camp, its "Room 101," is the punishment block. In a symbolic twist, it was built by Shukhov's work team. "The walls were stone, the floor cement, there were no windows at all, the stove was kept just warm enough for the ice on the wall to melt and form puddles on the floor. You slept on bare boards, got three hundred grams of bread a day, skilly only every third day."[105] One recalls Milton's description of the damned "starving in Ice."[106] Ten days in the "hole" mean that one's health is ruined for life. Fifteen days spell death. This is where Buynovsky is sent for confronting the malevolent Volkovoy when the latter conducts a body search out in the freezing outdoors: "You don't know Article 9 of the Criminal Code! ... You aren't real Soviet people!"[107] The wolfish warder might have let Buynovsky's barrack-lawyer comment slide, but the bit about not being a true Soviet gets his goat. For this is how he sees himself, as a true and perfect Soviet; and he is right.[108]

There exists a curious subset of sources, memoirs or interviews in which Solzhenitsyn's prototypes give their impressions of the writer and comment about the way he depicted them. Tracked down in 1964 by an enterprising reporter, Captain Boris Burkovsky (ret.), the inspiration for Captain Buynovsky, agreed that his fictional counterpart as well as Tyurin, Tsezar, Alyosha, and Limpy, the brutish mess orderly, "very much resemble the actual individuals."[109] He also recounted what happened after his time in the "hole" was over: "I came out of the punishment block, as we prisoners used to say, 'transparent and shaky.' I was unsteady on my feet. But when I returned to the barrack dozens of hands stretched out toward me holding pieces of bread, lumps of sugar, rolled cigarettes."[110] These words constitute an extra-textual, uplifting epilogue to the tale, or at least to the Buynovsky plot line.

The real-life Burkovsky went on to give this description of the author as he had known him in the gulag:

> I spent some four years in the same barrack with Solzhenitsyn. He was a good comrade and an honest person. He was taciturn and tended to avoid noisy conversations. I remember that when lying on his bunk he would often read a well-thumbed copy of Dahl's dictionary, now and again jotting down something in a large notebook.[111]

This perspective might just as well be the fictional Buynovsky's. It is almost as if the empirical naval officer enters the fictive world and goes back in story time to throw a glance across the barrack at the untalkative prisoner with the notebook who will script him one day.

With the captain no longer an *authorized* source of light relief, what drollery remains occurs betwixt the interstices of the text, as when a prisoner remarks that Buynovsky's wartime association with the British was "quite enough for them to pin twenty-five on you," and the former naval person indignantly responds, "Sorry, I don't go along with all that destructive liberal criticism. I think better of our legal system."[112] There are even a few smiley faces, though not all of them are human: "One dog bared its teeth as though laughing at the zeks."[113] The dog is, of course, a German shepherd, and there are several such carceral canines about, which assist the dozens of soldiers guarding the camp. Before marching the prisoners to the work sites these brave warriors hold them "in a semicircular embrace, automatic weapons leveled":[114] an unemphatically realized iteration of the demonic symbolism of the circle or wheel.

Still, if this place is Hell, it is a peculiarly Soviet one, with all the corruptions and inefficiencies characteristic of the communist system. The bosses embezzle, the zeks pilfer: the former to feather their nest, the latter to survive. The camp has an air of impermanence: other than the massive punishment block, its infrastructure is shoddy and its economic output borderline useless. In this place of detention, as in the planned economy of which it is a part, "more depends on the percentages than the work itself."[115] The construction site, with its scruffy workforce, ramshackle sheds, and abandoned industrial parts, is a scene familiar to anyone who has visited the Soviet Union (or post-Soviet

Russia). And beyond the misery of camp life there is the pervasive poverty in the country at large: the free workers employed on the site are so destitute that they steal the zeks' bowls if these are left unattended. Even the warders have to go without, as we infer from a conversation among four of their number that takes place while Shukhov is washing the floor in the guard house: "Rice, man! There's no way you can compare it with millet!"[116]

Some of the absurdities of the penal regime are intentional: they are a form of punishment. In the Special Camps, notes Solzhenitsyn in *The Gulag Archipelago*, the warders would take down the numbers of prisoners who were guilty of some infraction and then demand an explanation in writing, "although pens and ink were forbidden and no paper was supplied."[117] It is precisely such explanations that Tsezar and Buynovsky must provide at the end of Shukhov's day and it is precisely this objection that the foreman, Tyurin, makes to warder Snub Nose on their behalf.

Implied counterfactuality, with its *what if?* questions that invite the receptor to visualize alternative human and historical scenarios, is a feature of *The First Circle* and *The Red Wheel*. Such phantom hypotheticals or, to use Gary Saul Morson's term, "sideshadowings," which carry "the sense that actual events might just as well not have happened,"[118] are also present in "Ivan Denisovich." In this subtextually speculative regard, observes one commentator, Solzhenitsyn's tale echoes the narrator's lament in *The House of the Dead*:

> How much youth had been buried in vain within these walls; how much power and strength had perished here for nothing! For the whole truth must be told: all these men were quite remarkable. They were perhaps the most gifted, the strongest of all our people. But mighty powers had perished in vain, perished abnormally, unlawfully, irrevocably. Yet who is to blame?[119]

As a reader, I found myself wondering how differently things might have turned out if the personalities in "Ivan Denisovich," who are as humanly varied and individually remarkable as Dostoevsky's convict characters, had never been sent to the gulag but had been allowed to lead normal, unexceptional lives in a normal, unexceptional country. In a world thus conjectured, Tyurin and Shukhov might be prosperous peasants, Kildigs a well-to-do smallholder, Eino a successful commercial fisherman, Buynovsky a naval officer of flag rank, Der a loudmouthed foreman on some showpiece construction project, and Fetyukov a moderately crooked company director or industrial manager. As for Tsezar, he would be busy making films in discreet or overt homage to his idol Eisenstein. Beyond such pragmatic scenarios, one thinks of the suffering Shukhov and his comrades would have been spared, the children they might have had, the ordinary human happiness they could have known.

But then, the Stalin regime allowed its subjects no private space in which they could live, work, or love free of its totalizing presence. The danger of arbitrary arrest, or worse, was always there. Sedulous conformity offered no protection. As Tyurin observes, "Proletarians or kulaks, it made no difference in '37. Or whether or not they had a conscience."[120] Under Stalin, the possibility of alternative worlds and lives of the kind imagined by Dostoevsky's narrator was canceled, or relegated to the realm of private fantasy.

5

History shows that the fall or death of a long-lived dictator often marks the end of a cultural period, which may then recede into the historical distance with extraordinary speed. In his preface to "Ivan Denisovich," Tvardovsky commented that the events of "the time of the personality cult ... seem to us to belong to a distant past,"[121] yet the tale was written just six years, and published just nine years, after Stalin departed this world for the next one.

"A prison camp as seen through the eyes of a peasant, a work in which you could hear the voice of the Russian people"[122] was the one-sentence précis that Anna Berzer, the *Novy Mir* staff member who was the first to read the unsolicited manuscript, used to pique Tvardovsky's interest. These were well-chosen words. As Solzhenitsyn put it, "The muzhik Ivan Denisovich was bound to arouse the sympathy of the superior muzhik Tvardovsky and the supreme muzhik Nikita Khrushchev."[123]

Tvardovsky's response to the tale was rapturous. It was not just literary and editorial, but even physical: during his initial encounter with the text he actually had to change his position *bodily*:

> But after two or three pages he had decided that he couldn't read it lying down. He had got up and dressed. While the household slept, he had read through the night, with breaks for tea in the kitchen—read the story once, then reread it.... So the night passed, and what for peasants are the early morning hours arrived—but for literary persons it was still night, and Tvardovsky had to wait a little longer.[124]

Now, Khrushchev never actually read Solzhenitsyn's tale. But he *heard* it. The last person in the chain of individuals who by chance or design played their part in bringing the text to the Leader's attention was his cultural advisor,

Vladimir Lebedev. This bespectacled, urbane apparatchik owed his association with the First Secretary to the latter's habit of having literary works read aloud to him,[125] a fact that indicates Khrushchev's connections with the traditional practices of Russia's oral culture as well as the burden of a busy schedule, compounded by his advancing years. "Let my eyes rest and yours do the work," he would tell his son-in-law Aleksei Adzhubei, who often acted as his reader.[126]

"Sometime between 9 and 14 September 1962,"[127] while Khrushchev was holidaying at Pitsunda on the Black Sea, Lebedev took up his duties as the premier's *assistant de lecture*: "We read the first part during his rest period but then he pushed aside all his papers and told me to go ahead and read the whole thing."[128] The advisor knew what made his boss tick, so "for his main emphasis" he chose the passage in which Shukhov and his friends are building the power station.[129] One detail reported by Solzhenitsyn lends this version of the event a special ring of truth: "[Khrushchev] of course liked particularly the 'labor' scene, in which Ivan Denisovich was 'so careful with the mortar.'"[130] The author wryly acknowledges that the responses of this empirical reader—empirical listener—were adequate to the text: the First Secretary "listened carefully to this entertaining tale, laughed in the right places, groaned and grunted in the right places."[131] In fact, Khrushchev, always an impulsive soul, was so bowled over that he "wanted to invite Solzhenitsyn down to his dacha right then and there but thought better of it."[132] It is a pity the invitation never went out, for who knows what might have transpired from such an encounter? Solzhenitsyn, at least, thought that a one-on-one meeting with the supreme leader might have had historic consequences (another, extra-textual, counterfactual). A year later, in December 1962, Tvardovsky introduced the author to Khrushchev at a Kremlin gathering of the "creative intelligentsia," and the two men exchanged a few words:

> I felt a surge of gratitude, and so as we shook hands I simply gave voice to what I felt: "Thank you, Nikita Sergeich, not from me, but the millions who suffered." I thought that his eyes grew moist. He understood what he had accomplished, and he liked me for telling him so. . . . I should have requested an audience, even though I had no idea what form such a conversation might take. . . . I should have spoken to Khrushchev frankly! He was a man who liked to make his own decisions, so it is quite possible I could have persuaded him to consolidate what he had started. But I failed to rise to the moment, this instant when for the first time I came into direct contact with the course of Russian history.[133]

After he became a published author, Solzhenitsyn lived with the confident knowledge that his writings possessed a special transformative power that impacted national and international audiences. A month before he was deported to West Germany, he told a supporter that his "Letter to Soviet Leaders," a plea to the Politburo to abandon its Leninist ways, was sure to change the collective mind of Brezhnev and co. and show them how they should act in the country's true interest.[134] This "characteristically enlightened faith in the word" struck that interlocutor, a former member of the *Novy Mir* staff, as "childlike and at the same time magnificent."[135] Even after his arrest on February 12, 1974 Solzhenitsyn wondered if he would be taken "to see the government, that very Politburo of theirs [to] have our first—and last—discussion";[136] and in *Between Two Millstones* he recounts at some length his efforts to school President Yeltsin, by letter and via the telephone, in the lessons of Russian history. There were factual reasons for Sozhenitsyn's belief in his powers of writerly persuasion, and they had to do with the manner in which "Ivan Denisovich" saw the light of day, and the role played in its release to the public by Khrushchev.

The First Secretary was certainly the most important reader Solzhenitsyn ever had, even if Khrushchev was not much of a reader. His cultural knowledge did not extend "beyond the limits of classical Russian literature and Russian history,"[137] according to Milovan Djilas, who first met the future premier in 1945. He liked his Tolstoy and Turgenev, his Leskov and Kuprin, and that was that. Nothing wrong with Khrushchev's choice of books, though it is a pity that these private preferences shaped the government's treatment of the writers and poets in its purview. The irony of it is that Solzhenitsyn's model receptor is one who reads not for pleasure or even intellectual stimulation but to learn "the truth," like the characters Kostoglotov and Podduev in *Cancer Ward*, or Nerzhin and Volodin in *The First Circle*. For such a reader engagement with a literary text must be direct, powerful, possibly traumatic, but also enlightening and morally uplifting. In other words, not unlike Khrushchev's at Pitsunda.

Years later the fallen Soviet leader recalled his impressions of the tale:

> It is very heavy, but it was written well, in my opinion. The life of Ivan Denisovich and his surroundings are well described and deeply disturbing. This is the main quality required in a work of art. It evokes revulsion toward what existed in the camps and the conditions under which Ivan Denisovich and his friends lived while they served their terms in the camp.
>
> I know that readers really went after this book and devoured it with pleasure. It was as though they were searching for something. They were

looking for an explanation of what had happened. They were trying to find an answer to how Ivan Denisovich, an honest man, could find himself in such conditions in our socialist time, in our socialist state. I think that this already says something good about the author. He made people aware of how many had been in the camps.[138]

Khrushchev's take on the novella may strike us as jejune, "on the level of an intermediate party school," to quote Djilas once again.[139] Yet this evaluation of "Ivan Denisovich" fits in well with the concept of a reader's "horizon of expectations" developed by Hans Robert Jauss. Such a literary horizon is a function of

> first, ... the familiar standards or the inherent poetry of the genre; second, ... the implicit relationships to familiar works of the literary-historical context; and third, ... the contrast between fiction and reality ... which ... includes the possibility that the reader of a new work has to perceive it not only within the narrow horizon of his literary expectations but also within the wider horizon of his experience of life.[140]

In Khrushchev's case, this experience was unusually broad and varied. It included work as herdsboy, followed by industrial labor and, after the revolution, rapid advancement from humble Party cadre to the highest positions in the Stalinist state, with related administrative duties as well as mass murder in Moscow and the Ukraine; and service as a political commissar in World War II, including the battle of Stalingrad.

The Leader's self-described reader response to "Ivan Denisovich" fulfilled all three of Jauss's criteria, with the last one clearly paramount. This is confirmed by the premier's private comments as recorded by Tvardovsky:

> Yes, the material was unusual, and I would add that the style and language were also unusual, so I couldn't get into it immediately. Still, I think this is a powerful work, very powerful. And despite the nature of the material, it doesn't make you depressed, although there is a great deal of bitterness there.[141]

Now, most people do not spend a lot of time worrying about where they stand in relation to history. Politicians or intellectuals, however, tend to think about this sort of thing constantly, and usually in concrete, self-specific terms.

Khrushchev certainly did. Edward Crankshaw begins his biography of the first secretary of the Soviet Communist Party with this anecdote:

> One evening when Khrushchev was at the summit of his power he was holding forth in one of his more ebullient moods to a group of Western diplomatists at a reception in Moscow. Suddenly, irritated by their professional coolness and evasiveness, he checked himself and exclaimed, "When I find myself talking to you gentlemen, I also find myself wondering.... You all went to great schools, to famous universities—to Harvard, to Oxford, to the Sorbonne. I never had any proper schooling. I went about barefoot and in rags. When you were in the nursery I was herding cows for two kopeks. I had no diplomatic training.... And yet here we are, and I can make rings round you all.... Tell me, gentlemen, why?"[142]

The biographer calls this story "partly apocryphal." In fact, as a text, or rather as a fragment of an as yet unwritten—un-tape-recorded—autobiographical narrative, it operates on the level of heroic self-presentation. Khrushchev's question, "Why?", is less a rhetorical query than a rhetorical prompt. The Soviet premier wanted his listeners to conclude that the reasons for his worldly success lay not in the advantages of birth-given social status or an expensive education, which he did not possess, but in his own talents and determination. Nowhere does he refer to communism or the Bolshevik Revolution. The anecdote allows us a rare glimpse into Khrushchev's reading of his own self, as that of a man who by dint of innate ability rises from darkest obscurity, from basest poverty to bestride the international scene. He is the waif made good. In this Soviet version of the Horatio Alger story, the barefoot Boy Nikita lifts himself up despite his lack of the proverbial bootstraps. There is a fairy-tale quality to the First Secretary's words: we catch a hint of the folk character Ivan the Fool, the crafty simpleton who outwits many a prince or a wizard, just like the rustic Khrushchev who knows how to trick those preppy Harvardians and effete Oxonians. The connection to the humble yet sly hero of Solzhenitsyn's tale offers itself.

In a speech given soon after the publication of Solzhenitsyn's tale Khrushchev made a revealing slip of the tongue, referring to the writer as "Ivan Denisovich."[143] In the premier's mind, the central character had become conflated with the figure of the author: an indication that Khrushchev's reception of the text, despite his functional awareness of the conventions of imaginative literature, took place on a sub-literary plane, where a work of fiction is seen as a mask for the man who wrote it and the events it describes don't just have the ring of truth, they *are* the truth. Metonymy to the max!

In retirement the former Soviet ruler was introduced to some of Solzhenitsyn's other books. Sergei Khrushchev, Nikita Khrushchev's son, recalls: "Included in Father's reading were Solzhenitsyn's *First Circle* and *Cancer Ward*, and also Orwell's *1984*." These works Khrushchev read in samizdat form. "He didn't like them," Sergei states tersely.[144] Or maybe he did. In the spring of 1969 Sergei's half-sister Yulia "phoned *Novy Mir* to convey greetings from her father who after reading *The [First] Circle* had declared Solzhenitsyn to be a writer of genius."[145]

During his incarceration in the gulag and for years thereafter the writer operated under a moral imperative: to bear witness on behalf of those who had perished in the torture-chambers, prison cells, and barracks, "the millions whose last whisper, last moan had been cut short on some hut floor in some prison camp."[146] Khrushchev's reforms gave the millions of zeks and exiles their freedom. One of them was Solzhenitsyn. This was the First Secretary's finest hour. The decision to bring the prisoners back was his and his alone. The author terms this act "Khrushchev's 'miracle,'"[147] although he takes care to enclose the qualifying mythogenic noun in inverted commas. Nonetheless, the First Secretary made Solzhenitsyn possible as (subsequently) the public purveyor of novels and stories and (eventually) as a heroic artist for the twentieth century.

6

Khrushchev reading of the tale was primarily political; secondarily, self-referential; and, by his lights, sympathetic. But of course there were as many responses as there were readers. This is how one contemporary, Ilya Zilberberg, describes his first encounter with the text; and let me note that this informant is generally hostile to its author:

> I felt I was being gradually transported to another world. Yet the manner in which I was being transported there was unlike the manner in which one willingly immerses oneself in a world of pleasurable impressions, or when strong impressions intrude into one's own world and fill it. I entered this other world on my own, slowly and with difficulty, forcing my way past the stylistic structure and unfamiliar language forms, cutting through the spiritual fabric separating our two worlds, which was braided with barbed wire and covered with icy growths, as I overcame the shock and

bemusement caused by the strangeness of that world, its inhabitants, their thoughts and deeds, their life (their *non-life*!). ... This was so hard that after a while I was physically unable to continue. I raised my eyes from the book and looked around: here I too was surrounded by lights and by people, but instead of the camp compound with its scurrying zeks I was sitting inside a well-lit reading room filled with calm and thoughtful readers. I was unable to remain in place and left the room. ... I went back to my reading and again after a while I had to interrupt it in order to collect myself. This happened several times.[148]

Zilberberg experienced the condition that Samuel Coleridge famously described as the "willing suspension of disbelief,"[149] that wonderful state of receptivity and credulity in which a person curled up with a book finds himself prepared, nay, anxious to embrace the contingent authenticity of the characters, events, and settings it contains. Sometimes, however, this readerly procedure can become distressing or even harrowing, as in the case of Varlam Shalamov's *Kolyma Tales* (*Kolymskie rasskazy*; 1978), which are set in the terrible work camps of the north. These stories are so wrenching, the world they depict is so utterly bereft of any kindness or hope that, though exquisitely formed and structured, they never generate "pleasurable impressions" for their readers. Soon after the publication of "Ivan Denisovich," Shalamov sent Solzhenitsyn an encomiastic letter which contained this obliquely critical observation: "The camp is a school of negative knowledge [*otritsatel'naia shkola*] from the first day to the last for any man."[150] The fictive (rather than ethical) incompatibility between the two writers, Solzhenitsyn and Shalamov, was noted by Alexander Etkind, who observes that they "distrusted one another because they introduced the world of the gulag from two opposing perspectives, of a survivor and a soon-to-be-dead."[151]

Yet the effect of "Ivan Denisovich" on Zilberberg was just as disturbing. His very surrender of disbelief was too distressing for him to endure for more than a few minutes at a time, even though he was ensconced in an institutional environment—a library reading room—expressly designed to facilitate the evolvement of that normally agreeable hallucinatory state in a reader. Instead, cognitive trauma induced him repeatedly to interrupt his lecture by physical motion (we recall Tvardovsky's body movements during his first encounter with the tale) in order to take a break, not from reality but its simulacrum. He found himself in need of empirical reassurance that his own self, his own body, and the world wherein they dwelled, were all still there, intact and un-subsumed by the terrible power of Solzhenitsyn's prose. The impact of such a supremely intense trans-literary experience is akin to the effect produced on a pre-modern religious believer by an artistic depiction of the Apocalypse or Hell.

Those readers who had actually been imprisoned in the gulag experienced a reaction that was no less emotional, though very different in kind. One former zek wrote to Solzhenitsyn:

> I had no intention of paying you a compliment. But I must say that when I read your "Ivan Denisovich" I had the impression that I had once again found myself in the camp, even if for just two hours. All my camp friends had the same impression.[152]

This is suspension of disbelief with a vengeance: a literary experience that re-inserts the receptor into the distressing state he had once known and which he thought he had escaped forever. Yet unlike Zilberberg, the ex-prisoner felt no need to interrupt his lecture of the tale. If it took him two hours to go through the sixty-six pages of print in his issue of *Novy Mir*, then this works out at just under two minutes per page: an indication of a calm, controlled engagement with the text.

According to Viktor Erofeyev's imaginative formulation, Shalamov, who spent altogether seventeen years in the gulag, "was not an Orpheus who descended into Hell but a Pluto who rose from Hell and realized the 'illusory and onerous nature of hope.'"[153] To extend this allegorical assessment, Solzhenitsyn was not a Pluto, but an Orpheus. Before they fell out, Shalamov told Sozhenitsyn, "The tale is like verse, everything in it is perfect and appropriate to its purpose [*tselesoobrazno*]."[154] Perfection of form is, by the very nature of things, impossible to prove or quantify, yet over the years many readers and critics have seconded that opinion.[155] It is, I confess, one that I share.

So far I have quoted reader responses that were laudatory, even encomiastic, but there were others that were hostile, and often ferociously so: a fact that in its own way testifies to the power of Solzhenitsyn's writing. Of these antipathetic reactions surely the most grotesque one belongs to Grigory Trofimovich Zheleznyak, a bullet-in-the-back-of-the-head specialist, and proud of it: "We, the executors, were also human, we were also capable of heroism: we did not shoot every fallen prisoner, and by not doing so risked our posts."[156] In a similar vein, here are a few selections from a critique by Anna Zakharova, a functionary of the Ministry for the Protection of Public Order and a Party member in good standing:

Please explain how the officials and officers denigrated by former prisoners, even if the latter were unjustly sentenced, are to blame.... They merely did their duty according to the regulations, instructions, orders, and so forth, as would be the case in any office, factory, or industrial plant.... I am certain that all the officials who have read these works feel outrage, to the very depths of their souls. They have not offered a response either because they are unable to express themselves on paper, as is also true of myself, or because they are too busy, since the work of re-educating convicts takes up so much time.... Clearly, the hero of the work, Shukhov... looks to the sick bay in the sole hope of shirking work as well as his duty of redeeming his guilt before the Motherland. He may be innocent, but since he is incarcerated in a corrective labor camp, as a Soviet man and a communist he ought to set an example to his fellow-prisoners and fill them with enthusiasm, rather than grow more deviant himself and contribute to the deviance of others.[157]

Picture Comrade Zakharova in her moment of truth, moment of hate. A real-life Rosa Klebb, rimless spectacles a-glinting and garish medals a-tinkling, she pours over her well-thumbed copy of *Novy Mir* seeking out evidence of subversive intent. Usually a recipient of denunciations, she is now writing one herself. But let us be clear: in spite of its absurdist, farcical overtones, her diatribe demonstrates a genuine engagement with the text. Zakharova registers details; analyzes descriptions; evaluates characters and ideas. Now the dangers of such engagement for a Soviet true believer become apparent, for with their logical lapses and clashes of incompatible ready-made utterances, her comments keep collapsing into semantic chaos. The tale failed to induce a suspension of disbelief, whether willing or unwilling, in this adversarially minded receptor; it did not change her mind or her heart; instead, it effected the disintegration of her small portion of the Soviet discourse, if not of her own totalitarian self.

7

Solzhenitsyn, that skilled geometer, covers all the angles. Occasionally the adumbration of space proceeds on the minutest of scales, one not of yards but of inches. In the sick bay, Shukhov watches Kolya Vdovushkin, a young medical orderly, "writing lines of exactly the same length, leaving a margin and starting each one with a capital letter exactly below the beginning of the last. He knew right off, of course, that this wasn't work but something on the side."[158] What

Kolya is doing, of course, is writing poetry.[159] The informed reader sees him through the eyes of the uninformed Ivan Denisovich, and we have an instance of that Tolstoyan trope, "making it strange." More exactly, periphrastic defamiliarization. A couple of pages later, Vdovushkin's status as a poet is confirmed when we learn that the camp doctor, Stepan Grigorich, had got him onto the hospital staff in order to preserve him for the cause of Russian literature:

> Vdovushkin was now practicing intravenous injections on ignorant prisoners and meek Lithuanians and Estonians, to whom it would never occur that a medical orderly could be nothing of the kind, but a former student of literature, arrested in his second year of university. Stepan Grigorich wanted him to write in prison what he hadn't had a chance to write outside.[160]

Here is a passage rich in sinister meanings. The professionally unqualified figure in a "crisp white gown"[161] jabbing inmates with a hypodermic needle calls to mind Hitler's *Konzentrazionslager*, even if the impulse behind *this* medical practice is entirely literary: a reminder that, in Bataille's phrase, "literature is not innocent," and neither are those who make it. In fact, the poetic ephebe Vdovushkin is not even a quack like the good Grigorich, who treats infectious diseases by forcing patients to shovel snow in sub-zero temperatures: *Arbeit macht gesund*. He is a complete medical fraud. On the other hand, one recalls Shalamov: he was saved from death by starvation by a camp doctor who got him an appointment as a hospital attendant. There he recovered and wrote his poems.

So, what price poesy? What price art?

These problematics of artistic morality are made explicit when Shukhov overhears Tsezar and one of his intellectual interlocutors, Prisoner Kh-123, discussing the film *Ivan the Terrible* (1944) directed by Tsezar's idol, Sergei Eisenstein. When Kh-123 declares, "A genius doesn't adjust his treatment of a theme to a tyrant's taste,"[162] the cineaste's response is as Modernist as it gets: "Art isn't what you do, it's how you do it."[163] Meanwhile Shukhov, who has brought the Eisenstein aficionado a bowl of gruel, listens patiently, uncomprehendingly to this "educated conversation."[164] The hero is equally ignored by the artistic moralist Kh-123 and the artistic amoralist Tsezar, who "held his hand out for the bowl, without even looking at Shukhov—the gruel might have traveled through the air unaided—then went back to his argument."[165] Tsezar has managed to objectify Shukhov, not by word of mouth but manual motion.

As the only intellectual with a prominent textual presence, the Eisenstein-worshipping film director attracted a fair amount of comment from reviewers and critics. Yet, despite his amber cigarette holder, aesthetic airs, and patronizing attitude to those less cinematic than himself, Tsezar is as decent a member of camp society as most, and more so than some.[166] And speaking of Tsezar, the framing reference to his ethnic identity, articulated in Shukhov's homely accents, amounts to a wry meta-joke: "Tsezar was a mixture of all nationalities. Not knowing whether he was Greek, Jew or gypsy."[167] If Tsezar is to be the victim of Stalin's anti-cosmopolitan drive, then Solzhenitsyn will turn him into a true cosmopolitan! One should add that with his mustache and pipe and mock-power name, the cineaste is a parodic quasi-stand-in for the Generalissimo himself, who otherwise is mentioned but once, when an anonymous zek sneeringly refers to "Old Man Whiskers"[168] (*bat'ka usatyi*).[169] The passage was added at the behest of the Central Committee official, Lebedev. He seems to have cottoned on to the political meaning of the tyrant's textual absence, "an unusual polemical device directed at those who explained all the horrors of totalitarianism by referring to the Leader's demonic role,"[170] and persuaded the author to insert a reference to the dictator in order to bring the tale into conformity with the current party line.

As for Vdovushkin, neither Longinus nor Burke nor Bataille nor even Solzhenitsyn himself can help us decide how good or bad a poet he is: there are no Vdovushkin quotes in the text. It is up to us, the readers, to make that determination. Still, somehow one doubts that the lit. student with the syringe has succeeded in accessing the sublime. Besides, there are clues. The name Vdovushkin (Little Widower) positively offers itself up as an aptronym. To Russian ears and eyes, it is irresistibly reminiscent of Makar Devushkin (Blessed Maiden), the hero in Dostoevsky's first novel, *Poor Folk* (*Bednye liudi*; 1846). Makar is a myopic, genteel forty-seven-year-old clerk, a bit pompous, a bit sentimental. He is an epistolarian in an epistolary novel, but not an artist, and his name reflects his "ageing girly syndrome."[171] Yet if Devushkin is old-maidish, then what is the figurative meaning of Vdovushkin's viduage? Who is his dead wife?

I submit she is one of the Muses, perhaps Calliope, the patroness of epic poetry: the text Vdovushkin is copying out when Shukhov enters the sick bay that morning is a "new long poem"[172] (*novoe dlinnoe stikhotvorenie*).[173] Yet although the poet's muse is dead, his art has not been harnessed to the service of the terror state. A graphomaniac Vdovushkin may be; enjoying the patronage of a medical crank he most certainly is; but he is not churning out SocRealist tripe for the amusement of the Party bosses or the motivation of the hoi polloi.

Beyond the parameters of the narrative, Vdovushkin and his calligraphically executed manuscript serve as a contrastive reminder of a famous episode in Russian literary history. I refer to another gulag poet, a zek on general duties who carried a rosary, its beads fashioned out of prison bread, as a mnemonic aid while he composed and memorized thousands of lines of iambs, trochees, dactyls, anapests, and amphibrachs: Aleksandr Solzhenitsyn himself.

8

As the hero prepares to smuggle a broken blade into the camp, he offers a desperate prayer, lest he be given ten days in a punishment cell for this act: "Save me, Lord! Don't let them put me in the hole!"[174] The warder who pats him down fails to find the precious contraband. Yet Shukhov's religious sensibility, such as it is, is essentially pre-Christian. He asks Buynovsky, Gang 104's in-house atheist, "How can anybody not believe in God when it thunders?"[175] The peasants back home, he tells his astronomically informed interlocutor, figure that God breaks up the moon to make stars. The captain has little patience with such superstitious hooey and expresses his disapproval in suitably naval terms: "I never met a sailor as stupid as you.... What savages!"[176] A Russian reader might be reminded of Ivan Turgenev's novel *Fathers and Sons* (*Otsy i deti*; 1862), in which the main character, Bazarov, a free-thinking medical student, mocks the local peasants for believing that thunder is generated by Elijah the Prophet as he rolls across the heavens in his chariot. In fact, and in part, Shukhov was pulling Buynovsky's leg: the peasant likes being "playful"[177] with this prison newbie who "knows science,"[178] in the same way that the villagers in *Fathers and Sons* see the protagonist as an eccentric at best, and ridiculous at worst. Solzhenitsyn's prose works abound in encoded commentaries, polemical, interrogative, or supportive, to the classical texts of Russian literature.

Shukhov may be able to account for the relationship between God, the moon, and the stars, even if on the plane of magic, but he does not have an explanation for the way the unlimited goodness of the Deity can be reconciled with the reality and prevalence of evil in this world. But then he does not spend much time worrying about such things. He is even skeptical of the efficacy of prayer. "Prayers are like petitions—either they don't get through at all, or else it's 'complaint rejected,'" he tells Alyosha the Baptist[179] (naturally, the latter disagrees). Again, this is an entirely pre-Christian stance, reminiscent of Epicurus's belief that the gods do not concern themselves with human affairs.

With this theodicean exchange between Shukhov and Alyosha, the text alludes to—but does not formally pose, or answer—the central question of the twentieth century: "Where was God at Auschwitz?" On first reading, the answer seems to be negative: in the Special Camp there is no God. We learn that after a few weeks there, the Ukrainians of the Eastern Catholic rite lost the habit of crossing themselves when sitting down to a meal while "the Russians don't even remember which hand you cross yourself with."[180] We all know that Hell is a place of eternal punishment where the sinner's soul shall know no surcease from its torments. Shukhov's words to the sweet-tempered Baptist can be taken to mean that the two of them are in just such a place. But unlike those terrible Siberian camps in the *Kolyma Tales*, the Special Camp, though at times and in places hellish, is not a dark, closed universe of unremitting human horror. It is a locus of pain; but also of life; and even, sometimes, of happiness, however fleeting. Shalamov's disagreements with Solzhenitsyn, which eventually led to an open break between them, hinged on this very point: "The novel is dead. ... A reader who has witnessed Hiroshima, the gas chambers of Auschwitz, and the concentration camps, will find plots that were invented offensive."[181] For Solzhenitsyn's gulag "brother,"[182] a literature of the imagination was no longer possible, and so instead he asserted his faith in a literature of the documented and documentary truth, in a world where evil had triumphed, perhaps for all time.

Solzhenitsyn's *best* heroes always possess the quality of psychic health, gifted to them by a writer whose personality, like Goethe's, exhibited a rare degree of inner balance. Shukhov can still love and he can still hate, without second thoughts or hesitation. He and his fellow-zeks, the groveling Fetyukov excepted, have the strength of spirit to function as thinking, feeling, empathizing human beings. As well as the strength of body. This is important, for a valid moral stance requires a minimal level of biological viability, a point expressed with flamboyant over-emphasis by Nietzsche: "All credibility, all good conscience, all evidence of truth come only from the senses."[183] With his Tolstoyan interest in the functions and malfunctions of the biological self, Solzhenitsyn never lets us forget that the prisoners are not just mind and feeling, but also skin and muscle and bone. Survival is hard work. In this cold, colorless hell, Shukhov has learned to endure by using his wits and skills. He knows how to utilize his physical body in the most efficient way possible. This is the *how* of his heroism. "Survival ... is an act of refusal and resistance; and the survivor's capacity to bear inhuman hardship, his small victories against the monolith of destruction, are the forms of life-inspired stubbornness."[184]

So, where is God in all this? Flinty Tyurin has his own notion of providential justice. The officers who discharged him from the army and turned him into a starving pariah were shot during the Great Terror. When he learned this, he recalls, "I crossed myself and said, 'So you're up there in heaven after all, Lord. You are slow to anger, but you hit hard.'"[185] Meek Alyosha's faith is very different from the foreman's muscular variety: "We must pray for spiritual things, asking God to remove the scum of evil from our hearts."[186]

Tyurin's harsh words are dangerous, in more ways than one. His is the language of retribution, not repentance; of rage, not forgiveness. Solzhenitsyn recalls that just before the issue of *Novy Mir* went to the printers, the sympathetic apparatchik, Lebedev, asked for this passage to be removed. "But what they were suggesting was that I should make concessions at the expense of God and of the peasant, and this I had vowed never to do."[187] The passage stayed; God and peasant remained textually intact. Leona Toker's suggestion that *The Gulag Archipelago* constitutes a call to revolt[188] is also applicable to "Ivan Denisovich," if we accept—as we must—that Tyurin's voice is authorially privileged within its spectrum of articulated viewpoints.

As for Shukhov, he finds the idea of God as judge or redeemer utterly foreign: "I'm not against God, see. I'm quite ready to believe in God. But I just don't believe in heaven or hell. Why do you think everybody deserves either heaven or hell?"[189] Solzhenitsyn's hero may be confined in a place designed by evil minds to operate according to "the law of the taiga,"[190] the wolfish rule that man shall abuse and torture man, but he cannot accept that any human being deserves eternal damnation, or for that matter, eternal bliss. He has known too much pain and too little happiness to be comfortable with such neat notions. His quiet, questioning words are an expression of an instinctive defiance—of God, perhaps; but certainly of the System that brutally separated him and his fellow prisoners from their loved ones, erased their identities as farmers or soldiers or artists, and consigned them to this icy inferno.

The novelist Valentin Kataev, a postrevolutionary Modernist who became a Stalin-era literary journeyman and then a Thaw liberal (such a banal progression!), did not think much of Shukhov because he "does not dare to protest, even from under his blanket."[191] His colleague Kornei Chukovskii, to whom these words were spoken, offers an astringent comment: "But how much did Kataev protest under the Stalin regime? He composed slavish hymns, like the rest of them."[192] Or consider this comment by Dmitry Bykov, perhaps Russia's most influential literary critic, who suggests that

Ivan Denisovich is not Solzhenitsyn's favorite hero. Moreover, he is not a typical hero. He is a patient sufferer [*terpila*]. This is a hero who is part of the majority, but does not embody the essence. Whereas the captain or little Alyosha are heroes whom Solzhenitsyn loves. ... Solzhenitsyn does not love the patient sufferer, he loves those who are capable of defending their honor, who have the strength not to break. Like the captain or little Alyosha. Solzhenitsyn is interested in those who mounted rebellions, like the one in Kengir. Americans, I feel, make the same mistake as some Soviet critics, by assuming that Ivan Denisovich is a representation of the Russian soul.[193]

Actually, hyper/hypocritical Kataev and even thoughtful Bykov failed to pay attention, for Solzhenitsyn's hero is not always patient and biddable. It's just that he knows when to pick his moment. In the early hours of the morning Shukhov commits an act of sabotage, a covert deed that did not escape that professionally alert reader, Officer Zakharova: "We can immediately recognize what sort of person this Shukhov is when, having washed the floors in the warders' room, he tosses the unwrung wash rag behind the stove and pours the dirty water onto the path where those in authority walk."[194] A climatic reminder. In the frigid temperatures of wintery Kazakhstan water turns to ice in seconds and "those in authority" are apt to slip and break a neck or limb as they strut down the ice-covered path, which of course is the idea.

> The Earth that wakes *one* human heart to feeling
> Can centre both the worlds of Heaven and Hell,

wrote Emily Brontë. Ivan Denisovich Shukhov's heart is never dead to feeling. He shows the nobility of human survival under inhuman conditions. More than that, in a manmade hell he has retained his moral autonomy and personal dignity and has become a resister: he is a free man.

CHAPTER THREE

"Turgenev Never Knew": The Shorter Fictions of the 1950s and 1960s

Anyone who manages to experience the history of humanity as a whole as his own history will feel in an enormously generalized way all the grief of an invalid who thinks of his health, of an old man who thinks of the dreams of his youth, of a lover deprived of his beloved, of the martyr whose ideal is perishing, of the hero on the evening after a battle that has decided nothing but brought him wounds and the loss of his friend. But if one endured, if one could endure this immense sum of grief of all kinds...

—Friedrich Nietzsche, *The Gay Science*

The enormous tragedy of the dream in the peasant's bent shoulders...
—Ezra Pound, Canto LXXIV

Life is a train station.
—Vladimir Sorokin, "A Month in Dachau"

1

The 1960s were the time when Solzhenitsyn emerged or, rather, erupted from his carefully constructed literary underground and became a cultural celebrity, and soon thereafter the leading opponent of the Soviet government inside the country. Yet where his evolution as an artist was concerned, these developments were almost entirely incidental. An emphatically self-contained personality, the author honed his craft in his own way and at his own pace. Both then and later his creative dynamic bore little relation to what he was doing in the public sphere, let alone the rise and fall in his standing with the critics or even the readers. In this narrow sense, literature was *not* impacted by life. Of course, after the success of "Ivan Denisovich" Solzhenitsyn was determined to spread his message of remembrance and resistance to a national audience. He was now writing with a view to publication, whether in *Novy Mir*, samizdat, or abroad. He tested new ways of scripting new readers, principally by extending the range of his social and historical subjects. Formal experimentation was confined to the successive redactions of *The First Circle* particularly its final, "atomic" version, which marked the beginning of Solzhenitsyn's authorial transition to a maximal diegetic stance.

The shorter works of the 1950s and 1960s hew mostly to nineteenth-century thematic and structural models, so there have been frequent critical comparisons that remark on this very point:

> In Russia ... peasant women have taken the place of the muzhiks, for they possess a strength that their slavish menfolk have lost. Solzhenitsyn investigates the nature of that strength in "Matryona's Home," just as Tolstoy did so for all his female characters.[1]

Or:

> In the sketch "A Reflection in the Water" [sic] ..., like the Russian poet Tiutchev, Solzhenitsyn passes from a short description of nature to a philosophical aphorism.[2]

The work mentioned in the quotation above belongs to the first cycle of "Miniatures," written between 1958–1960, which display an elegiac, anti-industrial aesthetic that would have been recognizable to John Ruskin. These seventeen "microstories"[3] and one "Prayer" started circulating in samizdat almost as soon as their author became a public figure and they remain among Solzhenitsyn's best-read works, at least in Russia. The "Miniatures" represent his divagation into the genre of the prose poem, artistic territory once staked out by Ivan Turgenev and subsequently explored by a succession of authors, nature lovers of the same melancholic bent. They bear resemblance in theme and tone to Ivan Bunin's prose fragments of 1930, for example, "The Idol" ("Idol") and "The Calf's Head" ("Teliach'ia golovka").[4] The ultimate generic referent, however, is the *petits poèmes en prose* by Charles Baudelaire (1869), the inventor of this "oxymoronic genre,"[5] although his settings were entirely urban. That said, while Baudelaire's prose poems are "recognized as [his] breakthrough to poetic modernity,"[6] Solzhenitsyn's own exercises in this formal vein constitute something entirely different, a topically themed experiment in the archaization of the literary text.

The "Miniatures" show an ever-enduring Russian space, which the communist project had tried to level and then to rebuild as a technocratic utopia. Nostalgic and often mournful, they rue the Soviet uglification of the countryside, anthropomorphize trees and animals, and occasionally feature individual characters or relationships. The autobiographical imperative that operates across Solzhenitsyn's oeuvre remains in evidence: the "Miniatures" are a record of the author's peregrinations, by train, cycle, and on foot, across the Soviet Union. In this itinerant sense, they anticipate the descriptions of the countryside around the village of Rozhdestvo in *The First Circle*, where he lived in the 1960s, or even the appreciations of the Swiss and North American landscapes in *Between Two Millstones*. A metonymical stress on the historical and the actual is blended with an elaborate, metaphor-rich descriptive style to produce discrete meditations on life, death, history, nature, and beauty. Like other pre-modernist artists, Solzhenitsyn is sentimental in the sense of Friedrich Schiller: "The sentimental poet is always concerned with two opposite forces, has two modes of representing objects to himself, and of feeling them; they are, the real or limited, and the ideal or infinite; and the mixed feeling that he will awaken will always testify to this duality of origin."[7] The "Miniatures" are suffused with both attitudes, which the stories and novels contain in more expansive form.

When the author showed his prose poems to Tvardovsky the latter was unimpressed, dismissing them as "jottings on your scribbling pad, for future use":[8] in effect, an editorial rejection. Hurt but not discouraged by this verdict, Solzhenitsyn began to distribute the pieces privately "to good people."[9] As a result, they were among the first of his texts to circulate in samizdat, where they enjoyed an immediate success. This kind of landscape writing has always evoked a sympathetic response with Russian readers, although a non-nature-loving receptor might find the "Miniatures" a touch too maudlin, too saturated with pathetic and affective fallacies, too prone to moralize the countryside and its people—the finer feelings pervading them redolent of William Wordsworth in full Lake District flow. Yet Solzhenitsyn's sentimentalism, unlike Wordsworth's, never turns into self-preoccupation or self-pity.

These static or moving pictures in words depict forests, fields, rivers and lakes, historic churches and bell towers, villages nestling in the folds of a gently undulating landscape, a garden after a summer shower, a puppy playing in the snow, a duckling squeaking for its mother. The geography is central or northern Russian, although "A Storm in the Mountains" ("Groza v gorakh") offers a

bombastic celebration of primordial nature in the Caucasus: "Like the arrows of the Lord of Hosts the lightning flashes fell."[10] "The City on the Neva," a much superior production, is a reluctant paean to St. Petersburg, an ekphrastic sketch of the city skyline that treats it as an instance of pure architectural form: beautiful but heartless. The imperial capital, the authorial voice reminds us, was built by eighteenth-century slave labor: "The bones of our forefathers caked and fused and petrified into palaces—yellowish, reddish, chocolate, green."[11] There is no mawkishness here, just a terrible sadness about the millions of lives sacrificed throughout Russian history on the altar of the state's ambition. St. Petersburg is but a cemetery resting on unhallowed ground.

More typical is "Along the Oka" ("Puteshestvuia vdol' Oki"), where the traveling persona contemplates a succession of riparian views and identifies village churches, now fallen into ruin, as the cynosure of a quiet, wounded beauty. In an arresting death image, these decaying houses of worship with their missing crosses and "gaping holes between … rusty ribs" are likened to cadavers greeting the traveler from afar.[12] The piece ends on a wistful note, which is disrupted by the rattle of raucous modernity:

> Our forefathers put all that was finest in themselves, all their understanding of life, into these stones, into these belltowers.

Ram it in, Vitka, give it a bash, don't be shy! Film-show at six o'clock, dancing at eight.[13]

Always when thing Soviet, things modern intrude into Solzhenitsyn's bucolic spaces, the mood darkens. The poetic/prose persona shudders at the sight of an automobile, a rubber-pawed, smoke-spewing monster that is a ghastly replacement for a horse or a camel, "that two-humped swan."[14] Solzhenitsyn disliked mechanical conveyances of every kind other than trains and, by extension, streetcars. Death is a frequent subject: in "The Elm Log" ("Viazovoe brevno"), a piece of firewood about to be sawed up is likened to a man with his head on the execution block, and "The Fire and the Ants" ("Kostër i murav'i") describes a colony of the tiny insects perishing when they swarm into the flames "as though some force was drawing them back to their abandoned homeland."[15] There are Tolstoyan resonances here. One thinks of the scene in *Childhood* (*Detstvo*; 1852) where little Volodya Irtenyev is distracted by the sight of worker ants going about their business on the forest floor, though as creepy-crawly symbols Solzhenitsyn's emmets carry a heavier burden of meaning. The aforementioned "Reflection in Water" ("Otrazhen'e v vode") is a stark statement of religious faith that could have come from the pen of Tolstoy in one of his bleakest moods: "If, try as we may, we never have been and never shall be able to see, to reflect the truth in all its eternal fresh-minted clarity, is it not simply because we are still in motion, still living?"[16] "The Old Bucket" ("Staroe vedro"), on the other hand, is wistfully self-referential. The narrator takes a walk in a Byelorussian forest that holds traces of wartime trenches and dugouts, which remind him of "another wood like it nearby"[17] where he had seen action many years ago. "A Poet's Ashes" ("Prakh poeta") describes an abortive visit to the grave of Yakov Polonsky, a nineteenth-century lyrist. The Solzhenitsyn persona is told that the ancient monastery where the gentle Romantic was entombed is now a jail, and thus out of bounds:

"You can't get to Polonsky. He's in the *zone*. You can't get to him. And anyway, what's there to see? Just a broken-down memorial. Wait a bit though." The camp-guard turned to his wife—"Didn't they dig Polonsky up?"

His wife, cracking sunflower seeds on the porch, nodded: "Of course. He was taken off to Ryazan."

The camp-guard couldn't stop laughing. "Got his release, eh."[18]

This is the only flash of humor in the entire cycle. The joke, though macabre, is not bad, even if it is articulated by one of those squat servants of the gulag who in the good old days used to torment the zeks with wolfish dedication. In the exchange, the authorial persona is pointedly civil, employing the grammatically correct language of the city gentleman or intellectual, while his interlocutor, a prison guard, uses jailhouse jive. Ortega y Gasset's *el hombre masa* has learned to speak Russian.

The shortest and strangest of these very uneven pieces is "Approaching the Day" ("Pristupaia ko dniu"), where the sight of some thirty young people "bending, squatting, bowing" in a forest reminds the poetic/prose subject of a religious congregation.[19] Upon closer inspection he discovers the secular truth of the matter: "No, they weren't saying their prayers. They were doing their morning exercises."[20] The temple of nature has been converted into a gym, in keeping with the modern cult of the body: an offensive development on a variety of fronts.

By way of contrast, the cycle ends with an actual "Prayer" ("Molitva"), penned just after the publication of "Ivan Denisovich." In this orison, the writer (the empirical, believing Solzhenitsyn) gives thanks to God for allowing him "to send mankind a reflection of your rays"[21] (*ia smog poslat' chelovechestvu / otblesk luchei Tvoikh*),[22] a phrase that echoes, perhaps inadvertently, Akhmatova's identically titled poem of 1915:

> After mass, thus I'm praying, impassioned,
> After so many tormented days,
> Let the menacing cloud over Russia
> Shimmer brightly in glorious rays.[23]
>
> *Tak molius' za Tvoei liturgiei*
> *Posle stol'kikh tomitel'nykh dnei,*
> *Choby tucha nad tëmnoi Rossiei*
> *Stala oblakom v slave luchei.*[24]

This coda to the cycle adumbrates a theodicean connection that aligns the tragic history of twentieth-century Russia to the Creator's Plan, with the writer assuming, humbly or otherwise, a mediating artistic function between God and country. The "Prayer" is an intensely personal statement of faith, as prayers often are, but there is more to it than that. Personal, yes, but not private: this is a published text, after all.[25] Tzvetan Todorov reminds us that prayers "[coincide] with a speech act that also has a nonliterary existence,"[26] and the religious poetry of St. John of the Cross, John Donne, and Akhmatova herself is a case in point. A literary prayer or a prayer that becomes a fact of literature invites an exegetic treatment that must be supported by two different conceptions of the text, as an expression of a believer's faith and an aesthetic production. Since Solzhenitsyn's "Prayer" constitutes part of, or is at least formally appended to, a published *literary* whole, it qualifies on both counts.

In the "Miniatures" the author is writing *against* the twentieth-century loss of faith in nature as a site of transcendent beauty and source of spiritual solace. This numinous stance is in evidence even—especially—when the places he visits have been poisoned and wounded by politics or war. Here, as elsewhere in the oeuvre, his reception of the countryside rests on a traditionalist acceptance of the national value of landscapes and the living things that inhabit them. How very different from the "wakeful" and "hopeful" wanderers on the beach in Virginia Woolf's *To the Lighthouse*, with their modern (modernist) "imaginations of the strangest kind—of flesh turned to atoms which drove before the wind, of stars flashing in their hearts, of cliff, sea, cloud, and sky brought purposely together to assemble outwardly the scattered parts of the vision therein."[27] Solzhenitsyn's own vision is of a natural world that remains unatomized and unscattered, and always very Russian.

At the same time, the "Miniatures" all touch upon themes that are central to this writer's prose: history, tyranny, people in nature, people in confined spaces, the poetics of the body, the ethics of artistic creativity, as well as the presence or absence of God in the lives of his countrymen. But for the references to the Soviet here and now, there is nothing in these texts that would have startled or puzzled the very same Turgenev or Bunin. So, generically and stylistically, the pieces are out of time, though not out of place, which makes them the most problematic of Solzhenitsyn's literary creations. In our knowing, quotational culture his prose poems will tempt some receptors to approach them with tongue firmly planted in cheek or fingers tightly crossed: to consume them as pastiche. And yet, the narrative/poetic voice is so ingenuous, the works so patently defenseless against a mocking reader response that, perhaps, they remain invulnerable to such sly treatment. Perhaps.

2

The seven stories I shall discuss next were written in 1959–66. Four of them—"Matryona's Home," "Incident at Kochetovka Station," "For the Good of the Cause," "Zakhar-the-Pouch"—appeared in *Novy Mir*, and for that reason they remain the best-known. These works were sharply critical of Soviet reality but got past the censor thanks to Solzhenitsyn's post-"Denisovich" glow and Tvardovsky's political pull. The other three stories were unpublishable in the Soviet Union.

The series shows Solzhenitsyn at his confident, writerly best, a master storyteller with an anthropological eye for human and social detail. He displays a sure knowledge of the cultural codes that defined the speech, clothing, bearing and even facial language of mid-twentieth-century Soviet men and women. Strong sociological content is combined with direct moral engagement, which on occasion becomes polemically actualized. There is much wagging of the authorial finger, and not every twenty-first-century reader, whether Russian or Western, will necessarily enjoy these pedagogical prompts. Nevertheless, they are integral to the fictive package, so there can be no suspension of disbelief without an acceptance of the message or at least its presence in the text.

Solzhenitsyn paints a grim picture of socialism in one country, from the cretinous economics of collectivized agriculture to the stultifying effects of an ossified ideology. Trumping these concerns, however, is his Tolstoyan investigation of goodness and truth and their place in the human condition. Yet if the edifying message is always present, it is balanced by the author's equally Tolstoyan skill at fashioning magically believable characters and lives. The works possess a formal tightness and balance which led certain critics to propose that Solzhenitsyn is a better short story writer than novelist, a view that has remained current in some quarters to this day. At the same time, none of the stories is a psychological study, even if some of the characters, such as Lieutenant Zotov in "Incident at Kochetovka Station," are multilayered personalities with secret complexities. They have depth, but it is of a cultural, rather than psychological, kind.

Set in periods and places that are filled with human suffering, the stories describe what are sometimes horrifying instances of cruelty or injustice. Several of the texts, however, also contain a situationally unexpected instance of generosity, kindness, or personal decency: an uplifting surprise. Let us recall Solzhenitsyn's comment that "a piece only gained, that its effect was heightened, as the harsher tones were softened." Traces of that harshness are still present, but there is also a consonance between the meta-rhetoric of denunciation and repentance and the intricate literary structures that support it. This goes even for "The Easter Procession," a polemical tour de force that lacks a protagonist or even identifiable characters as such, unless a bawling band of blasphemers can be described as a collective personality: the Swinging Sixties, Soviet-style. Some of the fictional presences are sketched with the lightest of touches, for example the dying Red Army veteran in "The Right Hand" or fugitive Anna in "What a Pity," who calls to mind Chekhov's genteel heroines. Other personae are endowed with a remarkable richness of texture, such as Matryona in the eponymous story, whose furrows and wrinkles are as memorable as those of the equally rustic, equally pre-modern Ivan Denisovich, while her timber cottage, with its almost living walls and fittings, is the most vividly described domestic interior in the whole of Solzhenitsyn, a writer who more than most was interested in the materiality of the home.

Other than "Zakhar-the-Pouch," each piece is organized around one of those familiar closed/open space binaries: the massive building of the cancer hospital vs. the verdant park that surrounds it ("The Right Hand") or the hyper-elongated rectangular form of a Moscow boulevard vs. the sprawling urban expanse on either side ("What a Pity"). "Matryona's Home" and "Zakhar-the-Pouch" are suffused with a dolorous love of Russia, its people, and its landscapes; and feature mythic topoi, such as a pair of brothers who pay court to the same woman ("Matryona'") or a battle between an army of the righteous and a barbarian horde ("Zakhar"). "An Incident at Kochetovka Station" and "For the Good of the Cause" are, in places, almost dramaturgical, with sustained stretches of demotic conversation that frame the action while serving as a culturological snapshot (snap-record) of the sociolects of the age. With their staccato rhythms and vernacular twists, these dynamic exchanges anticipate the daytime, nighttime dialogues in *The First Circle*. And if "The Right Hand" shows male bodies injured by history and ravaged by disease, elsewhere there are touching depictions of wounded femininity: gentle Anna in "What a Pity," who is frightened of every man wearing a uniform or brandishing a briefcase, and elderly Matryona, who never married her true love and lost every one of her children to poverty.

This is classic middle-period Solzhenitsyn: minimal-narrator, maximal-content, and only occasionally and only covertly experimental. As is the rule in his worlds, the action of history upon the individual is brutally, irreducibly direct, while the characters are shown at their most politically, domestically, or biologically vulnerable. Yet, whether these stories treat forbidden themes overtly, as for example "The Easter Procession," or obliquely, as happens in "The Right Hand," they all attack the ideological and aesthetic codes of the day or the era, sometimes to devastating effect. The only exception is "For the Good of the Cause," an uncharacteristically cautious treatment of hypocrisy and corruption among government bureaucrats in the post-Stalin period. In several of the stories trains figure prominently. As Solzhenitsyn explained many years later: "I have loved railways from childhood, and I perceive their disappearance as a loss second only to that of horses. I find it painful."[28]

One last point. "The Right Hand," "Matryona's Home," and "Zakhar-the-Pouch" form a trilogy of sorts, discrete installments in a fictionalized autobiography, though only in "Matryona" is the first-person narrator identified by name or, rather, patronymic, as Ignatich (see Isaevich). A pensive, reticent soul, the autobiographical hero has done time and is a cancer survivor. He has few friendships and connections in the "free" world. Preternaturally observant and curious about people, he lives a full life of the mind but does so privately, almost asocially. In "The Right Hand," set in 1954, we find him recuperating from a malignant tumor in the same Tashkent hospital where Oleg Kostoglotov, the hero of *Cancer Ward*, will receive treatment a few months hence, albeit along a different fictive timeline. "Matryona's Home" shows him a couple of years later, after he takes a job as a schoolmaster in a remote village. In "Zakhar-the-Pouch," where the action is set circa 1964, he is a bicycle-riding explorer of Russia's cultural sites, now perhaps a bit more outgoing but still watchful, still reserved: a hermit on the road. The narrator does not explicitly self-identify as a writer, though he spends the nights working on his manuscripts ("Matryona's Home"). But in each case, he never dominates the fictive proceedings. Instead, he occupies a fabulaically subsidiary position as he reports on an encounter with another character who is the real protagonist. Even in "The Right Hand," where at least half the text is devoted to the narrator's medical situation, the figure of the dying Red Army veteran overshadows everyone and everything else.

3

Upon reading "The Right Hand" Tvardovsky told the author, "All in all, this is the most terrifying thing you have ever written."[29] A larger-than-life personality, the editor was often flamboyant in his pronouncements, and he had not yet been introduced to *The First Circle*, the novel in which Solzhenitsyn's transgressions against the SocRealist rulebook were far more spectacular. Still, Tvardovsky had a point. For this work to have been published in Khrushchev's Soviet Union, let alone Brezhnev's, would have been an aberration even greater than the cause célèbre that was "Ivan Denisovich." "The Right Hand" challenges the significant myth of the revolution as a world-liberating event while sharing tropes and topoi with the works that Solzhenitsyn published in *Novy Mir* between 1962–66. Tvardovsky found the story terrifying because on many levels it seemed so familiar.

"The Right Hand" is an intensified anecdote, a compact narrative whose plot centers round a paradox of injustice and in which a discrete human predicament is historicized. The narrator, a former political prisoner, is a recovering patient at the Tashkent Oncological Clinic. As he is relaxing in the hospital grounds on a balmy spring afternoon, he meets a very sick man who has reached the Uzbek capital after one of those exhausting bureaucratic odysseys that are a frequent occurrence in Russian literature. The narrator, himself barely ambulant, offers to accompany the new arrival to the hospital building. Shuffling their feet and frequently pausing for breath, the two men make their way there. But when they reach reception, the duty nurse, an insipidly pretty Komsomol, refuses to sign the admission forms: the small-mindedness of the paper shuffler compounded by the callousness of youth. In an attempt to change her mind, the stranger produces his certificate of military service, a dog-eared document attesting that in 1921 this pasty-faced man with a monstrously distended belly was a member of "the distinguished 'World Revolution' Special Detachment of____Province eliminating large numbers of surviving counterrevolutionary vermin with his own hand"[30] (*i svoei rukoi mnogo porubal ostavshikhsia gadov*").[31] It identifies the bearer as a Comrade Bobrov. We infer that the former world revolutionary saw action in the wooded regions near the central Russian city of Tambov, the scene of the country's largest peasant uprising since the eighteenth century, which was suppressed by Mikhail Tukhachevsky, the future marshal and future victim of Stalin.[32]

The ending is abrupt. We never find out if the old cavalryman manages to gain admission to the clinic, though the mark of death is stark upon his ruined body. One almost has the sense that Solzhenitsyn, guided by considerations of narrative economy, clipped off the final paragraph with a pair of authorial scissors, à la Chekhov. As for the narrator, the reader may assume that the coming de-Stalinization campaign will end his "perpetual" exile.

Within the corpus of Solzhenitsyn's prose this short story constitutes a companion piece to *Cancer Ward*, though it was composed some six years before that novel. The two works share the same raw medical content and both are set in the Uzbek hospital where he was treated for seminoma. There are other cross-textual congruences. In "The Right Hand," the narrator tries to intimidate the duty nurse by adopting the guise of a hardened hood, and in *Cancer Ward* the hero, Kostoglotov, employs the same subterfuge to confront an amnestied criminal at the Tashkent railway station. As the narrator in the story blusters and glares, he takes on the appearance of a "gorilla":[33] Kostoglotov's textual totem is the macaque.

Most of the action in "The Right Hand" takes place in the leafy park adjacent to the clinic, which contains a kiosk selling office supplies, a fruit stall, a native tearoom, and an alabaster bust of Stalin "grinning sarcastically behind his stone whiskers,"[34] the iconic rictus that ornamented so many of the Leader's likenesses. Now, the autobiographical imperative that operates across Solzhenitsyn's fictions meant that their plots and settings were subject to a rigorous authorial fact check. We can be certain that the appearance of the park and the hospital as well as the narrator's sensations and perceptions are mnemonically accurate. In this narrow sense, the story is a dramatized record of one day in the life of Aleksandr Isaevich. He even bestows upon his alter ego a cherished private ambition, which was realized only after the author moved to Vermont: "All my life I had wanted to play tennis, but I had never had the chance."[35] As for the Central Asian venue, its sights and sounds serve as a contrastive backscreen for the very Russian figures of the veteran and the exile. The latter's generalized sense of estrangement from the world is compounded by the sunlit strangeness of his surroundings. That said, one can easily imagine the same events taking place somewhere in central Siberia or central Ukraine circa 1954. In other words, the Soviet trumps the subtropical, which is also true of *Cancer Ward*, where the local color receives much greater textual prominence.

The exile's personal situation is defined through a succession of negations:

> I was like the sick people all around me, and yet I was different: I had fewer rights than they had and was forced to be more silent. People came to visit them, relatives wept for them, and their one concern, their one aim in life was to get well again. But if I recovered, it would be almost pointless: I was thirty-five years of age and yet in that spring I had no one I could call my own in the whole world. I did not even own a passport, and if I were to recover, I should have to leave this green, abundant land and go back to my desert where I had been exiled "in perpetuity."[36]

This is not mawkish self-pity but a matter-of-fact recognition on the narrator's part that he exists in a social void. Rightless, friendless, womanless, he is utterly bereft. He is terminally poor: he cannot afford the apricots, raisins, and cherries on sale, those fruity markers of the Asian locale. The negative quality of the ex-prisoner's state of being is not just personal but generational, as when he recalls his "contemporaries, frozen to death near Demiansk [site of a Red Army defeat in 1942], incinerated at Auschwitz, harried to exhaustion in Djezkazgan [site of the Kengir labor camp], or dying in the wastes of Siberia."[37] Welcome to the bloodlands of Eurasia.

Ссыльный учитель.
Кок-Терек, 1953

At the same time, the story conveys an intoxicating sense of physical renewal. The narrator is radiantly happy, for he has escaped death. Yet joy is tempered by resignation: "The clearer it grew that I was recovering from the disease, and the more certain I became that I would remain alive, the more wistfully I looked around."[38] The authorial alter ego is acutely aware of his biological contingency: "In my wildest dreams I still measured my extra span of life not in years but in months."[39] His health may be on the mend, but he looks terrible: his face is lined, his complexion greenish, his posture bent.

With physical restoration comes physical need: the ex-prisoner is overwhelmed by a terrible, pulsating sexual longing. The park is a locus of medical femininity, its paths and alleyways pullulating with "women—women, women! … young doctors, nurses, laboratory assistants, clerks, housekeepers, dispensers, and relatives visiting patients."[40] A list of identities and professions: catalogue prose with a hint of objectification. The sight of these nubile bodies wearing white coats or draped in gaudy, gauzy dresses of silk and cotton tantalizes the exile. He watches, and covets. "Each one, as she flashed past, momentarily made up a complete plot for a novel: her past, the (nonexistent) chance of my getting to know her."[41] He is, after all, a writer, whether former, actual, or would-be. From unattainable objects of desire the women are transformed into unrealized subjects of literature.

Fictive circumstance affords Kostoglotov and Vorotyntsev, two of Solzhenitsyn's manliest protagonists, the opportunity to study from up close female faces and bodies that are in the same room, the same bed. Visually or by touch the heroes erotically fracture their partners into sets of eyes, lips, arms, ankles, feet. Not so this character. He is separated from the enchanting figures he so wistfully watches by distance. He is never in a position to focus his fragmenting gaze on the flesh underneath those bright dresses. It is true that the narrator objectifies the women in the park, yet the effect is touching, because he is so powerless, both as a cancer survivor and an ex-convict. He others them, but with his wilted physique, "clown-like striped jacket,"[42] and dangerous past he is *painfully* aware of his own otherness in this sunlit, feminized space. Or rather, it is the narrator's later, healthier self in the untextualized here and now that realizes his old self's incongruousness in the textualized there and then: "Not one of these women would have dared to walk beside me. But I could not see myself."[43]

Solzhenitsyn gives us the bare minimum, so we learn little else about this frail ex-prisoner; little, that is, except that he has a bit of a temper, when he faces down the unsympathetic receptionist. As for the dying cavalryman, he is reticent and distracted, his spirit crushed by the disease. Throughout the story he is always acted upon, a passive object of another's individual or institutional will. Even the narrator, sickly though he is, quickly assumes authority over the new arrival:

"Do you happen to have a cigarette, comrade?"
"You can forget that idea, old fellow," I barked at him. "You and I haven't got a hope unless we give up smoking."[44]

The veteran shows a flicker of vitality just once, when he haltingly relates that many years ago Sergei Kirov, a leading Bolshevik of the early Soviet era, had shaken his hand (that right hand!). The ashes of ideological ardor still glow red inside that ruined frame.

If the narrator is but an autobiographical outline, the figure of the ailing cavalryman is an imagined silhouette. His fictive presence is a function of physiology, political belief, and war memory. We always see him from the outside, that is, through the ex-prisoner's tired eyes. The latter acts as his guide, a role also played by *Cancer Ward*'s Kostoglotov, who counsels and assists his fellow patients.

The quintessential charismatic cavalryman in Russian literature is Vasily Denisov in *War and Peace*, the hard-drinking, hard-fighting hussar with a "sinewy hairy hand and stumpy fingers in which he held the hilt of his naked saber."[45] The Red Army veteran's hand, we learn, is also small, but once upon a time it must have been just as muscled and strong and capable of martial prehension:

"And I remembered the way horsemen used to strike down men on foot with a single, sweeping backhand stroke."[46] These days, however, this semiotically weighted extremity is morbid, like the rest of Bobrov's ravaged body. Of course, as a *beau sabreur* the gallant Denisov stands far above Tukhachevsky's mounted butcher, that whilom minion of the Red Terror.

Now, the right—left binary is a fixture in the world's mythological and folklore systems, as noted by Yuri Lotman: "The asymmetry of the human body constituted the anthropological basis for its semiotization, because in all human cultures, the semiotics of right vs. left possess the same universal character as the opposition up vs. down."[47] As an anthropological norm, right-handedness is commonly privileged over left-handedness.[48] In Russian, the title of the story is *"Pravaia kist'"*, and as is the case in English, the word *pravyi* or "right" also means "just." And so, we read: "With a great effort he raised one clenched hand, and I pulled a sweaty, crumpled piece of paper out of it"[49] (*On s trudom pripodnial odnu kist', szhatuiu v kulak, i ia vytianul iz neë potnuiu izmiatuiu bumazhku*);[50] this is the ex-trooper's *hand*written admission request. Bobrov's listlessly raised fist turns into a parody of the *Rot Front* salute, favored by communists in the 1920s and 1930s. If we accept that the former cavalryman wielded his sabre in an unjust cause, then "the just hand" is, or was, the hand of injustice.

The old trooper's service has long been forgotten by the regime for which he once killed and bled: "Now they don't even acknowledge my existence. Some of the records were burnt, others were lost."[51] The man with the right hand is one of those Solzhenitsynian characters whose battered frames are a chronicle of twentieth-century Russian history: living physiological archives. Perpetrator or victim, the body is the message; and for the time being, the message remains extant.

This is not the whole story, however. Bobrov may have earned his spurs by putting peasants to the sabre, his brain may be addled with Bolshevik bromides, but even as his body festers, his spirit endures. He remains recognizably (admirably?) human. He bears his awful disease and those bureaucratic outrages stoically, even heroically. The unselfconscious decorum with which the old man conducts himself transcends his tired fanaticism in a manner that Dostoevsky would have recognized.

Still, Solzhenitsyn never lays it on with a trowel. The descriptions of the dying veteran are carefully neutral in tone even when he is shown at his most pathetic: "A small, ungainly man who looked like a beggar was addressing the crowd from time to time in a voice gasping for breath: 'Comrades… Comrades…'"[52] Bobrov asks the narrator for three rubles, which the latter, desperately poor though he is, gives him after the briefest of hesitations. In this connection, other Dostoevskian associations suggest themselves, for instance, with the protagonist of *The Idiot* (1869): "The topos of humility may take the form of dressing so badly that the holy man is mistaken for a beggar, as Myshkin is on arrival at the Epanchin household."[53] In the *Life of St. Feodosy of Pechersk* (c. 1088), a hagiographic work that did much to embed the topos of the holy beggar in medieval Russian culture,[54] "the kenotic ideal finds expression both ideologically and pragmatically,"[55] in the latter sense, when the faithful mistake the saint for a common mendicant. Of course, Bobrov is neither a holy man nor a hagiographic hero, yet his presence carries identifiable kenotic overtones.

While the old veteran's revolutionary certificate may be a literary creation, the introduction of this scrap of vintage newspeak anticipates the methodology of *The Red Wheel*, which incorporates hundreds of archival documents to illustrate the military and political events described while conveying the discursive flavor of the times. In "The Right Hand," however, the larger historical picture remains untextualized. True, there are echoes of the foundational violence that brought the Soviet state into being, for example, the bureaucratic endorsement of Comrade Bobrov's military service as a form of political pest control. The subject at *hand*, however, is the Soviet present with its routine injustices but also its plenitude of people who are fair-to-middlingly happy. These untroubled souls are merely walk-ons and walk-offs: the players on the tennis courts next to the clinic and the fashionably dressed women crisscrossing the park.

The portrait of Bobrov reminds us of the "creatural dignity of every human individual," which Erich Auerbach identified as the topic of central concern in Russian literature. Clearly, the narrator does not love the revolution or its works, and his political take on the ailing Red Army veteran remains unstated, but then, he has no political take, for he sees and treats the veteran as, first and last, a fellow-suffering, fellow human being.

4

Tvardovsky may have been "terrified" by "The Right Hand," but another empirical reader, a poet far more famous than he, used similar language to describe "Matryona's Home," which she found "more terrifying than 'Ivan Denisovich.'"[56] That reader was Akhmatova: textual horror is in the eye of the receptor. The grand matriarch of Russian literature was awed by the story's "amazing details" and its evocation of a happier past before Matryona's village was "pulverized" by the "locomotive" of modernity.[57]

In 1964, Ilya Ehrenburg (not a writer Solzhenitsyn especially admired) offered this opinion: "['Ivan Denisovich'] is beautifully written [*eto masterski napisano*], but I understand how it was done, whereas with 'Matryona's Home' I cannot."⁵⁸ In other words, the story is an architectonic mystery, so much of a piece, so excellently crafted, that this reader's sharp eye was unable—reluctant?—to penetrate its structures and textures. Epics, being pre-literary, authorless, and culturally whole, display the same order of resistance to analysis, and "Matryona" is pervaded by an epic authorial sensibility. In effect, Ehrenburg was saying that Solzhenitsyn had achieved formal perfection or had come as close to it as is artistically possible. These were large claims to make, even for a work that had entered the canon almost at the instant of publication, and anyway, perfection is unsusceptible to critical quantification.

We observe a different readerly dynamic when we examine Tvardovsky's initial response to "Matryona's Home," which came while "Ivan Denisovich" was still finding its tortuous way onto the pages of *Novy Mir*:

> He went around in circles, first talking about the story, then making some general observations, then returning to the story, then going over his general observations again.... A true artist himself, he could not reproach me with not telling the truth. But to admit that it was the whole truth would have undermined his political and social beliefs at their foundations.⁵⁹

A few months later, however, "Ivan Denisovich" was published, to near-universal acclaim. Tvardovsky now overcame his ideological scruples and guided the story into print, thus giving Solzhenitsyn his second publication, which demonstrated that the tale about the Russian peasant in the Special Camp was no flash in the pan.

Ehrenburg and Tvardovsky's takes on "Matryona," with their respective emphasis on Solzhenitsyn's writerly technique and his truth telling, offer a good point of departure. So, let us get started.

In the summer of 1956 the authorial narrator, here named Ignatich, leaves a "hot and dusty desert" (that is, southern Kazakhstan) to travel to "the central belt ... close to the leafy mutterings of forests."⁶⁰ A man wounded by history, he is fleeing bad places and bad memories. A couple of clues give us to understand that the narrator is a war veteran and former prisoner who has been freed as a result of Khrushchev's liberalizing reforms. Ignatich longs to "efface" and "lose" himself in "deepest Russia."⁶¹ Like so many itinerant characters in Russian literature, he is engaged in the pursuit of authenticity, the pursuit of difference. He will find plenty of both.

Yet, this is not how "Matryona's Home" begins. First, there is a preamble that adumbrates the axes of time and space and action:

> A hundred and eighty-four kilometers from Moscow trains were still slowing down to a crawl a good six months after it happened. Passengers stood glued to the windows or went out to stand by the doors. Was the line under repair, or what? Would the train be late?
>
> It was all right. Past the crossing the train picked up speed again and the passengers went back to their seats.
>
> Only the engine-drivers knew what it was all about.
>
> The engine-drivers and I.[62]

This proem combines cryptic observations ("only the engine drivers knew"), geographical references ("a hundred and eighty-four kilometers from Moscow"), and quotidian details ("passengers stood glued to the windows"), with the narrator's somber tones constituting the common diegetic denominator. His status as the omniscient textual authority is put on record, and the setting is spatially fixed, perpendicular to the steel track that runs for hundreds of miles from the fabled capital into an untextualized distance. Moscow may be the heart of Russia and its literary spaces, but this story is set *elsewhere*, at some other point in the limitless expanse of the nation's symbolic geography. There is also a hint at the contingency of all imaginative literature, a veiled caveat: like those train passengers, we the readers will be intrigued and absorbed, but only briefly, for the duration of the story's discourse time, thereafter free to continue on our non-readerly way, though perhaps a little sadder and a little wiser.

So, Ignatich arrives in this region of forests and marshes, ironically by train, and sets the plot in motion. He obtains a job as a math teacher and takes lodgings with Matryona Grigorieva, a widow who lives in the small village of Talnovo. The site of an impoverished collective farm, it lies a short distance away from the mainstays of the local economy, the railway itself and the polluted settlement of Torfoprodukt (Peat Product). "Turgenev never knew that you can put words like that together in Russian," the narrator ruefully comments, and he is, of course, right.[63] (Granted, *The Brothers Karamazov* is set in the town of Skotoprigonyevsk, or Cattle Station.) Every place name here, however noxious, is taken from real life: as is always his practice, Solzhenitsyn fictionalizes to a minimal degree.

Matryona's cottage has the battered appearance typical of the impoverished villages of central Russia. As Ignatich walks up to it for the first time, he is his usual observant self. One can imagine him writing down his impressions that same evening after he moves in:

> Its row of four windows looked out on the cold backs, the two slopes of the roof were covered with shingles, and a little attic window was decorated in the old Russian style. But the shingles were rotting, the beam-ends of the house and the once mighty gates had turned gray with age, and there were gaps in the little shelter over the gate.[64]

Our narrator notes that the roof extends over part of the yard and remarks on the three flights of stairs in front: one leading to the landing, another to the attic room, which is separate from the rest of the structure, and another down to the basement. The geometry of the domestic space is thereby delineated, for future readerly reference.

Every important event in Matryona's life happened inside this four-windowed house and it seems to have acquired a personality of its own, one of which Ignatich is instantly aware. As the tale unfolds, the cabin, from its sagging ceilings and crooked floors to the tattered furniture and crowded kitchen, becomes a co-participant in the fictive proceedings. Throughout the story Ignatich describes the function of every part of the dwelling with ethnographic precision, but also with palpable affection. Of course, it takes him some time to get his domestic bearings, and he does so by stages, in the same way that he gets to know his landlady.

The peasant name "Matryona" derives from the Latin *matrona*—"venerable woman": an onomastic hint. In fact, the heroine is a few months short of sixty, which in this country and era qualifies her as unambiguously old. In appearance Matryona is that national archetype, the head-scarfed babushka, and so the description we get is correspondingly brief: she has faded blue eyes in a "roundish face"[65] and suffers from an unexplained ailment, "a wicked disease" that comes upon her every few months.[66] Her voice is lilting and soft and reminds the narrator of a grandmother in a fairy tale. Matryona is one of those rare characters in Solzhenitsyn who smiles, and smiles well—so well, in fact, that Ignatich makes repeated attempts to capture that gently radiant expression on film, though he manages to take just one picture that does it justice.

Matryona is hardworking, uncomplaining, unselfish, and so very, very kind. Her neighbors take advantage of the old woman, as do the collective farm bosses, and they all look down on her as a bit of a fool who can be easily ordered or induced to work for free. Ignatich's landlady has three younger sisters who are reluctant to visit because, he suspects, "they were afraid that Matryona might ask them for help,"[67] a passing comment that is harrowing in its implications. On the whole, the villagers are a decidedly unattractive lot, "with everyone a degenerate or a vampire," as one of Solzhenitsyn's biographers puts it, with just a small degree of exaggeration.[68]

The main body of the text is built around Ignatich's curious relationship with his landlady: not quite friends, not quite confidants, these two very different personalities quietly rub along and quietly grow fond of each other. The former prisoner does not dwell on the bond between them: it is an evolving narrative given, and anyway, Ignatich tends to be guarded where private matters are concerned. Part of the story's appeal is its Chekhovian reticence about the subtleties of human interaction, which contrasts with the lively account of the passions and compulsions swirling elsewhere in the village. Ignatich is an exemplary pedagogue *and* an exemplary narrator.

With the ex-prisoner now a tenant, the cabin's single room is informally divided into two halves: Matryona's, which contains a bed between the corner and the stove, and nothing else; and Ignatich's, with a camp bed and small desk next to a couple of windows. The sleeping areas, hers and his, remain ungendered, a mimetic blank that fits the nature of the relationship. It is more like that of a couple of friends living companionably under the same roof than that of a mother figure and a son figure, which would have been the more obvious fictive treatment. The little kitchen, where the old woman employs her limited cooking skills with the few edibles she is able to procure, is the only feminized space in the house.

The cabin is a little planet with its own humankind (Matryona and Ignatich), fauna (a goat, a cat, a population of mice, and a teeming multitude of cockroaches), flora (Matryona's favorite rubber plants, a whole "forest" of them),[69] and microclimate: "The freezing winds could not blow the warmth of the stove away all at once, though it was cold by morning, especially when the wind blew on the shabby side."[70] Each of the classes of living things that populate the cottage occupies its own domestic niche. The goat, a scrawny animal with twisted horns, supplies the household with milk. The cat's job is to catch the mice, which it does well, even though it is lame. That gammy leg is nicely textualized: "When she jumped from the stove she didn't land with the soft sound a cat usually makes, but with a heavy thud as three of her feet struck the floor at once."[71] The mice are described through the same medium of sound. They are never seen but always heard as they scurry between layers of wallpaper, the cat tracking their invisible progress with an angry eye. Even the cockroaches, which after dark cover the kitchen floor, table, and walls in a moving mass of brown carapaces, receive the same aural treatment. It is beautifully enhanced by means of a defamiliarizing simile, one of which Tolstoy himself would have been proud:

> At night, when Matryona was already asleep and I was working at my table, the occasional rapid scamper of mice behind the wallpaper would be drowned in the sustained and ceaseless rustling of cockroaches behind the screen, like the sound of the sea in the distance [*kak dalëkii shum okeana*].[72] But I got used to it because there was nothing evil in it, nothing dishonest. Rustling was life to them.[73]

Another narrative strategy the author employs is one that is often found in travel writing. After all, our narrator is a wanderer of sorts. Matryona and her neighbors speak in dialect, while urban, educated Ignatich, who likes to use local words when referring to local realities, acts as a linguistic mediator between the rustic characters and the non-rustic model reader. These diegetic procedures endow the text with just the right degree of lexical exoticism. One is almost tempted to call "Matryona's Home" a stationary travelogue, in which the narrator ranges far and wide on his mental excursions through culture and history.

Both Ignatich and his landlady value their privacy:

> All the Talnovo women kept at her to find out about me. Her answer was, "You want to know—you ask him. All I know is he's from distant parts." And when I got round to telling her that I had spent a lot of time in prison she said nothing but just nodded, as though she had already suspected it.[74]

For his part, the narrator does not "try to rake up her past,"[75] even though he is curious about it. In any case, several weeks pass before Matryona opens up to him. Taciturn Ignatich is a good listener and Matryona has plenty of tales to share. Little by little, he learns about her life, a succession of losses and tragedies that go back to World War I.

Now, imagine being born in Russia circa 1900. Nobleman or peasant, merchant or priest, capitalist or worker, right-thinking communist or wrong-writing intellectual, your time on earth—should you be fortunate to live out your allotted biological lifespan—would have been shaped by wars, revolutions, and political terror, before it reached those thawing, briefly cheering Khrushchevian times and then, if your weary body held out, the sluggish years of the Brezhnev era.

> Few of them made it to thirty.
> Old age was the privilege of rocks and trees.[76]

There is a universality in Matryona's harrowing experiences, though Solzhenitsyn is careful to show the interplay of the historical and the personal in the choices she made or that were made for her by others.

Matryona's cottage was built by the family of Faddei Grigoriev, the man to whom she was once betrothed, and the two young people meant to live in the attic room after they were married. It was not to be. Conscripted into the imperial army at the start of the Great War, Faddei went missing in action, and after the passage of three years and two revolutions his younger brother, Yefim, came courting: "They were short-handed. I got married."[77] Then Faddei, who had been taken prisoner, reappeared and in his jealousy and rage uttered the words that would hang over Matryona for decades, like a curse: "If it wasn't my own brother ... I'd take my axe to the both of you."[78] The axe, that Russian weapon of rebellion and revenge ...

Driven by a twisted need to possess his beloved at least in name, Faddei took to wife a girl also named Matryona, though she looked nothing like his lost sweetheart. (He loves the signifier, not the signified.) Years passed; the sinister parallels continued. The first Matryona had six children, all of whom died in infancy, while the second Matryona, constantly abused by hate-filled Faddei, also bore six children, all of whom survived. Faddei beat his wife, Yefim cheated on his. In 1941 Germany invaded Russia, Yefim went off to war and went missing in turn, but *he* never came back. Later lonely Matryona "begged from the other Matryona, the cruelly beaten Matryona, a child of her womb (or was it a spot of Faddei's blood?)."[79] This is her adopted daughter, Kira.

Actually, not everything in the protagonist's life is darkness and sorrow. Kira is now grown up and married to an engine driver from a nearby village: a good match. She loves her foster-mother and helps her out as much as she can, while Matryona's best friend, Masha, often has her over in the evenings when the two women sit together gossiping and chewing sunflower seeds. Soon after Ignatich moves in, his landlady obtains a widow's pension, and the rent he pays is a welcome addition to these meager sums. For the first time in years Matryona can afford new clothes: a pair of felt boots, a jerkin, and an overcoat made out of her son-in-law's railwayman's greatcoat: the Soviet Union was big on uniforms. She sews two hundred rubles into the lining for her funeral; cue Shukhov's habit of keeping a bit of paper money similarly concealed. The villagers, small-minded as ever, are envious of her good fortune, but Matryona is quietly happy: "Now my mind's a bit easier, Ignatich."[80]

Talnovo is a rural backwater in the middle of a Soviet nowhere: a good place in which to lie low for a while. Ignatich, who has the intellectual's penchant for inquiry, becomes a student of the village and its inhabitants. As autumn turns to winter he gets an education in the bleak realities of country life: the medieval living conditions, ruined environment, backbreaking labor, demographic decline, and cross-generational alcoholism. The villagers, collectivized subjects of the Soviet modernization project, are beholden to the state in the manner of latter-day tenant farmers or serfs: "So just as in the old days they used to steal the squire's wood, now they pinched peat from the trust."[81] Yet traces of the old ways survive in the Talnovites' cultural practices and speech patterns. These vestiges fascinate the narrator, who in a surge of anthropological enthusiasm buys a camera to record the peasants' customs: "I wanted to take a photograph of somebody at an old-fashioned handloom. (There were looms still standing in two cottages in the village; they wove coarse rugs on them.)"[82] He meets the local characters, including the hunchback tailor, a half-witted shepherd, and the battle-axe wife of the collective farm chairman; and as the new schoolmaster who is always snapping pictures, he turns into a local character himself.

Still, Ignatich spends most of his time inside the cabin. Its interior is dominated by the traditional Russian stove, a massive adobe-covered brick structure used both for heating and cooking, and with a sleeping berth on top. Instead of wood, the stove is fueled with the ubiquitous peat. It is there that the narrator first encountered Matryona, who was feeling poorly that day, "lying... under a heap of those indeterminate dingy rags which are so precious to a working man or woman."[83]

In cultural texts, the Russian stove is a marker of cozy, rustic authenticity. It often features in fairy tales where it is known to bake scrumptious pies all by itself and even to operate as a supernatural conveyance in the manner of a magic carpet. Solzhenitsyn, however, refuses to sentimentalize this hoary fixture. The Noble Engineer, as Gore Vidal called him, liked to show how things work and how they don't, and so the narrator carefully lists the stove's pros and cons, doubtless articulating the author's empirical experience:

> When I got to know it I saw that the Russian stove was not convenient for cooking: The cook cannot see the pots and they are not heated evenly all round. I suppose the stove came down to our ancestors from the Stone Age because you can stoke it up once before daylight, and food and water, mash and swill, will keep warm in it all day long. And it keeps you warm while you sleep.[84]

The encyclopedic Ignatich not only lists the fixture's functions but traces its origins back to prehistoric times. As well he might, for Matryona lives outside of history, even if she is its object and victim. Indeed, she has more in common with those Upper Paleolithic men and women than the self-reflective, class-reflective, or God-reflective people of today. The heartwarming wonder of it is that the narrator, whose nostalgia for "deepest Russia... if it was still anywhere to be found"[85] defines him as a recognizably modern sort, is able to connect with an elderly peasant widow, whose identity, though deeply Russian, belongs to a yet deeper past.

As for Matryona's "Stone Age" stove, though it may not be "convenient for cooking" or even for heating the cabin, it has another, secret, function. According to Mercia Eliade, "The man of traditional societies could only live in a space opening upward, where... communication with the *other* world, the transcendental world, was ritually possible."[86] In Talnovo, as Ignatich discovers, the rituals have been half-forgotten and the magical space is now *flattened*, but the unmentioned chimney, which rises from inside *Matryona's home* to point at the heavens, still serves as an occult funnel or conduit, a "passage from the virtual to the formal, from death to life,"[87] to use Eliade's terms. The stove "cosmicizes"[88] her humble living space, materializing the conceptual axis that connects Solzhenitsyn's "deepest Russia" to the empyrean regions up above.

Ignatich is a night owl, spending hours behind the little desk in his part of the house. "I ... was working in a silence broken only by the rustling of the cockroaches and the heavy tick of the wall-clock."[89] Here a Russian reader might nod knowingly, for this passage represents a prosaic counter-allusion to one of Pushkin's darkest poems, "Lines Written at Night during Insomnia" ("Stikhi, sochinënnye noch'iu vo vremia bessonitsy"; 1830):

> I can't sleep, there is no light;
> darkness and dull sleep around me.
> Dreary ticking of the clock
> somewhere nearby me sounding.
> Girlish babblings of the Parcae,
> flutters of a somnolent night,
> the mouse-like commotion of life...
> Why disturb me with your strife?[90]

Unlike Pushkin's nocturnal subject, Ignatich finds the domestic darkness soothing. Anyway, if the narrator stays up late, it is *because* he is writing—secret chronicles of the gulag, no doubt—rather than receiving visitations by the Fates or the Norns. A trained mathematician, he is a secularist who does not believe in things that go bump in the night. His very interest in the villagers' customs and superstitions, which is so clearly intellectual in nature, demonstrates a disassociation from the otherworldly that is the mark of the modern mind. For the people of Talnovo, however, the magic, white and black, is all around, and as the narrator conducts his researches he writes down every item of newly acquired esoteric knowledge.

Ignatich's chief informant on the local varieties of the supernatural is, of course, his landlady: "You mustn't go into the garden on the feast of St. John or there would be no harvest next year. A blizzard meant that somebody had hanged himself. If you pinched your foot in the door you could expect a guest."[91] As for science, it's just another kind of witchcraft: "There was a program about the seeding of clouds from airplanes. Matryona ... shook her head, 'Oh dear, dear, dear, dear, they'll do away with one of the two—summer or winter.'"[92] She utters this objection from atop the stove, a fabulous object capable of manned and unmanned flight, if only in fairy tales. But then, Matryona is like a storybook grandma, or so we are told.

Gabriel García Márquez once explained, in language which Solzhenitsyn would have appreciated, that he wrote his novel *One Hundred Years of Solitude* (*Cien años de soledad*; 1967) "simply by looking at reality, our reality, without the limitations which rationalists or Stalinists through the ages have tried to impose on it to make it easier for them to understand."[93] Of course, Talnovo is nothing like Macondo, and not only because the weather is miserable and the air is heavy with peat smoke rather than the aroma of coffee beans. "Matryona's Home" scarcely qualifies as an example of magical realism, a literary practice that posits a "reconciliation... between congruent concepts: natural and supernatural, realist and fantastic."[94] In Solzhenitsyn's story, mystical perceptions are the attribute of the heroine and her neighbors, but the narrative is shaped by Ignatich's secular perspectives. If Matryona displays the same quality of magical imagination as Ivan Denisovich, Ignatich's scientific outlook recalls Captain Buynovsky, though our narrator chooses to give voice to it in tones that are far less strident. To quote Harold Bloom on one of Solzhenitsyn's favorite writers, Dickens, we are dealing with "an art in which fairy tales are told as though they were sagas of social realism."[95] Though not Socialist Realism!

Solzhenitsyn's shorter prose often features some cultural object that is metonymically privileged and refers the reader to a particular period in Russian history. Thus that leering bust of Stalin in "The Right Hand." Here the historical prop is a wall poster, of the same political vintage, showing a "crude beauty... forever reaching out from the wall to offer me Belinsky, Panferov, and a pile of other books."[96] The free-thinking critic Vissarion Belinsky (1811–48), much honored in Soviet times, was the author of a celebrated "Letter to Gogol" ("Pis'mo Gogoliu"; 1847), in which he declared that the Russian people is inherently revolutionary and inherently godless, a view enthusiastically adopted by later generations of radicals from the Populists to the Bolsheviks. Fyodor Panferov (1896–1960), a SocRealist drone with two Stalin Prizes to his name, won fame with the novel *Bruski* (1928–37), an account of the campaign to collectivize the countryside, narrated in ideologically correct terms. We can imagine where Ignatich stands on all these points!

One might be tempted to conclude that the garish image on Matryona's wall indicates a naive belief in the Soviet message, with all that this implies. "Characters who accept any fictionalized version of reality uncritically and unquestioningly (like citizens who accept the dictates of politicians without challenge) are rendered incapable of effective action in the real world,"[97] in the stern words of an American scholar. In fact, Solzhenitsyn's heroine keeps that silly picture to add a bit of color to her darkish cottage. She shares the universal human need to enhance the home, so how can we blame her if she lacks her tenant's informed artistic sense? At the same time, mention of the poster directs the reader to a celebrated passage in Nikolai Nekrasov's long poem *Who Is Happy in Russia?* (*Komu na Rusi zhit' khorosho*; 1869–77):

> Oh, may it come quickly
> The time when the peasant
> Will make some distinction
> Between book and book,
> Between picture and picture;
> Will bring from the market,
> Not picture of Blücher,
> Not stupid "Milord,"
> But Belinsky and Gógol!
> Oh, say, Russian people,
> These names—have you heard them?
> They're great. They were borne
> By your champions, who loved you,
> Who strove in your cause,
> 'Tis their little portraits
> Should hang in your houses![98]

Panferov is certainly a poor substitute for Gogol, but the larger, implied point is that a century after Nekrasov, the same kind of cultural ignorance that his poem so *liberally* lamented continues to be on full display in these Russian houses, even if the reactionary Blücher has been replaced by the revolutionary Belinsky.

Be that as it may, the picture belongs to a set of cultural referents that mark Matryona's attitude to high and low art. As the narrator discovers, she has her own aesthetic, which does not quite conform to the Nabokovian notion that farmers are fine with true beauty whereas philistinism is an attribute of the urbanizing rustic, that is, "a peasant has to become a townsman in order to become vulgar."[99] On one occasion, Ignatich's landlady listens to a radio program of Russian folk songs performed by the famous bass Feodor Chaliapin, and offers this comment:

"It isn't our sort of tune, and he's tricky with his voice."[100]

(Nabokov would not have approved.)

Later she is moved by the romances of Mikhail Glinka: "That's our sort of singing."[101]

(Nabokov would have approved.)

Another telling domestic detail is the faded wallpaper, laid down in five separate layers "back in the good old days"[102] (*eshchë po khoroshei zhizni*).[103] This homely phrase takes us back to the 1920s, a time of relative prosperity, or even to the years before the revolution, which constitute the text's referential rural idyll, when Matryona for the last time knew real happiness, or so Ignatich imagines, in a land that was peaceful and prosperous, or so he believes. In an access of nostalgia for this fabulous Russia that once was (or was not), he is visited by a vision:

> And suddenly the blue and white and yellow July of the year 1914 burst into flower before my eyes: the sky still peaceful, the floating clouds, the people sweating to get the ripe corn in. I imagined them side by side, the black-haired Hercules with a scythe over his shoulder, and the red-faced girl clasping a sheaf. And there was singing out under the open sky, such songs as nobody can sing nowadays, with all the machines in the field.[104]

This hallucinatory sundering of the fictive here and now marks a momentary shift from minimal narrator to maximal narrator mode. Social realism cedes place to social surrealism. Once again, Ignatich (a secret writer) affirms his in-text status as the custodian of diegesis. The Herculean figure in his Arcadian tableau, so reminiscent of a rural painting by Zinaida Serebriakova,[105] is Faddei, the man to whom Matryona was once plighted. And on the mimetic plane, Ignatich's picture in words introduces a second explosion of color into the story's monochromatic palette, after the cartoonish poster with its book-loving siren.

Forty years on Faddei, though purblind and stooped, is still a vigorous, impressive-looking man. If Matryona is the personification of goodness, this dark-visaged paterfamilias is a malevolent ogre, a vibrantly drawn money-grubber who bears comparison to some of the most memorable evildoers in Russian literature. Among his lesser defects is the fatherly pride he takes in disciplining his son for poor school grades: "I beat him every week now. And I've got a heavy hand."[106] Granted, that plump, indolent boy is no David Copperfield: Ignatich's worst pupil, he displays an ignorance of decimals that would put a squirrel to shame.

Faddei has brooded over Matryona for decades, but he is just as obsessed by the house that the Grigoriev menfolk built all those years ago. In the dead of winter the grasping old fellow, who, it seems, still has a place in Matryona's heart, persuades her to give up the top room, which he proposes to dismantle into its constituent timbers and transport to Kira's village of Cherusti. "To get and keep a plot of land in Cherusti the young couple had to put up some sort of building," explains the narrator,[107] by now thoroughly familiar with the affairs of the Grigoriev clan. If he cannot have the whole house, reasons the pernicious patriarch, he will make sure that at least a piece of it remains in the family—*his* family. Matryona's relations on both sides, though poor in absolute and relative terms, have tangled property interests the intricacy of which, and the angry passions they engender, would not be out of place in a Balzac novel. Actually, Matryona has already left the room to Kira in her will, and her foster-daughter is in no hurry to claim ownership, but in the eyes of the law she is still Faddei's child.

It is a snowy, ice-cold February day. While the tractor-drawn sledge carrying the disassembled attic is stuck at a railway crossing, a pair of locomotives slams into it, killing Matryona, one of Faddei's sons, and the tractor driver. Eager, as ever, to help, even though her help was not needed and her agreement to the property transfer had been secured, she had decided to accompany Faddei and his drunken auxiliaries and had tarried on the steel tracks as the men were attempting to mend the towrope. Matryona's abode and refuge, the house she loved so much, becomes the instrument of three deaths, including her own.

A cozy little world is demolished by ancient resentments and modern greed. Industrial, linear time cuts through tribal, cyclical time, unraveling it into a mess of loose temporal threads. This violent event occurs at a mythical locus, a crossroads, at a hinge moment in the fictive proceedings: the story's climactic chronotope. Pre-modern Matryona dies a technological death at the spot where the steel tracks of the railway, that symbol and agent of progress, fatally bisected a snow-covered country lane which must have been there since before any of the characters, or their parents, were born.

Yet even after Matryona is gone, Faddei is heard muttering that he had "nursed every bit of timber here in his arms."[108] A week later the old brute triumphantly takes possession of that coveted attic, his grief over the death of his own flesh and blood superseded by the thrill of material possession, long-deferred but finally attained. Like a malevolent demon, Faddei harms and destroys life wherever he goes, whatever he does. He is Matryona's human antithesis, and one wonders if they ever could have been happy had they married.

In the days before house-hunting Faddei puts his plan into action, Matryona feels increasingly bereft and even levelheaded Ignatich gets a bad feeling. The cabin starts to emit alarming portents and signs. The cat goes missing and the mice grow restless, scampering and squeaking in a way that strikes the narrator as "defiant."[109] After the heroine perishes these tiny house spirits get into a frenzy: "They were running furiously up and down the walls, and you could almost see the green wallpaper rippling over their backs."[110] No wonder: like every other living thing in the cabin, the mice will soon be dead or dispersed. If Matryona's home is a tiny planet or a Noah's Ark sailing the seas of the Russian twentieth century, then its destruction is an extinction level event.

The postmortem section of the story features a displacement of the accents: an instance of diegetic syncopation. Instead of scripting Matryona's funeral as a grand finale, Solzhenitsyn keeps it offstage: "The priest and the deacon waited inside the church and didn't come out to Talnovo to meet them [the mourners]."[111] The interment is bookended by a pair of extended multi-character scenes: the formal lamentation and the wake, both of which occur inside the wounded house. These set pieces are gendered: women perform the funerary incantations and men do the funerary drinking, with the ubiquitous Ignatich present on both occasions.

First, the lamentation. Following tradition, the wooden coffin holding Matryona's broken body is placed under the icons in the single room of the cottage and the entire village comes to pay its respects. Once again, the narrator provides an anthropologically correct account of a popular ritual while carefully noting the hierarchies of sorrow, real or feigned, displayed by the mourners. But this is not all. Beneath the threnodic crying and keening and the customary expressions of grief, observant Ignatich discerns a second, materialistic discourse that denotes competing property interests: "I realized that a lament for the dead is not just a lament, but a kind of politics."[112] Even as they chant the prescribed words, Matryona's sisters and the Grigoriev family are negotiating over the disposition of her house and chattels. Among those present, only the second Matryona, "wailing and sobbing over the coffin in her simplicity,"[113] a nameless old woman who comforts her, and Kira, the heroine's adopted daughter, are genuinely distressed (also, Kira's engine driver husband must now go on trial). Like the narrator, citified Kira is a stranger to these country rites: she "didn't follow the ritual, but wept straightforwardly, in the fashion of our age, which has had plenty of practice at it."[114]

The wake takes place a few days later in Matryona's kitchen. Raucous voices sing half-remembered hymns and copious quantities of vodka are consumed. There is bad food, strained laughter, and listless gossip. This alcoholic feast goes on for hours, and one wonders how the narrator is able to sit it out. Although sit it out he must, in keeping with his duty as the custodian of diegesis.

With the funerary rites over, Faddei and the three sisters carry out an ill-tempered division of Matryona's earthly goods. After the part-destroyed house is part-inherited by her covetous relatives, Ignatich rents a room from one of Matryona's sisters-in-law, a sharp-tongued biddy who fills him on the details of the dead woman's marriage while subjecting her character to waspish commentary. It is only then that the narrator realizes his former landlady's true human worth.

The "terrifying" aspects of the story, to use Akhmatova's term, call to mind Tolstoy's play *The Power of Darkness* (*Vlast' t'my*; 1886), even if its lurid plot, with seduction followed by murder and murder followed by infanticide, exceeds the horrors shown in "Matryona's Home" by a dramatic margin. Nonetheless, this may be Solzhenitsyn's most Tolstoyan work, in the sense that it contains the largest number of fictive and thematic connections to the master's oeuvre within the shortest length of text. Moreover, while in the other fictions such linkages are often polemical, such is not the case here. Take, for instance, the train theme that looms so large in the text. The obvious parallel is with *Anna Karenina* and the heroine's awful death under those iron wheels. However, the destructive impact of the railway on the countryside is the more pertinent link. Tolstoy's hero, Konstantin Levin, associates trains and the tracks they move on with immorality and believes that railway construction is destroying the social and moral integrity of rural life.[115] Although Solzhenitsyn was very fond of trains, "Matryona's Home" depicts them and their infrastructure as un-*naturally* ugly, in keeping with the work's programmatic de-aestheticization of Soviet modernity. The rustic heroine is afraid of fire, lightning, but most of all, trains. "When I had to go to Cherusti the train came up from Nechaevka way with its great big eyes popping out and the rails humming away—put me in a proper fever," she confides.[116] Her artless comment, with its whiff of supernatural fear, confirms that the railway is this fictive world's axis of doom and connects the story to Dostoevsky's novel *The Idiot*, in which, as one scholar notes, "a full disclosure of the railroad motif" reveals its apocalyptic connotations.[117]

Matryona's analeptic statement of dread is also a proleptic token of the horrors to come. The route she traveled on that occasion, from Talnovo to Cherusti, happens to be the same one that Faddei's sinister little caravan would follow at the hour of her death. As for the toponym "Nechaevka," which like every other place name in the story is taken from real life, it makes one think of Sergei Nechayev (1847–82), the fanatical revolutionary who served as a model for Petr Verkhovensky in Dostoevsky's novel *Devils*. The famous terrorist's shadowy presence, if only as an onomastic cognate referent, adds to the sense of foreboding conveyed by Matryona's words.

The heroine attends church once in a while, keeps icons in her house, and lights the icon-lamp on feast days, but it would be wrong to call her a practicing Christian. Or even a Christian as such. The analytical Ignatich concludes, "If anything, she was a heathen [*iazychnitsa*],[118] and her strongest beliefs were superstitious."[119] However, the narrator abandons this anthropological stance when he notes that "she had fewer sins on her conscience than her gammy-legged cat. The cat did kill mice."[120] But this second comment does not change the essential truth: Matryona, that most Russian, most moral of Solzhenitsyn's creations, is not a believer in the conventional or even unconventional sense.

So was the atheistic Belinsky right after all when he declared that Russianness is next to godlessness? Not if Solzhenitsyn has anything to say about it. While "Matryona's Home" begins with a narrative proem that is designed to draw us in, it ends with a moral lesson meant to remain with us after we turn the last page. As the narrator or now, perhaps, the (implied) author puts it in the magniloquent passage that closes the story,

> We had all lived side by side with her and never understood that she was that righteous one without whom, as the proverb says, no village can stand.
> Nor any city.
> Nor our whole land.[121]

In rhetorical terms, what we have here is a *sententia*, the adduction of a maxim or wise saying that gives shape to a conclusion. Like most great endings in most great works, these three sentences carry important implications. They elevate the narrative purport to that of national identity and national survival. The final, extradiegetically formatted message both synopcizes and transcends the social situations and historical realities depicted in the main body of the text.

Now, Solzhenitsyn was very fond of Russian proverbs, which he collected all his life in emulation of Vladimir Dahl (1801–72), the celebrated lexicographer who was one of his cultural heroes. In many of the fictions these folksy one-liners serve as oral indicators of a character's rootedness: Matryona herself is *literally* proverbial in her speech, as Ignatich duly records. In a characteristically didactic moment, the author had originally titled his story "No Village Can Stand Without a Righteous One" ("Ne stoit selo bez pravednika"), after the saying in the afore-quoted passage, a choice wisely nixed by Tvardovsky. The notion of "a righteous one" (*pravednik* or *pravednitsa*) is present in many of the world's religions, although Solzhenitsyn's frame of reference is always Christian and always Russian.

"Blessed are the pure in heart: for they shall see God" (Mathew 5:8). Indeed, every one of the Beatitudes pronounced by Jesus in the Sermon on the Mount[122] applies to Matryona, even if she had never read it or even heard it recited from the altar. The heroine is, after all, a "heathen," or so we are told.

For just as, according to Eusebius and St. Augustine, there were Christians before Christ,[123] the story posits that, in some mystical Russian sense, there can be Christians after Christ, but without Christ. Like Dostoevsky, who "constantly aspired … to fathom all kinds of complexities, be they complexities of thought or complexities of life,"[124] this author practices a religious dialectics that is meant to explain the spiritual lapses and discontinuities of *his* time and place by means of paradoxes and aporias which are grounded in the minutiae of everyday life, as lived by everyday people. At the same time, the portrait of Matryona is suffused with the spirit of kenoticism, the practice of "unceasing self-humiliation as a means of transcendence,"[125] which earlier writers such as Dostoevsky and Nikolai Leskov fixed in their readers' minds as the "most Russian of existential approaches."[126]

To venture a *sententia* of my own, I am reminded of Nietzsche's insight that

> only Christian *practice*, a life such as he *lived* who died on the cross, is Christian. Such a life is still possible today, for certain people even necessary: genuine, original Christianity will be possible at all times. Not a faith, but a doing; above all, a *not* doing of many things, another state of *being*.[127]

So, behold Matryona the Righteous One, who may yet be the salvation of her family, her people, and her country.

Or may not.

5

"An Incident at Kochetovka Station" was the first work of fiction Solzhenitsyn wrote with a view to publication instead of "for the drawer." The plot is based on a wartime memory, albeit one that was not the writer's own but belonged to one of his friends.[128] Before the piece appeared in *Novy Mir*, the titular toponym was changed to avoid antagonizing Vsevolod Kochetov (1912–73), a SocRealist panjandrum and notable opponent of Tvardovsky and his journal.

Thus, "An Incident at *Krechetovka* Station." In time the author restored the original title, evidence of his determination to reverse every textual compromise, however minor, that was forced upon him when he lived in the Soviet Union.[129]

As often happens in Solzhenitsyn's stories, the narrative situation is organized around a dynamic interaction between a pair of individuals who meet inside a densely coded physical space where history intrudes and moral choices loom. The two main characters are Lieutenant Vasily Zotov, a young officer in charge of the eponymous station, and Igor Tveritinov, a middle-aged soldier who is the survivor of a catastrophic Soviet defeat. Although Zotov develops a liking for Tveritinov, when the latter misspeaks he decides the older man is a spy and hands him over to the secret police. Much of the action takes place inside Zotov's office, a cramped corner room with a portrait of Lazar Kaganovich, Stalin's Commissar for the Railways (another artifactal marker from the nation's past). The historical event that casts its dark shadow over the two men is Operation Typhoon, the German drive on Moscow in October 1941, when the story is set. At this point in the war things are going badly for the Red Army: the Wehrmacht has broken through and looks like rolling all the way to the capital. Indeed, just a few days earlier "a couple of crazy German motorcyclists" had shot up Kochetovka[130] and the station itself was bombed by the Luftwaffe.

In the first half of the story, we learn a good deal about Zotov, his team of subordinates, the families in the adjoining settlement, and the manner in which the Red Army is fighting back against the Nazi onslaught. Kochetovka is an important junction on the railway network supplying the front, and the protagonist spends much of his time meeting with military train commanders and dealing with their (invariably urgent) requests. The lengthy preamble that leads up to Zotov's encounter with Tveritinov amounts to a succession of narrative openings and closings which, in almost kaleidoscopic fashion, give us a sense of what life was like during these first, calamitous months of the war.

The Kochetovka scenery is grimly industrial: station platform, storage sheds, locomotives, rail cars. Nature is present in the form of cold autumn winds and slanting sleet. Other than the characters themselves, the only living thing present is a leafless oak sapling outside Zotov's window. There is another tree, with buds showing on its branches, which can be glimpsed in a photograph of Tveritinov's daughter: a token of more clement times.

An ardent Soviet patriot, Zotov despairs over the Red Army's reverses more than he does about the fate of his pregnant wife, stranded behind enemy lines in Byelorussia. He is prim, pedantic, and puritanical, in other words, not unlike Solzhenitsyn himself at age twenty or twenty-two. A recent graduate of a textile machinery college, the lieutenant has had minimal exposure to the arts: his favorite writer is Maxim Gorky, but Chekhov and Ibsen are a closed book. As for his discursive habits, they are those of any rank-and-file Komsomol: he thinks in clichés and speaks in platitudes: "He must do all he could and do it as well as he could, especially now that the twenty-fourth anniversary of the revolution was so near at hand."[131]

Not all or even most of this is Zotov's fault, and Solzhenitsyn is careful to let the hero's voice be heard, whether by showing him in conversation with the other characters or via free indirect discourse. As for the narrator, he asserts his perspective only occasionally and only briefly, as in this moving passage, which features a diegetic shift from the private and personal to the epic-historical, and back to the private:

> Since then tens of thousands of gun barrels had thundered and millions of fountains of black earth had erupted and millions of people had been whirled as if by a monstrous roundabout; people had walked from Lithuania, people had come by train from Irkutsk. And now at this station, with a cold wind whipping up the snow and rain, with trains standing idle and people milling aimlessly by day and by night, sleeping hugger-mugger on the black floors, how could one believe that that little garden, that child, that dress still existed?[132]

(Tveritinov has just shown Zotov his family photos.) The "monstrous roundabout" (*prokliataia karusel'*)[133] is a variant of the giant wheel figure that operates as an organizing metaphor for historical evil across the oeuvre.

The lieutenant is the cynosure of a small group of personalities that are lightly drawn human or professional types: a dispatcher, blonde, coquettish Valya; a clerk, sharp-tongued Frosya, "one of those tough, weather-beaten, middle-aged Russian women who are used to having things their own way both at home and at work";[134] and a grizzled veteran of the steel tracks, Kordubailo, who started work under the tsars and is wise about the ways of the world. There is also sly Sergeant Guskov, who has little time for the boyish officer and is not afraid to show it. As history at its most brutal unfolds just a few miles away, these disparate characters perform their duties with varying degrees of competence, gossip, bicker, and worry about the little things.

Earnest Zotov is puzzled that his subordinates

seemed to have something more to live for than the news from the front; they had their potatoes to lift, their cows to milk, their wood to saw, their windows to seal. They talked about these things most of the time and were much more preoccupied with them than with the news from the front.[135]

Flaxen-haired Valya, who has set her cap at the lieutenant, tries to explain: "And in the meantime we're only human, we must live."[136] This Tolstoyan life-goes-on message is present across Solzhenitsyn's fictions, where it acquires a special resonance when set against the horrors of the Russian twentieth century. Though tempted by the blonde's open interest, Zotov wishes to stay faithful to his wife and anyway, he is emotionally drawn to Paulina, a young mother from Kiev with whom he feels "a sacred bond of grief."[137] Meanwhile, the station commandant must put up with Antonina, a voluptuous bed-hopper who once tried to seduce him before taking up with "an ugly great stallion of a man."[138] Their boisterous lovemaking in the next-door room distracts the hero from his nighttime reading, Marx's *Das Kapital*, which otherwise is a bit of a snooze.

It is not that this stuffy officer, with his unflattering crew cut and glasses perched on a lumpy nose, is irresistibly attractive to the opposite sex. In wartime, however, social barriers break down and affairs are begun and ended without much ado. Besides, Zotov has the kind of awkward charm that women find appealing. His palpable naivety may raise the hackles of his men but it softens the hearts of the Kochetovka women, the man-eating Antonina excepted. This jejune quality, of which the lieutenant is painfully aware, is reminiscent of young Nikolai Rostov in the early chapters of *War and Peace*. Another leitmotif is Zotov's sonorous northern accent, with its clearly pronounced unstressed *o*'s. It becomes especially prominent when the young officer is excited or stressed and shows that he hails from a region of the country that Solzhenitsyn always considered the repository of authentic Russianness.

There are similarities between bookish Vasya Zotov and bookish Gleb Nerzhin in the unfinished novel *Love the Revolution*, which shows Solzhenitsyn's autobiographical hero going to college and going to war. Zotov's study of the Marxist classics, his shyness around women, and his vulnerable masculinity are pure Nerzhin. Indeed, when working on "Kochetovka" the writer used *Love the Revolution* as source material, borrowing scenes and themes from that novel. In addition to the whole young-man-goes-to-war topos, these include the terse exchanges between Zotov and the train dispatchers that open the story (wartime railroading at its rawest) and some lines from an execrably bad Leninist poem declaimed by a "thin, pale-faced lieutenant with lanky hair"[139] (the historical Aleksandr Solzhenitsyn c. 1941, but promoted in rank for the occasion). The poem keeps running through Zotov's prosaic head as he broods over the German advance. The citational element in question is a nice piece of meta-irony: an invented character appropriating a piece of conspicuously defective verse penned by his empirical creator at an earlier moment in authorial time, with Solzhenitsyn's secret alter ego, that skinny lieutenant, acting as the agent of this textual transmission from bad poet to bad reader (or rather, listener). On the other hand, unlike young Nerzhin, who feels an instinctive revulsion from Stalin, Zotov is secure in his adoration of "the omniscient, omnipotent Father and Teacher who was always there, who foresaw everything, who would do all that had to be done."[140] This is Stalin (satirically) coded as a divine figure or, not to be too blunt about it, as God Himself.

A few lines of dialogue reveal the textures of civilian life in the midst of war. Frosya feels class envy toward the "rich" evacuees with their "greedy mugs" who "want a boiled chicken—nothing else will do."[141] Yet she feels compassion for Paulina and her child, billeted on Frosya by the authorities: "'Look,' I says, 'there you are, there's potatoes, there's pickled cabbage, help yourself, and I don't want anything for the room, either.'"[142] Like most people, the sharp-tongued clerk is a mixture of the good and the bad, though in her case the good predominates.

Of course, this is not just any country but that shabby, tyrannous place known as the Soviet Union, its injustices and inefficiencies compounded by the trauma of war, and so early in the story we get a sense of the political context. The day before, starving Red Army troops released from German captivity had looted a supply train, and one of them was shot by a guard, who was nearly lynched as a result. Pretty Valya and loudmouthed Frosya have little sympathy for the former POWs, but old man Kordubailo begs to differ: "Then you've never seen hunger, my dears."[143] He tells a bemused Zotov that he has taken the oath of loyalty five times, all the way back to Tsar Alexander III: a witness to history who is there to remind us that governments come and go but decency and common sense are always of value.

Later in the story Zotov must deal with a couple of escort commanders, Sergeants Gaydukov and Dygin, whose respective train journeys are mini-epics in themselves. Gaydukov's rail car is transporting twenty conscripts and a consignment of horses to the front, while Dygin and his men are taking a load of entrenching tools to Tbilisi, a city hundreds of miles away from the nearest German: a wartime snafu. Gaydukov, just nineteen years old but already a frontline veteran, "not only knew the rules; he also knew the proper way to break them."[144] He does everything he can to keep his troopers comfortable, trading favors for moonshine and turning a blind eye when the soldiers bunk down with the girls who have climbed aboard along the way. Unlike the inhabitants of Gaydukov's "uproarious carriage,"[145] forty-something Dygin and his men have had a rough time of it: without rations for eleven days, their only sustenance was some pilfered beetroot. At the end of his tether, Dygin, recently called up from the factory floor and not yet used to army discipline, shouts at the bewildered station chief, "We're not dogs!"[146] There are several instances across Solzhenitsyn's oeuvre where a character defiantly proclaims his humanity to an authority figure, and this is one of those occasions: we note that Dygin speaks up not on his own behalf, but of the soldiers in his unit.

The lieutenant's spell of duty is about to end when a man unlike any other he has met in his young, by-the-numbers life enters his ken. The stranger's large features, "rich and deep, aristocratic yet controlled"[147] voice, and odd little habit of gesturing with his fingers make an immediate impression. He wears a weird mixture of military and civilian clothing covered with a sprinkling of coal dust from the locomotive tender in which he has been riding. This unusual-looking figure is Tveritinov, the man Zotov is fated to betray.

The newcomer seeks the commandant's assistance to catch up with his assigned train and soon the latter is half-apologetically examining a couple of family snapshots, which he had asked to see as a way of verifying Tveritinov's identity.

> There was a special quality about the whole family. Zotov himself had never met any families like that, but little fragments in his memory—from the Tretyakov Museum, from the theatre, or from books—had gradually built up in him the idea that such families existed. Looking at these photos, Zotov sensed an atmosphere of cultured security.[148]

The two men get on well, with the lieutenant clearly starstruck: "I've an idea I do know your name. Aren't you an Honoured Artist?"[149] (he isn't, of course.) As Zotov questions Tveritinov, at first more or less officially but then in an increasingly friendly fashion, it emerges that this unlikely soldier is a member of a Moscow theatre troupe who had joined the People's Militia[150] just a few weeks earlier:

> "Did you get any military training?"
> "A few days. Bayonet practice. With sticks. And how to throw grenades. Wooden ones."

"Then what—did they arm you?"
"They chucked us a few rifles when we were already on the move."[151]

Tveritinov is a survivor of the encirclement at Vyazma, where four Soviet armies were destroyed by the Germans earlier that month as they began their drive on Moscow. Brief though it is, his account of the fighting completes the grim picture of the Red Army at war.

In the course of the conversation the generational and intellectual gulf between the two men becomes clear, not perhaps for the lieutenant but certainly for the actor. To Zotov the year 1937 means the Spanish Civil War and little else: "The International Brigade! Guadalajara, Jarama, Teruel!"[152] For the thoughtful thespian, it is a time best left undiscussed, at least with *this* interlocutor. Yet Zotov grows so comfortable with Tveritinov that he gifts him his tobacco ration, which the actor, a nicotine addict, gravely accepts: "You have warmed me, literally and figuratively. You are a kind man."[153] The officer makes the travel arrangements Tveritinov requested and they are about to part ways, when the actor commits a toponymical mistake, using the pre-revolutionary place name "Tsaritsyn" instead of the communist-style "Stalingrad." That slip of the tongue triggers an ideological tripwire in Zotov's vigilant brain: "So he wasn't a returnee. He was a plant, an agent. With those manners, most likely a White émigré."[154] Under a manufactured pretext, the lieutenant leads Tveritinov to the guardroom and puts him under arrest, all the while feeling strangely uncomfortable about the whole business.

The story's climactic passage describes the moment just after the betrayal: as happens elsewhere in this writer's prose, the narrative emphasis falls not on the hinge event itself but the rippling effect of its consequences:

> Zotov could not help looking back once more—for the last time in his life—to catch a glimpse of that face in the dim light of the lantern, the despairing face of King Lear in the burial chamber.
> "What are you doing, what are you doing," shouted Tveritinov in a voice that rang like a bell. "You're making a mistake that can never be put right!"[155]

This is one of the very few times that we find an explicitly referenced Shakespearian trope in a Solzhenitsyn text; the reference itself, so appropriate when applied to a professional actor, belongs not to the lieutenant but the extradiegetic narrator, and so does the elucidative "for the last time in his life."

Tveritinov's anguished words register with Zotov, but the deed is done. Yet after the actor is taken away, the lieutenant feels something very much like remorse. Twice he tries to learn the fate of the man he briefly met in the room with the Kaganovich portrait. On the second occasion, a testy security officer informs him, mangling the actor's name and controverting that last heartrending cry: "Your Tverikin's being sorted out all right. We don't make mistakes"[156] (*u nas braka ne byvaet*).[157]

The two main personalities are scripted discursively and sociologically. Tveritinov's old-world, otherworldly persona is utterly unlike Zotov's, with his politically pre-determined words and actions. The languages of their bodies are just as different, though this is to be expected, for Tveritinov's distinctive mannerisms are due as much to his stage experience as his genteel upbringing. Zotov is what he is: a subaltern ideologue who is comfortable in his certainties, though one who in time might change for the better. Courteous, cultivated Tveritinov, however, is a rare bird in Stalin's Soviet Union, an autonomous individual who is unable to disguise his autonomy. He may be an actor, but he would rather not lie or dissemble. When a dangerous subject like the Great Terror comes up he prefers to keep silent and steers the conversation to the next topic.

Although Zotov is a bit of a stuffed shirt there remains something likeable about him, a quality felt by the discerning Tveritinov before that act of betrayal. Where the reader is concerned, the sympathy one feels for the young officer stems from the sense one has that he possesses the potential to evolve. He lacks "a past," as the narrator observes,[158] but he may have a future—perhaps an ethical future—should he survive the war. Conversely, one can easily imagine Zotov puttering through the years and decades to come, visited by second thoughts and late regrets but never truly apprehending the black enormity of what he did. Plenty of characters in Solzhenitsyn and plenty of people in real life have but half a conscience and do just fine.

6

"The Right Hand" and "Matryona's Home" may be among the most "terrifying" of Solzhenitsyn's productions, but "For the Good of the Cause" is the most conventional.[159] Like all great artists, this writer liked to take risks. Remarkably, as he grew older he tended to do so more, not less. Here, however, there is no risk. As Solzhenitsyn later explained,

> In the spring of 1963 I wrote a story for *Novy Mir* which I felt no inner compulsion at all to write: "For the Good of the Cause." It seemed

reasonably hard-hitting, yet viable. ... But I found it pretty hard to write (a sure sign of failure) and it didn't go very deep.... The publication of this story left a nasty taste in my mouth. True, when almost everything was banned, even this provoked a great deal of lively comment. But in "For the Good of the Cause" I was beginning to slip: a telltale trickle underfoot showed that I was slithering toward conformity.[160]

This harsh self-evaluation almost invites one to examine the story as a collection of codified conventions sourced from official Soviet literature. This time the writer's mastery of the SocRealist arts, which normally he employed to subvert that model, produced an outcome that was neither polemical nor parodic. "For the Good of the Cause" may be the only politically correct item among Solzhenitsyn's prose works, a period piece from a time when Khrushchev was f(l)ailing as a reformer and the word *tineidzher* had yet to enter the Russian language. In this regard, there is a parallel with Tolstoy's story "Albert" (1858), which Boris Eikhenbaum describes as his "only fabricated [*fal'shivyi*] piece of prose, a transcript of someone else's words which is articulated in a voice not his own."[161]

The plot might have come from a muckraking article in *Pravda*. Students and staff at a provincial technical college are about to move into a new building, which they have jointly renovated over the course of many months. When an official commission visits the old, cramped premises, a member, the scheming manager of an electrical relay factory, informs the principal that the restored structure has been reassigned to a secret research institute "for the good of the cause."[162] The principal seeks help from his wartime friend Grachikov, the secretary of the city Party committee, who tries to get the provincial Party chief, Knorozov, to intercede: "Communism will not be built with stones but with people!"[163] But stony-hearted Knorozov is unmoved, and the handover of the new school building goes ahead.[164]

All the events take place in the public sphere. Central to the story is the difference between the "right" and "wrong" method of partocratic governance. The former is exemplified by honest Grachikov, who prefers to explain and persuade rather than issue blunt orders, the latter by the despotic Knorozov, an exponent of "the 'strong-willed' style of leadership,"[165] who rules over his fief like a little Khrushchev, or a tiny Stalin. So far, so SocRealist.

In fact, schools were a favored locus in official literature, in which patrilineal and matrilineal teacher-pupil relationships and the collaborative environment of the classroom represented "the symbolic family of the state,"[166] which all Soviet art was expected to depict. "For the Good of the Cause" hews to this fictive pattern. Solzhenitsyn's junior college is a benignly totalizing environment. These preteens and teens study, play, eat, and sleep *inside* the college complex under the watchful eye of their surrogate parents, the teachers. The students' primary identity is institutional, as is that of their instructors. An admiring Georg Lukács called the college "a genuine collective ... bound by mutual trust, indeed love."[167] Certainly, every teenager and teacher is trustworthy and lovable and shimmering with sentimental schoolroom shine. As is to be expected, the spheres of good and evil are geometrically adumbrated. If the school is populated by the dedicated and the diligent, and functions like a cozy household, in the world beyond its cramped walls hypocrisy reigns and careerists prosper. This notion of the classroom as an idyllic niche was very personal to the author, who used to be a schoolmaster himself, and by all accounts a very good one. When he obtained a position at a Kazakh village school upon his release from the camp, "every lesson brought a throbbing happiness."[168] And he had a special fondness for the teaching profession, which is reflected throughout the oeuvre.

Although "For the Good of the Cause" is a by-the-facts fictionalization of a real-life event which Solzhenitsyn himself did not witness, it contains the usual autobiographical component, for the student characters are variously modeled on the writer's college friends from Rostov and the pupils he taught at School No. 2 in Ryazan.[169] In the first few pages, the pupils' disembodied voices offer boisterous, slangy comment on the goings-on in their lives. Yet once the adults—the teachers and officials—take center stage, these adolescent descants and sopranos vanish from the text and the action turns decidedly middle-aged.

The students are silhouettes. We encounter instantly recognizable, conspicuously gendered types: jock, jokester, nerd; beauty, flirt, frump. Some of the kids cultivate an early sixties look, with the boys sporting gaudy Hawaiian shirts and the girls showing off their seemingly "unkempt and half dishevelled but in reality elaborately contrived" hairdos[170] à la Jackie Kennedy. The story's most memorable presence is scruffy Chursanov, a youthful version of the scientific Bazarov in Turgenev's novel *Fathers and Sons*. With his patched collar and brusque, misanthropic manner, he jumps off the page, even if the sum total of his textual presence amounts to just a couple of paragraphs. A son of poverty whose widowed mother works as a street sweeper, Chursanov is a brilliant radio technician but disdains the arts, to the distress of Lydia Georgievna, the enthusiastic literature teacher who is popular with her pupils, especially the boys. Even churlish Chursanov is not immune to her pedagogical charms. Lydia wears her "thick fair hair brushed back,"[171] which leaves her forehead idealistically bare, like that of a Komsomol belle in a 1930s film. Although her students may not have attained the Mods vs. Rockers transgression quotient, the starchy schoolmarm worries about their waywardness. She fears that the boys' interest in clothes and habit of accepting female attention as their due means that they are "losing something psychologically important to them"[172] (here one discerns the author's fatherly take on things). Anyway, although literary Lidia is a bit of a priss and geeky Chursanov a bit of a boor, they are more than a bit sympathetic.

The school principal, Fyodor Mikheevich, the grizzled war veteran, tries to act as the focal point for the student body and teaching staff, rather than a stern authority figure. No wonder he and Grachikov get along so well. Other than Chursanov, only this thoughtful Party administrator sticks in the reader's mind. With a face "so expressively Russian that had he been dressed in a foreign suit or uniform, one still would have immediately recognized him as a son of Russia [*rusak*],"[173] he has an emblematic national presence: in Solzhenitsyn's book, always a good thing (see Frosya in "Kochetovka," "one of those Russian women"). Early on in the story, Grachikov is shown reminiscing about a wartime incident when he risked a court martial by stopping a general from crossing over a bridge out of turn. But that was then, and this is now. Party discipline is more onerous than the army kind, especially when imposed by someone like Knorozov, an iron-visaged monument to himself: "His face always looked as if cast in a mould. ... A smile would have upset its balance"[174] (a comment applicable to most Soviet functionaries).

In addition to the Stalinist Knorozov and the anti-Stalinist Grachikov, the officials shown include the industrial director Khabalygin, a tubby picaroon who hopes to land a job at the secret institute, and two anonymous Moscow apparatchiks, one "decently plump," the other "slim, good-looking, and fashionably dressed":[175] a bureaucratic double act. There is one semi-farcical scene, which occurs in the school's tiny preparation room, "a narrow crack between two rows of shelves which reached up to the ceiling."[176] Inside this attenuated locus of learning the chubbier of the two Muscovites espies a photo,

> a colourful, bosomy pin-up, carefully cut out round the curves of her body. Without the caption, it was impossible to make out whether this creature had been cut out of a Soviet magazine or a foreign one—she was just a beautiful woman with dark-brown hair, in a blouse with a red frill that emphasised her figure. Her chin was resting on her folded arms, which were bare to the elbows; she was holding her head slightly to one side and giving the young lab assistant and the experienced comrade from the Ministry a distinctly unofficial look.
>
> "You say you haven't any space here," he growled, finding it hard to turn around to get out, "but look what you hang on your walls, for God's sake!"[177]

It's a trap! The bureaucratic male gaze is held, deflected, and defeated by a countervailing female gaze, even if that "distinctly unofficial look" is just so many micro-dots of cyan, magenta, yellow, and black. No wonder the naughty picture makes Ministry Man shake his flab: those nubile, transnational forms challenge him on several fronts, not all of them ideological.

In a sense, "For the Good of the Cause" is the story of one man's disillusionment. Originally an admirer of Knorozov, whose take-charge attitude used to impress him, Fyodor Mikheyich now realizes that the Party's high representative just doesn't care. However, the author leaves the last word not with the educator, but the crook. Khabalygin, reveling in the success of his intrigues, tells the school principal, "It must be done like this, comrade"[178] (*Tak—nado, tovarishch dorogoi*).[179] In this country, at this time, in this place, he is right.

7

In 1963 Solzhenitsyn began work on *Cancer Ward* while continuing to refashion *The First Circle*, so his mind was now on larger formats, bigger things. "Zakhar-the-Pouch" joins together historical facts, rural realities, and national mythology into a multipronged fictive continuum. Still searching for cultural authenticity after all these years, the authorial narrator once again encounters a rustic figure who resides at the intersection of pre-history, history, and modernity. In comparison with "Matryona," however, this story textualizes a remoter past but a less traumatic here and now.

Solzhenitsyn's alter ego is cycling across Russia with a companion, perhaps his wife, perhaps a male friend, and the diegetic voice is in the first person plural.

The narrator and his escort are on a cultural pilgrimage to Kulikovo Field where on September 8, 1380 a Russian army defeated the Mongol host of Khan Mamai. Hymned in medieval chronicles and modern poetry—the text is saturated with uncoded and encoded literary citations—this famous victory marked the beginning of the end of Muscovy's vassalage to the Golden Horde. The site, located between the rivers Nepryadva and Don, to the southeast of the city of Tula, is a sacral space of the nation's imaginary, although the precise location of the battlefield, and even the size and composition of the opposing forces, remain a matter of conjecture. In Russia, Kulikovo is remembered as a world-historical clash of arms like Gaugamela (331 BCE), Châlons (451), Tours (732), Lepanto (1571), or Vienna (1683), or as the narrator puts it, "a battle nor merely between principalities or nation-states, but between continents."[180] Indeed, he has a penchant for patriotic hyperbole: "Almost a quarter of a million Russians ... an army that size staggers the imagination"[181] or, "With faces contorted with blood lust, they trample on the Russian infantry."[182]

Solzhenitsyn considered the Mongol conquest of Kievan Rus a catastrophe of the same order as the revolution of 1917. However, "Zakhar-the-Pouch" is not a meticulous literary investigation of a turning point in the nation's existence à la *The Red Wheel*, nor could it be, for the fourteenth century was too remote from the Soviet present or the author's intellectual interests for such an exercise in dramatized historiography. His point of departure may be historical, but his point of arrival is demonstrably contemporary: mythscape vs. Sovspace, or patriotic memory vs. cultural entropy. This commemorative treatment of the Field recalls the "Miniatures," as does the emphasis on twentieth-century ugliness encroaching on nature and architecture.

The (very) imaginatively reconstructed martial scenes contrast with the peaceful late summer vista in the here and now: fields of buckwheat, clover, and rye "as far as the eye could see,"[183] and in the midst of this collective farm plenty, a historic church and a cast iron obelisk, a marvel of Victorian engineering. The ripening crops serve as a ready source of similes: "Our men were mown down like wheat"[184] (*I my lozhimsia, kak skoshennyi khleb*).[185] In these passages, the diegetic *we* undergoes a semantic shift and acquires a nationalizing ring. The same wheat imagery is present in *The Tale of the Battle against Mamai* (*Skazanie o mamaevom poboishche*; c. 1400), a vivid contemporary account.[186] Solzhenitsyn's other source was Sergei Solovyov's magisterial *History of Russia* [*Istoriia Rossii s drevneishikh vremën*; 1851–79], which he follows closely, even uncritically, taking its fanciful description of the battle and dubious casualty figures as a factual given.

Alas, upon inspection it turns out that the church was looted by local peasants, the obelisk has been defaced, and the dirt road that leads to the latter is rutted and overgrown with weeds. The graffiti marring the monument stand in cretinous contrast to the narrator's hidden borrowings from the *Tale* and overt quotations from Aleksandr Blok's verse cycle *On Kulikovo Field* (*Na pole Kulikovom*; 1908).

In an annotation to that sequence of poems, Blok described Kulikovo as "one of the symbolic events in Russian history. Such events are destined to recur. The divination of their true significance lies still in the future."[187] The battle, he hints, was an event of eternal return, mythic or otherwise. Solzhenitsyn, who had already developed his nodal reading of the historical past, follows Blok in suggesting that this continental clash of arms may one day repeat itself: "What happened here was a turning point in the fate of Russia. For our invaders have not always come from the West..."[188] Later the author explained that this passage was an "anti-Chinese mine," a coded warning to the Soviet leadership about the gathering threat from Maoist China.[189] Eventually capitalist developments behind the Great Wall would deactivate that hidden explosive charge, but at the time of writing Solzhenitsyn was trying to speak truth to power, even if subtextually. He would do so super-textually seven years later, in his "Letter to Soviet Leaders," which identified "war with China, and our destruction, together with Western civilization, in the crush and stench of a fouled earth," as the twin perils facing his homeland.[190]

Still, the main category of receptors scripted into the story is of a different order from Brezhnev and co. "Zakhar-the-Pouch" reads like a poetically structured, imaginatively formatted history lesson. Some of the pedagogical tropes are diegetically laid bare. At one point, the narrator comes across three motorbike-riding working-class youths, who join him on the observation platform at the top of the obelisk. In return for the bikers' informed explanation of how it was constructed, he gives them an account of the battle: an exchange of cultural expertise. There are other teaching moments, as when the authorial alter ego summarizes the political situation in fourteenth-century Russia or reports on a toponymically themed conversation with a local resident: "You don't say Kulikóvo, you say Kulíkovo. The village of Kulíkovka is right next to the battlefield, but Kulikóvka's over there, on the other side of the Don."[191]

The narrator and his companion decide to stay overnight. As darkness falls, the modern age with its airplanes and cars recedes and the site is illuminated by a full moon. The Field is transformed into a mystic locus where past and present are one and the words of the poet assume material form: "From the river Nepriadva came the sound of swans, just as Blok had described."[192]

The main appeal of the story, however, lies in the portrait of the steward of Kulikovo, the eponymous Zakhar, a quirky character of a kind one occasionally encounters in Solzhenitsyn's worlds. Zakhar is a true eccentric, that is, a person who thinks other people are very odd. A lanky, disheveled figure with an aggressively proprietary attitude toward the site, his is not a welcoming presence, or not at first. The tetchy custodian would rather there were no tourists at all. But soon he warms to the narrator and tells him about the depredations inflicted on the Field by both visitors and locals. Touchingly, the keeper shows him a page torn from an exercise book "on which was written, in capital letters and in complete disregard of the ruled lines, a copy of the monument's dedication to Dmitry Donskoi and the year—1848."[193] It turns out that a farmer from a neighboring village had carted away the plaque to decorate his house, so that the law-abiding Zakhar had to resort to extra-legal action: "I made him give back some of the letters."[194]

There is a Dickensian quality to the portrait, a succession of fictive snapshots enhanced by bits of dialogue. The narrator picks out a few physical details such as the keeper's red hair which sticks out from under his cap, or a mysterious scratch across his unshaven cheek. The burden of characterization, however, is carried by Zakhar's surly speech patterns, which convey his custodial gruffness, sometimes to comic effect: "Well, they won't let me have a gun. They say I might shoot the visitors."[195] These threatening words are in keeping with the keeper's misleadingly martial appearance: he wears an old pair of officer's breeches, an army belt with a five-pointed star, and sports a Lenin badge that looks like a military decoration (a little in-joke: the badge is a facsimile of the Lenin Literature Prize medal that Solzhenitsyn was *not* awarded in 1964). He also has a limp, "a souvenir from the war,"[196] or so he claims. Zakhar's mock-warrior status is enhanced by the axe he carries under his jacket. The concealed weapon is held in place by a couple of loops. Cue Rodion Raskolnikov in *Crime and Punishment*, who goes about his murderous business similarly accoutred: "As for the loop, that was an ingenious device of his own. ... He could hardly carry an axe in his hands through the streets."[197]

Zakhar may give himself official airs, but he is also a rebel, always a privileged personality type in Solzhenitsyn's worlds. A rebel in word, and perhaps in deed: "'I'll bide my time, then I'll walk right through the regional department of culture. ... I'll take leave and I'll go to Moscow, right to Furtseva, the Minister of Culture herself. I'll tell her everything.'"[198]

Like his earlier iteration in "Matryona's Home," the autobiographical narrator is an inquisitive sort. He displays the same quasi-academic urge to record the things he sees and hears. He jots down notes and takes dozens of snapshots, though Zakhar refuses to allow himself to be photographed, mindful perhaps of the dignity of his office. Or is it that he shares the tribal superstition that a portrait "contain[s] the soul of the person portrayed"[199]? The authorial persona questions him about his circumstances and is surprised to learn that the keeper is paid twenty-seven rubles a month when the legal minimum is thirty. By way of comparison, in the early 1960s Solzhenitsyn earned a salary of sixty rubles as a part-time schoolteacher. As he observes in *The Oak and the Calf,* "Figures of this sort are below the threshold of comprehensibility for writers who are paid as much for a review a few lines long."[200]

Perhaps appropriately, Zakhar's given name means "The Lord Remembers" (Hebrew), while his patronymic, Dmitrievich, represents a connection to Dmitry I, the Muscovite prince who led the Russians to victory at Kulikovo all those centuries ago. As for the keeper's strange nickname, The Pouch (*Kalita*), the narrator bestows it because of the peasant sack Zakhar carries everywhere he goes. The moniker is also a tongue-in-cheek reference to Prince Dmitry's grandfather, Ivan I (1288–1341), who had the same cognomen. Ivan was the first in a line of rulers who brought Moscow to prominence, in his case, by acting as a sedulous agent of his Mongol overlords. As for the sack itself, it contains empty glassware left behind by visitors to the site, which Zakhar collects with a view to a refund, as well as a bottle of water and two loaves of bread. The narrator, wise in the ways of his countrymen, speculates that "on some days [Zakhar] probably carried a precious quarter bottle of vodka in there or some canned fish."[201] Yet there is more to the keeper's "inexhaustible sack"[202] (*meshok-samobranka*)[203] than its utilitarian or alcoholic functions. It is an object of mystery within whose canvas depths lurk secret meanings, a homely yet magical symbol that invites readerly *input*.

At one point, Zakhar is seen sleeping off an afternoon tipple, as we learn from a mock-heroic passage that gently parodies the medieval account of the battle cited earlier in the story.

> One fallen warrior was lying there this very day, not far from the monument, face down on mother earth—his native land. His bold head had dropped to the ground and his valiant limbs were spread-eagled; he was without his shield or sword and, in place of his helmet, wore a threadbare cap, and near his hand lay a sack.[204]

Yet for all his faults and fantasies, Zakhar does his duty conscientiously, spending the days and nights guarding the Field against intruders. He is the right man for the job in a country where all too often the job gets done badly or does not get done at all.[205]

8

The figure of the dutiful, honorable keeper of order is also present in "What a Pity," though this piece is a very different kettle of fiction. Written in 1963–5, for some private authorial reason the story—the shortest one in the oeuvre—was published thirteen years later. Like "Kochetovka," it dramatizes an event that Solzhenitsyn had learned about from an informant; the original facts are described in *The Gulag Archipelago*. After his release from the camp in 1953, the writer befriended another exile, Vladimir Vasilyev, a "sphinx-like" septuagenarian who had been one of the country's most eminent hydrographers.[206] The two men conversed at length, which is where Solzhenitsyn got his plot:

> Not so long ago V[ladimir] A[leksandrovich]'s daughter had stopped at a newspaper window on the Arbat in Moscow to look at *Trud*. A devil-may-care correspondent was lavishing well-paid words on a rousing account of his journey through the Chuisk Valley, which had been irrigated and brought to life by creative Bolsheviks. ... And suddenly ... he ended with this: "But very few people know that all these transformations are the realization of the dream of the talented Russian engineer Vasilyev, who found no support in old bureaucratic Russia. How sad that the young enthusiast did not live to see the triumph of his noble ideas!" The precious lines in the newspaper blurred, swam, Vasilyev's daughter tore the newspaper out of its case, pressed it to her breast, and carried it off, with a militiaman blowing his whistle after her.[207]

The differences between this factual, though imaginative, treatment of the incident and its full fictionalization in "What a Pity" are instructive. In the story, the professor's daughter, now evocatively renamed Anna Modestovna (Anna—"gracious" in Hebrew, Modest—"shy" in Latin), purloins the article not in the famous shopping street of Arbat but on one of Moscow's boulevards, tree-planted, sand-lined alleys that form a partial ring around the city center and carry a plethora of literary associations, most famously with Bulgakov's novel *The Master and Margarita*.[208] The heroine is an embodiment of old world gentility who seems entirely out of place in Stalin's Ozymandian capital. A working mother, she is using her lunch break to pick up a *spravka*,[209] or official document, from a nearby office: quite likely, to help her exiled father. Strolling down the boulevard in a state of gentle abstraction, she pauses to finger some overhanging branches, collecting raindrops in a whimsical game of her own device. The sudden appearance of a swaggering "young man … carrying a bulging bright-yellow briefcase,"[210] a garish marker of bureaucratic manhood, startles her from this strange diversion, but the Soviet salaryman saunters past, paying no heed to the furtive heroine. After his triumphant strut through the text we half-expect another encounter with an authority figure, which duly occurs when Anna, having alighted upon the newspaper with the precious article, attempts to detach it from the display board. She hears "the piercing staccato of a policeman's whistle,"[211] but instead of running away like her real-life prototype, stays meekly put to await her fate. The vigilant cop, however, is not a disembodied human alarum, as in *The Gulag Archipelago*. A solid, florid member of Soviet law enforcement, he has a "pink, broad-nosed face" and is "fit and strong."[212]

> He'd been on duty a long time and it had been raining. It would be nice to take the woman back to the station, along with her newspaper. While he filed his report, he'd dry out a little. But he wanted to understand. A respectably dressed woman, middle-aged, not drunk.[213]

Tremulously, Anna explains about the article and her father, but omits the fact that he is a prisoner. In the end, the policeman not only lets the heroine keep the newspaper but becomes her co-conspirator: "All right then, but don't do it again. Take it quickly, before anyone sees."[214]

The narrative diction is spare, the descriptive passages brief to the point of schematicism, in contrast to the extended quotations from the article, a bombastic example of high Stalinist journalese, for example, "this grandiose and majestic transformation of an entire region of nature."[215] The excerpts, interpolated by the narrator's sardonic comments, take up about a fifth of the story. The quotes inject an element of cultural commentary, reminding us that much of Soviet reality consisted of words, words, words that were lies, lies, lies. The intermittent references to Anna's hands and fingers (also her gloves) form a manual/digital leitmotif: her raindrop frolic is a case in point. During her conversation with the policeman the heroine sucks, childlike,[216] on a bleeding finger which she had cut on the glass-covered display case, and the manly cop first takes *pity* on girlish Anna because of her injury. The two characters' appearance, speech, and body language are nicely class- and gender-coded. The genteel heroine accompanies her apologies by "some kind of wriggle or bow,"[217] while the policeman has a peasant's "large, simple face"[218] and the stiff body language of a Soviet panjandrum (think Molotov or Gromyko). Throughout the encounter he remains completely motionless, never changing his expression. He speaks with his lips "barely parted," and as Anna expresses her gratitude for the fifth and final time, he merely nods, "standing alongside her" but not looking at her directly.[219] The patrolman is like a statue come to life or a living person that has been statued. At the same time, the cop on the boulevard may be the only sympathetic policeman in the Russian canon, if one excludes, as one must, the eight-foot-tall Uncle Steeple (*Diadia Stëpa*) in the cloying children's poem by Sergei Mikhalkov (1936) and the absurdist "militia-man" (*militsaner*) in Dmitry Prigov's Conceptualist verse cycle (1978). Anna's benign policeman, "the kind of man to drag people out of blaze or carry out an arrest without using firearms,"[220] is an abbreviated version of Mikhalkov's skyscraping hero who rescues a schoolboy from drowning and eighteen pigeons plus sparrow from a house fire. Solzhenitsyn knew his Soviet stuff and knew how to make fun of it.

And so, from Mikhalkov's doggerel to Nabokov's *délices*. It is hard to identify any "Nabokovian" passages in Solzhenitsyn's prose, though the author of *The Gift* (*Dar*; 1937–8; 1952) was one of his favorite writers. Having conducted numerous textological trawls across the length and breadth of his fictions, the only instant I could find occurs in this story.

Let us recall that gentle Anna is a collector of raindrops: "Each drop was also a convex mirror. In this mirror, against a light background of cloudy sky, she could see dark shoulders in a coat, and a head in a woollen hat, and even the interwoven branches above her head."[221] The authorial eye discerns with scientific detachment the operation of fluid statics (the behavior of fluids at rest) in these tiny watery globules, whether pendant from the integument or resting cohesively on Anna's fingertips. Another branch of physics, optics, is also brought into play. On the branches overhead, the droplet shows "silvery-white,"[222] but once deposited on Anna's skin, and depending on the angle of light, it becomes either transparent, acting as a liquid loupe through which she observes those delicate dactyloscopic lines and whorls, or reflective, turning into the "convex mirror" that holds a tiny (twisted) likeness of her face: a pair of luminous micro-images. The unconventional arboreal perspectives and the instantly materialized metaphor of the angle-surfaced mirror bring to mind one of the opening lines of *The Gift*: "Lindens of medium size, with hanging droplets of rain distributed among their intricate black twigs according to the future arrangement of leaves (tomorrow each drop would contain a green pupil)."[223] No less apposite is Kornei Chukovsky's point that the "the drops of water on the boulevard were created by a Tolstoyan hand."[224] Still, the passage in "What a Pity" contains vernacularisms of a kind that Nabokov would certainly have curled his lip at: *suchochki* (twiglets*), ssochilas'* (trickled down), *pliushchilas'* (slightly flattened itself).²²⁵

9

"The Easter Procession" is a dramatized eyewitness account of a Paschal celebration at a suburban Moscow church in AD 1966 and its violent disruption by a youth mob: Christians and louts. The disciplined fury of the narration is reminiscent of *The Gulag Archipelago*, which Solzhenitsyn was writing during the same period, while the story's state-of-the-world topicality recalls Turgenev's *Literary and Autobiographical Reminiscences* (*Literaturnye i zhiteiskie vospominaniia*), particularly "The Execution of Tropmann" ("Kazn' Tropmana"; 1870), a piece of literary reportage that describes the guillotining of a French mass murderer and the behavior of the attendant crowd.

The story begins rather oddly, with an astringent aside directed against, of all things, Cubism. The authorial voice deprecates the modernist rejection of the old representational ways and identifies mimetic realism as being supremely adequate to his purpose:

> Connoisseurs tell us that an artist should not paint everything exactly as it is. They say that color photography does this and that by means of curved lines and combinations of triangles and squares we should convey the essence of a thing rather than the thing itself. But I do not see how color photography could pick out what is significant among the faces in an Easter procession at the patriarchal church of Peredelkino²²⁶ half a century after the Revolution and compose them meaningfully into a single picture. Depicted in conventional terms (even without the aid of triangles), a present-day Easter procession can tell us a great deal.²²⁷

This obiter dictum may be discrepant to the body of the work, and of arguable conceptual validity, but it does the job of setting the geographical and temporal parameters for the events described.

Next comes a group portrait of the juvenile blasphemers, enhanced by dollops of Solzhenitsyn's patented (paternal?) sarcasm. This is the most powerful section of the piece. The youths are thuggish, their dates sluttish, with both sexes carrying on a peripatetic orgy. The hoodlums and hussies swarm around the church and dart in and out of the courtyard, "jigging"²²⁸ to transistor radios or strutting and sashaying, as the gendered case may be. Slack mouths ooze foul obscenities:

a form of "hearty Russian conversation," the narrator acidly comments.[229] These collective displays of depravity are quantified in mock-epic terms: "About one in four has been drinking, one in ten is drunk, and half of them are smoking—in that repulsive way with the cigarette stuck to the lower lip."[230] There is plenty of rough lovin'. "Some of them kiss their girlfriends [*marukhi*],[231] who are then pulled from one boy to another, staring aggressively around as though the knives may come out at any minute"[232] (to clarify the translation, the staring is done by the toughs, not the tarts). The point has been made, with abundant emphasis, but the narrative voice makes sure to ram it home: "An insult to the Passion of Christ..., snotty hooligans [who] come to watch how the old folk still practice the rites of their forefathers."[233] In this account of intergenerational aggression, the narrator reveals his own notional years when he offers a simile that harks back to the Jazz Age: "They crowd together as if waiting for a foxtrot to begin."[234]

Unlike the swivel-eyed mob, the congregants, two dozen or so in number, are lightly individualized. An elderly churchwarden's palpable terror contrasts with the "unworldly gaze" and "pure and bright" faces of the ten women, two of them young girls but the rest much older, who follow him out of the church holding candles and singing.[235] The little column has its own sacral, linear geometry that separates it from the crowd's Brownian motion, with its hint of a demonic circularity.

But what are these *droogs* and their *koshki*, to use the correct *Clockwork Orange* terms, doing here in the first place? The narrator, a worldly presence who keeps abreast of the sports calendar, explains: "The ice-hockey season on television is over, the football season has not started yet, and what brings them to church is sheer boredom."[236] Yet the vibrating malice that drives the teenage desecrators seems to be engendered by something other than teenage angst. Certainly, this much is suggested by the writing, which is graphic and expressive and focuses on the facial, bodily, and violent. The two groups, which are always in motion, seem to belong to different human species and even their languages are mutually incomprehensible, if one may describe Solzhenitsyn's jabbering blasphemers as language practitioners.

Also present is a third category of characters, the militiamen or police, who "smile amiably at the rising generation."[237] Agents of an irreligious government, these *millicents* (q.v. *A Clockwork Orange*) give tacit sanction to the mob by declining to intervene even at the most outrageous disturbances of the peace, though they make sure that blasphemy does not turn to battery.

In Solzhenitsyn's worlds, bells and belfries can uplift the spirit in ways both religious and aesthetic, as may be seen (and almost heard) in "Along the Oka," the "Miniature" quoted earlier in this chapter. Bells ring out in "The Easter Procession" as well, "but there is something false about it; the chimes sound somehow tinny instead of deep and sonorous."[238] Still, the demonic is kept, barely, at bay *outside*, for somehow the mob never dares to come into the church itself.

As the congregants exit that place of worship, they are trailed by the jeering crowd, now brandishing lighted candles in a parody of the sacred ritual: "A religious procession without worshippers, without people crossing themselves, a religious procession of people with caps on, smoking cigarettes, with transistors in their breast pockets."[239] The scene presages one of the organizing interpretative figures in *The Red Wheel*, in which the revolution triumphant turns into a mock-Paschal street party, its gullible acolytes celebrating victory with cries of "Christ is risen!"[240]

The celebrants, some of them terrified for their lives, complete the ceremony and thereby gain a moral victory of sorts, but the narrator is full of dark forebodings. One day, he warns, the bestial crowd will "turn and trample on us all," including the nameless persons "who urged them on to this."[241] Things, however, would turn out differently. These days Russian Orthodox activists attack rock musicians and their fans or disrupt stage productions of *The Ideal Husband* to protect their wounded faith[242] while the *militsiia*, now rebranded as the *politsiia*, piously look away. History repeats itself, the first time as thuggery, the second time also as thuggery.

There is a passage in the *History of Rome* (*Res Gestae*; c. 378–91 AD) by Ammianus Marcellinus that describes the arrest of the rabble-rouser Petrus Valvomeres by the prefect Leontius during a city riot. Auerbach treats this scene as an example of "a somber and highly rhetorical realism."[243] "On one side there is a pure mass of bodies, stupid and full of effrontery, like a crowd of juvenile delinquents, and on the other imposing authority, fearlessness, instant decision, flogging."[244] And: "[Ammianus] does not make the populace talk ... instead, he clothes the whole incident in the somber splendor of his rhetoric, which is as distant from popular style as possible."[245] And: "This element of the sensory and the gestural."[246] And: "A haunting and gruesome distortion of reality."[247] Each of these tropes is present in "The Easter Procession," but there is no "imposing authority" that can bring the rabble to heel or correct the gruesomeness and the distortion it generates. The Easter celebrants must rely on their spiritual courage as they confront the braying mob. Nonetheless, post factum and fictively, Solzhenitsyn assumes the part of the imposing Leontius by administering a literary flogging to these street toughs and skanks and, with an extra flick of his writerly wrist, to the partocrats who let them loose upon the faithful.

CHAPTER FOUR

Meteor Man: *Love the Revolution*

Convictions are more dangerous enemies of truth than lies.
—Friedrich Nietzsche, *Human, All Too Human*

We learned that a bright button is weightier than four volumes of Schopenhauer. At first astonished, them embittered, and finally indifferent, we recognized that what matters is not the mind but the boot brush, not intelligence but the system, not freedom but drill.
—Erich Maria Remarque, *All Quiet on the Western Front*

From my long experience of associating with soldiers, I knew that among the lower classes the shameless discussion of the intimate side of life fulfils approximately the same function as conversation about the weather for the upper classes.
—Victor Pelevin, *Buddha's Little Finger*

1

When an unfinished text by a famous writer appears in print, this is usually the doing of his literary heirs or some dedicated scholar who has spent a lifetime mining the archives. The case of *Love the Revolution* is different. Begun in the Marfino science prison and rewritten in Ryazan ten years later, the novel came out in 1999, in a collection of early works supervised by the author which also included the epic poem *The Road* and his prison and exilic verse.[1] In one sense, this was a matter of rounding out the published corpus of texts. In another, of giving a final shape to its automythobiographical component. It was as if the novelist was responding to one of his biographers, who had perceived a very un-Tolstoyan lacuna in the oeuvre:

His self-representations are of the fully grown man—soldier, writer, *zek*; not, however, husband or lover, with rare exceptions; and for any "portrait of the artist as a young man" or as a child we look in vain. Instead of any clear statement of where and when he was born, there is a sense of confused, almost mythic, birth.[2]

By releasing *Love the Revolution* and *The Road* to the public, Solzhenitsyn finally made available the two opening sections of the multigeneric Gleb/Sergei Nerzhin saga, which show this fictional alter ego emerge from the chrysalis of childhood and adolescence into young adulthood in a time of war. Whether *Love the Revolution* ought to be considered the first or second installment in the series is moot: "While the work has sometimes been referred to as a 'prose sequel' to *The Road*, it is in fact focused on the period *preceding* the wartime episodes included in the autobiographical poem."[3] To be precise, the novel fills in the narrative gap between chapters four and five of the latter text, thereby constituting its *midquel*.

Now, not only is *Love the Revolution* uncompleted, but it is also abridged. While its first two chapters as well as chapter four are included *in toto*, chapters three and five are chopped off in mid-text, or mid-draft, and chapters six and seven are but short fragments. The excisions are indicated by rows of dots. One is reminded, and perhaps meant to be reminded, of the manner in which the absence of stanzas or lines is marked in Pushkin's verse novel *Eugene Onegin* (*Evgenii Onegin*; 1825–32), the paradigmatic *Bildungsroman* of Russian literature. In that work, the dotted textual blanks function as a "compositional device."[4] Chapter seven, or rather a two-page extract therefrom, is followed by an outline of subsequent chapters, perhaps unwritten, perhaps half-written, which would have described the hero's experiences as an artillery cadet and his first weeks at the front. This précis also lacks a proper ending, concluding instead with a set of omission points: "Positional fighting at Novosil.—The Battle of Oryol.—The capture of Oryol..."[5] The interested reader is thereby referred to chapters five to eleven of *The Road*, which tell the story of Nerzhin's frontline service from the defeat of Operation Citadel to the invasion of East Prussia. In fact, "Solzhenitsyn's original intent was for *Love the Revolution* to be an account of his entire military career."[6]

The first time I opened *Love the Revolution* I, for one, was struck by its combination of the familiar and unfamiliar. Here was a work containing many of the elements I had learned to recognize and appreciate in Solzhenitsyn's prose, yet others were missing and there were formal features that seemed unique to this novel. Doubtless, its empirical audience is very different from that of, say, *The First Circle*. One assumes that readers come to the text prepared, that is, possessing prior knowledge of some or all of Solzhenitsyn's more famous productions. By releasing this *essai de plume*, the author invited his best-informed receptors to judge it against the corpus of his writings. Indeed, the novel's ostentatious incompleteness of form positively directs the reader to look to the other four Nerzhin texts for explanations and elucidations.

So let us begin at the beginning, or even before the beginning. In order to do so, we shall briefly examine aspects of the novel's peritext. Gérard Genette coined this term to describe a book's title, epigraph, chapter headings and other framing elements; together, peritext and epitext, or authorial "interviews, conversations and confidences" relating to a given work,[7] make up the paratext, which is a "vestibule" to the narrative as such.[8] As Genette puts it, "Limited to the text alone and without a guiding set of directions, how would we read Joyce's *Ulysses* if it were not entitled *Ulysses*?"[9]

Following Solzhenitsyn's usual practice with his works-in-progress or works-in-abeyance, he had kept the manuscript under wraps, but eventually its title became public knowledge, giving rise to rumors that this was a youthful exercise in the SocRealist manner. After all, the formula *Love the Revolution* evokes the bombastic titles of early Soviet novels featuring de-individualized zealots, such as Aleksandr Serafimovich's *The Iron Flood* (*Zheleznyi potok*; 1924) with its ardent Red Army soldiers, Valentin Kataev's *Time, Forward!* (*Vremia, vperëd!*; 1932) with its ardent construction workers, and Nikolai Ostrovsky's *How Steel Was Tempered* (*Kak zakalialas' stal'*; 1932) with its ardent revolutionary Pavel Korchagin, who is also an ardent piece of cardboard. In fact, Solzhenitsyn borrowed the titular phrase from the short story "Marina" (1923) by another writer, Boris Lavrenyov. In the prewar period his action-packed tales, with their iron-jawed commissars and lethal Bolshevik beauties, were hugely popular with Soviet readers. One of them was Sanya Solzhenitsyn, who in 1938 even sent the author a fan letter.[10] As Genette points out, "quotation-titles" possess special "connotative values": "These are ... echoes that provide the text with the indirect support of another text, plus the prestige of a cultural filiation, and do so as effectively as and more economically than an epigraph (which often, as a matter of fact, completes them)."[11] Indeed, serving as the epigraph to the novel is the full, slightly altered Lavrenyov quotation: "Young boy! Love the Revolution! It is the only thing in the whole world worthy of love!"[12] By dropping the exclamation mark from his title, Solzhenitsyn ironized the eponymous imperative, turning the strident slogan into a meta-comment or meta-query or, perhaps, a meta-lament: an instance of titular dialogism. Other than *The Red Wheel*, this early work is the most peritextually coded of all his productions.

Clearly, by the time Solzhenitsyn had (un)finished the novel his attitude to Lavrenyov's Red melodramas had changed. *Love the Revolution* shows how Nerzhin learns by painful and difficult stages that there are many things in the world worthy of love, though he is yet to realize that the revolution itself is *not* worthy of it. Gleb's epiphany will take place in the play *The Love-Girl and the Innocent*, set in 1946. In any case, this portrait of the autobiographical hero between the ages of twenty and twenty-two is far from complete. The novel mentions Nerzhin's late father but briefly, shows his mother in the shadowiest of outlines, and omits more than it reveals about his two most important relationships, his friendship with the equally revolution-loving Andrei Kholudenev and his marriage to pretty, romantic Nadya. Where these details are concerned, *The Road* tells us a great deal more.

Although incomplete and abbreviated, *Love the Revolution* contains hints of an epic vision of a country at war. The action moves from Moscow, where Gleb arrives to take up his studies at the Literature Institute on the day of Hitler's invasion, to his native city of Rostov in the south and the town of Morozovsk nearby, to the former Land of the Don Cossack Host through which the hero passes with his unit, to the frozen landscapes of east Russia whence he makes his way first to Stalingrad (half a year before the famous battle), and then to the town of Semyonov in Gorky Province to train as an artillery officer, his cherished ambition all along. The novel is part travelogue, for in six of the seven chapters (chapter two is the exception) Gleb is on the (rail)road. Here and there we encounter nicely crafted historical snapshots, as in the scenes of Red Army conscripts taking drunken leave of their loved ones at provincial train stations in the summer of 1941, a "timeless picture which became fixed in Nerzhin's memory."[13]

There are no scenes of combat. Nevertheless, *Love the Revolution* is very much a war novel, one that refutes all those SocRealist productions about heroic soldiers, led by a heroic Party, who do glorious battle against the Nazi hordes. The Red Army men shown are unheroic but very human, while the Party as such lacks any presence in the text, though some characters are members and several communist officials are shown, albeit of low rank. As for the Germans, the only one depicted, or rather mentioned, is the elderly artist Hermann Koske, a lifelong resident of Rostov who is arrested in the first days of the war on some trumped-up charge. Where the Supreme Leader is concerned, the work negates a statutory SocRealist topos: "Since in actual fact Stalin was not very much in evidence at the front, his usual role in war fiction was to deliver one of his major war time speeches over the radio."[14] And so the General Secretary's address to the nation on July 3, 1941, celebrated in hundreds of novels and memoirs, is dismissed by the narrator as an "absurd speech ... with periods of breathlessness and the gurgling of water."[15] Instead, it is an earlier speech by Stalin's number two, Vyacheslav Molotov, in which he informs the nation of the German attack, that receives textual prominence, but not as one of the mythical "Great Moments" of the Great Patriotic War[16] that were an obligatory ingredient of the Soviet war novel.

The passage in question occurs just a few pages into chapter one. The omnipotent author brings together a group of young men in a student dorm on Moscow's Stromynka street: five Muscovites plus Gleb, who has arrived in the capital a few hours earlier. The time is noon; the date, Sunday, June 22, 1941. Nerzhin and his roommates have just finished listening to a news bulletin, with reports of Soviet economic successes, a strike in Puerto Rico, a demonstration in Brazil, and British colonial misdeeds in India: details that give evidence of the remarkable quality of Solzhenitsyn's authorial memory. There is not a hint that the Soviet Union has been at war since the early hours of the morning.

Then Molotov's reedy voice comes on to make the fateful announcement.

> It was as if the six beating hearts of these future historians and economists were jolted by the kind of electric charge that bonds metals. In a single convulsive movement, they jumped to their feet and remained motionless where they stood, listening and from time to time exchanging worried looks. Long black clouds streamed across the murky sky like enemy divisions rushing into the breach. The well-ordered, logical, and comfortable world had cracked and was now divided by a yawning crevice, which the rickety little bridge named *our just cause* could not hope to span.[17]

The phrase "Our cause is just" came at the end of the speech and was much quoted by Party propagandists during the war.

The students' reception of Molotov's statement is conveyed through a form of free indirect speech that is collectively denotational: Nerzhin and his roommates are as one in their enthusiasm for what they imagine will be a short and victorious struggle. In the last sentence, however, a diegetic change occurs. The sense of history articulated here is the narrator's, as is the disdainful treatment of Molotov's concluding sound bite. The tone is still world-historical, but the metaphorical register is now polemical/satirical. We are given to understand how perilous the situation really is and by implication, how clueless the six Komsomols are about the trials that await them. The passage as a whole is figuratively framed by the contrasting images of the "bonding," that is, *joining*, of metals, with its SocRealist associations (see *How Steel Was Tempered*), and the "crack" or "crevice" *cleaving* the world: an imaginative binary. As for the speech itself, it is "rickety" because the man giving it, a colorless partocrat known for his sedulous servility to the Leader, is utterly incapable of any sincerity or originality or passion.

The passage is also a proleptic, cross-textual pointer to chapters forty-nine to fifty of *The First Circle*, which show another student sextet, the young women who will be living in the very same dorm four years after the war's end (Room 318 with "the big square window").[18] One of them is Nadya Nerzhin, who pines for her husband, serving time in the Marfino science prison just a few miles away.

2

There is a concordance between the textual and the authorial: inside this fictive world Nerzhin is beginning to realize himself as a personality while his creator is beginning to realize himself as a writer. The diegetic diction is more conventional than in the later works. Most of the time it relies on a kind of standard literary Russian, one taught at the Moscow Literature Institute attended by Nerzhin in the novel and by Solzhenitsyn in real life. As a rule, creative writing courses do not encourage original self-expression, and SocRealist ones least of all. Yet once in a while we come across a passage that looks forward to the terse, discontinuous textures of *The Red Wheel*. Here is an example. In the first weeks of the war farmers, worried about the looming shortage of animal feed, slaughter their livestock: "The market, red with veal carcasses, was like world gore two" (*Bazar, dostoinyi vtoroi mirovoi boini, byl krasen ot goviazhikh tush*).[19] Or take this intricately metaphorized scene in which the protagonist experiences a traumatic loss of identity as he awaits induction on a miserable autumn day:

> Names were called out, faces flickered, numberless like raindrops, and Gleb imagined that amid those slanting flickers the tiny, insignificant droplet named "Nerzhin," which only yesterday morning had fancied it held within itself the earth and the sky, might be lost forever.[20]

To call *Love the Revolution* multivocal, let alone polyphonic, would be an unsustainable terminological stretch. The diegetic mode is minimal narrator, the narrative emphatically functional, to use the Barthian term, that is, metonymically informational about *doing*. Most of what we learn about the protagonist and the men and women in his life comes from conventionally formatted colloquies, descriptive passages, and framed digressions. The narration mostly takes the form of free indirect speech that reflects the hero's point of view, so no surprises here. The occasional transitions from this Nerzhin-centered perspective to that of some other character and back can be abrupt, particularly in the first two chapters where he is shown in a variety of situations meeting a variety of people. On his return journey to Rostov, Gleb encounters a military pilot, a manly figure "who somehow quietly combined the strength, good humor, and ironic intellect of our middle Russian type."[21] Next comes a paragraph baldly detailing the pilot's anxious thoughts about the parlous state of the Red Air Force, whereupon the strong, good-humored flyer disappears from the novel forever and the narrative resumes its Nerzhinian course. The same jerky diegetic to-and-fro occurs on a couple of other occasions, for example, in the segments detailing the thoughts/feelings of Dr. Dovner, a no-nonsense city health official, and Nerzhin's best friend, Kholudenev, who shares his Marxist ideals and his love for Nadya. Kholudenev is another of those Solzhenitsyn characters that migrate from text to text: he is present in *The Road* as well as the play *Prisoners*.

Evident throughout the novel is an authorial awareness of the processes of history and their directional, vectored nature. Every important character is historicized: private lives, experiences, thoughts, and hopes are always shown against the backcloth of events current or past. People's fates are shaped by political and military realities beyond their control and, in the case of the rustic soldiers in Nerzhin's platoon, their comprehension. The hero, on the other hand, is keenly aware that he lives inside history, even if at this stage his understanding of it is distorted by Marxist dogma leavened with a dollop of Komsomol romanticism: "Their entire generation was born to carry the Revolution from their one sixth of the earth to the rest of the earth."[22] Emblematic historical developments, above all the brutal, bloody war against the Germans, are stripped of their mythical gloss and fictively reconceptualized. A key instance is the depiction of the popular response to Hitler's attack. Even as Molotov is still speaking, Nerzhin is appalled to see that "crazed people—our Soviet people!—were rushing to the banks, pulling their savings-books out of their pockets as they ran."[23] Rostov's febrile mood in the first weeks of the invasion is summed up in an evocative sentence: "They counted out their breaths in minutes, not yet understanding that they should count them out in years" (*Dyshali minutami, eshchë ne poniav, chto nado dyshat' godami*).[24] The phrase is derived from "We

Shall Pull Through" ("My vystoim!"; 1941), an Ehrenburg article which Nerzhin reads, and quotes, later in the novel, as in, "We must count out our breaths not in days but in years'" (*Perevesti dykhanie s dnei na gody*).[25] This doubling of a borrowed metaphor may have been meant to perform some indicial function, but is left hanging: a rare lapse.

Most of the people Nerzhin comes across in Moscow, Rostov, and even in the army react to the invasion in ways that are utterly non-ideological but all too human: Dr. Dovner displays a calm resolve to do his medical best; Zozulia, a venal Party functionary, quakes with animal fear; foppish Lieutenant Brant delights in his tailored uniform; while the peasant soldiers Dashkin, Trukhachyov, and Podriadin view the war as a calamity to be survived or avoided, their military oath furthest from their thoughts. As Private Nerzhin does the rounds of various headquarters trying to obtain that coveted transfer to the artillery, he meets officers who are variously competent or cretinous or martinetish, as has been true of all armies back to the beginning of time. Moreover, not every communist in the novel is a thug or a fool. Commissar Petrov, a political officer whose quiet manner belies a thoughtful intelligence, would rather speak to the men about the true situation at the front than lecture them on Lenin's greatness or goodness.

Occasionally the novel's demythologizing message is directly articulated by individual characters who despise the regime, and for good reason. One such figure is the genteel engineer Illarion Diomidov, whom Gleb and Nadya meet in Morozovsk. He is a middle-aged, middle-class survivor from tsarist Russia who has done time in the gulag. His name, with its classical connotations (that is, Hilarion Diomedes), is suggestive of a civilized Hellene toiling in the service of some barbarian potentate; his fragile, much younger wife Nina, the flaxen-haired daughter of an exiled priest, loves him "for his suffering," and he loves her "for her compassion."[26] The engineer describes to Nerzhin the reality of the camps "in inhuman detail"[27] and is secretly thrilled by each new Soviet defeat. Saturnine Trukhachyov, a private in Nerzhin's platoon, is another hater of the Bolsheviks who would gladly "shoot down the whole lot of them,"[28] though "behind this darkness Nerzhin sensed there was a good man."[29] He may sense it, but we do not, and as a character Trukhachyov is all the more memorable for it. The Cossacks, traditional enemies of the Soviets, watch with "somber joy"[30] as the retreating transport unit passes through their villages and consider the Red Army men ethnic and military strangers, referring to them as "the Russians":[31] an ethnographic motif that will resurface in *March 1917* where Zinaida Altanskaya, the lover of the writer Kovynev, is seen by her fellow Cossacks as a "Russian woman."[32]

Here and there, as the author reaches for a descriptive *mot juste*, he borrows the diction of other writers, chiefly Tolstoy. Upon his return to Rostov, Gleb, standing peaceably in a bread line, is pulled in by the police who are anxious to meet their quota of arrests for panic-mongering. His situation is perilous: he is liable to be sent to the gulag. The narrator comments, in earnestly Tolstoyan tones, "But Nerzhin's understanding of things was too complicated for him to understand a simple thing like that."[33] Another Tolstoyan moment involves a humorous instant of emotional eavesdropping which comes after a passage that describes Private Nerzhin's experiences cleaning the transport unit's stables: "As always happens when you are doing new, unfamiliar and exhausting work, the manure would not leave Gleb alone even when he was sleeping."[34] Solzhenitsyn's skill at reproducing various sociolects and categories of the vernacular is already displayed to full storytelling advantage. Examples are the phone conversation between Dovner and Captain Maksimov of the Rostov police when with a few casual words-to-the-wise the good doctor rescues Nerzhin from that one-way trip to Siberia; the staccato phone exchanges among harried train dispatchers; the folksy speech of the soldiers in Gleb's unit; or Lieutenant Brant's colorful Odessa accents.

Numbers of tropes, themes, and scenes anticipate those in the more famous works. After Dr. Dovner's intercession with Soviet law enforcement, we encounter what is the first appearance in any Solzhenitsyn text of his organizing metaphor for historical evil: "A gigantic wheel had rolled by, almost squashing him into a pulp, but Gleb never even knew that the wheel was there and that it kept on rolling."[35] Flaccid Zozulia (the Morozovsk Party boss), his sheep-faced daughter, and the town's hunchback NKVD chief belong to the same subspecies of *homo sovieticus turpis* as the grotesque Stalinists in *The First Circle*. Nerzhin spends a good deal of time pondering the gulf between those who read books and those who raise crops, a subject that will preoccupy him at the Marfino science prison, again as shown in *The First Circle*. Or what about the bond between the hero and cheerful, homely Podriadin, the peasant soldier who becomes his teacher of all things equine and practical? Surely, it foreshadows Nerzhin's friendship with the yardman Spiridon at Marfino, while Podriadin himself is scripted as a twentieth-century Platon Karataev, in overt tribute to *War and Peace*.[36] Later Solzhenitsyn would assign the same Karataevian traits to the hero of "Ivan Denisovich," but do so with a much lighter touch.

Some of the linkages to the other four works in which Nerzhin is a character are intricately coded. As the protagonist wanders the streets of Moscow on the second day of the war, he comes across "a tall elegant building that served an unknown purpose, but ... somehow he recognized that this was the ministry of foreign affairs."[37] Nerzhin has just seen the place where the idealistic diplomat Innokenty Volodin will have his office in *The First Circle*. In that novel, Volodin and Nerzhin, its two main characters, never meet, so it is fictively fitting that this younger version of the latter declines to approach the building: even intertextually, the trajectories of their lives must remain separate. Note that the narrator calls the institution in question a ministry, yet in 1941 it was still known as the People's Commissariat of Foreign Affairs: the name was changed five years later. This anachronistic detail becomes a proleptic clue. A more obvious instance of cross-textual foreshadowing occurs when Nerzhin and Kholudenev promise to write to each other while on active service, and Andrei says: "The censors will make sure we don't give the unit designation, the number of artillery pieces, the names of villages or roads, but there's nothing to stop us from discussing ideas of general interest."[38] That decision will turn out to be fateful one, for the letters the two men exchange at the front will be intercepted by SMERSH, the Red Army's counterintelligence branch: Nerzhin's arrest is depicted in chapter ten of *The Road*, while Kholudenev's prison experiences are shown in the play *Prisoners*.

There are plenty of other subtleties. During his walk around Moscow, Nerzhin looks in on Alexander Scriabin's house in the Arbat district. The composer died there while working on his symphonic work *Mysterium* (1915), the performance of which was meant to usher in the end of the world, in the most direct, apocalyptic sense: a hint to the wise and the musical that Nerzhin's world is about to experience a terrible cataclysm. The hero, that head-in-the-clouds young man who teaches high school astronomy, is astrally coded, as he is in *The Road*. Here Gleb is associated with the stars Vega, Deneb, and Sirius as well as the constellations of Cygnus and Orion, and the Pleiades. In one of the few passages where we are given Nadya's own starry-eyed take on things, she thinks of her husband as an "incandescent meteor"[39]—an ironized meta-quote from Napoleon who described geniuses as "meteors that are destined to burn up to light up the age."

With the astronomical Nerzhin, one is reminded of the allegory of the pilot in *The Republic*, who steers his ship by the heavens. The sailors mocked him as "a prater, a star-gazer, a good-for-nothing,"[40] but they were ignorant and wrong, and he was wise and right. For the pilot represents Plato's notion of the philosopher, for whom "courage, magnificence, apprehension, memory" are "his natural gifts."[41] But Plato also says that "the finest natures, when under alien conditions, receive more injury than the inferior"; and that "the most gifted minds, when they are ill-educated, become pre-eminently bad."[42] Solzhenitsyn's star-counting hero, a philosophical Marxist mocked by the unphilosophical, is proud of the books he has read and the thoughts he has thought, yet his higher truth is a lower falsehood and the Marxian absolute he apprehends is but a distorted version of the relative and the contingent. (Nonetheless, the constellation of Cygnus is also known as the Northern *Cross*.) Still, whatever the merits of this Platonic reading of Nerzhin's intellectual conceits, the novel contains plenty of satirical send-ups and lampoons of a more direct kind. Solzhenitsyn claims author's privilege to take a swipe at several pet hates such as Mikhail Sholokhov, living classic of SocRealism; Ilya Ehrenburg, wartime propagandist to the brainwashed; and Sergei Eisenstein, that cineastic fragmenter of history and its meanings.

At the same time, some character descriptions are schematic or, as in the case of the protagonist, virtually non-existent. Almost the only thing we learn about Nerzhin's appearance is that his hair is parted in the middle and that he is taller than Lyalia Brailovsky, the sister of one of his childhood friends. We never find out if he is fair or dark, or the color of his eyes. In fact, we are told more about the faces and bodies of secondary personae like Trukhachyov, Petrov, and especially Lieutenant Brant, that personification of theatrical, martial masculinity. But then, readers already familiar with Nerzhin from *The First Circle*, with its famous portrait of the hero as a wanly handsome prisoner, may not notice the omission. As for Lyalia, "the sensitive, delicate queen of [Gleb's] childhood,"[43] the story of her tragic romance with the mysterious Italian-Russian Aleksandr Gemelli (also present in *The Road* as a lionhearted anti-Stalinist) and her subsequent marriage to the crass bureaucrat Brailovsky amounts to a narrative detour that is (deliberately?) cut short. Neither sweet-tempered Lyalia nor her glamorous lover nor her vodka-swigging, card-playing spouse have any connection to the rest of the novel. The presence of such extraneous passages is due to the author's chosen strategy of meticulously fictionalizing not just his own younger self but an entire nexus of related life experiences and social situations; and also, to the novel's status as an incomplete, and therefore formally unrealized, production. The effect is quasi-Tolstoyan, in the sense that these seemingly inapposite scenes add variety and color to the textures of the narrated world. Solzhenitsyn employs a similar practice in *The First Circle*, where the autobiographically sourced, but fabulaically supernumerary characters, episodes, and details tend to be more fully integrated into the fictive proceedings.

3

So, what is this youthful Nerzhin like?

To begin with, while the Gleb of *Love the Revolution* is readily recognizable as the Sergei of *The Road*, the psychological and intellectual continuity between these two early Nerzhin iterations and the one so memorably enacted in *The First Circle* is much less obvious. But then, between 1941 and 1949 Solzhenitsyn's autobiographical hero would go through two life-changing experiences, war and prison, and become a very different personality, with a very different outlook. Moreover, as a *Bildungsroman*, *Love the Revolution* is the story of a young man's self-genderization, his continuous endeavor to construct a masculine identity adequate to his sense of self and the world he lives in. Here Solzhenitsyn is beginning to explore the themes of male self-expression and self-assertion that will figure so prominently in *The First Circle* and *Cancer Ward*. All three novels are androcentric productions, though their rhetoric of masculinity is very different from, say, the loud-mouthed, strutting variety in Mayakovsky's verse or the pugilistic, tauromachian one in Hemingway's prose.

Actually, at this stage in his life our hero is not a particularly likeable fellow. Introverted, humorless, and rather stuffy, he lives in a permanent state of intellectual abstraction. He sleeps six hours a night, determined to put every waking minute to productive ideological and philosophical use: "To save time and to compress it was Gleb's urgent motto since he was a schoolboy."[44] A Type A personality if there ever was one, he is always systematizing, prioritizing, multitasking. He is an idealist, yes, but his ideals are arid notions, for example, the victory of labor over capital or the liberation of mankind. His wisdom, such as it is, is entirely derived, from bad (and good) writers and bad (and good) philosophers, and he knows more about the rise and fall of the Roman Empire than the recent Soviet past. He imagines he has agency as a class warrior in the "coming great battle that will inevitably result in a World Revolution,"[45] but in reality his choices are predetermined by the terror state he serves and the Marxist discourse he employs. This subaltern of the Soviet imaginary is also an ideological snob who admires Lenin but considers Stalin "dim,"[46] though this is as far as his critical judgment will take him. Still, now and then Gleb shows an incipient capacity for independent thought: "He had regarded the strident clownish boastfulness of the prewar period and the crude falsehoods in literature and the arts as suspect two years ago."[47] So, Nerzhin is beginning—but only just beginning—to develop a nose for the Lie. We also learn that somewhere deep inside he retains memories of a childhood belief in God. Miserable after a particularly hard day in this man's army, he recalls the words of the Lord's Prayer and marvels at its "disinterestedness": "Little man was asking his Great God for one thing only: a bite to eat on this day."[48] These are pointers to the spiritually questing Nerzhin of *The First Circle*. And of course, Solzhenitsyn's hero dreams of being a writer, even though at this stage his knowledge of literature is characterized less by what he has read than by what he has not, while the poetry he writes is simply terrible:

> *Esli Lenina delo padët v eti dni,*
> *Dlia chego mne ostanetsia zhit?..*[49]
>
> [Should Lenin's cause concede defeat,
> my life will never be complete.]

This is the same bit of doggerel that Zotov obsessively recites to himself in "Kochetovka."

Stalin-era precarity... Although like every other subject of the Soviet state Gleb lives at its sufferance, apt to be deleted from civil existence at the whim of any Party boss or secret policeman, he is clueless about this truth, even after that narrow shave at the police station.

He is also clueless in matters of the heart. The reasons for this go back to childhood:

> He had never learned, and because he never had a father there had been no one to tell him, that there is such a thing as male good looks or that one should make an effort to be presentable. He grew up a pale, thin, unprepossessing youth, entirely preoccupied with his inner world and unconcerned about the way he dressed, not that he had much choice in the matter. He did not know how to make himself liked or how to court, and every time he developed a crush he would confine himself to writing in his journal and constructing fragile, kaleidoscopic pictures of love.[50]

Twenty-two-year-old Gleb is, to coin a word, under-gendered. He is, we are told, a "philosophical greenhorn" (*telënok ot filosofii*),[51] a metaphor that hints at a degree of sexual or metaphysical infantilism. Not surprisingly, this bookish youth married the first girl he kissed. The passages describing the Nerzhins' life together are brief, the details cursory. We learn that during two years of frustrating courtship, Gleb "left these trysts unsteady on his feet, never having experienced the free movement of requited feeling":[52] passion on his part, hesitation and second thoughts on Nadya's. Her favorite literary character is Pechorin in Mikhail Lermontov's novel *A Hero of Our Time* (*Geroi nashego vremeni*; 1841), but if there is anyone less like its broodingly charismatic hero, it is stick-in-the-mud Gleb. Once Gleb and Nadia are married, she finds herself baffled by her "meteor" of a husband, with whom she tries but fails to keep up emotionally and intellectually. After the outbreak of war she clings to Nerzhin with housewifely desperation, and she tends to find him most approachable when he is most depressed: a bad sign in any marriage. As if all this were not enough, here and there we are given to understand that her feelings for her husband are still not as deep as his are for her.

No doubt the clinging, conventional Nadya of *Love the Revolution* is very different from the touchingly vulnerable, lovingly loyal wife in *The First Circle*. For a fuller picture of the Nerzhins' marriage we must turn to *The Road*, where we learn that the fault may not be entirely her own. On their honeymoon, for instance, Gleb behaves more like a nerd of the revolution than a passionate lover, as his young bride ruefully acknowledges:

> Yet, you will deceive me: the circle
> of my arms you will break at dawn,
> now a stranger, indifferent, you will leave
> to read Karl Marx on the porch.[53]

No cigarettes or cuddles in bed *afterward*: another bad sign.

This topos of a young connubial love, curtailed, is reminiscent of the Soc-Realist novels of the Stalin period, which suffered from a serious sex deficit. Their heroes and heroines are too busy making five year plans to make out. In Veniamin Kaverin's trilogy *The Open Book* (*Otkrytaia kniga*; 1948–56), the heroine, a budding biologist, and her equally biological husband travel to the Sea of Azov to celebrate their nuptials. In these balmy climes the two eggheads behave in an impeccably collegial manner, discussing epidemiological research and other scientific topics. Still, their time at the seaside is not without its thrills: he puts his arm around her, she kisses him on the cheek, and they meet a local fisherman who reminisces about his exploits as a Red Army soldier in the civil war.

Back to Nerzhin. His friendship with the former zek, Diomidov, is the unconscious expression of a fatherless youth's need for a paternal mentor. Be that as it may, the enlightened engineer chooses to share his dangerous confidences because he sees the protagonist as something more than a cookie-cutter Komsomol:

> He had long known he had nothing to say to this generation, which considered denouncing someone to the NKVD an act of valor. With the advantage of age and experience, he could see right through Gleb and his ideological commitment that made him merciless toward himself and others, toward friends and strangers. It would have been madness to try to change this young man's mind. But prolonged suffering endows one with an irrational sense of what lies in another's heart.[54]

The engineer is being somewhat unfair to Nerzhin, if not to his demographic cohort. Solzhenitsyn's hero may be a stuffed shirt, but he is no snitch. When he refuses to join Dashkin in going AWOL—"I wouldn't advise it," he declares with his usual self-righteousness—the latter threateningly asks if he means to inform on him.[55] "I have never gone in for that sort of thing," replies Gleb, stiffly.[56]

Still, Diomidov is right to assume that Nerzhin is representative of his generation. He is, after all, a rather Tolstoyan character, with the emblematic averageness of a Dmitry Olenin or a Nikolai Rostov. Another Tolstoyan motif is the hero's problematic relationship with his platoon's equine component, which like every other experience he has in the novel is entirely autobiographical: "This was a period of overwhelming frustration for Solzhenitsyn, as he struggled to deal with the entirely unfamiliar ways of horses."[57]

4

The novel picks up in chapter three, once Gleb, newly drafted into the Red Army, leaves a heartbroken Nadya behind and is assigned to that transport detachment. To his abiding regret, he is ineligible for officer training because of a precancerous abnormality of the groin (another and very important autobiographical detail), which is why he is so ingloriously sent to this rear echelon unit where the men are not even issued uniforms. The chapter is titled "The Pechenegs" ("Pechenegi"), after the tribe that roamed the southern Russian borderlands in early medieval times: a hint that as Nerzhin's battalion, with its complement of 250 carts, 500 soldiers and 1000 horses, trundles eastward across those same steppes it resembles nothing more than a nomadic host or caravan.

Nerzhin's fellow conscripts are a mixture of peasants and Cossacks, all of them a good twenty years older than he. Thrust into this coarse, profane mass of soldiery, our hero is utterly lost. He lacks the indelicate, unreflective masculinity of the other men or even the delicate, "flamboyant"[58] variety of Lieutenant Brant, who arrives to take command of Nerzhin's platoon in chapter four. And how could it be otherwise when the soldiers see Gleb as a "ridiculous teacher in an adolescent's worn fur coat clutching a briefcase."[59] In other words, a child playing grownup; or a puerile pedagogue. The unfortunate briefcase, which holds a copy of Friedrich Engels's *Revolution and Counter-Revolution in Germany* (*Revolution und Konterrevolution in Deutschland*; 1852), as well as a few items of a domestic nature, will accompany him everywhere for the rest of the novel: a marker of Gleb's unmartial, civvy-street identity.[60] The results of all of this are predictable: "Nerzhin, profoundly offended by such injustice, insensitivity, and ignorance, sat down in the sun and rested his head on his knees. He felt that his life was over."[61] The scene is one that is replayed in hundreds of books and films about a raw conscript who must learn to be a man by learning to be a soldier. "You're in the army now," and so forth. More specifically, the figure of the introspective, intellectualizing outsider trying to fit in among rough men and their horses makes one think of commissar Liutov in Isaak Babel's *Red Cavalry* cycle of stories (*Konarmiia*; 1926), minus that character's Jewish identity and homoerotic fascination with the buff bodies of his troopers. But most of all Nerzhin recalls Paul Bäumer, the hero of *All Quiet on the Western Front* (*Im Westen Nichts Neues*; 1929), who after he joins the Imperial German Army finds himself resenting that "a braided postman should have more authority over us than had formerly our parents, our teachers, and the whole gamut of culture from Plato to Goethe" and who cannot accept "a renunciation of personality such as one would not ask of the meanest servants—salutes, springing to attention, parade marches, presenting arms, right wheel, left wheel, clicking the heels, insults, and a thousand pettifogging details."[62] Solzhenitsyn had read Remarque's novel before he went to war, and had been impressed, but his own experience of combat taught him that its author "had a very narrow, tendentious view" of army life.[63]

The soldiers find the educator in the too-short coat a comic figure and they rag him mercilessly, but they do not harass or haze him. These are family men with settled personalities and plenty of life experience, so they no longer have that youthful, brutal need to abuse the one who is weird, the one who is weaker. Even the platoon sergeant, whom Nerzhin naturally regards as having been put on this earth to be his personal tormentor, actually goes easy on him, as the hero later realizes. Still, there are plenty of cultural clashes and misunderstandings. Priggish Gleb is shocked by the men's sexual banter and obscene comments about women, including their own wives. During one bull session he tells the others of his "sacred faith" in Nadya, and is met with cynical laughter.[64] And then there is that Engels book. Every time Nerzhin curls up with his revolutionary tome there is some interruption, so he never gets past page five. One day his codriver, Dashkin, notices the title and not being up on the Marxist classics goes into a blue funk:

> "Are you crazy, keeping a book like that in my cart? ... That "counter" bit, tear it off! You can leave the "revolution," though. ... Wait a minute, what's Germany got to do with it? Do you want to see me go before a court martial? En-gels, you say? Show me the whole thing. ... It is En-gels. ... Now, there's a clever man. ... Let me tell you, brother, my fists got bloody smashing all those contras, so I don't need no book to tell me what's what."[65]

As he angrily studies, word by word, the Engels peritext, Dashkin inadvertently acts out the part of a Soviet censor, even if his ideological interdictions carry no political sanction: a moment of secret satire.

The hero's first weeks in the service are tough not only because he sticks out like a sore bookworm. With the Red Army reeling before the German onslaught, the supply system has broken down and the soldiers must live off the land, that is, the local Cossack villages. A famished Nerzhin makes do with what he can cadge or steal. As he proceeds on his unheroic anabasis to the River Don and beyond, cherished ideological beliefs and assumptions clash with the countervailing evidence of his eyes and ears. Gleb's political understanding may not have been changed by his brush with the Rostov police or even his conversations with Diomidov, but now he begins to *learn*.

His chief informant about the facts of Soviet life is foulmouthed, ill-tempered Miron Dashkin, the kind of Solzhenitsynian character whose life story is meant to illustrate the twists of twentieth-century Russian history (there is usually one such figure in every long or longish work). Many years ago, boasts Miron, he was "the chief revolutionary of Bobrovsk District,"[66] in which capacity he murdered the local landowner in front of his family: "To kill a man is easy, it's like wetting your fingers when you pee."[67] He did his bit in the civil war: "I must have shot a hundred of those White bandits with my own hand, and that's the effing truth."[68] Just another veteran of the class struggle, like the old man with the *right hand* in the eponymous story. In the 1920s Dashkin held a succession of entry-level political jobs including that of collectivization commissar, when he was nearly lynched by a mob of enraged village women, but later his career stalled and he ended up working as a stable hand for the district administration. His heavy drinking, which has given him an ulcer, may be the reason why the prickly "chief revolutionary" never rose high, or even low, in the service of the Party.

Malevolent Miron hates dour Trukhachyov, another soldier in the platoon, as a "Siberian kulak"[69] (he refused to join a collective farm) and the Cossacks for being "White bastards."[70] And he does not have much time for Nerzhin. After they are assigned to the same cart as codrivers, Dashkin spends hours mocking him as a hoity-toity city boy, useless with the carthorses and every kind of manual labor. Yet though Miron seems thoroughly Sovietized, he holds the Party bosses in contempt, all the way up to Joseph Stalin himself, encouraged in these seditious opinions by the Red Army's disastrous defeats. As the transport unit nears the Don river he concludes that the communists are done for and makes plans to desert: "The whole of Russia is on the run. What fool is going to look for us? ... Who knows, a week from now the war may be over."[71]

Dashkin is a genuinely bad man, but an interesting one, and the best realized character in the novel. Solzhenitsyn takes great care to make him believable, even providing a framing comment that explains why Dashkin's own yarns show him in such an unflattering light. "Although he had that almost universal human tendency to boast, his stories were unrehearsed, which may be why they did not sound crudely vainglorious."[72] This former peasant and former Red Guard is representative of a certain national type whose set of opposing qualities has fascinated Russian writers since Pushkin: calm resourcefulness and self-satisfied ignorance; innate common sense and an utter lack of imagination; raw courage and grasping selfishness; distrust of authority and hatred of the successful; salty humor and casual brutality. Here everything works, from Dashkin's earthy speech with its semi-assimilated party jargon and juicy expletives to his baffled, contemptuous attitude toward the protagonist, who for his part regards Miron with a mixture of ideological snobbery and male envy. The "chief revolutionary" is also the only source of comic relief in what is otherwise a very serious novel. "If you want to know, I sacrificed my nerves for the revolution," he informs Nerzhin on one occasion,[73] echoing unbeknownst to himself, and the author, Mrs. Bennet's wifely lament to Mr. Bennet in *Pride and Prejudice*: "You have no compassion on my poor nerves."[74]

Hungry, exhausted, and verminous, the ramshackle column finally reaches the village of Durnovka on the Buzuluk river as winter sets in. Here Nerzhin settles into army life. He acquires a uniform, albeit a secondhand one, learns to ride a horse, and even wins a measure of respect from the men when Lieutenant Brant tasks him with giving regular talks about the military situation.

5

The narrative is cut off just as the hero is about to realize his dream of becoming a gunner. Commissar Petrov gets him an assignment as a messenger to district headquarters in Stalingrad where Gleb must try to gain admission to the artillery school. Once again he is on the road, traveling along those wide-gauge steel diagonals and radii that run through so many of the spaces of Russian literature. Briefcase in hand, he hops freight trains and marks time at nameless stops, shivering amid the same snows and blizzards that doomed the Nazi advance on Moscow. With the chaos of wartime unfolding around him, the journey, a hallucinatory odyssey of chance encounters, interrupted conversations, and strange portents, takes days instead of hours. Nerzhin is shaken by the sight of a trainload of emaciated refugees from the besieged city of Leningrad and almost dies under the wheels of a rail car as he scrambles to climb on board, but is pulled to safety by a handsome old man with a long beard and clear blue eyes. His rescuer is dressed like a peasant but resembles a prophet. "He looked at Nerzhin strangely, as if forgiving him for something he had done. When he saw Nerzhin look down to examine his legs, he said, 'Someone's been praying really hard for you, my reckless friend. God must be keeping you safe.'"[75] The hero never learns the old man's name, though "later—much later—he guessed what it was."[76]

So can we. The mysterious graybeard may be wise old Kordubailo from the yet-to-be-written "Incident at Kochetovka," who is of the same appearance and age. Or perhaps he is Nerzhin grown old. No longer a young Komsomol in a hurry, he is the beatific bearer of a higher understanding that he shares with his uncomprehending younger self, whose life he has just saved by reaching out from the future into the past. Or one can be more fanciful still and propose that the stranger is a projection into venerable old age of the author's middle-aged self: a theurgic intrusion into the fictive world of its real-life, real-time creator, disguised as a patriarchal wanderer or even—to go out on a speculative limb— as another writer, Solzhenitsyn's peasant-faced, prophet-like "teacher," Tolstoy, in whose fictions trains carry lethal associations.

At district headquarters an exultant Nerzhin obtains permission to enroll in a school for artillery commanders where the other students all hold commissions: something much more prestigious than a mere officer training course.

As for the city itself: "What was there to see in Stalingrad? Nothing at all, obviously, a city like any other."[77] A moment of ironic prolepsis: another German offensive, another winter, the greatest Russian victory of all time, and the name will go down in history.

Then it is back to the transport battalion to obtain the necessary authorization from the CO, an elderly, androgynous colonel with a "woman's gray locks,"[78] whom one of Nerzhin's protectors among the officers tricks into signing the requisite piece of paper.

Just before he reaches his destination, the town of Semyonov where the artillery school is located, the hero is detained by a couple of hulking NKVD noncoms. They are looking for an escaped prisoner: "Come with me, I said! … You want to keep your teeth? Now move."[79] Fortunately, Gleb's papers are in order: "Alright, you can go, just make sure I don't see your face again."[80]

One last instance of foreshadowing, for artillery captain Nerzhin will be arrested at the front in 1945: third time unlucky. But that is another story.

CHAPTER FIVE

Helots and Heroes: *In the First Circle*

> As at all times, so now, too, men are divided into the slaves and the free; for he who does not have two-thirds of his day to himself is a slave, let him be what he may otherwise: statesman, businessman, official, scholar.
> —Friedrich Nietzsche, *Human, All Too Human*

> The scientists are in terror and the European mind stops.
> —Ezra Pound, Canto CXV

1

The First Circle is a portrait of Russia at the mid-point of the twentieth century, in the year, month, and week that the Soviet Empire celebrated Joseph Stalin's seventieth birthday.[1] Put succinctly—though like many a Russian novel, this work is gloriously, epically unsuccinct—it describes three days and nights in the life of a group of prisoners held at Marfino, a sharashka or secret science prison, their wives, lovers, and jailers, as well as assorted members of the communist *nomenklatura* all the way up to the Generalissimo-Secretary himself. The narrative sweep, multiplicity of plot lines, elaborately crafted set pieces, and vast array of human types and experiences give the book a markedly Tolstoyan quality, while its "many serendipitous encounters and coincidences are Dostoevskian,"[2] as is its gamut of distinctive and memorable character voices. Like "Ivan Denisovich" and the stories of the 1950s and 1960s, the novel is formatted in ways that connect it to the nineteenth-century classics, yet it anticipates the experimental diegetic practices of *The Red Wheel*, particularly in the sections that the author added in 1968, just before he began work on his saga of the Russian Revolution.

At the center of *The First Circle* are two men, Gleb Nerzhin, an imprisoned mathematician who is a nominally disguised version of the author circa 1949, and Innokenty Volodin, a high-ranking diplomat who has come to loathe the Soviet regime. The multiethnic cast of characters includes Slavs, Jews and Germans as well as two Tatars, two Bashkir girls, and a Mordvin; but there are no children. Or rather, the children are dead, like optical physicist Illarion Gerasimovich's little boy and girl or engineer Ivan Dyrsin's two youngsters; or fictively dematerialized, like design engineer Dmitry Sologdin's son, whom he has never seen. True, hovering just beyond the novel's margins are the young daughters of Colonel Yakonov, the ambitious sharashka director, and the three-year-old son of his deputy, the sympathetic Major Roitman, but they appear only in the affectionate thoughts of their fathers. The striking absence of children in what is, among other things, a family novel is a function of the zeks' tragic lives. As Solzhenitsyn told me regarding the low incidence of such junior characters in his prose, "Where this is appropriate, there are children, of different ages."[3] In this narrated world, the children have appropriately gone missing.

In addition to the dictator and his secret police chief, Viktor Abakumov, both of whom are major presences, other historical figures also make an appearance, among them Abakumov's predecessor, Lavrenty Beria, "a simpering person in pince-nez,"[4] and Stalin's *chef de cabinet*, the cowering Aleksandr Poskryobyshev. The scales of political evil are balanced by the ample figure of Hermann Goering, who waddles in and out of the text when Bobynin, one of the Marfino prisoners, recalls meeting him as a captive scientist in a German design bureau, a Nazi analogue of the sharashka.

So much for the fictive fundamentals, but what about the novel's place on Solzhenitsyn's authorial timeline? In fact, *The First Circle* had the most complicated textual history of any of his productions.

"Written: 1955–8. Distorted: 1964. Restored: 1968,"[5] *The First Circle* exists in several published forms. In 1962, the year in which "Ivan Denisovich" became a fact of literature, fewer than a dozen people knew that Solzhenitsyn had a completed novel lying in his metaphorical desk drawer. Having decided to offer the manuscript to *Novy Mir*, he pruned and reshaped the work with a view to getting it past the censors, but even so, publication proved to be impossible in the Brezhnevized Soviet Union of the mid-1960s. For almost fifteen years this self-bowdlerized version was the only one available, first in samizdat form and soon thereafter in foreign-published editions. The "restored" text, which was actually much modified as compared with the old master copy, appeared in 1978, in volumes one and two of the Vermont *Collected Works*.[6] But even this definitive iteration turned out to be not so definitive, for 2006 saw the publication of an annotated edition that contained hundreds of corrections, some of them substantial, as well as a selection of excerpts from earlier redactions.[7] Harry Willetts's new English translation, which came out in 2009 under the title *In the First Circle*, a more faithful rendering of the Russian *V kruge pervom*, is based on this authorized final version.

It was the 1964 variant, submitted by Solzhenitsyn to Tvardovsky's journal and subsequently smuggled out of the Soviet Union, that Heinrich Böll, François Mauriac, and Graham Greene received rapturously and the Swedish Academy cited when it awarded Solzhenitsyn the Nobel Prize. There was, however, a twist. In 1968, the same year that the self-censored text was brought out by Nikita Struve's YMCA Press in Paris, a British-based literary bootlegger and KGB asset, Alec Flegon, released a garbled version of the "distorted" version to steal a bit of the writer's thunder (and royalties).[8] Here I shall be looking at the 1968/2006 restored "atomic" version.

Flegon's fraud aside, what are the chief differences between the two variants, respectively nicknamed *Circle 87* and *Circle 96* by their creator? (The figures refer to the number of chapters.)

In *Circle 87*, Volodin phones the wife of a distinguished physician, Professor Dobroumov (Kind Mind), to warn her that the latter is in danger of being arrested for planning to hand over an experimental medical drug to a French colleague. *Circle 96* has Volodin calling the American embassy with a message that Soviet intelligence is about to obtain "important technological information about the production of the atomic bomb."[9] In both versions, the MGB orders Nerzhin's friend, the communist idealist Rubin, to identify the caller from a recording of the phone call. Rubin methodically narrows down the list of suspects until Volodin is arrested and taken to the Lubyanka. Thus, the plot in *Circle 96* revolves around two signature devices of the twentieth century, the telephone and the atomic bomb.

Now, Solzhenitsyn once claimed that when revising his prose works he was "always trying to condense."[10] If so, then *The First Circle* was an exception. It started as a wordy, sprawling production, and grew wordier and more sprawling through its eight—or nine, or ten—redactions. In "restoring" the text the writer did a great deal more than go back to the original storyline and reinsert the deleted sections. He refashioned the chapters devoted to Stalin, the women in the Stromyanka dorm, and the Makarygin family, and added three new ones: forty-four (Volodin and his sister-in-law, Klara Makarygina, visit the village of Rozhdestvo), sixty-one (Volodin calls on his Uncle Avenir in Tver), and ninety (Nerzhin debates politics with another prisoner, Gerasimovich). The name of the sharashka was corrected from the made-up "Marvino" back to the historically accurate "Marfino." However, the sections set in the science prison "did not undergo any serious polishing or even stylistic correction" except for the passages showing the relationships between the prisoners and the women in their lives, or those depicting the "ideological jousts" among the zeks.[11]

As to which of the two versions is superior, opinions differ. Georges Nivat prefers *Circle 96* for its broader historical scope and "mesmerizing tension."[12] Lev Loseff likes its style, which is free of the "prettified clichés" found here and there in *Circle 87*, but thinks it inferior in fictive value: Rubin has less psychological depth, Nerzhin is now his "one-dimensional ideological opponent," and Volodin is reduced from tragic rebel to a "heroic kamikaze."[13] Viktor Chalmaev goes further, finding that Volodin has become "just another defector."[14] The release of a successful TV miniseries based on the novel (2006) gave the debate a new impetus. For Vladimir Berezin, *Circle 96* is "a substitute for Sartre ... (anti)Soviet existentialism,"[15] while Alla Latynina suggests that it is "richer in content, more vivid, more complex" than *Circle 87*, though the "atomic" plot had grown "less brilliant with the passage of time, unlike the 'genuine and eternal' conflict in the medical version."[16]

My own conclusion is this: When placed side by side, the two alternative texts constitute a dynamic literary dyad or dialogic continuum in which the virtues of the "atomic" variant (cor)respond to the flaws in the "medical" one, and vice versa. 87 and 96 are each other's hypotext and hypertext. This binary fictive whole generates a composite meta-narrative that continuously interrogates itself. In order to fully appreciate either variant, it is necessary to read its counterpart, in a Postmodern procedure similar to that posited by Milorad Pavic's "lexicon novel" *Dictionary of the Khazars* (*Hazarski recnik*; 1984), which was written and published in two complementary versions, one male and one female, and expresses "the complex interaction of the apparently mutually exclusive forces of constant fragmentation and the recreation of totalities."[17] In both Solzhenitsyn's and Pavic's case, complementary or contrastive—take your pick!—intertextual distribution enhances the pleasure of the text while intellectually disciplining the pleasure-seeking reader.

2

The First Circle is saturated with conversation. Its captive scientists are tireless talkers, inveterate debaters. Their minds, ever questing, ever curious, seek solutions to the problems of the universe, the world, the country, the self. Most of the novel's intellectual content is contained in these intense, wide-ranging dialogues: daytime, nighttime prison symposia. (Chapter three, in which a group of zeks from the strict regime camps of the north is shown arriving at Marfino, is entirely in dialogue form, showcasing Solzhenitsyn's skills as a dramatist.)

Alone among the chatterers and polemicists, Gleb Nerzhin, Solzhenitsyn's mathematician hero, is tight-lipped, reticent, guarded. He may know a great deal about Russian history or Hinduism, but unlike his two best friends, the aristocrat-of-the-mind Dmitry Sologdin and the Bolshevik-of-the-heart Lev Rubin, he is still working things out. So usually he bides his time, while all around prolix, passionate talk ebbs and flows: he would listen, rather than vituperate. Still, from time to time Gleb lets himself go rhetorically, when the topic under discussion is "really satisfying."[18] On one such occasion, he suggests that scientific and artistic progress are two very different things. Sooner or later every theory and discovery becomes obsolete, but art possesses a value that is timeless and absolute:

> The seventeenth century had Rembrandt, and Rembrandt's still here – just try and go one better today![19] Whereas seventeenth-century technology seems primitive to us now. Or think of the great inventions of the eighteen seventies. To us they look like children's toys. Yet those were the years in which *Anna Karenina* was written. If you know of anything finer, I would like to hear about it![20]

Rubin objects: "You do at least leave us with some progress in engineering? You don't call that meaningless."[21] Another prisoner, the Trotskyist Grigory Abramson, employs his dialectical skills, honed in hundreds of political debates, to issue a challenge: "Your argument can be turned inside out. It can be taken to mean that scientists and engineers have done great things over the centuries and made progress, while the art snobs have obviously just been playing the fool."[22] Whereupon Sologdin pipes up in his sarcastic way, "In it for the money!"[23]

The exchange, in which the mathematician Nerzhin extols the arts while the philologist Rubin acclaims technological achievement, contains an echo of the cultural disputation between scientists and humanists, or in its Soviet version, "physicists" and "lyricists," which was a memorable feature of the 1950s and 1960s, and which resumed thirty years later in the form of the "science wars" of Western academia that pitted "scientific realists" against postmodernist professors. This interdisciplinary confrontation was formally inaugurated by C. P. Snow, like Solzhenitsyn a scientist-turned-novelist, in his 1959 Rede Lecture "The Two Cultures":

> A good many times I have been present at gatherings of people who, by the standards of the traditional culture, are thought highly educated and

who have with considerable gusto been expressing their incredulity at the illiteracy of scientists. Once or twice I have been provoked and have asked the company how many of them could describe the Second Law of Thermodynamics. The response was cold: it was also negative.[24]

Now, Nerzhin and his interlocutors would have no trouble reciting the Second Law of Thermodynamics, or indeed the First or the Third. With the exception of a few bohemian or proletarian souls, most of the zeks hold advanced science degrees. And even those who, like Rubin, hail from the humanities, know more than their share of scientific formulae and theorems: polymaths through biographical circumstance or their own intellectual curiosity. *The First Circle* is, among other things, an account of the manner in which the scientific and humanistic imaginations converge and interact within a single cultural space.

As is often the case with true believers, Rubin has something of the child about him. He spends his spare time drawing up plans for a chain of communist temples served by white-robed priests and acolytes, in the vein of Campanella or William Morris. Once he completes his utopia, which bears the title "Proposal for the Establishment of Civic Places of Worship," he intends to submit it to the Party's Central Committee. All this is not very scientific and goes to show that Rubin is anything but the coldly analytical, rigorously empirical intellect he imagines himself to be.

Nerzhin's panegyric to Rembrandt is, first of all, polemical. Normally Solzhenitsyn's quiet hero eschews verbal effusions of any kind. But art, whether visual or literary, is his passion. Later we learn that during his years in prison he has kept a book of poems by the peasant poet Sergei Yesenin: a kind of talisman. The political syllogisms of *Revolution and Counter-Revolution in Germany* have been superseded by the bucolic melancholy of verses like "The golden birch-tree grove has fallen silent..." Yesenin, that quintessentially folkloric, rural figure, is Nerzhin's new literary marker. The hero's life experiences may have made him a thoroughly, tragically twentieth-century character, but his aesthetic tastes are of the past. Modernism and its works, one imagines, would hold no appeal for this mathematician-turned-writer—including avant-garde music such as the compositions of Schoenberg and Webern, even if their atonal strains had been allowed to disquiet the ears of Soviet audiences.

In this regard, as in every other, Nerzhin's artistic preferences are always the author's. Reshetovskaya records that during his incarceration at Marfino, Solzhenitsyn made a number of musical "discoveries" via the radio, which included "two marvelous sonatas that he had not known, Beethoven's

Seventeenth and Schumann's F-Sharp minor [Piano Sonata no. 1]."²⁵ These details recur in *The First Circle*. In chapter five, the hero enters the acoustic lab, to find that it has become a den of din. Three radio receivers are playing, respectively and simultaneously, a jazz number, "songs from the Eastern European democracies," and Beethoven's Seventeenth Sonata, while the big band fan and bon viveur Valentin Pryanchikov is crooning, "Boogie-woogie, boogie-woogie."²⁶ The lab is a locus of a (hierarchically coded) cacophony. But in the end, Beethoven defeats his twentieth-century *counterpoints* when earnest Gleb asks raucous Valentin to cease and to hush, and "the limpid melody of Sonata No. 17 poured out unhindered."²⁷

3

Professor Chelnov, the elderly scientist who is the sharashka's presiding intellectual presence, is surrounded by an austere academic aura:

> His long, oval face, his sharp profile, his authoritative way of speaking to the administration, and that faint blue haze in his faded eyes, which is peculiar to those capable of abstract thought, made Chelnov strangely like Descartes or perhaps Archimedes.²⁸

When he composed this description Solzhenitsyn may have been thinking of Plutarch's portrait of Archimedes, who "possessed such a lofty spirit, so profound a soul, and such a wealth of scientific theory"²⁹ that he valued the pursuit of knowledge above all other things—even his life.

Uniquely among the inmates, Chelnov is allowed to wear clothing of his own choice, but the professor has an Einsteinian disregard for sartorial display and so he dresses in a cheap suit, felt boots, and an odd woolen cap that might be a man's or a woman's. Yet for all his brilliance and all his quirks, Chelnov is still a zek, no less a helot of the terror state than the peasant bricklayer Shukhov in the wastes of Kazakhstan.

Nonetheless, although the researchers at Marfino are slaves of science, acts of resistance do occur, as when Nerzhin rejects Colonel Yakonov's offer of a cushy assignment, Gerasimovich refuses to design a spy camera for the secret police, or another prisoner, Khorobrov, insists that he will work only twelve hours a day "according to the Constitution."³⁰ And at the end of the novel the Marfino zeks expose the informers in their midst in a collective gesture of defiance. However, these are exceptional events. Like humble Ivan Denisovich,

Chelnov and his colleagues assert their human dignity through work, but they do so in a manner that is entirely self-aware. They cherish their status as thinking, creating men, in the full knowledge that their labors are directed by, and conducted for, the benefit of a tyrannical regime. This ethical aporia is an important theme. Chelnov, we learn, "had applied the fine point of his pencil to many technical inventions, from the continuously operating boiler to the jet engine, and had invested a bit of his soul in some of them."[31] A hint that the professor has mortgaged that Archimedean part of himself in a succession of Faustian bargains.

The First Circle makes it plain that the thrill of generating knowledge can seduce even the purest of spirits for the foulest of reasons. Take Rubin. As the bearded scholar pores over his voice prints, he imagines himself to be the founder of a new discipline, phonoscopy, by equivalence to dactyloscopy, even as he is hot on the audio-trail of the enemy of the people, Volodin; while heroic, handsome Sologdin, a more conventionally ambitious soul, sees in his own professional success the promise of early release, but also of fortune and fame.

As a state organized on the allegedly scientific principles of Marxism-Leninism, the Soviet Union proclaimed the supremacy of science and devoted vast resources to pure and applied research. Like the factory, the hydroelectric dam, and the kolkhoz, the science *institut* was a fixture of its symbolic landscape. Following the subjugation and part-destruction of the old technical intelligentsia, the communist powers-that-be set out to construct the New Soviet Scientist, a pioneering social type intended to complement other progressive human variants such as the New Soviet Working Man, New Soviet Peasant, New Soviet Writer, and even New Soviet Priest. Yet, once Stalin's terror state swung into action, scientists, whether bourgeois or Bolshevik, found themselves persecuted as much as any other group. NKVD Lieutenant Aleksei Khvat's jeering words to Russia's greatest geneticist, Nikolai Vavilov, "You're not an academician, you're a piece of shit,"[32] sum up the brutality of this persecution and the human worth of its perpetrators.

In the aftermath of World War II, "Soviet Communism ... entered the ... final phase of its history ... an imperial stage"[33] and the regime started to ooze its own peculiar form of Marxist obscurantism. The oozer-in-chief was Joseph Stalin, the man with the "low, retreating pithecanthropoid brow,"[34] who in *The First Circle* is allowed to express his scientific fantasies at some length:

> He could, of course, make ... a contribution to biology, but he had entrusted work in that area to that honest and energetic man of the people,

Lysenko. In any case, Stalin found mathematics or perhaps even physics more alluring. All the Founding Fathers had fearlessly tried their strength in those sciences. He could not help envying Engels when he read his bold ratiocinations on zero, or on the square of minus one. Stalin was equally enthralled by the resolute way in which Lenin had plunged into the thickets of physics and left neither hide nor hair of the scientists, proving that matter could not be converted into any form of energy.

He himself, though, however often he paged through Kiselev's *Algebra* or Sokolov's *Physics for Upper Forms*, found them uninspiring.[35]

Clearly, the brain behind that angled brow was deteriorating. On Stalin's initiative entire branches of science were banned, among them Einsteinian physics, cybernetics, and something called "Weismanism-Morganism," that is, genetics. Practitioners of these forbidden disciplines were sacked, jailed, or murdered and their place taken by crackpots and conmen, for example, the neo-Lamarckian agronomist Trofim Lysenko, Stalin's frisky "man of the people."

Needless to say, characters like the scatological Khvat were not to be found in novels and stories by official Soviet writers (though he is present, as a master torturer and "living legend of the MGB,"[36] in Vladimir Sorokin's Postmodernist or post-Rabelesian novel *Blue Lard*; *Goluboe Salo*; 1999). Structured and styled according to a set of prescribed rules, these didactic productions formed a single authoritative corpus. In fact, all the works of SocRealist literature were canonical, by virtue of their existence in print. "Nearly every book of any size got a prize the year after it appeared. Forty or fifty prizes popped up every year," wonders a character in *Cancer Ward*.[37]

In her typology of the SocRealist novel, Katerina Clark lists six categories thereof, including "the novel about a worthy intellectual or inventor," which

> usually follows much the same plot outline as a production novel (the hero's "task" being, in this instance, to write or invent something or to get a new idea approved), except that more attention is paid to the hero's struggles with the enemies of the "truth" than to his encounters with the practical problems of task fulfillment or with natural disasters.[38]

Veniamin Kaverin's trilogy *The Open Book* shows how these topoi work. His heroine, Tatiana Vlasenkova, is born into a life of Dostoevskian poverty, but the October Revolution makes it possible for this daughter of a seamstress to become a professor of microbiology. Years before Alexander Fleming discovers penicillin, she writes a monograph on the bactericidal properties of mold, which is suppressed by a scheming rival. Prim, plain, and utterly joyless, Tatiana stoically endures numerous trials, including her husband's wrongful arrest, and eventually is hailed as a luminary of Soviet science. With its middlebrow readerly appeal, abundance of hospital detail, and strong social optimism, this microbiological saga recalls A. J. Cronin's medical novels (minus the romance), popular with English-speaking readers in the mid-twentieth century. Another SocRealist work, Daniil Granin's *Those Who Seek* (*Iskateli*; 1955), tells the story of Andrei Lobanov, an inventor and war hero who develops a leak locator for the electrical industry while bureaucrats obstruct and establishment scientists sneer. Professor Vlasenkova and Dr. Lobanov are grinds with good ideas and a collectivist mentality whose dedication to the cause stands above personal ambition or hurt. Bravely, they struggle with human and institutional obstacles in order to do good socialist research; and in the end, they always succeed.

Like their SocRealist counterparts, Solzhenitsyn's captive professors and PhDs are hindered by malevolent outsiders, but his scientists are individualists, not collectivists, and the obstruction theme is twisted around. *The First Circle* allocates the topos of anti-scientific sabotage to the MGB officers who guard, monitor, and harass the zeks. By making their lives miserable, these vigilant snoops impede the very research that their captives conduct for the benefit of the secret police. As the outspoken Bobynin tells General Abakumov,

> That's one parasite, the security officer at the workplace; then there's the other parasite, the security officer in the prison block, making nervous wrecks of us with his conduct reports and dirty tricks. What the hell to you expect all these security operations to produce? ... Are you trying to skim cream from shit?[39]

Another category of SocRealist narratives was "the villain or spy novel."[40] These Soviet page-turners contained an element of adventure, criminal detection and even the "picaresque."[41] They "entail a positive hero who is learning to be sufficiently strong to combat the foe, that is, Western decadence or his love for an alien," while at the same time acquiring a higher Party consciousness.[42] *The First Circle* everts this convention as well. Volodin learned to appreciate Western political freedoms during a posting in France. A series of flashbacks show how the diplomat's communist convictions wilted and died by discrete stages until he was transformed into that classic literary type, a seeker after the truth. Eventually he will be hunted down by the zek Rubin, whose Party consciousness has remained intact even in the gulag.

Thus, *The First Circle* is an anti-Soviet thriller. It is also a Stalin-era campus novel. We meet a range of faculty types: brilliant researchers, scientific eccentrics, academic careerists. Solzhenitsyn even gives us a philosophical windbag, the Marxist lumpen-lecturer Shamsetdinov, a speaker so soporific that he sends to sleep not just his audience but even himself. There is a good deal of intramural intrigue and several lab-room adulteries. In this sense, Marfino is less a concentration camp than a concentration campus.

Rubin, who used to teach German literature before the war, is a case in point. Early in the novel we see him walking to his worktable "holding the Mongolian-Finnish dictionary and Hemingway down low. White cake crumbs had lodged in his wavy beard."[43] Dishevelled Lev displays those markers of the college professor, thick tomes and absentmindedness. He tutors the German POW, Max, on Pushkin, and Nerzhin on Goethe. There is a neat symmetry here: a German prisoner learns about Russia's greatest poet while a Russian prisoner studies his German analogue, both instructed by the same informed source. Nerzhin's encyclopedic friend is also a pioneering linguist: "Rubin had been busy for two years with a grandiose work in the spirit of Marx and Engels, tracing all words in all languages to the concepts 'hand' and 'manual labour.'"[44] The implicit, and satirical, parallel is with Stalin, who is seen editing the ghost-written pages of his latest treatise, *Marxism and Problems of Linguistics* (*Marksizm i problemy iazykoznaniia*; 1950). As one biography puts it, "Stalin was a creative personality in the sense that he wrote his articles and speeches himself, in his own hand, while sitting at his desk."[45]

These educational and collegiate themes are also present elsewhere in the novel, as when Nerzhin reminisces about his math teacher at the University of Rostov, Professor Goryainov-Shakhovskoy, who once devised a mathematical proof of the existence of God.[46] We are shown a "red professor," Dushan Radovich, a veteran Bolshevik who used to teach at a long-defunct Marxist crammer, and a fake professor, Foma Oskolupov, an MGB general who likes to pass himself off as a distinguished scientist when he is on vacation.

Of course, there can be no campus novel without students, and so in chapters forty-nine to fifty we encounter a community of six female postgraduates who live in the university dorm on Stromynka Street. One of them is Nadya Nerzhina. These fledgling scholars are writing dissertations on topics that are variously anodyne or obscure such as "Hamlet and Don Quixote Principles in Man" or "The Nineteenth-Century Russian Political Economist Sluzhaila-Olyabyshkin":

Solzhenitsyn's choice of name for this nonexistent luminary is a rare moment of Gogolian whimsy. A member of the group, pretty, bubbly Olya, has been the victim of that unfortunate campus phenomenon, sexual harassment:

> When she entered the History Department, ... her young (and married) supervisor, for whom she wrote a term paper on Kievan Russia, had begun to press his attentions on her and was very insistent that she should specialize in medieval Russian history as a graduate student. Olenka had taken fright and defected to the Italian Renaissance, but the Italian Renaissance man wasn't old either and, when alone with her, behaved like a true Renaissance man. Whereupon Olenka, in despair, asked for a transfer to the decrepit professor of Iranian Studies and was now writing a thesis under his supervision.[47]

It is a special strength of this novel that together with the cruelties and tragedies of the Stalin period, it depicts the textures of ordinary life, with all its surprises and joys and disappointments.

4

Like its prequel *Love the Revolution*, *The First Circle* is a dramatized autobiography. Faced with a choice between a mnemonic adherence to the factual, or fictive elaboration, Solzhenitsyn almost always opts for the former. In the sharashka chapters, he cleaves to his prison experiences, compacting the 33 months he spent at Marfino in 1947–50 to just three days in December 1949: emplotment by temporal contraction. Physically, psychologically, and intellectually, Nerzhin is a self-portrait in time. Most if not all of the Marfino characters—inmates, guards, free workers—are also autobiographically sourced. Nadya is a *faithful* representation of the author's first wife, Natalya Reshetovskaya. Even Volodin, an entirely invented personality, comes as a bearer of treasured authorial memories, conveyed through his disorienting impressions of the village of Rozhdestvo, where Solzhenitsyn lived in the 1960s, and his terrifying experiences in the Lubyanka.

The people on whom Solzhenitsyn modeled three of the novel's most important personalities, Lev Kopelev (Rubin), Dmitrii Panin (Sologdin), and Natalya Reshetovskaya (Nadya), later wrote memoirs in which they confirmed its factual accuracy.[48] Panin even entitled his reminiscences *The Notebooks of Sologdin* (*Zapiski Sologdina*; 1973), an acknowledgment by this eccentric philosopher that in some sense, his fictional identity loomed larger than his material one. It is as if Andrei Bolkonsky or Natasha Rostova had real-life counterparts who composed commentaries on *War and Peace* that vouched, Tolstoy got it right! It's all true!

The Marfino Special Prison, Stalin's secret residence outside Moscow, the student hostel on the Stromynka, and the Makarygin family apartment at Kaluga Gate, are the four narrative loci. The dramatis personae form four corresponding nexuses, each centered round a single figure: Gleb Nerzhin and his fellow prisoners; Joseph Stalin and his cohorts; Nadya Nerzhina and the five other women in the Stromynka dorm; and Innokenty Volodin, his sexy, scheming wife Dotnara, his Stalinist father-in-law, General Makarygin, and the Makarygin family and retainers.

The Kaluga Gate building is a hub of strange concurrences and coincidences. Major Roitman, the sharashka's deputy director, lives downstairs from the Makarygins, whose daughter Klara is employed as a free worker at the science prison, where she has fallen in love with one of the inmates, Ruska Doronin, Nerzhin's young protégé. When he was a camp laborer, Nerzhin had laid the parquet floor in the Makarygins' apartment. Prior to moving into her new home, Mrs. Makarygina complains about a creaking floor block and months later Klara confronts her father over his hypocritical politics, standing "with one shoe on and one stockinged foot" on the parquet.⁴⁹ The philanderer Shchagov puts the moves on Nadya and next attends a party at the same apartment, "in which four years earlier the man whose wife he had just nearly stolen had crawled on his knees in ragged quilted trousers laying the parquet floor."⁵⁰ These chevron-patterned hexahedrons of polished oak serve as an artifactal indicator that the characters in question are *connected* by one or more degrees of *separation*, whether moral or political.

The three set piece social occasions, a Christmas dinner held by the German POWs (chapter four), Nerzhin's prison birthday party (chapter fifty-eight), and the high-Stalinist jamboree at the Makarygins (chapters sixty-two to sixty-four), are densely coded and include important encounters and conversations. They occur in the novel's diegetic present, unlike the two New Year's Eve parties of 1930 respectively recalled by Gerasimovch (chapter forty-one) and Abramson (chapter fifty-six). At the first of these festive gatherings, which took place in Leningrad, Gerasimovich met Natasha, his wife-to-be; his arrest soon thereafter marked the beginning of their family Golgotha. The second party, held in the snows of Siberia, was in actual fact a disguised "conference of exiles on their country's situation"⁵¹ and featured as its keynote speaker a fanatical Trotskyist with the Dostoevskian name of Satanevich. In the novel, the year 1930 carries an emblematic meaning as one of "the knots of history"[52] (*uzly mirovoi istorii*),[53] when Stalin attained dictatorial power and collectivization got going in earnest.

Of the novel's cast of characters, some twenty or so enjoy a substantial textual presence. Among the signature traits Solzhenitsyn assigns his creations are Rubin's bushy black beard which in the course of the novel evolves into a kind of permanent prop; Sologdin's white teeth and eccentric idiolect; Potapov's granny glasses and habit of quoting Pushkin; Pryanchikov's youthfulness; Spiridon's shortsightedness; Abakumov's animal strength; Makarygin's flapping ears; Yakonov's soft flesh; Innokenty's delicate build; Dotnara's erotically charged body; Nadya's faded beauty; Simochka's bird-like frailty; Agnia's wanness; Saunkin-Golovanov's rectangular shape; Radovich's desiccated head and torso. Curiously, the only major figure that lacks a textual leitmotif is the authorial alter ego Nerzhin, even though in *Love the Revolution* he was humorously themed by means of that unmartial briefcase.

There are several allusions to works by Tolstoy. The title of chapter twenty-six, "Sawing Wood" ("Pilka drov"), points to "The Woodfelling" ("Rubka lesa"; 1855), one of his early stories, but its content has a different Tolstoyan referent: the rapture of physical labor felt by Nerzhin as he wields a bucksaw in tandem with Spiridon on a crisp winter morning evokes the celebrated scene in *Anna Karenina* where Levin joins a team of peasants to mow a meadow on his estate. The satirical treatment of Stalin recalls the irreverent portrayal of Napoleon in *War and Peace*, and the glittering party in Prosecutor Makarygin's apartment is hypertextually connected to the opening pages of the same novel, which describe the glittering salon of Madame Schérer.

Frequent analeptic detours sketch out the characters' personal histories. Some of these divagations push the novel's time frame back to the year 1900 and even earlier and take up entire chapters, such as the story of Yakonov's love for the ethereal Agnia or Stalin's nocturnal recollections of his life and crimes. And the novel is nothing if not topical where international politics is concerned. It conveys the author's belief that the West's chances of success in the Cold War were problematic at best, an opinion to which he later gave a polemical expression in his American speeches of the 1970s. Stalin mentally sneers at Churchill and Roosevelt as "that pair of fools,"[54] Volodin dismisses his Western counterparts as "trusting babes" and "stupid donkeys,"[55] Rubin joyfully marks the victories of Mao's troops on a map of China, and Yakonov places his bet on the worldwide triumph of the Soviet cause, though in his heart he roots for the capitalist enemy.

Several professional or aspirant men of letters are present. Volodin's brother-in-law Nikolai Galakhov is a wicked parody of Konstantin Simonov, a SocRealist stalwart. Nerzhin, of course, is working on a large-scale study of the revolution of 1917. Potapov, the pedantic electricity specialist, co-authors with him the story "The Buddha's Smile," embedded in mid-text, and Rubin is an amateur poet. So is Colonel Mamurin, the spectral ex-Chekist incarcerated in the sharashka. There is also the engraver, a prisoner with a young face but gray hair that "made him very good-looking."[56] This handsome figure composes secret chronicles of his prison experiences. As he is about to undergo a body search, his fellow writer, Nerzhin, watches him with a metatextually knowing eye:

> Nerzhin had a good view of the engraver, who was nervously pacing, and guessed why he was agitated. He had discovered in prison a talent for short-story writing. He wrote about life in a German POW camp, about his cellmates, about his appearances in court. ... Some old man, a friend of the family, had read them and let the author know through his wife that even in Chekhov such consummate and eloquent skill was rarely encountered.[57]

The details pertaining to Nerzhin's mysterious literary confrère amount to a set of encoded authorial self-references, see the miniature manuscripts, the narrow readership, the "microscopic script."[58] Even the fact that the engraver's first wife was also his third is suggestive, for Solzhenitsyn's own marriage to Reshetovskaya occurred twice, before and after his incarceration. We never learn this character's name: he remains anonymous because he is a fragment—figment—of the author. Of course, there are differences. The engraver is older than Nerzhin/Solzhenitsyn and looks nothing like him; he is a womanizer; he is vain. Yet, "whether it was done well or badly, the engraver was preserving the truth for all time, the cries of tortured souls, what Stalin had done to millions of Russian POWs."[59]

The fictive world includes not only live people, but dead books. For prisoner Khorobrov, Vasily Azhaev's unthrilling thriller *Far from Moscow* (*Daleko ot Moskvy*; 1948), which depicts Komsomols laboring on a showpiece construction project, is "a pie without filling, a hollow egg, a stuffed bird"[60] (*pirog bez nachinki, vytekshee iaitso, chuchelo ubitoi ptitsy*),[61] a sequence of metaphors that neatly reverses the usual process of turning fowl into food. Prisoner Dvoetyosov, working-class and therefore less highfalutin, offers a more pungent critique of SocRealism. Upon coming across another zek poring over a volume of Gorky, he jibes, "You'd be better off in the shithouse, communing with your soul."[62] Stylish

Sologdin, on the other hand, is too refined even to comment on such unstylish literary fare. He employs books by Mayakovsky and Ehrenburg as window props, a broad artifactal hint that their works are pulp doggerel or pulp fiction.

In general, the SocRealist classics come in for a rough time. These ponderous statements of the Soviet imaginary are disimagined at multiple points in the novel. Take Volodin's brother-in-law, the establishment writer Galakhov. Not without talent, capable on occasion of self-reflection, he has transformed himself by stages from a youthful enthusiast for the Five Year Plan into a lavishly remunerated hack. His character's textual status as a Simonov caricature contributes to the work's *roman à clef* quality. Swarthily good-looking like his real-life prototype, Galakhov also shares his life story: he won fame as a frontline correspondent and is a lyrical poet, novelist, newspaper columnist, and playwright, though his three Stalin Prizes pale in comparison with Simonov's six.[63] One should add that Dinera, Galakhov's glamorous actress wife, bears more than a passing resemblance to the film star Valentina Serova, a Soviet Betty Grable.

In inventing Galakhov, Solzhenitsyn tried to get inside the mind of an intelligent, self-aware practitioner of the gray arts of SocRealism:

> Whenever he started on a new, large work, he was full of fire and swore to himself and his friends that this time he would make no concessions, that he would write a real book. He sat down enthusiastically to write the first pages. But he soon began to notice that he was not alone, that an image floated up and hovered ever more distinctly before him, the image of the one for whom he was writing and with whose eyes he willy-nilly reread each newly written paragraph. And this one was not the reader, his brother, friend, and contemporary, nor was he a generalized critic, but for some reason always the illustrious critic in chief, Yermilov.[64]

Vladimir Yermilov, Galakhov's model or nightmare reader, ruled the SocRealist roost for forty years, making and destroying reputations and sometimes ruining lives. As for the empirical consumers of those "large works," we are shown two, and what a study in contrasts they are! For the acerbic Khorobrov, Galakhov's *Selected Works* is "meretricious trash."[65] The same hefty tome inspires a very different reaction in Nadya's roommate Erzsike,[66] a starry-eyed Hungarian communist:

> This book was her introduction to a world of lofty, noble characters whose flawless integrity astounded Erzsike. Galakhov's personages were never

shaken by doubt as to whether they should serve their country, whether or not they should sacrifice themselves. Erzsike still had a rather poor knowledge of the country's language and customs, which must be why she had yet to see such people for herself, but that only made it all the more important to learn about them from books."[67]

Even Dinera, Galakhov's cinematic wife, sees the limitations of the SocRealist model and directs a few barbs at Vsevolod Vishnevsky, the Racine of the Stalinist stage: "The dramatis personae are all faceless – three Party secretaries, seven senior officers, four commissars. It's like the minutes of a meeting."[68]

Galakhov is not the only SocRealist present. One evening Klara Makarygina goes to a boring play with a boring date. The performance that leaves her glassy-eyed is Gorky's drama *Vassa Zheleznova* (1910) and her companion on this occasion is Ernst Saunkin-Golovanov, a literary critic with a body out of Zamyatin: "a rectangular forehead and a rectangular head on a rectangular trunk."[69] That is, a triple square. The critic's name is a piece of linguistic camouflage draped over smelly etymon: in German, *ernst*—"serious," and in Russian, *golova*—"head" and *GOloVaNOv*—*govno*—"shit." In other words, *ernsthafte Scheisse*, or a headful of serious… The rectangular critic explains to Klara that though the men incarcerated at Marfino may be innocent, they still belong behind bars, as units of human "material."[70] The term in question was central to the Leninist discourse, as this passage from Nikolai Bukharin, one of its relatively benign practitioners, shows: "Proletarian compulsion in all its forms, beginning with shootings and ending with labor conscription is, however paradoxical it may sound, a method of producing a communist humankind out of the human material of the capitalist era."[71] So when later in the novel the classist Sologdin imagines the common people as "the formless raw material of history, from which the sturdy, crude, but indispensable legs of that Colossus—the Spirit of Man—are molded,"[72] this self-declared foe of Bolshevism displays an impeccably Bolshevist pattern of thought.

5

The two co-protagonists, Nerzhin and Volodin, are "questers,"[73] that is, seekers after the truth. Though destined never to meet, they are "united in a kinship of revolt."[74] Their parallel, alternating presences shape the flow of the narrative: point, counterpoint.

Ever since Nerzhin was arrested as a frontline Red Army officer, he has been steadily building a worldview to replace the romantic Leninism of his youth, for he no longer *loves the revolution*. In a series of flashbacks, Volodin is shown moving from a comfortable acceptance of his comfortable life to a revulsion against the terror state. Despite the distance between them in space and status, the two characters' textual presence obeys a shared fabulatory rhythm. Nerzhin declines to join a science project that will enable him to remain in the haven that is the sharashka at almost the exact moment that Volodin makes his fateful phone call; Nerzhin and friends celebrate his birthday with prison food and drink while Volodin attends the glitzy gathering at the Makarygins; Nerzhin experiences a resurgence of his love for Nadya just as Volodin renews his connubial bond with Dotnara; and at the end of the novel both men undergo routinized prison processing: Nerzhin prior to being transported to a work camp, Volodin as a new arrival at the Lubyanka.

Their personal philosophies echo each other as well: the mathematician Nerzhin, influenced by the books of Sankhya, espouses the ascetic notion that "the happiness of total satisfaction ... is the death of the soul,"[75] while the diplomat Volodin proclaims himself a follower of Epicurus because "he says that in reality man needs very little, and for that very reason his happiness is not at fate's mercy."[76] The novel's twin heroes are entwined with cultural texts that are thousands of years old. The same contrapuntal pattern is evident in their friendships. Nerzhin has a protégé in the sharashka, young Rostislav (Ruska) Doronin, an anti-Soviet Scaramouche who spent years on the run. For his part, Volodin acts as a mentor to his sister-in-law, Klara, an ethically aware young woman who happens to be in love with none other than the colorful Ruska.

Unlike Nerzin and Volodin, classic in-between characters who ponder and execute difficult moral choices, most of the other personalities have settled worldviews. Their opinions cover a wide spectrum. The old Bolshevik Radovich and the old Trotskyist Abramson, the middle-aged utopian communist Rubin, and the young Hungarian student Erzsike who adores everything Soviet, represent three generations of true believers. These Leninists of the heart are outnumbered by a herd of dogmatic Stalinists, who are variously (in many cases simultaneously) careerists or fools. In the latter category, two dunces loom especially thick whilst generating a measure of comic relief: Boris Stepanov, the under-educated party secretary who raises pigs at his suburban Moscow home, and Rakhmankul Shamsetdinov, the over-educated party lecturer who has bored hundreds of audiences up and down the country.

Like the communist idealists, the opponents of the regime fall into three generational categories. The austere Chelnov, Marfino's most brilliant mind, was arrested in 1932 for criticizing Stalin, while Volodin's uncle, the noble-born Avenir, displays a noble disdain for the tawdry reality of Soviet life; the middle-aged zeks Bobynin, Khorobrov, Potapov, Gerasimovich, and Sologdin, all of them accomplished science professionals, have arrived at a loathing of all things Soviet by a variety of life paths; thirty-one-year-old Pryanchikov, once a prisoner of the Nazis and now a prisoner of the Soviets, as well as boyish Ruska hate the tyrant with a youthful ardor.

Ruska contrives to get himself recruited as a stool pigeon in order to sabotage the prison surveillance system as a kind of double or triple agent. Isaak Kagan's motives for becoming a snitch are very different. This former storeman had once refused to inform on his co-workers because "the idea of denouncing people who were kind to him, or neither kind nor unkind, nauseated him,"[77] but after his arrest he became a stoolie out of simple fear. Two other finks, blue-blooded Artur Siromakha and athletic Viktor Lyubimichev, are driven by cold-hearted calculation. The same attitude typifies the sharashka director, Colonel Yakonov, who is happy to serve the Party if this will ensure his physical survival (in the early 1930s he was a zek himself) and, as a bonus, afford him an agreeable standard of living. Colonel Klimentiev, the by-the-book prison commandant, and Captain Shchagov, an ambitious war veteran, are honorable military men who behave dishonorably in the line of duty (Klimentiev) or personal advancement (Shchagov), though in the end both do the right thing. Another semi-sympathetic character is Yakonov's Jewish deputy, Adam Roitman, a courteous military engineer very much in love with his wife, whose Volga accent is a linguistic marker of authentic Russianness. Though *technically* one of the jailers, Roitman is granted the realization that "he had slipped ... from the role of creator to that of a supervisor of creators."[78] There is even a Nazi, hatchet-faced SS-Obersturmbannführer Reinhold Zimmer, who despite years spent in Soviet prisons has retained the repulsive aura of the true Hitlerite.

Although the men and women in *The First Circle* live in a society where the Party's presence extends into the most private areas of life, many of them have identities that are entirely apolitical. Ippolit Kondrashov-Ivanov (in real life, Sergei Ivashev-Musatov), the sharashka's resident "serf-artist,"[79] supplies "pictorial adornment"[80] for the homes of the MGB *Polizeibonzen*, but in his spare time paints for himself. Kondrashov's canvases are as realist, but un-Socialist, as anything that came from under the brush of a nineteenth-century Itinerant, yet his *Castle of the Holy Grail* (*Zamok sviatogo Graalia*), which provides one of the novel's organizing images-in-words, is marked by a Wagnerian symbolism that evokes the Russian Silver Age.[81] The peasant yardman Spiridon Yegorov, who is a kind of ambassador for Russia's rural masses in what is a largely urban text, displays an indifference to the totalitarian ideologies of the left and right but loathes Stalin and all his works. The two women in Nerzhin's life, Nadya, his wife, and Simochka, his prison girlfriend, love him no matter what. For Simochka, Gleb is a tragic war hero and so she likes to imagine her sweetheart in his officer's uniform standing tall amidst the bombs and the explosions, his auburn locks in martial disarray; the older and more sophisticated Nadya compares herself to the Decembrists' wives who followed their husbands, nineteenth-century rebels, against the autocracy, into Siberian exile.

As is the rule in Solzhenitsyn's fictions, masculine perspectives predominate. During a nighttime conversation between Nerzhin and Ruska, the latter, overwhelmed by the kind of white-hot sexual longing felt only by very young men, exclaims:

> "The one and only thing that the Big Chief could do to hurt us was to deprive us of women! So that's what he has done. For twenty-five years! The swine! I wonder if anybody realizes," he said, beating his breast, "what a woman means to a prisoner?"
>
> "You can go mad that way!" Nerzhin protested, but a sudden warmth welled up in him when he thought of Sima and her promise for Monday evening.[82]

For Rubin and Sologdin, "an unfaithful wife can't be forgiven but an unfaithful husband can,"[83] a rare point of agreement between these political adversaries. Sologdin, an accomplished lady-killer who just a few hours earlier had consummated an agreeable extra-marital encounter, explains: "The very structure of the body and the means of coupling show that there is an immense difference!"[84] Thoughtful Nerzhin, however, begs to differ: "If nations are equal and human beings are equal, surely men and women must also be equal. In all respects."[85] Ever calm and ever reasonable, he is the keeper of the threesome's friendship.

Now, *The First Circle* is a work in which the fictive balance palpably favors men and women of high intellect and high education over the less cerebral, less credentialed personae (*The Red Wheel* is another). This is to be expected in a novel about physicists, mathematicians, and engineers. Some of Solzhenitsyn's heroes proclaim their opposition to the people's state in starkly classist terms. Volodin's uncle, the degraded nobleman Avenir, regards the proletariat with contempt and execrates the idiocy of slum life. Working class people, he declares, are "barbarous," with vulgar life styles and tastes, unlike peasants who "commune with the soil" or intellectuals who "are engaged in the noble work of thinking."[86] Haughty Sologdin and mild-mannered Gerasimovich, both accomplished science professionals, would certainly agree. The former preaches a nostalgic, feudal vision of Russia but thinks of his countrymen as a "lost," "debauched," and "godless" nation.[87] For his part, Gerasimovich dreams of an authoritarian technocratic regime that would guarantee "equitable inequality ... based on talent, natural or cultivated."[88] The two elitists find themselves challenged on the main points of their doctrines, by Rubin and Nerzhin respectively. In the course of his climactic quarrel with the former, Sologdin concedes that his neo-Slavophilism is just a pose, while Gerasimovich's vision of a Russia governed by those fit to govern is calmly refuted by Nerzhin a dozen chapters later. Even so, when Gerasimovich declares that supreme power ought to be held by "us, the Russian technical intelligentsia"[89] and not "the asinine hoi polloi,"[90] Nerzhin feels world-historical shivers run down his spine. The misanthropic cogency of Gerasimovich's technocratic elitism makes it perhaps the most seductively dangerous doctrine enunciated by any Solzhenitsyn character anywhere, even if Nerzhin does his levelheaded best to make the contrary, technocratically egalitarian case.

Some of the tragic topoi that comprise the Gerasimovich plot line are duplicated in a section depicting another married couple, the Dyrsins. The husband, Ivan, is also a prisoner, but unlike the optical engineer, he is not a "genius."[91] Of working-class origin, he has "high cheekbones, sunken cheeks, thick speech, and a comic surname."[92] The economy of description is functional, because Ivan Dyrsin is but a *pre*-text, here to serve as the recipient of his wife's heartrending confidences, which take the hypodiegetic form of three letters. They are composed in spare, matter-of-fact language, like the speech of suffering children in Dickens or Chekhov:

> Granny died on November 26, 1949, at 12:05 p.m. When she died, we didn't have a single kopeck, but Misha, bless him, gave us two hundred roubles; it didn't cost a lot, but of course it was a pauper's funeral, no priest and no music; they simply took the coffin to the cemetery on a cart and tipped it in the hole.[93]

The novel's most unusual character is Lieutenant Nadelashin (*nadelal del*—Now He's Done It!), one of the Marfino guards. Fussy and teetotal, the lieutenant is utterly lacking in the jackbooted masculinity of the secret policeman. He "minces"[94] rather than struts and looks "a little eunuchlike."[95] Despite these trespasses against Soviet gender norms, Nadelashin has a wife and children. His secret passion is sewing, that marker of old-world femininity: he would rather be a tailor than a turnkey and so he makes clothes for himself and his family. There are other transgendered moments. The lieutenant is "moon-faced,"[96] and since in Russian folk culture, like many others, the moon is associated with the modalities of femininity, his lunar mien is an indicator of Nadelashin's epicene nature. So is the way he salutes, "like an old woman," in the words of his commanding officer.[97]

Now, Solzhenitsyn was in some ways a rather Victorian writer. In his writings, the masculine/feminine boundary is firmly drawn and functions as a heteronormative textual given. His representations of the erotic are usually shaped by a male character's perspective; when shown, intimate relations and intimate congress are invariably heterosexual. The only overt reference to Uranian practices occurs in *The Gulag Archipelago*, where the narrative voice comments ruefully on the way male and female prisoners would form same-sex relationships in the camps: "The walls grew—and Eros dashed back and forth. Finding no other sphere, he either flew too high—into platonic correspondence—or else too low—into homosexual love."[98]

Secret androgyne or not, like every other character in the novel Nadelashin has a fixed ethical identity, and his is definitely on the positive side. He is polite to the scientists he guards and is privately impressed by their fortitude and intelligence. As a warder in the Lubyanka, he used to eavesdrop on the zeks' conversations and "would have liked ... to listen to somebody's story from beginning to end without interruption, to hear how he had lived before and what he had been jailed for."[99] In other words, he would have liked to be the novel's model reader, or listener. Still, courteous and cheerful though he is, Nadelashin must monitor the inmates' conversations and report on them to his less courteous, less cheerful superiors: duty calls.

So what is it about the Lubyanka and MGB androgyny? Upon his arrival at that notorious jail Volodin encounters one of Nadelashin's former colleagues, "a face that was neither masculine nor feminine, a flabby, boneless face with a big red scald mark, and lower down a lieutenant's golden epaulets."[100] And lower done, *nihil*? A head and shoulders combo, satirically scripted and ambiguously sexed—or unambiguously de-sexed. Solzhenitsyn enjoyed turning the *odd* Chekist into a eunuch, whether sympathetic or otherwise.

6

Nerzhin's status as the authorial alter ego makes him the novel's principal personality, although Natalia Solzhenitsyna suggests that in the fictive scheme of things he is "no more important than Gerasimovich, Rubin, Sologdin."[101] Be that as it may, *this* Nerzhin is older, sadder, wiser than the jejune and self-absorbed hero of *Love the Revolution*. No longer a young Komsomol in a hurry, there is little in him now of the "incandescent meteor" that Nadya married all those years ago.

When the reader leaves him at the end of *Love the Revolution*, or that unfinished novel leaves the reader, Solzhenitsyn's hero was beginning to abandon his bookish ways. The narrative poem *The Road* and the plays *Victory Celebrations* and *The Love-Girl and the Innocent* record the subsequent changes. Nerzhin's two years at the front saw him "regenerated" by war "the way motherhood regenerates women"[102] (a Nietzschean dramaturgical moment). Slung into a work camp, Gleb gained in moral and political understanding: "What a brothel of a country we fought for!" he says, wonderingly,[103] and he now believes that one's conscience is "the most valuable thing we have" (*The Love-Girl and the Innocent*).[104]

The Gleb Nerzhin of *The First Circle* is Solzhenitsyn circa 1949: "His auburn hair, parted in the middle, was still thick, but there were crow's feet around his eyes, little wrinkles around his mouth, and furrows across his brow. His skin was affected by the lack of fresh air, and his face had a wilted look."[105] (The only discrepancy: Solzhenitsyn was blond. He darkened Nerzhin's hair to differentiate him from the fair-haired Sologdin as well as the empirical authorial self.) The hero is sparing of speech and gesture: "But what above all made him seem older was the economy of his movements: that economy by which nature conserves the flagging strength of prisoners in the camp,"[106] a carceral trait he shares with Ivan Denisovich. Nerzhin was never an ebullient personality, but the gulag years have taken their toll. There is something tired, even wan about him: it is as if he has been dipped in narrative gray. Simochka's impressions of Gleb are a case in point. In the way of those who are in love, she spends hours surreptitiously observing the man of her dreams, who appears to her "old, gray-faced, and haggard"[107] as he sits across from her in the lab thinking or writing, though his features turn "youthful"[108] when he becomes absorbed by some interesting project. The second and last time we see Nerzhin through the eyes of another is when during his meeting with Nadya at the Lefortovo jail she decides that "being in prison suits him."[109] As a *physical* presence, therefore, Nerzhin is undernarrated, in contrast to the extended, and frequent, descriptions of his friends, Rubin and Sologdin, and his enemy, Yakonov: it is Gleb's moral and intellectual existence, rather than his physical or even emotional self, that is diegetically privileged in the novel.

Gleb is still married to Nadya, his student sweetheart, who waits for him ever-patiently, ever-longingly as the years pass by and she moves from the bloom of girlhood into the sterility of enforced spinsterhood. In a letter written from prison he had released her from any marital duty of obligation: "There is no need for your life also to be ruined. You must marry someone else."[110] This was less a noble gesture on Gleb's part than a sober recognition that there could be no future for them together, in this country, in this period of historical time. And the intensity of intellectual life at Marfino, the pleasure he derives from his secret literary endeavors, and his burgeoning romance with Simochka all serve as distractions.

As a ladies' man, however, Nerzhin is not in Sologdin's league. His experience with the opposite sex is limited to the few months he and Nadya spent together as newlyweds (*Love the Revolution, The Road*), a fleeting sexual encounter with a terrified German woman in war-torn East Prussia (*The Road*), and a brief, doomed romance with the camp "love-girl" Lyuba (*The Love-Girl and the Innocent*). He courts Simochka with no second thoughts, and as a second choice: "Any other woman at the next desk, whatever she looked like, would have done just as well as Simochka."[111] The young woman may be in love with Gleb, but on his side the relationship is an entirely a selfish one: the hero is as flawed a human being as any other. Yet when he is unexpectedly granted a meeting with Nadya—thanks to a chance encounter she had with the dour jail commandant, Klimentiev, who was moved by Nadya's desperate pleas—Gleb's feelings for her return and he is reminded of the marital loyalty she has kept. Unlike Sologdin, who idealizes his wife even as he enjoys his prison dalliances, Nerzhin is not a man to compartmentalize his heart. Accordingly, he tells his almost-but-not-quite lover, with something of the younger Gleb's self-righteousness, that sleeping with her would make him feel remorseful: "Just so long as I have nothing on my conscience"[112] (*Lish' by menia ne gryzlo*).[113] Simochka, now gently, shyly in love, is crushed, a victim of Nerzhin's masculine self-realization project.

Beyond these internalized dynamics of sex and gender, Gleb has wide-ranging, even unusual intellectual interests, in contrast to his narrowly Marxist predilections before the war. Debating Rubin, he discourses knowledgeably on Taoism and the Vedas and has much to say about a great many other cultural subjects. His friend calls him, not unfairly, "an eclectic."[114] If so, it is an eclecticism born of experience. "I draw my conclusions not from the philosophical works I've read but from the life stories I hear in prison," Nerzhin explains:[115] the modus operandi of a real(ist) writer. Solzhenitsyn's hero never reads for pleasure (though that volume of Yesenin may be an exception): books are "allies" or "enemies,"[116] as they were for the man who invented him. And Gleb is utterly lacking in liberal guilt, Russian-style:

> Unlike the educated gentlefolk of the nineteenth century, the zek Nerzhin could descend without dressing up in strange clothes and feeling with his foot for the ladder; he was simply slung bodily into the mass of the people, in ragged padded trousers and a patched tunic, and given a daily work quota. Nerzhin shared the lot of simple people not as a condescending gentleman, always conscious of the difference and so always alien, but as one of themselves, indistinguishable from them, an equal among equals.[117]

Nerzhin may have molded himself into a man of a calm, contemplative disposition, but in his personal relationships the mathematician acts on instinct, as when he conceives an immediate liking for the young adventurer Ruska and the optical expert Gerasimovich. If Rubin and Sologdin, who are a bit older, treat Gleb with a certain condescension, in his friendship with Ruska he in turn adopts the part of mentor.

Nerzhin, Rubin, and Sologdin form the novel's "central triad."[118] I like to think of the three men as color coded, even if the symbolic spectrum in question is monochromatic. While tired-looking, self-denying Nerzhin is *gray*,[119] swarthy, sable-bearded Rubin is *black*, and the aggressively blond Sologdin is *white*. The two older men bear names which hold secret meanings. "Rubin" is a near-homonym to "Rudin," hinting at the sympathetic, doctrinaire and very talkative hero of Ivan Turgenev's eponymous novel (1856). Like Dmitry Rudin, a Heidelberg graduate with an enthusiastic attachment to the philosophy of Hegel, Marfino's Marxist maven has a connection to many things and thoughts German. And if one were to shift the stress in *Rúbin* to the second syllable, one would get *rubín*, Russian for "ruby," with its connotations of the electrified red stars atop the Kremlin; while *Sologdin* calls to mind *sol'nyi* (solo) or *sol'* (salt), appropriately so in the case of this individualistic and acerbic personality. We also note that his name is co-sonorous with *Solzhenitsyn*.[120]

With Rubin, the writer succeeded in creating a textured character with some very believable contradictions and quirks. He is, in Solzhenitsyn's own comment, "a profoundly principled man, an honest communist and a patriot."[121] A Party loyalist from youth, he steeled himself to do his political duty even if this meant denouncing a cousin as a Trotskyist or forcing a reluctant village to collectivize. Yet, he is loyal to his friends, contemptuous of the secret police, always mentally alert and socially engaged. Rubin has never quite assimilated the situational immorality of the true Stalinist. During the war he served as a psychological warfare officer, a sort of highbrow commissar, but was sent to prison for protesting Red Army atrocities in Germany. An essentially kind and decent man, his personality is better than his politics.

Sologdin is a very different proposition. He is scripted as the personification of charismatic, heroic masculinity. "With his little blond beard, his bright eyes, his high forehead, and his regular features, Sologdin was like an Old Russian knight [*drevnerusskii vitiaz'*][122]—and unnaturally, indecently handsome."[123] In his youth, we learn, he was a (Dostoevskian) mixture of things, "sincerely devout," "hopelessly vain," "fond of money," and equally attracted to and revolted by revolutionary violence.[124] He became first a Komsomol, next a skilled engineer, only to be arrested in one of the Stalin-era sweeps. He has spent twelve years in prison, including a stretch in the terrible mines of Vorkuta; he has never seen his son, born after his arrest; his wife no longer writes for fear of losing her job. An accomplished lady-killer, he seduced the girlfriend of the camp commandant, who knocked out some of his teeth in revenge. In the sharashka he sleeps with sultry Larisa, an MGB wife, less because he finds her sexually enticing than to drive home a political point: by screwing her, Sologdin is screwing the System. Rubin, who is not without male envy, accuses him of "pretending to be Alexander Nevsky,"[125] but actually Sologdin looks like Nikolai Cherkasov, the actor who played the medieval warrior prince with over-the-top theatricality in Eisenstein's famous film (1938). Rubin's jibe is a subtextual clue: as we know, the director and his productions stood low in Solzhenitsyn's esteem.

A scion of the (very) minor nobility, Sologdin likes to give himself aristocratic airs: "There goes Count Sologdin."[126] His primary marker, however, is lexical. A self-proclaimed traditionalist, he speaks in something he calls the Language of Ultimate Clarity (*Iazyk predel'noi iasnosti*), a form of Russian purged of all foreign words. He carries on in this weird, labored idiolect, often incomprehensible to Sologdin's fellow prisoners, and sometimes the reader, for page after page, with obsessive-compulsive persistence.[127] Nevertheless, Solzhenitsyn assigns the novel's most powerful arguments against the Marxism-as-science notion to this hero, crank, and poseur.

Sologdin's critique, which he puts forward in an epic debate with Rubin, employs many of the same arguments and even terminology as Karl Popper's confutation of Marxism in *The Open Society and Its Enemies* (1945) and *The Poverty of Historicism* (1957), although Solzhenitsyn was certainly unfamiliar with these works at the time he was writing (and rewriting) *The First Circle*.[128]

Popper:	Marxism is a "prophetic religion."[129]
Sologdin:	Marxism is a "blind faith."[130]
Popper:	The methods of science "always consist in offering deductive causal explanations, and in testing them."[131]
Sologdin:	"In true science all propositions derive directly from a strictly defined starting point."[132]
Popper:	"As opposed to the intellectual irresponsibility ... of an oracular philosophy which escapes into verbiage, modern science enforces upon our intellect the discipline of practical tests."[133]
Sologdin:	"Concrete knowledge is validated by the ability to apply its findings in practice."[134]

Popper:	"If we are uncritical we shall always find what we want: we shall look for, and find, confirmations, and we shall look away from, and not see, whatever might be dangerous to our pet theories."[135]
Sologdin:	"You don't want to argue with me because you don't know how to. None of you do, because you avoid people who think differently, and you won't risk denting your nice, tidy ideology!"[136]
Popper:	"Is it true that the workers' victory must lead to a classless society? I do not think so. ... The most likely development is, of course, that those actually in power at the moment of victory ... will form a *New Class* ... a kind of new aristocracy or bureaucracy."[137]
Sologdin:	"You crucified yourselves to do away with oppression, but you inflicted worse, far worse oppressors on us. ... Is there or is there not a new class, a ruling class?"[138]
Popper:	"The principles of dialectics would suggest that a new antithesis, a new class antagonism, must soon develop."[139]
Sologdin:	"You know that a society free of contradictions is an impossibility, yet you shamelessly promised it."[140]
Popper:	"Dialectics is sufficiently vague and adaptable to explain anything at all."[141]
Sologdin:	"This [negation of the negation] is one of the three laws by which you explain absolutely everything."[142]

Rubin, another character who is in error about some things but right about others (privately, he concedes there is "a grain of truth" in what Sologdin says),[143] is bested rhetorically but counterattacks, dissecting his opponent's aristocratic pretensions and patriotic conceits. Sensing that Rubin is winning the day (or rather, night), a flustered Sologdin gives up his Slavonic calques and cognates, goes off on an extended rant, and ends up declaring that "cock-eyed" Russia would have been better off had it become Catholic and that the Language of Ultimate Clarity is just a "game."[144] And so, Sologdin is busted: shown up as a snob and a fraud. The "honest communist" Rubin deconstructs the fake aristocrat Sologdin while ever-reasonable Nerzhin tries to stop the quarrel lest his two friends are overheard by the guards, by repeatedly uttering the safe word "Sense!"[145] (*Razum!*)[146]

Flanked as he is by two such forceful personalities, Gleb's own qualities of thoughtfulness and moderation are overshadowed at times. Unlike Rubin or Sologdin, he is a character in transition who does not have all the answers.

Still, the intellectual and emotional compatibilities between Gleb and his two confidants are eminently believable. The same cannot be said about the affinity between Sologdin and Rubin, which seems psychologically unlikely. The author was aware of possible readerly skepticism on this score and sought to preempt it by having the following thought occur to another zek, Abramson: "Strangely enough, Rubin and Sologdin were supposed to be friends, perhaps because they had been neighbors on the bedboards at Butyrki."[147]

The optical designer Illarion Gerasimovich is also an important contributor to the multivocality of the text. Like Nerzhin and Bobynin, he challenges the jailers directly; like Rubin and Sologdin, he is the bearer of a distinctive political message, which he articulates at considerable and often persuasive length.

The initial description of Gerasimovich invokes the visual clichés of Soviet propaganda, not in order to encode this character but to decode him: portraiture via counter-semiosis. The scientist is "a short, narrow-shouldered man with a markedly intellectual face and pince-nez, the typical spy portrayed in Soviet posters,"[148] and later there are references to him as "a puny sparrow of a man"[149] and a "little fellow"[150] (*malysh*).[151] Gerasimovich shares his diminutive build with his slip of a wife, Natasha: their common spousal trait. Natasha is 37 but looks older and has "the austere face of a nun"[152] (*strogoe litso monakhini*):[153] one of the few clichés the author failed to catch when he was carrying out the definitive redaction.[154] The story of these native Leningraders is tragic almost beyond imagining. In the 1930s they endured Siberian exile, the death of their two children, and grinding poverty. During the war, they lived through the terrible siege of their city, only for Illarion to be sent to prison on another false charge. But whether together or apart, they persevered; they survived. Now, however, Natasha is at the end of her tether. At a meeting with her husband in the Lefortovo prison she erupts in a stream of reproaches and imprecations. She no longer has the strength to endure persecution by the lumpen-neighbors in her communal apartment or to put up with her relatives' insults. In childlike language, Natasha begs: "Invent something for them, so that they'll leave you in peace. I know you've got something for them right now! Save me! Sa-a-ave me-e-e!!"[155]

As it turns out, this is something the engineer cannot, or will not, do:

> Gerasimovich rose, looked contemptuously at the barrel-bellied, flabby-cheeked, pig-faced degenerate wearing a general's hat, and said in a ringing voice: "No! It isn't what I was trained to do! Putting people in prison isn't my trade! I am no fisher of men [*lovets chelovekov*]![156] It's enough that we've been imprisoned ourselves."[157]

The phrase "fisher of men" derives from Mathew 4:19: "And he saith unto them, Follow me, and I will make you fishers of men" / *i govorit im: idite za Mnoiu, i Ia sdelaiu vas lovtsami chelovekov*. And so, Gerasimovich rejects the demonic eversion of that biblical command.

Yet, wrenching and heroic though these details are, they do not entirely blend with the representation of the Gerasimoviches' bodies and personalities. Instead, they are enumerated in discrete stretches of text and pasted onto husband and wife. Solzhenitsyn *tells* us, he doesn't *show* us; he waxes indignant, not indicial. Illarion and Natasha are animated biography and history, unlike more fictively integrated creations such as Rubin, Volodin, Nadya or even General Makarygin, those Tolstoyan simulacra of living, breathing, feeling human beings. But to repeat, *what* Gerasimovich says constitutes one of the novel's most interesting discursive components; and in any case, the deployment of characters as historiographical functions was a technique the author would develop further in *The Red Wheel*, where it is one of that saga's defining tropes.

This relative fictive flatness is brought into sharp relief when the narrator shows us the object across which husband and wife face each other during Natasha's prison visit:

> That clumsy little table had more of a history behind it than many a human life contains. Generations of prisoners, men and women, had sat there sobbing, numb with fear, fighting against murderous sleeplessness, some still proudly defiant, some signing trivial denunciations of family and friends. They were not usually allowed to handle pencils or pens, except for the few required to make depositions in their own handwriting. Those few had contrived to leave their marks, those peculiar absentminded scribbles and scratches that mysteriously preserve the tortuous workings of the unconscious.[158]

Here a tired piece of furniture contorts and emotes, like the domestic fittings in the stories of Bruno Schultz. A thing made of wood speaks to us of human suffering and human terror. The passage is almost, but not quite, prosopopoeic, that is, although the little table does not speak itself, the extradiegetic narrator speaks *for* it, to touching effect. The little table is now in semi-retirement, no longer employed as a torture prop, but it still has its jailhouse uses. It is more vivid, more memorable than brilliant, brave Illarion or poignant, childlike Natasha, so that the opening sentence of the description becomes an inadvertent warning to the reader.

Certain of Gerasimovich's opinions have a distinctly Solzhenitsynian ring, so there is a measure of meta-fictive irony in the fact that the optical expert gives voice to these ideas as he argues with the author's alter ego, Nerzhin:

> We have been starved of freedom, so we think that freedom should have no limits. But unless limits are set to freedom, there can be no well-adjusted society.[159]

And:

> We have deserved our regime and leaders; we got ourselves into this mess, and we must get ourselves out of it. ... We can see for ourselves how our people have degenerated, how uncouth they have become, how indifferent they are not only to the fate of the country, not only to the fate of their fellows, but even to their own fate and that of their children. Indifference, the organism's last self-preservative reaction, has become our defining characteristic. Hence also the popularity of vodka – unprecedented even by Russian standards.[160]

Yet the soft-spoken scientist does not merely offer harsh and informed criticism of the benighted masses. He goes a step further. He proclaims his right, indeed his obligation as an intellectually superior being to hold sway over the lowbrow and the downscale. He and his gentle wife, Natasha, have endured terrible suffering, inflicted upon them by agents of the proletarian dictatorship. Gerasimovich wants to pay the proletarians back. His anti-populist authoritarianism is a form of revenge on Stalin's ochlocrats, who lord it over the clever, the sensitive, the cultivated. In effect, Solzhenitsyn takes his own notion that those who are ethically and historically aware must bear a special duty of care for the people's wellbeing, and hyperbolizes it into a program for the enlightened repression of a corrupted nation, along the lines of José Ortega y Gasset's *The Revolt of the Masses* (*La rebelión de las masas*; 1930):

> [The mass] has come into the world in order to be directed, influenced, represented, organised—even in order to cease being mass, or at least to aspire to this. But it has not come into the world to do all this by itself. It needs to submit to a higher court, formed of the superior minorities.[161]

Inevitably, we must agree with Nerzhin that Gerasimovich's neo-Platonic state where the professors rule and the proles obey is the bookish fantasy of a despairing intellectual, no less naive than Rubin's communist utopia with its toga-wearing apparatchiks. Still, it is pleasant to visualize coarse, unevolved creatures like Abakumov, Bulbanyuk, and Oskolupov, the novel's presiding trinity of Chekist generals, stripped of their gaudy uniforms and flapping potbellies and doing hard, honest work with their hands at the direction of their intellectual betters. Or, dream of dreams, to picture Stalin as a wretched vagrant skulking in some Circassian cave or city cellar in a counterfactual Russian Empire of the imagination!

As the conversation between Gerasimovich and Nerzhin draws to a close, the latter prophesies that "noble people will suddenly spring up" like mushrooms after a rainstorm, unexpectedly, "mysteriously," and their voices shall "shatter concrete."[162] Yet Solzhenitsyn leaves the last word with the older man, who gives Nerzhin's homely simile a sinister twist: "Before that happens, your noble people will be carried away in hampers and baskets – weeded out, chopped up, short of a head."[163]

7

The First Circle is high in hypodiegesis. Not only does it contain multiple life stories that are formatted as discrete narrative excursuses, but it includes two embedded texts that are co-authored by the secret writer, Nerzhin. These occur at a midpoint in the novel, in chapters fifty-five and fifty-nine, which are respectively titled "Prince Igor" and "The Buddha's Smile."

First, fifty-five. Infused with a jaunty spirit of fun, Rubin and Nerzhin stage a mock trial of the twelfth-century Prince Igor Svyatoslavich, conducted according to the kangaroo-court norms of Stalinist jurisprudence. The prince is the hero of *The Lay of the Host of Igor* (*Slovo o polku Igoreve*; c. 1185), an anonymous epic which most Russians regard, despite lingering doubts about its authenticity, as "the only literary masterpiece" of the Kievan period.[164] The *Lay* tells the story of a doomed military expedition against the Polovtsians, or Cumans, a Turkic tribe of the southern Don region, and Igor's defeat and capture at the end of that campaign. The epic was adapted by Alexander Borodin for his opera *Prince Igor* (*Kniaz' Igor'*; 1890), and so holds a doubly canonical status. Therefore, in addition to the original East Slavonic text, the Rubin-Nerzhin performance has a second, musical, referent. Beyond this parodic connection to the nation's cultural tradition, the Nerzhin-Rubin theatricals reflect the prominence that the *Lay*, or rather its modern translations, enjoyed in late Stalinist Russia as a "formal," "stylistic," and "thematic" model for SocRealist war fiction.[165]

The two dramatists twist and paraphrase the texts of Borodin's libretto and the *Lay* itself into the wooden language of high Stalinism, a diegetic device also employed in *The Gulag Archipelago*, viz., "the anachronistic application of camp terminology to a discussion of the Decembrists' interrogations and imprisonment."[166] Nerzhin and Rubin mount their show inside the semicircular second floor dorm of the sharashka, with actors and audience distributed around this narrow, curved space, which with its tiers of bunks takes on the appearance of a tiny, constricted amphitheater. The players are Rubin (prosecutor), Nerzhin (judge), Bulatov[167] (usher), and Zemelya (juror), while the audience comprises Sologdin, Potapov, Khorobrov, Prianchikov, Dvoetyosov, Kagan, Chelnov, Ruska, and even the yardman Spiridon. Of the actors, only Rubin is in costume, having draped a blanket round his shoulders in the manner of a judicial robe. He also has use of the only prop, a locker that serves him in the office of a dais. The spectators frequently interrupt the performance, bantering with the players in a manner reminiscent of English panto or American vaudeville. In these meta-dramatic exchanges, the cast members never break character. Even Spiridon, for whom such cultural jollities should be utterly alien, enters into the spirit of the proceedings, smiling "a crafty peasant smile."[168] Strictly speaking, the yardman is surplus to requirements: he has no business being here and is included only because his presence gives the theatricals the requisite universalizing meaning. See the Christmas show mounted by the convicts in *The House of the Dead*, which is the counter-referent for the Nerzhin-Rubin play. In Dostoevsky's novel, the outsider in the mixed audience of prisoners, wardens, and townspeople is the gentle-born narrator, who "was better equipped to judge than they"[169] the quality of the performance, and does so approvingly.

As an "insulting parody of Soviet judicial procedure,"[170] in MGB Major Shikin's not inaccurate assessment, the play mocks the same Stalin-era legal travesties that elsewhere are satirized in the characters of prosecutors Makarygin and Slovuta. And like the lecture on Marxism-Leninism in chapter eighty-eight, it was designed as a sustained moment of comic relief in what is otherwise a very serious novel. In addition, this dramaturgical event discharges several other fictive functions. It is an act of (c)overt resistance by the zeks; a carnivalesque extravaganza through which the prisoners effect an imaginative escape from the carceral present by transforming themselves into simulacra of their political masters; and in a supra-meta-textual twist, a reminder of the contingency of all art, including *The First Circle* itself.

To this reader, the play calls to mind Mayakovsky's drama *Mystery-Bouffe* ("*Misteriia-Buf*"; 1918/1921 and his long poems *150,000,000* (1919) and *Very*

Good! (*"Khorosho!"*; 1927), celebrations of the October Revolution that employ the forms of literary parody and rely on the same canon-twisting, genre-bending treatment of politics as heroic history crossed with slapstick. The last of these agitprop productions employs a famous passage from *Eugene Onegin* to lampoon a trio of anti-Bolshevik figures, turning the elderly socialist Ekaterina Kuskova into a geriatric Tatiana Larina; the Liberal leader Pavel Milyukov, her "mustachioed he-nurse";[171] and prime minister Alexander Kerensky, a limp-wristed version of Onegin himself. This stab at political burlesque may be charitably described as broad humor. The Rubin-Nerzhin theatricals share Mayakovsky's satirical obviousness. The mock trial also carries a whiff of the gag-playing (*khokhmachestvo*) typical of Soviet student and prison life,[172] and this is where it fails to convince. Nerzhin may have accumulated much knowledge and life experience since his days as a "philosophical calf," but he has not changed in this regard: he is no more humorous now than he was then. So how can we accept his sudden transformation into a jailhouse jokester?

Although to my mind this episode does not really work, many readers have been known to split their sides laughing. If so, more laughter to them! Interestingly, however, Tvardovsky and Yevgeny Yevtushenko both recommended the chapter's removal, as did the philologist Mirra Petrova, a particularly sensitive reader.[173]

In contrast, "The Buddha's Smile" is much more of a piece. This is a fantastic tale written by Nerzhin and, less believably, the aloof engineer Potapov. Set in the immediate postwar period, it purports to describe a visit by Eleanor Roosevelt to the Butyrki Prison, which the authorities turn for the occasion into a showpiece Potemkin penitentiary. Four inmates are selected to play the part of happy *cons*. They are bathed, manicured, pedicured, perfumed, costumed, and given wigs to cover their shaved heads. As Mrs. Roosevelt looks on benignly, the zeks are served a gourmet lunch by a bevy of pretty waitresses, leaf through American magazines, and are confessed by a priest; all of this simultaneously. Here the prisoners are, once again, the players; the warders, the stage workers; the Chekists, the directors; and Mrs. Roosevelt plus entourage (a secretary, interpreter, and "two respectable matrons of the Quaker persuasion"),[174] the uninformed audience. Enthroned in a very theatrical armchair (the cell has been suitably furnished for the occasion), the former First Lady questions the four lags about prison conditions. They make the prescribed responses, variously embellished or edited by her MGB interpreter, while the Chekists and screws glare at the performing zeks from behind Mrs. Roosevelt's back. As soon as the presidential widow leaves, the inmates' bodies are stripped of their costumes, the props removed, and normal prison life resumes. But a small bronze

Buddha that was part of the décor is accidentally left behind and becomes a souvenir of the occasion, "enigmatically smiling in his niche."[175] Despite this Orientalizing formula, on some gossamer-thin textual plane the little figure is transformed into the novel's organizing symbol of wisdom and enlightenment, like the Buddha statue with its "golden smile"[176] in Yevgeny Zamyatin's dystopian novel We (My; 1920; publ. 1924). As for the ex-FLOTUS, she is a stand-in for every credulous cultural tourist who went to the Soviet Union and saw a paradisal present or a future that worked.

The two prison plays form a hypodiegetic binary: free theater vs. slave theater. Rubin and Nerzhin are uninhibited performers whose jailhouse improv is an act of imaginative rebellion, whereas the quartet of zeks are objectified into performing automata programmed to follow a script laid down by the secret police, on pain of death.

Lastly, "The Buddha's Smile" represents one more eversion of a SocRealist master plot. Take, for example, the play *I Want to Go Home* (*Ia khochu domoi!*; 1948) by Sergei Mikhalkov, a literary carthorse of the Stalin, Khrushchev, Brezhnev, Andropov, Chernenko, Gorbachev, Yeltsin, and Putin eras. The setting is postwar Germany. British intelligence imprisons a group of Soviet children in a dungeon-like orphanage, complete with punishment cell. The tragic tots are starved, abused, forbidden to speak Russian, and forced to attend Catholic services (sic!). Yet still they resist. An American journalist, the wickedly named Miss Dodge, tours the facility and watches approvingly as the hungry waifs are fed porridge and butter for the occasion; of course, all ends well and the patriotic orphans are reunited with the Motherland.

8

Room 318 in the student dorm on Stromynka Street is an alcove of femininity in what is a mostly masculine novel. Like the Marfino zeks, the women who inhabit these cramped quarters form a little society with its own hierarchies, friendships, and enmities. Nadya, of course, is one of this work's principal characters and the story of her love for Nerzhin has always been central to its appeal. Yet in this space, this group, she is a woman with a secret, for she dares tell no one that her husband is a political prisoner. Guarded and reticent, she is the outsider among her roommates, each one of whom represents a recognizable type. Fetching, fizzy Olya is excited about a new boyfriend; plain, thirtyish Muza is kindhearted and clever; slinky, blonde Lyuda nurtures the "primitive belief" that a woman's sex life *is* her life;[177] rustic Dasha would gladly swap her dissertation for a husband and child; stylish Erzsike, a starry-eyed Hungarian communist and true believer, is perplexed by the gray reality of Moscow, the capital of progressive mankind. All these personalities have voices and choices of their own but remain peripheral figures, walk-ons or look-ins who lack the textured presence of Nadya, Klara, or even Dotnara. The women in Room 318 are also sharers of a tragic gender destiny: "Where there should have been men their own age, or ten to fifteen years older, moving and smiling, the war had left nothing but gaping black holes."[178]

With their emphasis on the distribution of material objects and boundaries along the three spatial axes, Solzhenitsyn's descriptions of his interiors often read like stage directions. The opening of chapter forty-nine includes this floor plan in words:

> The long sides of the room went from window to door, and on each side three iron beds, head to foot, hugged the wall, with three rickety sets of wicker bookshelves between them. Two tables stood in line in the middle of the room, leaving only a narrow passage on each side between themselves and the beds. The one nearer to the window, heaped with books, exercise books, drawings, and reams of typescript, was the "dissertation" table; the other was for general purposes.[179]

(One can just see Natalya Reshetovskaya describing or perhaps sketching the room's well-remembered layout for her husband.)

Another typical Solzhenitsynian trope governs his depictions of female characters inside their private spaces, where they are invisible to the prying male gaze. When thus cloistered, they are often shown performing traditional feminine tasks or otherwise behaving in an overtly gendered manner. As the chapter opens, Olya and Lyuda are getting ready for a night out. The former is ironing while Lyuda preens in front of the mirror and admires her blond curls, thinking to herself that "any one of them would be enough to ensnare a poetic youth."[180] She is meeting a young Spaniard, a poet brought to the USSR as a child during the Spanish civil war. After the fall of darkness lubricious Lyuda plans to play the part of a timorous virgin, the better to seduce her exotic date, as she sneeringly informs the other women. This pretty, predatory girl is a Moscow Medusa Gorgon, her golden ringlets the serpents of sex, although in a departure from the legend, Lyuda's reflection does not kill her but makes her sultrier. The Spanish poet, however, may be in carnal peril, or so Freud warns: "The terror of Medusa is … a terror of castration. … The hair upon Medusa's head is frequently represented in works of art in the form of snakes, and these once again are derived from the castration complex."[181] Of course, Lyuda's roommates, being female, are immune to *that* danger. In any case, the head of curls floating in the dormitory mirror is surrounded by a nimbus of myths or a halo of hypotexts, confirming a recent scholar's well-researched observation that

> Medusa is transformed into an image, inserted into the order of designation; henceforth, she will serve primarily as the support for a long chain of discursive and figural events, beginning with Perseus's own account of his triumph over Medusa (recounted by Ovid), including the famous Roman mosaic depicting Perseus with Medusa's severed head (the prototype for countless depictions of the myth in the history of Western art), and extending into our [twentieth] century with Ferenczi's, Freud's and Hélène Cixous's psychoanalytic accounts of the myth.[182]

Meanwhile Muza is brooding about an incident that happened a couple of days earlier when she was approached by a pair of MGB officers who invited her to become an informer. After she demurred, they threatened her with a pistol and promised to run her out of the university. The gun may have been an over-the-top gesture straight out of a gangster movie—were the two Chekists really prepared to shoot her right then and there?—but the threat to destroy her academic career was very real. Pure-of-heart Muza is crushed: "What she felt was deep disgust, as though she had smeared herself with something obscene that could not be washed away or concealed or shown—something that made existence impossible."[183] The language here is coded to evoke the trauma of rape, in implicit contrast to Lyuda's self-presentation as a vestal Komsomol. Muza has three days before she must decide whether to accept the MGB assignment: another one of those momentous, dichotomizing choices that the characters in this novel so often face.

If Muza is ethical but apolitical, Erzsike, a former member of the Hungarian Resistance, is that classic figure, the guileless foreigner discombobulated by the realities of Russian life. With her red-tinted view of the Soviet Union, Erzsike finds it hard to believe that Moscow girls may marry for money and is enthralled by Galakhov's potboilers. Nonetheless, the recent execution of László Rajk, communist Hungary's foreign minister, has cast a shadow over her love for all things Soviet.

Enter Dasha, who has just had an amusing encounter with a would-be suitor on the tram, which she relates to the other women: girl talk, nicely formatted. Cattily, she advises Lyuda to wash her feet. For the preening blonde is a slattern: her bed is always in disarray, like her sex life, whereas high-minded Dasha's is "as neat and pretty as any shrine."[184] *She* is the truly vestal one, or so the simile suggests.

Into this maximally feminized space Solzhenitsyn introduces manly Captain Shchagov, who comes to Room 318 to pay court to Nadya. An ex-soldier with a distinguished war record, he has made a conscious decision to seek social advancement in the grubby, corrupt Soviet Union of the postwar period, where patriotism has been superseded by a lust for material success and aspirational members of the Party are undergoing "embourgeoisement,"[185] and having a good time as they do so. Shchagov is a veteran on the make, scheming to marry a relative of the Makarygin family for advancement and to seduce Nadya for some fun on the side. Yet despite his cynical schemes he is a fundamentally decent sort. In one of the novel's most moving scenes, Nadya confesses to Shchagov that her husband is in prison, whereupon the captain gives up his amorous designs and offers a toast: "'All right, then, soldier's wife!' he said roughly, cheerfully. 'Don't let it get you down. Take hold of this glass. Keep your head and all may be well. Let's drink to the resurrection of the dead!'"[186] Later that evening, however, Shchagov makes his way to the house at Kaluga Gate to play footsie with the Makarygin girl and ingratiate himself with the host, in another of the novel's Tolstoyan life-goes-on narrative moments.

9

The tough, wily yardman, Spiridon, is the novel's only peasant character. A severely shortsighted but vigorous fifty-year-old, he is red-haired (like Lenin) but going gray. Solzhenitsyn gives him an amazing life to live and a great deal to say, most of it to Nerzhin, who gets to know him out of an anthropological sense of curiosity and ends up becoming his friend. The mathematician even introduces Spiridon to his favorite poet, the rural bard Yesenin, though with uncertain results (we recall Ignatich's efforts to enlighten Matryona musically). The yardman's name is his message. "Spiridon" derives from the Greek word for "spirit," whereas "Egor" is a demotic version of Georgii, the name of one of Russia's patron saints. Thus, Spiridon Yegorov—Spirit of St. George. And of course, "Spiridon" rhymes with "Platon," an onomastic pointer that links this gruff character to the gentle peasant in *War and Peace* scripted by Tolstoy as an embodiment of the kenotic virtues.

Spiridon is a late addition to the gallery of canonical muzhiks in Russian literature, which includes Karataev and assorted Tolstoyan rustics, as well multiple characters in Turgenev's *Sketches from a Hunter's Album* (*Zapiski okhotnika*; 1852), the hero in Dostoevsky's story "The Peasant Marey" ("Muzhik Marei"; 1876), and Luka in Gorky's play *The Lower Depths* (*Na dne*; 1902). Like these wise and sometimes mystical graybeards, Spiridon has traits and life experiences that are universal. A devoted family man who would do anything for his wife and children, he lives a private life of courage and decency, but in the public, historical sphere his choices are invariably misguided and sometimes completely wrong. He is a *homme-type*, a stand-in for the common people whose pre-modern mindset and narrow moral outlook compounded the nation's tragedy, or so the author believed. Veniamin Kaverin, an establishment writer but also a strong Solzhenitsyn admirer, offers this verdict: "A truly Russian personality that is capable of achieving everything, yet will never achieve anything, because he always remains true to himself."[187]

Spiridon's life is a chain of historical topoi. He became the head of the household as a young boy, when his father was killed in World War I; fought successively for the Greens (peasant guerrillas), Whites, and Reds in the civil war; was a ploughman and a proletarian; a prosperous farmer and a collectivization commissar; a camp inmate and a camp guard; a soldier and a deserter; a slave laborer in Germany and a slave laborer in Russia. Like Ivan Denisovich or the peasant soldiers in *Love the Revolution*, Spiridon never became one of the nationalized Soviet masses. Drafted into the Red Army in 1941, he made his way back to his village after his unit was scattered by the Wehrmacht and began to farm for himself, until the fortunes of war turned and he fled westward with the retreating Germans.

"Horrifyingly ignorant"[188] of high politics and high art, indeed of every intellectual topic explored in the novel, Spiridon is supremely commonsensical, though he suffers from the "reckless fatalism" of the true Russian,[189] a trait that led him to consume raw alcohol in an American DP camp. As a result, he lost much of his sight. The MGB officers treat the purblind peasant with lordly disdain; the captive scientists ignore him or, like the snob Sologdin, view him as an amusing exotic. In a passage suffused with a Tolstoyan sense of how two individuals can fall victim to complete mutual misapprehension, we learn that

> each man believed himself superior to the other: Sologdin because he knew all about mechanics, the resistance of metals, and other scientific matters, and also because of his broad grasp of social issues; Spiridon

because material objects always obeyed him. Sologdin, however, patronised the yardman openly, while Spiridon hid his feelings.[190]

The design engineer, who likes to put on aristocratic airs, has an imperfect grasp of what constitutes good breeding, for a true gentleman accords all those he meets, whatever their social status, the same degree of courtesy. But that's Sologdin for you: despite his personal courage and professional brilliance he is pretty clueless about a great many things, including the rules for being upper class. As for Spiridon, in the way of the Russian peasant he keeps his counsel whenever he comes into contact with an authority figure, whether aspirant (Sologdin) or actual (Major Shikin). It is just as well that they remain ignorant of what's on his mind.

For like the techno-elitist Gerasimovich, Spiridon nurtures dreams of retribution, though of a much most merciless kind, as when he tells Nerzhin that he wants to see "old Daddy Whiskers and their entire set up" wiped out by an atomic bomb, even if it also incinerates Spiridon's own family "and a million other people" (see chapter one of this study). In "Ivan Denisovich," we recall, Tyurin articulated this stern notion of providential justice: "So you're up there in heaven after all, Lord. You are slow to anger, but you hit hard." Spiridon formulates his notion of good and evil with no reference to God: "Killing wolves is right; eating people is wrong."[191]

10

Not all readers will agree with Michael Scammell's assessment that this novel displays "a perfection of artistic form akin to that of 'A Day in the Life of Ivan Denisovich.'"[192] *The First Circle* may be a kind of thriller, but it is far from taut, even in a digressive, polyphonic Dostoevskian sense. In an effort to remain true to the facts, Solzhenitsyn crammed as many real-life personalities and events into the Marfino chapters as his chosen novelistic format would allow:

> When I was writing *The First Circle* ... it was as if I was assailed from every side by facts, faces, incidents, statements, comments, somebody's words, all those friends who were imprisoned in the sharashka with me, so that I could barely deflect this mass of detail: no, I don't want this, or this, or this, it's too much for one chapter—there was such a profusion of material.[193]

Sometimes it shows, when factological exactitude and moral messaging trump good old narrative value. In the Marfino chapters, the author cleaves to the autobiographical record so faithfully that the thicket of characters and character situations, each one derived from personal knowledge, can become an obstacle to readerly reception. Again and again, the implied author jabs the implied reader in the chest or drags him by the collar out of his cozy, implied armchair, anxious to demonstrate the enormity of the Soviet tragedy by showing another life maimed or ruined by the terror state; or by displaying another secret policeman for our revulsion. There are costs to all this. The story lines involving two of the most intriguing characters, Yakonov and Roitman, peter out, while less interesting personalities usurp the fictive space. The narrative's universalizing function is undermined by its mnemonic, localizing focus.

For instance, the two resident MGB officers at the sharashka, Major Myshin (in charge of security at Marfino Prison) and Major Shikin (in charge of security at the Marfino research center), may be *respectively* redundant. Shikin has a large head, gray hair, and strangely small hands and feet, while Myshin is "unhealthily obese" and "violet-complexioned."[194] Despite these nominal stabs at characterization, the majors are fictive blanks. The zeks bestow upon them the collective nickname "Shishkin-Myshkin," a hint that we should regard the malevolent pair as a composite personality or duo, like Salii and Zamalii, the "indistinguishable pair of Tartar Red Army soldiers" in the comedy *Victory Celebrations*.[195] These twinned security honchos are the bane of the Marfino prisoners, but as comic figures they lack the key quality of contrastively framed absurdity. They harass and insult, snoop and spy, but somehow they fail to gel, separately or with each other. Clearly, Myshin and Shikin are based on actual Chekists the author encountered at Marfino. One wonders why he did not substitute the former for the latter, or vice versa: fuse the fiends. The same question might be asked about another Stalinist pairing, that of Stepanov, the Party secretary at Marfino, and his predecessor and then deputy, Klykachev. Elsewhere, however, we encounter an MGB duo that is grimly comedic, Lieutenants Tyukin and Kuleshov, responsible for monitoring calls to the US embassy. The "very polite"[196] plainclothes officers Nikolai Ivanovich and Sergei Ivanovich, who try to recruit Muza at gunpoint, are just as grotesque and just as Gogolian, even though their textual presence is limited to a few sentences. Mirra Petrova speculates that the novel's character dyads, which she classifies into "analogue pairs" such as Shikin and Myshin, and "antipode pairs" such as Radovich and Slovuta, were meant to refer us back to the story of the Flood and the beasts that "went in two and two unto Noah into the ark" (Genesis 7:9; see the title of chapter fifty-three, "The Ark").[197] Perhaps so.

Still, Myshin and Shikin, the novel's Rosenkrantz and Guildenstern,[198] are no more than supporting players. If they fail to register with the reader, this matters little in his readerly scheme of things. Elsewhere the costs of fictive redundancy are higher. Thus, two of the Marfino zeks, embittered Khorobrov and cerebral Potapov, are important contributors to the novel's anti-Stalinist discourse. Yet, set next to the tragic Gerasimovich, stern Bobynin, or exuberant Pryanchikov, let alone Nerzhin, Sologdin, and Rubin, they appear under-differentiated, even anonymous, despite all the interesting things they have to say. Still, as *voices* rather than *presences*, they do the fictive job.

The novel's anti-Marxist sections have their problems as well. It is not that they lack satirical punch. Those in the early to middle part of the text are often very funny and to the point. Lieutenant Tyukin dreads his mandatory Marxism-Leninism study sessions, for he

> was certain to be asked in next Monday's politics class "who are 'the friends of the people' and how do they fight against the social democrats," why we had to break with the Mensheviks at the Second Congress and had been right to do so, why we had reunited at the Fifth Congress, again acting correctly, then at the Sixth Congress had again gone our separate ways and yet again had been right to do so.[199]

In the Stalin chapters, we observe the dictator laboriously generating Marxian analyses, some mental and some written, of the past, present, and future of the universe. The epic quarrel between Rubin and Sologdin begins with "an honest debate"[200] about the dialectic and is a rhetorical tour de force. Later on, however, the anti-Marxist satire grows tired. The entirety of chapter eighty-eight is devoted to a political lecture by the world-historical bore, Shamsetdinov. Taken on its own, this ex cathedra performance is a hilarious send-up of Soviet ideological claptrap. Solzhenitsyn wickedly mocks the clunky jargon in which it was couched and the intellectual lunacy that it conveyed, all this with a parodic verve reminiscent of the opening pages of Dostoevsky's *Devils*. When making a secret recording of the chapter, he actually had to take periodic breaks in order to laugh.[201] Yet Shamsetdinov's talk adds nothing to the notion, well established in the Stalin sections and at other points in the novel, that by 1949 the Progressive Worldview had become a dead letter, in fact, thousands of volumes of dead letters. For once, the author's distinctive technique of mnemonic reconstruction lets him down, leading him to saturate eighty-eight with extraneous, though doubtless accurate, detail. For example: "Thanks to the exertions of

Stepanov and his whippers-in, all the rows were filled by 6:15 except the second and third, where no one could sit, because they were wedged tightly together and jammed against the front row."²⁰² Those rows two and three are furniture clutter that distracts rather than informs.

In a larger sense, the novel's ideological bias undoubtedly dates it to some extent. For while varieties of Marxism still inspire mass movements in geopolitically peripheral locales such as South Africa or Nepal, these days its main presence in the Western cultural space is as a minority interest discursive practice, confined to the college campus and the political journal, with the flamboyant exception of Slavoj Zizek and his Lacanian-Leninist theatrics, which are appropriately performed in art galleries as well university lecture halls and also cemeteries.²⁰³

That said, we should keep things in perspective. The novels of Tolstoy and Dostoevsky, or George Eliot and James Meredith abound in references to the intellectual fashions of the day, which does not preclude engagement with the texts by twenty-first-century readers. Pierre's masonic experiments in *War and Peace* or Levin's agricultural researches in *Anna Karenina* constitute but a segment of the grand narrative whole, a few dozen pages in a thousand-page work, which by retarding the narrative drive enhance its epic scope. Even when these cultural detours become a distraction, they never distract us for long, because soon the heroes get on with their loves, their wars, their lives. So do Solzhenitsyn's. Besides, if Stalin's catechistic tracts or Simonov's wooden tomes are no longer much read, or read at all, this is in no small measure due to Solzhenitsyn himself, indeed to the very novel I am discussing.

11

The governing metaphor in *The First Circle* is derived from Dante's multi-layered, upturned-cone representation of Hell, which the narrative sources as the framing referent for all the personalities and most of the personal situations depicted: when he began work on his novel, Solzhenitsyn used the code word "Dante."²⁰⁴ References to circles, circumferences, and spheres abound, and the association is invariably sinister, that is, infernal. The first word in the first chapter is a cognate to *krug* (circle): *Kruzhevnye strelki pokazyvali piat' minut piatogo*²⁰⁵ ("The filigreed hands pointed to five minutes past four").²⁰⁶ The clock in question, an ornate object of gilt and bronze, stands on Volodin's office shelf. From this point forward, the hero is accompanied, or haunted, by a private circular motif. At one point he tells Klara, as he draws a pattern of lines in the ground (the Russian soil itself a symbol) with a broken stick (that fracture itself a symbol),

> "You see this circle? That's our country. That's the first circle. Now here's the second". A circle with a larger diameter. "That is mankind at large. You would think that the first forms part of the second, wouldn't you? Not in the least! There are barriers of prejudice. Not to mention barbed wire and machine guns. To break through, physically or spiritually, is well-nigh impossible. Which means that mankind, as such, does not exist. There are only fatherlands, everyone's fatherland alien to everyone else's."[207]

Volodin's dark cartography implies that the gulag, Soviet Russia, and humanity as a whole are disconnected and circumscribed by concentric rings of evil, multiple infernos in an infernal universe. Here, as well as elsewhere in the text, we see a connection to Gogol's novel *Dead Souls*, in which Russia is transformed into a universalizing allegory of Hell derived from the same source, the *Divine Comedy*.

Yakonov invites Nerzhin to join a cryptographic project that will enable the mathematician to remain in the haven that is Marfino, yet "his heart said 'get thee behind me, Satan!'" (Mathew 4:10; 16:23): a literary, as well as a religious, injunction. Nerzhin refuses the offer. "You've traded the food of the gods for a mess of porridge," Yakonov hisses,[208] his own reference appropriately pagan. So when Solzhenitsyn's hero exclaims to his friend Rubin, "You struggle to believe in the triumph of your infernal Communism [*torzhestvo vashego chertovogo kommunizma*],[209] but try as you may, you don't believe,"[210] this is no throwaway trope.

The building at the Kaluga Gage where the Makarygins have their apartment is "semicircular"[211] (*polukruglyi*)[212] and so is the dormitory cell in Marfino Prison.[213] Nerzhin warns Nadya, whose "life, like his, had been crushed beneath the wheel of the gray prison truck,"[214] that his prison sentence may "escalate in a spiral."[215] Rubin and the Chekists Bulbanyuk and Smolosidov listen to the recording of Volodin's phone call in awestruck silence: "Everyone felt the touch of the fiery wheel."[216] The three men are using a magnetic tape machine whose twin reels, though left unmentioned, look like spoked wheels. Lieutenant Smolosidov, a dark-haired, dark-visaged creature, was once an MGB executioner. He is the novel's most emetic presence. As the mixed Chekist-zek threesome hearkens to the sound of Volodin's voice, the saturnine spook crouches like "a sullen black dog"[217] or "a black dragon."[218] Demon and hound, Smolosidov squats at the intersection of two figurative codes. The tape that is transmitting heat from "the fiery wheel" prompts thoughts of *Faust* and the black dog who "winds in wide spirals ... with a swirl of fire ... behind his track,"[219] the form in which Mephistopheles first manifests himself to Goethe's hero. Wheels and spirals and flames!

Gerasimovich and Bobynin walk in the exercise yard debating their predicament as the slaves of science while the extradiegetic narrator monitors their movements inside this constricted locus: "three-quarters of a circuit," "a quarter circle," "a half circle," "a full circle," "an eighth of a circle," "another circle," "another incomplete circle—a horseshoe."[220] Spatially and figuratively, the two men are talking in circles. And no, horseshoes are not always a talisman of good luck.

Even the contours of a woman's body or dress can be sinister in a circular, sexual sort of way. Promiscuous Lyuda's flaxen curls are "snares" that she casts for her male victims. More minatory still are the skirts of General Makarygin's wife, the covetous Alevtina. As the Makarygins arrive to inspect their new home, she stomps by a female prisoner washing the stairs on her hands and knees (the diegetic angle is that of her daughter, the empathetic Klara):

> The procurator's wife went past, almost brushing the charwoman's face with her heavily perfumed pleated skirt. Perhaps because the silk and the scents were too much for her, the woman, still bent over her bucket, raised her head to see whether there were many more of "them." To Klara that look of searing contempt was like the touch of red-hot metal. The expressive face smeared with dirty water was that of a sensitive and educated person.[221]

Those fragrant domes of silk draping Alevtina's flabby thighs hide bunches of petite demons.

On a related Dantean note, in the *Inferno* the poet arrives at the gates of Hell "in the middle of the journey of our life."[222] By the same token, *The First Circle* is a novel of captive middle age.

Volodin is thirty-years old, while Nerzhin turns thirty-two on Sunday, December 25, 1949, day two of the fictive proceedings;[223] Nadya is the same age as her husband, so is Pryanchikov, and Sologdin and Rubin are thirty-six. In fact, most of the zeks are in their thirties or forties, though several younger personalities are also present, notably Ruska, Simochka, and Klara. Three septuagenarians figure prominently, Professor Chelnov, Uncle Avenir, and Generalissimo Stalin. They are the elders of this fictive world: two good, one a ghoul.

As is the rule in Solzhenitsyn, much of the text takes the form of free indirect speech, while the extradiegetic narrator is a voice in his own right: sometimes sorrowful, sometimes ironic or humorous, and with a marked fondness for metaphors and similes. Only very rarely does he, or the author, go a trope too far, as in this description of a despairing Nadya: "She stood as though crucified on the black cross of the window frame"[224] (*Ona stoiala kak raspiataia na chërnoi krestovine okna*).[225]

Present in Yakonov's office when the colonel makes his offer to Nerzhin is one of the mathematician's former teachers at the University of Rostov, Dr. Verenyov. As the hero gazes at this figure from the past, he thinks back on his life's journey. Here his indirectly rendered thoughts segue into a threnodial reverie about the suffering of millions:

> To Nerzhin, set as he was in his prison ways, this pale man in the twinkling glasses was like a ghost unlawfully returning from a forgotten world, separated from today's world by the forests around Lake Ilmen, the hills and ravines of the Orel region, the sands and marshes of Belorussia, prosperous Polish farms, the tiled roofs of little German towns. Other memories were engraved on this nine-year interval between meetings: the bright, bare boxes and cells of the Lubyanka, the grime and stench of transit prisons, stifling compartments in prisoner-transport trains, cold and hungry zeks out in the biting wind of the steppes.[226]

The place names and geographical references in the opening sentence are arranged in an east to west sequence that adumbrates the itinerary of Nerzhin's frontline service: Lake Ilmen in Novgorod province was the scene of heavy fighting in early 1943, Oryol was liberated in August following the Battle of Kursk, Byelorussia and Poland were cleared of German troops in 1944, and Germany itself was invaded in early 1945. The hero and the author's respective military journeys are identical. Gleb's second, carceral, west to east itinerary also coincides with that of Solzhenitsyn, but only in part, and the chronologies now diverge: while the hero was transported from conquered East Prussia to the Lubyanka, thence to a camp in the Asian steppes, and *then* found himself assigned to the sharashka, Solzhenitsyn own gulag journey took him from the same German parts and via the Lubyanka (winter-spring-summer 1945) to two work camps in Moscow (1945–6), next to the sharashkas at Rybinsk and Zagorsk (1946–7) and then Marfino (1947–50), and finally to the Special Camp at Ekibastuz (1950–53).

To Prisoner Nerzhin, Verenyov is not quite real: a specter from a former life. The theme of two separate worlds recurs when the mathematician is driven to meet Nadya at Lefortovo Prison. Once again, the Nerzhin-inflected narration acquires a threnodic ring of sorrow, but now it is the zeks who are the ghosts, as we learn from this beautifully executed passage:

> These meetings were rather like those ancient Greek stelae, columns with bas-reliefs on which the deceased and their living relatives who had set up the monument were depicted together. But there was always a little space between this world and the world beyond the grave. The living gazed lovingly at the dead, while the dead looked toward Hades, with eyes neither cheerful nor sad, empty eyes, eyes that had seen too much.[227]

At the end of the novel Nerzhin and several other Marfino inmates are taken to the transfer jail in a van disguised as a meat delivery vehicle, and the narrative voice waxes epic, extradiegetic one last time:

> Yes, what awaited them was the taiga and the tundra, the Cold Pole at Oymyakon, the copper mines at Dzhezkazgan. What awaited them yet again was the pickax and the wheelbarrow, a starvation ration of half-baked bread, hospital, death. They could look forward to nothing but the worst.
> Yet in their hearts they were at peace with themselves.
> They were gripped by the fearlessness of people who have lost absolutely everything—such fearlessness is difficult to attain, but once attained, it endures.[228]

These words echo a theme that was voiced by two different characters earlier in the novel. The tough Bobynin warns General Abakumov: "The man from whom you've taken everything is no longer in your power; he is free again."[229] Even more striking is a throwaway remark by Gerasimovich: "There's probably only one way to make yourself invulnerable. . . . That's to kill all your affections and suppress all your desires."[230] Such is the essence of zek Buddhism: we recall the little statue in Nerzhin's story. The men in the prison van are "at peace." They have attained the transcendent state of which Gerasimovich spoke, a gulag nirvana.

Still, Solzhenitsyn prefers to end his novel on a wry, ironic note. As the prisoners are driven through Moscow in that cynically camouflaged conveyance, it is spotted by the correspondent of *Libération*, a Paris newspaper. The

Frenchman is on his way to an ice hockey match. (While it is unlikely that a son of Gaul would have any interest, personal or professional, in this sport, for Solzhenitsyn it was emblematic of the regime's bread and circuses policy.) At the sight of the van with the word "Meat" emblazoned on its sides in four languages—one of *several* such vehicles he has seen that day—he jots down the thought that "the capital's food supplies are extremely well organized."[231] The informed reader might assume that this is a dig at Jean-Paul Sartre, the founder of an identically titled paper, and a writer who was the object of Solzhenitsyn's particular "aversion."[232] The informed reader would be wrong: Sartre started his revolutionary broadsheet in 1968. In fact, Solzhenitsyn merely wanted to give the Frenchman's fellow-traveling publication a name with a "generically" progressive ring:[233] an instance of anti-Sartrian serendipity, but nothing more.

12

The characters' ethical and physical selves are scripted by means of two supercodes, one demonic/angelic (binary), the other, zoological/ornithological/botanical (multifactorial). They mark the men and women depicted as good or evil or, middlingly, both, ranking them within and across their institutional, social, and family environments. Over the length of the novel these metaphorical valuations aggregate into a hierarchic schema that frames every persona's words and deeds, as well as the political causes they serve, support, or oppose.

The first code is derived from the controlling literary referents, Dante's *Inferno* and Goethe's *Faust*, as well as the realms of religion and myth, and usually denotes ethical darkness. For Nerzhin and Volodin, the Soviet terror state is, respectively, a "dragon"[234] or a "Leviathan";[235] prisoner Potapov warns prisoner Khorobrov, who is impatient to "clear off" work, not to "tease the dragon";[236] and in a Herculean moment of self-delusion, Stalin imagines his enemies as a many-headed "hydra":[237] the aging tyrant is a legend in his own mind.

The second code is unique to the text, and is directly descriptive of the characters' appearance and behaviors. In his character portrayals, Solzhenitsyn usually confines himself to describing the upper third or half of the body, so as the reader works his way through these 700 pages he encounters dozens of bizarrely shaped faces, necks, torsos, and bellies that might have been drawn by a Hogarth or a Cruikshank.

Now, among the great tyrannies of the twentieth century, the Stalin's Soviet Union was as personalized as Hitler's Germany. In discourse and deed, the men populating the hierarchies of power were but proxies and simulacra of the supreme leader, and presented themselves as such. Accordingly, Stalin, the arch- or alpha-fiend of the novel's infernal world, is served by a coterie of grotesque familiars. His Chekists and partocrats are variously bovine, bestial, or demonic, with the notable exception of lavender Lieutenant Nadelashin. We meet dozens of Stalin stooges, metonymically or metaphorically configured, as they go about their bad business, while the old man in the generalissimo's uniform presides over it all from his armor-plated citadel in the darkened Russian countryside.

And so, on to those bods and phizogs.

Saussurian semiotics posits that the relationship between a sign and the real-life or lowlife object it signifies is not natural or causal, but arbitrary. Yet sometimes an insult or slur can seem significantly fitting. Discussing what he calls Hermetic semiosis, that is, signification through similitude, Umberto Eco observes that

> the word *pig* is neither similar to a swine nor to Noriega or Ceausescu; nevertheless, on the grounds of a culturally established analogy between the physical habits of swine and the moral habits of dictators, I can use the word *pig* to designate one of the above-mentioned gentlemen.[238]

If anything, Eco is too circumspect. Analogies and allegories are culture-specific; physical resemblances, less so. The visual record shows that tyrants and their minions often have faces or bodies that are porcine; saurian; batrachian; piscine; even vermicular. Volodin thinks of Andrei Zhdanov and Aleksandr Shcherbakov, two (peacefully) deceased members of Stalin's leadership group, as "greasy swine."[239] He is spot-on, snout-on: one need only take a look at Zhdanov's official portrait, which shows a coarse-featured man with a mustache, his skin glistening with sebaceous oil. Fugly, blubbery Shcherbakov is just as pinguid, so Volodin scores semiotically there as well.

Clearly, Solzhenitsyn had a thing about political bad looks. He was fascinated by totalitarian faces and bodies and enjoyed imaginatively reconfiguring them as indicators of their owners' unworth: *ad hominem* elides into *ad bestiam*. In his programmatic statement on this subject, the writer makes a point similar to Eco's, emphasizing the semantic or narrative economy of this kind of second-order signification:

> I have long had a dream: what if some photographer were to put together an album entitled **The Dictatorship of the Proletariat**. No captions, no

text, just **faces**: two or three hundred conceited, well-fed, somnolent or fierce **mugs**, getting into cars, climbing onto podiums, ensconced behind their desks.[240]

Solzhenitsyn's satirical physiognomics of tyranny work just as well for Nazi Germany or Democratic Kampuchea or the Central African Empire, or the despotisms of our own twenty-first century. All one needs to do is go online and pull down a few photos from a few government websites.

So much for Stalinist phizzes, but what about Stalinist names? Here, too, real life seemed to generate its own mordant commentary, as we learn in *The Gulag Archipelago*. The empirical perpetrators of the regime's crimes, Solzhenitsyn discovered, came onomastically pre-coded:

> One might almost think they were hired because of those names. For example, in the Kemerovo Provincial State Security Administration, there were: a prosecutor named *Trutnev*, "drone"; a chief of the interrogation section Major *Shkurkin*, "self-server"; his deputy, Lieutenant Colonel *Balandin*, "skilly," and an interrogator Skorokhvatov, "quick-grabber." ... Are we to assume that nothing is at all expressed in people's family names and such a concentration of them?[241]

In *The First Circle*, Stalin is attended by his personal dogsbody, Aleksandr Poskryobyshev, a historical figure who was the general secretary's secretary. "There were four short knocks, or rather not so much knocks as a muffled sound, as if a dog was pawing the door."[242] We behold, or hear, a cringing cur, with the surname Poskryobyshev (Scratch-A-Bit) reconfigured as a serendipitous aptronym. The historical Poskryobyshev had much to cringe about. The generalissimo's bureaucratic batman, he was widowed in 1941, when his wife was shot by the secret police, but he carried on doggedly at the highest levels of government, until he lost his job and nearly his life shortly before Stalin's death, a victim of an intra-Party intrigue.

We get our first glimpse of the specimens staffing the secret police in chapter two. Lieutenants Tyukin and Kuleshov monitor all calls to the US Embassy. The two officers are units of bureaucratic freight: in Russian, their names are cognates to, respectively, *tiuk* (bale) and *kul'* (sack). While Tyukin's appearance is anonymous, his only physical peculiarity being a (syphilitically) flat nose, Kuleshov, a curly-haired, chubby-chinned fellow, suffers from an unusual skin condition:

Kuleshov decided to take a look at the sores on his left leg. They kept breaking out again and again for unknown reasons. They had been dressed with "brilliant green" zinc ointment and a streptocidal preparation, but instead of healing, the sores had spread under the scabs. The pain had begun to make walking uncomfortable.[243]

Kuleshov is a secondary or tertiary character, but here his all-too-human flesh comes alive, pathologically. The lieutenant's cutaneous lesions are symptomatic of leprosy; specifically, its most common form, multibacillary Hansen's disease. This is an encoded Dantean moment: in the *Inferno*, Canto XXIX, the poet observes leprous sinners who furiously scratch at their scabs. The author's decision to make his cherubic Chekist a victim of this medieval curse is the first in a long succession of body blows that the novel inflicts upon its Stalinist thugs and hacks. Most are monsters: bestial brutes, atavistic throwbacks, odious freaks, nightmarish goblins and orcs. Kuleshov, however, is not imaginatively deformed, but imaginatively diseased: political degeneracy, medicalized. Far more sinister than the leprous spook is that other Chekist, the loathsome Smolosidov, who is, we recall, a dog *and* a dragon, while Major Shikin, Marfino's security officer, is revoltingly canine *and* revoltingly scaly. "What a snake you are! What a dirty dog!" Spiridon thinks to himself as the major prepares to put him to the question.[244] Quentin Crisp once observed, "However low a man sinks he never reaches the level of the police." He forgot the qualifier "secret."

The folksy yardman's nickname for Major Shikin's colleague Major Myshin is The Snake.[245] Shikin approvingly (!) thinks of the snitch Siromakha as a "businesslike reptile."[246] Professor Chelnov was arrested for calling Stalin "a slimy reptile."[247] The dictator broods, then loses his train of thought: "He caught a brief glimpse of it, like the vanishing tip of a snake's tail."[248] When Nerzhin and Simochka exchange their first kiss, we encounter the novel's most romantic metaphor: "So the steel chain forged with such reptilian cunning snapped at the link that had been fashioned from a woman's heart."[249]

These ophidian motifs are first of all Biblical: "Upon thy belly shalt thy go, and dust shalt thou eat all the days of thy life" (Genesis 3:14). Secondly, they are Dantean, referring us to Canto XXIV of the *Inferno*, where snake-shaped devils torment the bodies of the damned: "…I saw a fearful throng of serpents and of kinds so strange that the memory yet chills my blood."[250]

For readers not prone to herpetophobia, Solzhenitsyn populates his novel with other categories of human/non-human hybrids.

Minister Abakumov, the owner of a "bull head"[251] on a muscular body, is a Stalinist Minotaur; the Marfino Special Prison is staffed with "the best security officers and archivists, the old bulls of the MGB herd";[252] General Oskolupov glares at Yakonov like a "maddened bull."[253] A minor referent in the novel is a book by Hemingway about "poor bamboozled bulls"[254] (perhaps *Death in the Afternoon*; 1932), as an unimpressed Nerzhin-Solzhenitsyn puts it to that Hemingway enthusiast, Rubin-Kopelev. A guard at the Lefortovo prison who has never heard of Hemingway is a "bull-necked gangster"[255] (*gangster s sheei pikadora*).[256] It is therefore zoologically significant that old-maidish Nadelashin's imprecation of choice is "a bull should toss you!"[257] (*byk tebia zabodai!*).[258] He knows whereof he curses. Occasionally a Stalinist zoomorph projects its inhuman nature upon the captive humans in its charge, as when Major Shikin warns the free workers about the prisoners' "reptilian interior."[259]

Back to the novel's herd bull, General Victor Abakumov. He enters the text as a shiny synecdoche, a "pair of golden shoulder-boards"[260] glittering importantly at the far end of his lavishly carpeted office: a massive, meaty ungulate in fancy dress, or dress uniform, his bureaucratic pasture a Persian rug.

The swine are more numerous than the bulls and the dogs, for in the novel's imaginative scheme of things the porcine trumps the bovine or the canine. The quondam Marxist, Nerzhin, recalls that once upon a time he used to "[wallow] in the dialectic like a piglet burying its snout in muck."[261] Stalin, he scoffs, is a "hog's brain"[262] (*borov tupoi*).[263] When Gleb is visited by a nightmare vision of a communist world government, he sees "Party hogs" living it up "behind ten fences in the gardens of California."[264] Think Comrades Eugene Dennis and William Foster at a new address in Beverly Hills. It is therefore fitting that Stepanov, the Marfino Party secretary, is a pig farmer on the side. California, here I grunt!

The novel's system of body signs includes a botanical sequence. General Bulbanyuk has a head "like a grotesquely overgrown potato with three bulges for ears and nose."[265] The charmless Chekist is a human vegetable, but the Russian text, though not the English translation, also tells us that his neck is like that of an ox (*volov'ia sheiia*),[266] so he is both tubular and taurine. This ruminant potato head is no figure of fun. When Bulbanyuk tasks Rubin with identifying the caller to the US embassy, the general first employs positive reinforcement, appealing to the philologist as "a Communist once" who may become "a Communist again someday," but goes on to warn him that should Rubin reveal the secret, he will be "annihilated."[267] Carrots and sticks, or beef and potatoes, MGB-style.

And then there is ex-Colonel Yakov Mamurin.

Formerly the head of the communications department at the interior ministry, this officer fell victim to the materialization of the tyrant's word:

> One day the Leader of All Progressive Mankind, on the telephone to the Chinese province of Yenan, had been annoyed by interference and crackling in the receiver. He rang up Beria and said in Georgian:
> "Lavrenty! What sort of idiot is in charge of communications in your department? Remove him."[268]

The onetime communications chief is a rum-looking cove. A working-class prisoner feels disgust at his pale eyes, lemony skin, and skull-like head: "Vermin! Like something out of a lab jar!"[269] Mamurin, it turns out, is in a triple textual bind, for not only does the sharp-tongued zek call him a fetus in a flask, but the other inmates nickname him the Man in the Iron Mask, while the narrator describes him, with a hint of pity, as a "pale ghost."[270] In the sharashka, the ex-colonel enjoys certain privileges. He resides in a room, not a cell, with a few sticks of furniture and a potted plant, but the window has bars. Once a month he is allowed to spend a night with his family in their apartment. In a Dantean universe where every man and woman occupies an assigned infernal or terrestrial slot, Mamurin is that impossible thing, a liminal figure: "The world of free men had rejected him, and he was too fastidious to join the world of zeks."[271]

Mamurin still adulates his "god," Joseph Stalin.[272] So what is a neglected, tyrant-worshipping ghost to do? Seek solace in literature, of course. Like the medical versifier Vdovushkin in "Ivan Denisovich," the cashiered Chekist is a prison poet:

> At first, he read a great deal in his solitude: *The Struggle for Peace; Knight of the Golden Star; Russia's Glorious Sons;* then the verses of Prokofiev and Gribachev and ... he underwent a miraculous transformation: He began writing verse himself! It is well known that poets are born of unhappiness and spiritual torment, and Mamurin's torments were more agonizing than those of any other prisoner.[273]

To quote Oscar Wilde, all bad poetry is sincere. Still, it is a totalitarian truth not universally acknowledged that with the right motivation, even the bluntest of pens can produce poetry for the ages. For didn't Yuri Andropov, the cadaverous KGB chief, enjoy rhyming in his spare time? Or what about Anatoly

Lukyanov, the chairman of the last Soviet parliament and anti-Gorbachev conspirator-in-chief? As lyrical as Andropov, this jowly apparatchik wrote reams of sentimental doggerel during his incarceration after the failed communist putsch of 1991, which he later published under the alias Osenev, or Autumn Man. The autumn of the partocrat... As for the books that specifically inspired Mamurin's literary metamorphosis, they form part of the anti-bibliography of SocRealist literature continually scripted in the novel.

The ghoulish Mamurin's verselets are as repulsive as the man himself. Upon reading them Rubin is so appalled that he begins to avoid the Iron Mask. Alas, we are never shown a sample of the ex-colonel's collected works. But we can picture the product: crude iambs crudely strung together, a base imagination struggling with hackneyed metaphors, in the manner of Russian literature's most celebrated bad poet, Captain Lebyadkin in *Devils*, a novel about an earlier generation of political fiends.

We saw how the text's monstrological and animal codes come together to shape its representation of the Stalinists. In the case of Simochka, Nerzhin's prison love interest, a different figurative conflation takes place: she is both "sparrowlike"[274] (*pokhozhaia na ptichku*)[275] and angelic (see her full name, Serafima). Simochka's avian traits are vested in her tiny body and frail bones, which "might have been filled with air; ... she was as weightless as a bird that looks bigger because of its feathers."[276] Nerzhin calls her his "little quail"[277] (*perepëlochka*).[278] She wears shawls, variously described as goat's-hair or mohair.

That bird-like quality and those shawls connect her to etheral Agnia ("chaste" in Greek, but also homophonically close to the Russian *angel*—"angel"), the "girl from some other world"[279] who many years ago was engaged to Anton Yakonov. Wandering the streets of the capital after a brutal conversation with Abakumov, the sharashka director recalls her gazing upon old Moscow and its domed, doomed churches, when she was illumed by their "golden radiance ... a yellow shawl around her shoulders, screwing up her eyes at the sun and looking golden herself."[280]—"And there appeared a great wonder in heaven; a woman clothed with the sun" (Revelation 12:1). As this otherworldly girl listened to her worldly boyfriend making plans for the future, "the transparent yellow shawl ... slipped down over her bent elbows and looked like a pair of delicate golden wings."[281] Yakonov remembers that "sometimes, when she was talking, her brows and nostrils quivered as though she were about to take flight."[282] That conversation with Agnia occurred "two days before the Nativity of the Mother of God,"[283] and the Woman Clothed With the Sun is traditionally identified with the Virgin Mary.

Agnia of the golden wings is a sister to golden-haired Nina Diomidova in *Love the Revolution*. One scholar speculates that Agnia's conventual quality links her to Liza Kalitina in *Home of the Gentry* by Turgenev.[284] Perhaps he is right: Yakonov's former fiancée would certainly be happier in a nunnery, whither the tragic Liza withdraws at the end of that novel, than married to the fleshy, pleasure-loving military engineer. Yet Liza is also passionate and sensual, whereas Agnia is strangely enervated. There is a listlessness about her that suggests she is not long for this (Soviet) world. A walk uphill or even an animated conversation can leave her exhausted, and when she submits to Anton's advances her kisses are "slack"[285] and she finds the physical side of love revolting. "... I just don't want to live," she explains.[286] Her boyfriend, we infer, is drawn to her by her unsoiled, spiritual quality, but what it is that attracts Agnia to him remains a mystery. Yet love him she does: "Every morning she looked apprehensively for any change in the way he behaved toward her."[287] She tells her baffled gallant that she dislikes Natasha Rostova in *War and Peace* "because she wouldn't let Pierre join the Decembrists" (she means, after the novel ends).[288] Solzhenitsyn's heroine explains herself through Russian literature, a favored trope in Russian literature. Indeed, this melancholy creature has nothing in common with Natasha in either of her iterations, as Tolstoy's eternal adolescent feminine or his exemplary fecund matron, for they inhabit different bodies, different texts. And once Yakonov emerges from his reverie, Agnia evanesces somewhere beyond the fictive horizon. Perhaps like the fallen angel in H. G. Wells's novel *The Wonderful Visit* (1895), she saw the earth as an ugly Land of Dreams[289] inhabited by "mythical monsters,"[290] of which Solzhenitsyn's fictive worlds have so many.

Volodin is also associated with avian themes, a kind of legacy from his late mother. The handwriting in her diaries looks "as though a wounded bird had skimmed the page and scratched an erratic trail with its faltering claw."[291] As the diplomat contemplates the possibility of arrest, "he threw back his head as a bird does to let water trickle down its taut throat."[292] The gesture recurs when his fears come to pass and he lands in the clutches of the MGB. Summoned to his first interrogation, "Innokenty put his hands behind him, and with his head thrown back, like a bird swallowing water, walked out of the box."[293] Gerasimovich, we recall, has his own bird-like body signature as "a puny sparrow of a man," though inside him beats "a heart as big as a cat"[294] (*serdtse s koshku*).[295] This last line, derived from a Russian proverb (*Sam s vorob'ia, a serdtse s koshku*[296]—"As small as a sparrow, but with a heart as big as a cat"), alludes to the authoritarian nature of his political views, for in the novel cats number among the top metaphorical predators. Other than stouthearted, cat-hearted Gerasimovich, feline imagery is associated with the MGB and its minions. Oskolupov has "green cat's eyes,"²⁹⁷ Abakumov's scheming aide Mikhail Ryumin "walk[s] as noiselessly as a kitten,"²⁹⁸ and the sleazy snitch Siromakha scurries about "in a series of catlike jumps."²⁹⁹

At the other end from the dragons and the snakes, the bulls and the pigs, the dogs and the cats are Solzhenitsyn's "rabbits," the term used in *The First Circle* and *The Gulag Archipelago* to describe the prisoners of terror state. When the Marfino zeks mount a mini-rebellion, exposing Major Shikin's informers, that is, *rats*, the narrator comments, "This was an exceptional event not just at the Marfino Institute but in the whole history of the security services. Rabbits had every right to die. They had no right to fight back."³⁰⁰

But the "rabbits" do fight back and win a small victory. Defiant humanity trumps the bestial and the demonic. And so, hope endures.

13

Heinrich Böll compared *The First Circle* to a cathedral.³⁰¹ If he is right, then it is a cathedral in which the gargoyles loom larger than the saints, and the grossest of these grotesques is Stalin. Not that his predecessor, Vladimir Lenin, lacks a presence in the novel, but this is invariably transitory or derived. Then he scurries across the page like a troll, only to vanish into the shadows. Arguing with Rubin, Nerzhin criticizes the coarseness of Lenin's jibes against his liberal opponents: "'Paladins of logorrhea'! [*Rytsari slovobludiia!*]³⁰² It makes you sick to say it. Liberalism means love of freedom."³⁰³ Like the artist he is, Solzhenitsyn's hero has taste: to him, the Leninist style is as ugly and charmless as the physical man himself.

Stalin, on the other hand, is a major presence. Chapters nineteen to twenty-three, which show the aging despot brooding and scheming in his armorplated keep, are almost a novel-within-the-novel, the dark hub of *The First Circle*. There was a time when the author, carried away by the promise of Khrushchev's reforms, imagined them "cheerfully splashed ... over the pages of *Pravda*" under the title "One Night in the Life of Stalin."³⁰⁴ Such are the flights of fictive fancy.

Solzhenitsyn was right to be proud of his nocturnal study of the dictator. The only portrait by another writer that even comes close in capturing his grisly essence is the chapter about Stalin and his dentist in Anatoly Rybakov's novel *The Children of the Arbat* (*Deti Arbata*; 1987). Rybakov, however, gives us the tyrant in murderous middle age: Stalin the five-year planner, collectivizer, and purger. In *The First Circle*, the General Secretary is a couple of decades older, decaying inside and out, and preoccupied with thoughts of death, even if the will to slaughter still throbs within him.

In one provocative reading, *The First Circle* is an extended horror tale, with Marfino prison a sinister castle and Stalin "a traditional gothic villain of the vampiric kind":[305] a different kind of gothicism from the one so elegantly, if implicitly, adduced by Böll. There may well be something to this Stalin-the-undead interpretation, for what are the bloodsucking cadavers of legend if not the ultimate outsiders, outlanders of power?

In Russia, an autocrat may enhance his power mystique if he has a whiff of the Other about him. With the exception of the Polonized False Dmitry I (reigned 1605–6), the first example of this foreigner-as-ruler phenomenon was Peter the Great. In their transmission through the layers of national culture, the tsar's body image (great height, shaven face), European dress, and half-foreign speech, peppered with Dutch and Latin words, were transmuted into the composite figure of a gigantic, gibbering alien whom his terrified subjects identified as a forerunner of the Antichrist or even as the Son of Satan himself. Yet the vast majority of the population never saw their tsar or even his likeness. They acquired their sense of his foreignness at second remove, through rumor, travelers' tales, and for those who could read, seditious pamphlets and leaflets.

Stalin, however, had total control over his public presentation. Film and radio made his persona utterly familiar to the Soviet masses. A sallow-faced, heavily mustachioed Georgian who spoke with a thick Caucasian accent, he was visibly, audibly a foreigner. Unlike Peter, he did not emphasize his alien traits—on the 1937 census form he even identified himself as Russian—but ever the pragmatist, he put them to good use. His infrequent public speeches were an essential element of his pubic presentation, with each radio-transmitted pronouncement a vocal reminder of the terrible power behind the muffled mountain voice.

In *War and Peace* Tolstoy directs his authorial ire as much at Napoleon the *hero* as at Napoleon the *man*. Solzhenitsyn follows that precedent by first dismantling the Stalin myth and then tackling the historical, empirical Stalin. Indeed, there was much to dismantle. Seventy years ago, the Soviet dictator was the cynosure of all meanings, a communist master of the universe. Stories of him were everywhere, saturating the discursive spaces of the USSR to the exclusion of every other ideological narrative, including that of Vladimir Ilyich Lenin, or the Great October Socialist Revolution, or the Great Patriotic War. Or to put it differently, those narratives were subsumed into the Stalin legend, which covered factories, farms, institutions, social structures, artistic productions, scientific activities, landscapes, cityscapes, inscapes, outscapes, and outhouses in a fulvous fug of words and images, so that all these places and things were reduced to mere appurtenances of the Leader's life story. Stalin was the transcendental signifier of the past, present, and future. Madame de Staël's description of Napoleon as "the man who was going to take the place of everyone else and render the human race anonymous"[306] is much more applicable to the Soviet ruler, even if his intellectual and charismatic gifts were vastly inferior. Unlike the famous conqueror, however, the General Secretary had access to the technologies of modern propaganda, which transformed his biological body and political self into a glamorized cultural product, disseminated worldwide for consumption by the fanatical and the credulous.

In the opening lines of chapter nineteen the narrator lists the Leader's graven images, stressing their multiplicity, ubiquity, material form, and semiotic equivalence:

> On the ottoman lay a man whose likeness has been more often sculpted, painted in oils, watercolors, gouache, and sepia; limned in charcoal, chalk, and powdered brick; pieced together in a mosaic of road maker's gravel, or seashells, or wheat grains, or soybeans; etched on ivory; grown in grass; woven into carpets; spelled out by planes flying in formation; recorded on film… than any other face ever has been in the three billion years since the earth's crust was formed.[307]

(In a meta-proleptic twist, the ottoman happens to be the one on which Stalin expired by painful, urine-soaked stages on the night of March 5, 1953.) After this cleverly crafted stretch of catalogue prose comes a description of the physical person:

> Yet he was only a little yellow-eyed old man with gingery (not pitch black, as in his portraits), thinning (luxuriant according to his portraits) hair, with deep pockmarks in a gray face and a sagging dewlap (these last features were not portrayed at all), with uneven, blackened teeth, a mouth smelling of pipe tobacco, and fat, moist fingers that left marks on documents and books.[308]

This is Stalin redux, as eyes, hair, teeth, epidermis: a biological specimen. The aging partocrat, all flaccid septuagenarian flesh, is nothing like his coded likenesses. Instead of an icon of wisdom and power we behold a personage that is unimpressive and *insignificant*. In fact, twentieth-century tyrants, from Francisco Franco to Boleslaw Bierut, from Augusto Pinochet to Robert Mugabe, tended to be unprepossessing figures, puny bodies crowned with puny mustaches, whose official portraits must perforce beautify and enhance. By depicting Stalin as a pigeon-chested, oily-skinned old bod, Solzhenitsyn restores the physiological record. He extracts the human meat from inside the exoskeleton of myth. As depicted in *The First Circle*, the public Stalin is all text, but in his private, protected environment he is all flesh, a totalitarian oyster whose ancient tissues groan under the weight of his legend. It was canonized in the *History of the Communist Party of the Soviet Union: Short Course* (*Istoriia VKP(b). Kratkii kurs*; 1938), which the tyrant is shown perusing with acute readerly or writerly pleasure: large sections of the book were composed by Stalin himself.

The portraits in shells and soy beans and airplanes mock-solemnly enumerated by the narrator signified the mythical "Father of the Peoples of East and West," "Inspirer and Organizer of Victories," and "Coryphaeus of Linguistic Science"—just some of the dozens of Stalin cognomens that crop up in *The First Circle*. This treatment of Stalin myth is not just satirical, but dialogical, for as Solzhenitsyn later explained, it was meant to invite our readerly input: "The author's right, the author's duty, is to give his own picture and stimulate the reader's imagination."[309] We are prompted to match the glamorizing agricultural or aeronautical signifiers of Generalissimo Joseph Stalin against the *man* Joseph Dzhugashvili. And when we oblige, the Stalin sign collapses, having been rendered ridiculous, false, absurd, from the Latin *absurdum*—incongruous. The transcendental signifier is transcended!

What Solzhenitsyn gives us next, however, is not a historicized portrait but a historicized lampoon, albeit one with plenty of wit and range. Entombed in his aboveground bunker, wallowing in self-secreted malice and hate, attended by quailing cohorts, the geriatric Generalissimo calls to mind the most famous tyrant of them all, Adolf Hitler, who died a nocturnal, technological death in a similarly secret, hermetic environment. Stalin skulks and sulks, prowls and ponders inside his dimly lit lair. We learn his dismal thoughts, inner resentments, and (ir)rational fears. In this land of political contingency, where all live upon the Leader's sufferance, he too is contingent, prey to private terrors and phobias that gnaw at him daily, or rather nightly. The devil is in the details, as when we are shown the symptoms of the tyrant's lophobia, or fear of poison: "With a little key that he carried in his waistband, Stalin unlocked the metal lid of a decanter, poured himself a glass of his favorite cordial, drank it, and locked the decanter again."[310]

While much of what Stalin thinks and says and writes is either a direct quotation or a pastichean extrapolation, Solzhenitsyn permits himself considerable authorial licence. Notably, he infuses this dropout seminarian with a residual *timor Dei*, by showing him "praying properly," out of simple, stark fear, after the German invasion of 1941:

> At that time he had made a vow to God: If the danger passed and he survived in his post, he would restore the church and church services in Russia and would not let believers be persecuted and imprisoned. (It should never have been allowed in the first place; it had started in Lenin's time.) And when the danger was over, when Stalingrad was behind him, Stalin had done all that he had vowed to do.[311]

So, in a darkly Dostoevskian twist, the Church is restored by demonic fiat and the Generalissimo of Lies keeps his promise to the Lord of Hosts. Solzhenitsyn turns his Stalin, who dreams of becoming the "Emperor of the Planet" or "Emperor of the Earth,"[312] into a parody of Constantine the Great, the pagan Roman ruler who after defeating his rival Maxentius allowed Christian worship throughout his dominions. Eusebius tells us that after his victory, Constantine "continually made progress in piety towards God,"[313] but Solzhenitsyn's godless global emperor makes progress only toward Hell.

Stalin muses about his successes and failures as a double agent for the Okhrana, the tsarist secret police. Whether he ever was a spy—many scholars have their doubts—is beside the point. Solzhenitsyn is getting back at the despot in any way he can, by being fanciful as well as factual. The diarist Aleksandr Gladkov commented:

> Everything here rings true, with the exception perhaps of the psychological portrait of Stalin, who after all was a more complex personality, more complex in a Shakespearean sense: he was an evil-doer [*zlodei*], but a complex and unique one, whereas Solzhenitsyn, who hates him, simplifies him. Yet this is not a flaw but a certain artistic inevitability.[314]

Or as the writer later explained, "My view was that Stalin should reap the harvest of his secretiveness. He had lived mysteriously—so now anyone was entitled to write about him as he thought fit."[315]

There are some grimly funny moments, as when we learn that "a group of Moscow journalists had even suggested renaming the Volga and the moon after

[Stalin]"³¹⁶ or observe the Soviet autocrat toying with the idea of bringing back serfdom:

> Why not write it into the statutes of each collective farm that since the land belongs to it in perpetuity, everyone born in a particular village automatically acquires membership in the farm at birth? Represent this as a right and an honor. Launch a public-relations campaign immediately: "A Further Step along the Road to Communism," "Youth's Inheritance—the Collective Granary," ... well, the writers would find the best way to put it.³¹⁷

If in strictly historical terms Solzhenitsyn's Stalin is something of a chimera, language-wise he is pitch-perfect. The author does a wickedly accurate job of reconstructing the tyrant's idiolect with its simplified, Basic Russian vocabulary and catechistic cadences, what Arthur Koestler called "Djugashvilese." This is the voice that numerous Stalinists, from General Abakumov to Major Shikin, ventriloquize elsewhere in the novel. In some passages of direct speech, Solzhenitsyn employs enallage by phonetic transcription to reproduce that famous Georgian accent, with its stressed initial syllables and stretched *a*'s. This, though, may be a reconstruction too far, for it makes one think of those Hollywood films where a carpet-chewing Hitler rants in Teutonic English.³¹⁸ Still, the tyrant's Caucasian vocals are so textualized on only three or four occasions, as when he summons his servile Cerberus, Poskryobyshev, into his presence or lays down the law (or lack of it) to the quaking secret police chief, Abakumov.

The appetites of the flesh, which Stalin used to indulge freely, are now quiescent. Yet once in a while the Draculean drives that have propelled him so high and low can still flare up: "This was how he had celebrated his birthday. On the evening of the twentieth, Traicho Kostov had been done to death. Only when the dog's eyes glazed over could the real celebrations begin."³¹⁹ The unsympathetic Napoleon of *War and Peace* becomes sympathetic whenever the narrative focus shifts to his physical form, as in the scene of his matinal massage before the battle of Borodino. Solzhenitsyn's Stalin lacks a single attractive trait. Rubin may insist that the Soviet leader is "at once the Robespierre and the Napoleon of our Revolution,"³²⁰ but he is more sociopath than socialist, and a senile one at that, his best years and crimes behind him. Vampire or mortal, *this* Stalin has lost his style.

And so, he reminisces. His memories are a succession of self-glorifying or self-pitying projections of his decrepit present self into the recent or distant past. Once again, Lenin sneaks into the text, the object of Stalin's retrospective resentments and jealousies as his onetime "rash and superficial" patron.[321] As for Trotsky, the Generalissimo remembers him as a "clown"[322] with "oratorical pretensions."[323] However, the dictator has a soft spot for another former adversary:

> There was one man he had trusted, and only one, in a life free of trust and mistakes. In the eyes of the world, that man had seemed so firm in friendship and in enmity, he had swung around so sharply and held out his hand in friendship. This was no windbag; this was a man of action!
> And Stalin had believed him!
> That man was Adolf Hitler.[324]

As one historian puts it, "Thus did Hitler's psychopathic mendacity trump Stalin's pathological mistrust."[325]

No doubt Solzhenitsyn's paranoid, lophobic Stalin is quite mad. The Generalissimo's nostalgic regrets about the rupture of the Nazi-Soviet pact, like so much else in this novel-within-the-novel, are fictional, in both senses of the word. Still, they have the ring of truth. Svetlana Alliluyeva reports that as World War II was drawing to a close, her father would often say, "Alas, together with the Germans we would have been invincible."[326] Indeed, the tyrants of that generation had a collegial appreciation of each other's genocidal professionalism, sharing a "system of values that calibrated morality by degrees of perceived ruthlessness."[327] In 1920, Mussolini referred to Lenin as "an artist who has worked in men as others have worked in marble or metal"[328] and two years later Lenin returned the compliment by describing him as "a first-rate man who would have led our party to power in Italy."[329] In 1938 the Duce declared that Stalin had "transformed itself into a fascist,"[330] while during the war Hitler hailed Stalin, albeit in private, as "one of the most extraordinary figures in world history"[331] who deserved "unconditional respect" and "in his own way is a hell of a fellow."[332] Earlier, the Soviet leader had been impressed by the Fuehrer's actions during the Night of the Long Knives: "Some fellow that Hitler! Splendid! That's a deed of some skill."[333] And then there is Stalin's notorious toast of 1939, offered at a Kremlin reception for Joachim von Ribbentrop, the Nazi foreign minister, and quoted in the novel: "I know how the German people loves its Führer, and I therefore drink to his health!"[334] Even after the Soviet victory, Stalin retained his respect for the late Reich Chancellor: "I agree that he was an adventurer but I can't agree he was mad. Hitler was a gifted man. Only a gifted man could unite the German people."[335] (What a pedestrian comment, you might say. But then, as Perry Anderson writes, "Banalities are by definition accurate,"[336] and the Stalin we meet in the novel is nothing if not banal.)

Solzhenitsyn's Stalin is associated with the East: *The Gulag Archipelago* describes him as a "Khan" with an "out-and-out Oriental character,"[337] and *The First Circle* follows the same interpretation, as can be seen from its parodic reproductions of the Generalissimo's Caucasian vocals. In "March the Fifth" ("Piatoe marta"; 1953), a poem that is the most extreme instance of Russocentric othering in any Solzhenitsynian text—it was composed days after the author's release from the special camp and conveys a hatred of the tyrant that can only be understood in that context—the poetic subject expresses mixed feelings about the passing of "the Great Mogul," or "pockmarked Yusuf":

> I feel joy and relief, but also regret: you escaped Russian vengeance,
> you outwitted us, my Georgian chum![338]

The five Stalin chapters, and the novel wherein they are encased, are a literary act of "Russian vengeance," long deferred, but finally inflicted.

... And eventually, amended. In the *Literary Collection*, Solzhenitsyn speculates that Stalin's fondness for Mikhail Bulgakov's play *The Days of the Turbins* (*Dni Turbinykh*; 1925), which he saw performed nineteen times, might be taken as evidence that the dictator, surrounded as he was by Party sycophants and "the distorted and flattened scene that was Soviet dramaturgy and literature," "occasionally felt a compensatory need to see for himself that independent, proud people do exist."[339] The writer's admiration for his "brother," Bulgakov, led him to concede the possibility, however faint, that even Stalin's totalizing cynicism had its limits.

14

If there is a category of characters in Solzhenitsyn's fictions who rank as low as secret policemen and their snitches, it is members of the procuracy, those goldbraided perpetrators of Stalinist injustice. He holds them in the same contempt that Tolstoy reserved for his judges. Pyotr Makarygin, a prosecutor in political cases and Volodin's father-in-law, is among the novel's least sympathetic presences. He has consigned hundreds of men and women to the gulag. Yet callous and brutal though he is, he is also one of this writer's most memorable creations, a character of Tolstoyan vividness whose very coarseness, human and behavioral, is meticulously scripted. The Makarygin story line was Solzhenitsyn's first attempt to show a multi-generational family and to describe the private lives of the Soviet elite, a novelistic line of inquiry continued in *Cancer Ward* with its depiction of the personnel director Pavel Rusanov with wife, children, and pet Alsatian.

The patriarch of the Makarygin clan enters the fictive proceedings in a stately manner, introduced as he is by his full name, military rank, academic qualifications, and professional experience:

> Major General Pyotr Afanasyevich Makarygin, candidate in Juridical Sciences, had behind him a long career as prosecutor in "special cases," meaning those of which the public was for its own good best left in ignorance and which were therefore dealt with discreetly.[340]

This judicial brute boasts the same heavy build as the other middle-aged Stalinists in the book, but his appearance is far from anonymous. The general's blunt head is decorated by a pair of large and drooping ears weirdly reminiscent of "the wings on a sphinx,"[341] a trait that calls to mind another important bureaucrat in another famous work. Tolstoy's Aleksei Karenin also had funny ears, although despite his marital shortcomings he was an altogether more attractive human being. Or what about Senator Ableukhov in Andrei Bely's novel *Petersburg*, whose "pair of protruding ears were of a distinct, and not altogether pleasant, pale-green color: his ears looked as though they belonged to a corpse"?[342] Or the "pink ear-wings" of the Guardian S-4711 in *We*?[343] It would be plausible to conclude that when we encounter a high official in a Russian novel, it's all outside the head, and *August 1914*, with its portrait of Konstantin Pobedonostsev, the notorious Procurator of the Holy Synod, confirms this deduction: "Hollow cheeks ... big glasses ... ears sticking out as though aghast at the growing wickedness of this hopeless world."[344]

Nietzsche's Zarathustra *spoke* out *thus* on the subject of otic hypertrophy:

> And when I came out of my solitude and crossed over this bridge for the first time I did not trust my eyes and looked and looked again, and said at last, "An ear! An ear as big as a man!" I looked still more closely—and indeed, underneath the ear something was moving, something pitifully small and wretched and slender. And, no doubt of it, the tremendous ear was attached to a small, thin stalk—but this stalk was a human being![345]

In light of these literary and philosophical associations, Makarygin's last name is apt: in Serbo-Croatian, the native language of his friend Radovich, *magarac* means "donkey." I should add that General Abakumov is another figure whose hearing organs are a deaf giveaway. In Stalin's presence, they invariably "filled with blood and became red hot, and whenever this happened, Abakumov feared that his continuously burning ears would arouse the Boss's suspicion."[346]

Unlike the cerebral Karenin or skeletal Ableukhov, sphinx-eared Makarygin is a bon vivant who enjoys the Soviet good life, and he has much to enjoy. The prosecutor's zek-built apartment is crammed with the kind of massive furniture and heavy rugs typical of prosperous homes of the period, whether in Moscow, Chicago, or Buenos Aires. Presiding over this cluttered domestic environment is Makarygin's dough-bodied wife, Alevtina Nikanorovna, whose plebeian name is a sure indicator of her rustic or lower-class urban origins. Alevtina is a Stalinist *Hausfrau* with a craving for shiny things such as silver cutlery and cut glass, as well as bed and table linens, oriental carpets and antiques, "never missing a good buy—at closed auctions, in the private shops for employees in the procuratorial and judicial system, in commission shops, or in the flea markets of 'newly incorporated territories.'"[347] The apartment and the plethora of objects inside it must be cleaned, dusted, and polished, to which end the general's wife employs a Bashkir maid whom she directs with a firm if pudgy hand. Actually, Alevtina happens to be the second Mrs. M. Her predecessor in matrimony, a "proficient" machine-gunner whose "life was regulated by the latest instructions from her Party cell,"[348] died giving birth to Klara, the youngest of the prosecutor's three daughters.

As a character, Pyotr Makarygin comes into his own in chapters sixty-two to sixty-four, which describe a reception in his apartment "given ... with classically bourgeois luxury" (Heinrich Böll)[349] after he is awarded the Red Banner of Labor (yes, there is some irony here). In truth, by this time the Red Banner was seen as a middling honor.[350] Mikhail Gorbachev, seventeen, received one for his exploits as a combine harvester driver on a collective farm that very same year. Still, the order was large and garish, like most Soviet decorations, and was designed to appeal to the homespun tastes of the New Soviet Man or Woman. It certainly fills the prosecutor, as vain as the next Stalinist, with not-so-secret joy.

In addition to Comrade and Mrs. Makarygin, present that evening are the two sons-in-law, Galakhov and Volodin, with their wives; Makarygin's colleague Slovuta, another major-general-at-law, fresh from conducting a show trial of Japanese "war criminals" in the Far East; Makarygin's chum Radovich, the old-time, old-line Bolshevik; the prosecutor's young female relative whom Shchagov hopes to marry; Shchagov himself; Klara Makarygina's occasional escort, the critic Golovanov; Klara herself; a few of her former fellow students, including a shy, pretty girl and a communications expert employed jamming Western radio broadcasts; and a balding fellow in his twenties holding high rank on the staff of the Supreme Soviet, whom Mrs. Makarygina would dearly love to see as Klara's husband.

As a set piece social occasion, the three chapters are a homage to *War and Peace*, for the Makarygin reception is hypertextually modeled on the soirée in the salon of Anna Schérer described in the opening pages of that novel. Meant by the general to play the part of in-house celebrities for the evening—the role assigned by Madame Schérer to the Vicomte de Mortemart and the Abbé Morio—are his two sons-in-law:

> It was for Slovuta's sake that they had invited Innokenty so pressingly, insisting that he should come in his diplomatic uniform, with the gold braid, and so, together with their other son-in-law, the celebrated writer Nikolai Galakhov, make the occasion no ordinary one.[351]

Volodin enters this festive gathering "sour faced,"[352] almost the picture of jaundiced Prince Andrei surveying Madame Schérer's guests with misanthropic disdain. A day has passed since the diplomat's fateful phone call and he is oppressed by a sense of foreboding. He also feels estranged from his wife, again like Andrei. Still, his mood soon improves and he engages Galakhov in animated conversation. The exchange, in which Volodin's brother-in-law does his best to justify his status as a living classic of SocRealism, is the only instance in the novel when a servant of the terror state attempts to explain himself to a critically minded interlocutor.

While Galakhov and Volodin sit there talking, Dotnara or Dotty, as the diplomat's beautiful wife prefers to be known, walks over to join them. This evening she is not her usual exuberant self. She seems shy, even timorous. Volodin's husbandly eye picks out a tiny tremor in her upper lip. He knows that this is a sign she is feeling amorous, and although he has not slept with her for months, he finds that trembling "doe-like" lip and her "meekness" toward him erotically enticing.[353] Physically the blonde and voluptuous Dotty is very different from darkly pretty, pregnant Lise Bolkonsky, but that tiny cervine detail links her across texts and centuries to Tolstoy's "little princess" whose "pretty little upper lip ... was too short for her teeth, but ... lifted all the more sweetly."[354]

The whilom proletarian Makarygin may not have Madame Schérer's aristocratic French or aristocratic manners, but his modest social skills are more than adequate for this social occasion. He carefully monitors the behavior of the invitees (the rustic Alevtina would have been utterly useless in this regard): "Makarygin had been desperately maneuvering to prevent Radovich from firing off some provocative remark, to keep Slovuta happy, and to make sure Galakhov was not bored."[355] We recall Madame Schérer invigilating her guests as she "moved about her drawing room, approaching now a silent, now a too-noisy group, and by a word or slight rearrangement kept the conversational machine in steady, proper and regular motion."[356] That lady was particularly concerned about Andrei's friend Pierre Bezukhov, a serious young man with serious ideas, and watched him with a beady eye lest he launched into some inappropriate disquisition upon Napoleon or the Concert of Europe. Here Pierre's counterpart is Radovich, a serious old man with serious ideas. An unreconstructed Leninist who used to teach at the Institute of Red Professors, he is out of place, out of time at this Stalinist soirée. At one point the host actually shakes a beefy prosecutorial finger in his direction, warning him to toe the party line.

If Makarygin intends for Volodin and Galakhov to serve as the evening's social ornaments, twenty-four-year-old Vitaly, the Supreme Soviet staffer, is the invited man of influence, a youthful analogue to Prince Kurakin, the courtier whom Princess Drubetskaya successfully importunes to obtain a posting for her son with the Guards. As the party gets going, the balding sub-parliamentarian finds himself on the receiving end of a great deal of attention from Klara's pretty friend. She flirts a little, then pulls him aside to ask if he could arrange the release from a Siberian work camp of her father, who was recently paralyzed by a stroke. Unlike Kurakin, however, "the budding statesman"[357] Vitaly is unwilling to help. He articulates his refusal in judiciously heartless tones: "'If we take that line, what will be left of the whole legal code?' He grinned. 'After all, he was duly tried and found guilty! Just think! What if he does die in the camp? People die in camps just like anywhere else.'"[358] These words and that grin qualify the milquetoast apparatchik as one of the novel's most hateful presences.

Dushan Radovich, on the other hand, is considerably more sympathetic. To a Russian ear, his authentically Serbian name is irresistibly reminiscent of the phrase *dusha raduetsia*—"the soul rejoices." Yet the name is a wry joke. There is nothing soulful, nothing joyful about the Red Professor, a desiccated twig of a man. "Radovich was wearing a threadbare semimilitary tunic, and his skin was dark parchment stretched over a blocky head."[359] Later we learn more about the political history of this Bolshevik body:

> He had a splinter from one of Kolchak's shells in his chest, he had suffered from a duodenal ulcer for fifteen years, and every morning for many years

past he had carried out the excruciating procedure of irrigating his stomach through the esophagus, without which he could not eat and go on living.[360]

In one of the novel's quasi-Pasternakian coincidences, Radovich had got to know Abramson during the war, when the veteran Trotskyist had enjoyed a few months of freedom. He told the Serb about the interrogation methods of Stalin's secret police, thereby convincing the old Bolshevik that the revolution had indeed been betrayed.

As often happens with elderly radicals whose time is past, Radovich is both tragic and ridiculous. He stalks the Makarygins' model apartment like a stiff-limbed mummy from some dusty political tomb. Still, he has his hopes. The fanatical Red Professor looks forward to the approaching war between the United States and Britain "over markets," impatient to see the triumph of world communism ensue dialectically from this preordained clash of imperialisms.[361]

A detail of clothing illustrates the way things have changed for the socialist Serb. For many years come rain or shine he had worn his old Budenny helmet, the spiked Red Army cap of civil war vintage, until the police began pulling him in as a suspicious character: following the Soviet Union's Winter War with Finland (1939–40) the *budenovka* had been scrapped, a change in the regime's artifactual lexicon. Totalitarian fashions are politically seasonal. In 1949 a sartorial anachronism like Radovich's might have had consequences as grave as Tveritinov's slip of the tongue in "Incident at Kochetovka Station." The Red Professor, however, was wise to the danger and got rid of his revolutionary headgear.

The presence (and absence) of the *budenovka* on Radovich's leathery head has a transtextual polemical function. The Thaw period, during which the first versions of the novel were written, witnessed a short-lived re-mythologization of early Soviet history by a younger generation of artists for whom the Red Army helmet of yore became a neo-Romantic symbol. In the song "Sentimental March" ("Sentimental'nyi marsh"; 1957) by the guitar bard Bulat Okudzhava, the lyrical/revolutionary persona imagines his heroic death in some future war of national or proletarian liberation: "And commissars in dusty helmets will lean in silence over me."[362]

In addition, the *budenovka* held a private mnemonic resonance for the author. His earliest memory was as a three-year-old, when "the Chekists wearing their pointed caps [*ostrokonechnye shapki*] entered the Church of St. Panteleimon in Kislovodsk, stopped the service, and with a thunderous clamor marched to the altar, which they then looted."[363] *The Road* describes how in 1932 his grandfather Zakhar Shcherbak decided to give himself up to the "Spike Heads" (*ostrogolovye*), that is, the Chekists, and walked into their Rostov headquarters wearing "a wooden cross over his shirt."[364] In Russian folklore, notes Solzhenitsyn's commentator, demons are depicted as having prong-shaped heads.[365]

Presently Makarygin, Slovuta, and Radovich repair to the study, a constituent element in the novel's hierarchy of political loci which also includes, in descending order of power projection, four other offices: Stalin's at his dacha, Abakumov's at the ministry of state security, Yakonov's at the sharashka, and Volodin's at the foreign ministry (Makarygin's office ranks between those of Abakumov and Yakonov). The prosecutor is a collector of rare tobaccos, a fact that gives this room, in which the narrative brings together the codes of political power and domesticity, its distinctive Makaryginesque character: the workspace as puff-space. We are shown

> a small, oval table of dark wood, placed conveniently in the study to hold cigarette papers and a roller for filling them, a selection of pipes in a rack, and a mother-of-pearl ashtray. Near the table stood a tobacco cabinet of Karelian birchwood with numerous drawers containing a variety of cigarettes with cardboard mouthpieces, cigarettes without mouthpieces, cigars, pipe tobaccos, and even snuff.[366]

The room contains other emblematic objects. Occupying fully half the desk is a colossal inkstand in the shape of the Kremlin, with tower and turrets. We may assume that this bureaucratic toy is of a piece, architecturally speaking, with another Soviet-themed gewgaw, the "massive writing set—a model of the Kremlin" owned by Aleksei Tolstoy in "Apricot Jam."[367] Also on display are the volumes of law books that Makarygin never reads and his decorations, among which the newly minted Order of the Red Banner, as big as a saucer, dazzles the eye. Completing the decorative details are a portrait of Stalin in his generalissimo's uniform, a bust of Lenin on a shelf, and next to it a photograph of the first Mrs. Makarygina brandishing a Mauser pistol in classic revolutionary fashion.

As Makarygin, Slovuta, and Radovich draw on their cigars, the two generals exchange the kind of self-satisfied banter typical of successful middle-aged men everywhere. Meanwhile the Serb seethes amid the clouds of smoke, trying to restrain himself from interrupting that pair of Stalinists with some anti-Stalinist jibe. For Radovich is an idealist in a country ruled by cynics. As a soldier of the Party, he was sustained by a conviction that in the midst of hunger, the revolution's supreme leader and supreme ascetic, Vladimir Lenin, "refused to eat butter."[368] After the sinister Slovuta leaves, the Red Professor makes this point to Makarygin, but the well-informed prosecutor promptly disabuses the Serb of his Leninist dietary notions: "There was a pretty good staff dining room in the Kremlin even in those days."[369]

Unlike Rubin, who is just as passionately devoted to the communist cause, the ex-professor lacks the ability to step outside himself: he has no imagination. Yet there is something ineffably likeable about this mummified paleo-Bolshevik, who must live "the subdued life of an invalid"[370] to avoid arrest by the regime for which he fought and bled all those years ago. Now he is utterly remote from the centers of power, the centers of evil, and so the gloomy Serb enters and exits the fictive world as a survivor and witness, rather than a perpetrator.

15

Lev Loseff notes that free-willing Volodin stands apart from the other characters, who inhabit a world governed by "extreme determinism," and compares him to Pierre Bezukhov in *War and Peace* and Nikolai Stavrogin in *Devils*, European travelers who return to Russia to act as "dramatic catalysts" in their respective texts.[371] To this one might add that Volodin has style. With his fluent French and languid demeanor, he is the picture of upper-class privilege. Where the counterfeit Count Sologdin primps and pretends, always trying that little bit too hard, the cultivated diplomat carries himself with effortless superiority. Always elegantly turned out, he wears his tailored suits well, in contrast to the Chekists and apparatchiks with their ill-fitting uniforms and mesomorphic torsos. As early as chapter one, Innokenty is assigned traditional anatomical markers of aristocratic breeding: "tall and narrow-shouldered,"[372] "nervous fingers."[373] Volodin, Dotnara, and the rest of the Makarygin family could be characters in a novel of manners about Soviet high society.

In fact, Volodin is the product of two antagonistic class bloodlines. During the Bolshevik takeover his father led a detachment of Red sailors and between shootouts and executions found time to marry the beautiful daughter of a noble family. Volodin Sr. went on to serve in the Cheka, Lenin's secret police, but perished in the civil war and was posthumously accorded the status of a revolutionary hero. Innokenty was brought up by his mother.

The diplomat's wife is one of Solzhenitsyn's most memorable female characters. A sensual beauty who is the embodiment of statuesque "Russian womanhood,"[374] she looks and whores like Hélène Bezukhov in *War and Peace*. Dotnara's voluptuous figure is much appreciated by the womanizer Shchagov as his hungry gaze palpates her contours: "Padded shoulders were very much in fashion, but Dotnara looked all the more feminine for refusing to hide the delicate curve of her upper arm."[375] The account of the unraveling of the Volodin marriage employs another Tolstoyan motif. In *Anna Karenina*, Mr. Karenin is newly displeased by his adulterous wife's habit of slurping her tea. For his part, Volodin grows irritated by the soon-to-be-faithless Dotnara's masticatory mannerisms: "Had she only recently acquired or had she always had, unnoticed by Innokenty, that unpleasant way of chewing, or rather chomping, especially when she ate fruit?"[376]

Dotnara's sister, Dinera, is the epitome of blonde cinematic pulchritude. The eldest of the Makarygin girls, this star of the screen has led a life of Hollywoodian flamboyance. Her first husband was a film director who put her in the movies, her second was a general, while her current spouse is the SocRealist celebrity Galakhov. Together, Nikolai and Dinera constitute the novel's one and only power couple.

The junior member of this non-Chekhovian trinity of sisters is Klara. "Neither beautiful nor even just nice-looking,"[377] she is pure of heart and strong of will. Klara still lives at home and works at Marfino as a free employee with the rank of MGB lieutenant. Celluloid Dinera (Child of the New Era) and statuesque Dotnara (Daughter of the Toiling People) have made-up names typical of the 1920s, markers of their parents' youthful ideological fervor that tell their own satirical story. In contrast, "Klara" is semantically loaded (The Clear One) but politically neutral, for the youngest Makarygin daughter came into the world after the revolution had run its bloody course.

Plain, principled Klara is a very different personality from her selfish and pleasure-loving sisters. She admires Innokenty but loves Ruska, the handsome young prisoner. Her moral education began in Tashkent, whither the Makarygin family were evacuated on the third day of Hitler's invasion: a class privilege. In the Uzbek capital, "Klara had an unverifiable feeling that the city around her was awash in sewage and that heroic purity and spiritual nobility had withdrawn to some place five thousand versts away,"[378] that is, the Eastern Front. At the University of Tashkent, she studied "old Gorky, with special reference to his influence on Uzbek literature,"[379] an academic experience that prompted her to switch to engineering. But it was Klara's encounter with the female slave worker washing the stairs in the Kaluga Gate apartment house that affected her the most:

> She remembered the exact spot, on the next to last step of a long flight, and whenever she passed it, on days when she did not use the elevator,

she remembered the crouching gray figure and the upturned face full of hatred. Afterward, she always kept close to the banisters, fearing that she might step on the cleaning woman. She could neither explain this superstitious impulse nor repress it.[380]

Klara and Innokenty's friendship begins when she acts out the scene for him, "with many gestures,"[381] on those very steps, a dramatized performance that functions as a second-order chronotopic event (the chronotope is, of course, the staircase). As he watches and listens, the diplomat undergoes a transformation from a "glamorous Westerner" into someone "looking humble and rather lost, and for some reason hat in hand."[382] The doffing of that hat is the single most poignant instant of physical movement depicted in the novel, or perhaps the whole of Solzhenitsyn.

Like the Galakhovs and the Nerzhins, Innokenty and Dotnara were married shortly before the war.

> For six of the best years in a man's or a woman's life, each gave all that the other could ask. Six years that largely coincided with those in which much of mankind were saying heartbreaking farewells, dying on the battlefield or under the rubble of shattered cities, years when crazed adults were stealing crusts of bread from children. The world's grief did not pale the cheeks of Innokenty and Dotnara.[383]

Eventually Volodin began to feel a very Tolstoyan dissatisfaction with his life of privilege, life of lies. Looking for answers, he went through his late mother's papers and realized that the quiet, loving figure he always took for granted had possessed intellectual and artistic depths of which he had been utterly unaware: a charming child of the Silver Age. He also discovered that she had secretly been in love with a man other than his father. These are the family lessons he learns, but there are historical ones as well. In the course of his researches, Volodin concludes that the February Revolution was a far more important event than the one of October, which came about as a result of a "narrow conspiracy"[384] (an interpretation of the year 1917 that is the organizing historiographical concept of *The Red Wheel*). Innokenty realizes that "he was a savage, reared in the caves of social science, clad in the skins of class warfare."[385] His subsequent ethical actions, which culminate in that call to the US embassy, are his act of rebellion against a troglodytic state: "Puny, milk-and-water Innokenty had tried to save civilisation!"[386]

Volodin's attempt to halt the Soviet nuclear program is his one-man *mission civilisatrice*.

16

The First Circle is a prison cum urban novel in which the characters, whether convict or free, live in environments of brick and concrete. Of the novel's ninety-six chapters only one, chapter forty-four, is set in the countryside. Here Volodin and his sister-in-law, Klara, venture out into the rural open, an expedition that becomes an important stage in their respective moral quests.

In "Matryona's Home," we recall, Ignatich longs for a place of refuge "somewhere where the trains don't run."[387] The same fictive orientation *away* from those steel tracks, which intersect so many of Solzhenitsyn's imagined worlds, is evident on this occasion. Innokenty and Klara's day in the country is a journey back in time: once they alight from the train, they move from modernity to pre-modernity. Their progress, or regress, through the countryside is scripted as a succession of chronotopes: the two young people cross a field, walk down a path, wander through a cemetery, pass by a church, rest under a tree, traverse a stream, drink from a spring. Etiolated Volodin is winded by all this ambling and rambling, an inadvertent textual disclosure of the author's own physiological state circa 1968: he "overburdened Innokenty... with the heat exhaustion he experienced during a bicycle tour of the area... that year the fifty-year-old writer experienced a worsening of his hypertension."[388]

"Is this Russia, then? Is this the real Russia?" wonders Westernized Volodin as he gazes upon an expanse of forest and field where "there was no one and nothing else to be seen or heard: no human being, no farmstead, no trailer, no abandoned haymaker, nothing but the warm reveling of wind and sun, and birds lost in the void."[389] Klara, who has a bit of a crush on the handsome diplomat, tells him he looks like "Yesenin coming home from Europe to his native village,"[390] and Innokenty obligingly recites a couple of half-remembered lines by the peasant bard. By doing so, he unknowingly confirms a textual connection to his co-protagonist, Nerzhin, who carries with him a volume of Yesenin everywhere he goes: simple verse for complex minds.

In the course of their excursion the two friends come across upon a village. Other than the Lubyanka, this is the most terrible place described in the novel, a locus of human and environmental devastation:

Neither the ill-fitting, matchwood doors, which seemed to belong to chicken coops rather than houses, nor the unopenable double windows without ventilation panes looked as though human life could be concealed behind them. The traditional pigs and poultry were nowhere to be seen or heard. Only the wretched rags and blankets hung out on clotheslines in one of the yards showed that someone had been there that morning.[391]

The visit to this derelict habitat has the quality of a nightmare. Klara and Innokenty meet a half-deaf babushka clutching a dead chick and a slow-witted man with a wooden leg. The third figure they encounter, a dwarfish female with a wicker basket, is particularly grotesque: as she approaches the two wanderers, she undergoes a succession of sinister shifts of shape and identity:

"Little girl …," Innokenty began, but quickly realised that she was older than he had thought. "Er … young lady …" But by now she was almost upon him, and it turned out that she was a woman of nearly forty, remarkably small and with cataracts on both eyes.[392]

The villagers' poverty is medieval; their master, the modern terror state. The same impersonal forces of history that exalted the Volodin and Makarygin families have mangled and maimed the bodies of these farmers. "Power relations have an immediate hold upon [the body]; they invest it, mark it, train it, torture it, force it to carry out tasks, to perform ceremonies, to emit signs," observes Michel Foucault.[393] And if, as the French post-structuralist posits, such acted-upon and thereby "marked" physical forms perform and signify, then here their message is: despair, depravity, death.

In a corner of this post-apocalyptic scene the visitors glimpse a familiar shape:

Then a cat slunk out of the thistles, stalking something, no longer a domestic animal. It did not turn its head to look at the two human beings but sniffed the ground all around and went on, toward the no-less-dead main street, on which this one abutted.[394]

Cats, as we know, are symbolically ambivalent. They can be signifiers of cozy domesticity or occult danger. The mangy grimalkin gliding through that wretched hamlet is a figure from an allegory yet to be textualized, which will acquire fictive form after Volodin finds himself a prisoner of the MGB a few months later and is given a drink of water:

The mug's capacity was three hundred grams; it was enameled, greenish, with a strange picture of a cat wearing glasses, pretending to read a book, but furtively eyeing a cheeky bird hopping around nearby. They couldn't, surely, have chosen this picture especially for the Lubyanka? But how apt it was! The cat was the Soviet regime, the book the Stalin Constitution, and the sparrow a thinking individual.[395]

The village church, overgrown with moss and weeds, was converted into a warehouse to serve some industrial or agricultural interest. The churchyard has been ploughed over by tractors and trucks. "The sick, mutilated earth was covered with incrustations of mud like hideous gray scabs and putrescent puddles of leaden sludge."[396] Fragments of marble—floor tiles? gravestones?—are strewn along the church wall or lie scattered in the road. A foul stench pervades the air, of stagnant water or dead animals or raw sewage.

> "What's that smell around here?" Klara asked.
> "Eh?" The one-legged man was surprised. He thought a bit. "Ah ... must be from the cattle yard. ... Our cattle yard's just over there."[397]

Somewhere beyond the margins of the narrative, lies an *animal farm*.
From the stunted woman with the cataracts the visitors learn that the village is called Rozhdestvo, which means "Nativity." Can a toponym be more pregnant with meaning?

> And what rough beast, its hour come round at last,
> Slouches towards Bethlehem to be born?

Yet, the two church crosses are still in place, just as they were fifty years ago, before the twentieth century came calling. (In "Along the Oka," one of the "Miniatures," the narrator remarks that when the crosses are knocked off those onion-shaped domes, a village dies.)

No longer able to bear the sights and smells, Klara and Innokenty flee this Stalinist anti-Bethlehem and re-enter a piece of the "real Russia" that had so enchanted them:

> They stopped in the spreading shade of the first, huge willow and looked around. Away from the stench, all was moist and green and fresh, and they could see the church up on the hill, but not the dreadfully mutilated

earth around it, only the dots that were birds darting and sailing around the belfry.[398]

In Canto XXXI of the *Paradiso* Dante paints his vision of Heaven: fire-faced, white-bodied angels flying on golden wings in and out of the petals of a white rose. And so, after walking through the demonic village, Innokenty (The Innocent One) and Klara (The Clear One) are—perhaps—rewarded with a glimpse of the Divine. In a universe that contains a hell or even multiples thereof, one expects or, at least, one hopes that there is also a heaven, however remote or unattainable.

Volodin's second out-of-Moscow excursion is a trip to Tver where he visits his maternal uncle, Avenir. In the decades before the revolution, this ancient town, which lies some 100 miles north of Moscow, was a center of the *zemstvo* (local self-government) movement, which the author considered one of the most admirable and hopeful civic developments in late imperial Russia. Of course, the revolution put paid to all that. Between 1931 and 1990 Tver was known as Kalinin, after the titular head of state under Stalin. In the novel, however, it is referred to by its hallowed, historical name.

Uncle Avenir lives in ungenteel poverty with his humble-born, warm-hearted wife in a shabby wooden house, which, like Matryona's cabin, constitutes a rickety place of refuge from the depredations of Soviet modernity. Behind the house is a lovingly tended garden. We are never provided with a picture-in-words description of this leafy space, even though in the "Miniatures," for example, Solzhenitsyn showed that he enjoyed constructing verdant verbal landscapes. Instead the narrator gives us the garden's dimensions (300 square meters) and matter-of-factly lists the plant species growing there: catalogue prose is among this writer's favorite devices. So what might have been an island of color and life amidst the novel's succession of gray cityscapes, officescapes, and prisonscapes remains a mimetic blank scripted as a horticultural gesture of defiance. Avenir *cultivates his garden* as part of a lifelong privacy project, his endeavor to separate himself from the Stalinist state and its Stalinized masses. The little orchard is a materialized metaphor that remains tantalizingly immaterial.

Inside the cabin things are even more interesting. Over the years and decades Volodin's uncle has accumulated thousands of issues of the Party newspaper, *Pravda*, placing them in elaborately designed, cunningly masked vertical and horizontal arrangements in every room and corner of his home:

> … The swatches of yellowed newspapers hung up out of the sun and dust were just a noncriminal way of preserving the most interesting news from

times past.... He couldn't mark them, but he knew by heart what he could find in any one of them. They were hung up in such a way that the interesting bits could be got at without undoing a whole bundle every time.[399]

An informed syllogomaniac, or collector of rubbish, Avenir wishes to preserve the historical record by keeping track of the changing lies of the regime. This eccentric recluse, whose Biblical name (see Abner) coincidentally means "future" in French, is the novel's most *passé* figure, a custodian of analepsis in a proleptically vectored text. As Innokenty and Avenir sit talking into the night inside this strange, crooked house filled with newsprint and history, the uncle describes the Founding Father's satanic sniggers as armed sailors disrupted the first, and last, session of the Constituent Assembly in 1918. This is a glimpse of the Lenin of *The Red Wheel*, the goateed fanatic writhing and vibrating with nihilistic passion.

The faded broadsheets the uncle collects, *dated* units of newspeak that are continuous historically but discontinuous materially, transform the cabin into a house of secret knowledge, a fragile labyrinth of esoteric texts externalized and extended into physical space, as in Jorge Luis Borges's story "The Library of Babel" ("La biblioteca de Babel"; 1941). In fact, Avenir is like a character in Borges or Nabokov, whose heroes inhabit a "fantastically reduplicated reality,"[400] though *this* hero retains the ability to transit at will between the two realms and to assess the degree of duplication or distortion present in either. In the narrated universe of *The First Circle*, he is its best-informed reader.

As for the novel's best-informed or best-intentioned writer, this is Nerzhin. His secret manuscript, the "reflections on the Russian Revolution hidden away in his desk,"[401] contains the following passage, which with its geometrical imagery anticipates *The Red Wheel* while recalling the mathematical modeling of the text in Zamyatin's novel *We*:

> The history of 1917 holds no surprises for a mathematician. A tangent soaring at ninety degrees toward infinity at once plunges into the abyss of minus infinity. In the same way, Russia, taking off for the first time toward a freedom never before seen, immediately came to an abrupt stop and plunged into the worst of tyrannies.[402]

Nerzhin's abyss or pit is national, unlike Nietzsche's individualized existential void: "And when you look long into an abyss, the abyss also looks into you."[403] That word, "abyss" (*bezdna*, with its near-synonym, *propast'*), occurs at intervals throughout the novel, although its figurative function varies.

Usually this is carceral, but at other times it has a recognizably Nietzschean ring, as when Nerzhin tells Simochka, "We are people of the abyss."[404] It is fitting therefore that the name Solzhenitsyn chose for his autobiographical hero is suggestive of the Russian word *net* (no), just as Nietzsche liked to imagine that his surname was a cognate with the Polish *nie*. On the other hand, the egocentric sharashka director, Anton Yakonov, has a last name that hides within itself the pronoun *ia* (I), while his initials, A. Ya., represent the first and last letters of the Russian alphabet. "I am Alpha and Omega, the beginning and the ending, saith the Lord" (Revelation 1:8). We discern a hint of the ultimate conceit or ultimate blasphemy or, perhaps, the ultimate hope. And so, as Nerzhin confronts Yakonov and tells him he is resolved to depart the first circle of this gulag inferno for the abyss below, the text actualizes the polemical conjunction of two encoded ethical meanings: an onomastic, binary, liturgical drama that reads, "not I."

Nerzhin and Volodin's self-chosen fate is to be sovereign, choosing human beings.

> For some people the day comes
> when they have to declare the great Yes
> or the great No.[405]

CHAPTER SIX
Rebel versus Rabble: *Cancer Ward*

In what does one at present believe more firmly than in one's body?
—Friedrich Nietzsche, *Beyond Good and Evil*

What does man actually know about himself? Is he, indeed, ever able to perceive himself completely, as if laid out in a lighted display case? Does nature not conceal most things from him—even concerning his own body—in order to confine and lock him within a proud, deceptive consciousness, aloof from the coils of the bowels, the rapid flow of the blood stream, and the intricate quivering of the fibers! She threw away the key.
—Friedrich Nietzsche, *On Truth and Lies in an Extra-Moral Sense*

Illness is not a metaphor.
—Susan Sontag, *Illness as Metaphor*

1

Every historical period has a thematic disease. A pathological condition seizes hold of the cultural imagination and becomes richly, sickly textualized. It is depicted in works of art and, mediated through the medical practices and discourses of the age, acquires symbolical, allegorical, ideological meanings. These endure even after the aesthetic that generated them is superseded by a new one. A cure may be found, the myths and signs may lose their currency, but the art remains.

The Middle Ages dreaded the plague. In the early nineteenth century, the Romantics feared and exalted consumption, the symptoms of which appealed to their notions of beauty, even when it was the artist himself that was stricken, as John Keats's odes show. (The dangerous glamour that TB held for that epoch calls to mind the heroin chic of our own popular culture.) Syphilis, whose victims included two of the fathers of the Modern, Charles Baudelaire and Friedrich Nietzsche, was an obsession for the Victorians and Edwardians. During this "golden age" of Western venereal anxiety,[1] it was conceptualized as both sinister and insidious, a thing of horror secretly gnawing away at the victim's vitals for years and even decades, before it manifested its tertiary phase and deprived him of his looks, his mind, his life. In the twentieth century, cancer became culturally preeminent in the urban societies of the first and second worlds, though for a while its place in the public imagination was taken by AIDS.

Cancer Ward tells the story of a group of patients variously dying or recovering from malignant tumors, and the medical personnel who attend them. The setting is a hospital in an unnamed Central Asian city, readily identifiable as Tashkent, the capital of the Soviet republic of Uzbekistan. Yet this is much more than a medical novel, for the range of subjects covered is vast: in addition to cancer itself and the invasive and noninvasive treatments of it, there is the revolution of 1917 and the civil war; World War II; Tolstoy's teachings; Gorky's writings; Lenin's libels; Stalin's crimes; the planned economy and the black economy; socialism and communism as theoretical constructs and political realities; the social status of women; ethnic identities and relations; sexual function and dysfunction; sport; classical music; arts and crafts. Even Bollywood films and rock and roll get a mention.

Of all of Solzhenitsyn's fictional works, *Cancer Ward* is the most explicit in its depiction of human suffering. "While TB takes on qualities assigned to the lungs, which are part of the upper, spiritualized body, cancer is notorious for attacking parts of the body (colon, bladder, rectum, breast, cervix, prostate, testicles) that are embarrassing to acknowledge."[2] Still, the novel does not always follow Susan Sontag's dark formula: while most of the characters, including the protagonist, Kostoglotov, suffer malignancies of the lower regions, the callous bureaucrat Rusanov has cancer of the neck and the sweet-natured Ukrainian, Proshka, has cancer of the heart. Of the dozen or so patients who figure in the novel by name, several die or are about to die, the prospects of some are uncertain, but others return to health, among them the two main characters, Kostoglotov and Rusanov. Yet more often than not, even a cure entails the maiming of the body. The perky teenager Asya undergoes a mastectomy, the shy dreamer Dyoma loses his leg to amputation, and the elderly Bolshevik Shulubin, should he survive, will have to spend the rest of his life attached to an ostomy bag, an object of revulsion and pity to those around him.

There are descriptions of malignant tumors and the procedures for treating and excising them. The clinic's senior surgeon is in the habit of saying that "if all the breasts she had cut off were collected together and made into a pile, the result would be quite a small mountain."³ Passages such as these shocked "the Victorian sensibilities of Soviet readers,"⁴ with their inhibitions about the human body and its functions and malfunctions. Soviet writers were equally unnerved. One of them complained that the novel "contains descriptions of disease in pathological terms, and the reader inevitably succumbs to the dread of cancer—a phobia that is already widespread in our century."⁵ Such psychosomatic squeamishness recalls the demonization of illness in pre-modern societies. As Foucault writes of the lazar houses of medieval Europe, "These low places and these rites ... were intended, not to suppress [leprosy], but to keep it at a sacred distance, to fix it in inverse exaltation."⁶ Western audiences, inured to depictions of bodily horror by the conceits of Modernism or the excesses of popular culture, did not have the same reaction to the novel as the SocRealist worthy I quoted. It is also true that the author, a former oncological patient himself, felt a certain grim satisfaction in reminding his well-appointed empirical colleagues of the contingent nature of the socialist good life. "Some of those present may soon perhaps find themselves in a cancer ward and realize what sort of symbol this is," he warned a meeting of the Secretariat of the Writers' Union in 1967.⁷

Actually, the supposed symbolism of cancer in this work has been the subject of considerable debate. Critics drew parallels between *Cancer Ward* and Anton Chekhov's novella "Ward Number Six" (1892), formerly known as "the most terrible production in the whole of Russian literature."⁸ In Chekhov's provincial asylum, which is even shabbier than Solzhenitsyn's oncology clinic—for once, a tsarist institution surpasses a Soviet one on the misery index—a charming, truth-seeking paranoiac confronts a hypocritical doctor. The charismatic madman, Gromov, raves about "human viciousness, ... brutality trampling on justice, ... the heaven on earth which will come to pass."⁹ The doctor, Ragin, is uninterested in his patients and preaches a sort of bastardized Stoicism that denies the reality of pain and advocates non-resistance to evil.¹⁰ An unscrupulous medical rival has him imprisoned in the asylum, where he is beaten by a brutal orderly and dies. The story may be read as an attack on Tolstoyanism, which Ragin's doctrine somewhat resembles, a meditation on the collapse of bourgeois certainties about religion, culture, and the sciences (there are hints of Nietzsche in Gromov), or an allegorical depiction of Chekhov's doomed homeland. This last interpretation, which gained favor as soon as the story appeared, was summed up by the writer Nikolai Leskov in the formula, "In 'Ward No. 6' all our customs and characters are depicted in miniature. Ward No. 6 is everywhere. This is Russia ..."¹¹

Similarly, many readers were tempted to view Solzhenitsyn's cancer clinic as a metaphor for the Soviet Union. One of them was Tvardovsky, who fretted that the title "might be interpreted as political and allegorical."[12] His suggested alternative, *The Building at the End of the Alley*[13] (*Korpus v kontse allei*), may have contained "more semantic play than the blunt *Cancer Ward*,"[14] but Solzhenitsyn stuck to his authorial guns, sustained by the conviction that Tvardovsky's journal suffered from a preference for "anodyne, watered-down surrogate titles."[15] An American scholar discerns in the novel a "symbolism" that is "organic" or even "pathological"[16] (there's that word again!). The author himself, though, was firm on this point: "The texture is too dense, there are too many medical details for [cancer] to be a symbol."[17] The implication is that, as scripted in the text, the hospital is not a second-order figure but a first-order metonym for the country's health care system or, more broadly, for Soviet society circa 1955.

Still, even if one refrains from apprehending the totality of the novel as a meta-allegory, it holds discrete imaginative meanings that discharge an organizing function at many points in the narrative. It could not be otherwise in a work written by an author whose invariable practice when composing his longer works was to conjoin the descriptive and diegetic aspects of the text through an integrating hierarchy of metaphors, as is the case in *The First Circle*, *The Gulag Archipelago*, and *The Red Wheel*, whose very titles are figuratively formatted historiographical definitions. Crucially, it is the main character, Kostoglotov, who employs his disease as a figure of speech, or rather, thought. As he wanders the streets of Taskent at the end of the novel he says to himself: "A man dies from a tumor, so how can a country survive with growths like labor camps and exiles?"[18] Kostoglotov's status as a cancer survivor and a former prisoner gives his image special significance. Whether the hero's somber speculations should be taken as the novel's programmatic message is for the reader to decide. The narrationally unemphatic way in which they are presented suggests that perhaps they should not.[19] Yet, even if the oncological hospital or the disease itself is not a symbol, there are individual malignancies that are symbolically scripted, such as the liar Podduev's cancer of the tongue, greedy Chaly's cancer of the stomach, and pretty Asya's cancer of the breast.

Another example of medical imagery is the partocrat Rusanov's temperature when he enters the clinic, 37 °C (99 °F), an impeccably Stalinist value that evokes 1937, the year of the Great Terror. Much later in the proceedings we encounter a second totemic number: after he is discharged, Kostologlotov must pay "fifty-eight rubles and a few kopecks" for a prescription.[20] Now, fifty-eight is the number of the article in the penal code under which he received his sentence. "The fact that at every stage in his life he was pursued by the figure 58 did not surprise him one jot," notes the Kostoglotov-inflected narrative voice.[21] The baring of the device is *informationally* superfluous, for by this point in the novel we are well aware of the details of Oleg's prior prison experiences. Still, the wry comment reinforces the hero's textual status as a man of (difficult) destiny.

Georges Nivat identifies a "network of secondary signs" that links the characters,[22] such as Tchaikovsky's ballet *The Sleeping Beauty* (*Spiashchaia krasavitsa*; 1889; Kostoglotov had dreamed of seeing it, Vera, the woman he loves, listens to music from it as she thinks about him) and, of course, the fabulous uriuk or Asian apricot tree. "There was no time more beautiful than when the apricot trees were in bloom in town," we read.[23] The uriuk, Nivat explains, is a "marvel of the Orient, this immense ... tree blossoms forth in an enormous pink ball, six meters across."[24] Here is an arboreal fact that clearly situates the locus far away from frigid, unexotic Russia. The tree is first mentioned when Kostoglotov recalls his surrogate parents, the Kadmins; later Vera goes looking for it in the city, but fails to find it; finally, it is discovered by the hero himself on the day he leaves the clinic, the first day of the rest of his life. For Vera and Oleg, the apricot tree is a symbol of hope, love, rebirth: their bilateral signifier. Like the old oak on the Bolkonsky estate in *War and Peace*, it is this fictive world's tree of life.

2

One commentator calls these 500-plus pages a "short tale" (*nebol'shaia povest'*).[25] He is taking the author at his word, for Solzhenitsyn, with his characteristic dislike of the word "novel," preferred to describe his creation as exactly that, a tale. Yet one suspects that if asked to choose between the terms "novel" and "tale" most readers, whether Russian or foreign, would opt for the former rather than the latter. Still, whatever its nomenclature, *Cancer Ward* exhibits a remarkable structural and textual tightness. This work is *polished*. It displays an unfaltering balance between the historical and the literary, the political and the private, while sharing with Solzhenitsyn's other long or longish fictions their encyclopedic reach, quasi-dramaturgical multivocality, plenitude of subplots, and complexity of cultural codings. At the same time, the authorial diction is markedly restrained and unobtrusive, especially when compared with the stylistic flamboyancies of *The First Circle* or *The Red Wheel*.

"My habitual and 'saving' device is to rearrange all events along the axis of time," Solzhenitsyn once remarked.[26] As in *The First Circle*, the temporal rearrangements here comprehend an autobiographical time shift. Although the text employs the writer's experiences as a patient at the Tashkent oncological clinic in 1954, Solzhenitsyn moved the action forward by a year. "The beacon of the Twentieth Congress [which] initiated the great progressive movement of our day"[27] is just around the corner. At that gathering Nikita Khrushchev, the new Soviet leader, would give his Secret Speech, soon to become not-so-secret, dealing a mortal blow to the cult of Stalin and, in a wider sense, to the doctrine and practice of communism itself. The narrative offers up portents of the soon-to-come period of national cleansing, such as the sacking of Stalin's Supreme Court, the dismissal of Georgy Malenkov, his onetime heir apparent, from the premiership, and the first prisoner releases from the camps. As he regains his health, Kostoglotov's thoughts turn toward the future and the choices he must make in the days and years to come. There is a whiff of freedom in the air and the hero can feel it tickling his nostrils.

As so often happens in Solzhenitsyn's prose, anachrony rules. *Cancer Ward* opens with Rusanov's arrival at the Medical Center and his ceremonial induction into the ranks of the diseased. During this process Rusanov, an important servant of the state, receives every institutional courtesy. Then we go back in time to the night when a moribund Kostoglotov staggered into the clinic and unceremoniously fell down on the floor, violating the protocol of admission, to the dismay of the duty orderly. Distributed across the length of the novel are other analeptic excursuses, often in the form of a character's recollections of his or her past deeds or misdeeds. These digressions may predate the main narrative by years or decades. In *The First Circle*, the ultimate historical reference point is the 1910s and the seductions and wonders of the Silver Age, but here it is the Russian Revolution and its attendant brutalities, which degraded Kostoglotov's middle-class parents and in which Podduev and Shulubin were enthusiastic participants. Nevertheless, the controlling fictive orientation is proleptic. As the patients in Wing No. 13 worry, suffer, die, recover, relapse, repent, argue, and fall in love, the vector of history is slowly shifting, preparatory to Khrushchev's shattering revelations.

In addition to "Ward Number Six," *Cancer Ward* has been compared to Thomas Mann's novel *The Magic Mountain* (*Der Zauberberg*; 1924). Although Solzhenitsyn had never read it,[28] such a comparison is not without merit. Both works are large-scale narratives that are set in the confined space of a medical establishment and cover a wide range of cultural and historical themes. Both describe the quest for enlightenment of an intelligent and passionate hero who eventually leaves this hermetic space to resume his life's journey in the social and historical sphere. Both display an anticipatory narrative alignment, although in *The Magic Mountain* this conveys a sense of foreboding, for looming over the textual horizon and casting a shadow over the protagonist, Hans Castorp, is the catastrophe of World War I. Like the International Sanatorium Berghof,

Solzhenitsyn's Medical Center is a world complete unto itself, a societal microcosm at a hinge moment in historical time. The two novels' respective locales, the Swiss Alps and the Asian city of Tashkent, are geographically remote places that were traditionally depicted as exotic or picturesque, but which are consistently deromanticized in their respective texts. The cast of characters in *Cancer Ward* is as ethnically, politically, and culturally diverse as the one in *The Magic Mountain*. It includes Russians, Germans, Uzbeks, Kazakhs, a couple of Ukrainians, a Greek, a Crimean Tatar, a Karakalpak, a Korean, an Armenian, and a Jew. There are communists, non-communists, ex-communists, and anti-communists; intellectuals; workers; peasants; soldiers; crooks.

Of course, no writer, not even the integrating- and holistically minded Solzhenitsyn, could hope to cover every facet of twentieth-century Soviet history in a single work. Chief among the events that remain unmentioned is collectivization, the Stalin regime's violent transformation of the countryside that changed the face of the country. And even though the characters grapple with difficult moral issues, religion is not a major presence in their lives, which was to be expected in this ideologically secularized society. The only two believers shown, the Orthodox Christian Aunt Styofa and the Muslim Mursalimov, are old and rural and remain on the novel's margins. As for Kostoglotov, he acknowledges his lack of faith almost *en passant*, referring to himself in the second person: "You've never counted yourself a Christian, indeed the very opposite sometimes."[29] Yet the veteran Bolshevik Shulubin who, we may assume, began his political career as an atheist, tells him at one point: "Sometimes I feel quite distinctly that what is inside me is not all of me. There's something else, sublime, quite indestructible, some tiny fragment of the universal spirit. Don't you feel that?[30] If cancer is cellular chaos, then this work overwrites it medically *and* ethically.

As a hospital novel, *Cancer Ward* depicts familiar institutional types: the manly surgeon; lonely female doctor; bossy matron; sexy nurse; saucy cleaning woman; incompetent administrator. (Several of the dramatis personae were autobiographically sourced.)[31] There is even a medical *femme fatale*, a scheming junior physician in love with the hunky sawbones. The work is a useful guide to mid-twentieth-century clinical practices. "I have asked some leading cancer specialists for their view of the story, and they have acknowledged that from the medical point of view it is impeccable, and abreast of modern knowledge," the author proudly noted.[32] Like Tolstoy and Mann, he enjoys showing the minutiae of social and institutional life. Medical machines, devices, and procedures are described in expert detail. There is a good deal of professional dialogue among the doctors. The hero, Kostoglotov, is determined to keep control over his body and so he challenges and questions his physicians at every turn on the details of his treatment. As he learns, so do we, the readers.

The Medical Center is not a showpiece facility. It is ramshackle and dirty, like so many of the locales in Solzhenitsyn, who is always attuned to the dingy, entropic quality of the Soviet cityscape. The patients, many of them in extreme pain, crowd not only the wards but the corridors and stairwells. A few of the new admittees lack even beds: Kostoglotov spends his first night at the clinic lying a bench. One commentator, who underwent treatment in the same institution a decade before Solzhenitsyn, recalls: "I was a patient there in the spring of 1945. Only for a few days, however. A dark, shabby building. A thick layer of dirt in the wards. But it was surrounded by a beautiful park. A remainder from those times when it was a *zemstvo* [tsarist-era local government] hospital."[33]

The important presences number about a dozen. Taken collectively, they exhibit a balance of the sexes. While the doctors are mostly female, one of them is a man; while the patients are mostly male, one of them is a woman. These two exceptions are the surgeon, Lev Leonidovich, and the teenage breast cancer sufferer, Asya. Each has a strongly gendered presence and is scripted as a representative practitioner of a medical specialty (Lev) or a representative member of a generational cohort (Asya).

During the Soviet period the health care professions were overwhelmingly female, and so the clinic is largely served and run by women. Hence the healthcare maternalism that pervades it. The three most important medical personalities are Ludmila Dontsova, the no-nonsense head of the radiology department, Vera Gangart, her skilled and beautiful acolyte, and Zoya, a vivacious part-time nurse. The director of the clinic may be a pompous, paper-shuffling male, but the manner in which this institution functions is shaped by the dynamics of socially active and interactive femininity. The women radiotherapists trained by Dr. Dontsova think of her as "Mother" and so does the dying Sharaf Sibgatov, a simple-hearted Tatar whose worldview is tribal and ahistorical; and the women physicians and nurses relate to each other as ranked females in a gendered hierarchy of power, as when Vera Gangart instructs the nurses or Zoya sets straight the sluttish cleaning woman, Nellya. In fact, the hospital is something of a matriarchy, a self-contained island of female authority and expertise. Surrounding it on every side, however, are the institutions and practices of the Soviet state. That patriarchal polity's designated representative in the novel is the unmanly Rusanov, who personifies male privilege, Stalin-style, even as a cancer patient.

The ward where Kostoglotov spends most of his time is a space within a space within a space. It is a room on the second floor of Wing No. 13 of the Medical Center, which is situated on the city's outskirts. The protagonist shares this locus with eight other men. To the left of the door stands a stove, giving the room an asymmetrical shape. The spatial irregularity functions as a perceptual prop, helping the reader to visualize the scene of the action. As Kostoglotov's fellow patients die, go under the knife, or are discharged, theirs beds are freed, to be taken by new arrivals. Also, in the course of the novel some patients, like Rusanov or the young Ukraininan, Proshka, move from bed to bed. These *in-ward* movements are meticulously recorded. Inside the ward's sociographically scripted environment, the patients act and interact territorially, ranking and re-ranking themselves within the resident male group. Rusanov, for instance, is furtive and surreptitious, his bed a burrow wherein he hides whenever the tough Kostoglotov speaks too loudly or approaches too closely. For his part, the hero dominates the room, stomping up and down between the row of beds or perching on the window sill from whence he holds forth to anyone who will listen. As his health improves, he shows a marked tendency to adopt characteristically masculine, almost simian, poses, always within those same four walls, as in: "Kostoglotov was lying diagonally across his bed, his feet up on the rail and his head hanging over the mattress into the aisle."[34]

Although many of the most important scenes take place in the ward, other areas in the Medical Center, such as the transfusion unit, the x-ray room, and the doctors' offices, feature as well. On the whole, the hero's relationship to the space surrounding the clinic building—the park and the city beyond—is as "monotonous" as that of Hans Castorp to the Alps.[35] Occasionally Kostoglotov takes walks in the hospital grounds. Most of these *promenades du malade* are routine excursions, but there are two exceptions. The first is a long conversation the hero has with Shulubin about politics and history, the second an episode where he empties his bottle of mandrake root infusion to please Dr. Gangart's medical scruples. Once in a while Kostoglotov visits a nearby bazaar, accessible through a broken section of the surrounding wall.

The space that is external to Wing No. 13 is described in a passage which, with its references to windows, lights, and ambient temperature, is structured along the same *lines* as the opening paragraph in "Ivan Denisovich". Winter in balmy Tashkent, however, could not be more different from its counterpart in the freezing Kazakh steppe, as the very first climatic negative in a sequence of such negatives indicates:

> There was no wind or frost. Reflected in a windowpane [Kostoglotov] could see a nearby puddle. There was no ice on its black water. It was only the fifth of February and already it was spring. He wasn't used to it. The fog wasn't fog: more a light prickly mist that hung in the air, so light that it did not cloud but merely softened and blurred the distant lights of street lamps and windows.[36]

(The counter-affirmative textual connection to "Ivan Denisovich" recurs a page or so later, when Kostoglotov looks forward to seeing "stars that were not blinded by prison-camp searchlights,"[37] a sentiment he will also express in his letter to the Kadmins, which opens part two of the novel.)[38]

The clinic contains two women's sections. The larger of these, a "great nest of sick women,"[39] holds more than thirty beds. Their occupants spend much of the time talking, although their converse is far from elevated: "Prices, goods, furniture, children, men, neighbors, right down to the most shameless subjects imaginable."[40] Some of the male cancer sufferers, even terminally ill Proshka, may appear outwardly healthy, but the female patients look drab or unkempt, with the single exception of the teenage beauty, Asya. Certain Russian readers were upset by the images of diseased or maimed womanhood in *Cancer Ward*. Yet, it is doubtful if these depictions are any more graphic or explicit than the ones found in Dostoevsky's novels. The difference is that most of his damaged women suffer in fictively traditional ways, as madwomen, consumptives, or prostitutes. They retain their femininity, however wounded or distorted, unlike the women sufferers in Solzhenitsyn's hospital, whose bodies are medically altered or de-sexed: as Sontag tells us, "Cancer is a demonic pregnancy."[41]

In *The Magic Mountain*, the inner lives of the characters, particularly their subconscious drives, are privileged over the operation of social or cultural forces. Such is not the case in *Cancer Ward*. The staff members and patients are shaped by history rather than Freudian psychoanalytic theory, the element that more than any other dates Mann's novel to the time it was written.

The heroes, heroines, and villains of *Cancer Ward* have lived through some of the most terrible events of the twentieth century. Shulubin and Podduev took part in the revolution and the fratricidal, nationwide violence that followed. Kostoglotov and Chaly fought against Hitler. Dyoma's father was killed in that war, as was Vera Gangart's fiancé. Zoya's family fled central Russia from the invading Germans. Yet, it is Stalin's tyranny that looms darkest in the novel's historical scheme of things. There is scarcely a character that did not suffer because of it or take part in perpetuating it (in the case of Shulubin, both). The Volga Germans Mita and Federau and the Crimean Tatar Sibgatov were deported, together with the entire populations of their republics, to Central Asia, in 1941 and 1944 respectively. Kostoglotov was arrested and handed a lengthy prison sentence for holding political discussions with his college friends. The daughter of Elizaveta Anatolievna, the cultivated cleaning woman who likes to read French novels,[42] died in exile; Elizaveta's husband is a prisoner in the gulag. The Kadmins spent years in the camps apart from each other before being reunited in Ush-Terek. In contrast, over a period of three decades or more the bureaucrat Rusanov has brought misery, and sometimes death, to dozens of people; and there are other Stalinists whom we meet in the course of the novel.

3

The narrative is shaped by the conflict between two antagonists, the former political prisoner Oleg Kostoglotov and the Party placeman Pavel Rusanov. Kostoglotov is the angular, angry truth-seeker; Rusanov, the flabby, coldhearted servant of the state. Theirs is a clash of wills, moralities, personalities, life experiences, languages. Stricken by the same disease, they find themselves in the same institutional space, where they come face to face with death. Yet Party man Rusanov is much more than just a pudgy foil for Kostoglotov. As one commentator notes, "They share a peculiar relationship whereby one implies the other."[43] Mr. K. and Comrade R. are in contrastive fictive distribution: taken on his own, neither man makes anything like the same sense as when he is considered next to his adversary.

I should like to begin with Rusanov, for there is a quantifiable, finite quality to this dramatis persona, which distinguishes him from the complex and ever-changing Kostoglotov. Rusanov is of a piece, and a nasty piece of work he is.

From the Soviet Union to the Libyan Arab Jamahiriya, from the Islamic Republic of Iran to the Bolivarian Republic of Venezuela, revolutionary states have never been able to sustain the initial impulse of pure belief that brought them into being. In time, the frenzy fades. Utopian fervor is replaced by bureaucratic routine. The fanatics grow flaccid, potbellied, dyspeptic. The heady days of violent struggle fade into memory, even as its rhetoric remains. Visions of a paradisiacal future are replaced by a preoccupation with the here and now. Instead of the new millennium, there is the five-year plan.

Rusanov is the man in the gray Stalin tunic, the paunchy five-year-planner. He belongs to the stratum identified by Robert Service as the one group in society [that] was certainly indebted to Stalin. This was constituted by the high and middling ranks of the bureaucracy in the ministries, the party, the armed forces and the security organs. The material assets of functionaries were small by the standards of rich in the West. But they knew how hard life was for the rest of society; they also understood that, if they were unlucky in some way in their career, they might suddenly enter prison despite being innocent of any crime. Immediate pleasure was a priority for them.[44]

The head of the personnel department at an unnamed industrial enterprise, the novel's antihero is one of those Stalinist middle managers. Every factory and construction project, every research institute and government office had a "cadres section" that vetted and monitored employees. Ensconced behind his desk, the pallid partocrat enjoyed a "mysterious, isolated, almost supernatural position in the general production system."[45] After all, one of Stalin's best-known apothegms was "Personnel is the deciding factor" (*kadry reshaiut vsë*). And so, among the nicknames Rusanov's fellow patients bestow upon him is Personnel (*Kadr*).

This Soviet HR specialist represents a transnational, trans-ideological type. He is every totalitarian pen pusher who "makes the little children cry" while leading a family life of cozy domesticity. With his Himmler-like spectacles and Himmler-like physique, Rusanov is a "scrubbed little man," "milksop,"[46] "Whey-face,"[47] "bald pate,"[48] whose expression conveys a terrible blankness. At the same time, he contrives to project a gravitas of a falsely bookish kind, like General Oskolupov in *The First Circle*, so that rough-hewn Poddéev starts calling him "Professor" as soon as he arrives in the ward. This pedagogical motif resurfaces on a subsequent occasion: "Sitting up sternly in bed, bald, in his skullcap and glasses, Pavel Nikolayevich looked rather like a schoolteacher."[49] Indeed, the bureaucrat loves to instruct and to pontificate, as a means of self-assertion and self-validation.

A wise historian once observed that secret police chiefs tend to look like dedicated schoolmasters. Although Rusanov never managed to get into the GPU, or NKVD, or MGB, the principle still applies. And then there is the simple, honest pleasure of telling others what to think. If the intellectually inquisitive Kostoglotov is always seeking to learn new things, Rusanov is serenely confident he knows all that there is worth knowing. He revels in his privileged access to the creeds of Marxism-Leninism and is certain that they make him an authority on every subject, even though he has had only six years of schooling.

Pavel Nikolaevich Rusanov's name is a collection of clues. To begin with, it is an ironic nod to the two fictional Pavels that loomed large in the SocRealist canon. They are the martyrs Pavel Nilin in *Mother* (*Mat'*; 1907) by Maxim Gorky and Pavel Korchagin in *How the Steel Was Tempered* by Nikolai Ostrovsky. Both novels, which are structured and coded in accordance with traditional hagiographic patterns, portray an ideologically unformed proletarian who becomes a revolutionary hero, performs a succession of valiant deeds, and in the end dies for the cause. The bureaucrat's patronymic is one of Solzhenitsyn's onomastic jokes: Nikolaevich—son of Nikolai (Ostrovsky). The family name, Rusanov, carries its own message. It means "of Russia" and is a marker of degraded nationhood. By way of fictive confirmation, ever so seldom the bureaucrat displays some authentic national trait, as when in a devil-may-care moment he downs a shot of vodka "like a true Russian,"[50] contrary to his doctors' dire warnings.

The world as seen by this Stalinist HR manager is a bleak and barren but connected kind of place:

> As every man goes through life he fills in a number of forms for the record, each containing a number of questions. A man's answer to one question on one form becomes a little thread, permanently connecting him to the local center of personnel records administration. There are thus hundreds of little threads radiating from every man, millions of threads in all. If these threads were suddenly to become visible, the whole sky would look like a spider's web, and if they materialized as rubber bands, buses, trams and even people would all lose the ability to move, and the wind would be unable to carry torn-up newspapers or autumn leaves along the streets of the city.[51]

This is the geometry of a bureaucratic hell or, in the words of Jorge Luis Borges, "Soviet Russia [as] an indecipherable labyrinth of state offices."[52]

As he rose from factory worker in White Russia to provincial functionary in Uzbekistan Rusanov destroyed numbers of lives. His first victim was his neighbor Rodichev (Native-Born), whom he denounced to the secret police, obtaining his share of their communal apartment as a reward. Later he deleted from civil existence a "bourgeois" engineer who publicly, and correctly, called him a fool, a stenographer who "distorted" the speech of an important official, a "pigheaded" accountant (was Rusanov fiddling his expenses?),[53] and the entire Yelchanski family, which he destroyed by betraying first Mr. Yelchanski and then Mrs. Yelchanski, whereupon Rusanov dispatched their infant daughter to an orphanage. On another occasion, he threatened to have a young woman charged for concealing her mother's arrest: she took poison as a result. The partocrat is particularly proud of the years 1937–38. He remembers them as an "excellent and honorable time [when] the social atmosphere was noticeably cleansed and it became easier to breathe."[54] For Pavel, the Great Terror was a good year at the office.

A veteran inhabitant of the cubbyholes and ratholes of power, Rusanov is adept at playing those little office games in which a subordinate may be instantly reduced to size by a targeted signal from the power-bearing body: pausing before returning a greeting, drawing one's eyebrows together, half-turning one's head toward one's interlocutor or not turning it at all.[55] He even excretes judiciously, making a point of avoiding the staff lavatory in favor of a restricted access facility on another floor. Workers of the world, evacuate!

But all of these fun and games are now in the past. Like the desiccated judge Ivan Ilyich in Tolstoy's novel, Pavel is torn away from the abstractions of bureaucratic existence by life-threatening illness and must deal with raw, terrifying biological reality. As the diegetic voice informs us in appropriately Tolstoyan tones, "He had as good as lost all his personal status, reputation and plans for the future—and had turned into one hundred and fifty-four pounds of hot, white flesh."[56] Yet, if Rusanov is a Soviet analogue of Ivan Ilyich, he is one that is in no way redeemed or enlightened by suffering. He does not slough off his official identity as he writhes in pain on his hospital bed, he does not contemplate the black nothingness of the void. Instead of dying, he recovers, although if anyone deserves a cringing, squalid demise, it is Pavel Rusanov. Besides, throughout his hospital stay the personnel director remains close to his family, unlike Tolstoy's alienated jurist whom cancer drives ever further away from his wife and daughter.

Rusanov has a cancer of the neck. The bureaucrat's sickly scrag is his secret anatomical link to Chekhov's Dr. Ragin, who has "a small growth on his neck which prevents his wearing hard, starched collars."[57] In the course of the novel Rusanov never changes, never evolves, except in a physiological sense, and he leaves the hospital exactly the same man he entered it. "The tumour under his jaw, the size of a fist,"[58] knocks him down for a while, but it does not knock him out. Yet the reader has little reason to rejoice on his behalf. If Stalin, as depicted in *The First Circle*, was the grand paranoiac of the Soviet Union, Stalin-worshipping Pavel is a petty, puny version of the late Leader. He is always looking for evidence of sabotage or wrecking by those more educated than himself, in spite of his own massive ignorance about medicine, chemistry, physics and, indeed, every other scientific subject. He even suspects that Dr. Gangart, an ethnic German and thus, by his lights, a likely Nazi spy, is plotting to poison him, and watches her with a baleful eye.

None of this means that Pavel is a white-hot fanatic or even an ice-cold one. Instead, he is a drip: a whiner, a shirker, a coward. Lacking as he does in kindness or imagination, he feels no sympathy for anyone other than his wife and children, whom he views as socially valuable extensions of himself. As for the men, women, and children outside his family circle, he judges them according to their membership in their respective socio-political groups and standing with the Party. In the course of the novel he manifests a liking for exactly two people he meets, the pretty nurse Zoya and the crook Chaly. On his first day in the ward Rusanov is disturbed by the Uzbek Mursalimov "whispering—prayers or something, probably, the old fool."[59] The partocrat tells him to shush, for why should another man's desperate orisons have any meaning for Pavel, who holds sacred only Stalin and the other gray divinities of the communist pantheon.

The antihero is one of the novel's most talkative presences, and his talk is hideous to hear. He speaks in a mixture of propaganda clichés, half-baked quotations from SocRealist writers, and pious references to the eternal verities of Marxist-Leninist theory. This is the sociolect of Stalinism, and Solzhenitsyn lampoons it brilliantly. Pavel's Soviet-speak exemplifies what the writer considered the great crime of the communist regime against the Russian language, its wholesale impoverishment and rigidification by ideological and cultural hacks.

Once upon a time there were voices that prophesied the appearance of grotesque mutations like Rusanov. "The moral hypocrisy of those commanding," warned Nietzsche, would entail their "[borrowing] herd maxims from the herd's way of thinking, such as 'first servants of the people' or 'instruments of the common weal.'"[60] In these politically incorrect terms, the HR director, a quondam proletarian turned lumpen ideologue, is a ripe-for-the-reaper embodiment of the herd principle. Speaking or thinking in his wooden Russian, Rusanov delivers himself of a succession of herd maxims that refer the reader to the slogans and catchwords of the Stalin Text.

As soon as he arrives at the hospital, he is displeased by the standards of patient care:

> Nobody had given him any medicine. Assassins in white coats [that is, the falsely accused physicians in the manufactured Doctors' Plot of 1953]—that was well said. They'd just hung up a temperature chart for idiots to

look at. The orderly hadn't even come in to make his bed. He had to do it himself! My word, our medical institutions still need a great deal of smartening up!⁶¹

Asked by a despairing Podduev what he thinks people live by, he replies, without interrupting his matinal feeding (on the menu that day, home-cooked chicken): "There's no difficulty about that. ... Remember: people live by their ideological principles and by the interests of their society."⁶²

Rusanov's flesh has its own story to tell. His blank features, pale skin, and portly build call to mind his namesake Pavel Chichikov in Gogol's *Dead Souls*. Chichikov is a conman who roams the length and breadth of Russia buying up titles to deceased serfs in a scheme to defraud the government. He is, suggests Vladimir Nabokov, "a traveling salesman from Hades" (see chapter two), whose chthonic nature is revealed in his vermicular appearance: "Rotund Chichikov may be said to be formed of the tight folds of a huge flesh-colored worm."⁶³ In fact, Solzhenitsyn's antihero once worked in a macaroni factory. Picture white, maggoty Rusanov kneading gooey dough to turn it into white, maggoty food: like manufacturing like.

Chichikov is a paragon of *poshlost'*, a word which Nabokov amusingly renders into English as "poshlust."⁶⁴ *Poshlost'* is of "a world where nothing spiritual remains."⁶⁵ It is "not only the obviously trashy but also the falsely important, the falsely beautiful, the falsely clever, the falsely attractive."⁶⁶ A *poshliak* is not quite the same as a philistine, a person who is "preoccupied with the material side of life and believe[s] only in conventional values,"⁶⁷ a description that fits the covetous Chaly, Rusanov's sole friend in the ward. *Poshlost'* also happens to be "one of the main attributes of the Devil."⁶⁸ Nabokov provides a list of characters in world literature personifying this tawdry trait, among them Gertrude, Claudius and Polonius in *Hamlet*, Marion Bloom in *Ulysses*, Alphonse Berg in *War and Peace*, and even Aleksei Karenin in *Anna Karenina*.⁶⁹

Solzhenitsyn waged passionate war against the world-principle of *poshlost'*, and not least its artistic pretensions.⁷⁰ The garish posters and inane radio programs that so appalled Ignatich in "Matryona's Home" are examples of *poshlost'*, and so is the novel *Far from Moscow* cited in *The First Circle*, whose author is "a barefaced liar."⁷¹ As late as 1997, Solzhenitsyn gave voice to his anti-*poshlost'* campaign during a round table discussion at the Russian Academy of Sciences, when he excoriated—what else!—Hollywood movies: "The vulgarity [*poshlost'*] of a perverted art, which long ago turned into a pseudo-art, waxes triumphant without any constraint, maims the public's aural and visual perceptions, and soils people's souls."⁷²

Rusanov, his soul soiled with no input from the American film industry, oozes *poshlost'* from every flabby pore, though of a homespun Soviet rather than a globalizing Hollywood variety. Slug-like, he crawls through the novel, his trail signposted by his relentlessly banal and relentlessly uplifting observations on life, history, literature and every other topic under the sun.[73]

Of course, Chichikov is a confidence trickster who is conducting an elaborate scam for the prosaic purpose of self-enrichment, whereas Rusanov is an ideological communist who hates black-marketeers so much that he "dreamed, literally *dreamed*, of introducing public executions for speculators. Public executions would speedily bring complete health to our society."[74] Such stern sentiments notwithstanding, the Rusanov clan is not entirely pristine on the greasing-the-palm score. While her husband is in the clinic, Mrs. Rusanova pays the workers remodeling the family apartment extra, although he considers these informal emoluments "petty-bourgeois."[75] She even tries to slip a backhander to the head nurse, Mita (the offer is declined). And when Rusanov meets the wheeler-dealer Chaly, who uses the absurdities of the centrally planned economy to make a fast ruble, he takes a shine to the smooth-talking crook and happily takes him up on his offer to obtain hard-to-come-by tires for the family automobile.

Solzhenitsyn's fictive worlds, set as they are in the shabby spaces of Soviet Russia or Asia, seldom contain shiny new things, sleek consumer products, or brand name goodies. Rusanov is the only character in the novel who lives the Soviet dream, with its "to each according to his work" motto. If the objects a man owns may be said to describe him, then the partocrat's sealskin hat, new green-and-brown pajamas, fur-trimmed slippers, electric razor, and fountain pen, "the one with the enclosed nib, the new kind,"[76] do so, abundantly. The signs are there for all to read: a peasant visiting the clinic is about to ask Rusanov for directions but then takes one look at the sealskin on his head and walks away without a word.[77] What a contrast to ragged Kostoglotov, who owns just one new material object, a winter hat several sizes too small.

Still, the personnel director finds himself in this rundown facility because he is unable to obtain specialist treatment in Moscow, a fact that reflects his geographical and political distance from the centers of power. He may be a big rigatoni at the plant where he watches over the employees' files, but he does not belong to the Party's upper echelons. He laments that he will not receive the coveted personal pension, an amenity reserved for important members of the nomenklatura. Rusanov believes that he missed out on this boondoggle because he had once passed up the opportunity to join the secret police (in *The First*

Circle General Makarygin, a full nomenklatura member, has similar regrets). Still, this was perhaps to the good, he reasons, in view of "the unstable situation during the last two years,"[78] his way of referring to the execution of Beria and his cohorts, ordered by Khrushchev and his cohorts.

Several commentators have sought to compare the antihero to some of the characters in Tolstoy. "In his encounter with the unknown," suggests Kathryn B. Feuer, Rusanov "recalls Tolstoy's other great bureaucrat, Karenin."[79] Now, I have always felt that Anna's stick-in-the-mud husband has had a bad press. Nabokov, for instance, indicts him as "a dry righteous man, cruel in his theoretical virtue, the ideal civil servant, the philistine bureaucrat who willingly accepts the pseudo-morality of his friends, a hypocrite and a tyrant."[80] Yet surely Russia would have done much better historically had there been more such ideal civil servants running the place, whatever Karenin's deficiencies as a husband or cuckold. It is capable and honest administrators that country has always lacked, whether in its imperial, Soviet, or post-Soviet iterations. Judging from the way Solzhenitsyn privileges prime minister Stolypin in *The Red Wheel*, this was the writer's view as well.

James M. Curtis adduces a different Tolstoyan prototype, Karenin's philandering brother-in-law Stiva Oblonsky, who "although not a bureaucrat in spirit ... is a bureaucrat in fact."[81] He discerns an equivalence between charming Stiva's self-centeredness and repulsive Rusanov's moral coarseness. "He cannot repent of the social injustices that he has committed, any more than Stiva can repent of his infidelity."[82] The parallel may be a bit of a stretch, but the obliviousness toward others that Curtis detects in these two characters is a shared human flaw. Moreover, he is surely right that *Cancer Ward* shows the influence of Tolstoy's "later works about love and death,"[83] that is, *Anna Karenina*, *The Death of Ivan Ilyich* and, of course, "What Men Live By," the story that changes the dying Podduev's entire outlook when the construction foreman reads it at Kostoglotov's behest.

Yet, if the sage of Yasnaya Polyana is, in some extratextual sense, gazing down upon the comings and goings in the cancer hospital, if he is the totem of this narrated universe, then Rusanov is guilty of the ultimate blasphemy. "The mirror of the Russian Revolution? Rice croquettes? Your namby-pamby Tolstoy, there were plenty of things *he* didn't understand," he sneers.[84] Every Soviet reader could recognize this statement as a string of quotes from that noted literary critic, Vladimir Lenin.

Back to the flesh.

Pavel has always been lacking in the manly virtues. As a thirteen-year-old he was bullied at school, as a young factory worker he was "a weakling" too "shy" to touch the rock-hard bicep of "the sun-tanned healthy he-man" Rodichev.[85] He had a good war, in the sense that he never went to war: as "a valuable, experienced official,"[86] Rusanov spent those terrible years taking care of his files far away from the fighting. In fact, the personnel director is a coward, pure and simple. Brooding on his hospital bed in the dead of night, he has this one thought: "He was not afraid of being brought to justice, or of the judgment of society, or of disgrace, but simply of being beaten up."[87] Nevertheless, as a cancer patient—a cancer survivor—the partocrat displays a measure of resilience, aided as he is by his lack of imagination and his abiding will to (Soviet) power.

Still, perhaps I am being a bit unfair to Rusanov the Red-blooded male. After all, his wife, the formidable Kapitolina, has borne him four children. The novel's antihero may not possess the aggressive masculinity of a Chaly or a Podduev, but his sexuality is far from stunted. After his arrival in the ward he ogles Zoya appreciatively, his rheumy eyes lingering on her perky bosom. Still, Rusanov's *tendresse* for the voluptuous nurse lasts but a couple of minutes, for he is not a tender man, although he is at his most human when he is leering at her from under the covers.

Other than his roving eye, Pavel has no redeeming traits. He is a walking, talking, eating, drinking, secreting, excreting (the text is not sparing of detail) specimen of *homo sovieticus turpis*. Clearly, he does not possess the layeredness of characters like Kostoglotov, Podduev, Vera Gangart, or Dr. Dontsova. However, the author thoughtfully provides his antihero with a nightmare, in which the plump partocrat crawls down a claustrophobic concrete tunnel or pipe, as if traveling through the birth canal, and emerges at the other end to be confronted by the ghosts of his victims. The uterine/parturient image reminds us that the HR specialist does look a bit like a human embryo.[88]

The fictive long and short of it is that Rusanov is a preprogrammed practitioner of the political and discursive practices of the Soviet state: half man, half manual. How ironic, then, that when *Cancer Ward* was discussed by the leadership of the Writers' Union in 1967, so many of the comments could have come straight from his mouth. One pictures the assembled hacks in their imported suits glibly pontificating on a work that was entering the canon even as they droned. Particularly gormless are the comments by two writers, Kerbabayev and Sharipov. They speak up, then fall silent for all eternity. "Why does the author see only the dark side? Why don't I write about the dark side? I always strive to write only about joyful things," quavers Kerbabayev.[89] "Let him repudiate *Cancer Ward*. Our republic has reclaimed virgin and long-fallow lands and is going forward from success to success," sputters

Sharipov.⁹⁰ Poor Kerbabayev! Poor Sharipov! Quoted in *The Oak and the Calf*, they were immortalized as the Tweedludum and Tweedledee of SocRealism, comical extras in the Legend of Solzhenitsyn.

    Certainly, *Cancer Ward* is at its most tendentious when the narrative focuses on the personnel director, as Solzhenitsyn himself acknowledged. After all, Rusanov is a lampoon, a parodic citational entity in a maximal mimetic novel, so he obeys different textual rules from other, more nuanced fictional presences, as is also true of the propagandist Shakhmetdinov in *The First Circle*.

    Pavel is proud of never having been unfaithful to the redoubtable Kapitolina: "During all these years no difference of interests had developed between himself and his wife. Their proletarian sympathies did not change."⁹¹ In fact, Mrs. Rusanov and the four junior Rusanovs, the biological outcomes of those sympathies, are scarcely more appealing than the family patriarch.

    As was the unwritten rule for Party wives, Kapitolina is considerably larger than her spouse: "Kapa, with her broad figure, her two silver-fox furs, her large handbag the size of a briefcase and her shopping bag full of provisions, was taking up at least three places on the bench."⁹² As stupid and ignorant as her husband, this giantess communicates in the same ghastly Sovietese: "Doctors are a detestable race, anyway. How dare they talk about production achievement when it's living people they're processing?"⁹³ Kapitolina, the daughter of *Das Kapital*, is an expanded, meatier version of Alevtina, General Makarygin's covetous better half in *The First Circle*. Even the names of the two consorts rhyme across the texts and decades, a hint that as readers, we should look for parities between these Stalinist matrons.

    Potbellied Pavel and broad-in-the-beam Kapitolina have done their procreative bit for the CPSU. The two eldest children, Yuri and Aviette, are important presences in the novel. Yuri has recently received an appointment as a prosecutor, but Rusanov is not entirely happy with firstborn, sensing that the young man is too faint-hearted for the job. He is right to be concerned. In an effort to keep up with the more enlightened legal practices now being instituted, Yuri eschews the traditional ruthlessness of the Soviet lawman, suspending, for example, the prison sentence of a lorry driver convicted of stealing a case of macaroni: a supple intratextual connection to Dad's first job as a macaroni maker.

    But it is the partocrat's eldest daughter, Aviette, who is "the pearl of the Rusanov family."⁹⁴ As is true of Dinara and Dotnara in *The First Circle*, the name Aviette, or She-Aeroplane, nicely dates her conception, gestation, and parturition to the early socialist period. And like the Makarygin sisters,

Aviette has enough sense to be ashamed of her ridiculous moniker, preferring to be known as Alla. Pretty in a permed, scrubbed sort of way, she is a fourth-year journalism student in Moscow, a Stalinist version of a Midwestern coed. Aviette has been on the right side of history ever since she popped out of Kapitolina. The She-Aeroplane performed her first act of political activism at age five, when mum and dad dispatched the tiny tot to goad the imprisoned Rodichev's pregnant wife as a way of expediting her departure from the living space they coveted. In the years since, Aviette has evolved into an aspirant poetess who likes her tetrameters ideologically sound but also just a little bit sexy, provided the naughty bits are enhanced by "really progressive ideological thinking."[95]

Although she has found the path to Parnassus, Aviette is still daddy's little girl and shares his diehard outlook and nostalgia for the good old days. Seething with indignation, she tells him about the judicial reviews of Stalin-era persecutions now underway in Moscow: "As if the wheel of history can ever be turned back! Who could do it? Who'd dare?"[96] There's that fateful (Red) wheel again.

Like her father, Solzhenitsyn's anti-heroine has strong opinions, as may be seen from her comments on the right and wrong way of writing literature and reciting poetry:

> There's this long, lanky fellow Yevtushenko, a complete unknown, no rhyme or reason. All he has to do is wave his arms about and yell, and the girls go mad...[97]

And here is another ideological effusion, one of which the sunny Kerbabayev would have been proud:

> Why does truth suddenly have to be harsh? Why can't it be radiant, uplifting, optimistic? Our literature ought to be wholly festive. When you think about it, it's an insult to people to write gloomily about their life.[98]

Addressing a meeting of the Moscow branch of the Writers' Union in 1966, the author confirmed that his progressive poetess was a unit of discursive practice, SocRealistSpeak made flesh:

> They say she is a lampoon—I agree. They say she is farcical—I agree. But the thing is, I didn't invent the lampoon or the farce. If you like, I could

take the speech by Aviette and demonstrate that this was said by this critic, and that was said by that critic. All I did was simply quote from them."[99]

But what about Aviette's two younger siblings?

Seventeen-year-old Lavrenty or Lavrik, named after the now disgraced Beria, is a good athlete but a mediocre student. He enjoys siccing the family Alsatian on random passersby, dreams of becoming a Red Army officer, and is thrilled to have the use of Dad's car, a miniscule Moskvich. "A handsome and sporty young man in a new blue suit. ... He kept proudly swinging the car key on a little strap round his finger."[100] All in all, a Stalinist version of a prom king. The youngest child, Maya, twelve, is a curly haired micro-cipher that rounds out the number of the Rusanov children. Their collective presence points to a question that hangs over the entire work: what kind of world is this where deficient human beings like Pavel and Kapitolina reproduce in multiples while heroes like Kostoglotov are left without issue?

4

A state that claims to be the most just and best governed in history, ruled by an autocrat whom poets hail as the greatest genius that ever lived, sends a young soldier off to war against a fierce foe. The soldier suffers a wound and attains noncommissioned rank. His mother, grandmother, and sister die in a brutal siege. In the fullness of time the foe is vanquished at an incalculable cost in blood, and the soldier is discharged and returns to his studies. But a few months later the state arrests him on a false charge and gives him a seven-year sentence. He serves out its entire length, collecting a second honorable wound in the process, and is banished to a remote and arid region. His girlfriend, imprisoned in another camp, prostitutes herself in order to survive. They will never meet again. A few months into his exile the ex-soldier contracts cancer and is told by his doctor that he has three weeks to live. At the age of thirty-four, he resigns himself to dying. Broken in body, wearing the remnants of his army uniform, he makes his way to a medical facility hundreds of miles away, only to collapse in one of its public areas.

On a rainy January night, a harried orderly asks Dr. Vera Gangart to deal with a newly arrived patient who is "making a scene."[101] Sprawled on the floor next to the main staircase she finds "a lanky fellow dressed in a pair of high boots, a soldier's faded greatcoat and a civilian fur hat with earflaps."[102] It takes the physician one look to realize that this hospital interloper is almost *in extremis*.

"Who are you?" she asked him.
"A human being [*che-lo-vek*],"¹⁰³ he answered quietly, unperturbed.¹⁰⁴

And so Vera, whose name means "faith," *beholds a man* (John 19:5).

Oleg Kostoglotov had spent the day wandering the city in a kind of farewell tour of the non-carceral world, for he expects to die within the week. When he arrived at the clinic, he was told to come back later: "'There's no room,' they said. 'You'll have to wait a few days'"¹⁰⁵ (Luke 2:7).

Actually, we first encounter the hero a good fifty pages earlier, when Rusanov enters the ward and, vigilant as always, takes a good look at him. The personnel director conceives an immediate dislike for the younger man, fastening onto what he perceives as Kostoglotov's wild, woolfish mien: "a villanous cutthroat's mug" with a deep scar, "black, uncombed hair standing up on end," a "coarse, tough expression,"¹⁰⁶ "large rough hands."¹⁰⁷ The hair, the hands, the scar will recur, again and again. They form, together with the hero's bony build, his physical leitmotif. Soon thereafter we get Zoya's take on him. The no-nonsense nurse notices the same details, but her attitude is not unsympathetic: "gangling frame," "unkempt coal-black hair," "large hands."¹⁰⁸

Cancer Ward, writes one commentator, marked a departure from Solzhenitsyn's practice of portraying his empirical self in the guise of the hero or the narrator: "He changed the color of Kostoglotov's eyes and hair (brown and black, respectively), changed his age, profession, and so forth"¹⁰⁹ Rangy, scarred Kostoglotov is angular in more ways than one, while his surname, which means "bone-swallower," has intimations of spines and skeletons. Geometry was his favorite subject in school and throughout the novel he is accompanied by geometrical themes. A onetime geodesy student, Oleg works as a land surveyor in Ush-Terek, his place of exile: see Kok-Terek, where Solzhenitsyn served out his banishment. He helps young Dyoma with his stereometry studies, expressing a fondness for axioms and theorems in an almost lyrical fashion. Like D-503 in Zamyatin's novel *We*, the hero sees other people as mensural forms. As he stares at Zoya's pert breasts he imagines picking up a ruler and placing it on top of them,¹¹⁰ and he thinks of her bosom as "elliptical" (*tëplye ellipticheskie kronshteiniki*);¹¹¹ he perceives Vera's body as triangular and her neck as a nexus of "thin, defenseless lines."¹¹² Recalling his childhood, "Oleg shot up and flew in a crazy parabola."¹¹³ In his letter to his surrogate parents, the Kadmins, the hero writes of his frustration at the doctors' refusal to give him the truth about the radiation treatment and says he wants to "smash this vicious circle"¹¹⁴ (*razorvat' etot krug*).¹¹⁵ The phrase is not just a common figure of speech but an iteration of his geometrical motif, with a hint of the demonic circle or wheel that is a recurrent presence in Solzhenitsyn's texts. See Vera's thoughts of "this notorious cancer circle"[116] (*preslovutyi rakovyi krug*)[117] and Rusanov's notion that the crook Chaly "was a good fellow, but they moved in different circles"[118] (*khoroshii byl chelovek Chalyi, no vsë-taki drugogo kruga*")[119]—different circles of we-know-what, that is.

In "Ivan Denisovich," the hero's hands, face, teeth, and jerkin are markers of his carceral experiences. Kostoglotov comes into the novel bearing his own material record of privation. Oleg's boots, greatcoat, and belt with the Red Star emblem are part of his old army uniform, which like many veterans in this impoverished land he continued to wear after the end of the war (so does Shchagov in *The First Circle*). His kitbag is of the same military vintage. It is covered in grease-stains, with a shrapnel-hole and a burn-hole from when he was fighting the Germans. He bought that "wretched tight black hat"[120] after his release from the camp. He got his angry facial scar in jail defending Japanese prisoners-of-war from a gang of criminals.

Raw-boned, hard-featured Kostoglotov is not one of life's beautiful people. I imagine him looking like a young Lincoln, as in this description of the sixteenth president left by a contemporary:

> The face of Lincoln told the story of his life—a life of sorrow and struggle, of deep-seated sadness, of ceaseless endeavor. It would have taken no Lavater to interpret the rugged energy stamped on that uncomely plebeian face, with its great crag-like brows and bones.[121]

Throughout the novel we never see the protagonist to his physical advantage: an eversion of the topos of heroic masculinity. His posture and gait show the effects of disease, and in the presence of Vera Gangart he often displays a certain shyness. A man bedecked in women's clothes is one of the oldest tropes of humor, yet poverty has forced Kostoglotov to cross-dress: to be able to walk outdoors, he gets hold of a badly cut woman's dressing gown, which combined with his old army belt gives him a "really comic" appearance.[122] By contrast, Professor Chelnov's woolen traveling rug looks like "a woman's warm shawl"[123] but makes him "a majestic figure" (*The First Circle*).[124]

Conscious of his rough edges, in his relationship with Zoya and Vera, the two women in his (restored) life, Kostoglotov tries to be especially civil. He speaks to Zoya "as gently as he could, almost singing the words."[125] Once he realizes that Vera is not a medical iron maiden, he makes a point of addressing her "politely and in his normal urbane manner. He was the first to say good morning, and would even greet her with a friendly smile."[126] Even his body language changes in her presence. On one occasion, as Vera approaches Oleg's bed during her rounds, the latter, "not knowing how best to show his respect for the doctor, drew up his long legs."[127]

Kostoglotov's shabby attire and odd headgear invite associations with the hero of a celebrated novel, another onetime student who attended the same university in the same city, albeit some sixty cross-textual years earlier:

> He was so wretchedly dressed that anybody else, however used to them, might have hesitated to go out in daylight in such rags. . . . A drunken man . . . suddenly yelled as he went by, "Hi, you in the German hat!" and went on pointing at him and bawling at the top of his voice. . . . It was a high, round hat . . . now all rubbed and rusty with age, stained and full of slits; what remained of its battered brim was cocked up grotesquely at one side.[128]

Pages later Rodion Raskolnikov experiences a "very unpleasant incident,"[129] when he is almost run down by a carriage and struck by the coachman's whip.

The hero of *Cancer Ward* encounters several such Raskolnikov moments. As Lavrik Rusanov drives his father from the clinic, the thuggish youth beeps the horn at Kostoglotov and then swings the car toward him, pretending to run him down. A few hours later when he is visiting the city zoo, Oleg fails to notice a group of children gaping at him: "For them he was an animal too, an extra one free of charge."[130]

Of course, Kostoglotov is not a split personality like Raskolnikov, although he has his dilemmas, but this ex-prisoner's will to freedom is equal in intensity to that of Dostoevsky's hero. He must resist anyone who demands that he obey, submit, succumb. His rebel spirit makes him question his doctors on every medical point even as he secretly doses himself with an infusion of mandrake root in case conventional treatments fail. By showing Kostoglotov as a patient who insists on the right to know his prognosis and wants a final say over what is done to his body, the novel transcends the hospital ethos of its day and anticipates modern clinical practices as described by the columnist and AIDS activist Andrew Sullivan:

> The first generation of AIDS patients and HIV-positive men and women transformed the role of the patient from passive recipients of pity and medicine to active, angry participants in their own care. For the first time

we saw dying people not just living but fighting aggressively for viable treatments and even a cure.[131]

Even in the army, an institution predicated on a soldier's unquestioning obedience to his superiors, Kostoglotov "tried to spread democracy," as he self-deprecatingly puts it.[132] That is, he talked back to his officers: clearly, a barracks lawyer. Like Raskolnikov, and Bezukhov, and Zhivago, he is one of Russian literature's great asker of questions. The young geologist Vadim may claim, "We aren't robots.... We don't take anything on trust,"[133] but like the dedicated communist he is, he accepts the regime's ideology as a scientific given, beyond doubt or dispute. In this regard, Kostoglotov is Vadim's antipode, as he is that of every communist believer in the novel. Intellectual curiosity and independence of mind are his defining traits. In a state that demands total obedience from its subjects, they can also be dangerous ones. In this sense, he is not just an outsider, but an interloper.

When Rusanov smugly declares that Marxism-Leninism holds the answers to all the questions that were ever asked or ever will be asked, Kostoglotov issues a challenge: "No one on this earth ever says anything 'once and for all.' If they did, life would come to a stop and succeeding generations would have nothing to say."[134] The implication is that the Progressive Worldview leads to intellectual stasis and death and that its adherents are dead intellects: there can be no life of the mind without a dialogue of minds. Kostoglotov's position is the classic Nietzschean one: "'This is *my* way; where is yours?'—thus I answered those who asked me 'the way.' For *the* way—that does not exist."[135]

Early in the novel, Kostoglotov is in a debilitated physical state: another parallel with starving, feverish Raskolnikov. When he arrived in Wing No. 13, the hero was on his last legs, but soon thereafter, as his body responded to the doctors' ministrations, his health began to improve. Kostoglotov's recovery—after twelve days of x-ray therapy he is ambulant, argumentative, and once again attracted (and attractive) to women—is a "miracle," or so Zoya tells him.[136] For the next several weeks he continues to undergo x-ray treatment and receives other kinds of clinical care. While all this is happening he ponders and argues about issues of a philosophical, political, or artistic nature, to which his existential predicament has given an urgent, life- or death-affirming quality. "For a typically healthy person... being sick can even become an energetic *stimulus* for life, for living *more*."[137] Thus Nietzsche. Thus Kostoglotov.

Solzhenitsyn's unyielding hero represents the highest type of human being in the writer's ethical hierarchy, a sovereign, free-thinking personality who is defiant in the face of mortal danger, is not afraid to hate, but would rather love, and with a passion. Like Nerzhin in *The First Circle*, he is engaged in a continuous process of self-construction and self-enlightenment while facing down the forces of history. By the end of the novel Kostoglotov has reconstituted himself physically, as a recovering cancer patient; discursively, as a dedicated controversialist who for the first time in his life can publicly speak his mind; and attitudinally, as a man who, though in love with an intelligent and beautiful woman, refuses to exchange his status as an autonomous subject for domestic bliss. In many ways, he is kin to another character in the Russian canon, the loudmouthed, adamantine, yet emotionally vulnerable Yevgeny Bazarov in Turgenev's *Fathers and Sons*.

Like Bazarov, Kostoglotov has the defects of his virtues: he is obstinate and proud and can be abrasive, even rude, to his friends as well as adversaries. He is the captain of his fate and so with an almost pagan nobility he reserves for himself the option of suicide should the pain become unbearable, as he confides to Vera when she discovers the mandrake infusion hidden inside his bedside table. To quote Nietzsche one more time: "The thought of suicide is a powerful comfort: it helps one through many a dreadful night."[138]

Kostoglotov's originality of mind and temperament is reflected in his speech. It is a mixture of literary Russian, folksy expressions, and camp slang, with the occasional obscenity thrown in for gruff measure. Here Solzhenitsyn's hero also recalls Bazarov, that colorful and subversive ranter.

The author gives Kostoglotov the best lines in the novel.

"… Man is a complicated being, why should he be explainable by logic? Or for that matter by economics? Or physiology?"[139]

"What's so terrible about moral perfection? … It can't harm anyone—except someone who's a moral monstrosity!"[140]

"He's not a proletarian, he's a son of a bitch."[141]

The protagonist is a linguistic subversive, as is true of any thoughtful, articulate person who lives under a system that tries to control all public forms of expression. If Bazarov deliberately eschews the language of the academy or the salon, Kostoglotov refuses to have anything to do with the obligatory discourses of Marxism-Leninism. Just as he will not accept the state's monopoly on truth, he will not accept its monopoly on words. "Every time someone disagrees with you, you call it ideological sabotage!" he sneers at Rusanov,[142] throwing the partocrat's own cliché into his well-fed face. Still, he can be verbally judicious, as well as aggressive. He makes sure he employs the correct medical terms when speaking to his doctors. By trespassing into their discursive space he challenges the physicians' authority as sanctioned healers who in the way of 1950s medicine claim absolute decision-making power over their patients' bodies. It is therefore ironic that the hero's knowledge of Latin, a smattering of which he picked up in the camp from a former classical scholar, lands Oleg in a situation that puts *him* in a position of medical power. Asked by the Ukrainian, Proshka, the meaning of the words *tumor cordis, casus inoperabilis* on the latter's medical certificate,[143] the protagonist decides not to tell him that they stand for "tumor of the heart, case inoperable."[144] Erudition, it turns out, carries with it ethical responsibilities, no matter how or where it was acquired.

The hero is a man who inspires respect and even affection in others. He may be ill, dressed in rags, and socially marginalized, but he has winning ways. To the Kadmins, the elderly married couple, he is almost a son. Young Dyoma looks up to him and hangs on his every word; cynical, despairing Podduev respects his judgment; the tough-minded surgeon Lev Leonidovich speaks to him not as doctor to patient, but man to man. Following her interactions with Kostoglotov, Dr. Dontsova begins to question her assumption that "any damage to the body was justified if it saved life."[145] Beyond all that, two young and accomplished women on the clinic staff develop feelings for him.

Mann's hero, Hans Castorp, is "an ordinary young man,"[146] an upper middle-class German whose conventional nature and desire to be liked give his character a Tolstoyan universality. The grizzled war veteran and camp survivor Kostoglotov may appear to have little in common with callow Castorp, whose own experience of combat lies beyond the parameters of *his* text. Yet both characters possess those special qualities of thoughtfulness and curiosity about ideas and people that turn their respective institutional stays (two months in Kostoglotov's case, seven years in Castorp's) into journeys-to-knowledge full of adventures of the mind. Moreover, both men have an ardent, sensual nature, and their relationships with women are an important factor in their texts. There is also the coincidence that the two heroes hail from an important maritime city, Hamburg in Castorp's case, Leningrad in Kostolgotov's.

Cancer Ward presents Kostoglotov's life story prior to his arrival at the Medical Center in discrete, anachronous segments. Most of this biographical information is supplied by the protagonist himself in his conversations with Dr. Dontsova, Zoya, Vera, and other sympathetic characters, and in his letter to the Kadmins at the beginning of part two. We learn that Kostoglotov is *déclassé*, in a representatively Soviet way. Born in 1922, he is the son of a former merchant, a moderately prosperous man of affairs and as such a member of a social category targeted for elimination by the Bolshevik regime. Nevertheless, Oleg received the rudiments of a bourgeois upbringing, for his dispossessed parents insisted on teaching him "how to behave properly and answer politely."[147] As is also the case in "Ivan Denisovich," the novel posits an implied counterfactual. We can imagine that had there been no revolution, Kostoglotov would have been comfortably well off, systematically educated and, in all probability, married and a father. However, *that* life never happened. Born and raised in the straitened circumstances shared by most Soviet urban dwellers, as a soldier and then a prisoner Kostoglotov knew deprivation and danger of the most extreme kind. He is beyond poverty, for poverty presupposes the ownership of something, and he owns but "a pair of patched boots and a hole in a doughnut."[148] As well as that ridiculous hat.

There are certain years associated with loss of faith by the adherents of communism: 1956 (Khrushchev's Secret Speech, the Soviet invasion of Hungary), 1968 (the Prague Spring), 1973 (the publication of Solzhenitsyn's own *Gulag Archipelago*). On this apostatic timeline, Kostoglotov gives up on the doctrines of Marx and Lenin at a remarkably early point, during his service in the Soviet Union's Winter War with Finland (1939–40), as he reveals to Shulubin.

Like every character in every Solzhenitsyn story or novel, the protagonist is historically contextualized, with all that this implies by way of cultural beliefs and biases. Take, for example, his view of the sexes. He respects Dr. Dontsova for her professional competence but also her "masculine decisiveness."[149] Even so, he trusts her colleague Lev Leonidovich, "a man who meant business" (*delovoi muzhik*),[150] more than any of the "women doctors," Dontsova included.[151] Many of his assumptions about men and women and their respective social roles, which he holds as self-evident givens, might strike today's reader as quaint, or worse. Yet they are of Oleg's time, place, and people.

Kostoglotov reads and studies whenever he gets the chance, but is not an intellectual; he argues against the communist creed, but is not an ideologue; he accepts the reality of absolute good and absolute evil, but is not a believer, "indeed the very opposite sometimes." Perhaps most important, he is a man who would like to play by the rules, provided they exist and they are fair. This civic attitude of mind is evident in the hero's very last social interaction in the novel, when he intervenes to prevent a criminal from jumping a queue at the city railway station: "He wanted things done honestly and in the proper way."[152] Not a bad motto for a man to have.

I mentioned Kostoglotov's newfound opportunity to say what he thinks within the social space he inhabits. As soon as Rusanov arrives in the ward, the hero is rhetorically hitting him where it hurts: "They'll write you an obituary: Party member since the year zero. As for us, they'll just carry us out feet first."[153] Sometimes Kostoglotov's sallies convey a between-the-lines message that is even more subversive. During another argument with the HR honcho he jibes, "You even started to lift a log during Saturday Work, only you stopped halfway,"[154] a mocking reference to an iconic image of Soviet propaganda, the photograph of Lenin hoisting a length of timber on a besuited shoulder for the inaugural all-Russian Day of Saturday Work in 1919.

For the first time in decades Rusanov finds himself confronting an opponent of inferior status who is not afraid of him. An ideological fish out of water, the bureaucrat flounders discursively whenever Kostoglotov addresses him in the direct language of the street and the camp or mocks him with one of those cutting comments. Despite all his efforts, the personnel director never gets the better of the younger man, and how could it be otherwise? Kostoglotov has attended the symposia of the cells and the barracks where he was taught by Russia's best minds. As the former zek argues with Rusanov in their climactic debate, the gaunt figure in the too-short hospital jacket is transformed into an orator hearkening to the march of history:

> Suddenly furious, he threw himself raging into debate just as he'd done dozens of times in prison. His mind overflowed with phrases and arguments he'd heard from other men who were probably no longer alive. In the heat of the fray the scene seemed to shift in his mind. The crowded, enclosed room, crammed with beds and people, became a prison cell.[155]

... But also, a public square.

The diegetic fusion of the fictive present with the fictive past via a character's prison memories was a device employed in *The First Circle*. And in *The Oak and the Calf* Solzhenitsyn describes his state of exultation on November 30, 1966, when he addressed an audience at Moscow's Institute of Oriental Studies in one of his first unsanctioned public appearances: "To enjoy my proud and open defiance, my acknowledged right to think for myself!" And: "I ... awoke one morning a free man in a free country!!!"[156]

Toward the end of the novel a minor revelation takes place. When Oleg returns to the ward from his last session of radiation therapy he overhears another patient, Ahmadjan, a cheerful young soldier, excoriating the prisoners in the gulag as layabouts and malingerers who should be given "shit to eat"[157] (see the warder in "Ivan Denisovich" for whom the zeks "aren't worth the bread we give them. Feed them on shit, I would").¹⁵⁸ Jolly Ahmadjan, it turns out, is a camp guard, the Soviet equivalent of an *SS-Totenkopfverbände* member. This moment of recognition is spelled out in a single, beautifully structured sentence: "He seemed to be seeing him for the first time, and yet he had seen him for years, framed by the collar of a sheepskin coat, carrying an automatic rifle":¹⁵⁹ another integrating diegetic shift from the hero's here and now, to his carceral past. Challenged by Kostoglotov, Ahmadjan expands upon his comment in broken Russian: "They no human beings!"¹⁶⁰ (*Oni—ne liudi!*).¹⁶¹ With this declaration, a fictive prefiguration is completed, for it refers us back to the exchange between Vera and Oleg on his first night at the clinic: "Who are you?"—"A human being." The two contrastive statements, the *ecce homo* and the anti-*ecce homo*, adumbrate the novel's secret Christological theme.

Nonetheless, Ahmadjan, that happy Soviet who is "uneducated above the checker-playing level,"¹⁶² recovers his health, just like the party hack Rusanov or the spiv Chaly. There is no biological justice in this novel, just as there is none in the real world.

5

The human body has been rewritten many times, from the Greeks to the Arabs, from the schoolmen of medieval Europe to the medical researchers of the modern age. During and after the Renaissance, it was anatomically cut open, turned inside out, and put on public display. Where the religious mind once imagined an imperfect reproduction of a perfect *corpus dei*, there emerged over the course of six centuries a complex, dynamic amalgam of systems (skeletal, respiratory, circulatory, alimentary, excretory, reproductive, nervous), tissues (epithelial, connective, muscular, nervous), biochemical and bioelectrical processes, and genetic codes. As an object of scientific study and clinical treatment, the body was mapped, categorized, and taxonomically catalogued. Its internal organs and structures are familiar presences to us; formerly secret and mysterious, they have now been entered into the cultural record.

During his stay at the sanatorium the hero of *The Magic Mountain* visualizes the body of the woman he loves by mentally dissecting or, rather, peeling it open, tissue by tissue. His vision is informed by extensive (excessive?) reading in anatomy, physiology, and biology (classical and evolutionary):

> Hans Castorp understood that this living body—with its mysterious symmetry of limbs, nourished by blood through a network of nerves, veins,

arteries, capillaries, all oozing lymph; with its scaffold of bones, some of them tubes filled with marrow, some like blades, some like bulbs, some torqued vertebrae, but all originating in a gelatinous base that with the help of calcium salts and lime had grown firm enough to support the rest; with its joints made of tendons, cartilage, and slippery, well-oiled balls and sockets; with its more than two hundred muscles; with its central system of organs for nutrition and respiration, for registering and transmitting stimuli; with its protective membranes, serous cavities, and glands pumping secretions; with its complicated interior, a network of pipes and crevices, including openings onto the world outside—understood that this self was a living entity of a higher order, far removed from those simple organisms that breathed, fed, even thought, with just the surface of their bodies.[163]

As medical novels, *The Magic Mountain* and *Cancer Ward* belong to a literary tradition whose origins go back to the Renaissance. François Rabelais's duology, *Gargantua* and *Pantagruel*, combined late-medieval and early humanistic attitudes to the corporeal self in order to provide an "aesthetic representation of carnival motifs."[164] The extravagant descriptions of the two giants' physical forms feature narrative tours of their anatomical spaces that take place along the alimentary/excretory axis. These fantastic and farcical excursions occur at both ends, as it were, and are informed by the author's training as a physician. In the centuries since a surprising number of important writers also happened to be doctors: Tobias Smollett, Friedrich Schiller, Arthur Conan Doyle, Anton Chekhov, Somerset Maugham, Mikhail Bulgakov, Louis-Ferdinand Céline, William Carlos Williams, Kobo Abe, Vasily Aksyonov, and Stanislaw Lem. Some of these authors' most celebrated works were shaped by their experiences as certified healers and include medical textualizations of the body as well as depictions of physicians and hospitals. Less common are writers who acquire their somatic knowledge from under the stethoscope or the scalpel, that is, as patients. The man who wrote *Cancer Ward*, one of the most famous cancer survivors in history, was of course just such a figure. His novel is concerned with twentieth-century medicine as much as twentieth-century tyranny. The work contains descriptions of medical loci (patient ward, x-ray lab), procedures (injections, biopsies, histological tests, blood transfusions), and practices (pharmacological, radiological, surgical). It explores the institutional conventions of the health care professions, their view of the human body (reductionist, materialist), and attitudes to alternative medicine (hostile, dismissive), while interrogating the status of the physician (the omniscient subject) versus that of the patient (the compliant object).

The language and methods of medicine are among the topics in Solzhenitsyn's continual intertextual polemic with Tolstoy. With the sublime confidence of a man who enjoyed excellent health all his life, the laird of Yasnaya Polyana took a dim view of doctors and their works. His fictions mock their jargon—"morbid irritability,"[165] "floating kidney"[166] and the like—in a manner that resonates with modern readers, who can only agree that these terms sound ridiculously bizarre. Tolstoy's physicians and surgeons are almost always quacks. In *Anna Karenina*, Prince Shcherbatsky is "neither a fool nor an invalid" and consequently "did not believe in medicine."[167] He treats the medical celebrity brought in to examine his daughter as a charlatan. In the same novel, Tolstoy's alter ego, crusty Konstantin Levin, adopts an even more proactive stance: at the spa in Carlsbad, his biceps bulging from weight-lifting exercises, he threatens a tiresome German doctor with a cane. The medical practitioners in Solzhenitsyn's novel, however, enjoy a palpable degree of implied-authorial sympathy, just like the other categories of credentialed experts depicted in his works (always provided, that is, they know what they are doing and that they are doing it for the public good). If there is a profession that gets short shrift in his fictions, it is the legal one: "Lawyers in Russia seem to breed like flies, if you'll excuse the expression," a wise army *doctor* informs the law graduate Sasha Lenartovich in *August 1914*.[168]

Like Molière or Tolstoy, this writer proceeds from an awareness that the authority of doctors rests on their use of a professional language inaccessible to outsiders. In *Cancer Ward*, the nomenclature of body parts, diseases, and clinical procedures figures prominently throughout the text. The novel contains a great deal of information about oncological treatments, much of it conveyed through conversations among the hospital staff or between its members and the patients. However, Solzhenitsyn's reading of the dynamics of clinical practice is subtler than Tolstoy's. The conversation between Kostoglotov and Dr. Dontsova in chapter six is a case in point. Professionally anxious to learn all she can about the origin of his disease, she questions him on his medical history. As Kostoglotov recounts his experiences in the camp hospital, the terrible story of that part of his life begins to emerge. But the doctor is only interested in "the essential,"[169] that is, the type and quality of patient care he received. The horrific details of Kostoglotov's prison experiences are, from her clinical perspective, "superfluous."[170] So, he concludes that whatever he tells her about the gulag, this intelligent and otherwise empathetic woman will never understand or rather, will never hear. The discussion develops into an argument about the hero's desire to have a say over what Dr. Dontsova and her colleagues are doing to his body. Oleg is determined to negotiate his status as a coequal participant in his treatment, rather than be objectified into a "monkey"[171] or "a grain of sand."[172] Dr. Dontsova may consider him an "importunate"[173] patient, but having been the victim of those exercising unlimited power, this old zek is unwilling to cede control of his physical self to anyone, even a votary of the Hippocratic Oath: "A man can dispose of his own life, can't he? You agree I have that right?"[174] The hero's stance is non-medical, post-Christian, in effect, Nietzschean or Kiplingesque, as in: "No price is too high to pay for the privilege of owning yourself."[175]

Ever since he learned he has cancer, Kostoglotov has kept himself informed about the nature of the disease and the purpose and side effects of the treatments he receives. "I'm like an intelligent soldier who has to understand his mission before he'll fight," he explains to Vera Gangart in a characteristically soldierly turn of phrase.[176] At the regional hospital where he was diagnosed he demanded to know his prognosis. The surgeon who conducted the examination told him he had three weeks to live. Zoya, studying to be a doctor, is horrified by this professional violation, but Kostoglotov disagrees: "He was a good man. A human being! [*Chelovek!*[177]]"[178] There's that word again.

The hero's moral philosophy of the body, his "physiology of optimism,"[179] combines scientific, vitalist, and traditional folk notions. It is an original construct. It is also a fantasy:

> "I wouldn't be surprised," Kostoglotov continued, "if in a hundred years' time they discover that our organism excretes some kind of cesium salt when our conscience is clear, but not when it's burdened, and that it depends on this cesium salt whether the cells grow into a tumor or whether the tumor resolves."[180]

(Although as he knows only too well, some men have no conscience.)

At times Kostoglotov seems to be on the same page as Tolstoy. "Why should every medicine be given by injection? You don't see anything similar in nature or among animals, do you?" he asks Dr. Dontsova.[181] Still, on the whole he eschews the Tolstoyan "physician, heal thyself" stance. After all, he is a son of the twentieth century who has studied the quantifiable disciplines at one of his country's finest universities. He has been taught to analyze, hypothesize, verify. When the medical professionals he respects—Dr. Dontsova, Vera, Zoya—take the trouble to explain what they are doing to his body, he accepts their ministrations, drawing the line only at the hormone therapy that would emasculate him.

In *The Red Wheel*, Vorotyntsev, the informed career officer, disproves Tolstoy's view of war by word and deed; likewise Kostoglotov, the informed hospital patient, disproves Tolstoy's view of medicine by knowledgeably participating in the medical care he is given.

Still, our skeptical hero is reluctant to pin all his hopes on the doctors. As a passionate anti-dogmatist, he refuses to concede a monopoly on truth to these white-gowned authority figures. In this contrarian spirit, he seeks out non-medical alternatives such as the mandrake root and the birch-tree fungus. He even tells Dr. Dontsova that he entered the clinic merely as a form of insurance, the root being his primary, preferred method of treatment, but this is laying it on with a trowel, an attempt to shock the stern oncologist into seeing things his way. In fact, rather than achieving a full recovery, the protagonist would be happy just to see his cancer go into remission. Using another one of his military analogies, he explains: "As far as I'm concerned, it's enough that you've driven back the tumor and stopped it. It's on the defensive. I'm on the defensive too. Fine. A soldier has a much better life in defense."[182] Beyond Kostoglotov's fondness for martial references, the image he employs performs a culturally endorsed mimetic function. As Sontag reminds us, "The controlling metaphors in the descriptions of cancer are, in fact, drawn ... from the language of warfare."[183]

6

Cancer Ward is the most erotically charged of Solzhenitsyn's fictions. Kostoglotov enters the Medical Center in the expectation that he will not leave there alive, but recovers his health and as he does so, rediscovers his sensual, sexual side. He becomes romantically involved with two female staff members, Zoya, a nurse in her early twenties, and subsequently with Vera Gangart, a thirty-one-year-old radiotherapist. The hospital, a place of maimed and dying bodies, is transformed into a locus of love and desire. Bataille posits that eroticism "is the assenting to life even in death,"[184] and Kostoglotov is a case in point. Yet while Oleg and Zoya have a passionate, though brief, affair, the hero's relationship with Vera never acquires a physical expression. It remains an unspoken, wistful mutual longing that brings them ever closer, spiritually, emotionally, and intellectually, but at the end of the novel Kostoglotov rejects the possibility of its domestic consummation. Eros vanquishes Thanatos and then for good or *ill*, sense of self, or pride of self, supersedes Eros.

The two female figures to whom Oleg is drawn are a study in contrasts. Zoya, whose name means "life" in Greek (as she is fond of telling others), is a sexy blonde with the compact, curvaceous body of a Russian peasant girl and lots of common sense. Vera is darkly beautiful, the embodiment of sophisticated, introspective womanhood. Her cultural horizons are broader than Zoya's: where the fair-haired nurse grooves to Bollywood soundtracks, Vera listens to classical music, particularly Tchaikovsky.

As a story of men and women occupying the same institutional space and interacting *freely* by day and by night, *Cancer Ward* marks a departure from *The First Circle*. Although Vera, Zoya, and Dr. Dontsova show a correspondence to recognizable feminine archetypes (wife, lover, mother), they are strong and complete personalities who share the defining traits of professionalism, self-reliance, and self-discipline. They have known tragedy in their time and have had to negotiate barriers and overcome obstacles, and as a result have acquired a great deal of practical wisdom. Granted, the two younger women are Tolstoyan in the sense proposed by Kathryn B. Feuer, as "wonderfully individualized heroines who nevertheless exist most powerfully in the novels as objects of temptation or tenderness or saving love for the men," and discharge the equally Tolstoyan function of fulfilling a "custodial role"[185] (think Maria Bolkonsky in *War and Peace*). This is not to imply that Vera and Zoya are *fictively* contingent on the man in their life. In *The First Circle*, Nadya and Serafima, and Dotnara and Klara are female character pairs that always move within Nerzhin's and Volodin's respective textual orbits. *Cancer Ward* relies on a different storytelling logic, one that accords its important female personalities a marked degree of fabulatory autonomy. Even the bubbly teenager Asya is a self-sufficient presence: it is Dyoma that is attached to her, textually as well as romantically, and not the other way round. Of course, *Cancer Ward* is shaped by this author's customary patrilineal structures. The largest portions of story time and discourse time are allocated to male characters such as Oleg, Rusanov, and Dr. Oreshchenkov. In essence, this is a novel about Kostoglotov and his quest for life and truth, so *his* masculine themes and concerns predominate. Traces of this androcentric bias manifest themselves even in those passages where no male character is present. We have already seen that in Solzhenitsyn's worlds, when women retreat into their private spaces away from prying (male) eyes, they engage in the secret rites of womanhood. In the chapter that shows Vera alone in her room, we see her dusting the furniture and dancing like a ballerina, just as in *The First Circle* the female residents of Room 318 did the ironing, whispered confidences, or posed in front of the mirror, hidden in their segregated feminine world: a fictive purdah.

No other character in Solzhenitsyn is as desperately, passionately male as Oleg Kostoglotov. This rugged former soldier and prisoner is full of an elemental sexual longing. Having been deprived of female companionship for longer than he cares to remember and having faced the prospect of an early, painful death, he thirsts for a woman's touch. There is nothing more important in his life than women, he tells the surgeon, Lev Leonidovich. Yet Oleg's raging desire is not just a function of biology. It is also a spontaneous assertion of his personhood, for he comes out of the cruel gulag system where men and women were commodified into units of industrial production and treated as chattels of the state. There, we recall, "Eros dashed back and forth" inside the barbed wire. If human beings are choosing beings, then the hero's decision to refuse the hormone treatment, which will destroy his libido and strip away his sexual identity, is one of the two most important decisions he makes in the novel: "Seven years in the army and seven years in the camp, twice seven years, twice that mythical or biblical term, and then to be deprived of the ability to tell what is a man and what is a woman—is not such a price extortionate?"[186] (The seven years Castorp spends in the sanatorium are "no round number for devotees of the decimal system" but "a mythic, romantic bundle of time.")[187]

There is something in Kostoglotov of Jack London's adventurers and explorers, those larger-than-life figures that Solzhenitsyn read about as a boy. Like London's Smoke Bellew staggering out of the taiga after surviving the Arctic winter with its wolves, blizzards, and terrible silences, Oleg is greedy for life and the pleasures it offers. Yet, it is not just the softness and heat of a female body he craves. What he sees as truly erotic is the possibility of being completely unguarded, completely relaxed with a woman, to let her see him and love him just as he is. If he owns himself in the Nietzschean sense, he would like to share that ownership with a female other. As he falls in love, Kostoglotov discovers that "it was the greatest pleasure in the world to be able to trust, to give himself to trust."[188] That said, the hero also displays the traditionalist belief that "only with men could a man have long-standing, even normal relationships."[189]

It was while he was writing *Cancer Ward* that Solzhenitsyn concluded that he lacked a "specifically feminine point of view."[190] Having identified this deficiency, he set out to correct it by doing what he always did when faced with a dearth of knowledge: carrying out research. He acquired a female informant, Mirra Petrova, a literary scholar who became his go-to source on femaleness and femininity. Dr. Petrova was, by the writer's own admission, the first artistically kindred spirit he had ever met.[191] Solzhenitsyn, who tended to be reticent about the minutiae of the creative process, says little concerning the exact nature of the things his source told him, merely noting that her comments ranged "from disapproval of insufficiently high-minded depictions of women to objections that the portrayal was inadequately sensuous."[192] One is tempted to speculate. Did the novelist and his consultant discuss female psychology, sensibility, body language? Did they talk about the female sexual impulse and response?

Certainly, the manner in which women are depicted in *Cancer Ward* shows a new degree of sophistication. There is a heightened authorial awareness of the way a woman daydreams or worries, shops or does housework, looks at an attractive man or perceives her own physical form. As Zoya sits at her desk chatting with Kostoglotov she fluffs her hair, unconsciously preening herself, and later in the same scene she steals a quick look at his body, her eyes tracing its contours in a characteristically feminine way: "Those raw-boned arms and shoulders ... but that was the disease."[193] Occasionally, however, this gynocentric point of view, point of feeling can be overstated, as when a few lines later Solzhenitsyn has the nubile nurse palpating the protagonist "with her womb"[194] (*vsem lonom oshchushchaia ego*).[195]

A more spiritual, more eternally feminine personality than earthy, uterine Zoya, Vera too is an integrated character in whom intellect, emotions, and the physical self coexist in a believable fictive balance. Like many shy people, the enchanting physician possesses an uncommon degree of self-awareness. At one point in her life, Vera had wanted to adopt a son or a daughter, but then she changed her mind: "There was a great danger—she might stop loving it later. And a greater danger still—it might grow up a stranger to her."[196] Vera senses that Kostoglotov has the mature man's "unwieldy heaviness" that gives a woman that cherished sense of security[197] (Zoya also looks upon him as a potential protector). Her body is textualized with the same metonymic precision as Zoya's: when Vera sits down in an armchair to relax, she "curled her stockinged legs up underneath her"[198] in that unique double-jointed way women have.

Some of the other female portraits also include evocative descriptions of gendered body language. The refined orderly Elizaveta Anatolievna speaks to Dr. Dontsova "slightly twisting her body in apology [*chut' izgibaias' v izvinenie*],[199] as excessively polite people sometimes do":[200] a posture identical to that of the equally cultivated Anna Modestovna in "What a Pity," who when confronted by the patrolman, we recall, performed "some kind of wriggle or bow [*nemnogo izgibaias' ili nemnogo klaniaias'*]."[201]

Was Solzhenitsyn inspired by one of his favorite writers as he was thinking up Zoya and Vera? After all, they show an intriguing physical resemblance to the two heroines in Yevgeny Zamyatin's dystopian novel *We*. Curvaceous Zoya of the round eyes and pouting lips resembles the woman-child O-90, D-503's state-approved sexual partner, who is "sort of rounded all over, and the pink O of her mouth."[202] Willowy Vera, on the other hand, calls to mind lithe, dark-haired I-330, the revolutionary with whom D-503 falls in love, though Solzhenitsyn's heroine lacks her sexual or political daring. I-330 has a face that is doubly triangular: "Her dark eyebrows pulled up high toward her temples, they made a sardonic sharp triangle; and the two deep lines running from her nose to the corners of her mouth made another, this time with the point up."[203] Vera's body is the sum of two metaphors, "two triangles, set apex to apex, the upper one narrow, the lower one broader."[204] In "The Easter Procession," the authorial voice deprecated the artistic practice of using "curved lines and ... triangles" to describe faces and events, but here Solzhenitsyn employs it with no second thoughts.

Now, the triangle is a symbol of male sexuality when pointed upward and of female sexuality when pointed downward. Plato's *Symposium* tells of a primordial race of androgynes who were cut in two by Zeus and then refashioned by him and Apollo into men and women:

> So Eros for each other is inborn in people ... and he unites their ancient nature, undertaking to make one from two, and to heal human nature. Each of us then is but the token of a human being, sliced like a flatfish, two from one; each then ever seeks his matching token.[205]

In this Platonic sense, the triangular contours of Zamyatin and Solzhenitsyn's supremely feminine heroines are tokens of a token, biologically actualized forms that clue us to that fabulous unity of the sexes which the male characters long for and project onto the bodies of the women they desire, who in turn recognize and reciprocate that integrating, healing erotic impulse.

As for Kostoglotov, he is strangely reminiscent of D-503: the two characters are almost the same age (thirty-four and thirty-two years old respectively), are surrounded by mathematical formulae and associations, possess a hirsute, simian masculinity (see D-503 "hairy, shaggy"[206] and "ape-like"[207] hands), and their faces bear a deep scar (Kostoglotov) and "a vertical crease" which is "like a scar" (D-503).[208]

Zamyatin's labially obsessed hero imagines that "all women are lips, nothing but lips."[209] Kissable synecdoches, in other words. It has been noted that "in some of Solzhenitsyn's works certain parts of the female body, most commonly the breasts and lips, attract heightened attention."[210] Thus, Zoya and Vera. The nurse's full lips turn modernistically "flame-colored"[211] (*ognevatye*)[212] when she is aroused. Vera's delicate lips remind Kostoglotov of "little wings"[213] (malevolent Rusanov thinks of them as "thin")[214]; I-330's lips are knife-like.[215] According to the natural philosopher Pavel Florensky, "The lips ... being the most revealing of the depths of the will, are considered among oriental peoples to be the most intimate part of the body."[216] Whether or not Russians are of the East—and the novel is certainly set in those much-imagined parts—Kostoglotov, who frets that the lipstick Vera uses "coarsened her, it spoiled her delicacy,"[217] probably would have agreed.

Born in Smolensk in the heart of Russia, Zoya was evacuated to Tashkent in the first year of Hitler's invasion and knew much hardship during the long trek to Asia by cattle car and barge, and in the hungry years thereafter. Her mother is dead. She has no contact with her father. Zoya's only other living relative is an elderly grandmother with whom she shares two rooms in a communal apartment. A twenty-three-year-old student at a medical college, the part-time nurse takes her hospital duties seriously, even if she is not consumed by her job like Dr. Dontsova or Dr. Gangart: "As a rule Zoya felt everyone had a right to his share of freedom and that when one came to work one was under no obligation to work oneself to death."[218] Her dreams are domestic: a home, a husband, children. By the same token, Zoya's knowledge of the world is limited and her thinking is conventional. When Kostoglotov suggests that Stalin was as much to blame for the siege of Leningrad as Hitler, she finds this observation astounding. She has no awareness of the extent and brutality of the gulag. Yet despite her professionally brisk manner, Zoya is thoughtful and kind. She makes a point of being cheerful around the patients, even those who annoy her, like Rusanov. She is also a hard worker, a quality that is always privileged in Solzhenitsyn's worlds: Kostoglotov nicknames her "the bee with the golden fringe" (*pchëlka s chëlkoi*).[219] Zoya is clever about people and knows how to exercise or delegate authority. When the slatternly Nellya orders a dying patient to carry a bowl with a medical solution, she easily puts the work-shy wench in her place. She haggles confidently with the native sellers in the market and is a skilled seamstress, having learned dressmaking not by attending a class but by watching her friends.

Most of all, in the midst of all this suffering and death, Zoya is defiantly, radiantly alive. She has an exuberantly healthy body, "down to the last pore of skin and the tiniest toenail."[220] Her joyous sense of her physical self calls to mind Tolstoy's most memorable creations. She is conscious of her beautiful breasts, "their weight as she leaned across the patients' beds and their tremor when she walked quickly."[221] The curvy blonde is the type of woman that men invariably find attractive: she exudes sex appeal. More than that, Zoya is one of the most eroticized female presences in all of Solzhenitsyn. She is so sexy that even flabby

Rusanov perks up when she enters the ward. In fact, it is through the medium of his eyes and ears that we first meet her (as we do Kostoglotov): a "pleasing," "delicious" voice, "a trim, firmly-built girl," "golden hair,"[222] "dainty little finger," "generous, tightly-laced figure."[223] By ogling the pretty nurse with such relish Rusanov performs a service for us, the novel's receptors: his prurient gaze maps Zoya's face and figure, cataloguing her attractions for our readerly reference. Whenever she makes an appearance, one or more of the physical details that so pleased him are mentioned or elaborated upon, so that eventually we learn she has "enormous," slightly protruding eyes,[224] that her lashes are blond, and the texture of her hair is fine.

Zoya is naturally flirtatious, knowing just how to pout, twinkle, and smile at a man. She may be the only female character in the Russian canon who can roll her eyes. She has had several affairs, an experience which taught her to keep control of her passions. In a society where private morality is relaxed and contraceptive techniques are medieval, this is a wise course of (in)action for a young single woman to adopt. So if Zoya goes to a party on one of her "unsafe days," "she [is] as alert as a sapper walking through a minefield":[225] a defamiliarizing military image of a type often encountered in this novel. When a young man she fancies fondles her breasts, she enjoys the sensation yet retains enough of a detachment from the pleasure of the moment to be annoyed by his "silly, vulgar" chatter about Indian films:[226] in Solzhenitsyn's world, Bollywood is as bad as Hollywood.

The attraction between Kostoglotov and Zoya grows quickly, with Kostoglotov playing the traditional male role of initiator and pursuer at every stage. When they are not flirting or making out, he tends to assume a paternal tone, speaking to his girlfriend "as one would to a much younger person."[227] From the very beginning, the relationship is charged with an erotic tension enhanced by the thrill of forbidden knowledge shared and exchanged. Now that Zoya knows about the gulag she is in peril, the hero tells her earnestly. In turn, the nurse lends him a medical textbook so that Kostoglotov might research his disease, even though patients are strictly forbidden to possess reading materials of this kind. Later Zoya reveals that the hormone therapy Oleg is receiving will suppress his sex drive and, eventually, destroy his reproductive capacity. She thus becomes the agent of the hero's difficult dilemma, the medical choice he must confront: pharmacological castration versus the possibility of death.

Soon the gaunt patient and the sexy nurse almost, but not quite, fall in love. The initial stages of the affair are described in a trinity of scenes that spans a single week of story time. Thereafter the relationship is kept under narrative wraps, for even while Kostoglotov continues to see Zoya, he finds himself increasingly drawn to Vera.

Scene One.

It is a Thursday evening. Kostoglotov makes his way to the corner in the corridor where Zoya sits at the duty nurse's table. His motives for doing so are mixed: he wishes to learn more about his condition but he would also like to spend some time with a pretty girl. In a sense, this is a typical first date. Having made each other's acquaintance in an institutional setting, a man and a woman switch social contexts and begin the getting-to-know-you process. Yet even as Oleg is chatting Zoya up, history and death are part of the conversation, for this is Russia at the midpoint of the twentieth century. They talk about their families (most of them died in World War II), their interests (his is cancer, hers, embroidery),[228] the time that they first met (he was "writhing about on the couch right here in the hall" with "a face like a corpse"),[229] former relationships (his college girlfriend has "perished,"[230] as he puts it; later we learn that she became a camp prostitute), their homes (his lies in a barren desert; later we learn he is a political exile). The two feel the rush of mutual attraction and "the gay, multicolored wheel of their game" begins to roll.[231] In Solzhenitsyn, material or metaphorical wheels often have sinister connotations, but this one does not—indeed, quite the contrary. Meanwhile Sibgatov, the terminally ill patient whose every movement gives him pain, is laboriously washing himself in the ward behind them. Zoya does not see him, but Kostoglotov does; and ignores him, as he must.

Scene Two.

Sunday afternoon. At Kostoglotov's request, Zoya is wearing the same gray-and-gold dress that she had on during their first meeting. He asks her—directs her—to undo the top button, and she complies: the first, faint ping of sexuality.[232] They repair to the doctors' staff room, which with its soft armchairs becomes a private refuge. Yet even as they talk and flirt and gaze at each other in this temporary *endroit d'amour*, Kostoglotov and Zoya cannot quite escape to never-never land: "There was nothing to remind one that this was a hospital except for a newsletter, *The Oncologist*, pinned to the wall."[233] Dated November 7, the anniversary of the Bolshevik Revolution, the medical bulletin carries a secret satirical message. Again at Oleg's command, Zoya takes off her white hospital gown and sashays before him in the manner of a model. She poses and dances, her movements reminiscent of a burlesque performer, not that she, or Kostoglotov, has ever seen one. Carried away by the excitement of the dance and her burgeoning feelings for the rugged figure sprawled before her, Zoya writhes provocatively, crooning a song from one of those Bollywood movies.

The spell is broken. Austere Kostoglotov is shocked by this blatantly erotic display and angered by the glamorization of criminals in the film from which the song is taken. As a prisoner in the gulag he fought them for his life, and has the scar to prove it.

Scene Three.

Tuesday evening. Again, there are the conversational preliminaries that are such a pleasurable prelude to physical intimacy. Kostoglotov and Zoya walk over to a nearby corridor where she must refill a lung cancer patient's oxygen balloon. One of those unfortunate souls waiting for a place in a ward, he lies, gasping for breath, on a camp bed in a corner of the landing. He remains anonymous: when Zoya says his name, Kostoglotov does not hear it. The details of the patient's appearance are generically morbid: "yellow-looking," "pinched nose," "wheezing in his chest."[234] This uninformed perspective reflects Kostoglotov's perceptual stance, or rather his lack of one. Filled with desire for the blonde nurse, he barely notices his surroundings.

As Zoya fills the balloon from the cylindrical—phallic—oxygen tank, Kostoglotov pulls her close. The passage that follows proved to be among of the most controversial in the novel. Yet all that Oleg and Zoya do is kiss, three separate times. It was not the nature of the encounter that unsettled some readers but its correlation to the spatial frame within which it occurs, for the latter is explicitly and disturbingly clinical. During much of the scene Zoya's hand continues to rest on the tap of the tank as she controls the flow of oxygen into the balloon. Once again, sexual play and mortal illness are contiguous, and once again, Eros is oblivious to Thanatos.

As the two lovers cling to each other, they gasp for breath, like the dying man choking nearby. Their osculations are lengthy: a full page of text for just three kisses. Nowhere else in the novel, or even in the whole of Solzhenitsyn, do we find such an extreme degree of narrative retardation, which is generated via extended dialogue and elaborately structured descriptions. The first kiss lasts "two centuries,"[235] that is, 200 years of story time, if we take the image at face value. The second kiss is likened to a plunge into the ocean by a diver searching for a pearl, a trope with a distinctly erotic resonance (a few moments later the metaphorical geography turns mountainous when Kostoglotov imagines that Zoya's kisses "had just dragged him along the top of the Caucasus").[236] The lovers whisper endearments and talk about a future together, which is when Zoya reveals the truth about the hormone injections. As the two of them walk back to the landing after that passionate clinch, they are "holding not hands but the balloon, now inflated like a football; through it each jolt was conveyed from him to her."²³⁷ The coital connotations are there for us to decode. But what of the dying patient on the camp bed?

> Sitting among his pillows, traces of a neat parting still left, he had stopped coughing and was beating his forehead against his raised knees as if they were a wall.²³⁸

A sentence that is Dostoevskian in its horror: a scene of utter, mortal despair. That poignant parting in the man's hair reminds one of the pathetic little bun worn by the holy fool Maria in *Devils*, while the rhythmic knocking of his head recalls the doomed consumptive prostitute in *Notes from the Underground* (*Zapiski iz podpol'ia*; 1864), slumped on a dirty city pavement and endlessly beating it with a dead fish.

In *Death and Sensuality* (*L'érotisme*; 1957), Bataille conceptualizes the sexual act as a moment in biological time when a man and a woman's²³⁹ subjective "knowledge of death" forms a "potential continuity" with its objective reality.²⁴⁰ As they make love, the partners' physiological, sensory, and emotional state becomes death-accepting or even death-affirming:

> Mortal anguish does not necessarily make for sensual pleasure, but that pleasure is more deeply felt during mortal anguish. Erotic activity is not always as overtly sinister as this, it is not always a crack in the system; but secretly and at the deepest level the crack belongs intimately to human sensuality and is the mainspring of pleasure. Fear of dying makes us catch our breath and in the same way we suffocate at the moment of crisis. ... Beyond consent the convulsions of the flesh demand silence and the spirit's absence. The physical urge is curiously foreign to human life, loosed without reference to it so long as it remains silent and keeps away. The being yielding to that urge is human no longer but, like the beasts, a prey of blind forces in action, wallowing in blindness and oblivion.²⁴¹

In the oxygen tank scene, Kostoglotov and Zoya do not, as yet, became intimate in the full physical sense, but the organizing elements in Bataille's erotic schema are all there, diegetically actualized and redistributed along the axes of carnal desire and physical suffering inside a discrete unit of space. Even his beasts are present: "Close, unbelievably close, [Oleg] saw two tawny eyes, almost predatory-looking"²⁴² (*dva eë zhëlto-karikh glaza, pokazavshikhsia emu khishchnymi*).²⁴³ Unbeknownst to the two lovers, unbeknownst also to himself, the terminally ill patient lying nearby becomes a third party to their tryst and the bearer of its death-dealing aspect. It is he who feels a *mortal anguish* and a *fear of dying*, and *suffocates* as he does so, while Oleg and his girlfriend give in to the procreative urge that is *foreign to human life*, in this case, the life of this unseen and unheeded Other.

As Kostoglotov follows Zoya back to the ward he is already devising a way of getting "this woman, this 'bit of skirt'" to see him later that night.[244] In this he will be, surely, successful. As we find out, several other encounters take place subsequently. A malicious tattle-tale in the women's ward informs Vera Gangart about the amorous goings-on next door: "You take that scruffy one, the one with the belt round his middle—every night duty he gives that nurse Zoya a bit of a cuddle!"[245] This piece of gossip leads to an estrangement between Vera and Oleg, one that puzzles him greatly, for he does not know that Vera knows.

It is in the nature of the male to compare the physical attributes of the women to whom he is attracted. Once he develops an interest in Vera, the hero starts looking at Zoya's body with a newly critical eye. As she walks up the stairs in front of him after their second date he notices that her legs are "a bit thick," unlike willowy Vera's lissome limbs.[246]

The Kostoglotov-Zoya plot line is abruptly canceled when the hero realizes that he has fallen in love with the dark-haired physician. A brief paragraph in which the medicalized phallic motif is restated forms a narrative coda for Oleg's affair with the nurse. "Everything that had grown up between them, taut and strained like the oxygen balloon they had once carried together, had suddenly subsided little by little, until there was nothing."[247] This is known as tying up loose ends, or loose balloons, and Solzhenitsyn does a creditable job. Thereafter Zoya evanesces, except for one farewell appearance. On his last full day in the hospital Kostoglotov and his former girlfriend bump into each other and she invites him to stay with her: the romance may not be entirely over, at least on her side. The hero, who a few minutes earlier had received a similar invitation from Vera, is baffled, in that classically clueless male way. "It is easier to find your way in the *taiga* forest than to know where you are with women," he mutters to himself, manfully, as he takes his leave of the fetching nurse.[248]

If the connection between Oleg and Zoya is primarily sexual, his relationship with Vera functions on several different levels. The Russian-German physician is a more complex personality than vivacious, homemaking Zoya. She is Kostoglotov's generational and intellectual peer, although in his letter to the Kadmins he comments condescendingly, "She's still a young woman, younger than I am.... She seems to have a schoolgirlish belief in book-learning."[249] At this stage,

Oleg is reluctant to admit to himself, let alone his surrogate parents, how much this woman means to him. In fact, Vera is not at all the medical *ingénue* he imagines. The war and the gulag, those crucibles of Kostoglotov's fate, determined the course of her life as well. Her brother was arrested just before the German invasion and died in prison, and her fiancé was killed fighting the Nazis. Vera's mother survived her son by only a few years. These tragedies are compounded by the suspicion the doctor's ethnicity brings upon her in postwar Russia. Thus, Rusanov mistrusts Vera because of her German name, but at least he does not use his fancy pen "with the enclosed nib, the new kind" to shoot off a denunciation to the local KGB office. On an earlier occasion, however, a driver for the secret police who was a patient accused Vera of plotting to poison him, just because she was German. (Un)fortunately, he lived. Those lying words, uttered by one of Stalin's sedulous slaves, are an instance of willful, stubborn ignorance displaying itself to full moral disadvantage when in the presence of a superior human being. Solzhenitsyn's fictions abound in such revelatory moments.

Vera is an accomplished medical specialist, a pupil of Dr. Oreshchenkov and Dr. Dontsova, and a highly regarded member of the hospital staff. She is comfortable exercising authority in the institutional environment of the clinic, in spite of her quiet and reclusive nature. In fact, when Kostoglotov and Vera first met, he saw her, and resented her, as exactly that, an authority figure. Yet even then, as he lay on the hospital floor close to death, he noticed "her slender, gazelle-like legs":[250] the male gaze refusing to be dimmed by the encroaching darkness.

For Kostoglotov, Vera is mysterious, fascinating, and not a little intimidating. His attitude toward her is very different from his simple, pulsating desire for Zoya, expressed in Oleg's confident instructions to her to dress up or down for his pleasure. While the hero's liaison with the nubile nurse proceeds in a linear fashion, its progress and regress shaped by the dynamics of sexual desire, his relationship with Vera develops by fits and starts and is hindered by mutual misapprehensions and even suspicions. These two mature, self-aware personalities must negotiate multiple barriers of private identity and life experience before they can understand, let alone trust, one another; before they can discern within each other that Platonic missing half of the complete erotic self. Yet, as we watch the feeling between them grow, we realize that Oleg and Vera are wonderfully compatible, even on the scale of their individual chronologies: his "seven years in the Army and seven years in the camp" are exactly matched by her "fourteen deserts," her "years of faithfulness" to the memory of her fiancé.[251]

In contrast to sexy Zoya, Vera is surrounded by a special aura of purity. Early in the novel, as Kostoglotov watches the brown-eyed physician ministering to her patients, his male instinct tells him that she is chaste, perhaps even a virgin. In fact, years after her fiancé died Vera had one, unsatisfactory, affair. Her room in a shabby communal apartment is a "convent cell,"[252] its windows covered with bars, its walls decorated with a picture of the Peter and Paul fortress, the sinister prison which used to hold so many rebels and writers. Inside her private space she listens to music from *The Sleeping Beauty*, a ballet that tells the story of a princess awakened to life and to love by a handsome knight-errant.

Important mythological and musical meanings attach to the private name Kostoglotov gives Vera after he falls in love with her. He calls her Vega, after the brightest star in the constellation of Lyra, which represents the harp of Orpheus, who descended into Hades to bring back his wife Eurydice: *Vega* is the zeugma of Kostolgotov's love. In *Cancer Ward*, this celestial object stands as a sign of beauty and life, as it does in Solzhenitsyn's post-carceral poem "Return to the Stars" (*"Vozvrashchenie k zvëzdam"*; 1953) where it appears as "boiling, unimaginably white Vega."[253]

Cerebral, romantic Vera is associated with works of high art. They are her source of knowledge about men, women, and the ties that bind them. Sitting in her lonely room she ponders the swaggering masculinity of Hemingway's heroes and the aggressive sexuality of Bizet's Carmen who, she senses, is but "a man in woman's clothes."[254] The idea that Carmen is a guy in drag is not without wit. One can imagine Solzhenitsyn chuckling to himself as he bestowed this insight upon his heroine. Still, the lovely doctor is not so ethereal that she cannot take pleasure in the reality of her own physical self, although such enjoyment is mediated through the forms of music: "Vera took delight in every new movement. It was like changing step during a dance."[255] If Zoya twirls, nay, gyrates for a male audience of one, Vera does her pirouettes in secret, within the four walls of her "cell." Yet the male qualities she values, "attention and tenderness and a sense of security,"[256] are not very different from those treasured by Zoya.

The scene in chapter twenty-five where Vera daydreams at home after doing the cleaning and skipping to the strains of *The Sleeping Beauty* invites closer examination. Tired after all that dusting and dancing, the heroine sinks into her mother's armchair (intimations of a comforting maternal embrace). Later she picks up a picture of her dead fiancé: "The neat face of a young boy: those unclouded, vulnerable, inexperienced eyes; the tie hanging down over the neat white shirt, the first tie he'd ever worn. It was his first suit too."[257] Screwed into his lapel is "a severe-looking little badge" with Lenin's profile.²⁵⁸ Gradually, the careful reader sees Solzhenitsyn's own youthful features come into focus, for this ekphrastic passage describes a studio portrait of the writer which dates from the time when he was a student, though *that* photo shows him wearing a dark shirt and tie.

As Vera lets her mind wander, it is Solzhenitsyn's own eyes that are watching her from the framed photograph she holds. He has made his beautiful heroine fall in love with his younger self, somewhere in the novel's untextualized past, in the guise of her boyfriend who went to war and fell fighting the Germans. And Solzhenitsyn loves her too, a secret rival to his own created hero, Kostoglotov. All this shows that between the interstices of the text lurk some very private and very intricate writerly meanings. They encipher the relationship between author and text, while reminding us of the contingent status of both.

A precedent for this arrangement may be found in *Anna Karenina*, where Tolstoy inserts himself into the narrative not only autobiographically, in the guise of Levin, but also cryptically, through the medium of Anna's subconscious. At periodic intervals in the novel she is troubled by visions of a dishevelled French-speaking muzhik hammering a piece of iron, and as she lies dying under those terrible wheels she catches a final glimpse of the same mysterious figure. But is not this apparition Tolstoy himself, the Gallicized aristocrat who dressed like a peasant and liked to work with his hands, haunting his alluring and errant heroine in order to punish or warn or protect her?

Vera is a woman of science and so she understands that "the laws of tissues, the law of hormones and the laws of growing old [are] indisputable."[259] Still, with the exception of that one brief and unsatisfactory relationship, she has kept herself to herself. Her romantic notions stop where biology and physiology begin, or at least before she finds herself drawn to Kostoglotov. "I believe in systematic science, practically tested," she tells him primly,[260] an attitude that explains her decision to subject him to the hormone therapy without his knowledge, which he considers a personal betrayal.

Again, as a practising physician Vera has no time for alternative medical practices. When she discovers Kostoglotov's mandrake infusion, she tells him to get rid of it. They step outside the clinic building and he pours the potion on the ground. The act turns into a shared ritual, an unspoken libation to Moist Mother Earth, the pagan Slavic divinity, even if here the soil in question is Asian instead of Russian.

The episode with the potion prefigures Kostoglotov's blood transfusion, performed by Vera later in the novel, which marks the turning point in their relationship. The scene showcases Solzhenitsyn's skill at scripting and interrelating bodies, psychologies, and physical phenomena inside a single fictive space, one that in this case happens to be a thoroughly and, for Kostoglotov, a disorientingly feminized one.

It is now spring, and the hero's health is definitely on the mend. He is summoned to the transfusion room by a doctor he has never seen before, a plump, apple-cheeked young woman. Ornery as ever, he is unwilling to allow yet more things to be done to his body without explanation or justification. He shares the other patients' irrational beliefs about the "old blood" and "bad blood" that the hospital supposedly uses, an endearing sign of childlike magical thinking in this otherwise self-confident, sober-minded figure. In fact, Kostoglotov has not abandoned his medically informed approach to the treatments he receives, but he has seen how botched procedures can result in hematomas, and wishes to avoid that risk. Besides, he takes an immediate and visceral dislike to the strange doctor with her "impatient, pink, puffy, goose-pimply arms":[261] on some private level of perception, those flabby, coarse-skinned limbs set off his sexual alarm bells.

As Oleg lies on the transfusion cot, still refusing to allow the transfer of the suspect blood into his circulatory system, his eyes are staring upward:

> The sun had come round to the side of the building where the dressings room was. It didn't come straight in through the windows, but two of the panes were shining brightly and part of the ceiling was covered by a large patch of light reflected off something shiny.[262]

Just then Vera walks into the room and he consents to the procedure, gratified to learn that the label on the jar with the blood is dated March 5, 1955, the second anniversary of Stalin's death: a reminder that the Draculean dictator is no longer around to feed on his subjects' life essence. While the dark-haired physician, aided by a young nurse, sets up her equipment, Oleg falls into a semi-trance, fatigued by weeks of x-ray treatments and lulled by Vera's comforting presence. Now, Tolstoy's narratives are often wrapped in the edges of sleep, as when Nikolai Rostov dozes in his homebound sleigh (*War and Peace*) or Anna Karenina daydreams in the train that carries her away from Moscow and Vronsky, an unread English novel in her hand. In this strange, hypnagogic state, the character's self-awareness recedes to the margins of the narration and is replaced by a collage of memories, reveries, and half-registered sensory impressions. So it is with Kostolgotov:

> The large patch of sunlight on the ceiling, weak as though filtered through lace, formed an uneven circle. This patch, reflected off he didn't know what, was contributing to his happiness and beautifying the clean, quiet room.[263]

For weeks now the hero has been brooding about the hormone injections. As the blood begins to flow into his body, he reproaches Vera for hiding the truth about them. She does not answer, but in one of those phallocentric passages that occasionally snake their way into the novel, her fingers stroke the cannula carrying the blood into Kostoglotov's vein: "It was as if they were helping to remove all obstructions in the tube."[264] Still silent, Vera steps out of Oleg's field of vision.

> It meant that the only things in sight were the instrument stand, the bottle of brown blood, the shiny bubbles, the tops of the sunlit windows, the reflections of the windows with their six panes in the frosted glass of the lamp globe, and the whole expanse of ceiling with its shimmering patch of faint sunlight.[265]

A catalogue of details, most of them with ocular values and meanings: angles of vision, light, and reflectivity.

Staring at the ceiling, Kostoglotov begins to think out loud: "First my own life was taken from me, and now I am being deprived even of the right... to perpetuate myself. I'll be the worst sort of cripple!"[266] This is one of the hero's most direct expression of self in the novel. The very feminine Vera now knows how much his biological maleness matters to this very masculine personality. Meanwhile —

> That patch on the ceiling—from time to time it seemed to quiver, to contract at the edges. It was as if a frown was passing over it, as if it too was thinking but couldn't understand. Then it would become motionless once more.[267]

The mutable spot of light overhead, which is visible only to the supine protagonist, is not unlike a child's smiley-face drawing of the sun, although *this* solar visage seems pensive rather than happy. The luminous flecks and dots Kostoglotov espies are a reflection of something, but of what we do not yet know, and nor does the hero.

Still out of sight, Vera says, her voice breaking with emotion, that she cannot believe Oleg feels this way. By uttering these words, she concedes that she is no longer just his physician and he is no longer just her patient: the renegotiation of their relationship is at hand. Concerned about the emasculating effects of the hormone treatment, Kostoglotov brings up the writings of an early twentieth-century sexologist he had read as a boy and describes the revulsion he had felt at their coldly mechanical representation of the act of physical love: "Such consistent, logical, irrefutable materialism. ... You see, that sort of attitude destroys everything human on earth."[268] Whereupon Vera reenters his line of sight and says, her face wearing "the usual friendly smile": "I don't want you to accept it either."[269] This is the breakthrough moment. A new and more intimate connection is formed, though it occurs as a meeting of minds, not bodies, in contrast to the passionate gropings and explorings Oleg and Zoya conducted over the oxygen tank (another medical device) earlier in the novel.

As the transfusion nears completion, the hero watches Vera rearranging the medical cushion that supports his elbow where the catheter is joined to the median cubital vein, and adjusting the wad of cotton wool around the entry point, and her fingers once again caress the rubber tube. These are no longer *clinical* manipulations by a doctor conducting a medical procedure, but beguilingly feminine gestures of affection, even if they occur at one physical remove. Custodial care is transformed into the protective and tender concern of one proximate lover for another.

But what about the mysterious patch of light?

> The strange patch of pale sunlight on the ceiling suddenly began to ripple. A flashing cluster of silver spots appeared from somewhere. They began to move about. Oleg watched the fast-moving ripples and wavelets. He had finally realized that the mysterious nebula [*tumannost'*][270] high up on the ceiling was no more than a reflection of a puddle, a patch of ground outside the window by the fence that hadn't dried up yet.[271]

Beams of light traveling from the sun, a star like the refulgent Vega-Vera, illumine the pools of rainwater outside and are reflected onto the ceiling above Kostoglotov's head. From there the light strikes his cornea, which draws the beams together, and then they are refracted in the aqueous humor. The lens of the eye brings them into focus on the retina, whence the image is transmitted via the optic nerves, through the optic chiasm, to the thalamus and from there to the cerebral cortex. The word "nebula" underlines the *nebulous*, inchoate nature of the light patterns on the ceiling while also evoking the Andromeda Nebula, the great spiral galaxy in the eponymous constellation and one of the farthest objects in space visible to the naked eye. The transfusion room is a planetarium of the imagination. Beyond these astronomical connotations, hovering on some allusive plane of meaning is the myth of Perseus, the prince who flew on winged sandals to save chained

Andromeda from the monstrous whale Cetus. The same topos of rescuing warrior and rescued maiden is present in the ballet *The Sleeping Beauty*, with which Oleg and Vera were separately identified earlier in the novel. Yet in the transfusion scene the topos is inverted, for chaste Vera's medical ministrations to Oleg, a former soldier who is immobilized by that phallic tube, make *her* the rescuer.

The physical nature of the scintillating reflection is no longer a mystery, but it remains semiotically opaque, for we sense that this projected image has meanings beyond the environmentally descriptive. The patch of light is a flickering, floating signifier, an unrealized metaphor or an uncoded symbol.

This imaginative geometry of light—optical axes and vectors, astronomical values and references—points to a reality more exalted than physiology and sex, blood and hormones, even biological life and death. Like Plato's image of the sun, the deity who "is not only the author of visibility in all visible things, but of generation and nourishment and growth,"[272] Solzhenitsyn's luminous reflections and refractions clue us to the Forms of Good and the Reality of the Ideal.

Plato, in *The Republic*:

> Now take a line which has been cut into two unequal parts, and divide each of them again in the same proportion, and suppose the two main divisions to answer, one to the visible and the other to the intelligible, and then compare the subdivisions in respect of their clearness and want of clearness, and you will find that the first section in the sphere of the visible consists of images. And by images I mean, in the first place, shadows, and in the second place, reflections in water and in solid, smooth, and polished bodies and the like.[273]

Kostoglotov's love for the beautiful doctor, and hers for him, extends far beyond the realm of "logical, irrefutable materialism," to those sunlit spheres described by the Greek philosopher. From that sublime perspective, whether Oleg and Vera's bodies will be joined together in a physical union is, truly, *immaterial*.

7

Brusque and direct in speech and manner, Lev Leonidovich is a man's man, and the only Jewish character in the book.[274] He boasts a power name that carries regal overtones (see King Leonidas of Sparta): Lev (from the Latin *Leo*)—lion,

Leonidovich is the patronymic form of Leonid (from the Greek Λεωνιδας)—lion-like. Therefore, the surgeon, a son of Leonid, is leonine to the third power! Graceful Vera, however, privately thinks of her hirsute, barrel-chested, long-armed colleague as a "gorilla," albeit an "amiable" one.[275] He gives his young patient Dyoma the same mixed, manly simian vibe, which the fatherless boy finds comforting as he pictures himself being operated on by those "hairy, ape-like hands."[276]

Lev Leonidovich comes into the novel equipped with his personal stalker, the ironically named Angelica. A red-haired harpy three years out of medical school, she pursues the brawny surgeon with diabolical determination, employing every trick in the handbook of sexual harassment to get him into her bed or if that fails, into trouble with the hospital bosses. An incident in which the red-head, in full stalking mode, uses a lab report to drape herself over the surgeon is witnessed by Kostoglotov: now that his health is on the mend, the hero is preternaturally alert to signs of sexual tension in his surroundings.

> She went on talking and talking (and it was true, her right shoulder *was* pressing against Lev Leonidovich's arm!). The paper Lev Leonidovich had begun to write on was lying there. His pen was hanging idle, upside down between his fingers.[277]

That drooping pen is a phallic signifier of Lev's lack of lust: once again, provocative Angelica has failed to provoke the shaggy surgeon.

This gruff character meets with Kostoglotov's approval *because* he is a man. Yet when the hero seeks out the surgeon to ask him for advice about the hormone therapy, they misunderstand each other as *men*. The surgeon, who has been tailed by amorous Angelica for years (!), asks Oleg, "Do you really think women are the flower of life? You know, you can get fed up with them after a while... All they do is stop you achieving anything serious."[278] The hero, however, is unconvinced, though he keeps his doubts to himself: "What an absurd idea, to live to see the day when women seem superfluous! Surely a man should never let himself go like this!"[279] In fact, the four super-masculine characters in the novel, Kostoglotov, Podduev, Chaly, and Lev Leonidovich (all of them hirsute, that is, "simian"), are, or were, surrounded by nubile women. Kostoglotov's romantic involvement with Zoya and Vera we have already discussed; Podduev was a serial womanizer; the wheeler-dealer Chaly is a bigamist with a girl in every (black) market town. Lev Leonidovich, who must fend off his unangelic stalker, is the only one of the four who is chaste.

If the supernally named Angelica is a petite demon, sixteen-year-old Asya, a new arrival in the clinic, looks like a "delicate yellow-haired angel"[280] and a "film star,"[281] at least to the virgin eye of Dyoma, with whom she forms an unlikely friendship.[282] As these romantic notions suggest, the smitten youth sees the pert teenager as the embodiment of exquisite, unattainable womanhood. Until he met Asya, Dyoma was revolted by the very notion of sex because of his widowed mother's casual promiscuity. In fact, Asya is a girl of her time and place, a Soviet version of that universal type, the high school beauty queen. Fun-loving and popular, she is also a varsity pentathlete. Like Rusanov and, once upon a time, Shulubin, Asya believes in the principle preached by SocRealist writers, "life is for happiness,"[283] although she infuses the formula with mawkish adolescent sentiment: "What is there in life except love?"[284]

Asya may be just a year older than Dyoma but she has had lots of boyfriends, or so she says, and has made out lots of times, or so she claims. She tells the bemused boy about the new dance of rock and roll fashionable in distant, fabulous Moscow[285] and employs a signature qualifier of the period when she boasts about her sexual escapades: "Why wait? It's the atomic age!"[286]

During her first days in the hospital Asya is oblivious of her disease, a cancer of the breast, but then is informed she must have a mastectomy. When we meet her next, she is no longer an empty-headed bobbysoxer but a frightened young girl who cannot imagine herself so maimed, so de-feminized. In a wrenching passage that features one of those stretches of catalogue prose Solzhenitsyn occasionally favors, a despairing Asya takes leave of her body as she knows it:

> She began to imagine bathing dresses in different styles—with or without shoulder-straps, one-piece or two-piece, every contemporary and future fashion, bathing suits in orange and blue, crimson and the hue of the sea, in one color or striped with scalloped edges, bathing suits she hadn't yet tried on but had examined in front of a mirror—all the ones she would never buy and never wear.[287]

On the eve of the operation she seeks out her shy admirer and invites, nay forces him to play with her doomed breast: "No one but you will ever kiss it! Dyomka, *you* at least must kiss it, if nobody else!"[288] This is how Dyoma, who has just lost a leg to cancer, receives his sexual awakening. The relationship between the two teenagers never blossoms into romance, or at least we never learn if it does: Asya disappears from the novel as suddenly as she enters it. If *Cancer Ward* contains a male counterpart to the pretty pentathlete, it is not bookish Dyoma but that son of privilege, the all-Soviet high school jock Lavrik Rusanov. But loathsome Lavrik and lovely Asya's paths never cross, which is a good thing.

Next. While doctors like Chekhov's Ragin enjoyed high social status in late imperial Russia, during the Soviet period theirs was not a prestigious or remunerative calling, a fact reflected in the straitened circumstances of physicians like Dr. Dontsova. Outside the clinic walls this skilled medical professional who has saved hundreds of lives is just "a person in a queue,"[289] in the words of one commentator. Here the point made explicitly and at length in *The First Circle*, that the Soviet Union was a place where the qualified and the intelligent mostly go unrewarded, while their moral and intellectual inferiors rule the roost, is presented obliquely, and is all the more effective for it. Foucault shows that in the Age of the Enlightenment doctors began to acquire a position of political eminence owing to their new status as "programmers of a well-ordered society."[290] In the nineteenth century these medical experts came to enjoy an "accumulation of economic and social privileges" as authorized and increasingly effective healers.[291] On this analysis, Soviet physicians were de-privileged because in 1917 the programming of society was taken over by pure ideologues, votaries of a scientific doctrine that subsumed and redefined all other professional practices and disciplines. Prophylactic care and therapeutic or surgical treatments of the body were subordinated to new political imperatives that aimed at the construction of a perfect society populated by perfect people by means of economic restructuring and social engineering.

As it turns out, Dr. Dontsova's professional dedication may have cost her her life. When she started working in the radiology section, the x-ray machine lacked a shield, a typical omission in an economy where shortages reign and the individual is but a disposable unit of socialist production. Eventually a shield was installed and the medical personnel were issued protective clothing, but even so, Dr. Dontsova spent far more time in the radiology room than was safe. Over the years she suffered appallingly high levels of exposure to ionizing radiation. The result is that this cancer specialist develops the disease herself: another tragic irony in a novel where illness strikes the sympathetic and unsympathetic alike and one's chances of recovery have nothing to do with one's human worth or membership in a social category. (The topos of the professional healer who contracts a life-threatening illness is a common one in medical narratives.)[292] Sontag makes the point that unlike epidemic disease, which destroys communities, cancer is selective, so that "the judgment tends to fall on the individual rather than society."[293] In *Cancer Ward*, this social truth is diegetically framed by means of two defamiliarizing descriptions that occur at separate points in the text but share a brutally graphic, Tolstoyan quality. Just as cancer has turned Rusanov into "one hundred and fifty-four pounds of hot, white flesh," it transforms Dr. Dontsova into "a helpless sack crammed with organs."[294] She devolves from healer to patient: her institutional status is inverted, like Dr. Ragin's, though unlike him, she may yet live.

As happens in *The First Circle*, *Cancer Ward* offers up a rustic figure that connects the urban and institutional situations depicted to pre-modern patterns of life and belief. Spiridon's counterpart here is the elderly female patient, folksy Aunt Styofa. Together with the tribal Sibgatov and Mursalimov, she is an outsider in the world of twentieth-century medicine and twentieth-century tyranny. As a mother *and* a grandmother, Aunt Styofa is a doubly maternal character. She belongs to a large and loving family whose members often visit her and bring her treats, which she shares with lonely Dyoma. If Kostoglotov acts as the boy's stand-in "elder brother"[295] and Asya as his surrogate sister (that one kiss of the breast excepted), Aunt Styofa becomes the youth's substitute materfamilias. Deeply devout, she has retained the traditional Christian beliefs of Russia's peasant masses, much more so than her cross-textual coeval Matryona. She is upset by Dyoma's godless ways and tries to teach him the rudiments of religion while urging him to forgive his mother's promiscuous behavior. When Dyoma asks her that terrible Why Me? question, the old woman has the faith but not the words to give him the answer he craves: "It depends on God. … God sees everything. You should submit to him."[296] To which the schoolboy replies, by his own lights, reasonably: "If he can see everything, why does he load it all on one person? I think he ought to try and spread it about a bit …"[297] This colloquy calls to mind the conversation between Shukhov and Alyosha about divine justice in "Ivan Denisovich." Like the sweet-natured Baptist in that tale, Aunt Styofa bears the novel's theodician message, although as in Alyosha's case, it is structured so as to be *textually* less persuasive than her life's example.

As for Dyoma, he is the novel's student-in-residence, poring over his textbooks and learning new things from those he meets, in a procedure that replicates Kostoglotov's hungry acquisition of knowledge in the camps and in the clinic. And so, Oleg gives him geometry lessons. Aunt Styofa provides him with a smattering of religious knowledge and, perhaps more importantly, with an awareness that the Komsomol certainties he was taught are irrelevant to his life situation. Asya teaches him about girls. And even though Dyoma loses his leg to cancer, he gives every indication of being a survivor, in the full sense of the word. Unlike so many others in this novel, he has a future.

Now, the notion of time as a precious commodity not to be misspent or squandered was central to Solzhenitsyn's sense of self from early youth. For him, time was the currency of virtue. His life is an amazing example of every hour and every minute employed in the performance of urgent literary and extra-literary tasks, sometimes to the detriment of personal or family relationships. In his fictive worlds, characters like Ivan Denisovich or Georgi Vorotyntsev, who are constitutionally incapable of twiddling their thumbs, enjoy special authorial favor. Yet no other character in Solzhenitsyn is as conscious that *tempus fugit* as Vadim Zatsirko, a patient in Kostoglotov's ward who is dying of a melanoblastoma. Vadim is a geologist in his late twenties who was stricken by cancer just as he was trying to develop a new method of finding iron ore in the ground: the outline of a classic SocRealist plot. He is also a doctrinaire communist and an unreflective philistine who considers Rabelais "obscene."[298] Nonetheless, Solzhenitsyn bestows on this rather unsympathetic and even frightening figure something of himself as a young man: "From his earliest days this demonic, insatiable hunger for time had been part of his make-up."[299] An entire page is devoted to a description of Vadim's temporal obsession. When he was a schoolboy he would plan his recesses more meticulously than his teachers planned their lessons. As the tumor grows, the young scientist increases the tempo of his researches, determined to "bequeath the people a new method of discovering ore deposits."[300] With his flat passions, arid views, and fatal disease, the young geologist resembles any number of exemplary protagonists from Soviet propaganda novels such as Nikolai Ostrovskii's steel-tempered hero, Pavel Korchagin. Yet even Vadim's industrial fanaticism is unable to overcome his growing awareness of approaching death, and in the end he abandons his feverish geological inquiries in favor of a stoical acceptance of his fate.

The scenes in which this character is a central presence are scripted to confute "the novel about a worthy intellectual or inventor,"[301] one of the six categories of SocRealist prose identified by Katerina Clark. It is as if Solzhenitsyn had plucked Vadim from some different, drier text and *embedded* him in a fictive environment where he could finally resign from Korchagin's phalanx of true believers.

While Vadim is a recognizable SocRealist type, albeit with an interesting temporal twist, no Soviet novel could be expected to contain a character like the construction foreman Yefrem Podduev, another of Kostoglotov's neighbors in the ward. A sullen, rough-spoken fellow in his fifties, he is guilty of many bad things: wife beating, child abandonment, serial fornication, casual brutality toward those weaker than himself. Although essentially apolitical, as a teenage

Red Army recruit during the civil war he shot seven adherents of the Constituent Assembly, a youthful killing that recalls Dashkin's execution of the landowner in *Love the Revolution*. Let me elaborate. Thirteen-year-old Yefrem is the morally derelict peasant child who symbolically murders Russian democracy by slaughtering the defenders of its first freely elected parliament (the number seven has mythical overtones). By extending the chain of Podduev's dark deeds back to early Soviet times the author keeps faith with his cold-eyed view that the Russian nation was the agent of its own twentieth-century degradation and enslavement. Arguably, the passage that describes Yefrem's foundational crime is fabulaically superfluous, its conceptualizing function too obvious. But then there is Yefrem's participation in the gulag system as a supervisor of prison labor. As he casts his mind over the past, he recalls three prisoners, a peasant, an ex-officer, and a frail youth, whom he forced to work past all endurance on one of his building sites (three is another mythical number). The youth warned Podduev, "All right, chief. It'll be your turn to die one day."[302] This earnest of retribution, all the more chilling for being uttered not by a somber graybeard but a downy-faced adolescent, is realized with Old Testament severity. Tyurin in "Ivan Denisovich" would have understood, and approved.

Released from the clinic as an incurable case, Podduev ends his days at a railway station, a favored tragic locus in so many Russian novels. By then he has realized the error of his ways, thanks to Tolstoy's story "What Men Live By," which Kostoglotov persuaded him to read: the protagonist as a facilitator of a fellow human's moral awakening, via a canonical text written by the novel's presiding literary presence.

Another notable patient is Maxim Chaly. A small dynamo of a man, he bursts into the ward on a gloomy rainy morning in a whirlwind of jokes, ditties, and salutations. Although he suffers from a stomach tumour, "there was nothing of the exhaustion of cancer on his face."[303] He travels light, a razor and a pack of cards his only possessions. The date on which this strange little fellow makes his appearance is March 5, 1955: two years to the day when Stalin died. The name Chaly, which means "roan," calls to mind the colloquial *shalyi*, that is, "unhinged" or "crazy." Thus, Maxim Chalyi—Maximum Madness! But the most remarkable thing about Solzhenitsyn's Mad Max is his nose, a "great, soft, reddened" organ which "gave his face its simple-hearted, attractive and open quality."[304] Chaly's fondness for card games, the way that he thrives on chaos and entropy, and most *prominently*, his rampant red flag of a proboscis call to mind the braggard Nozdrev (Mr. Nostril) in *Dead Souls*, that "nasty noisy nosey swindler"[305] whose nasal passages are bristly twin tunnels leading straight down to Hell.

Gambler, prankster, drinker, lecher, Chaly flaunts all manner of sins. As the sluttish Nellya gets ready to clean the ward, he engages with her in what is known in twenty-first-century America as inappropriate sexual banter. The flirtation is crude and explicit on both sides:

> "Come on, hurry up then, get down and wash the floor, we want to inspect the façade!"
> "Look as much as you like, we don't charge for that."[306]

Minutes after he is admitted, Chaly puts together a poker game consisting of himself, Rusanov, and Ahmadjan. The black-marketeer, the bureaucrat, and the camp guard ante up on the anniversary of Stalin's death: how more pettily demonic can you get! The party continues as Rusanov, saddened by the absence on this mournful occasion of the Generalissimo's portrait in the newspaper (an omen of the political changes underway), shares a bottle of vodka with his new friend. The "artful dodger"[307] Chaly explains to the glum partocrat his uncomplicated life's wisdom: "Let the others croak if they want to. You and I'll have a good time!"[308] He tries to convince a boozy Rusanov of the merits of the black-market economy. Here he actually talks sense, waxing indignant about the authorities' practice of posting guards to catch illegal tomato traders instead of sending those sentinels of socialism to pick the vegetables themselves. And all the time Aleksei Shulubin, the Old Bolshevik who out of love and fear of Stalin gave up, one by one, his political ideals and moral principles, stares at them unblinkingly with blood-red eyes from the corner of the room: the whilom leader of the masses contemplating mass man in all his glory.

The personnel director finds that thousand-yard stare unnerving: "He was an eagle-owl, that's what he was."[309] The sentence may be read as an extadiegetic allusion to that famous line from Hegel, "The owl of Minerva spreads its wings only with the falling of dark": philosophy is always just that one historical instant too late to tell us what *will be*, it can only explain what *was*. When later in the novel Shulubin selects Kostoglotov as the recipient of his confidences, it is to make philosophical and historical amends, to conduct a cleansing of his polluted soul, long after the fact.

Chaly emerges from his operation as hearty as ever. When Rusanov leaves the hospital, wife on arm, the jolly crook is standing at the entrance to Wing No. 13, his hand raised in a clenched fist salute: the iconic gesture of the revolution stripped of political meaning and turned into a palsy greeting. Chaly promises Rusanov to get new tires for the family Moskvich, and so the friendship between the two men, two sub-demons, is sealed. In this tentative alliance of the communist and the crook we see much of Russia's future history adumbrated, down to the ochlocrats and oligarchs of the post-Soviet transition.

The novel's most important intellectual exchange occurs in chapter thirty-one, where Kostoglotov and Shulubin have their conversation about the past and its meanings. They argue whether the Russian people was complicit in Stalin's crimes. Shulubin, with a bitterness that comes from a deep, terminal self-loathing, is harsh: "The people are intelligent enough, it's simply that they wanted to live. There's a law big nations have—to endure and so to survive."[310] But the price of survival was too high, he adds, quoting Pushkin to illustrate his point: as so often happens in Russian novels, the great poet is the ultimate authority on matters of love, life, and history:

> In our vile times
> ... Man was, whatever his element,
> Either tyrant or traitor or prisoner![311]

These are the only three choices available to a subject of the terror state, avers the Old Bolshevik. The former zek Kostoglotov is more forgiving. He agrees that most Russians sought to survive, but refuses to condemn them as a people: "Pushkin was too rash."[312] That phrase, with its transgressive ring of skepticism about Russia's national genius, is classic Kostoglotov. Besides, while it is hard to imagine the hero adopting the survival-at-any-cost position, his is the same stance as Nietzsche's, who proclaimed that "the only thing which can prove today whether one has worth or not—that one holds out."[313]

The two men go on to discuss Shulubin's doctrine of "ethical socialism," which rejects the false "idol" of happiness[314] (he is a follower of Francis Bacon and his theory of the idols) in favor of "a society in which all relationships, fundamental principles and laws flow directly from ethics, and from them *alone*."[315] Here Shulubin is on shakier ground. He may be able to quote from Pushkin and Georg Herwegh, to adduce Prince Kropotkin and Vladimir Solovyov, but his perfect society seems drably smug and insipidly totalizing in its rigid reliance on a communally endorsed hierarchy of moral values and practices. "One should never direct people toward happiness.... One should direct them toward mutual affection," he explains.[316] This notion may be derived from the *Essay on the History of Civil Society* (1767) by Adam Ferguson, the Scottish Enlightenment thinker:

If, in reality, courage, and a heart devoted to the good of mankind, are the constituents of human felicity, the kindness which is done infers a happiness in the person from whom it proceeds, not in him on whom it is bestowed; and the greatest good which men possessed of fortitude and generosity can procure to their fellow-creatures, is a participation of this happy character.[317]

Although the ex-Bolshevik rejects the use of violence and coercion as a political instrument, both are implicit in the practicalities of his project. Yet his strictures against private felicity as the be-all of human existence are in line with the Harvard Address, where the writer controversially stated: "Even biology tells us that a high degree of habitual well-being is not advantageous to a living organism. Today, well-being in the life of Western society has begun to take off its pernicious mask."[318] Still, the novel's democratically structured multivocality leaves it to us, the readers, to weigh the respective merits of Shulubin's and Kostoglotov's systems, shaped as they are by their tragic life experiences on either side of the barbed wire fence: the former's decades-long, soul-sapping fear of arrest, the latter's years of struggle in the gulag.

The Harvard Address saw Solzhenitsyn express disdain for the "pursuit of happiness" formula of American political discourse. Yet his views about what constitutes an ethically valid public stance show some nuance. In the essay "Live Not By Lies!" he concedes that only exceptionally brave or desperate individuals, the Kostoglotovs of this world, are capable of "self-immolation or even a hunger strike."[319] By the same token, "civil disobedience à la Gandhi" is not an option for most people.[320] So instead, in the eponymous formulation, one should "live not by lies."

One character in *Cancer Ward* has done precisely that.

Dormidont Tikhonovich Oreshchenkov is a seventy-year-old physician who lives in semi-retirement in the city's outskirts. Here is another speaking or even whispering name: Dormidont—Sleeper (Lat.), Tikhonovich is the patronymic form of Tikhon: see Tyche, the Greek goddess of fortune. Tikhon is also a near-homonym for the Russian *tikhii*, or "quiet." These are onomastic hints of Oreshchenkov's special status in this fictive universe. His is the unusual case of the honorable man who spends his entire life in plain view of a tyrannical state yet never sullies himself by being complicit in its works: his public conduct is always congruent with his private conscience. The doctor survived the revolution, the civil war, low Leninism, high Stalinism, World War II, and the regime's postwar retrenchment, thanks to his professional skills—he once saved the life of a high Party official—but also plain old luck. In this he resembles another fictional doctor, Yuri Zhivago, his cross-textual colleague and coeval. In the twilight of his career, Dr. Oreshchenkov maintains a small private practice as well as keeping a paternal eye on former pupils like Ludmila Dontsova. When the radiologist concludes that she might have developed cancer, she seeks him out for a second opinion, for the elderly physician has her complete and unconditional trust. Yet their professional and personal association carries a larger meaning.

In his comments on the nineteenth-century Russian classics, Auerbach suggests that "the born Orthodox Russians, throughout the entire country, and regardless of class distinctions,... seem to form a single ancient patriarchal family."[321] The fragmenting forces of revolutionary chaos and totalitarian control did much to dissolve those bonds of patrilineal allegiance and filial loyalty, but enough of them survived the violent action of history, especially in provincial backwaters like Tashkent. *Cancer Ward* features three patriarchal figures, all of them medical men: the brusque surgeon, Lev Leonidovich; Kostoglotov's replacement father, the exiled gynecologist Kadmin; and the wise old doctor, Oreshchenkov, although in fabulatory terms they are characters of secondary importance. Nonetheless, Dr. Oreshchenkov's presence—with a full chapter devoted to his life, times, and friendship with Dr. Dontsova—broadens the novel's social scope, adding to its typology of twentieth-century victims, perpetrators, and witnesses of tyranny.

The same is true of the episode that shows Rusanov's betrayal of Rodichev, his neighbor in the flat they shared in the 1920s. Rodichev is one of those enthusiastic, under-educated souls who were drafted into the Party after the revolution, supported Stalin in his rise to supreme power, and went on to implement his defining policies of collectivization and industrialization. Communists of his kind, ignorant but idealistic, coarse but caring, were wiped out in their tens of thousands by the Great Terror. Solzhenitsyn, who had known people like Rodichev when he was growing up in Rostov, portrays this political type, one that by the 1950s had long since passed into history, with a light touch. Rodichev speaks the right words, sings the right songs. At one point he hums a revolutionary ditty popular in the early years of the Soviet regime:

Blacksmiths we are, with hearts young and free.[322]

The effect is subtly comical, since he and Rusanov work in a pasta factory. Yet all the while Rodichev carries the mark of doom on his broad proletarian forehead, for the crooning communist will be denounced by his charmless, chinless chum, who covets his share of the apartment and resents his easygoing ways.

Solzhenitsyn has an occasional tendency to overpopulate his longer narratives, one that is noticeable in *The First Circle*. In *Cancer Ward*, too, the author seems determined to fill in as many sociological, ideological, and occupational slots as possible, in order to give his novel the desired panoramic quality. Thus, several of the personae carry minimal narrative value, for example, Yevgenia Ustinovna, the clinic's senior surgeon, and Olympiada Vladislavovna, a nurse. Both are fictive supernumeraries, included in the text to make a point. Yevgenia Ustinovna comes bearing a message that is directly derived from its literary totem, Tolstoy. Although a credentialed physician, she is sympathetic to alternative medical practices of the kind so fervently advocated by Kostoglotov: "She remembered and understood the words of Tolstoy's Cossack, Yeroshka, who said about West European doctors, 'All they can do is cut. Well, they're fools. But up in the mountains you get the real doctors. They know about the herbs.'"[323] (The reference is to the novel *The Cossacks*.)

Yevgenia Ustinovna is not just a quotation in a doctor's gown. She is depicted as going against literary type, having "none of the traits usually ascribed to members of her profession, none of the resolute look, determined lines across the forehead or iron clenching of the jaw."[324] Solzhenitsyn provides her with a body (though in her fifties, she is girlishly thin) and a mannerism (she is a nicotine addict who during her rounds "would sometimes raise her first two fingers to her lips").[325] As the head of the surgical staff, the chain-smoking surgeon is another female authority figure in the hospital's matriarchal chain of command, outranking her supermasculine colleague Lev Leonidovich, who seems comfortable with the arrangement. Nonetheless, Yevgenia Ustinovna's textual presence is no more substantial than her invisible cigarette fumes. Olympiada Vladislavovna, on the other hand, is not so much textually present as absent: she is called away from her job to attend a ten-day trade union conference, prompting the narrator to comment sarcastically on the waste of time prevalent in such meetings. That is all there is to her; and it is not a great deal.

8

In *The Magic Mountain*, the location of the sanatorium is symbolic, for Switzerland lies at the geographical center of the western half of the European continent. But what about Solzhenitsyn's cancer hospital?

If the Romantics glamorized places that were "remote, Asiatic, or ancient,"[326] then Uzbekistan, land of Tamerlane, and Tashkent, its capital city, qualify on all three counts. In *Cancer Ward*, however, both country and city are consistently de-exoticized; and when spaces and people are othered, this is a matter of a given character's angle of cultural perception. Fictively, the Uzbek capital functions as the novel's framing chronotopic locus, an open, unbordered urban venue that surrounds the concentric interiors of the Medical Center, the oncology clinic, and Kostoglotov's ward. The city is both anonymous and differentiated, Asian and Soviet, beautiful and ugly, familiar and strange. His writer's heart may lie in "deepest Russia" with its "leafy muttering of forests," but Solzhenitsyn is preeminently an urban novelist. The depictions of Tashkent, which is shown on three different occasions through the eyes of, respectively, Dr. Dontsova, Vera, and Kostoglotov, are a collage of urban images and happenings and anticipate the sophistication with which the writer would re- or de-construct the historical cities of Petrograd, Moscow, and Zurich in *The Red Wheel*.

A feminist scholar writes: "Whether or not all of us do both, women as a sex are institutionally responsible for producing both goods and human beings and all women are forced to become the kinds of people who can do both."[327] Nowhere else in Solzhenitsyn, or even twentieth-century Russian literature as a whole, are the joyless routines of urban womanhood more movingly described than in this novel. Chapter seven textualizes them in the form of one of those "day in the life" stretches of prose at which Solzhenitsyn excels, which describes the patterns of Dr. Dontsova's professional, administrative, and domestic existence. "Today had been typical,"[328] the narrator warns us in the accents of the doctor herself, and goes on to enumerate the succession of medical consultations, colleague-to-colleague discussions, patient examinations, administrative decisions, phone calls, and staff meetings that fill the physician's time at the clinic. She broods about the stomach pains she has been experiencing of late. On her way home she contemplates the chores that await her when she will get there, for she must cook dinner, clean the apartment, and do the washing, naturally, by hand: her husband and son are unwilling to perform such "repetitive, endlessly self-renewing work."[329] To top it all, she must worry about the threats uttered by Rusanov that morning, which she will "contemplate all evening and all night."[330]

Joseph Brodsky found this chapter particularly affecting:

> The description's flatness and monotony definitely matches the list of her tasks, epic in their length and idiocy, yet this list lasts longer than anyone's ability to sustain a dispassionate tone recording it: a reader

expects an explosion: it is too unbearable. And this is exactly where the author stops.[331]

As Dr. Dontsova is traveling home we get our first glimpse of Tashkent. In many ways, this a typical Soviet metropolis, with crowded trams, female shoppers carrying "big bags like small suitcases,"[332] sullen queues, and dingy shops with empty shelves. A longtime resident of the city, the physician is used to its sights, smells, and sounds, and has had a bad day at work. Her mind is elsewhere, so she pays no heed to details that might strike a Russian, European, or American reader as exotic. The only indication that Tashkent is located east of west is a reference to an Uzbek boy selling almonds next to a teahouse, but the doctor's tired eyes glide over this figure without registering its otherness. In *Cancer Ward*, only Kostoglotov's city impressions carry a sense of the unfamiliar.

If Tashkent is de-exoticized, so are most of the non-Russian characters. The cast of patients includes several Turkomans: the middle-aged Kazakh Egenberdiev, the elderly Uzbek Mursalimov, and the latter's youthful countryman Ahmadjan, the cretinous camp guard. Racial and national traits are noted but not dwelled upon. Egenberdiev sits on his bed "legs crossed as though he was sitting on a rug at home."[333] Mursalimov has "dark-bronze skin"[334] and wears a skullcap, the traditional headgear of his people. He looks like a "mummy,"[335] but the noun is an indicator of Mursalimov's emaciated condition rather than a fanciful intimation of pharaohs and pyramids. The Ukrainian Proshka, the youth who has cancer of the heart, speaks in an appropriately Ukrainian voice, using words like *harno* (good) and *trokhi* (a little), which to a Russian reader immediately fix him ethnically, just as an English speaker would consider "bairn" or "ken" standard markers of Scottishness.

At the same time, the novel conveys the subtleties of inter-ethnic (mis) communication, which expand the work's heteroglossic component. When Dr. Dontsova addresses the non-Russian speaking Egenberdiev, she does so in a loud voice, carefully articulating each word, as adults do with small children. The Kazakh Egenberdiev and the Uzbek Ahmadjan can just about make themselves mutually understood, "although each thought the other was murdering the language."[336] But Ahmadjan communicates with the Crimean Tatar Sibgatov (who is also Turkic) in Russian, because "their languages weren't much alike."[337] A historically ignorant soul, the camp guard is thrilled by the film *The Capture of Plevna* (*Vziatie Plevny*),[338] which is set during the Russo-Turkish war of 1877–8 and, as he puts it, shows "our Russian boys" crushing the Ottoman enemy.[339] Truly, he is a figment of Russia's imperial imaginary.

Nizamutdin Bakhramovich, the time-serving hospital chief, is another Uzbek, a beneficiary of the Soviet policy of nurturing "national cadres." A man of slender accomplishment but much self-importance, he directs the doctors to discharge dying patients to "increase the turnover of beds" and "help the statistics,"[340] in an echo of Kapitolina Rusanova's Sovietese ("it's living people they are processing"). His countryman, Dr. Halmuhamedov, is a complete medical fraud. Here the restraint with which the novel treats ethnic difference is abandoned: Lev Leonidovich, a Jew, others his incompetent colleague with contemptuous relish:

> He looked like an illustration from the travels of Captain Cook, a savage straight out of the jungle. His hair was a dense mat, his bronzed face was spotted with jet-carbon blackheads, his ferociously gleeful smile revealed a set of large white teeth—there was only one thing missing: a ring through his nose.[341]

"Of course it was not his appearance that mattered ...," the narrator adds piously,[342] thereby qualifying this lurid portrait as a hybrid utterance, but the damage is done: hapless Halmuhamedov enters the novel, only to exit it on the next page, in the guise of a South Seas cannibal.

The other ethnic cutout is a patient, Friedrich Federau, a Russian-born German. Although a Party member, he was deported to Kazakhstan in August 1941 together with the entire population of the German Volga Republic. *Treue Friedrich* remained loyal to his persecutors despite the many humiliations he suffered then and later. He continues to love the CPSU with the sedulous devotion of the terror-slave. His is a recognizable type, the political activist whose ideological commitment trumps all notions of morality, self-respect, or even common sense. Teutonically blond, Federau is pedantic, punctual, and "exact in everything he [does]."[343] He has the body language of a Prussian officer in a bad movie: when the chief surgeon arrives to examine him, "he [stands] up, thumbs down the seams of his trousers."[344] Were Friedrich not wearing hospital slippers, he would have clicked his heels.

Yet on the whole, when depicting his non-Russian characters Solzhenitsyn tends to privilege individuality over nationality. Federau may be a Teutonic piece of cardboard, but Vera Gangart, another Russian-German, is one of Solzhenitsyn's most memorably drawn heroines. To repeat, when indicators of ethnic otherness are present in the novel, they usually reflect a particular character's perspective. This fictive procedure is governed by the same narratological rules that prevail in Solzhenitsyn's other prose works. Much of the time the narration takes the form of free indirect speech, although the implied-authorial narrative voice may take over for discrete stretches of text. Take, for example, this scene, in which a supine Kostoglotov gazes longingly at sexy Zoya. The reader successively encounters two perspectives: the intradiegetic, where the hero examines a woman's face and body in mute masculine appreciation, and the extradiegetic, where the narrator adopts an explicatory and even ironic stance, almost but not quite polemicizing with the romantically enthralled protagonist:

> How pleasant and easy-going she was, with that golden hair and those great wide eyes.
>
> If only he could have seen himself, his hair, matted from lying on the pillow, sticking up in pointed tuffs all over his head, one corner of a coarse calico issue shirt showing with hospital informality from under his jacket, which was not buttoned up to the neck.[345]

The visual angle that underpins the gently mocking description in the second paragraph happens to be Zoya's, although this congruence between the implied-authorial (extradiegetic) and the Zoya-related (intradiegetic) points of view does not mean that it is her voice that is doing the mocking: at this stage in the proceedings, the nurse's attitude toward Kostoglotov is briskly professional. The authorial narrator may be giving the hero's hairy leg a gentle pull, but for the time being Zoya is keeping him at arm's (leg's?) length.

Upon his arrival in the ward, Rusanov sees the other patients as undifferentiated husks, "eight abject beings,"[346] and then proceeds to categorize them: "All the others there seemed either apathetic wrecks or non-Russians."[347] He dismisses Egenberdiev, a Kazakh, and Mursalimov, an Uzbek, as "two natives"[348] (*dva natsmena*)[349] and mockingly addresses the latter as "aksakal" ("village elder" in Uzbek).[350] Scripted as a bureaucratic stereotype, Rusanov stereotypes his neighbors. His white supremacist credentials established, he can now get on with the business of being the novel's irredeemable villain.

By contrast, Kostoglotov is completely lacking in such Great Russian chauvinism. When he was in the camp he had resented the Armenian prisoners who "had looked after one another jealously and always taken the best jobs," yet he realized that "they hadn't invented Siberia" and were just trying "to help and save one another."[351] During a bull session in the ward he suggests that judging a person's worth by his membership in a given economic class is a form of "racism":[352] a clever subversion of one Soviet ideologem, that of the defining nature of a person's social origin, by the application of another, that of the reactionary evil of racial discrimination. When the hero recalls Ush-Terek, his Kazakh place of exile, there is not a single detail of the local landscape or way of life that he remembers as exotic or "Oriental." At the same time, he is fully aware, indeed fascinated by, the ethnic and cultural realities he encounters in Uzbekistan, which is as different from Kazakhstan as, say, Slovenia is from Slovakia.

On occasion, however, Kostoglotov falls back on a cultural shorthand that scripts ethnic difference according to a Russocentric perceptual matrix. Just before he undergoes the blood transfusion the hero is struck by the beauty of the attending nurse, a young girl "with a dark complexion and a Japanese slant to her eyes."[353] The erotic promise of the East, cited. And as he travels across Tashkent at the end of the novel the protagonist observes an elderly passenger on the tram, "no ordinary Uzbek but a man with an air of ancient learning about him."[354] The wisdom of the Orient, cited.

9

In the final two chapters the narrative leaves the confines of the cancer clinic, that locus of life and death, history and medicine, politics and ideology. Kostoglotov, his health now on the mend, is discharged and ventures into the city of Tashkent. As heralded by the title of chapter thirty-five, this is to be his "First Day of Creation" (see Genesis 1:5), and therefore utterly unlike Oleg's other *first day*. "If you're thinking about that first day, ... I was a dying man,"[355] he tells Vera at the midpoint of the novel, and hours before he walks out of the clinic Zoya, whose name means "life," reminds him: "Try and remember your first day here, out on the landing. You didn't think you were going to last more than a week, did you?"[356] But then, chapter thirty-six, which concludes the novel, is entitled, "And the Last." The biblical allusions are plain: "And God blessed the seventh day, and sanctified it" (Genesis 2:3). "And the LORD God formed man *of* the dust of the ground, and breathed into his nostrils the breath of life; and man became a living soul" (Genesis 2:7).

On the eve of Kostoglotov's departure Vera and Zoya present him with two separate, unexpected invitations. Vera's offer is shyly and hesitantly phrased: "You know... there's no reason at all why you shouldn't stay ... at my place."[357] Zoya's is brisk, almost off-hand: "Hey, Oleg! ... Do you have anywhere to spend the night? Write down my address."[358] So as he walks out of the clinic, Kostoglotov is in a quandary. Inside the Medical Center the beguiling physician and the sexy nurse were the objects of his desire, female figures whose custodial power gave the hero's erotic longing that extra edge of transgression. Now they are holding out the promise of a new beginning, or rather, two different beginnings. His life's road is about to bifurcate or trifurcate, and Oleg must choose which direction to take.

The novel reverses the usual procedure in descriptive prose whereby a larger, framing spatial setting is defined or at least delineated before the action is set in motion. In *The Magic Mountain*, for instance, geography carries a prolegomenous narrative function. Castorp travels from his home in Hamburg to the Berghof sanatorium at Davos-Platz, a journey that takes up two days of story time. As he transits from north to south across a large stretch of Europe, we encounter references to "many a landscape,"[359] a body of water (Lake Constance), a mountain range (the Alps), a historical region (Swabia), and railway lines and stations. Once the protagonist arrives at Davos-Dorf station, space becomes localized. When he reaches the sanatorium, Castorp's cicerone, his cousin Joachim, even supplies him with the figures for its elevation. *Cancer Ward*, however, shows the clinic in its institutional and human complexity over hundreds of pages of text, and only then takes us outside for an extended look at its urban and ethnic surroundings. As the hero, having alighted from a clattering streetcar, makes his way across the city, he adopts "the changeless, unhurried manner of those about him"[360] (an instance of a Kostoglotov-inflected othering). Now at last Tashkent assumes a topographical and architectural concreteness. Together with the hero, we learn its layout: the slum-like outskirts, the showpiece center with its imposing buildings, and the Old Town, an Uzbek version of the casbah.[361]

Kostoglotov's progress across this urban landscape occurs on several planes of meaning. It is a reversal of his farewell walk on the day before he entered the clinic. It is a quest for the fabulous uriuk. It is a succession of sensory experiences that reintroduce him to the pleasures of seeing, hearing, smelling, eating, and drinking. It is an extended peripatetic meditation in the course of which he forms a life-changing decision. Leopold Bloom may be the paradigmatic twentieth-century city wanderer, but he is a fragmented character moving through a fragmented metropolis, Joyce's phantasmagorical version of Edwardian Dublin. Solzhenitsyn chops and distorts neither hero nor city. Yet, like Bloom, his protagonist is an Ulyssean traveler whose daylong journey is filled with portents, temptations, monsters, mirages, and mysteries.

Gazing out of the tram window Kostoglotov catches a glimpse of Zoya's house, but after the briefest of hesitations he stays in his seat and continues on his journey. He gets off in the Old Town and sets off to look for the mysterious uriuk. From the balcony of a teahouse he notices "something pink and transparent" showing above a courtyard wall[362] (in a foreshadowing moment earlier in the novel, Vera had hoped to see a blooming apricot tree "even if from a distance, or perhaps sheltered behind a fence or a clay wall").[363] The passage that follows reads like the ekphrasis of a genre painting:

> It was like a fir tree decorated with candles in a room of a northern home. The flowering apricot was the only tree in this courtyard enclosed by clay walls and open only to the sky. People lived in the yard, it was like a room. There were children crawling under the tree, and a woman in a black headscarf with a green-flowered pattern was hoeing the earth at its base.[364]

A tree in bloom attended by a mother figure, her black headscarf a sign of mourning, her grandchildren playing in the beneficent arboreal shade. Is this a hint of the life Kostoglotov never had, or never will have? A wife he will not meet, the children he will not father? The scene may also be taken as an allegorical representation of the human biological cycle: Insemination (the hoeing of the earth)—Birth (the tree blossoms, the mother)—Life (the children, the headscarf's green, flower-like motif)—Death (the headscarf's blackness)—Rebirth (the tree's deciduous nature). The uriuk's symbolic status is made explicit when Kostoglotov mentally compares it to a "fir tree decorated with candles." For believers (though Oleg is *not* such a one), the Christmas tree represents Christ as the true tree of life and the candles betoken "the light of the world" (John 8:12, 9:5; Mathew 5:14) that was born in Bethlehem. Alternatively, the green flowers on the woman's head covering may be read as signifiers of her Moslem identity.

Christmas trees are associated with children, and the Kostoglotov who wanders the city is a kind of child, "tottering on two uncertain legs."[365] Indeed, the sense of wonder that fills him during his odyssey is childlike. The hero's defamiliarizing take on the objects and situations he encounters are conveyed via diegetic, that is, periphrastic, shifts, as when Kostoglotov comes across a street stall selling shashlik, a dish he had longed to sample ever since he had heard about it in prison: "Across the grill and above the fire lay fifteen or so long, pointed aluminium sticks [*poltora desiatka dlinnykh zaostrënnykh aliuminievykh palochek*][366] strung with meat."[367] The stallkeeper tempts Oleg by waving a skewer at him "as one would to a child."[368] Later he eats some ice cream (an item on every kid's menu) and drinks a glass of wine, a truly ambulatory feast. It is not that the joys of food and drink are absent in Solzhenitsyn: Nerzhin's birthday party in the sharashka shows quite the contrary. Across the fictions, however, the characters' gastronomical pleasures tend to be a function not of plenty, but of want, as is the case here.

The uriuk may be a "pink miracle" sought and found,[369] and the eating of the shashlik an almost unbearably sensuous pleasure, but Kostoglotov's city tour has its darker moments as well. At the Central Department Store, a palatial emporium with broad staircases and parquet floors, he inspects himself in a gigantic looking glass:

> There was no trace of the military man he considered himself to be. His greatcoat and boots only vaguely resembled a greatcoat and boots. His shoulders had drooped long ago and his body was incapable of holding itself straight. Without a hat and without a belt he looked less like a soldier than a convict on the run or a young lad from the country in town for the day to do a bit of buying and selling. But for that you needed a bit of bravado, and Kostoglotov looked exhausted, devastated, fearfully neglected. … This terrible duffel bag on his back had stopped looking soldierly long ago, it now looked like a beggar's bundle.[370]

This is the first time in *ten years* that Kostoglotov has seen himself in a full-length mirror. Ten is, of course, another mystical number, while gazing at one's mirror reflection is an act that can have the gravest of consequences, for mirrors are magical things. "As some peoples believe a man's soul to be in his shadow, so other (or the same) peoples believe it to be in his reflection in water or in a mirror," or so James Frazer tells us.[371] The Central Department Store is a "cursed temple."[372] As he explores its gleaming halls, with their milling crowds and displays of unattainable goods—mock-sacred artifacts of some Stalinist cargo cult—Oleg is visited by a premonition that he and Vera are fated never to have a life together: "He… he had lost the impulse. He… he was afraid. They were separated by this department store…"[373]

But there is another way to read Kostoglotov's mirror scene.

The philosophical psychoanalyst or psychoanalytical *philosophe* who made mirrors a showpiece fixture in the dark, overfurnished house of the mind was Jacques Lacan. According to him, in their development children pass through three stages, the pre-mirror, the mirror, and the post-mirror. Of the second of these, Lacan writes: "The human child, at an age when he is for a short while, but for a while nevertheless, outdone by the chimpanzee in instrumental intelligence, can already recognize his own image as such in a mirror."[374] This is the time of *self*-creation, when the infant acquires the ability to distinguish between self and other; and subject and object. The French psychoanalyst compares infant specimens up to eighteen months old of the species *homo sapiens* to adult specimens of the species *pan troglodytes*: simian themes are important in *Cancer Ward*, where they are mostly associated with Kostoglotov. Eventually, Lacan's goggle-eyed baby peering into the looking glass graduates to a higher level of awareness and, having identified the reflected self, proceeds to share it with other, similarly self-discovered selves:

> This moment at which the mirror stage comes to an end inaugurates, through identification with the imago of one's semblable and the drama of primordial jealousy …, the dialectic that will henceforth link the *I* to socially elaborated situations.[375]

This, then, is how men, women, and children, whether physical or fictional, eternally invent and reinvent themselves through the eyes of others, and these others are reflections of still others, links in an endless karmic chain of human-to-human signification. Lacan writes of "a nursling in front of a mirror who has not yet mastered walking, or even standing."[376] On this "first day" of the rest of his life, we recall, Oleg had turned into a metaphorical toddler, "tottering on two uncertain legs."

So, here is the hero's predicament: the recently reborn (because recovered from near-mortal disease) man-child stands before a malefic mirror inside a sinister "temple," expecting to see his preferred self-image, that of a soldier. Yet instead of the super-masculine figure of the warrior, this Red Army veteran beholds an unmanly, mutable image: now a fugitive convict, now a hawker, now a beggar. A succession of ghostly, ghastly *non-selfs*. Somewhere over the years the empirical Kostoglotov became a chiral figure, that is, one that is asymmetric to its own reflection, like Nietzsche's Zarathustra: "But when I looked into the mirror I cried out, and my heart was shaken: for it was not myself I saw, but a devil's grimace and scornful laughter."[377]

Yet after that near-terminal *ecce homo* moment on the hospital floor, the protagonist had successfully negotiated numerous "socially elaborated situations" inside the Medical Center. There Kostoglotov's body was reconstituted, thanks to the custodial care given to him by a trinity of female healers, Ludmila Dontsova (with whom his relationship was institutional), Vera Gangart (whom he covets erotically), and Zoya (whom he possessed sexually). The names of the three women respectively mean "Beloved by People," "Faith," and "Life." However, despite receiving such loving, faithful, life-giving succor, the hero has a long way to go, a great deal to do before he can cease his existential totter and stand tall and proud, and see his mirror-self do the same.

Feeling faint from the wine and the press of the crowd, Oleg longs "to lie down somewhere in the shade by a stream, just lie there and purify himself":[378] hints of yet another mythical or poetic topos. He knows of no such idyllic spot and instead repairs to the city zoo, which he had promised Dyoma he would visit. The figurative man-child Kostoglotov sets off for a zoological garden, that favored locus of childhood, at the request of the physical boy-child Dyoma.

In any novel, a visit by the protagonist to a menagerie is certain to have special meaning and will often be designed to invite allegoresis (an allegorical reading) on the part of the receptor. Figuratively, animals may be textualized in one of several ways, as metaphors, symbols, emblems, or anthropomorphs. The section describing Kostoglotov's experiences at the zoo is informed by all these interpretational postures.

As seen by Kostoglotov, the Tashkent Zoological Garden contains the three categories of creatures described in medieval bestiaries, that is, beasts, birds, and reptiles. However, if "in a theocentric world animals were merely one part in the hierarchy that ranged from stones to angels and on to God himself,"[379] then Oleg finds no Christian-allegorical meanings here. Instead, this provincial attraction turns out to be a collection of squawking, squealing, screeching, snarling—or silent—therianthropes, which Oleg, as the newly enlightened hero of the text, is able to identify and interpret, despite, or perhaps because, "his brain was so twisted that he could no longer see things simply and dispassionately."[380] How so? As we saw, *Cancer Ward* contains a system of descriptive signs associated with animal life. Kostoglotov's totem is the rhesus monkey; the hospital surgeon, Lev Leonidovich, possesses an analogous simian quality; Vera is a "gazelle" and Zoya a "bee," while Rusanov is wormlike or worse. In the clinic, where he was textually surrounded by a plethora of zoological referents, some of which he generated himself, Kostoglotov learned the novel's imaginative codes by narrative osmosis, for he is the protagonist and this is *his* fictive world.

Now the hero is in a position to match these codes to the zoological specimens he sees. As he inspects the captive creatures in their cages, he perceives them as the signifiers of his current situation and personal history. He admires the "proud" spiral-horned goat,[381] which has "the sort of character a man needed to get through life,"[382] and pities the squirrel running endlessly in its wheel. When he looks at the vultures forlornly flapping their wings, Oleg's shoulder blades twitch in psychosomatic sympathy: at an earlier point in the novel, he assumed the figurative form of "a large bird whose wings have been unevenly clipped to prevent it from taking off into the air."[383] Most of the time, however, Kostoglotov's attitude is "perverse"[384] or "odd,"[385] shaped as it is by his gulag memories. Gazing at the nocturnal porcupine, he thinks of a prisoner who has been summoned to an interrogation in the dead of night. The badger's striped snout reminds him of "an old lag's clothes"[386] and a grizzly languishing in its cramped cage makes him picture a zek in a punishment cell. The monkeys on their plank beds are like inmates in a barrack. One of the strongest visual impressions Kostoglotov receives during his excursion is generated not by the sight of a living creature, but by the sign of its absence. A notice on an empty monkey cage reads: "An evil man threw tobacco into the Macaque Rhesus's eyes."[387] The hero, who has endured much pain at the hands of his fellow human beings, is astounded by the pure evil of this act, while his heart is touched by the "childish simplicity"[388] of the message. In an extra-textual comment, Solzhenitsyn explained: "The spiteful person who spills tobacco in people's eyes for the hell of it is meant to be Stalin specifically."[389]

The tyrant himself metaphorically materializes when Kostoglotov visits the beasts of prey. Gorging themselves on plentiful meat, they are like the "camp gangsters" he has known.[390] The apex predator here is the "expressively" bewhiskered "Mr. Tiger."[391] The former prisoner looks at him with hatred and thinks "strange thoughts"[392]—thoughts, we learn in the sentence that follows, of Joseph Stalin, the mustachioed, tawny-eyed despot. But Oleg may also have been reminded of Zoya's "predatory," "tawny" eyes when she kissed him for the first time and evoked in him a different, sensual kind of dread.

Presently the protagonist encounters his second "miracle"[393] of the day:

> ... The Nilgai antelope, light brown, on fine, light legs, her head keen and alert but not in the least afraid. It stood close to the wire netting and looked at Oleg with its big, trustful and ... gentle, yes, gentle eyes.
>
> The likeness was so true it was unbearable. She kept her gentle, reproachful eyes fixed on him. She was asking him, "Why aren't you coming to see me? Half the day's gone. Why aren't you coming?"[394]

By some magical process of fictive palingenesis, Vera, the woman Oleg thinks of as a gazelle, presents herself before him as the beautiful nilgai (the wire netting of the cage—the bars on Vera's window). For the protagonist, this is "witchcraft," "a transmigration of souls."[395] The Hindu connotations of that last phrase are remarkably appropriate: the home of the nilgai antelope lies on the Indian subcontinent. Or as Bataille would have it, "The image of the desirable woman as first imagined would be insipid and unprovocative if it did not at the same time also promise or reveal a mysterious animal aspect, more momentously suggestive."[396]

The sweet, tremulous eroticism of the delicate creature Oleg sees or imagines seeing is familiar to us from the sonnets of Petrarch:

> The pictured hind fancy design'd glowing with love and hope;
> Graceful she stepp'd, but distant kept, like the timid antelope.[397]

His erotic vision of Vera renews the hero's determination to seek her out. He departs the zoological garden for her apartment. He is about to knock on the front door when it is opened by one of her neighbours, a young man pushing a gleaming red motorcycle. "Snout-faced" and with a "flat, bashed-in nose,"[398] the fellow is bestial—zoological—in form, and he brushes past Oleg as if he were not there. Next he is confronted by a second grotesque, a jabbering female with "a low forehead and slanting cheekbones."[399] She barks at him that Vera is not at home and drives him back into the street. The motorized youth, the slope-browed harridan, the ear-splitting noise of the bike's engine starting and stalling outside are bad enough, but then Kostoglotov notices some bedding laid out on the railings in front of the building. "Those pillows, mattresses, blankets, envelope-shaped blanket-covers and banner-like sheets implied such stable, tested experience that he hadn't the strength to reject it."[400] The communal apartment is transformed into a domestic "fortress"[401]—*Festung Gangart*—which this onetime soldier realizes he lacks the strength to conquer. He turns and walks away.

Before departing the city Oleg writes to Vera to tell her that their love, had he succeeded in seeking her out, might have been destroyed by a "gray, decrepit yet ever-growing snake," and so he has decided to leave, forever.[402] He seems to be saying that a physical union between them, with its attendant domestic compromises and social obligations, would sully the Platonic or Petrarchan purity of feeling that exists between them. Perhaps he imagines the two of them as an Adam and Eve in some Eden of the heart, as lovers who must never heed the gray serpent, must never eat from the tree of knowledge, the beautiful apricot tree for which they separately and so wistfully yearned.

Kostoglotov's letter ends with these words, the hero's most touching expression of self in the entire novel:

> Now that I'm going away …, I can tell you quite frankly: even when we were having the most intellectual conversations and I honestly thought

and believed everything I said, I still wanted all the time, *all the time*, to pick you up and kiss you on the lips.

So try to work that out.

And now, without your permission, I kiss them.[403]

The wandering prince in *The Sleeping Beauty* (Tchaikovsky's ballet and Charles Perrault's fairy tale) kisses the sleeping princess, thereby awakening her to life and to love. Kostoglotov, also an itinerant figure though avowedly not a prince, brushes the lips of his beloved with his own lips only from a distance, and only on paper: a supremely romantic act by this supremely unromantic hero, the magic of which is mediated at second or third or fourth remove through music and folklore.

In the final analysis, we can only surmise and speculate, for Oleg's departure from the relationship and from the text itself is open to multiple and conflicting interpretations. His fictive exit is in keeping with the tradition of the Russian novel from Pushkin to Pasternak, in which a man and a woman seemingly destined for one another are kept apart by life, death, or history. As the train carries the hero back to his place of exile, his boots dangle over the corridor in the third-class carriage "like a dead man's."[404] Yet Kostoglotov's recovery of his health, though incomplete and provisional; his love for Vera, though troubled and unconsummated; the signs of a political liberalization, though partial and tentative, suggest new opportunities and new beginnings.

Part Two
THE WRITER EX SITU

CHAPTER SEVEN
Twilight of All the Russias: The Red Wheel

Madness is rare in individuals—but in groups, parties, nations, and ages it is the rule.
—Friedrich Nietzsche, *Beyond Good and Evil*

Socialist realism demands of the artist the truthful, historically concrete depiction of reality in its revolutionary development.
—Statutes of the Union of Soviet Writers

In order to believe in the Antichrist... you need not believe in God, immortality, or even the soul. All you need is to possess common sense.
—Valentin Sventsitsky, *The Antichrist (Notes of a Strange Man)*

What are we waiting for, assembled in the forum?
The barbarians are due here today.
—C. P. Cavafy, "Waiting for the Barbarians"

1

If Joseph Brodsky, like Conrad and Nabokov before him, was an exiled artist who tried "to cure himself of his country,"¹ then during his own separation from Russia Solzhenitsyn essayed an entirely different kind of reparative project, one that was directed not inward, but outward. Long ago the author had resolved to heal his homeland through the medium of imaginative literature, and he had composed his novels and stories and *The Gulag Archipelago* as a means to that end. Now he was engaged in a new creative enterprise that saw him depict the events of a remoter past in accordance with his evolving writerly aesthetic and conjectural reading of the historical process. He did this because, as Ortega y Gasset writes,

"Historical knowledge is a technique of the first order to preserve and continue a civilization already advanced."² Yet as Solzhenitsyn saw it, the year 1917 marked the *demise* of a civilization which, though already advanced, was also very imperfect. His demiurgic ambition was to resurrect it fictively via the medium of imaginative and historiographical prose, to examine the reasons why it fell, and to determine whether such an outcome could have been prevented.

Solzhenitsyn preferred to describe *The Red Wheel* as an epopee. His definition of the term is rendered in language that reflects his predilection for clear and detailed explanations, as one might expect from a former schoolteacher:

> This is a prose form next in order of magnitude after the novel. The individual fortunes of the protagonists are here not at the center of attention as in a novel. They are not even very important, because the field of vision is not limited to them, rising instead to a different level: to a depiction of the events of an era, of an entire nation, of individuals who are no longer fictional, and of their actions in real historical circumstances.³

The Red Wheel is a four-part, ten-volume account of World War I and the Russian Revolution, an intricately formatted synthesis of prose, documents, and analysis that transcends the grand sweep of this writer's earlier large-scale productions as it shows the fall of an empire and the corruption of its people: Solzhenitsyn's *Der Ring des Nibelungen*. An extended act of author-to-nation communication, this saga cum study poses the question, "Where did we go wrong?" and answers it in moral and political terms, but with a mystical twist that is unlike anything else in the oeuvre. In his Templeton Lecture, delivered when he was in the midst of writing the epopee, the author explained:

> If I were asked today to formulate as concisely as possible the main cause of the ruinous Revolution that swallowed up some sixty million of our people, I could not put it more accurately than to repeat: "Men have forgotten God; that's why all this has happened."⁴

The Red Wheel, though, is not concise—far from it—and in narrative terms, Holy Russia's abandonment of its holy ways is just one theme among many others. Indeed, the epopee is much more, and much more important, than a by-the-book demonstration of the perils of apostasy, whether national or individual. As I have tried to show, in Solzhenitsyn's fictional works matters of religion and religious faith are treated from a variety of angles and with remarkable subtlety. *The Red Wheel* is no exception. Two of the historical actors depicted here, Tsar Nicholas II and General Samsonov, are devout believers, yet fail disastrously in their public duty. The tsar is "a true Christian on the throne [who] diverged no farther from the mean of mediocrity than the average monarch."[5] Nonetheless, he dooms his empire to collapse through a long series of misjudgments and errors that culminate in the act of abdication, all the while seeking and, by his lights, achieving communion with the Godhead. The general is a brave and honorable soul but a feeble commander, who bears direct responsibility for the deaths of tens of thousands of soldiers he leads into battle, a failing he tries to expiate by the supremely un-Christian act of suicide.

Henry James once proposed that "the only condition that I can think of attaching to the composition of the novel is ... that it be interesting."[6] If *The Red Wheel* is a cycle of novels or even a "super-novel,"[7] then it most certainly is interesting, and often for those Jamesian reasons of high narrative value and memorable characterization. It is also cleverly structured and shaped. Again, let us consult the author, who in 1983 told the French reporter Daniel Rondeau, "In my epic I had to employ up to eight different genres...,"[8] though he forbore to explain exactly which ones he had in mind. Perhaps we can do it for him: war fiction, historical romance, family tale, key novel, docudrama, film treatment, political satire, and scholarly treatise, *The Red Wheel* is oriented toward multiple categories and forms but is not defined by any one of them. Lev Loseff, however, suggests that its "generic precedent" is the chronicle as an agglomeration of documents, "muddled eyewitness testimony," "pious hagiography," and "biting denunciation," through which "Biblical time" is recorded and interpreted.[9]

Like *The Gulag Archipelago*, *The Red Wheel* is a sui generis, compound production that subjects a particular time period to forensic investigation and moral review, but it is also, again like Solzhenitsyn's history of the camps, an authorial settling of accounts with the perpetrators and facilitators of a great evil. When prime minister Pyotr Stolypin, the saga's "beau ideal of a statesman,"[10] is shown warning raucous deputies in the Duma, "We shall answer to history for our actions at this historic moment, just as you will,"[11] the sourced quotation is transformed into a meta-statement of ethical purport.

Solzhenitsyn divided his master-epic, which bears the subtitle *A Narrative in Discrete Stretches of Time* (*Povestvovan'e v otmerennykh srokakh*), into four Knots, in keeping with his nodal reading of the events of the past. Each Knot covers a major inflection point in the nation's existence: the catastrophic Russian defeat at Tannenberg in the first weeks of World War I, with an embedded narrative about prime minister Stolypin and his death at the hands of the enigmatic terrorist, Bogrov, which takes the action back to the nineteenth century (*August 1914*; in two Books); the military and political developments leading up to the fall of the autocracy (*November 1916*; in two Books), with a phantasmagorical excursus that describes Parvus's political seduction of Lenin in a dank Zurich bedroom; the February Revolution, shown as the beginning of a great national unraveling that affected all classes of society and all regions of the country (*March 1917*; in four Books); and the immediate aftermath of these events, which laid the course for the Bolshevik takeover six months later (*April 1917*; in two Books). The first three Knots comprise Act One: Revolution (*Deistvie pervoe—Revoliutsiia*), while *April 1917* is the only Knot in Act Two: Popular Rule (*Deistvie vtoroe—Narodopravstvo*), which originally was also meant to include the unwritten Knots *June–July 1917*, *August 1917*, and *September 1917*. The term *narodopravstvo*, a calque of the word "democracy," carries a distinctly pejorative ring: *caveat lector*.[12] By way of illustration, here is a passage from one of the "Fragments of Democracy" ("Fragmenty narodopravstva") chapters in *April 1917*:

> Vasilyev, a homeowner from the Chistye Prudy district, did nothing to hide his support for the former regime and openly spoke at meetings to that effect. Several young men carrying knives called on him at his home and stabbed him to death.
> Nothing was taken.[13]

In accordance with the normal practices of historical scholarship, the epic employs unpublished documents which the author examined in the course of his researches in Soviet, Swiss, and American archives, such as participant accounts of the fighting at Skrobotovo in Poland, the correspondence of Aleksandr Guchkov, a onetime Chairman of the State Duma, and the private papers of the Cossack writer Fyodor Kryukov, who serves as the prototype for Fyodor Kovynev, an important presence in Knots II–IV. He is tentatively (counterfactually?) identified as the true author of *The Quiet Don*.[14] While he was still living in the Soviet Union, Solzhenitsyn interviewed the elderly Vasily Shulgin (1878–1976), a flamboyant personality with flexible right-wing views who was a member of the delegation of worthies that induced Tsar Nicholas II to abdicate. In the epic, Shulgin is portrayed as an "unbalanced,"[15] "romantic"[16] monarchist given to finding parallels between the Russian Revolution and its French antecedent, who "discovered that the masses had a single face, and it was a rather bestial one."[17] As I noted, *The Red Wheel* is part imaginative fiction, part work of history—including oral history.

In a 1980 interview with Hilton Kramer of *The New York Times*, the writer commented on this aspect of his epopee:

> I have collected almost 300 written [unpublished—HK] testimonies on the experience of the Revolution. These witnesses were not speaking about "historical" events but about personal experience. I learned what I could from witnesses in Russia, and then, when I came out, I had contacts with many survivors of the Revolution who are now in the West, where people could write about their experiences openly.[18]

Among the hundreds of printed sources that Solzhenitsyn consulted, many of them antiquarian or obscure, was a self-published memoir by Pavel Bogdanovich, a former officer on General Samsonov's staff.[19] His book is set in two different fonts and may have inspired the writer's choice of variable typographic formats,[20] a distinctive feature of *The Red Wheel*.

Although the epic is prodigiously long, as originally conceived it was meant to be much, much longer: in fact, at least five times its actual published size. "I did not realize that I would never have time for an undertaking of such scope," the author conceded.[21] The missing Knots V–XX (Acts Two—Five) are summarized in an appendix, "The Narrative Beyond the Point of Suspension" ("Na obryve povestvovaniia"), which is subtitled "Summary of the Unwritten Knots" ("Konspekt nenapisannykh uzlov"). The word *obryv* means both "cessation" and "precipice" and evokes the title of Ivan Goncharov's anti-nihilist novel of that name (1869). *April 1917*, the last novel in the tetralogy, ends with its chief fictional figure, Colonel Vorotyntsev, resolving to dedicate himself to the counterrevolutionary struggle as he stands on a "precipice"[22] high above the Dnieper, and the scene's paratextual counterpart, "The Narrative," follows a couple of pages later (one last prefiguration in a work featuring hundreds of others). This forty-page synopsis ends in 1922, when the ailing Lenin loses his power of speech and the leaders of the Tambov rebellion are shot by the Cheka; there follows a list of five Epilogues (Epilogi), the last of which carries the date 1945. "The Narrative" omits all reference to the fictional characters but extends the totality of the text to the end of World War II, thereby linking *The Red Wheel* to the other works in the Solzhenitsyn oeuvre.

The saga's gestation and realization took the best part of the twentieth century, from 1936 when it was conceived by a teenage Sanya Solzhenitsyn as he wandered the streets of Rostov, to 1991 when the septuagenarian writer, seeing out the last years of his domicile in Vermont, declared the project complete, only to prune and modify it one last time in the quiet of his suburban Moscow dacha in 2003–5. *The Red Wheel* exists therefore in *three* published variants (four, if one counts the 1971 edition of *August 1914*): that of the Vermont *Collected Works* (vols. 11–20; 1983–91), that of the Moscow *Collected Works* (vols. 7–16; 2006–9), which bears the mark of considerable revision, and an abridged four-volume version (2001)[23] intended "for those who would like to read [the entire text] but don't have the time to read all ten volumes."[24] These displays of authorial sovereignty, but especially the two redactions Solzhenitsyn carried out after the entire work had been released in multiple languages, have analogues in the writer's continual reworkings of his other fictions, notably *The First Circle*. The Russian composer Alfred Schnittke once remarked, "A work of art is a conception that became distorted,"[25] and the author's tweakings of the integral text were attempts to hone the conception and trim the distortions.

Still, whether tweaked or untweaked, *The Red Wheel* never produced the impact its creator intended, even if several of its meta-points soon became entrenched in the public mind. The reasons for the relative unsuccess of a work Solzhenitsyn considered his life's achievement are many and various. He had scripted its model receptor as being of an unusually diligent bent: "This book is not designed to be read through easily, for amusement, but to understand our history,"[26] so that each Knot and each chapter is an individual, "discrete" teaching moment, a study aid in a patriotic memory restoration project. Solzhenitsyn may have meant his master-epic to be accessible to the widest possible readership, yet it is anything but. We have the case of a writer misidentifying his empirical audience. How so?

First, there is the matter of sheer volumes. If, as the cult émigré writer Sergei Dovlatov once put it, "There's a reason every book, even one that isn't very serious, is shaped like a suitcase," then Solzhenitsyn had crafted a remarkably heavy set of luggage. The reader is confronted by thousands of pages of densely packed prose inhabited by hundreds of fictional and historical personalities, all of them with something to say, signify, or symbolize, who are situated in a variety of closely researched, painstakingly (some have suggested, pedantically) reconstructed social and cultural environments. Perhaps the only factual mistake to be found in the entire tetralogy occurs in *August 1914*, when Vorotyntsev notes that the spiked helmets worn by the Germans provide protection from bullets:[27] in fact, being made of leather, they did not.

Second, *The Red Wheel* is anything but a smooth read. The text is studded with this writer's signature neologisms, archaisms, and dialecticisms, rare and even non-existent grammatical forms, and syntactic inversions and omissions that recall the linguistic experiments of the Futurist poet Velimir Khlebnikov, the inventor of "trans-sense." The same elements are present in the earlier works, but here they acquire a new prominence and indicial importance, endowing the epopee with a conspicuously experimental quality that will inevitably deter the casual reader. Indeed, a particular sentence in *August 1914* prompted an otherwise encomiastic reviewer to complain, "Were you to hear something like this on a tram, you would be unable to identify the language spoken: clearly, you would say, it belongs to the Slavonic family, but which one is it?"[28]

Next, on the mimetic and storytelling planes we encounter a different order of complexity. The text oscillates between a hyper-realist metonymy and a quasi-poetic metaphoricality, preternatural concreteness of description and surreal estrangement. The modes of narration are just as variable: first-, second- and third-person points of view, reliable, unreliable and even mendacious character voices, streams-of-consciousness and streams-of-speculation, and diegetic blanks and ellipses. With each successive Knot, the narrative increasingly exhibits a fractured quality along both the syntagmatic (chains of meanings) and paradigmatic (patterns of meanings) axes, to better account for, and recount, the cultural and societal ruptures occurring in the fictive here and now. Then there are the mock-cinematic Screens—the epic's most conspicuously experimental element—the archival interpolations, and the dedicated chapters (or chapter sections) of historical analysis and appraisal, the first of which comes with an earnest warning: "The author ... suggests that only the most indefatigably curious readers immerse themselves in these details. Others can easily go straight on to the next section in larger print."[29] By virtue of this advisory, every one of the stand-alone historiographical segments is officially relegated to the paratext, confirming the truth of Genette's observation that "just as the presence of paratextual elements is not uniformly obligatory, so, too, the public and the reader are not unvaryingly and uniformly obligated: no one is required to read a preface ... and ... many notes are addressed only to *certain* readers."[30] Such self-selected "certain readers" will discover that the sections in question are written in careful prose saturated with facts and stats, though some, like the portrait of Trotsky in *April 1917*, are vibrantly drawn sketches of public actors or events. In addition, the non-fictional segments form islands of diegetic stability within the ever-mutable main narrative. Again, *caveat lector!* The saga tackles the problematics of history by employing the problematics of fiction.

Next, throughout the epopee the writing is weighed toward exposition and explanation, with *August 1914* constituting "an enormous preview"[31] for the other three novels. Some figures are given extended genealogies that go back several generations; in the case of Georgi Vorotyntsev and Sanya Lazhenitsyn, to the reigns of Ivan the Terrible and Peter the Great respectively. New faces and voices are constantly being introduced and set in the context of the times, often via Solzhenitsyn's favored trope of litotes (rhetorical negation), for example, "Lechitsky was not one of those dandified generals from the metropolis and had never enjoyed anyone's patronage. The son of a village priest, he had spent his whole career serving with the troops."[32] Many of these minor character portraits, like the one I just quoted, are overtly functional, that is, they *tell*, rather than *show*.

Indeed, *The Red Wheel* has a larger cast of characters than *War and Peace* and *Anna Karenina* put together. *August 1914* is populated by dozens of high-ranking military personages, so that upon meeting one of them Samsonov thinks this (parenthetic) thought: "Major General Shtempel (Samsonov wrinkled his brow—there were so many generals in his army: yes, of course, one of Ropp's brigade commanders)."[33] The reader wrinkles his brow in sympathy. *March 1917* and *April 1917* pullulate with revolutionaries and revolutionary enablers of every stripe such as the members of the Petrograd Soviet of Workers' Deputies, who are as numerous as Samsonov's generals.

Finally, there was the matter of timing. In Solzhenitsyn's homeland, the first two Knots had a severely restricted samizdat circulation, while the entire text only saw the light of day during and after the slow-motion collapse of the Soviet Union. By that time the nation's literary spaces had become filled, even cluttered, with a critical mass of hitherto suppressed works by classic authors as well as a huge profusion of new writings. The *Zeitgeist* had shifted and minds were on other things, though plenty of readers noticed the parallels between the imperial implosions of 1914–17 and 1985–91, as, of course, did Solzhenitsyn himself.

In the English-speaking world, the first version of *August 1914* enjoyed bestselling status, largely on the strength of the author's Nobel Prize-winning reputation, but was overshadowed by the appearance of *The Gulag Archipelago*, Volume I, three years later. Of the epopee's integral text, only *August 1914* and *November 1916*, both superbly rendered by H. T. Willetts, were eventually released, and their reception turned out to be more than a little cool, shaped as it was by some of the readerly challenges listed above as well as a firmly established misapprehension, à la Richard Pipes and Arthur Schlesinger Jr., that the author was a dour nationalist ill-disposed toward democracy and representative government. Elsewhere, however, the epic met with success, most notably in France, where Solzhenitsyn's personality and writings always enjoyed a special resonance.

The Red Wheel may not have acquired the mass audience that the author had hoped for, but its portrait of Lenin has proved influential, helped by the publication of *Lenin in Zurich* (*Lenin v Tsiurikhe*; 1975),[34] a collection of chapters plucked from Knots I–III of the as yet unfinished saga "like so many raisins from a cake."[35] This is a de facto novel, with the Bolshevik chief as a memorably malevolent, quirkily human antihero. Like its fictionalized Lenin, the epic's treatment of premier Stolypin as imperial Russia's last, lost hope was assimilated by broad strata of the culture, including the Putin-era powers that be.[36] The same is true of yet another meme, that of the February Revolution as the cataclysmic event from which all subsequent catastrophes necessarily followed: Russia's year zero. This, too, is now a commonplace in official and popular Russian interpretations of 1917.[37] Hence, Solzhenitsyn's ten volumes of literary historiography succeeded in generating three units of cultural transmission that have shaped the national conversation about the country's past.

2

The epopee's formal structures exhibit the acknowledged influence of the trilogy *USA* by John Dos Passos. Solzhenitsyn had read *1919* (1932), the second novel in the sequence, in the Lubyanka prison in 1945 and had been impressed by its Camera Eye and Newsreel segments, which he adopted for *The Red Wheel* when he resumed work on the saga many years later. In a 1976 interview with Nikita Struve, the writer's most wide-ranging statement on his literary techniques, he explained the differences between Dos Passos's experimental narrative devices and his own Glance at the Newspapers (*Vskol'z' po gazetam*) chapters and Screens (*Ekrany*). "When I create a newspaper montage, it is much stricter and tighter, it is composed much more with the plot in mind, because the course of history itself is reflected in these newspaper montages of mine."[38] Solzhenitsyn's *press précis* employ a variety of sources, including foreign ones: *March 1917* quotes German and Austrian news reports about the fall of the tsar, which are unanimous in their fair and balanced expression of *Schadenfreude*.[39] The period flavor is enhanced by samplings of yellow journalism: scare headlines, celebrity gossip, and lurid stories of crime and passion. There are also snippets of war propaganda, all of it witless, which evoke its Soviet analogue during World War II. Lastly, the "Glances" feature commercial advertisements, chosen for their qualities of coarseness or quaintness as Solzhenitsyn's historical gaze turned from the Soviet-era authorial *now* to the pre-Soviet, pre-authorial *then*. The adverts bear an amusing resemblance to their down-market counterparts in the post-communist era, for example, "ANY LADY *can have an* IDEAL BUST, *that glory of womanhood! Marbor pills! Strictly reliable! No one disappointed.*"[40] The same goes for the movie listings, which publicize box office attractions such as "LOVE'S ACCORD, THE MORPHINE GIRL, THE GOLDEN DREAM."[41]

Among the important characters, Sanya Lazhenitsyn is an early twentieth-century news junkie while Vorotyntsev happens to be the exact opposite, never even *glancing at a newspaper* until *November 1916*, in the entirely mistaken belief that politics is irrelevant to the military profession. Newspapers are "like spoiled food," sneers General Krymov,[42] an able commander, while the less than able Tsar Nicholas and Tsarina Alexandra dismiss them as "revolting."[43] For his part, the mage Varsonofiev, though he realizes that "no newspaper could ever clarify his or anyone else's thoughts," is addicted to such "simplistic and superficial" reading "like a habitual smoker or drunkard" is to his "craving."[44] A spectrum of reader receptions that adds to the other gradations of cultural engagement recorded in the epic.

Interestingly, when the writer redacted his saga in the early 2000s, the brunt of the excisions fell on the newspaper and "fragmentary" chapters in *March 1917* and *April 1917*.[45] After a decade or more of reflection, he had concluded that the press clippings scattered across the length of these novels were in many cases superfluous to his authorial purposes: "the course of history," it seems, had been adequately covered in the main narrative. Natalia Solzhenitsyna, upon whom the massive task of resetting the entire text inevitably devolved, likened the process to that of extracting individual bricks from the wall of a standing house and replacing them with new ones.[46]

The most eye-catching element, however, is the Screens, left-indented columns of text formatted as short film scripts. Thematically and figuratively connected to the main narrative, they depict violent events such as battles, riots, or pogroms. Solzhenitsyn explains: "Very dynamic and … basically mass scenes. … There aren't even any individual actors left anymore, just representatives of the masses."[47] His micro-scenarios, which are composed almost entirely in the present tense, pullulate with exclamation points and scan like blank verse. In cinematographic terms, the Screens are manifestation-oriented, that is, descriptive of the visual and audible components of each mock-film production. There are "long shots" and "close-ups," as well as an occasional "rear view," "full screen," and "pan shot." The sound component includes voices, songs, military marches, and audio effects such as gunfire, explosions, the trampling of feet, or on one occasion, the "crackle" of a fence crushed by a crowd of demonstrators.[48]

The only codified notation used is an equals sign, to indicate "cut to." Also, the Screens, perhaps anachronistically, connote a polychromatic color scheme, with shades of red predominating.

These quasi-film treatments are unlike anything else in Solzhenitsyn.[49] Overtly experimental, graphic in more sense than one, they disrupt the flow of the narrative while imaginatively enhancing it by zooming in on the brutality of combat or mob action as they hint at the mythical meaning of both via montage and metaphor. Ilya Kukulin comments that in the Screens, the writer references Sergei Eisenstein's films (more so than Dos Passos), and particularly his use of montage,[50] even entering into a "creative dialogue" with him.[51] Solzhenitsyn was famously critical of the famous director, but like the accomplished artist he was, he knew how to learn or borrow from what he considered an axiologically contaminated source. If he could bend the topoi of SocRealism to his own story-telling advantage, as he had done in his earlier fictions, then Eisenstein's tropes were there ready for the taking, and subverting.

One of the cinematic inserts describes the lynching of Admiral Nepenin, the commander of the Baltic Fleet, by mutinous ship crews. Here is the climactic passage, which with its staccato phrasing is typical of these "mini-scripts."[52]

> A shot!
> = Again, the admiral's face!
> a bewildered, innocent expression,
> now he understands
> now he grasps the truth he sought!
> = But he sinks from the frame.
> Falls.
> The press of sailors pauses.
> They look down at him. They are curious.
> They keep shooting into the recumbent body.
> A shot, and then another one.[53]

Like his "Miniatures," Solzhenitsyn's mock-film forays predicate a direct reader response: you either love them or hate them.

In the Struve interview the writer explained that the Screens "stress the symbolical movement."[54] One sequence of such figurative enactments extends across the length of the epopee: in the very first Screen (*August 1914*, chapter twenty-five), the revolving "red-gold" blades of a burning windmill take on the form of a Catherine wheel while evoking *Don Quixote*;[55] a second Screen

(*March 1917*, chapter 299) contains an analogous, spatially contracted transformation wherein the red butonnières worn by revolutionary officers metamorphose into spinning, fiery wheels;[56] and in the last Screen in the sequence (*March 1917*, chapter 453), the same thing happens to a "slightly crooked" Red Cross sign.[57] On each occasion we are referred back to the titular image and its counterpart, the Cross.

The proverbs that interpolate the narrative are another innovation, which represents a culmination of Solzhenitsyn's longstanding interest in paremiology. Alexander II reportedly said, "All other countries live according to the law, but Russia lives according to its proverbs and sayings,"[58] and here the writer was on the same page as the antepenultimate Romanov tsar. See *The First Circle*, where Nerzhin muses: "The folk were even more frank about themselves in their huge stock of proverbs than Tolstoy and Dostoevsky in their confessions."[59] Set in caps and centered on the page, each maxim functions as a snippet of terse commentary that broadens the saga's spectrum of voices by articulating the people's collective, ahistorical sense of right and wrong. After all, *The Red Wheel* is a work in which the accents of the city vastly outnumber those of the village, which nonetheless is identified as "the nodal point of Russia's destiny."[60] The proverbs right the balance. Some of the sayings are pithy: "When Moscow finds a husband, Petersburg gets a wife"[61] (revolutionary events in the two capital cities); or reference an important symbol or metaphor: "If you're sitting on a wheel, look to see what it conceals"[62] (see the epic's titular metaphor); or wax poetic: "Even a distant pine waves to its own copse"[63] (Pyotr and Nina Obodovsky's return to Russia from foreign exile); or rueful: "I had farther to go but the horses were slow"[64] (changes in the army high command on the eve of the revolution); or despondent: "It's with worrying and grieving I know I'm still living"[65] (trench warfare); or skeptical: "If you and I are both gents now—who'll be left to follow the plow?"[66] (the 1905 Revolution); or sinister: "Tsar and commoner—the grave awaits them"[67] (the surrender of General Klyuev and his troops); or sardonic: "If a villain you are, you'll get pretty far"[68] (the disarming of the Borodino Life Guards by pro-Duma troops).

Tolstoy knew a thing or two about these capsules of folksy wit. In *War and Peace*, the authorial narrator describes them as "those folk sayings which taken without a context seem so insignificant, but when used appositely suddenly acquire a significance of profound wisdom."[69] This is the formula employed in the epopee. The muzhiks Terenti Chernega and Arseni Blagodarev are casually proverbial in their speech, as are the more rooted of the non-peasant personae such as Kovynev. In the Struve interview, Solzhenitsyn explained: "I have a mental picture: among my readers I see a certain peasant—he may even be illiterate but he listens and listens to what's in the story, then out he comes with his proverb, just rattles it off."[70]

Yet, is this a reader too far? Solzhenitsyn's notional rustic receptor calls to mind the yardman Spiridon in *The First Circle* who, obedient to the author's sovereign will, wanders into the prison theatricals put on by Nerzhin and *company* and, unlikely though it is, hearkens smilingly to their stagey shenanigans: Spiridon is a literalist who loves literature. It is safe to say that *The Red Wheel* has had few, if any, empirical readers in the same category. Be that as it may, in the last two Knots the contra-distinctions between the folksy one-liners and experimental flourishes in what is now a maximal narrator text assume a new significance. The sayings signpost the cultural divide that separates the words and ways of the floundering elites from those of the peasant masses, who whether in or out of uniform have become terminally estranged from the powers that be. Meanwhile the epic's resident muzhiks, Blagodarev and Chernega, stride through the text in their no-nonsense way, scattering proverbs in their wake.

Set in bold print and distributed throughout the length of the work are the numbered Documents (*Dokumenty*), historical sources that are presented in full or in part, for example, diplomatic dispatches, military orders, revolutionary proclamations, and propaganda leaflets. Among these dry or demagogic texts there is one of mystical import, a letter from Grigory Rasputin to Tsar Nicholas of July 1914, in which the mad monk, blissfully ignorant of the rules of punctuation, warns his imperial acolyte of the dangers ahead: "Dear Friend again I say to thee there is a storm cloud over Russia disaster much grief darkness and no break in the cloud."[71]

Despite his psychic talents and eyes that purportedly glow red,[72] the saga treats the magic muzhik as a rustic mountebank, albeit one with flashes of rustic common sense. On a couple of occasions, the narrative even hints that Rasputin's mojo might, after all, be the real thing. See "Grigori's prediction that [Tsarevich Aleksei] will no longer suffer after he turns fourteen,"[73] that is, after the summer of 1918. Nonetheless, other characters have metaphysical inklings that possess a higher transcendental value, as when the dying Stolypin imagines telling his sovereign, "I have dark forebodings, Sire.... The year 1905 may repeat itself."[74]

3

David Remnick comments: "So vast is the project, so numerous are the characters, that one could more easily summarize *War and Peace* than *The Red*

Wheel."⁷⁵ The epopee's connection to that famous novel is one that Solzhenitsyn was happy to acknowledge. He first read it at the age of ten when, as he recalled, "I did not understand the personal side of the plot at all ... but I was completely caught up by the overall composition and the historical scenes."⁷⁶ That is, the war chapters.

Now, Tolstoy is a monologic writer whose fictions are suffused with a powerful author-centric discourse. Nevertheless, *War and Peace* is organized in a manner that permits and rewards selective reading. Its *overall composition* includes multiple self-contained narrative sequences, while Tolstoy's heroes and heroines, as Boris Eikhenbaum showed, are mutable psychological and emotional states of being who are textually restored or revised with each successive character iteration. Accordingly, a reader of *War and Peace* may choose to access the fictive world not through the elaborately carved front door that leads directly to Anna Pavlovna Schérer's drawing room, but by one of the side entrances which dot the length of the textual edifice. Such an alternative point of ingress is offered by the chapters devoted to the campaigns of 1805 and 1812, which ten-year-old Sanya Solzhenitsyn so enjoyed when he first opened the novel. By the same token, I have known female readers who as young girls were enthralled by the family sections, especially those where Natasha Rostova is the main presence. Tolstoy's fictive arrangements are adequate to the exercise of receptor bias, and not just by book lovers of tender years. The same is true of *The Red Wheel*, perhaps even more so, because the "discrete stretches" that make up the saga endow it with a programmatic narrative discontinuity, which positively invites one to dip and peruse.

In *War and Peace*, the three most important heroes, Andrei Bolkonsky, Pierre Bezukhov and Nikolai Rostov, are direct authorial emanations (albeit with all kinds of novelistic additions and refractions), with the sum of their presence forming a kind of composite personality that is approximately congruent to that of the empirical Tolstoy. In turn, the epopee features a trinity of male figures who periodically find themselves at the nexus of history and moral choice: the patriotic officer Vorotyntsev, the earnest truth-seeker Lazhenitsyn, and the political extremist Sasha Lenartovich. Together, they display a similarly broad range of authorially derived traits, even if the proto-Bolshevik Lenartovich happens to be the epic's most important fictional villain. The writer once told the Russian-American theologian Alexander Schmemann that Lenartovich had started as one of its "three prototypes," but "we had to go our separate ways, irrevocably," with Lenin added to that foundational threesome in his stead.⁷⁷

There are dozens of parallel or intersecting plots with hundreds of historical and imagined, public or private personalities that belong to every social class, cultural stratum, and demographic group under the setting sun of the Russian Empire. The tsar and his family, courtiers, ministers, political actors of every ideological hue and allegiance, military men of all ranks, businessmen and beggars, intellectuals and ignoramuses, workers and peasants, policemen and criminals, Russians and foreigners, Ukrainians and Cossacks, Christians and Jews, Realists and Modernists, Bolsheviks and Mensheviks, priests and atheists, ascetics and libertines, professors and students, teachers and schoolchildren, they are all here, as well as a patriarchal Tolstoy and several Tolstoyans, including an eccentric general and a pacifist peasant. There is even a Tolstoy double, a Moscow watchmaker called Petrov who likes to display himself to the public in the manner of a shop window attraction: "Pretending to have no idea why passersby paused to stare at him, startled by his incredible (and no doubt carefully cultivated) resemblance to Lev Tolstoy: it was as if the untamable old man had returned from the grave and was busy mastering yet another trade!"[78] (one of several meticulously researched instances of historical whimsy in the epic). The saga continually interrogates Tolstoy's status as a national fetish of culture and tourism, which he continues to enjoy in the twenty-first century.

Although at this point in its halting progress to modernity Russia was still an overwhelmingly agrarian society, and Solzhenitsyn had always looked to its rural population as the keeper of the nation's core values, members of the elites substantially outnumber the few rustics such as Blagodarev who are allotted a prominent part in the fictive proceedings. Filling in the sociological blanks, therefore, is a cluster of characters associated with his village of Kamenka in Tambov Province. Evpati Bruyakin, a "greatly respected"[79] shopkeeper, is unapologetically pessimistic about the way things are going. Another man of respect, Grigori Pluzhnikov, has his own take on the state of the nation: "The town's our enemy, and the landlord's our enemy."[80] Bespectacled Anatoli Zyablitsky, a "townie"[81] who is a frequent visitor to Kamenka, is active in the cooperative movement ("our founder, Robert Owen").[82] In human interest terms, however, these earnest figures are overshadowed by Kamenka's younger presences such as Vasya "Wet-leg" Tarakin. This plausible young man claims to be a conscientious objector, but he is disliked by the villagers, who mutter that he "acts the holy fool"[83] to avoid being called up. They are probably right, though Tarakin has a conscientious way with words: "Count Tolstoy ... has opened [my] eyes to the idea of Jesus Christ."[84] Wet-leg completes his conversion to Tolstoyanism by transitioning to a meatless diet, which he seems to enjoy more than Sanya Lazhenitsyn (see below). And on the non-pacific side, there is the "open deserter"[85] Mishka Rul, a local hoodlum with revolutionary leanings who comes into his own after the fall of the tsar and the subsequent breakdown of law and order in the countryside.

In the way of novelists from Tolstoy to Hilary Mantel, Solzhenitsyn asserts authorial ownership over the historical figures that populate his text. Victors, villains, or victims, they all come with an assigned historiographical valuation. In addition to Tsar Nicholas II (pious but weak) and prime minister Stolypin (the last great statesman of the Russian Empire), there is General Aleksandr Samsonov and his German opponent Hermann von François (bayonets vs. machineguns), the future head of the Provisional Government, Alexander Kerensky (a revolutionary charlatan), Vladimir Lenin (a brilliant nihilist), Leon Trotsky (a charismatic adventurer), and Joseph Stalin (already plodding his way to power). Two sinister subversives, the plus-sized Alexander Parvus and the diminutive Nikolai Gimmer, are Machiavellian figures operating in the shadows on behalf of a conspiracy so immense, they are unable to grasp its full extent or even their own part in it. Aleksandr Shlyapnikov, a prominent Leninist, receives surprisingly sympathetic treatment. From a family of Old Believers, he is a "genuine proletarian politician"[86] in a notionally proletarian party: a Lech Walesa type, but without the religious faith or street smarts. Alexandra Kollontai, the glamorous Bolshevik feminist who once took Shlyapnikov as a lover, is a fragrant presence, even though the saga satirizes her notion of the revolution as a sexually liberating enterprise:

> During the two days of her journey she thought a great deal, not about Shlyapnikov but Lenin. Not as a man, of course, for that would have been ridiculous, but about how she should justify to him—for such a conversation was inevitable—her new theory and its ideal. ... She was prepared to put up a fight on behalf of her brainchild: without the New Eros, the entire point of the revolution would be half lost. She was already seething as she imagined the inevitable clash: how could he be so unforgivably indifferent toward what was so clearly one of the essential tasks facing the working class, to coin a phrase?[87]

Despite Kollontai's refusal to accord Lenin the status of a desirable male, or even a male at all, he remains the most vividly drawn historical figure, and the most striking instance of characterization via diegesis in the whole of Solzhenitsyn.

The fictional characters interact with the heroes and antiheroes of history in the approved Walter Scott manner: the invented personae observe and transmit the appearance, words, and deeds of these public actors, that is, when the latter are not doing the transmitting themselves, as when Trotsky holds forth to the army surgeon Dr. Fedonin on a train that is carrying them back to Russia and its revolution. Professor Olda Andozerskaya, who loathes the Bolsheviks, is reluctantly impressed by Lenin's public displays of his will to power:

> When Lenin suddenly appeared and, standing on the balcony of the Kschessinskaya house, let out a whistle like Nightingale the Robber, which tore off the fig leafs from the Executive Committee [of the Petrograd Soviet], this was at least something real and terrible ... a naked dagger, openly displayed.[88]

That oratorical blade, we are invited to imagine, will next go to work on the feeble manhoods of Lenin's socialist rivals.

The epic's verdict on the tsar, which is delivered by Vorotyntsev, is unfavorable: "Mentally so limited, and so weak-willed. So inarticulate. And so inactive."[89] And, most devastatingly, a "childlike sovereign"[90] (*tsarstvennyi rebënok*),[91] in the judgment of Stolypin himself. According to the assassin Bogrov's revolutionary calculus, the premier is more deserving of death than Nicholas, for the latter is "a title, and no more. Not a worthwhile target. ... No successor would ever weaken his country more than this Tsar had."[92] Granted, Bogrov thinks this thought five decades before the accession of General Secretary Leonid Brezhnev.

In any case, the human appeal of Russia's last autocrat lies less in the kind of man he was than in what was done to him and his wife and children after the fall of the monarchy; but then, the terrible events of July 17, 1918 lie outside the work's descriptive perimeter. Though not entirely: the fatal bullets fired by Bogrov into Stolypin, we are told, "were the opening shots of the fusillade at Yekaterinburg."[93] So when the emperor thinks to himself, "There was truth in the saying that 'the Tsar's heart is in the hands of God' (*serdtse tsarëvo v rukakh Bozhiikh*).[94] Nicholas was also answerable to history—and history would understand the course he had taken,"[95] at this instant of discourse time the text engages with one of the essential historiosophical passages in *War and Peace*:

> "The King's heart is in the hands of the Lord [*Serdtse tsarevo v rutse Bozh'ei*]."⁹⁶
>
> A king is history's slave.
>
> History, that is, the unconscious, general, hive life of mankind, uses every moment of the life of kings as a tool for its own purposes.⁹⁷

The formula "the King's heart is in the hands of the Lord" derives from Proverbs 21:1: "The king's heart is in the hand of the Lord, as the rivers of water: he turneth it withersoever he will" (*Iakozhe ustremlenie vody, tako serdtse tsarevo v rutse bozhiei: amozhe ashche voskhoshchet obratiti, tamo uklonit e*). By means of this doubled, Biblical/Tolstoyan intertextual transaction, the epic polemically interrogates the tsar's stated sense of Christian resignation. A couple of sentences later, a moment of bathos: Nicholas's desire "to know God's will more clearly through the occult channels open only to the enlightened"⁹⁸ prompts him to retain the services of the mystical fraud Monsieur Philippe, a "doctor of medicine from Lyons"⁹⁹ but in reality a retired butcher. A lack of mental acuity transforms faith into gullibility. Nevertheless, the text grants Nicholas the realization "before God and himself" that he is "not only an unlucky ruler, but an unworthy one,"¹⁰⁰ while the chapters detailing his state of mind and way of life after the imperial family are detained at the Provisional Government's pleasure have a how-the-mighty-have-fallen appeal, so that the doomed tsar and his consort exit the text as largely sympathetic figures. As Solzhenitsyn told Struve, he prefers to treat his antiheroes of history with authorial "sympathy" (*sochuvstvie*), but *after* they have been "overthrown, shackled, or betrayed."¹⁰¹ Only in the abdication scene, where Russia's last sovereign is shown wrestling with his inadequacies and then resigning himself to his fate and his God, does he attain a measure of tragic grandeur:

> After all, no one had forced him to give the new government his blessing and to urge that it should be obeyed, but this he did...
> What else can one say.... He was a Christian.
> Too much of a Christian to sit on the throne.¹⁰²

Kerensky, whose swift elevation to the summit of power begins with his appointment as justice minister in the Provisional Government, receives more mocking treatment than any other figure shown. The leader of democratic Russia is the owner of an "adjustable"¹⁰³ dolichocephalic head sporting "long, curved lips,"¹⁰⁴ topped with a "bristly crew cut,"¹⁰⁵ and resting on a pair of "narrow shoulders"[106] which match his "wasp waist,"[107] so that the ministerial body constitutes "a straight line."[108] This historical *actor*, we are meant to understand, is an entirely two-dimensional personality. As a public speaker, Kerensky is a purveyor of "customary claptrap,"[109] "oratorical pirouettes,"[110] "cubic kilometers of verbiage,"[111] and "cascades of words,"[112] delivered in a "reedy,"[113] "ringing,"[114] or "piercing"[115] voice "with machinegun-like rapidity."[116] The Russian Revolution's would-be Danton,[117] Robespierre,[118] or Napoleon[119] is a political *enfant terrible*[120] or metaphorical "adolescent"[121] or sometimes "boy"[122] who alternatively froths at the mouth or falls into a pretty swoon. When he is *compos mentis*, he appears "immune to the force of gravitation"[123] and may be seen "taking wing! airborne! in flight!,"[124] hovering above the action "like some igneous bird"[125] or, perhaps, a populist pterodactyl, as when he "fold[s] his wings against his shoulder blades"[126] or "sprout[s] new wings from his back."[127] With his "neurotic jitteriness"[128] and segmented body, the future premier has something puppet- or toy-like about him. He is a "jack-in-the-box,"[129] a "harlequin,"[130] and a "clown":[131] in her journal of the revolution, a source the author undoubtedly consulted, the poet Zinaida Gippius compared Kerensky to Pierrot.[132]

Solzhenitsyn certainly would have endorsed Nietzsche's warning in *Beyond Good and Evil*:

> What happened most recently in the broad daylight of modern times in the case of the French Revolution—that gruesome farce which, considered closely, was quite superfluous, though noble and enthusiastic spectators from all over Europe contemplated it from a distance and interpreted it according to their own indignations and enthusiasms for so long, and so passionately, that *the text finally disappeared under the interpretation*— could happen once more as a noble posterity might misunderstand the whole past and in that way make it tolerable to look at.[133]

In this Nietzschean sense, *The Red Wheel* was an attempt to clear away the *interpretations* that had occluded the truth about what happened in 1917, and to restore the *text* by means of a bespoke, syncretic, fictive cum historiographical methodology. Indeed, one imagines that had *The Red Wheel* been published half a century earlier, its representation of the Russian Revolution might have become the defining one, foreclosing or at least fore-shaping all subsequent treatments. The splendor of the conception, the connections in style and theme to the Silver Age, and the text's temporal proximity to the events described would have all worked in its favor. Even so, in the years since its publication the tetralogy has become an essential point of reference for novelistic representations of the revolutionary period. *The Red Wheel* may be also considered the foundational Russian literary study of World War I, with Solzhenitsyn simultaneously acting as his country's Erich Maria Remarque and Ernst Jünger.[134]

As for Nietzsche's other point, about revolution as history's burlesque, the epic is on the same page. Take the (perhaps apocryphal) story about the Marquis de Sade in the Bastille. A few days before the citadel was stormed, or rather entered, by the mob, the sexual provocateur and all-round malevolent spirit could be heard yelling to the Parisians outside, for the sheer pleasure of goading their better angels, "They are killing the prisoners; you must come and free them" (whereupon he was moved to an insane asylum). In *March 1917*, we read:

> Kerensky vaulted up from the floor as if propelled by invisible wings and perched on the sill, grasping the casement handle with one hand and swinging the *fortochka* [ventilation pane] wide open with the other as he pressed his body against the awning and inserted his narrow rectangular head into … into … the *fortochka* itself, which was a good fit.
>
> Looking at the mad maelstrom in the square below, he cried out in the same fabulously resonant and penetrating voice he had used at the podium, though by now it had grown somewhat hoarse, "Look to your duty! Everyone to their posts! … Defend the State Duma! … It is I, Kerensky, who command this! They are shooting the Duma deputies!!!"[135]

The deputies, of course, are in no more peril than were de Sade's fellow prisoners: Kerensky is emitting his rant of the day in the excited knowledge that his fulminations are music to the sea of ears outside. To quote Nietzsche again, "Fanatics are picturesque; mankind prefers to see gestures rather than to hear reasons."[136]

Solzhenitsyn was always firm in his conviction that individuals, great and not so great, good and not so good, can have a quantifiable impact upon the fate of nations. Not-so-great and not-so-good Kerensky is a case in point, but then, he was a recognized political leader, however misguided and meretricious. Yet in certain circumstances, even an obscure or liminal personage who leads no one and commands nothing may dam(n) the flow of events. Stolypin's assassin, Bogrov, who exalts himself through a single violent act, is one such world-historical nullity. The twentieth century would know many such "psychopathic nerds,"[137] from Gavrilo Prinzip to Mark Chapman. In *August 1914*, Bogrov is shown as a tormented soul, a double or triple agent for the Okhrana with a "pampered body,"[138] a "melancholy gaze,"[139] and a "disciplined mind."[140] The son of a wealthy Jewish family, he looks like a "typical upper-class exquisite"[141] but is morbidly self-conscious, wears fashionable suits, and plays roulette at Monte Carlo while living the life of an international conspirator: Dostoevsky crossed with Ian Fleming.

The important fictional characters number some two dozen, with most of them based on real-life people. There is no protagonist as such, though Georgi Vorotyntsev, the career military man who strives to be the subject of history in spite of his complicated private life, comes close. Some commentators, however, would go further. "Vorotyntsev is the fictional hero of *The Red Wheel*, Stolypin its historical one," insists one reviewer.[142] In addition to the rugged colonel, there is his wife, the musical Alina, and his lover, sparkling, green-eyed Olda, an academic who is a passionate monarchist; "methodical,"[143] "quiet," and "thoughtful"[144] Isaaki (Sanya) Lazhenitsyn, a representation of the author's father who carries more than a hint of the young Solzhenitsyn himself, down to his "soft, corn-colored hair";[145] and Ksenia Tomchak, a lovingly drawn portrait of Solzhenitsyn's mother; good-looking, vainglorious Aleksandr (Sasha) Lenartovich, a hereditary radical who throws in his lot with the Bolsheviks; romantic, freckle-faced Yaroslav (Yarik) Kharitonov, a junior officer and eldest son of Ksenia's headmistress, the formidable Aglaida Fedoseevna; clever Fyodor Kovynev, a Cossack intellectual and aspiring novelist; and mystical Pavel Varsonofiev, a white-haired scholar with the gift of prophecy. Levelheaded Arseni Blagodarev, a soldier befriended by Vorotyntsev during the East Prussian campaign, is the work's most important peasant persona.[146] Quiet Vera Vorotyntseva (Georgi's younger sister), artsy Likonya (Lenartovich's elusive object of desire), prodigal Zinaida Altanskaya (Kovynev's passionate protégée), and earthy Katyona (Arseni's young wife) have a memorable textual presence and show that the writer had not lost his knack for depicting female characters in the first bloom of womanhood.

Some of the personae are assigned distinctive mannerisms or quirks. Sanya is in the habit of "tilting his head backward, half closing his eyes,"[147] Olda has a "characteristic pose" where she "arch[es] her small hands before her and strok[es] one with the other,"[148] and when we first meet Likonya she is an intricately designed concatenation of pouts, sighs, and sideways glances that men find enchanting and her elders, annoying. In a marital moment that recalls the patterns of Anna and Aleksei Karenin's mutual estrangement, Alina of the "translucent," "shell-like" ears[149] becomes worried by the unfaithful Georgi's newly acquired, or newly noticed, habit of emitting deep husbandly sighs.[150] A few minor characters have an equally vivid presence, notably Ensign Chernega. The owner of a "spherical head"[151] with a "snug covering of silky hair"[152] and a muscular body that has the appearance of a "rolling ball or a round loaf,"[153] he is nimble like a cat[154] despite his "knobbly" toes.[155] Chernega's bulbous form, so reminiscent of a very young, very Bolshevik Khrushchev, is appropriate in one fated to become a servant of the Wheel. Meanwhile, those lumpy lower digits wiggle at the reader to catch his attention. In *relative* textual terms, the corporeal *I* and its functions and malfunctions enjoy the same degree of prominence as in the earlier fictions.

Many of the principals are young or youngish and happen to be in excellent health. The teenage Ksenia is keenly attuned to her bodily sensations. An aspiring dancer, she takes a jaunty delight in her physical self: "A leap! Another leap! How beautifully she did it! She was like a bird. She had a remarkably small foot—a man could have hidden it in his hand."[156] Lenin is not just a political and discursive presence, but an anatomical one. He keeps a mental inventory of his (allegedly) "healthy heart, lungs, liver, stomach, hands, legs, teeth, eyes, and ears,"[157] though he worries that there may be something wrong with his "apparatus for adopting correct decisions,"[158] that is, brain. In fact, that organ is already showing the symptoms of arteriosclerosis, which in due course would terminally ossify it. The Bolshevik chieftain is textually unfolded from within, but he is also parsed from without. Thus, Lenartovich is disappointed by Lenin's "unheroic" appearance, especially his "crooked, uneven, and diseased teeth" and "morbidly asymmetrical cranium":[159] the "apparatus," it seems, is as crooked as its casing. The embodiment of charismatic revolutionary masculinity, socialist Sasha is believably mindful of the flaws in the Leader's physique, yet this budding extremist admires his informed ruthlessness and strength of purpose. Soon Lenartovich will decide that Lenin is a "superman" (*sverkhchelovek*),[160] becoming a Leninist even before he becomes a Bolshevik.

Among the epic's junior presences are Zinaida's baby boy Zhenya, dead at the age of six months, and Arseni and Katyona Blagodarev's toddler Savostyan and infant girl Proska. As for those awkward adolescent years, the text features a rough balance between the decent and the delinquent. The former category includes Kolya Stankevich, a Petrograd schoolboy who discovers that the insurgent masses are the instrument of a coarse and rampant evil, as do his two coevals half a country away, the Rostovians Yuri (Yurik) Kharitonov, fourteen (Yarik's younger brother), and Vitaly Kocharmin, sixteen. On the darker or redder side, we have the feral teens who are the revolution's gofers: "In

Teatralnaya Square a couple of brutes were pulling a small sled with the body of a policeman tied to it face up. . . . Two boys of fourteen ran after the sled, trying to insert a cigarette into the corpse's mouth."[161] Another fourteen-year-old, "big for his age"[162] Kolya Bruyakin, the son of the Kamenka storekeeper, is scarcely more sympathetic. This gilded village youth assumes leadership of the local gang, with which he commits a variety of felonious acts. In *April 1917* the overgrown adolescent takes to ogling Yulia Anikeevna, his former schoolteacher, filling the idealistic young woman with well-founded dread.[163] Depraved Kolya is the most vividly drawn pubescent character in the epic. Clearly destined to travel further down the path of vice and crime in the years of violence that are to come, this otherwise peripheral figure is one of the saga's proleptically plotted personalities, like Vorotyntsev and Lenartovich, whose textual presence contains clues about what will happen to them in the fullness of (Soviet) time.

In comparison with Solzhenitsyn's earlier prose there is a new awareness of the dynamics of gender and the misapprehensions that occlude the sexes' understanding of each other. Minor participants in the proceedings are coded with stenographic succinctness and, sometimes, mordant wit. The touring concert group that Alina joins to escape her crumbling marriage features a quintet of seedy male types plus three rather demure showgirls:

> There was a fat-faced funny man who did comic Ukrainian songs. A mustachioed quartermaster lieutenant colonel who sang baritone. A violinist of Mephistophelian appearance. A young lawyer's clerk who performed monologues. Two ladies who sang and one who danced. (All of these were regularly accompanied by the fair-haired fellow with the strong jaw who used to play the piano at the Union cinema.)[164]

The insightful Kovynev shares this thought with Vorotyntsev: "We don't read women's letters five times over, looking for coded messages between the lines. They turn our letters upside down, hold them up to the light . . . And what do we do? Pick out the tasty bits, squeeze the juice out of them—and pop the letter into a chest. We're differently constructed."[165] This Cossack knows his genderlects! Among the female personae, Susanna Korzner, the wife of a prominent Moscow lawyer, is distinguished by a high level of emotional intelligence or, as she puts it, her "delicate antennae alert to feelings,"[166] which most of the male characters lack, notably the hyper-masculine Vorotyntsev. Like Susanna, Vera Vorotyntseva is preternaturally aware of the hidden currents of attraction and tension between the sexes: her watchful, reticent nature makes her the saga's Fanny Price. At the political gathering where Georgi and Olda first meet, Vera realizes that her brother is drawn to the green-eyed professor even before he is aware of the fact. For her part, Olda takes an instant dislike to Vera for keeping him under scrutiny "as if she was his wife instead of his sister."[167]

D. M. Thomas asserts that "Eros...is almost absent from *The Red Wheel*,"[168] but this is far from true. Many of Solzhenitsyn's fictional men and women are involved in romantic relationships or harbor unrequited or secret feelings for each other. "It seemed people couldn't steer clear of these love affairs,"[169] reflects the austere Vorotyntsev days before beginning one of his own. The passages describing Zinaida's liaison with Kovynev carry a strong erotic charge, as do the scenes of Vorotyntsev's romance with Olda, and Likonya's with Gordey Polshchikov, a Volga businessman scripted as a polemical evocation of Foma Gordeyev in Gorky's eponymous novel (1899). Broad-shouldered, platinum blond Polshchikov, a "luminous eagle" of a man,[170] is a better businessman and lover than Gorky's sub-Dostoevskian protagonist, a libertine with mystical leanings who is not so much larger than life than larger than Gorky. Gordey's given name is a near-homophone of *gordyi*—"proud," appropriately so for one of Solzhenitsyn's most flamboyantly masculine heroes:

> Polshchikov was now just over forty years of age, but nothing in his appearance betrayed his years, neither his face, nor his figure, nor his eyes, nor his legs. A Volga native, captain, rider, and connoisseur of horse flesh, he was always quick to move and light on his feet. This past December he had rescued a drowning man from the icy waters off Astrakhan, after which he drank two glasses of vodka, chasing them down with a bottle of bubbly, and afterward was none the worse for wear. Lighthearted and quick with his tongue, he was liked by all sorts of women. True, he was married.[171]

(Once again we observe the employment of the rhetorical negative and functionally structured prose as a means of introducing a new character.)

Gordey is a laughing *Übermensch*, the personification of the *positive* ideal of "sex, the lust to rule, selfishness"[172] preached by Nietzsche's Zarathustra, and as we know, Nietzsche was the young Gorky's idol. Yet the charismatic entrepreneur combines a thirst for life and its pleasures with a sense of patriotic commitment. In a vatic moment, he dreams of building a great canal that will link the Volga with the Don,[173] a project that was realized only after World War II, and in considerable part by gulag labor.

There are other sightings of Eros in the text. Kolya Bruyakin, the shopkeeper's unruly son, loses his virginity to olive-skinned Marusya, Kamenka's resident village vamp:

> He ... abandoned himself to her tyrannical passion. She wouldn't even let him undress himself, she took off all his clothes, kissing him here, there, and everywhere, petting and teasing him, taking her pleasure in every way she could think of. Her eyes were like glowing coals, her lips brick red, and there was a deep flush on her cheeks. She licked the boy into shape and taught him all sorts of diabolical tricks.[174]

And while Katyona Blagodareva is entirely faithful to Arseni, she is also markedly sensual, inviting and receiving a sexy flogging at her husband's hand inside a Russian *banya* or sauna, a traditional locus of peasant sexuality.[175] That steamy encounter elevates their already happy union to a new height of conjugal passion. Unlike stalwart Arseni, Terenti Chernega has no respect for the institution of marriage, strewing illegitimate children on his life's journey like the egregious Yefrem in *Cancer Ward*, whom he much resembles in his casual cynicism and general disdain for humanity. In matters of sex, tumid Terenti is unenlightened to the max: "What makes them cheerful or glum, d'you think? It all depends on whether they've had it or not,"[176] his lecher's jive sending celibate Sanya into a state of priggish "dismay."[177]

As these details show, the epic's historiographical strand is supported by its plentiful human interest content. Several families are depicted, notably the wealthy Tomchaks, the Jewish-Russian Arkhangorodskys, and the Blagodarevs, the young peasant couple. The sequence of Tomchak/Lazhenitsyn chapters at the beginning of *August 1914*, in which husbands, wives, parents, and children are happy in the same way/unhappy in their own way, in accordance with that universal Tolstoyan law, constitutes an extended narrative proem that depicts the last days of peace in a distant and tranquil province of the empire. This is the lull before the storm, the hush before the explosion. Subsequent chapters and Knots will record other moments of felicity or hidden heartache in the midst of war and revolution, thereby confirming a second Tolstoyan truth, that the human need for passion or friendship will find a way even under the most traumatic historical circumstances.

Characters, singly or in groups, move in and out of narrative focus in a manner that recalls *The First Circle*, but on a much grander scale. Inevitably, the male personalities are *historically* more proactive than their female counterparts, though D. M. Thomas is wrong to suggest that "women play a very minor part" in the saga.[178] In fact, numbers of women are shown operating in the public sphere, notably the historical Kollontai and the semi-fictional Andozerskaya, two proto-feminists holding diametrically opposite views. The epic's treatment of extreme political violence is traced along what the author called "the female line" (*zhenskaia liniia*):[179] thus, the textual prominence enjoyed by the two retired terrorist aunties, Adalia and Agnessa Lenartovich, who are, respectively, of the populist and anarchist persuasion. In *April 1917*, Susanna Korzner, one of the epic's wisest voices, offers a prescient comment on the devolving state of the nation: "I believe… though I'm afraid to say it… that we can expect a brutal civil war…"[180] She goes on to lament the absence of a national figure that might warn the country of the coming danger: "Where are our prophets! [*I net—proroka!*]. It is a tragedy that Tolstoy didn't live to see these tragic times, for perhaps people would have listened to him."[181] To which Mrs. Korzner's interlocutor, a family friend named Shreider, replies: "Don't you know that prophets are heard only when the public finds their exhortations pleasing?"[182] (a nicely realized instance of authorial self-referentiality).

Several female characters are assigned to the educational field. In addition to Andozerskaya, they include stern Mrs. Kharitonova and altruistic Elizaveta Smyslovkaya, who gives private lessons to "anybody, anywhere—the children of the poor, neighbors' children, nephews, grandchildren, draymen, and most recently factory workers."[183] In fact, in this series of novels by a onetime pedagogue the teaching profession is remarkably well represented. Elizaveta'a father was once a headmaster, her brother Pavel is an instructor in a military academy, middle-aged Ensign Ustimovich, an officer in Lazhenitsyn's battery, is an ex-teacher who carries with him the aura of the classroom even in the trenches, and Kovynev used to teach in a girls' gymnasium, where Zinaida Altanskaya was his favorite pupil.

"Bold in her judgments,"[184] Zinaida intellectually outshines her mentor, who is some two decades her senior, an ex-Duma deputy, and a published author, though she lacks his literary gifts. Her character is one of Solzhenitsyn's most ambitious creations, an attempt to depict a multilayered female personality between the ages of sixteen and twenty-two from two contrary perspectives, her own and that of her proximate lover, Kovynev. The author sets out to make his heroine's complicated inner self believable in universalizing human terms (see Tolstoy) by framing her private aspirations against the quotidian contexts of the times (see Chekhov), depicting her transition from dreamy, sensual adolescence to ardent, sensual womanhood (see Bunin), and showing how her emotional traumas and spectacular reversals of fortune are caused by an addiction to hyper-intense experiences of the mind, spirit, and body (see Dostoevsky). Where Likonya carefully constructs for herself a persona as a Silver Age enchantress, Zinaida is naturally sexy, just as she is naturally brainy. But above all else, she is "a rebel pure and simple,"[185] and as we know, figures of this type are always privileged in Solzhenitsyn's fictions.

When Kovynev shares with Vorotyntsev the carefully edited story of the relationship, "the distant girl seemed to hover outside their compartment, speeding through dark space, borne along with the train. On feet? Wings? A broomstick?"[186] This comment, wherein two masculine perspectives merge in erotic wonder, holds hints of the bewitching Margarita in Bulgakov's novel *The Master and Margarita*, who flies over the rooftops of Moscow on her missions of rescue. But Zinaida, though scripted as an incarnation of the feminine Eros, refuses to be *her* artist's redeemer, just as she spurns the cultural conventions of the age. She is the opposite of Kovynev, who suffers from a lifelong habit of going with the flow, as his former pupil repeatedly points out, for she tries to right the generational imbalance in their association by means of constructive or even destructive criticism: "You adapt too readily to whatever company you find yourself in!"[187] Acid-tongued Altanskaya is her own woman, much more so than Fyodor is his own man or even his own writer.

The tragic disorder of Zinaida's personal life is due as much to her own passionate nature as to the Cossack litterateur's failings as a teacher, friend, and would-be lover. For six long years he blows hot and cold, toying with the idea of consummating the romance while she holds back and tests him, and herself, by acting the sardonic *femme d'esprit*. She tries to get him out of her life and her (intellectual) system when she takes up with a married engineer who shares Fyodor's quality of Chekhovian passive idealism, "eternally seeking but not striving to find."[188] As part of this erotic side project, Zinaida forces her meek engineering beau to confess all to his wife. She does this not out of some Tolstoyan commitment to truthfulness in all things but because it happens to be the most extreme choice. Then she gets pregnant and her lover goes back to his family. Following these developments and the birth of her son, Zinaida's relationship with Fyodor enters the physical stage, even as little Zhenya falls mortally ill in the village where she had left him in his nurse's charge.

Tanya Belobragina, an army nurse, represents the female side of the caring professions, as well as being the only Cossack woman depicted. This young woman, who is rebounding from a tragic love affair, "took her work very seriously … and showed a special interest in face and neck wounds."[189] She displays uncommon courage when during the catastrophe at Tannenberg she conceals a regimental flag on her person lest it be captured by the enemy. Tanya is next seen in *March 1917*, having spent two years in German captivity; she now wears a St. George's Cross. She becomes an appalled witness to the revolutionary chaos in her native town of Novocherkassk, the capital of the Land of the Don Cossack Host. Other female characters inhabit the realm of art, like lissome Likonya, the epitome of dreamy Silver Age femininity; or of nature, like the young peasant wife Katyona whose exuberant sexuality recalls that of Zoya in *Cancer Ward*. All these heroines are, or will be, impacted by the tragic march of history. As a romantic teenager, Ksenia Tomchak looks forward to a "higher happiness" that "did not depend on war or revolution, on revolutionaries or engineers."[190] She is fated to learn better, but only after the epic ends.

4

Each Knot contains its complement of dramatic episodes in which the epic's historiographical and mythical strands converge inside a clearly delineated, physically constricted, or imaginatively enclosed locus: a chronotope of nodality. Among these hinge happenings are Sanya's meeting with Tolstoy at Yasnaya Polyana, Bogrov's assassination of Stolypin at the Kiev Opera House, Varya Matveeva's sexual encounter with the anarchist Zhora inside his sinister smithy, Sanya Lazhenitsyn and Kotya Gulai's philosophical conversation with the seer Varsonofiev in a Moscow tavern, General Samsonov's suicide in a dark German forest, Sanya's nocturnal disputation with Father Severyan in a frontline dugout, Parvus's political intercourse with Lenin upon a floating *camp* bed, Zinaida's *confessio peccatoris* at the Utkino Church of Tambov, Obodovsky's inspection of an overturned streetcar on a Petrograd street, a Red Guard patrol's abortive attempt to arrest the monarchist Kutepov inside a Petrograd mansion, Nicholas II's abdication on the imperial train, Sanya and Ksenia's *promenades des amants* in revolutionary Moscow, Varsonofiev's anticipatory dreams of a national catastrophe, and the saga's concluding scene in which Vorotyntsev gazes into the future, darkly, from a high cliff above the Dnieper.

Short or elaborate *mises en scène* follow one after another, often accompanied by a plethora of backstories. Characters with various kinds of professional expertise take the floor to provide us with specialist or privileged information. Here is General Svechin briefing his friend Vorotyntsev on the improved performance of the Russian arms industry in the third year of the war:

This is for your ears only: right now we have as many three-inch shells in stock as we have expended all through the war! Machine guns? The Tula plant used to produce seven hundred a year, now it's a thousand a month! Artillery fuses—it used to be fifty thousand a month, now it's seventy thousand a day![191]

In a related statistical vein, there are numerous instances of catalogue prose, as in the index of Lenin's "exasperating opponents"[192] in the European and Russian socialist movements, its starkly denotational structure a wry meta-comment on the historical irrelevance of the figures in question: "Vandervelde and Branting, Huysmans and Jouhaux, Plekhanov and Potresov, Ledebour and Haase, Bauer and Bernstein, the two Adlers, even Pannekoek and Roland Holst."[193] In fact, Solzhenitsyn's actuarial Lenin is peculiarly prone to itemizing objects or people, especially if they are vessels of the "bourgeois spirit" (*burzhuaznost'*),[194] the definition of which changes as the *Weltgeist* moves him.

Occasionally a character is given a pithy line, for example, "Our age is a mere film on the surface of time" (Varsonofiev),[195] or "The people are the infantry" (Vorotyntsev),[196] or "Germans rely on heavy artillery, Russians on God"[197] (Kotya Gulai). Portions of the epic cover subjects that are obscure or arcane but expand its informational function. At one point, Kovynev, who obsessively collects facts and figures for future literary use, enumerates the career stages by which a junior railway employee may rise to the position of engine driver.[198] The fictive world is permanently under construction and we are right there on the building site. At the same time, one cannot help but be impressed with the way that the text employs a myriad social and cultural details, gathered over decades of dedicated authorial research, to fix the flavor of daily life in late tsarist and early revolutionary Russia. Here is Vorotyntsev trying to ring Alina after his arrival in wartime Moscow, which is overflowing with refugees from the western marches of the empire "When he had telephoned from the station the young lady had answered '*zajete*,' and only when he had asked her to repeat it did he realize that she meant '*zanyato*'. So there must be Polish girls working at the exchange."[199] Other samples of historical trivia that ornamentalize this fictive world include the tsar's articulated cigarette holder, composed of a cork section, "a gold ball," and an amber mouthpiece,[200] and his "ashtray in the shape of a little old-fashioned Russian ladle,"[201] or on a more voguish note, Mrs. Korzner's bracelet wristwatch, "the kind that was beginning to come into fashion."[202]

Descriptions of private spaces such as the Tomchak manor in the southern steppes, the Pervushins' noisy, cozy house in one of Moscow's historical districts, Andrei Shingarev's modest apartment, Olda Andozersky's Modernist flat, and Gimmer's conspiratorial den convey the textures of domestic life in the last years before the Bolshevik Revolution, which replaced these upper- or middle-class environments with shoddy barracks and communal dwellings, into which the country's inhabitants were crammed irrespective of their former or current social standing.

While the major heroes and heroines depicted in this "super-novel" possess abundant physical and psychological texture, as do some of the secondary and even tertiary figures, many of the epic's presences, whether real-life or invented, are only nominally or fleetingly individualized, and some appear as metonymical specimens that serve to denote a given social or ideological category of historical actors or subjects. By the same token, the plethora of senior officers depicted in *August 1914* or the dozens of revolutionary activists shown in the last two Knots often fail to gain fictive traction, yet their inclusion in the text is essential to its panoramic representation of the events of 1914–17. These men and women are not characters in a novelistic or even super-novelistic sense, that is, suspension-of-disbelief-inducing simulacra, but historiographical functions, and should be evaluated as such. In fact, "90% of the dramatis personae are historical figures, whether major or minor, but who did really exist," as Solzhenitsyn confirmed himself.[203]

By way of assisting the reader in negotiating his who's who of revolutionary politics, the author thoughtfully provides his public figures with a physical marker, often a beard, in keeping with the male fashion of the age. These facial ornaments are variously "Assyrian-black" (Nikolai Sokolov, unaffiliated social democrat),[204] "sparse, reddish and with patches of white" (Pyotr Struve, liberal intellectual),[205] "spade-like" (General Nikolai Ivanov),[206] "shapeless" (Nikolai Chkheidze, leading Menshevik),[207] "reddish" and "beautiful" (Yuri Nakhamkes-Steklov, unaffiliated social democrat),[208] "delicate" (Fyodor Valuev, head of the Northwestern Railways),[209] "bristly" (Boris Stürmer, the tsar's antepenultimate prime minister),[210] "like a highwayman's" (Vladimir Lvov, Procurator of the Holy Synod in the Provisional Government),[211] "unremarkable" (Maksim Vinaver, prominent Kadet),[212] "long" (Admiral Viktor Kartsev),[213] "disheveled" (Nikolai Kishkin, leftwing Kadet), "large" (Nikolai Chaikovsky, veteran revolutionary),[214] "curly" (Igor Demidov, leftwing Kadet),[215] "wedge-shaped" (Prince Dmitry Shakhovskoi, prominent Kadet),[216] "blond" (Viktor Chernov, Socialist Revolutionary leader),[217] "square" (Mikhail Liber, leading Menshevik),[218] or "unkempt" (Ivan Yefremov, liberal Duma member).[219] In *The Red Wheel*, history is a festival of beards. Then there is that famous pair of goatees, Lenin's "sparse" and "ginger-colored"²²⁰ and Trotsky's "hook-shaped."²²¹ A minatory mustache belonging to "sleepy-whiskered Stalin" (*tikhousyi Stalin*)²²² briefly bristles in *March 1917*. So does Gorky's droopier sub-Nietzschean, sub-labial production, on several occasions in the tetralogy. Among these hirsute revolutionaries, moderates and reactionaries, "clean-shaven like an actor"²²³ Kerensky cuts a theatrical figure. The phrase derives from Vladimir Nabokov *père*'s memoir of the February Revolution,²²⁴ though it is also present in *The Master and Margarita*, where Dr. Stravinsky, the director of a lunatic asylum, is "as carefully shaven as an actor."²²⁵ A hypertextual hint, perhaps?

The international conspirator Alexander Parvus is the epic's monster-at-large, a greenish-skinned, green-blooded "hippopotamus" cum "elephant"²²⁶ (*slonobegemot*)²²⁷ who is also piscine, as in "fishy eyes,"²²⁸ and even scyphozoan, as in "jellylike paws."²²⁹ Deputy interior minister Pavel Kurlov is a grotesque hybrid, a "polecat"²³⁰ crossed with a "boar."²³¹ Bogrov is ophidian, that is, demonic, as in, *terrorist, zmeias' chërnoi spinoi, ubegal*²³² ("the terrorist's black back was wriggling away up the aisle").²³³ Elsewhere on this speciesist spectrum we have a drake (plump, foolish Colonel Kulyabko of the Okhrana),²³⁴ ram (cretinous General Artamonov),²³⁵ billy goat (lanky General François),²³⁶ bear (heavyset General Samsonov),²³⁷ and bull (Chernega,²³⁸ Svechin,²³⁹ Pluzhnikov,²⁴⁰ Rodzianko).²⁴¹ Kovynev, a dedicated lady's man whose Cossack ways go with a certain suavity, is "catlike,"²⁴² and so is the skirt-chasing Chernega. The same is true of Nobs, a Swiss social democrat who has no interest in girls but happens to be one of Lenin's more witless disciples.²⁴³ Nonetheless, the zoo-metaphorical rankings are textually less prominent than those found in *The First Circle*.

Solzhenitsyn offers an imaginative, textured treatment of historical figures and events he finds *fictively* interesting, but on other occasions he foreswears such expansive storytelling practices, preferring to stick to the primary sources. Of *August 1914*, for example, Solzhenitsyn writes, and this is by no means a self-criticism: "The detailed descriptions of military operations, down to the fate of individual regiments and battalions, faithfully reproduce the historical record."²⁴⁴ Many of the imperial family chapters are but a lightly amplified paraphrase of the tsar's journals and correspondence and his courtiers' memoirs. In the same overtly documentary vein, the painstaking account of the functions and malfunctions of the Petrograd Soviet in Knots III–IV is an only nominally fictionalized exercise in historical writing, despite all those wagging beards. Nonetheless, the occasional longueurs and narrative troughs, which one almost expects to find in a work of this size, are redeemed by the distinctive authorial diction. It performs a constant aestheticizing and framing function that holds the whole thing together. But then, as is true of any idiosyncratic literary style, Solzhenitsyn's way with words will not be to every reader's liking.

5

In chapter one, I quoted Solzhenitsyn's words that "history is the result of the interaction of the Will of God and free human wills [and] is irrational, we can never truly understand it." *The Red Wheel* is a sustained attempt to explain the material developments that ensued from the successive fateful conjunctions of these two forces between 1899–1917. To that end, the author designed a new novelistic (epopean) discourse, and a format to go with it, which combined established and experimental tropes to adumbrate the historicized encounter of the human and the divine. Consequently, the text delves into the hidden side of things. It interprets the life of the nation and the individual through interlocking systems of images and topoi that have a mystical resonance and connect the narrative to the plane of archetype and myth. This discourse tends to the Menippean, in the meaning of the definition proposed by Julia Kristeva in *Desire in Language*:

> Menippean discourse is both comic and tragic, or rather, it is *serious* in the same sense as is the carnivalesque; through the status of its words, it is politically and socially disturbing. It frees speech from historical constraints, and this entails a thorough boldness in philosophical and imaginative inventiveness.... Phantasmagoria and an often mystical symbolism fuse with macabre naturalness. Adventures unfold in brothels, robbers' dens, taverns, fairgrounds, and prisons, among erotic orgies and during sacred worship, and so forth.[245]

All these locales and practices of transgression are present in *The Red Wheel*, including the carnal, as when Zinaida, desperately in love with Fyodor Kovynev, brings him to her parents' drawing room where she "walked around naked at his request while he lay on the sofa lazily looking over her with those ... emerald eyes."[246] Elsewhere, however, there are omissions and circumlocutions. In particular, the text draws a narrative veil over the revolution's violently erotic aspect, referring to the latter only intermittently and, in most cases, obliquely.

To repeat, Solzhenitsyn's master-epic is a work of symbols and portents. Its organizing image is the eponymous Wheel, which stands in satanic opposition to the Cross in a faith-based instance of contrastive distribution. "All the characters in *The Red Wheel* confront this choice, consciously or unconsciously,"[247] insists Svetlana Sheshunova. In a narrative moment of some considerable subtlety, the first, subtextual, iteration of the Cross vs. the Wheel antithesis occurs in the canned prose of an imperial manifesto, which is displayed in a "*cylindrically* unrolled" (my emphasis—RT) form on an advertising pillar: "Russia, answering the challenge of her foes, rises up to do battle, rises up to perform her feats of arms with steel in her hand and the cross on her breast."[248] At the risk of stretching the imaginative point, one might read the word "cross" as a signifier that becomes physically twisted or rounded by the pillar's circular surface, thereby acquiring a second, sinister signified. Chapters later we encounter another, this time explicitly formatted, Cross vs. Wheel antithesis when Mrs. Kharitonova is shown "laying out a game of patience, 'Cross Beats Crescent' [*Krest pobezhdaet lunu*[249]]."[250] The headmistress may be a "hard woman,"[251] but she is also a concerned mother who hopes to divine the fate of her son Yarik, an officer in Samsonov's army: two divergent card codes, the gaming and the fortune-telling, which now become conflated, a fictive trick also present in Pushkin's tale "The Queen of Spades" ("Pikovaia dama"; 1834).[252]

The final scene in *November 1916* describes Zinada Altanskaya's penitential visit to the Utkino Church, where she repents, confesses, and receives absolution. The episode is quantified and vectored along lines which, to this reader, recall Descartes's ontological proof of the existence of God in the Fifth Mediation: "Existence can no more be separated from the essence of God than can its having its three angles equal to two right angles be separated from the essence of a triangle."[253]

Contrary to the spirit of the age, Zinaida, although an unbeliever, is sympathetic to the Church, but in recent months, which saw her life devastated by the death of her "secret infant,"[254] Zhenya, she has found herself at the lowest point in her life: "Darkness. Silence. But this is not the grave. You are still alive."[255] On a desolate autumn day some mysterious force induces the young woman to make her way to the church—"her legs had brought her [there] unbidden"[256]— where matins is being sung. Zinaida does not join the worshippers in the side chapel but remains in the nave, still utterly dispirited and despondent. Her gaze travels along a vertical trajectory, focusing on an indifferently painted dome fresco of God the Father sitting in the clouds (even in this state of inner turmoil she retains her critical taste), and then along a horizontal one, fixing on an icon of Christ that shows "a completely human face, though its complexion was not of this world."[257] She becomes "a passive receptacle for the Divine Will,"[258] and the sound of the chant that is issuing from the chapel "removes some kind of block."²⁵⁹

Overcome with remorse, Zinaida mentally lists and numbers her transgressions:

> She thought that as the Church defined sin she was a sinner three times over. No, four. Five, even. ... She had seduced a married man [and] by insisting that he should "tell" had split that family irreparably. She had abandoned her dying mother. She had abandoned her son for her lover. She ... that made four. ... Her fifth sin had stuck to her, merged with her! She had stayed away from her aunt because she knew the answer she would get, and that it was not the one she needed.²⁶⁰

The heroine's aunt, a nun at a nearby monastery, had once invited Zinaida to stay with her there, but the young woman had felt that "God the Comforter is an absurdity."²⁶¹ The fifth sin is that of indifference or pride or despair.

The sacramental quantifications continue when in the presence of Father Aloni, the "broadshouldered and benevolent"²⁶² rector, Zinaida presses her forehead against "the tooled cover of the Gospel, and there was a crucifix to her right."²⁶³ As the priest hears her confession, the young woman haltingly negotiates five spiritual "thresholds,"²⁶⁴ which correspond to her five sins, while "another Breath, the Spirit, hovered over her and stole tremulously into her."²⁶⁵ After going through these discrete and difficult stages of repentance, the prodigal mother and daughter is granted divine forgiveness as laid down in the formula of absolution recited by Father Aloni, although the text replaces its concluding words, "in the name of the Father, and of the Son, and of the Holy Ghost. Amen," with omission points.²⁶⁶ For the reader already knows that the young woman had attained communion with the three persons of the Trinity: God the Father, as represented in the fresco, God the Son, as depicted on the icon, and God the Holy Spirit, as mystically apprehended by her conscience-stricken self.

Yet even after the priest has performed the sacrament, Zinaida still feels an overwhelming need to be reunited with her lover, Kovynev, and to bear his child. This *unspoken* desire, which has already caused her and several others great suffering, elicits this *spoken* response from the priest: "How can anyone forbid you to love when Christ said that there is nothing higher than love? And He made no exceptions, for love of any kind whatsoever."²⁶⁷ Aloni's justification by love, which concludes the chapter as well as the novel, explicitly comprehends *eros*, *philia*, and *agape* and is thereby rendered universal, in the sense of the text.²⁶⁸

Another symbolically weighted appearance of the Cross occurs in *March 1917*. Days after the revolution Vera Vorotyntseva and her beloved old nurse, Polya, attend a service in a packed church where "at the supreme moment of the liturgy" the priest carries a "large cross decorated with flowers" from the altar and solemnly places it on the lectern.[269]

> All of a sudden, with an instinctive confidence born of long experience everyone inside the church joined in with the choir, by some miracle neither outpacing, nor falling behind, nor overshadowing those beautiful voices but majestically magnifying them, and a thunderous chorus, so very different from the singers' exquisitely poignant chant, shook the air and made it reverberate with a swelling earthly force: "We bow before Thy Cross, O Lord!"[270]

This passage, as well as the chapter as a whole, is in dialogue with the scene in *War and Peace* where the Rostov family attend mass in the first month of Napoleon's invasion and a despondent Natasha, with "softened face and shining eyes"[271] recites the prayers, which fill her with "a devout and tremulous awe."[272]

In diegetic terms, however, the titular image is much more important. In a 1989 *Time* interview, the author commented on his epic's central metaphor, using the opportunity to take a swipe at that despised mechanical conveyance, the automobile:

> We are not talking about the wheels of a car, after all. We are talking about a gigantic cosmic wheel, like a spiral galaxy, an enormous wheel that once it starts to turn—then everybody, including those who turn in it, becomes a helpless atom. A gigantic process that you can't stop once it has started.[273]

(See *April 1917*, where Vorotyntsev thinks to himself, "We have been snared by the tail of a fiery Galaxy, which is now dragging us along.")[274]

The two primary figures of historicized geometry, the Cross and the Wheel, stand at the apex of an elaborately crafted system of in-text manifestations and actualizations while coexisting or combining with other archetypal references such as the World Tree and the three wells that lie beneath it. Refracted across the various narrative layers, each glyph in the organizing dyad generates explicit, but more often encoded, images and meanings. Cognates and synonyms of the words *koleso* ("wheel") and *krug* ("circle") are ubiquitous, in a procedure that recalls *The First Circle*. We encounter a plethora of actual, figurative, or lexically camouflaged wheels, red or un-red, solid or spoked. Balls, hoops, rings, disks, spheres, spirals, helices, cones, and cylinders of every material and metaphorical kind superabound. So do radii, diameters, circumferences, arcs, spirals, and parabolas. Also, whirlpools, funnels, pipes, merry-go-rounds, roundelays, and balloons. There is even a noose or two. The histrionic Bogrov imagines he is an acrobat climbing the pole in "a colossal *circus* with ... the whole world as the invited audience"[275] (my emphasis—RT), and the unhistrionic Lenin poses next to the "big red wheel of a train engine,"[276] which turns into a symbol of revolutionary modernity or modern revolution. One character, the transcontinental villain Parvus, is a human sphere, a "dome"-headed,[277] spongy glob of fat and tissue who lends a sagging shoulder to the many-wheeled revolutionary juggernaut as it gathers speed in the midst of a world war.

Sheshunova compares the tetralogy to J. R. R. Tolkien's neo-mythological saga *The Lord of the Rings* (1954)[278]—see its titular MacGuffin, the magical One Ring—and, intriguingly, G. K. Chesterton's Christian novel *The Ball and the Cross* (1910).[279] Then there is the revolution's proprietary color scheme, which in addition to red includes different shades of black. The homicidal anarchist Zhora is dark-haired and swarthy, the well-fed factory workers marching against hunger are "a mass of black and gray,"[280] the jubilant crowd that hears Pavel Milyukov announce the formation of the Provisional Government is a "gray-black sludge,"[281] and Aleksandr Kerensky, the socialist demagogue who dreams of becoming a democratic dictator, swans about in a black jacket of an aggressive cut.[282] To quote a famous title, it's *le rouge et le noir* all over again.

Like some of the other elements in this infrequently read epic, the titular trope entered the public discourse. Announcing his candidacy for a second term as president in early 1996, Boris Yeltsin declared, "We should try to do everything we can so that we Russians, and our country, do not perish under the red wheel of the past."[283] He may not have known that a year earlier Solzhenitsyn, who blamed Yeltsin's government for the chaos and poverty of the post-communist transition, had modified his metaphor to condemn the president himself: "The time will come and some other Russian writer, after carefully studying all the secrets of the 1985–95 decade, will produce an epopee about him, which will be entitled *The Yellow Wheel*."[284]

6

The Red Wheel abounds in references to the Eastern Orthodox liturgical year and its festivals, fasts, and saints' days. A scholar writes: "The text contains descriptions of religious services, icons, and the characters' state of being when they are at prayer ... the chronology of the religious calendar constantly 'intrudes' into the chaotic, febrile chronology of the revolution."[285] The church calendar also serves as a generating source for the implicit or explicit coding of the dramatis personae and their lives. For example, "Likonya," the name of the Silver Age nymph who is one of the epic's most intriguing female characters, is a diminutive of "Elikonida" (*Helikonida* in Greek) and is redolent of "an association between fire and water".[286]

> It is phonetically similar to *lik*, which is a synonym of the word *ikona* ("icon"). [L]*ikonia* also sounds like *ikona*. Lastly and most importantly, the character's full name, Elikonida ... (onomastically revealing of her origins as a merchant's daughter), is that of a female martyr of the third century. ... According to her hagiography, she was thrust into a cauldron of boiling pitch but an angel of the Lord appeared and put out the fire. After it was relit and burned all night, she emerged from the flames unharmed.[287]

The word *lik* occupied a prominent place in the lexicon of the Russian Symbolists, particularly Aleksandr Blok, whose poems are a hidden referent for the poetic Likonya in Knots I–II. Throughout the epic, the heroine's textual appearances are accompanied by water images and references. Of the two men in her life, the radical socialist Lenartovich and the Volga businessman Polshchikov, the former is associated with notions of fire ("a red glow, a star's explosion"),[288] but the latter is appropriately water-based and river-borne. Also, star-crossed Likonya came into the world on February 29 (OS), that is, "the unlucky Feast of St. Cassian, which occurred once every four years":[289] the heroine's quadrennially recurring birthday lies at a mystically inauspicious intersection of the church calendar with its secular (Julian) analogue.

Another instance of Christian time-reckoning involves the Blagodarev couple. In a very human, spousal moment, the recently married Arseni and Katyona had once made love at the time of the Great Fast, despite the Church's prohibition on such intimacies during the Lenten season:

> The rule was that even newlyweds had to take a break after Shrovetide. But Katya wasn't pregnant yet, and they were both hungry for it. So they told each other in whispers, "If we are committing a sin, maybe God will forgive us." And they kept it up until Palm Sunday. But God must have

forgiven them, because look what a fine son she'd borne! If they'd bowed to the law Katya might still have been childless when the war came.[290]

On an entirely different note, the revolutionary harpy Agnessa Lenartovich is also "superstitious about dates,"[291] giving voice to this insight: "Have any of you noticed on what day the war began? The day the Sveaborg rising was put down. History is exacting retribution!"[292]

In addition to Likonya, several other characters are calendrically coded, for example, "[Bogrov] was born on the day on which Pushkin died. The very day, only exactly fifty years later, when the century had turned half-circle."[293] This instance of celebrity hemerology, enhanced by the thematic circularity of the metaphor, frames the national genius Pushkin and the anti-national fiend Bogrov as a Manichean pair of exemplars: creativity vs. chaos, or art vs. cliché.[294]

Thus, the narrative unfolds along several timelines: one historical and linear, as in the "Calendars of the Revolution" ("*Kalendari Revoliutsii*") at the beginning and the end of *April 1917*; another, Christian and familial, as in the frequent references to the saints' days and feasts of the Church; and a third one that is ahistorical and cyclical, as in the patterns of life in Sanya Lazhenitsyn's village of Sablinskaya where "war and the recruiting officer's summons [were accepted] as acts of God, like a blizzard or a dust storm,"[295] or the patterns of thought inside Ensign Chernega's head, which reconfigure the world war as "a universal, lingering plague, with no possible sense or purpose."[296] At the end of the epic Chernega joins the Bolsheviks, at which point he exits cyclical time for linear time. Most of the rural characters, however, never abandon their timeless, mythological ways. These are described by the liberal Duma deputy Andrei Shingarev, a onetime country doctor with the eyes of "a good-natured bandit,"[297] in anthropologically vivid terms:

> You might be told that the cow had to be sold because its color didn't please the house sprite. ... Then if there was a cattle plague the women would plow the fields around the village naked. ... Then there was what some call "folk medicine." If a woman was having a difficult delivery they'd hang her upside down from the stove and a runner would be sent to the church three versts away to ask the priests to open the royal gates so as to ease the birth.[298]

(It turns out that the Russian stove, about which we learned a great deal in "Matryona's Home," possesses additional, obstetrical properties.)

Later in the epic, the thoughtful Pyotr Struve[299] tells Shingarev, "The people live from moment to moment, they inhabit the present, the past, and the future simultaneously [*Narod—zhivët srazu: i v nastoiashchem, i v proshlom, i v budushchem*]."[300] For his part, the "good-natured bandit" speaks of the peasants' ignorance and superstition "not contemptuously [but] sadly, pityingly."[301] He believes that if left to their own devices these rural folk will never rise above their pre-modern condition: "Only we can drag them out of the mire."[302] The policies advocated by this sympathetic parliamentarian, however, are a different matter, and his tenure as a minister in the Provisional Government will turn out to be far from stellar, as recorded in *April 1917* and "The Narrative Beyond the Point of Suspension."

A solar eclipse that occurs on day three of the Tannenberg campaign prompts superstitious dread among the marching Russian soldiery, who refuse to accept the astronomical explanations provided by their officers, among them Lieutenant Kharitonov: "It's a bad omen! It bodes no good!"[303] The distance that separates Russia's bearded masses, whether in or out of uniform, from the spheres of scientific knowledge is truly epic. The point is driven home a couple of pages later: "In the next village someone found a bicycle and wheeled it out and the whole company crowded around to look. Many of them were seeing this wonderful contraption for the first time."[304] No *wonder* that when the peasants contemplate action in the political here and now, their thinking is almost always muddled or magical. The same is true of the industrial workers shown in the last three Knots, who are but farmers in factory overalls. In spite of their urban domicile and employment in the mechanized production process they remain in thrall to the supernatural, just like Shingarev's village patients or the soldiers in Kharitonov's platoon. A carpenter at Petrograd's Obukhov factory explains the failures of the imperial government in these sword and sorcery terms: "Rasputnik [Rasputin] had some Jew working for him, Ruvim Shtein [Dmitry Rubinstein] or something, and this Jew had a horse that was as good as invisible, could gallop all the way to [Kaiser] Wilhelm and back in one shot."[305]

In fact, superstitious habits of thought and action pervade the entire social hierarchy. Some of the empire's most exalted personages think of themselves as second-sighted, when they are merely second-rate. Before they met Rasputin, the tsar and tsarina, we recall, employed the services of the fraudulent medium, Monsieur Philippe. Interior minister Aleksandr Protopopov, who with his belief in Tibetan gurus resembles some New Age crank, consults an astrologer to identify unpropitious dates on his official calendar.[306] Joan Quigley, anyone? In the same vein of wanton credulity, Alina Vorotyntseva has the habit of seeing the most mundane events and objects as "symbols,"[307] whether it is the sun peeping out from behind the clouds (good)[308] or a dish of overcooked rice (bad).[309] Alina's rival for her husband's affections, the donnish Olda Andozerskaya, also subscribes to this fashion for the unfathomable, though the besotted Georgi finds her fey ways charming: "Even the professor's belief in astrology, fortune-telling, and good and bad luck signs somehow did not seem incongruous."[310] And then there is Rasputin, whose real and alleged doings are discussed in salacious detail by a succession of democrats, demagogues, and demi-mondaines at discrete intervals in the epic.

Occasionally even sober-minded personalities with an entirely modern mindset seek to explain the difficult-to-accept or difficult-to-comprehend in otherworldly terms, for such is the tenor of the times. As the revolution unfolds, Captain Nekrasov, a disabled war veteran, articulates this piece of esoteric knowledge:

> Now, there's an old man who lives in Uglich, his name is Yevsei Makarych. After poring over the Holy Scriptures, last autumn he made a prophecy: soon Russia shall know great trials and tribulations. To save themselves, people will dress in rags and seek out places where no one knows them. There will be many years of famine. Thousands will be killed or desolated. Suffering will first befall some, then others, then all. Only in the seventh generation will people once again live well.[311]

As a writer, Solzhenitsyn is always aware that, to quote Horkheimer and Adorno, "the transposition of myths into the novel ... does not falsify myth so much as drag it into the sphere of time."[312] Jungian archetypes and their folkloric Russian cognates are encountered either on the plane of symbolically weighted description or individual character perception, as we saw with Nekrasov. Such references to magical figures and things always occur at appropriately chthonic moments in story time, as when a gang of revolutionary soldiers, high on the promise of "complete freedom" and a good lynching, emit "a whistle like Nightingale the Robber,"[313] a malevolent human/avian creature from the bylinas (medieval Russian tales).

The *mystical methodology* operating in *The Red Wheel* is associated with the epic's most eccentric presence, the "stargazer"[314] Pavel Varsonofiev. His surname conjures up the "half-holy foolish but very remarkable"[315] wanderer Varsonofy of Mount Athos, a fictional presence in Vladimir Solovyov's *Three Conversations on War, Progress, and the End of World History* (1900), a foundational text of

Russian eschatological literature,[316] or even St. Barsanuphius of Palestine, a hermit from the reign of Emperor Justinian. Varsonofiev is a widower aged "fifty-five in round figures,"[317] as he cryptically informs Sanya and his friend Kotya Gulai over some beers in a Moscow tavern. Indeed, the augur has much to be cryptic about, for he possesses the true gift of second sight. A former Duma member and a publicist of an enlightened conservative bent,[318] the mage is visited by precognitive visions of the chaos that is to come: the national catastrophe foreshadowed and fore-scripted as a sequence of symbolic intimations of the End. While Tsar Nicholas, Protopopov or even Olda Andozerskaya are in thrall to various forms of superstitious nonsense, Varsonofiev has apprehended, and not by any design of his own, the secret meaning of divine agency. The Stargazer possesses a higher degree of mystic acuity than Russia's salon occultists, let alone its illiterate hoi polloi, because he "was used to treating such dreams not as kaleidoscopic jumbles of incoherent fancies but as genuine spiritual encounters with the living or the dead, but always in code."[319] This working journalist is the epic's Prospero, with hints of Plato thrown in. The seer certainly looks the part: white-haired and white-bearded, he has "long white" fingers which look like "candles,"[320] a booming voice, and eyes that are "cavernous hollows,"[321] that is, Platonic, as in the Parable of the Cave. "I read certain books and write others. ... I read thick ones and write thin ones,"[322] he reveals (or, rather, does not). By way of confirmation, years after that beery conversation Kotya comes across "a little book by our Stargazer" on "the Ideal Society [and] how to inculcate virtue"[323]—themes that are perfectly, and identifiably, Platonic.

The procedures underpinning the epic's *analytical methodology* are articulated by Professor Andozerskaya, "the cleverest woman in Petersburg,"[324] who teaches at the Bestuzhev Courses, Imperial Russia's preeminent institution of higher learning for female undergraduates. The professor's field is medieval European history, which would appear to bear little relevance to the modern world, or so her students tell her, albeit with due deference. Like any academic challenged to justify her life's work, the clever medievalist has a great deal to say in defense of her subject. After pronouncing that in those feudal times "mankind had never experienced such an intense spiritual life,"[325] she offers this formula, delivered in judiciously maternal tones: "History isn't politics, my dears, with one loudmouth echoing or contradicting what another loudmouth has said. Sources, not opinions, are the material of history. And we must accept the conclusions as they come, even if they go against us."[326]

In keeping with its nation-building, nation-affirming orientation, the epic includes a cosmological narrative, which is given voice by Lieutenant Colonel

Aleksei Smyslovsky of the artillery (brother to the teacher Elizaveta Smyslovskaya), who has made "a special study of astronomy."[327] He explains that

> this whole earth of ours ... is the prodigal son of the ruling luminary. It lives only by the light and warmth its father bestows on it. But that diminishes from year to year, and the atmosphere becomes poorer in oxygen. A time will come when our warm coverlet will be threadbare, and all life on earth will perish...[328]

Shades of H. G. Wells's *The Time Machine*, perhaps, though the colonel's imaginative astrophysics also prompts thoughts of the cosmicism of Nikolai Fedorov, a proponent of the physical resurrection of the dead, and Konstantin Tsiolkovsky, the pioneering rocket engineer and space visionary, both of whom belonged to a Russian school of natural philosophy that ultimately derives from Aristotle. Smyslovsky is the bearer of the epic's astronomical code, which *The Red Wheel* shares with Solzhenitsyn's earlier novels such as *Love the Revolution* and *Cancer Ward*:

> In the whole dark expanse to the east, as far as he could see from the northern to the southern extreme, no light winked except Andromeda and Pegasus sprawled across the sky, and brilliant Capella had crept out in pursuit of sinuous Perseus, and the Pleiades clustered in their milky haze.[329]

As so often happens in Solzhenitsyn, the stars and galaxies with their exotic names and mythological associations become a source of figuratively formatted transfers of meaning, for example, metaphors and zeugmas, while serving as a fictive measure of the awesome distance between the materiality of human existence and the infinite vastness and majesty of the Creation.

Also present is "nature's calendar,"[330] which governs the lives of the peasants who till the soil and the soldiers who fight in the trenches. Or even the patterns of autocratic rule: "To Nikolai nature was one great living creature. His first waking thought was always about the weather."[331] The tsar was, after all, an English country gentleman who happened to be sitting on the throne of All the Russias, although the saga remains silent on this cross-cultural point.

The flora and fauna of this fictive world is far from abundant, in keeping with its preponderance of military and urban environments. *November 1916*, however, opens with an extended description of the forests of eastern Poland and the birds that live there such as crows, ravens, kites, song thrushes, white storks and a few pages later, a nightingale. In a recognizably Tolstoyan procedure, this autumnal landscape, which is shown via the melancholic perceptions of Lieutenant Lazhenitsyn, the saga's chief lover of nature, serves as a poignant frame for the scenes of trench warfare that follow. Also in the way of Tolstoy, and of epic narratives, the text correlates the characters' hopes and loves, thoughts and moods with the changing of the seasons or the state of the weather at a given moment of a given "discrete stretch of time." And so later in the same novel, we read:

> The day was dying without ever really dawning. An hour earlier there had been snow or rather a fine, frozen drizzle, and where no one had walked, and the heat from the buildings and the underground steam pipe had not melted it, a thin white coating remained to give the evening a wintry look. And it was getting chilly.
>
> Dmitriev was ill at ease.[332]

Mikhail Dmitriev, a reticent middle-aged engineer, is walking over to the Obukhov factory where he must persuade reluctant shop floor employees to work overtime for the war effort. As it turns out, his efforts are scuttled by a revolutionary agitator's "insolently mocking" voice,[333] presaging the screams and chants of the riots to come.

Anxious minds ponder the future. Vorotyntsev recalls a Chinese soothsayer's prediction that he is fated to die in 1945[334] (he will) and Bogrov wonders if "he might live to see what would happen in 1960"[335] (he will not). Vorotyntsev's premonition connects the epic's exemplary soldier to its exemplary statesman, Stolypin, who had "a resigned awareness that he would not die a natural death. (Warriors do not expect to.)"[336] And in another vatic moment, when discussing a notorious miscarriage of military justice with Svechin, the colonel imagines himself "wrongly condemned" and hanged:[337] see the play *Prisoners*, in which he is sentenced to this form of execution by the Soviet secret police.

One of the saga's most effectively realized moment of apocalyptically tinged prolepsis occurs in *March 1917*. On the day that news of the revolution reaches *Lenin in Zurich*, the Bolshevik chieftain, out on one of his mountain rambles, encounters a mysterious woman on a sorrel horse (*svetlo-ryzhaia loshad'*): "She emerged from the dark thicket, dressed all in red, and rode through the damp, clear, silent evening."[338] A lovelorn Lenin sees this apparition as an image of his revolutionary mistress, Inessa Armand, but we are free to choose a different reading: "And there went out another horse *that* was red: and *power* was given to him that sat thereon to take peace from the earth, and that they should kill one another: and there was given unto him a great sword" (Revelation 6:4).

The notions of historical and mythical time and the various cultural chronologies associated with them are present on almost every page. The titular month in Knot I is the birth month of Tolstoy (August 28 OS) and Napoleon (August 15). The mascot decorating the radiator of General François's staff car, a yellow toy lion captured by his troops from the Russians, serves as a materialized incarnation of Napoleon's astrological sign, Leo. The creator of *War and Peace* is the epic's literary totem and his novel serves as its textual foil, but Napoleon is François's ideal general as well as a prominent citational presence which is associated with several characters, among them Aleksandr Guchkov. In *March 1917*, the former Duma chairman, who has a Churchillian predilection for grand strategic projects and private military adventures, fantasizes about creating a new revolutionary army "with a Napoleonic spirit."[339] Still, it is the dopes and dunces of history that are especially, and absurdly, fond of comparing themselves to the French emperor. Upon attaining general's rank Kurlov concludes that his promotion is "rather reminiscent of Napoleon's rise,"[340] the assassin Bogrov displays a "Napoleonic hauteur"[341] at his trial, slow-witted General Zankevich plans to lead his troops against the rioting mob "in the manner of a Napoleon,"[342] and the braggadocious Kerensky imagines that his leadership style exhibits "the expressive terseness of a Napoleon."[343] To that end, the future premier wears "something like a work coat (which, it seemed, was meant to recall Napoleon's uniform)."[344] They are all wrong, and the martially accoutred Kerensky more so than the rest.

7

As so often happens in this writer's novels, there is much serious conversation, raucous argument, and public or private oratory. *The Red Wheel* is a study of the causes and course of the Russian Revolution, but also of the semiotics of revolution. The epic's dialogic discourse turns emphatically Menippean when it phantasmagorically reformats and satirically examines the mythology of violent social change and redemption, and its associated linguistic and symbolic practices. That mythology and those practices were born in France in 1789–99 and were adopted a century or so later by Russia's Populists, revolutionary socialists, anarchists, Bolsheviks, and their fellow travelers and liberal enablers.

Patterns of speech and thought are the chief instrument of characterization, most strikingly in the case of Solzhenitsyn's Lenin. He is largely derived from the fourth edition of his own collected works,[345] so that the Leader's bombastic, pleonastic idiolect becomes the instrument of his textual deconstruction. The preferred narrative mode is free indirect speech, that is, narrator-to-character or character-to-character paraphrase, with both moods (see Genette) generating hybrid utterances (see Bakhtin) by means of which the epic's multiplicity of voices is integrated into its anti-revolutionary discourse. *The Red Wheel* is a richly heteroglossic text. As the future Tsar Nicholas II travels across Siberia and the Urals, he enjoys a spot of sightseeing in "towns in which he never expected to find himself again: Irkutsk, Tobolsk, Yekaterinburg."[346] In 1917–18 the imperial family would be imprisoned in Tobolsk and Yekaterinburg, and murdered in the latter city.

Sometimes a single event is depicted from two or more character standpoints, as in the case of the Stolypin assassination at the Kiev Opera, which is shown through the eyes of Bogrov, Nicholas II, and the prime minister himself, prompting one of Sozhenitsyn's more thoughtful interviewers to think of "five or six film cameras [that] are positioned in different locations inside the theater."[347] In any case, every primary, secondary, or tertiary character is nationally or culturally representative, or both. These emoting, cogitating, talking metonyms (there is, to repeat, a great deal of talk!) sustain an overarching multivocality, with Lenin's taunting voice its most memorable component. The characters' "perceptual worlds"[348] variously remain separate, collide, draw together, or drift apart, underpinned by an implied-authorial assessment of how each personality is doing in both a historical and an ethical sense, so that at different moments in discourse time individual facts and lives may appear either fragmented or whole. These variable diegetic procedures distinguish the epic from the earlier fictions.

A passage in *August 1914* shows Vorotyntsev and Blagodarev's "perceptual worlds" in dialogue during the early stages of the battle of Tannenberg: the career officer knowledgeably assesses the enemy's tactics, and the peasant soldier, his agricultural practices: "Such beautiful potatoes! The Germans didn't let even gullies go to waste."[349] Elsewhere we observe the harmonious coalescence of two identities, usually in the case of a man and a woman who are in love (Arseni and Katyona, Pyotr and Nina Obodovsky, Sanya and Ksenia), or of two worldviews that meld into unanimity, though as a rule only briefly (Sanya and Father Severyan during their midnight conversation about the Church, Russia, and history).

Several of the principals have important things to say as direct articulators of the saga's anti-revolutionary discourse. They are *The Red Wheel*'s designated analysts whose views receive diegetic emphasis and, taken together, comprise a cumulative evaluation of the state of the nation. These bearers of insight each own an important part of the historical truth, which they express dialogically, that is, in conversation or debate with some other character. At the same time, they all have intellectual blind spots, with the exception of the sagacious Stolypin, Solzhenitsyn's ideal statesman. His one failing, if a failing it is, happens to be an excess of courage.

The military man, Vorotyntsev, cleaves to the uncomplicated belief that every man and woman owes the state a duty of allegiance, however ineffectual its rulers or troubled their own lives (but is a political naïf and a bit of a philistine). The university teacher, Andozerskaya, considers the autocracy the guarantor of the nation's existence even in the age of electricity and the airplane (but suffers from the academic tendency to overinterpret). The Cossack man of letters, Kovynev, rues the corruption and decadence that permeate all classes of society (but is prone to conspirological thinking). The industrial manager, Obodovsky, advocates the harmonious growth of the economy and civil institutions (but is too starry-eyed about Russia's capacity for change). The liberal, Shingarev, knows that the country is doomed unless the gulf between the rulers and the people is somehow bridged (but imagines that a revolution might be the "miracle" that will make it all come right).[350] The army chaplain, Father Severyan, regards the Church as the foundation of the nation's identity (but is unable to account for its institutional errors and crimes). The mystic, Varsonofiev, assigns blame for the looming catastrophe to the cultural and revolutionary elites as well as the Russian people itself (but supports the war). Soldier, professor, writer, engineer, priest, politician, mage: seven outlooks, one truth. These wise but imperfect figures personify Ortega y Gasset's ideal of the "excellent man" (or woman), who strives to serve a higher cause. Yet what may be the epic's most effective anti-revolutionary line belongs to evanescent Likonya, who has no political interests. As the country descends into fratricidal violence she asks the recently Bolshevized Lenartovich, "Why are you shooting at people?" (*Zachem v luidei streliaete?*)[351]

Occasionally the task of reporting *sequences* of specific events is delegated to some character in the "know," even if the know happens to be distorted by passion or partisanship. When this kind of personalized reportage occurs, diegetic irony is employed to counterbalance the speaker's bias, as when the two retired radicals, Adalia and Agnessa Lenartovich, narrate a potted history of the Russian terrorist movement for their niece Veronika's reluctant edification,[352] though later she will embrace the family tradition of revolutionary service.

March 1917 and *April 1917* are marked by a more assertive presence of the authorial voice, which drives home the meaning of what is happening in the country in no uncertain terms:

> In the early days of the revolution many people believed and said, and the newspapers so reported, that because the capital and with it the entire country had rid themselves of the tsarist regime, the police were no longer needed. Alas, the number of urban lowlifes turned out to be much larger than was thought. So now the militiamen were paid lavish wages that were three times the size of those earned by the policemen of old. (Which is why professional thieves and escaped convicts were eager to join their ranks.)[353]

While concealed speech serves as the chief source of diegetic irony, there are also instances of broad humor and even historical slapstick. Early on in the epic we are given this glimpse of the tsar pondering matters of state *en plein air*:

> Sometimes, when he was clearing the ice in the Winter Palace garden or taking a ride near Tsarskoye Selo, Nikolai strained his wits so much comparing the conflicting views picked up from subordinates or in actual conversation that if he could have transmitted all this tension into his crowbar it would have danced furiously on the ice, and if he could have communicated it to his horse it would have snorted and bolted.[354]

The implied notion of the imperial mount acting as a primal scream therapist to his conflicted master is a rare moment of light relief in the saga's Nicholas sections.

За работой с женой

The outbreak of war finds Lenin departing posthaste from the eastern marches of the Hapsburg Empire. Worried that he might be lynched by local Austro-Hungarian or Austro-Ukrainian or Austro-Polish patriots as a Russian spy, the Leader is reassured by the sight of a policeman: "Looked at dialectically, a gendarme is sometimes a bad thing and sometimes a good thing."[355] Later in the epic, the technocrat Obodovsky (modeled on a real-life figure) is importuned by a couple of "bothersome inventors," Podolsky and Yampolsky (real-life figures), who want to "build a gun fifty yards long operating on the magnetomotive principle and [with] a range of three hundred versts"[356] (a real-life project). The quantum of comedy generated by this Jules Vernian duo and their rhyming surnames is canceled, however, by an extended subsequent conversation between Obodovsky and Dmitriev concerning industrial relations at the Obukhov factory.

Among the other amusing bits are the portraits of Adalia and Agnessa, who preach the life-affirming principle of political assassination; the description of Ensign Chernega's stentorian snores as "the only sound to be heard anywhere on the Russo-German front";[357] and this news report, quoted in *March 1917*:

> PACHYDERMS ON THE MARCH. Yesterday an extraordinary procession took place on Tverskaya Street: two elephants and a camel wearing saddle cloths with slogans which hailed the principle of popular representation were followed by the famous clown and animal trainer Durov, who had suffered so much under the old regime, standing proud in a chariot.[358]

There are moments of gallows humor:

> On the Field of Mars everything was being readied for a mass interment of the revolutionary martyrs: fires were lit to thaw the frozen ground and sticks of pyroxylin were also used. But the funeral kept being rescheduled and rearranged. Another reason for the delay was the lack of dead bodies.[359]

Now and then we come across a passage that conveys a palpable sense of authorial joy at the business of storytelling, as when Yarik Kharinotov finds himself sharing a train compartment with an attractive, bubbly and extremely talkative army nurse, Natasha Anichkova. A member of "an insolvent branch of a large gentry family,"[360] she entertains him with a series of fantastic stories, from an account of how she had once danced the krakowiak on stilts to a potted history of the amazingly dysfunctional Anichkov clan:

There was a certain Ruf, who founded a masonic lodge in Moscow, and a certain Vereshchagin, who had a land surveyor thrown into a cold pond for failing to give him a low enough bow. There was a band of masked brothers who kidnapped a younger brother to extort money from their mother. A group of gentlemen from Tambov, tricksters who spent the nights carousing and turning over shop signs, then made their way to Moscow where they joined the Jack of Hearts Club, a meeting place of the city's gilded youth, and went on a crime spree leaving a jack of hearts as their calling card. On one occasion they placed a miter on the head of a shopkeeper who sold church utensils, before breaking into his cashbox. They also hoodwinked an acquaintance, the majordomo at the Moscow governor's residence, which was standing empty because of the holidays, and showed it to a succession of foreign buyers, executing the bill of sale at a fake notary's office and collecting the deposit. Upon graduating from the Corps of Pages in the reign of Nicholas I, another member of the Anichkov family had used a hand mirror to dazzle the empress and was denied a posting to the guards as a result. And a different Anichkov, whose mother would beat him and his brother, found work as a washerwoman's assistant and slept inside a straw-lined coffin at an undertaker's. Years later he became a deputy minister of education. Also, the assassin Karakozov was a distant relative.[361]

The tall tales told by this train-borne Scheherazade call to mind Pushkin and Gogol by way of Tynianov. They carry a sense of encroaching chaos, with the reference to Dmitry Karakozov, the fanatic who made an attempt on the life of Alexander II (1866), serving as a coda to these fanciful yarns of mischief and crime. In the epic, chaos comes in many guises and makes itself known in many accents.

8

The Red Wheel may be a novelistically formatted pre-history of the USSR, but its component Knots contain numerous passages that engage, usually indirectly, with aspects of the Soviet experience. Take, for instance, the impressions of Second Lieutenant Yaroslav Kharitonov upon crossing the German border, which elide into those of the peasant troops he commands:

> The villages of two-story brick houses, the stone byres, the concrete wellheads, the electric lighting (even in Rostov only a few streets had it), the

electrical installations on farms, the telephones in peasant houses, the cleanliness. ... Nothing left half done, nothing spilled, nothing out of place—and the peasants of Prussia certainly hadn't made everything so spick and span for the benefit of their Russian visitors! Beards wagged in Yaroslav's company—the soldiers couldn't make out how the Germans kept their farms so tidy. ... And why, when Germany was so rich, did Wilhelm covet Russian lath and plaster?[362]

For Lieutenant Kharitonov, read Captain Solzhenitsyn, for those rustic beards, shaven chins, and for Kaiser Wilhelm, Adolf Hitler, and there you have it: a neat account of how Red Army troops responded to the sight of Teutonic prosperity when they marched through the same alien regions in the last months of World War II. The critical treatment of the quality of Russian military leadership, down to the text's jaundiced take on the generals' stout physique, does extra-textual duty as a reminder of the repeated failings of Stalin's *Generalität* in 1941–2. The scenes of Russian surrender in *August 1914* invoke the tragedy of Soviet POWs captured by Hitler's Wehrmacht: "A novel solution! The con-cen-tra-tion camp!"[363] The same is true of the brutalities witnessed by Dr. Fedonin in a German *Stalag*. The liberal Korzner couple circulates typewritten tracts among like-minded friends in an early version of samizdat, as do members of politically active circles in Petrograd: "Copies—typewritten, cyclostyled, hectographed."[364] Or what about the description of Olda's eclectically decorated flat? With its "desk ... hidden under leaning towers of books,"[365] an icon of St. Olga displayed as "an ordinary picture,"[366] and quaint figurines distributed across the apartment's horizontal surfaces, it resembles nothing more than the home of a freethinking Leningrad intellectual during the Brezhnev era, but with nicer furniture.

Kovynev tells Vorotyntsev of meat rotting at a train station, kerosene shortages in Rostov,[367] and the practice of rendering precious butter into soap.[368] He could be discussing the inanities of the planned economy at any point between 1930 and 1990. Then there is the word *khvosty* ("tails"), which describes a new urban phenomenon, the crowds of shoppers lining up in front of food stores. Vorotyntsev sees his first queue when he arrives in Moscow after spending two years away at the front, and the colonel's defamiliarizing gaze interprets the sight in accordance with his military mindset:

People of different ages, mostly women, bunched together here and there, blocking the pavement, in a strange formation, each pair of eyes fixed on the back of someone's head. Like blind people waiting their turn for something, or soldiers standing with their mess tins ready when the field kitchen arrives—but there it was always quick. Here in the city it was weird to see one person studying the back of another's head."[369]

Under the Soviets, the *khvosty* would be renamed *ocheredi* and become a fixture of daily life. In the same passage, the colonel notices that the composition of the city's municipal workforce has altered: "Women tram drivers, women conductors, women changing the points. Women in place of yardmen. He caught a glimpse of a girl wearing a messenger boy's hat."[370] The feminization of much of the economy would be another, highly visible, feature of Soviet reality.

A revolutionary coinage invented by Robespierre and enthusiastically adopted by the communist terror state makes its appearance in *The Red Wheel* when a sinister cripple brings a group of detainees into the presence of a preening Kerensky: "I have the honor to report that I have captured, disarmed and delivered thirty *enemies of the people*."[371] Another, even more enduring term that repeatedly crops up in Knots III–IV is the adjective "Soviet" (*sovetskii*), which at this point in history denotes persons or actions pertaining to the Petrograd Soviet of Workers' Deputies.

Once in a while we encounter direct invocations of the Soviet future, as in the biographical chapter devoted to the beatific socialist Kozma Gvozdev, a historical figure and one of the few working-class characters in the epic: his Bolshevik adversary Shlyapnikov is another.

> Since then the first war had ended, the smoke of revolution had cleared, the country had been flattened by Soviet steamrollers (and the Cheka had shot Obodovsky), there had been another war, no happier for us than the first, and the Soviet steamrollers had rolled again, but all those who saw Gvozdev in the Spassk division of Steplag in the third decade of the captivity from which he would never escape say that even at seventy, with four numbers slapped on him, Kozma Antonovich preserved, in his eyes and on his brow, that peculiar childlike radiance, that look of startled vulnerability.[372]

Gvozdev, who is also present in *The Gulag Archipelago*, is a documented human link to Solzhenitsyn's chronicle of the camps, while in strange and atheistic way, the "childlike"[373] socialist recalls the "childlike sovereign" Nicholas II.

On a hidden satirical note, the author of record states apropos the unpretentious Stolypin, "In those days it was not the practice to trumpet the praises of statesmen throughout the land or to paste their portraits about the streets,"[374] a prompt to the epic's Soviet-era readers to take a closer look at the likenesses of Brezhnev and Andropov that decorated, so to speak, public spaces in every town and village.

Sasha Lenartovich's future life and death are adumbrated in two passages. At Likonya's name day party, he is visited by "an imperious sense of right: he had chosen her and she will be his, by his will and not hers!"[375] Such is the arousing promise of unbridled power not as yet won, but already there for the taking. Many chapters later, when Lenartovich conducts a search of Olda's apartment, she issues this warning: "A time may come when you will regret that these days ever happened."[376] We can imagine Sasha's middle-aged self recalling her words in 1937 or 1938, when he, like so many veteran revolutionists, will likely find himself lying on a prison bunk or being led into the execution cellar of the Lubyanka.

Although such prefigurations of the events and practices of the soon-to-arrive Soviet future receive considerable prominence, the epic's narrative logic hinges on a palpable, and intermittently articulated, sense of what *might have been*: an extended series of sideshadowings. In Solzhenitsyn's book, history does not carry a teleological sense and the revolution was not the ineluctable outcome of a chain of events stretching back to the beginning of time, or the beginning of Russia, and so the saga is suffused with a not-so-secret sorrow: had all those politicians and generals done things differently, and had the people held fast to its traditional values and way of life, his homeland would likely have avoided the disasters that befell it after 1914. Figures such as Colonel Kutepov, General Kornilov, and Admiral Kolchak, who became prominent White leaders in the Russian civil war, are scripted as tragic historical actors: they understand the catastrophe that has befallen their country and possess the will and the vision, but not the means, to stop the slide into chaos.

Solzhenitsyn's knots or nodes or loops in the fabric of time recall the points of divergence in speculative historiography and alternate reality fiction, two genres that began to acquire a wide audience in the English-speaking world around the time that the first version of *August 1914* appeared: Nabokov's novel *Ada* (1969) is a notable highbrow example. The sequence of implied counterfactuals distributed across the epopee's four constituent novels adumbrates a shadowy counter-plot set in an uchronia, or imagined time period, where there exists a Russia-that-never-was, a Russia-that-remained-itself.

Vladimir Sorokin, whose dystopian novel *Day of the Oprichnik* (*Den' oprichnika*; 2006) flamboyantly twists and braids the timelines of Russian history,[377] observes that counterfactual fiction can bridge the discontinuities in the nation's sense of self:

> Russia is fertile soil for alternative history. This is because in our country, no one, starting with the president and ending with the lowest hobo, knows what will happen next. So for a writer this is, without a doubt, an Eldorado. Such is the Russian metaphysics. As I have said many times, we live between the past and the future.[378]

Solzhenitsyn's hypotheticals occasionally acquire explicit form through a given character's comments or a suppositionally inflected passage, when hours or decades of alternative history are brought into fictive play. "If they acted without delay, on 27 August, they could smash the whole German center, after which no combination of moves could save the German army in Prussia,"[379] reflects General Martos, one of the few competent Russian commanders at Tannenberg. "Give us ten years of peaceful development and you won't recognize Russian industry or the Russian countryside,"[380] cries Obodovsky, an industrial organizer with the talent to be a second Henry Ford. This character is one of the saga's chief voices of counterfactuality, as demonstrated by his vision of a glorious future for his country and people, which he expresses in these recognizably Solzhenitsynian accents: "Russia's center of gravity will shift to the Northeast. That's a prophecy. ... Do you know Mendeleev's forecast that the population of Russia will be more than three hundred million in the middle of the twentieth century?"[381] To which Obodovsky's interlocutor, Arkhangorodsky, wise in the ways of their countrymen, replies, "Always supposing ... that we don't take it into our heads to disembowel each other first!"[382]

The "revolutionary and patriot"[383] Obodovsky and the Jewish progressive Arkhangorodsky are two of the epic's paragons, skilled engineers (a profession Solzhenitsyn always accorded special esteem) and good family men who combine a love of liberty with love of country. Yet what neither man realizes is that their homeland already stands on the wrong side of history and that the fateful deviation occurred on September 1/14, 1911, when Bogrov mortally wounded Stolypin.

The epic's uchronic strand is rendered explicit in the Stolypin-Bogrov embedded narrative, which takes up a large part of *August 1914*:

This program for the reconstruction of Russia by 1927–32, perhaps more ambitious than even the reforms of Aleksandr II, would have rendered Russia unrecognizable, enabling it to make full use of its natural and human resources for the first time. (… His project vanished, was never published, discussed, exhibited, or indeed recovered—all that survived was the testimony of the man who helped Stolypin to draft it. The communists may possibly have found it and used a distorted version of some of Stolypin's ideas for their own purposes.).[384]

At this instant of discourse time, historical time melds with hypothetical time and the seven decades of Soviet rule are reconfigured as a "distortion" of the fabulous uchronic epoch encoded into the saga. The lost or purloined document is a key to a future that might have, or would have, or should have been. Stolypin's memorandum is The Red Wheel's phantom manuscript or grimoire, the fairytale topos of a secret esoteric text that holds some momentous truth or revelation.

9

In one of the last letters he wrote, Nietzsche offered an angry, and prophetic, denunciation of the German people as civilizational dropouts on the grandest of scales:

This irresponsible race, which has all the great misfortunes of culture on its conscience and at all *decisive* moments in history, was thinking of "something else" (the Reformation at the time of the Renaissance; Kantian philosophy just when a scientific mode of thought had been reached by England and France; "wars of liberation" when Napoleon appeared, the only man hitherto strong enough to make Europe into a political and *economic unity*), is thinking today of the *Reich* …[385]

Russia, however, was thinking of revolution. The epic's treatment of the events of 1914–17 follows this Nietzschean logic: Solzhenitsyn traces, fictively and analytically, his countrymen's collective and individual historical irresponsibility, which is ascribed to a fatal distraction of the national mind. Long before he started work on the saga he had concluded that over the centuries the people and its rulers missed successive opportunities to realize the nation's world-historical potential, a position he expressed with frightening clarity in his short treatise *"The Russian Question" at the End of the Twentieth Century*.

The author held the view that the higher one rises in the affairs of man, the greater one's duty of care for the nation, and the saga's two sentinels of the *res publica*, the historical Stolypin and the fictional Vorotyntsev, exemplify the principle in question, though the latter attains a full understanding of his patriotic obligations only after his country succumbs to "this foul revolution."[386] Yet even then, the colonel's romantic and marital entanglements continue to distract him from pursuing what is the nationally responsible course of action. Stolypin, however, allows no private concerns to deflect him from his mission of national rescue.

The first of the dedicated historiographical sections and also the longest (*August 1914*, chapter sixty-five) is devoted to the famous statesman. Unlike any other public figure shown, he has the authority, the vision, and the organizing intellect to set Russia on the right path. He combines ruthlessness toward the enemies of the state with a sincere attachment to the principle of constitutional rule, or so the text would have us believe. He is the epic's clearest-thinking patriot, and this side of Stolypin's worldview is described in terms that resonate with Solzhenitsyn's own oft-expressed feelings for his native land:

> He had a constant anxious awareness of all Russia as though it were there in his breast. Unsleeping compassion, a love that nothing could alter. But though his love was all gentleness and tenderness, when anything threatened the things that mattered to him he was as unyielding as an oak.[387]

In confirmation of this authorial stance, over the length of the saga figures as different as the patriot Vorotyntsev, the liberal Shingarev, the right-wing republican Guchkov, the right-wing monarchist Aleksandr Nechvolodov, and the agrarian parochialist Grigori Pluzhnikov are all shown expressing admiration for the murdered premier.

Stolypin, we are told, was a "liberal-conservative prime minister"[388] who wished to bring into being "a state ruled by law,"[389] though the author concedes that his hero had a record of occasionally violating it: "That was the paradox: only by illegally changing the electoral law could the electoral principle and national representation be saved."[390] Solzhenitsyn shrouds this moment of inconsistency in a vivid parliamentary metaphor: "It was not Russia that Witte's electoral law had summoned to the Tauride Palace [the seat of the Duma] but a caricature of the country."[391] A structured argument is offered in support of Stolypin's harsh suppression of the revolutionary movement in 1906–7, his agricultural reforms, and Siberian resettlement program, which are identified as his greatest achievements. At the same time, Solzhenitsyn offers criticism: the prime minister did not appreciate the danger from the "court camarilla," "the retired bureaucrats" in the State Council, and the "diehards among the gentry,"[392] and sometimes he could be "too hotheaded and too stubborn."[393]

On the other hand, the chapter's treatment of Stolypin's foreign policy suggests, against the author's wishes, that the premier did not approach it with the same degree of nous as domestic affairs: "He was convinced that a ruler of the most mediocre intelligence could prevent war between nations at any time."[394] The prime minister is commended for his prescient understanding that "Russia simply could not go to war, and would not be ready to do so for a long time to come, that in her present state war would mean defeat, and that revolution would break out even before that happened."[395] Yet we are also told that "international problems seemed to him extremely easy to deal with compared with those at home,"[396] a statement that assigns the premier to the historical category of parochial politicians such as Neville Chamberlain who believed the same thing until events taught them otherwise. In a passage that discusses Russia's relationship with its partners in the Entente, we learn of Stolypin's conviction that "no one in Europe, or indeed in the world at large, had any use for a strong, nationalist Russia."[397] So stated, his position not only ignores Russia's longtime ally Serbia, fated to be the Central Powers' first victim in the Great War, but fails to differentiate between the diplomatic interests of France, which currently prioritized a strong Russia, and those of Great Britain, which historically did not. Instead, Stolypin decides that "England was alarmed by Russia's international strength, and would like to see her disintegrate,"[398] thereby demonstrating a conspirological misapprehension of centuries of British foreign policy. After meeting Kaiser Wilhelm II, Stolypin assumes that "relations with Germany could be put on as good a basis as anyone could wish,"[399] a dubious proposition in view of the identity of his royal interlocutor. If citationally accurate, this judgment would once again condemn the prime minister as a geopolitical naïf. Actually, the text offers support for just such a conclusion when we learn of his belief that "if a strong state *did not want* war, no one could force it to fight,"[400] a notion contradicted by the entire course of human history.

Yet despite these discontinuities in Solzhenitsyn's case for Stolypin, the portrait is a historiographical *tour de force* as well as an occasionally moving encomium that accords the premier heroic status in explicit and mythically charged terms: "In his tightly buttoned black coat, with his statuesque poise and mystical self-assurance,"[401] "a figure of epic presence,"[402] "a second Peter [the Great]."[403] In one of the subsequent fictional chapters, the mortally wounded prime minister is shown musing on his deathbed, "Enemies know the thing to peck out is the liver":[404] the second of the two bullets fired by Bogrov, which inflicted the fatal wound, had grazed that organ before lodging in the abdomen. Solzhenitsyn's Stolypin is nothing short of Promethean.

On the same Stolypinesque note of *pouvoir oblige*, the mage Varsonofiev tells Sanya and Ksenia that "power is a terrible gift" which demands from those who wield it "duty, responsibility, sacrifice."[405] Yet even men and women who do not hold public office have public obligations. "You must gear yourself to the laborious process of history: work, persuade others, and gradually change things,"[406] Arkhangorodsky explains to his daughter, a socialist zealot who impatiently awaits the coming of the revolution and its promise of a violent new beginning. But she refuses to listen, or if she listens, dismisses him as a reactionary enabler motivated by "slavish loyalism."[407] In the fissiparous society of late imperial Russia, its various groups speak languages that are mutually incompatible and, worse, incomprehensible. "Even the educated did not always understand each other,"[408] and the educated cannot get through to the uneducated, except for a few rooted souls like Vorotyntsev, who possesses "a smooth tongue, a talent for speaking to the troops,"[409] and the man of the people (or Cossacks) Kovynev. We also learn that Stolypin had the knack of "looking [the peasants] straight in the eye and patiently *explaining* things."[410] But then, a popular audience may respond to a non-explicatory rant in an equally gratifying manner, with or without eye contact. Kerensky displays a theatrical ability to stir the crowd, though only after the old order has disintegrated and the urban masses, or a large proportion of them, have lapsed into a state of collective bemusement and even "bestiality," as per Shulgin. On one occasion, Russia's self-described Danton is left unaware that his audience of revolutionary soldiers is taking his rhetorical flourishes as the literal truth:

> Next he said, stretching out his words, pausing to catch his breath, and stammering as he spoke, "Comrades, I speak to you from the very bottom of my heart. If it is necessary, I am willing to die!"
> Who were those evildoers? How could they bring him down so low?
> "Hey there, you must go on living!" they encouraged him, clapping their hands. Even from a distance they felt the pain filling this sickly, frail, pale fellow. He's at the end of his tether, it seems, and all because he's on our side.[411]

Sometimes hyperbole and pathopoeia (appeal to passion) can work only too well. Yet the joke is on the audience as well as the speaker: both are liberally, equally, and fraternally clueless.

10

The writer regarded nations as "generalized personalities"[412] with their own unique virtues, vices, and psycho-cultural inner core, and this essentialist doctrine shapes the epic's treatment of ethnic identity and difference. In *August 1914*, the authorial narrator ponders the faces of the Russian soldiers who fought and died in World War I:

> There are no photographs of them, and this is all the more regrettable because since then the composition of our nation has changed, faces have changed and no lens will ever rediscover those honest beards, those good-natured eyes, those relaxed and unselfish expressions.[413]

Those unphotographed peasants in their lumpy uniforms, we are invited to conclude, hail from a more nationally authentic time and place, which endowed them with an organic unity of self that was lost, perhaps irretrievably, during the decades of communist rule.

Zakhar Tomchak, a colorful rural entrepreneur who looks like a Zaporozhian Cossack, speaks exclusively in Ukrainian even though he is a character in a Russian novel.[414] Despite his practical sense and business acumen, the patriarch of the Tomchak clan has retained the magical thinking of his village origins: "He firmly believed that driving [an automobile] around the fields caused storms that beat down the crops."[415] The Cossacks themselves are metonymically typified by Fyodor Kovynev, the most *literary* member of this ethnos in Russian literature, as well as brave nurse Belobragina. Fyodor tells a surprised Vorotyntsev that "looked at from the Don, the Don is not Russia,"[416] an ethnographic point that was first explored in *Love the Revolution*. Representatives of the non-Slavic peoples of this polyglot empire appear only occasionally, as episodic and usually anonymous figures: after all, the epic's "true protagonist is Russia herself."[417] A Caucasian tribesman in full national dress walks down a street in Pyatigorsk, thrilling Varya Matveeva with his familiar otherness, a Tatar soldier is brought into a military hospital with a bullet in his spine but, mysteriously, no entry wound, a Georgian medical orderly joins the revolutionary commissariat for public order in order to sow the exact opposite, and another Caucasian brandishes a dagger as he "promise[s] to expel the Germans from Russia," winning a round of enthusiastic applause from the Petrograd Soviet.[418] An ethnographic box is ticked when we read that Pecherzewski, a soldier in Sanya's battery, boasts a "strong Polish accent."[419]

Vorotyntsev knows himself to possess the "German" traits of "efficiency" and "unwavering obstinacy," of which he is "secretly proud."[420] Still, the large number of Germans in government service, he feels, represent "a flaw in the system," though he concedes that the ones he knows are "honest professional soldiers."[421] For all his virtues, the colonel is a bit of a Blimp. Old man Tomchak, however, "had always respected the Germans" and believes that "instead of fighting Germany, all Russia should be learning from her how to work and prosper,"[422] a point that still holds true in the twenty-first century.

The Jewish question is addressed repeatedly, both by implication, as in Arkhangorodsky's comfortable combination of his religious identity with a patriotic loyalty to the empire, or directly, as when Vorotyntsev expresses what he considers a reasonable "middle view"[423] between "[handing] Russia over to the condescending leadership of the Jews" and "the desire to oppress them."[424] For her part, Susanna Korzner, an upper-class Jewish woman, refuses to be "a second-rate person ... a defenseless chicken,"[425] and Lazhenitsyn sets straight his friend, "bullet-headed"[426] Chernega, promoted from the ranks and cheerfully anti-Semitic:

> "Don't forget they're the ones who crucified Christ."
> Sanya removed his hand from his head and spoke sternly to the man up above. "Terenti, that's not a joking matter. Don't talk wildly. D'you think we wouldn't have crucified him? If he'd come from Suzdal instead of Nazareth, and come to us first, d'you think we Russians wouldn't have crucified him?"[427]

This is a recognizably Dostoevskian colloquy in what is otherwise a quasi-Tolstoyan text, enhanced by a cleverly coded allusion to Fyodor Tyutchev's poem "These poor villages ..." ["Eti bednye selen'ia ..."; 1855], in which "the King of Heaven in the likeness of a slave"[428] crisscrosses the land of Russia to give it his blessing.

As a voice-of-the-people xenophobe, Chernega is not alone. During Blagodarev's home visit to Kamenka, his fellow villagers inquire: "Was it true that the Frenchies had black devils fighting for them, in the flesh, not hiding themselves?"[429] In Petrograd, "yellow labor," that is, Chinese coolies employed in the wartime economy, breeds resentment across "the working class as a whole,"[430] while the anti-German pogroms in *November 1916* are scripted as a forewarning of the riots and lynchings to come, when Russian will turn against Russian.

Hermann von François, the dashing commander of the German I Corps, is the most important foreign presence (though Sir George Buchanan, the scheming British ambassador who makes an appearance in *March 1917*, runs him a close second). The general, who is of Huguenot descent, senses that "at heart he was still an ungovernable Frenchman."[431] The formula "an ungovernable Frenchman" (*neugomonnyi frantsuz*)[432] is, however, a *Russian* received idea. François's attitude toward his Russian adversary rests on a hackneyed sense of Teutonic superiority, one that would receive its comeuppance in the next world war: "Aversion to any sort of methodical work, absence of any sense of duty, fear of responsibility, and total inability to value time and use it to the full."[433] Actually, his chauvinistic views illustrate the pitfalls of ethnographic essentialism: Solzhenitsyn's fictions sometimes countermand the author's own stated opinions. Later in the epic, an angry Lenin rues his Russian roots: "A quarter of his blood, but nothing in his character, his will, his inclinations made him kin to that slovenly, slapdash, eternally drunken country,"[434] his inner rant echoing the general's *Ausländerfeindlichkeit* (dislike of foreigners). As we learn in the course of the saga, Lenin is its most anti-national, Russia-hating presence, whose only equal on this score is the cosmopolitan super-villain Alexander Parvus.

Colonel Knox, an Englishman with a Scots name, represents the Allies at Samsonov's HQ. A historical personality, he reappears later in the epic wearing a general's uniform. Knox is a cipher with the annoying habit of grinning often and inappropriately, in confirmation of the author's scornful attitude toward the airbrushed rictus of Western public discourse: "Samsonov disliked those artificial, ex officio European smiles."[435] Perhaps Solzhenitsyn should have given the colonel a stiff upper lip. Granted, *The Red Wheel* features at least one *Russian* grin that is just as insipid, the happy face in question belonging to the sovereign himself: "If [only] he wore the crown with suffering, and not with a sort of inappropriate smile,"[436] muses stern-visaged Vorotyntsev.

In addition to his physiognomic duties, the twinkling Knox has a textual job to perform by mangling the name of Generalissimo Suvorov, a celebrated eighteenth-century commander: "Your descendants will mention the name of Samsonov side by side with that of... er... Suvorov [riadom s imenem... *Zuvorova*[437]]."[438] Once again, the text is in dialogue with *War and Peace*, where during the campaign of 1805 Russian and French soldiers trade jokes and jibes under a flag of truce until a sneering Frenchman, ignorant of the generalissimo's death five years ealier, lets loose this taunt: "The Emperor will teach your Suvara as he has taught the others..."[439]

Once in a while a full ethnic stereotype enters the text, as in a comment by manly Colonel Vorotyntsev about his counterparts in the Romanian army: "Their officers are effeminate creatures who wear corsets and use face powder and lipstick."[440] The saga's chief fictional hero is sometimes chiefly wrong, which only makes him more believable as a son of his time and place. Still, it is the foreign presences in this Russian world that are the primary agents of xenophobia. During the February Revolution, a pair of British officers, one of whom is of a grotesquely elongated appearance—"everyone who visited the Astoria hotel knew his extraordinarily tall figure"[441]—watch as the mayor of Petrograd, Aleksandr Balk, and several tsarist generals are transported under armed guard to the Tauride Palace. The two Englishmen, but especially the extraordinary ectomorph, are turned into stand-ins for Western arrogance:

> He stopped, turned toward the people in the car and keeping both hands in his pockets and swinging his torso, chuckled, laughed and finally guffawed at the sight of the car and the arrested generals, and kept turning his head in order not to lose sight of this amusing spectacle. He even took one hand out of his pocket and pointed at them as they were being driven away.[442]

Though it may be hard to imagine a British officer of the period publicly conducting himself in so unrestrained and ill-bred a manner, the scene is lifted almost verbatim from Balk's memoir of the February Revolution as witnessed and survived by himself.[443]

11

As a historiographical production, *The Red Wheel* offers copious commentary on emblematic artistic figures, productions, and events from the diegetic present or historical past. Vera Komissarzhevskaya, a celebrated actress whose untimely death in 1910 occasioned an extraordinary outpouring of public grief, is present in the wistful recollections of Guchkov, who loved her when she was a young girl; Vsevolod Meyerhold's staging of Lermontov's drama *Masquerade* (*Maskarad*; 1835) at the Aleksandrinsky Theater becomes a dramatic marker of the nation's unfolding collapse; and Olda explains to a puzzled Georgi the aesthetics of Mikhail Vrubel's Art Nouveau painting *Pan* (1899), a copy of which hangs in her apartment.

Yet as a subject of historical appraisal, it is literature that takes pride of place over all other art forms, a reflection of the traditional logocentrism of Russian culture. In a topical sense, Solzhenitsyn's somber account of the Russian Revolution dialogically engages with earlier fictionalized treatments of these events. The works in question include the canonical, such as Mikhail Sholokhov's (?) *The Quiet Don* (*The Red Wheel* depicts the Cossacks as an ethnos in their own right); Aleksei Tolstoy's *The Road to Calvary* (*Khozhdenie po mukam*; 1921–40) (the epic supersedes its palpably pro-Bolshevik bias); Maxim Gorky's *The Life of Klim Samgin* (*Zhizn' Klima Samgina*; 1927–36) (the epic counteracts its anti-intellectual bias); and Boris Pasternak's *Doctor Zhivago* (*Doktor Zhivago*; 1957) (the epic privileges the tragedy of the nation over that of the individual, however sympathetic or sensitive); and the potboiled, for example, the novel *From Double Eagle to Red Flag* (*Ot dvuglavogo orla k krasnomu znameni*; 1921–22) by Pyotr Krasnov, an anti-communist Cossack general who refought the revolution on the printed page, and the trilogy *The Key, Escape,* and *The Cave* (*Kliuch—Begstvo—Peshchera*; 1929–32) by Mark Aldanov, an émigré writer whose pacey narratives won a mass audience in his native country after the fall of communism. As Solzhenitsyn told Struve, "Unhappily, the course of Russian history has been such, that in the sixty years which have elapsed since the events I am describing, not one substantial, coherent *literary* account has been written, nor a documentary one, for that matter."[444] *The Red Wheel*, which joins intricately structured prose with exhaustively sourced historiography into a syncretic megatext, was meant to fill that textual void.

Formally and thematically, the tetralogy constitutes a *summa summarum* of nineteenth- and twentieth-century Russian prose and poetry, in both their realist and Modernist phase. It anthologizes the national canon via a system of character portraits, direct quotations, encoded allusions, and borrowed tropes, with Tolstoy serving as the referent of referents. As actualized presences, the sage of Yasnaya Polyana and the books he wrote discharge a paradigmatic fictive function. Tolstoy is the first figure from history mentioned and the first one to appear as a character. *August 1914* has been compared to *War and Peace* and *November 1916* to *Anna Karenina*,[445] though whether those famous novels may truly be adduced as hypotexts for, respectively, Knots I and II of the saga is a different story. *August 1914* is programmatically counter-Tolstoyan in its representation of war, whereas *November 1916* depicts the same spectrum of familial, matrimonial, and romantic relationships that we find in *Anna Karenina*.[446] At one point, the unmarried, discreetly adulterous Olda briskly informs Vorotyntsev that Tolstoy's heroine "would not need to throw herself under a train nowadays but would get a divorce from a consistory court with no fuss, and marry Vronsky,"[447] but the colonel, clueless in matters of adultery and Tolstoy, fails to take the hint. On the other hand, the married and unimpeachably faithful Irina Tomchak "regarded Anna Karenina as the vilest of women."⁴⁴⁸ And in *March 1917*, as Vera Vorotyntseva contemplates the estrangement between Georgi and Alina, she formulates her own view of an ideal marriage:

> Vera believed that marriage was a mystery larger than the mere coming together of two people who were in love: a marriage entailed a different kind of life, the doubling of each personality and an ensuing completeness that could not be attained by any other means, a completeness that was perfect, in so far as human beings were capable of achieving perfection.⁴⁴⁹

Almost inevitably, the reader thinks of Konstantin Levin and Kitty Shcherbatsky.

One thing, though, is certain. Whenever the text touches upon Tolstoy's views on the Church, history, military affairs or even the moral diet, the narration invariably switches to the polemical register. Very occasionally, an anti-Tolstoyan point falls flat, as when the learned priest, Father Severyan, complains that *War and Peace* "takes on 1812, an epic year in the life of a devout people" and finds "plenty of room for Freemasonry—but for Orthodoxy? None at all."⁴⁵⁰ Actually, the balance between Freemasonry and Orthodoxy in the chapters devoted to the war of 1812 is exactly the reverse.

The Red Wheel refutes the sage of Yasnaya Polyana and his historiosophical stance even as it honors him intertextually. The epic's programmatic anti-Tolstoyan passage, articulated by the author of record, reads:

> We might look for consolation to Tolstoy's belief that armies are not led by generals, ships are not steered by captains, states and parties are not run by presidents and politicians—but the twentieth century has shown us only too often they are.⁴⁵¹

And by way of elucidation:

> We still hardly recognize how much great happenings in the history of nations depend on insignificant people and events.⁴⁵²

(Case in point: the neurotic nonentity Bogrov.)
And by way of elaboration:

> "So, we are in agreement, gentlemen." Prince Lvov gave a radiant smile. "Anyway, why do we need the police? Why should a free country have a police force? Surely an enlightened people has no need of one."

> For as Leo Tolstoy had taught, all unhappiness came from power. Therefore, power was no longer needed.
>
> There were no objections.[453]

This last passage describes the first cabinet meeting of the Provisional Government as chaired by its first prime minister, Prince Georgi Lvov, whom the text portrays, with full-Tolstoyan sarcasm, as a half-comic Tolstoy devotee.

Pushkin is also an important presence, beginning with that calendric comment about Bogrov's birthday coinciding with the poet's death day. On a related sepulchral note, as Petrograd finds itself in the grip of revolution, a rabble of mutinous soldiers swarms past

> the corner of the Moika Embankment between the round market building with the bas-reliefs of bulls' heads and the little cube-shaped church where Pushkin's body once lay ... that hidden corner from whence a single turn of the tramcar or one hundred paces will take you past the basement of The Comedians' Bivouac café of Silver Age fame (the old Stray Dog).[454]

The Stray Dog was an art cabaret of scandalous repute where Acmeists, Futurists and other members of the city's post-Symbolist scene met and performed in 1912–15. The site of Pushkin's obsequies and the avant-garde hangout nearby become a materialized point of divergence for the timelines and spaces of Russian literature, which are about to be altered, suppressed, or curtailed by the revolution and the dictatorial state it will bring into being.

In *November 1916*, Olda imagines that Nina Obodovsky, "with her dark hair and her quiet Russian, rustic even beauty," looks like the heroine of *Eugene Onegin*, "Tatyana Larina ... at forty,"[455] and in *March 1917* we learn that a unique collection of Pushkin's personal belongings was looted in Tsarskoe Selo, whether by revolutionaries or street criminals,[456] an act of sacrilege to shock any Russian's heart. In the trenches, Sanya finds time to read "tiny volume[s] of Pushkin"[457] and on a visit to Moscow Vorotyntsev is appalled to see the famous monument to the poet festooned with red flags, which are described as—what else?—"stick[s] with a long red pennon."[458] Back in Petrograd, "a group of revolutionary youths attempted to pull down the Bronze Horseman. The pranksters [*sorvantsy*] climbed onto the statue and struck at it with metal rods and a small crowbar, but to no avail."[459] An act of fetishistic violence that is subtextually reformatted into an allegorical assault on Pushkin's most famous narrative poem, *The Bronze Horseman* (*Mednyi vsadnik*; 1833); and beyond this, into a nihilistic rejection of the sacral status of literature in the national culture.

An earlier instance of cultural desecration, one wrought not by popular rage but popular neglect, is described by Olda: "On the twenty-fifth anniversary of Dostoevsky's death, out of the whole Russian reading public, out of all those in our enlightened capital city, from our proud student body—do you know how many people visited his grave? Seven! I was there..."[460] As textual referents, Dostoevsky's writings are present syntagmatically, that is, as sources employed to give an element of citational color to character voices such as Vorotyntsev's, or to shed light on some cultural or historical development. The colonel, we learn, appreciates the writer's advocacy of "an eternal alliance" between Russia and Germany[461] and Obodovsky approvingly refers to Dostoevsky's realization that the conquest of Constantinople was not a worthwhile national goal.[462] Apropos Bogrov's crime and the mindset that engendered it, the authorial voice posits that "Dostoevsky explored many a spiritual abyss, unraveled many a fantasy—but not all of them."[463] (In fact, the abysses and fantasies were entirely foreseen in his novel *Devils* with its *avant la lettre* terrorists for a utopian cause.) "It fell to Dostoevsky to observe the earliest years of this visitation and he understood it at once and warned us,"[464] observes General Nechvolodov, a military intellectual who on this point contradicts the author of record. A transtextual prefiguration is actualized when Irina Tomchak steps out onto her balcony at dusk and observes the bonfires built by local farmers to make potash out of sunflower haulm: "Suddenly—a vision: out there, countless nomads advancing on Russia like a plague of locusts had halted for the night, and these were their campfires."[465] An invitation to the reader to think back on those proleptically or prophetically configured national texts that describe an allegorical horde descending on Russia or Europe, for example, the Epilogue to *Crime and Punishment* or Blok's poem *Scythians* (*Skify*; 1918).

An anonymous letter to Alexander Herzen's newspaper *Kolokol*, possibly penned by the exiled revolutionary's lifetime friend and collaborator Nikolai Ogarev, supplies the epigraph to *Act One: Revolution*: "Only the ax can deliver us, and nothing but the ax... Russia summons us to the ax."[466] In *April 1917*, two idealistic schoolboys, Yurik Kharitonov and his best friend, Vitaly, make their way to a steep bluff that overlooks a collection of warehouses and wharfs and, beyond them, the River Don, which after the spring floods is "as wide as the sea."[467] There the pair "awkwardly [clasp] hands, right with left and left with right, so that their arms [form] a cross [*krest-nakrest*]" and swear an oath to "fight against everything that is base,"[468] that is, the revolution and its works. The *cross*-textual connection is to a passage in Herzen's memoir *My Past and Thoughts* (*Byloe i dumy*; 1852–70), which describes how as young boys, he and Ogarev, "suddenly embracing, vowed in sight of all Moscow to sacrifice our lives to the struggle we had chosen."[469] Yurik and Vitaly evert that famous pledge. The boys' paired names carry their own message: "Yurik"/"Yuri" is a Russian form of "George," viz. St. George the dragon slayer, and "Vitaly" derives from the Latin *vitalis*—"vital," "alive."

Herzen's successor as Russia's revolutionary writer-in-chief, Maxim Gorky, is deprecated on multiple textual occasions, as when during a performance of his drama *The Petty Bourgeois* (*Meshchane*; 1901), Altanskaya readily identifies its Nietzschean motifs but concludes that the play is a damp squib: "The big question—what is there to live for?—remains unanswered."[470] Her comment forms an appendix to the anti-Gorky critique in *The First Circle*, where another thoughtful young woman, Klara Makarygina, is dismayed by another Gorky production, *Vassa Zheleznova*. Gorky's status as one of the saga's negative cultural referents constituted a writerly act of readerly self-purgation: as a young man, Solzhenitsyn considered him a peerless talent.[471]

Roman Tomchak, Ksenia's able, abrasive brother, combines a flair for business with contempt for church and tsar, decorating the family home with two pictures of Tolstoy in celebrity agricultural mode, with plough and scythe respectively, as well as a likeness of Gorky, with "challengingly cocked head and squashed nose."[472] The latter's portrait is less an indication of Roman's literary tastes—actually, he has none—than his admiration for the "daring with which Gorky poured out his bile on industrial and commercial tycoons,"[473] that is, men like Roman himself.

Varsonofiev's apocalyptic dream of a boy with "a marvelously radiant face" inside the Petersburg stock exchange who clutches to his chest "some sort of small and shining object" that will produce "a terrible explosion for the entire world,"[474] that is, the Christ Child carrying an *infernal* machine, invites irresistible associations with Andrei Bely's Symbolist novel *Petersburg* and its time bomb in the shape of a "sardine tin with horrible contents."[475] The white-haired mystic's terrifying visions may also be read as counter-allusions to the four socialist reveries sequentially experienced by the ecstatic Vera Pavlovna in Nikolai Chernyshevsky's utopian novel *What Is To Be Done?* (*Chto delat'?*; 1863).

Duma deputy Shingarev's impressions of backwoods Russia bring to mind the story collection *A Young Doctor's Notebook* (1925–6) by Mikhail Bulgakov, another country physician who gave up medicine to pursue a second career. The epic's unique time frames and focus on the homicidal mythologies of terrorism hold parallels to Blok's unfinished narrative poem *Retribution*

(*Vozmezdie*; 1910–21),[476] a post-Symbolist attempt to descry the approaching catastrophe that was interrupted by its actual arrival, and his ballad *The Twelve* (*Dvenadtsat'*; 1918), which treats the revolution as the second coming, or second passion, of Christ; and in a broader sense, to the entire vatic strand in the writings of Russia's early twentieth-century Modernists who, like Blok, created a literature of dark, inchoate foreboding. "At the approach of the Master of Chaos the Russian eschatological consciousness experiences, as well as fear, something akin to bliss, for as the true Antichrist, he is the distorted reflection of Christ at the end of time," explains Lyudmila Saraskina.[477] From the very beginning, *The Red Wheel* depicts this mood of "fear" and "bliss" and shows how far it had spread across the strata of the culture, infecting minds that are as remote from poetry's ivory tower as it is possible to be.

At the outbreak of war, Sanya Lazhenitsyn (a Tolstoyan) and his friend Kotya (a Hegelian) feel "a fierce joy"[478] at the notion that they are privileged observers about to witness an exciting historical spectacle: "Perhaps disaster had already struck, perhaps the catastrophe was already being enacted, but—a discovery!—you could pass unharmed through the midst of disaster, conscious of its fearsome beauty."[479] The liberal opposition politicians Vorotyntsev meets in Petrograd share this positive expectation of a national cataclysm, but in what they imagine is a pragmatic sense: "Even a catastrophe will get us somewhere!"[480] And after the revolution happens, the teenage counterrevolutionary Yurik Kharitonov, overwhelmed by the excitement of war, girls, and spring floods on the Don, imagines that "there is something sweet in a catastrophe."[481] Events will show that these thrilled expectations are not so much wrong, as beside the point.

The Red Wheel historiographically annotates and axiologically confutes the doom-laden topoi of Silver Age literature. It administers to them an empirical test by historical evidence, thereby resuming the line of argument launched by Vasily Rozanov in his tract *The Apocalypse of Our Time* (*Apokalipsis nashego vremeni*; 1918):

> The candle went out. No, it wasn't God Who did this, but rather … a drunken wench was out for a walk when she stumbled and fell down flat on her face. How stupid. How revolting. "Enough of these tragedies, now play us some vaudeville."[482]

Sometimes a character will recite a passage, usually a piece of verse, to make a political or personal point: self-characterization by quotation (a familiar Solzhenitsynian device). In a poetic postcoital moment, a languorous Olda whispers a couple of lines by Tsvetaeva to a bemused Georgi, "From you, world-weary Anatomist, / I have learned how sweet evil can be."[483] The professor's pillow talk is erotic and pedagogical, in equal measure. A few chapters later Vorotyntsev's literary education resumes when he listens to salt-of-the-earth General Svechin deprecate "somnambulist poetry" and "those hysterics [Igor] Severyanin and [Aleksandr] Vertinsky,"[484] thereby conflating, perhaps appropriately, the flamboyant lyrist billed as the Russian Oscar Wilde and the cabaret crooner in his Pierrot costume. To prove his anti-avant-garde point, Vorotyntsev's chum goes on to recite some of Nikolai Gumilev's ("a fashionable poet")[485] less than impressive verses: "With Russian dead the foe must pave the way, or ne'er set foot in Paris."[486] In a fortuitous instance of cross-ideological solidarity, the revolutionary radical Lenartovich displays a similar disdain for the "disagreeable Modernist style,"[487] which he deems inferior to Semyon Nadson's cliché-ridden confessional verse. Bohemian Likonya, the object of Sasha's unrequited desire, declaims Gumilev's doom-laden poems, in keeping with her self-image as a mysterious enchantress (and also, to annoy the unenchanted), even if, as yet, she is deaf to their apocalyptic meaning.

In fact, when we first meet her, Likonya has all kinds of artistic interests. A fan of the stage director Meyerhold and the chansonnier Vertinsky (her catholic taste—bad taste), she is wont to say things such as "the cultural life of the nineteenth century was very humdrum."[488] In keeping with the aesthetics of the Silver Age, she turns herself into a living work of art: "she made great play with her voice, and even more with her eyelashes,"[489] "the hesitant, wondering turn of her head ... the thick black hair falling loosely to her shoulders,"[490] "fidgeting with [her shawl] to show off her narrow body."[491] The young woman's private domestic space is equally aestheticized, as Lenartovich learns when he finds himself alone in her room:

> It was as if he had dipped his two hands into Likonya, under her elbows, inside her sleeves, beneath the black locks that fell down to her shoulders. It was not just the tantalizing fragrance that filled the room—her perfume as well as some other scent—but all these various objects, scattered about or neatly laid out, the pieces and tokens of her life, the oval-framed silhouette in Chinese ink on the wall, the items of stage scenery—phe-ew, his head was starting to spin.[492]

The phrase "dipped his two hands into Likonya" (*obeimi rukami pogruzilsia v Likoniu*) re-actualizes the water symbolism associated with this character: on some subconscious level, socialist Sasha is attuned to his lady love's secret, free-flowing nature.

Yet after the exquisitely mannered heroine falls in love with Gordey she ceases to use literature as a lifestyle prop and instead seeks comfort in Tsvetaeva's passionate poetry, which speaks to her in the voice of tragic womanhood. Also, she now finds Vertinsky vulgar,[493] as indeed he was.

Another Gumilevian motif occurs at the beginning of *March 1917*, when Obodovsky, out for a walk in the imperial capital, comes across a tram that was pulled off its tracks by a rioting mob. The normally down-to-earth industrial manager finds the sight strangely unsettling:

> The streetcar was painted a natural green color, now grubby and reminiscent of the hide of some large animal. It slumped in the dirty snow like a massive work ox that was dying or already dead. Its glass brow was cracked: before the animal was brought down and butchered it had been struck on the head. The side on which it lay was mangled and dented, and shards of glass had cut into its body. The beast's trunk stretched out at an unnatural angle behind its back, with a length of rope attached. Its four cast-iron circular paws jutted out lifelessly parallel to the ground, and you could see how they had bent the track when they were dislodged from their sockets. The unfortunate creature's belly, which normally was hidden from sight, was now there for everyone to see and mock, showing its secret bulges splattered with street grime.[494]

The light rail conveyance is imaginatively animated and figuratively murdered, with the narrative conveying Obodovsky's unconventional perceptual stance: as an engineer with a social conscience, he has an affection for machines that serve the public good. The passage begins with a generic analogy ("reminiscent ... of some large beast"), then shifts to a simile derived from animal husbandry ("like a massive work ox") and a sequence of related anatomical metaphors ("brow," "head," "back," "belly"), which are controverted by the non-bovine images of the "trunk" and "paws," even as the fallen vehicle's mechanical nature ("cast-iron," "sockets") is acknowledged, in keeping with the hero's technocratic standpoint. Finally, the tram cum creature is discreetly gendered ("secret bulges"). Urban wreckage elides into urban whimsy in a quasi-hallucinatory procedure that recalls Mayakovsky's poem "Kindness to Horses" ("Khoroshee otnoshenie k loshadiam"; 1918), where a tired nag "topple[s]" on an icy "street, up-turned," causing the lyrical subject to feel "some kind of a universal, animal anguish."⁴⁹⁵ The governing referent, however, is another poem, "The Streetcar That Lost Its Way" ("Zabludivshiisia tramvai"; 1919) by Gumilev, which Roman Timenchik identifies as having "fixed ... the reception of this object of the urban landscape in Russian literature."⁴⁹⁶ A second scholar explains that

> The poets of the Silver Age depicted the streetcar as a necessary attribute of modern civilization, giving it animistic, natural-philosophical, and astral associations: somnolent or fatigued, possessed of a snout and eyes, endowed with a soul and the gift of speech, with the appearance of a mobile menagerie or comet or star, a dragon or a firebird, related to the elements, likened to the planet Earth, and driven by a carman who is Old Man Time.⁴⁹⁷

Every one of these associations is *canceled* in the passage I quoted. The tram is dead, and so is its magical status, celebrated by a literary tradition that is also fated to perish. The ruined streetcar becomes a foretoken of the destruction to be visited on Obodovsky's homeland and all its cultural productions. Yet across the spaces of poetic allegory and urban mythology, the hero's technocratic melancholia also connects him, via a cross-textual junction located in Weimar Germany, to the narrator in Nabokov's story "A Guide to Berlin" ("Putevoditel' po Berlinu"; 1925). In that early piece of prose by one of Solzhenitsyn's favorite writers, an exiled Russian voice celebrates the city tram's "old-fashioned charm" and imagines how a description of its "peculiar jolting motion" would delight "our great-grandchildren":⁴⁹⁸ a streetcar named nostalgia.

In addition to Tolstoy, several other literary celebrities are present, notably Zinaida Gippius and her husband Dmitry Merezhkovsky. They are lampooned as a "tall Symbolist poetess with a straight figure, domineering character, and a profoundly enigmatic gaze" and "a poet, prose writer, playwright, thinker, critic, and essayist who, though he spread himself a bit too thin, was also a genius, or something close."⁴⁹⁹ In the presence of a visiting Kerensky, the profoundly enigmatic Gippius lapses into a Dionysian frenzy, eulogizing the world war as "a sacrificial baptism, an ecstatic rite, a cleansing sacrifice to the Universal Fire, in which the Beauty of the World shall manifest itself"⁵⁰⁰ while her spouse looks pacifically on and the future premier reels in shock, despite his ambition to be the Danton of *this* revolution. Gorky, Solzhenitsyn's old bête noir, receives similar satirical treatment, albeit in the domestic register, when the allegedly proletarian writer materializes before the authentically proletarian Shlyapnikov in nocturnal dishabille: "Aleksei Maksimovich, dressed in a fleecy gown and looking displeased, stood stooping behind several women, wrinkling his spongy duck nose, the yellow mustaches hanging all the way down to his chin."[501] *The Red Wheel* features a selection of prominent noses, some of which might have come straight out of Gogol.

Vorotyntsev confides to Olda that he likes "nobody after Pushkin and Lermontov,"[502] thereby fixing himself textually as a cultural retrograde. Romantic Alina adores Lermontov's brooding hero Pechorin while regretting that her earnest husband is nothing like him, and Vera Vorotyntseva has decidedly sentimental tastes which include Dmitry Grigorovich's tale "Anton Goremyka" ["Anton-Goremyka"; 1847]—a meek serf is sent to prison on a false charge of robbery, and Ivan Turgenev's story "Mumu" (1854), in which a meek serf is forced by a cruel mistress to drown his little dog.[503] Alina is also a fan of Aleksandr Kurpin's mawkish novella "The Garnet Bracelet" ("Granatovyi braslet"; 1911), the story of a poor clerk who kills himself out of unrequited love, leaving behind a corpse whose face resembles "the death-masks of two great martyrs, Pushkin and Napoleon").[504] Adolescent Ksenia Tomchak is bibliographically coded as well, down to her muscle tone: "I've read all of Turgenev and got sick of him a hundred times over. Dostoevsky gets on my nerves, gives me the jitters [*ruki svodit v sudorogi*].[505] Hamsun and Przybyszewski and Lagerlöf none of us read,"[506] she tells Irina, her beautiful and aloof sister-in-law, though later Ksenia samples some Strindberg,[507] with unknown results. In contrast, Irina's secret hero from age nine was James Fenimore Cooper's "noble and fearless warrior" Natty Bumppo,[508] in emulation of whom she took up sharpshooting as a hobby. Theatre-loving Likonya sees her inamorato Gordey as "one of [Aleksandr] Ostrovsky's best young heroes,"[509] a notion which makes sociological sense, for the two lovers hail from the merchant class, whose ways and means that playwright had famously brought to the stage. With the revolution just around the corner, Tsar Nicholas, a conflicted soul who is one part autocratic and one part fatuous, pores over Caesar's *Gallic War* and L. Frank Baum's "The Story of Little Boy Blue."[510]

Stolypin is on some semi-mythical genealogical plane "related to Lermontov,"[511] during the battle of Tannenberg Samsonov lolls on a sofa like a latter-day Oblomov, Nicholas thinks of his chief of staff, General Alekseev, as a "Chekhovian man in a case,"[512] and Zinaida Altanskaya's first lover is "a pure Chekhov type," that is, "a shrinking violet, melancholy, a dreamer,"[513] or so her second lover, Kovynev, would like to believe. This last remark is addressed to Vorotyntsev, who happens to be just a bit Chekhovian himself, for his rank, temperament, and marital situation hold more than a hint of Colonel Vershinin in *Three Sisters* (*Tri sestry*; 1900). Even a well-known toponymical practice of the nineteenth-century Russian novel is brought into play: the name of the town where Vorotyntsev confesses his affair to Alina, a traumatic disclosure for both husband and wife, is given merely as "S." These overt or covert intertextual transfers, of which there are hundreds, position the tetralogy as an exegetic work that offers a discontinuous yet cogent commentary on the national canon.

Here is an example of how *The Red Wheel* hypertextually processes descriptive passages and diegetic tropes from two novels by two of Solzhenitsyn's predecessors, Tolstoy and Dostoevsky. In *August 1914*, Samsonov sends a report to army group HQ, in which he quotes "word for word" a dispatch by General Martos describing a "glorious episode" in which a regimental commander died a hero's death at the head of his color guard as it was putting the enemy to the bayonet, with the flag "now nailed to a Cossack lance."[514] Next, Samsonov relates this incident to Vorotyntsev, who "nodded repeatedly as though he had heard about it long ago."[515] The colonel nods because he has, of course, read *War and Peace*, where during the battle of Austerlitz Bolkonsky takes hold of a standard and charges against the French, suffering a near-mortal wound as a result. The fourth iteration of the "glorious episode" occurs a few chapters later when Sasha Lenartovich, a junior officer with revolution on his mind, sneeringly comments in a recognizably Tolstoyan, that is, defamiliarizing manner, "Imagine fighting for a bit of rag! And when that's done, for the stick it was tied to."[516] The ultimate reference, however, is to the short story "The Signal" ("Signal"; 1887) by Vsevolod Garshin: a switchman stops a train from crossing over a section of damaged track by brandishing an improvised flag, "a bloody rag on a stick" (*krovavaia triapka na palke*),[517] with the blood in question coming from a heroically self-inflicted wound. (As for the regimental colors in *August 1914*, they were rescued by Nurse Belobragina.)

On this occasion, the very unliterary Lenartovich discharges a double literary duty. His interlocutor is the army surgeon, Valerian Fedonin, who has spent the day operating on the Russian and German wounded: the doctor is one of those dedicated professionals who always receive sympathetic treatment in Solzhenitsyn's fictions. Sasha, however, has little time for such bourgeois do-goodery and emits a series of anti-patriotic rants: "The worse things are in this war, and the worse things are for Russia, the better!"[518] And: "Let the sufferings of the wounded be added to the sufferings of the workers and peasants."[519] And: "If you ask me, it's a pity Napoleon didn't beat us in 1812. He wouldn't have lasted long, and then we'd have been free."[520] The last of these diatribes, which may even contain a kernel of counterfactual truth, references a conversation in *The Brothers Karamazov* between that novel's bastard sibling, the loathsome Smerdyakov, and Marya Kondratyevna, the loathsome one's object of desire:

> In 1812 there took place a great invasion by the Emperor of the French, Napoleon I, the father of the one who reigns at present, and it would have been a good thing if those same French had conquered us: a clever nation would have conquered an entirely stupid one, miss, and joined it to itself. We'd have quite different manners and habits, miss.[521]

Tall, blond, and handsome, the law graduate Lenartovich happens to be superior in looks and learning to the semi-literate semi-Karamazov, who does not know that Napoleon III is the great Napoleon's nephew, but they are brothers in rage. Still, this is not all there is to the epic's most important fictional extremist. In the way of Dostoevsky's vocal articulators of evil, Lenartovich may be generally and particularly in the wrong, but he is right about some things: "The army on the Austrian front doesn't know a thing about us, and we know nothing about them. That's no way to fight a war."[522]

The Lazhenitsyn/Fedonin exchange represents an established type of intertextual transaction in Solzhenitsyn, whereby a unit of canonical text is dialogically adduced and diegetically reworded to discharge a satirical function in the fictive present. Lenartovich's paraphrase of Smerdyakov updates *The Brothers Karamazov* for the twentieth century while fixing the snooty socialist Sasha as a Russophobic antihero for the rest of the epic.

12

The saga's pre-autobiographical motif is initiated in the cluster of chapters at the beginning of *August 1914*, which introduce Sanya Lazhenitsyn and Ksenia Tomchak and show the wealthy Tomchak family at their functional or dysfunctional best or worst, and reaches its culmination in *April 1917*, where Sanya and Ksenia meet, fall in love, and plan a future together: Solzhenitsyn's parents fictionalized as he imagined they were *before* they became his parents. Clearly, the account is based on the stories the writer heard from his mother and her sister-in-law, Irina Shcherbak (Irina Tomchak in the epic). Ksenia's impressions of leafy Rostov, where "her heart always beat faster,"[523] are Solzhenitsyn's own, transposed a decade or more back in time from the 1920s and 1930s. So are those of teenage

Yurik Kharitonov, a child (or young adult) of that city. The tales of Lazhenitsyn's experiences at the front and Vorotyntsev's marital troubles rely on Solzhenitsyn's recollections of his service in World War II and his unhappy first marriage. One may safely assume that the colonel's austere temperament and dislike of empty socializing have the same authorial provenance: "Restaurants slow down the work in hand and increase the share of pleasure in life disproportionately."[524] Lenin's compulsion to put every moment to productive (that is, destructive) use recalls Solzhenitsyn's own lifelong *tempus fugit* obsession. Sasha Lenartovich's resentment of "blasted army regulations,"[525] his estrangement from the "uneducated and illiterate men"[526] in his platoon, and his reluctance to kill in battle all have the same authorial derivation. So does Sasha's knowledge of German and his habit of reading "German social democratic authors"[527] (see Nerzhin's forlorn attempts to plough through Engels in *Love the Revolution*).

This authorial-familial line of inquiry commences on the epic's opening page. Sanya Lazhenitsyn is traveling across his native steppe in a rickety cart a few days after Germany's declaration of war. A university student who grew up on a farm near the Land of the Don Cossack Host, he has decided to join up out of simple love of country: "I felt sorry for Russia."[528] The first sentence in this work of tens of thousands of sentences reads:

> The Caucasus loomed huge and elemental in a world of small man-made things. If all the people who had ever lived had opened their arms as wide as they could to carry all that they had ever made, or ever thought of making, and piled it up in swelling heaps, they could not have raised such an unbelievable mountain range.[529]

(In *November 1916*, Vorotyntsev and Andozerskaya will agree to disagree that "the problems of a colossus like Russia" are "like mountain peaks, visible from afar, and to many people,"[530] and the epic's first prefiguration will thereby be completed.)

The diction is, as ever, unmistakably Solzhenitsynian, but the mimetic tropes that support it carry a strong whiff of Tolstoy. Both this opening paragraph and the one that follows, in which the fabled massif is compared to a "celestial mirage,"[531] refer back to his novel *The Cossacks* (*Kazaki*; 1863), which records its itinerant's hero's *first* glimpse of the same mountain:

> The morning was perfectly clear. Suddenly, some twenty yards away, it seemed to him in that first moment, he saw the enormous, pure, white

masses with their delicate contours, and the fantastic, distinct, aerial line of their summits and the distant sky. And when he had grasped the whole extent of the distance between him and the mountains and the sky, the whole immensity of the mountains, and when the whole infinitude of that beauty had conveyed itself to his senses, he was afraid it was an apparition, a dream."[532]

Sanya, of course, hews to a reverse itinerary from Cadet Dmitry Olenin, lately a gentleman of the city of Moscow: the hero is traveling *away* from the empire's southern marches and *toward* its ancient capital. It will take him a week or more to get there, for Solzhenitsyn's homeland is a true "continent" (as we learned in "Zakhar-the-Pouch") or "almost a continent in size" (as we shall learn in *August 1914*).[533] Despite the picturesque views, the journey to the Mineralnye Vody station is an uncomfortable one, for whenever the horses break into a trot every turn of the (unmentioned) *wheels* makes Sanya bounce up and down like a yo-yo. Also riding in the cart is his half-brother Yevstrat, eight, who in the way of small boys is full of questions such as, "Why do you feel as if you're going backwards when you close your eyes?"[534] A narrative moment of literal and intertextual darkness, for it invokes, and inverts, a passage from *The Death of Ivan Ilyich* that records the protagonist's sensations just before his biological existence comes to a close: "It had happened to him as it had sometimes happened to him in a railway-carriage, when he had thought he was going forwards whereas he was actually going backwards, and all of a sudden became aware of his real direction."[535]

Sanya is "a child of the steppes with his deep tan and his slicked-down, corn-colored hair bleached from working in the fields [and] light brown mustache and the growth that was not yet a beard."[536] This is the hero as seen through the eyes of Varya Matveeva, a young woman of his acquaintance, who now crosses paths with him at the Mineralnye Vody station. Varya's impressions are an ekphrasis of one of the few extant photographs of Isaaki Solzhenitsyn, which shows him wearing his student uniform and looking both soulful and dashing.

Thousands of miles to the west, history is unfolding. The Russian army has crossed the German border and won a victory at Gumbinnen, as Sanya learns from a couple of newspapers which he "skip[s] from column to column":[537] an intra-textual pointer to the Glance at the Newspapers sections, the first of which follows a few pages later.

Also in chapter one, we are told about the hero's youthful attachment to the doctrines of Yasnaya Polyana, which "settled all things so convincingly, demanding only truthfulness."[538] Next, the text brings to bear upon Sanya's ethical views a succession of Tolstoyesque syllogisms:

> Tolstoy's truth made it necessary for him to tell a lie: having become a vegetarian, he could not possibly explain that it was for reasons of conscience without incurring the disgust and derision of his family and all the village. Instead, he had to begin by telling a lie: some German medical man had discovered that abstaining from meat ensured long life. When he had tossed enough sheaves around, his body craved meat, and it was hard work deluding himself that potatoes and beans were all he needed.[539]

The twice-repeated formula "to tell a lie" (repetition is a favorite Tolstoyan trope), the imaginary German doctor adduced as an authority on meatless diets (the great man hated doctors), and the hunger Sanya feels after a day's honest toil (cue Levin's *pleasurable* bodily sensations when scything with his peasants in *Anna Karenina*) are replete with cross-textual irony. If the description of the Caucasus and little Yevstrat's dream state are affectionate tributes from one writer to another, then this *truth is a lie* passage foreshadows the epic's critique of Tolstoy's intellectual system.

In chapter two, the author of *War and Peace* enters the fictive world in person. As Sanya lies on his bunk in a third-class carriage he lets his mind wander to the rhythm of the wheels, as rail passengers are wont to do in Russian novels (hypnagogia, here I go!). Four years earlier, at the height of his Tolstoyan phase, the hero had set off on a pilgrimage to the writer's estate in the same month of August, and now he reminisces about that earlier journey.

But first, let me make a couple of points.

August 1910 was not a happy time in the Tolstoy household. The writer's relationship with his wife had broken down and his flight to the "last station" of Astapovo was just two months away. Although this family drama remains unmentioned in the text, the informed reader will have knowledge of an entire literature of primary and secondary sources, which sets the context for young Sanya's encounter with his moral teacher. Such a know-it-all receptor might even recall the novelist's diary entries of the period: "Took a long walk in the morning" (August 2/15),[540] but especially, "Many tiresome visitors" (August 4/17).[541]

Like Kulikovo Field, Yasnaya Polyana is one of the nation's sacral sites. Its grounds include the famous "house that stands somewhat askew,"[542] an adjacent park, and a considerable expanse of field and forest. In Tolstoy's later years, this sprawling property was a demesne of reluctant ownership, its high land values and profitable rents a permanent affront to the great man's anti-materialistic principles. Among the many notables who called on the aging writer at his manor was Gorky. His *Reminiscences of Tolstoy* (*Vospominaniia o L've Nikolaeviche Tolstom*; 1919), a record of these visits, is a piece of early Gonzo journalism, breathless prose—"a Russian god,"[543] "Jehovah Sabaoth"[544]—leavened with dollops of gossip but also a commendable degree of self-awareness: "His interest in me is ethnological. In his eyes I belong to a species not familiar to him—only that."[545] The special aura surrounding Yasnaya Polyana was so powerful that General Guderian, whose Second Panzer Army briefly occupied it in 1941 during the German drive on Moscow, was later constrained to declare that whilst in possession of the estate his troops had behaved like knights in Krupp armor.[546] In fact, the Wehrmacht, history's most desacralizing army, remained true to form: the officers looted, the men vandalized, and a nameless Hun thrust his bayonet into the leather sofa on which Tolstoy was born: an ignorant *Landser*'s stab at immortality.

Sanya's visit to Yasnaya Polyana was the most important event in his life, so he remembers every detail. Having alighted at the local train station and obtained some difficult-to-follow directions, he set off for the sacred locale. There follows a succession of narrative retardations that defer the chapter's climactic encounter while introducing into the text Solzhenitsyn's beloved middle Russian landscape and giving texture to the hero's reflective personality: "Woods such as he had never seen in pictures and, living in the south, could never have imagined."[547] Presently Sanya reaches his destination, but he is too shy to enter through the main gate and instead makes his way to the park. There he finds himself in a section whose layout is linear (not circular): a "birch-lined avenue—*long, straight, and narrow* like a corridor" (my emphasis—RT), "*not altogether an open space* [*poliana;* my emphasis—RT] but a less thickly wooded *rectangular* [my emphasis—RT] area bounded by linden trees,[548] with paths running *lengthwise, breadthwise, and diagonally*" [my emphasis—RT].[549] Such is the verdant, diagrammatized locus in which the encounter takes place: a fictive zone that is neither enclosed nor unenclosed, and therefore exempt from Solzhenitsyn's usual spatial binarism. In this in-between place, the vectors of Sanya's ethical quest will drift and sag, for lack of a clear conceptual matrix. The park is a chronotope of incertitude.

Suddenly the diffident youth catches sight of the novelist conducting his morning constitutional and slips behind a linden tree in a private game of hide-and-seek. As Tolstoy draws closer, the novelist seems "shorter than he had expected,"[550] an instance of emotional eavesdropping that conveys the perceptual sine qua non of a dedicated fan coming face-to-face with his idol. Still, the writer is "so like his portraits that Sanya almost shook his head to make sure that it was not a mirage."[551] In the sunlight Tolstoy's head seems "*ringed* with a bright *halo*" (my emphasis—RT) as "he walked around all four sides of the *rectangle*" (my emphasis—RT).[552] A circle ("halo") that moves along a trajectory of right angles: hints of where the laird of Yanaya Polyana stands or promenades in relation to the epic's mythic coordinates, the Wheel and the Cross.

Our furtive pilgrim emerges from behind his tree of concealment and in a neat reversal of perspectives, it turns out that Sanya looks just as familiar to the great man, albeit in a generic sort of way: "Tolstoy had, of course, seen more than his share of visitors, schoolboys included. He knew the sort of thing they were likely to ask and had his answers ready."[553] Throughout the scene, *this* schoolboy's adrenalized brain generates a series of hoary archetypes, each one more evocative than the last: "the Gray-bearded One,"[554] "the Prophet,"[555] "the Lord of Hosts."[556] Sanya is channeling Gorky, even though he could not have read that colorful memoir, which was published a decade later. These tiny citational anachronisms illustrate the jejune, *derived* nature of Sanya's perceptions.

The ensuing conversation is brief and (not to) the point, depending on whether we choose to privilege Tolstoy's take on things or, as is more likely, Sanya's, with the novelist exquisitely polite and the schoolboy exquisitely shy. In truth, the exchange ends up going nowhere, for in response to his acolyte's eager questions Tolstoy merely quotes himself:

> "Have I understood correctly what you say about the purpose of man's life on earth?"
>
> ...
>
> "To serve the good. And so create the Kingdom of God on earth."[557]

Bashful Sanya begs to disagree: "Evil refuses to know the truth. Rends it with its fangs! Evil people usually know better than anybody else just what they are doing. And go on doing it."[558]

With these words, uttered by a character who is also, in an extra-fictive sense, his father, Solzhenitsyn addresses his reimagined Tolstoy across decades of history and libraries of books. For Sanya, too, is citing a body of texts, Solzhenitsyn's own, as in, "The world is being flooded by the brazen conviction that force can do all, and righteousness—nothing."[559] Or: "A timorous civilized world, faced with the onslaught of a ... snarling barbarism, has found nothing to oppose it with except concessions and smiles."[560]

The sage of Yasnaya Polyana is unconvinced by this line of reasoning, as of course he would be:

> "We must explain things patiently. Then they will understand. All men are born with the ability to understand."
> He strode off with his walking stick, obviously put out.[561]

Chapter two is a literary time machine, pre-tuned for a dialogic breakdown. As for truth-seeking Sanya, he belongs to a select category of characters, which also includes passionate Zinaida and poetic Likonya, who in the course of events undergo an ethical transformation, while remaining believably and appealingly human. In Sanya's case, we see him resiling from a schoolboy enthusiasm for the doctrines of Yasnaya Polyana to an informed patriotism that is very similar to Vorotyntsev's. Sanya's de-Tolstoyanization is signposted by the wide-ranging and intellectually weighty conversations he has with two of the epic's wise men, the augur Varsonofiev and the army chaplain Father Severyan, his friendship with Kotya Gulai, as well as his romance with Ksenia, whose quiet goodness complements his own restless, questing ways.

The young hero's Tolstoyan pilgrimage has automythobiographical implications beyond its status as a reconstructed episode from the life of Isaaki Solzhenitsyn. In August 1963, the writer went on a bicycle tour of central Russia in the company of his first wife, Natalya Reshetovskaya, during which they visited Kulikovo and Yasnaya Polyana.

В Ясной Поляне
с музейными
девушками-
практикантками.
1963

One can easily imagine the writer walking down the platform of the same rural station as Sanya, taking the same circuitous route to the estate, perhaps standing next to one of the lindens in the park, from whence he surveyed its alleys and lawns with an old gunner's eye. Beyond these speculations, the scene of Sanya's meeting with Tolstoy is suffused with a wry sense of writer-to-writer affinity. It becomes overtly textualized when the starry-eyed teenager thinks of Tolstoy as a "prophet," a term so often applied to Solzhenitsyn himself, or when the novelist recognizes his youthful visitor as one of those restless souls who "could read it all in his books if they cared to, but for some reason... insisted on hearing it from his own lips."[562] Not that Solzhenitsyn was ever as generous with his time when importuned by fans who appeared on his doorstep, whether in Ryazan, Moscow, or Cavendish.

But let us return to Sanya's journey to war. Upon his arrival in Moscow he meets Kotya Gulai, who has also decided to join up, and the two friends resolve to go on a "farewell tour"[563] of the city before reporting to the artillery school in which they have enrolled. We encountered the same topos of a wartime urban excursion in *Love the Revolution*. The differences, however, are telling. Moscow circa 1914 is nothing like the gloomy Ozymandian metropolis that Gleb Nerzhin explores on the day after Hitler's invasion. In *August 1914*, the ancient capital is a place of narrow, cozy streets and shady boulevards, with "a church at every bend in the road"[564] and throngs of people calmly, or excitedly, or briskly going about their business. It is a locus of spontaneous communal life, yet to be transformed by the bleak vision of Stalin's architects into a monument to a *radial* future: "Perhaps it is a good thing after all that the city was not built to a plan, that everyone raised his walls where he thought best, that no corner is like any other."[565] In *April 1917*, Sanya will wander the same streets, this time arm-in-arm with Ksenia, when instead of the peaceful bustle of yore they will encounter febrile crowds engaged in half-joyous, half-threatening displays of revolutionary enthusiasm: two young people in love who watch the flames rise as their country becomes hell's firewood.

By happenstance (*Doctor Zhivago*, anyone?) Sanya and Kotya bump into Varsonofiev, a distant acquaintance. They fall into a conversation in the middle of the street, in the course of which Sanya makes the programmatic announcement, "I am not a *pure* Tolstoyan anymore."[566] The three men repair to a nearby tavern to discuss this and other topics further, over a few beers. The exchange evolves into an intellectual Q & A session in which Varsonofiev asks most of the questions and supplies most of the answers. He is one of those learned patriarchs who enjoy holding forth, of whom Solzhenitsyn's novels have quite a few.

Having ascertained the two friends' intellectual outlooks, the mage comments on their declared desire to "struggle for the people":[567]

> And tell me, do the people themselves have obligations? Or only rights? ... Maybe your high moral level existed before the Mongol invasion. But since they started stirring the people up with the devil's mixer—you can date it from Ivan the Terrible, or Peter, or Pugachev, it doesn't matter when it began, it's gone on ever since, right down to our time, with its Black Hundreder tavernkeepers, and be sure not to leave out 1905— what is written on the people's invisible face and in their hidden heart? Take our waiter now—there's a pretty unprepossessing physiognomy for you. Up above us is the Union Cinema, a temple for the Antichrist of the arts, with a pianist playing in the dark—what, I wonder, is in his soul? I wonder what sort of bestial face will leer out from the Union one of these days? Why should we be expected to sacrifice ourselves for them all the time?[568]

(The piano-playing Kirk Douglas lookalike will later reappear as a member of Alina's touring concert show and will demostrate his wickedness when he hoots his support for an anti-German pogrom.)[569]

His fulminations against the wait staff excepted, Varsonofiev articulates a central tenet in the epic's conceptual scheme: the masses are no less to blame for Russia's ills than the politicians and ideologues, and these bad thoughts and behaviors have satanic implications. The intelligentsia, he declares next, is part of the people and carries no special obligation toward the latter: in *The First Circle*, Nerzhin reaches the same conclusion after his anthropological interactions with Spiridon. Also, public opinion is wrong to deny membership in the intellectual class to clergymen or educated persons who hold "retrograde" views.[570] On a more pedagogical note, the augur is doubtful that "students [who] fail their exams ... or have to rely on cribs"[571] belong in these exalted ranks. Varsonofiev's sociological opinions are Solzhenitsyn's own, including that bit about campus slackers. So is the mystic's belief that democracy is *not* the ideal form of government[572] because it is a utopian political dispensation and therefore never achievable, and anyway, "history is not governed by reason,"[573] a dig at Kotya, worshipper of the *Weltgeist*. Instead, it "grows like a living tree":[574] shades of Yggdrasil, one imagines. In the end, however, the Stargazer is unable to provide his mixed Tolstoyan/Hegelian audience with guidance of a practical sort, offering instead this gnomic observation: "The laws for constructing the best social order must be inherent in the structure of the world as a whole. In the design behind the universe and in man's destiny."[575]

There is something in Varsonofiev of Georgii Gachev (1929–2008), the Russian-Bulgarian scholar who belonged to the same distinctive tradition of speculative natural philosophy as Fedorov and Tsiolkovsky, and whose "original holistic system"[576] of "existential culturology"[577] was a self-described "mélange" of Proust, Spengler, and Rozanov,"[578] as in,

> The *fate* of a given people is the projection of its cast-mentality-disposition-character into the sphere of time. History (Life) is the factorization into a temporal sequence of what was integrally posited in the idea-principle-constitution of a given people (or person) in the form of a structure that exists in space."[579]

Be that as it may, the Stargazer approves of Sanya and Kotya's decision to go to war, because "Russia's back mustn't be broken."[580] As already noted, the epic's articulators of the authorial Truth are sometimes shown to be in the wrong, even on matters of the gravest import.

Two years later Sanya, by now a lieutenant and a combat veteran, tells Father Severyan, "I am no Tolstoyan. Not now."[581] Instead, he attends services and goes to confession, though as he also informs the chaplain, "I don't accept that Christ's teaching is a recipe for a happy life on this earth."[582] In the dugout he shares with Chernega, Sanya hangs up a Catholic crucifix, a detail that recalls the Elder Zosima's cell in *The Brothers Karamazov* where a similar object is displayed:[583] the epic's single most important instance of artifactal dialogism. Sanya has been awarded a St. George's Cross for bravery, but he has not rid himself of his introverted ways: "Lazhenitsyn somehow always felt guilty even when he had done nothing wrong,"[584] a Russian Orthodox version of Catholic guilt. On the other *hand*, he has learned to salute. (In Solzhenitsyn, the crispness or otherwise of this prescribed gesture is a marker of how well a young officer is adjusting to army life, viz. Ensign Lenartovich's floppy version in *August 1914*[585] and his snappier one in *March 1917*.)[586]

Father Severyan epitomizes Solzhenitsyn's notion of the ideal cleric: deeply devout, possessed of a critical intelligence, and with a library of books in his head. The Sanya/Severyan confab is one of those textual occasions when the Cross is present in material form, and the narration is structured so as to draw attention to this fact: "The priest crossed himself before the Catholic crucifix."[587] Father Severyan, we discover, holds strongly ecumenical views. His name is a Russian form of the Latin *Severus*, but it also recalls "Severtsev"—The One From the North," the surname Solzhenitsyn had originally chosen for the Vorotyntsev character.

Although he has now seceded from Tolstoyanism and receives the sacraments, Sanya is still searching for answers to the big questions and the priest, who is a decade or so older, offers an understanding ear. Their lengthy disputation, which takes place at the midnight hour, occupies a pivotal place in the epic's conceptual scheme. From a discussion of Tolstoy, church history, and religious doctrine, the two men inevitably move on to the destiny of Russia and the world. In form and tenor, their nocturnal tête-à-tête evokes Plato's Dialogues by way of Vladimir Solovyov's *Three Conversations*—with his "thick, wavy black hair,"[588] Severyan even looks like the famous theologian—while echoing in places Valentin Sventsitsky's *Dialogues on Faith and Unbelief* (*Dialogi o vere i neverii*; 1930), an influential tract that circulated among the faithful during the Soviet period. The interlocutors' individualized character voices—Sanya's courteous and sometimes hesitant, the chaplain's "weary"[589] and interrupted by occasional sighs—give their argumentative exchange the requisite novelistic flavor. So does the sound of distant explosions, the crackling of the stove, and Chernega's thunderous snores overhead: while officer and priest debate, that earthy soul lies slumbering in his bunk in stentorian dismissal of these intellectual proceedings. The sleep of Russia produces indifference.

Sanya's conversation with the chaplain witnesses the integration of two strong minds which become "united" in their "like-mindedness"[590] and coalesce into a single cogitating discursive whole. This is one of those occasions where we observe the complete convergence of text and author, for the thoughts the two men share with each other over the course of a dozen pages are manifestly Solzhenitsyn's own. In places, this composite implied-authorial monologue pertains as much to the realities of the Soviet period as to those of the year 1916. "Until we ask forgiveness of the Old Believers and are reunited with them Russia can expect nothing good" (Sanya);[591] "My own belief is that there was no schism.... In my heart it is as if all were united" (Severyan);[592] "In the last four centuries ... mankind has moved steadily away from God" (Severyan);[593] "An individual cannot escape paying for a grave sin, sometimes in his own lifetime, and still less can a society, or a people" (Sanya);[594] "Is the Church as such never to blame for anything?" (Sanya);[595] "The Church ... is now ... the state's captive" (Sanya);[596] "Icons, candles, incense, the blessing of communion bread ... the singing that rises up to the dome.... For my part I love all this" (Sanya);[597] Tolstoy "reproduces the most primitive variety of Protestantism" (Severyan);[598]

"The ordeal at the hands of a torturer" is "spiritually dirtier and more terrible than war" (Severyan);[599] "And why... when all the world is the loser, does every denomination insist on its unique and exclusive rightness? The Orthodox, the Catholics, and all the other Christians?" (Sanya).[600] In turn, the padre wonders if "there are only two of us Christians left in the entire world,"[601] a comment that references, perhaps inadvertently, Nietzsche's *The Antichrist*: "There was only *one* Christian, and he died on the cross."[602]

In the course of this quasi-Platonic dialogue, Sanya accuses the Church of failing to repent for the crimes it committed over the centuries: "Protestants and Catholics butcher each other, we butcher the Old Believers."[603] Of course, the correct ecclesiological position, as enunciated by Sventsitsky and countless other theologians—though, curiously, not by the chaplain—is that "the grave sins of individual representatives of the Church, even those who are members of its hierarchy ... are not sins of the Church, but sins against the Church."[604] Beyond this, the nocturnal colloquy holds a reflection of Solzhenitsyn's conversations with Fr. Alexander Schmemann, who summed up his differences with the writer in a pointed formula: "His treasure is Russia and *only* Russia, whereas mine is the *Church*."[605]

Now, as a younger man, Sanya was a bit of a party pooper. Like Fitzroy Darcy and Eugene Onegin, he attended dances in order not to dance, a lifestyle position for which he found support—where else?—in literature: "Sanya said that holding each other close in a waltz aroused desires before there had been time for any genuine feeling to develop and that Count Tolstoy thought this a bad thing."[606] In a subsequent and equally Tolstoyan development, the hero acquired a mistress, "black-haired Lyonochka with her guitar and love songs,"[607] and learned something about the ways of women, whatever the evolutionary state of his feelings. In *April 1917*, Lieutenant Lazhenitsyn's recession from his schoolboy Tolstoyanism is followed, as a kind of fabulatory reward, by his requited love for pure-of-heart, full-of-life Ksenia.

The heroine first enters the saga as a bouncy schoolgirl who dreams of becoming a free form dancer like her idol Isadora Duncan, but her father, the patriarchal Zakhar Tomchak, has other plans. He hopes to see Ksenia married, and soon, thinking to himself, "In a year's time I'd have a grandson, and in fifteen years, an heir."[608] Zakhar's projected marital timeline is fairly accurate, even if his assumptions about the disposition of the Tomchak fortune will be voided by the revolution.

When Ksenia turned thirteen, her father sent her to Mrs. Kharitonova's boarding school in Rostov, whose unofficial credo read: "The main purpose of education [is] to produce citizens—which mean[s] people hostile to authority."[609] There the young girl shone academically, showing a flair for foreign languages if not for the civic attitudes in question. She also developed an adolescent sense of estrangement from her family, ruing "the unrelieved uncouthness of her father's household"[610] and losing her childhood habit of daily fervent prayer. After leaving the school with a gold medal she moved to Moscow to attend an agronomy course, while secretly pursuing her love of dance.

One day, the heroine is walking in the Alexander Garden next to the Kremlin when she espies a group of children attended by their mothers, grannies, and nannies: "Her entire life to this point, all her studies and diversions, could only have had a single meaning and purpose. She knew without a doubt, she was absolutely certain, the only thing she wanted in this world was a son!"[611] The author's textual self just cannot wait to be born! And so almost as soon as Ksenia and Sanya meet and after the briefest of courtships become engaged, their thoughts turn to the child they will have when they are married (a parental dream that stands in contrast to Georgi and Olda's indifference to, if not dislike of, children):

> But Sanya had always wanted the very same thing! A son!
> And so they began talking about him, as if he were already here.
> They spoke of him as the inevitable one... [*o nepremennom nashem*]
> What happiness!*[612]

This is the epic's principal autobiographical passage: a proleptic inkling of the empirical Aleksandr Solzhenitsyn recorded in story time, before he came into the world in extra-textual time, before he carved out a presence in historical time. The writer's unborn and as yet unconceived future self is scripted as an "inevitable" child of destiny, mystically anticipated and imagined by his semi-fictionalized parents-to-be in Kremlin's shadow.

Shadow and light... According to popular Russian belief, to see a new moon over one's left shoulder constitutes bad luck: one time, Olda "throw[s] both arms around [Vorotyntsev] so that he would see the young moon... over his right, not his left shoulder,"[613] and on another occasion Sanya is "superstitiously happy he had seen the new moon over his right shoulder."[614]

These lunar motifs recur on the night that Sanya and Ksenia first meet:

> When the cabman made a turn, the full moon high above would shed its generous light on the couple, sometimes from the left, sometimes facing

them directly as if in greeting, then again from the left, occasionally disappearing behind the tall buildings nearby, and sometimes gleaming at them from across the river, so that they later remembered it all as an uninterrupted, smooth, and happy voyage under the moon.[615]

Here the moon's position relative to the two young people is sinistral, and therefore unpropitious: one more clue that their future life together will not bring them the "higher happiness" of which Ksenia had dreamed all those years ago.

13

Varya Matveeva is a plain orphan girl with a prim manner that hides a volatile nature. She attends the prestigious Bestuzhev Courses, her fees paid by a wealthy merchant who keeps dozens of waifs like her on his books. She is also a radical sympathizer, one of several aspirant revolutionists portrayed in the epic: Arkhangorodsky's fiery-tempered daughter, Sonya, is another. On the platform at the Mineralnye Vody station, Varya kisses Sanya with "sun-warmed lips,"[616] momentarily disturbing the hero's Tolstoyan commitment to chastity, and the two young people try to catch up. She is appalled to learn that the man of her dreams is joining the army and showers him with imprecations. Her jibes, "the idiot Emperor," "Black Hundred grocers," "long-skirted priests,"[617] convey both extremist fervor and left-wing snobbery. Then exit Sanya, on his mission to reminisce about Tolstoy and fight for Russia.

Varya reappears in chapter eight, which opens with a death scene out of Dickens, one of two *tableaux mourants* in the epopee (the other one shows the dying Stolypin). In a dark room smelling of "incense, dried herbs, and medicines"[618] she attends her terminally ill benefactor, a patriarchal figure with "big mustaches wearily drooping like a pair of damp tassels."[619] "God grant ... your schooling ... will bring good ... to you—and to other people. The light of ... learning ... is ... two-edged ...,"[620] he whispers. A murmured warning that will have a quiet resonance in subsequent chapters and Knots. Its implications will also be relevant for the heroine herself, and in a matter of minutes. But for now, Varya feels gratitude despite her patron's status as a "merchant, shopkeeper ... a Black Hundreder,"[621] that is, the class enemy. For all her revolutionary conceits, she is a warmhearted young woman.

After this memento mori, Varya emerges into the sunshine of her native Pyatigorsk, a picturesque spa town at the foot of the Caucasus, famously depicted in Mikhail Lermontov's novel *A Hero of Our Time* as a site of romantic intrigue and murderous passion. Fittingly for such a storied place, a Circassian in full tribal costume walks by, prompting Varya to think: "I'm home! This is my world (Although there was not a single highlander among her acquaintances)."[622] This snippet of land-of-my-fathers internal monologue, parenthetically conjoined with a skeptical, implied-authorial comment, is an early example of the epic's recurring diegetic shifts. Next, in a private "game"[623] that recalls Vera Gangart's *danse solitaire* in her lonely room, the heroine scampers over a hand-woven carpet spread out on the sidewalk in the traditional way of Asia's rug merchants. A fez-wearing storeowner follows her movements with "cunning and imperious"[624] eyes: the male gaze, Orientalized. We catch a whiff of the seraglio, enhanced by the display of halva and Turkish delight in the shop next door. All this brings to mind Ivan Karamazov's sinister comment, "As a matter of fact they say that Turks are very fond of sweet things,"[625] which comes at the conclusion of a graphic and detailed account of Ottoman atrocities that he relates to Alyosha in Book V of *The Brothers Karamazov*. As she continues on her way, oblivious of this alarming literary allusion, Varya idly inspects the row of stalls lining the street, but is brought up short:

> In the next booth was a tinsmith: a big galvanized basin hung above his counter by way of a shop sign, and the harsh, angry noise of hammer on tin from inside the booth made you want to cover your ears. Varya quickened her pace to escape from the din, but glanced sideways at the tinsmith as he paused and drew himself to his full height: a young man, wearing in spite of the heat a thick shirt the color of tin and a black apron standing out stiffly from his body. He was black-haired and swarthy like many southerners, and his one unusual feature was a pair of ears remarkably small for a head so broad at brow and chin.... The young man turned one eye on her, hammer in hand, showing ... sullen hostility.[626]

That crude sign is round in shape and therefore a symbolic clue, while the tinsmith's rudimentary ears instantly individualize the portrait (later we learn that another character, Chernega, also has "tiny ears,"[627] an otic detail that anatomizes the revolutionary connection between the glowering tinsmith and the roly-poly soon-to-be Bolshevik).

The metallic apparition banging away in the darkness turns out to be a figure from Varya's childhood, when she knew him as a hulking adolescent who was active in the anarchist underground and went by the name of Zhora. She recalls the revolutionary manifestoes that thrilled her as a schoolgirl: "Struggle with all acknowledged authority.... Blow up monuments."[628] Zhora's black cowlick, dark stubble, and "long, rigid (rubberized?) apron,"[629] markers of a proletarian masculinity, stir Varya's ideological passions. Despite her crush on mild-mannered Sanya, she prefers bad boys. The young woman engages the tinsmith in conversation, and Zhora reluctantly opens up. He reveals that he has done time for "polishing off" a prison warden[630] and barks out threats to the established order, punctuated by angry blows of his hammer: "We'll shoot the bastards one at a time!"[631] Varya is frightened and thrilled in equal measure. "It was as though the whole row of shops were spinning like a carousel and she was pinned by centrifugal force to the booth":[632] the same annular image will recur when prodigal Zinaida sleeps with her Chekhovian lover and falls "from a carousel in full career."[633] Varya offers no resistance as the anarchist with the "savage glare"[634] and "rampant apron"[635] pushes her into a cupboard at the back of the shed.

> She was breathing heavily with terror and from the heat in this tight black trap, this dark well.
> She felt the pitiless pressure [*neumolimoe davlen'e*][636] of his hands on her shoulders.
> Down, down, down.[637]

In the epic, wells are associated with female characters who have complicated or transgressive sexual relationships: as Father Aloni hears Zinaida's confession, she imagines she is "using the grapnel at a wellhead" to extract the "hot stone" of her sins from the blackness below.[638]

The "underground smith"[639] in his dark and noisy nook calls to mind the god Hephaestus. The patron of blacksmiths and metal workers, he was lame from birth, or so the *Iliad* tells us. So when stannic Zhora gets up "awkwardly, as though one leg had gone to sleep"[640] to drag Varya to that awful cupboard, this is an obliquely Homeric moment. His phallic work apron does duty for the chiton the god was traditionally depicted as wearing.

Also scripted into the episode is another, Tolstoyan, set of references. In *Anna Karenina*, the passage that describes the heroine's last moments reads: "... Something huge and implacable [*chto-to ogromnoe, neumolimoe*][641] struck her on the head and dragged her down on her back.... The little peasant, muttering something, was working over the iron."[642] See the phrase *neumolimoe davlen'e* in Varya's seduction scene. Next. Anna and Varya both carry a fashion accessory, a coded item of female adornment that functions as a mutable symbol. Before throwing herself under the train, Anna thrusts aside her little red bag, and when Zhora forces Varya into that black cupboard, "something knocked off her straw hat."[643] The mysterious ironworker of Anna's nightmares is reincarnated, less mysteriously, in the muscular form of the hephaestic ravisher banging away in that dark smithy. And on a non-Tolstoyan note, the errant straw hat is a marker of a woman's sexual abandon or surrender: in *November 1916*, as Vorotyntsev pushes Olda on a swing and kisses her for the first time, "her hat fell off, rolled away, and was carried off by the wind."[644] Within the hour, they make love.

Varya's encounter with Zhora may have been traumatic, but it seems she was not permanently traumatized. At the end of *August 1914* we find her cheerfully gossiping about her new professor, Olda Andozerskaya, and cheerfully discussing the French Revolution with the latter.[645] Volumes later Varya is shown managing a Red soldiers' canteen staffed by several women and girls, in which capacity she dislays "energy, organizational ability, meticulousness, and a practical sense":[646] there is more to this revolutionary fellow traveler than just an adolescent fascination with leather-clad macho anarchists. Yet the tin man's sexual degradation of Varya anticipates the carnal crimes and excesses of the coming revolution while "point[ing] to ... the scenes of the abuse and rape of the female body ... in ... *The Gulag Archipelago*."[647]

One last point. The name Zhora is a diminutive of Georgi, which makes the tumid tinsmith a namesake to the colonel, the epic's guardian of order and his political and ethical antipode. Their shared appellation is an indicator of difference, not similarity: "Vorotyntsev venerated St. George, who was his protector."[648] And yes, tin is a base metal.

14

Solzhenitsyn's battlefields are spaces transfigured, urban, rural, or natural environments that have shed their primary identity and are now a locus of mechanized violence, which alters or destroys their physical shape, sometimes in a fashion that can only be described as surreal. The epic's participant-observers are variously exhilarated, puzzled, stunned, terrified, or unconcerned by their experience of combat, as others in their field of vision are similarly affected or unaffected, or are maimed or killed. And though the movement of troops along the axes of advance or retreat seldom follows the geometrical patterns laid down in the orders they receive, these utterances of power have a mensurable impact on the fortunes of war, contrary to *War and Peace*. The generals' decisions always matter.

The tragic hero of *August 1914*, General Aleksandr Samsonov, enters the novel in a supinely non-martial manner, sprawled on a sofa at his headquarters: a materialized incarnation of the Russian phrase "a sofa general" (*divannyi general*)—an armchair general. From the very beginning, the narrative stresses Samsonov's "Kutuzovian" traits. The general is corpulent, torpid, and fatalistic, even though he is a dozen years younger than Kutuzov was in his Tolstoyan prime. Although Solzhenitsyn denied this,[649] I find there is also something in this character of the indolent, kind-hearted Oblomov in Ivan Goncharov's eponymous novel (1859), perhaps the most famous couch potato in world literature. For a Russian reader, the onomastic associations suggest themselves: Samsonov—Oblomov, Samsonov—*samoson* ("sends you to sleep"), a type of *sofa*. Upon meeting the general, Vorotyntsev thinks a worrying thought: "The lower part of Samsonov's face ... resembled that of the Emperor,"[650] with all the weakness-of-will implications that follow. Days later, however, the colonel is struck by the "unalloyed Russianness"[651] of the commander's features, and this quality of national authenticity, which holds a special value in Solzhenitsyn's texts, is confirmed by none other than the malevolent Lenartovich. He sees the general as "a big man on a big horse, looking like an ancient Russian hero in an oleograph."[652] (Solzhenitsyn was told by Samsonov's daughter that the novel showed him "just the way he was in real life,"[653] a reader response that must have pleased the author.)

Like Lord Marchmain in *Brideshead Revisited*, Samsonov is a nineteenth-century personality in a twentieth-century world, a living anachronism whose out-of-time status will have dire consequences both for the men he leads and for him personally. His life prior to assuming command of Second Army possessed a patriarchal, old Russian simplicity that left him entirely unprepared for the reality of modern warfare:

> During his long and successful career ... Cavalry General Samsonov had learned to carry out his duties in an unhurried and deliberate fashion, giving his subordinates to understand that each of us should follow the Creator's example, get through his work in six days, sleep quietly in his bed for six nights, and spend the seventh day in restful contemplation.[654]

As the strategic picture darkens and the general's mind grows increasingly disoriented, he obsessively repeats a German sentence about Napoleon standing at bay in conquered Moscow, which he had memorized as a schoolboy: *Es war die höchste Zeit sich zu retten*[655] ("It was high time to seek salvation"). A connection is thereby established between Napoleon's doomed invasion of Russia, its mythical associations from *War and Peace*, and the catastrophe that befalls Samsonov's army. On the same plane of character speech, defeat robs the commander of his knack of speaking to the troops, whom he addresses in the military bureaucratese of the age: "So be once again the brave soldiers you were! Be faithful to your colors and the famous names borne..."[656] But with the Russians comprehensively defeated, Samsonov regains the trust of his men, addressing them "quietly and kindly,"[657] as a tired old man: "What unit do you belong to, boys?... Were your losses very heavy?... You did your duty—thank you!"[658] By then François's scientifically led troops have reduced Second Army to a "melee of units"[659] and Vorotyntsev, who is not normally given to flights of fancy, imagines its commander as a "seven-pud sacrificial lamb."[660] This ovine motif periodically resurfaces in *August 1914*: the doltish General Artamonov is the proud owner of a cranium whose shape recalls the head of a sheep. The same order of imagery also, and cruelly, links the sympathetic Samsonov and cretinous Artamonov (note the onomastic rhyme) to that much-quoted apothegm attributed to a variety of great captains from Alexander to Napoleon: "An army of sheep, led by a lion, is better than an army of lions, led by a sheep." In a parallel metaphorical development, when Samsonov flees the field of battle his staff officers take to thinking of him as a "golden idol, the god of a savage tribe,"[661] that is, an oblation to some pagan divinity, Indra or Ares or Mars or Odin (most likely, the latter).

The general walks in the fear of the Lord, to the detriment of the suffering Russian soldiery: "What had happened was part of God's plan and men were not meant to understand it, or not yet."[662] Samsonov's war ends when he relinquishes responsibility for his army as well as what remains of his retinue of staff officers and Cossacks: a foretoken of the tsar's abdication in *March 1917*. The remnants of the group make their way into the Grünfliess forest where at one point Samsonov is seen sitting on "the low throne which the forest had grown for him"[663]—in reality, a tree stump—an image which profanes his status as a war leader while evoking a host of cultural texts that depict the woods as a place of magical metamorphosis, for example, Goethe's ballad "Der Erlkönig" ("The Alder-King"; 1782). Samsonov is now a mock-regal figure in a carnival of death. The phrase "forest throne" is also an allusion to Daniel 4:26: "And whereas they commanded to leave the stump of the tree roots; thy kingdom shall be sure unto thee, after that thou shalt have known that the heavens do rule." See Samsonov's notion of "God's plan."

Soon thereafter, the general shoots himself with his service revolver in the dead of night: "The sky had clouded over. Only one star was visible—obscured for a while, it peered out again. He sank to his knees on the warm pine needles. Not knowing where the east was, he looked up at the star as he prayed."[664] Samsonov's suicide is a fulfillment of a mystical vision he had experienced on the morning of that day, when an "inexorable angel" had told him he was fated to die.[665]

The German perspective on the battle is given via the character of General François, whom the epic correctly identifies as the true victor of Tannenberg, contrary to the official histories that assigned these laurels to Hindenburg and Ludendorff. That famous tandem is dismissed by the author of record as the embodiment of "mediocrity"[666] (*srednie liudi*),[667] an accurate judgment where Hindenburg is concerned.

The character portrait of the man who defeated Samsonov is delivered with a dose of Solzhenitsyn's patented irony:

> ... François still did not neglect to make sure that every decision he took was recorded and explained three times over: in orders to his subordinates, in reports to his superiors, and in a detailed account for the military archives (and, if he survived, his own book), an account not just of his actions, but of intentions on which he was not always authorized to act. Before the fighting began he wrote it all down himself, and afterward he invariably took a special aide-de-camp with him in one of his two cars—his own son, a lieutenant, whose job was to keep the general's diary and record his thoughts as they came to him.[668]

The pugnacious general textualizes himself three or four or even five times over! Yet despite his flamboyant ways and meretricious displays, the irreducible truth is that François is a brilliant commander.

Nowhere else in the epopee does Tolstoy's shadow loom larger than in the Tannenberg chapters. As noted earlier, *War and Peace* posits that history is "the unconscious, general, hive life of mankind," which is unsusceptible to the will of so-called great men, and reconfigures Mikhail Kutuzov, Napoleon's opponent in the war of 1812, accordingly. From the strategically clever, tactically ordinary, and habitually passive commander that he was, the elderly general is transformed into a fatalistic, "wisely Buddhist"[669] patriarch with an intuitive connection to the Russian masses. He knows better than to interfere with the march of events and affects a somnolent detachment from the military operations over which he presides. Napoleon, on the other hand, appears as a self-centered grotesque who takes "delight at the misery of others,"[670] even if his status as a world conqueror is an illusion in his own mind. The image of Kutuzov created by Tolstoy became entrenched in Russian culture, though not outside it, and in the fullness of time acquired the status of a national myth. Solzhenitsyn had considerable respect for the historical Kutuzov[671]—less so for the historical Napoleon—but considered the notion of the former as a mystical warlord risible.

Never a writer to leave his T's uncrossed, the author includes a chapter in which "Lev Tolstoy's theory is put to the test by General Blagoveshchensky."[672] The military figure in question (a real-life personage) may be the most literary commander in history, or historical fiction: "General Blagoveshchensky had read too much *War and Peace* and, being sixty years old, gray-haired, corpulent and lethargic, saw himself as a second Kutuzov, only with two good eyes."[673] The CO of a corps that is stationed "right on the Russian frontier,"[674] the general refuses to come to Samsonov's aid because, in his readerly judgment, under these circumstances a Kutuzov would have stayed put and mulled the flow of history. Blagoveshchensky refuses to bestir himself even when he hears "the low grumble of distant guns,"[675] a Napoleonic phrase that underlines his un-Napoleonic character. Here, as elsewhere, *Tolstoy's* Kutuzov is encoded into the text as the epitome of bad generalship. So when Samsonov worries early on in the campaign that "he was no longer a man of action but only the mouthpiece of events which took their course regardless of him,"[676] this is a bad sign. Later the epic subjects General Khabalov, the commander of the Petrograd garrison during the revolution of February 1917, to similarly skeptical treatment: "Khabalov felt that nothing mattered: what was meant to happen would happen, and the will of one general couldn't change a thing."[677]

August 1914 follows the Tolstoyan precedent in its from-the-ground-up depiction of combat as organized chaos at the level of the infantry firefight and cavalry charge. Now, however, the sphere of battle extends vertically to a height of several thousand feet: the Germans employ airplanes in a reconnaissance role, and so do the Russians, though with markedly less success, as Samsonov ruefully admits: "The planes are always grounded. Under repair. Or else there's no fuel."[678] Second Army has access to telegraph, telephone, and wireless communication, but his officers notoriously abuse the latter by transmitting their messages in the clear. Samsonov's chief of staff, even more clueless in matters of modern warfare than his master, offers an excuse: "We don't use ciphers. What does it matter? Those codes can be the very devil."[679] On the same note of professional idiocy, thousands of pages later Khabalov muses in his retrograde way: "These armored cars, they really are irksome. A fashion of some kind that doesn't fit into the old, well-established system of tactics, and there's even something indecent about them."[680]

Indeed, most of the generals shown in the epic are mediocre or worse, a feature *The Red Wheel* shares with canonical English, French, and German novels of World War I. When one of these martial duds, General Kluev, surrenders his corps to the Germans, he employs the physiognomics of power in a manner identical to Rusanov in *Cancer Ward*: "General Kluev's imperious stare, the awesome lift of his eyebrows. (Without which the men might stop obeying him!)."681 Like so many of the Russian commanders at Tannenberg, Kluev is a function of his own incapacity, a set of eyebrows in a gaudy uniform. On the other hand, Colonel (later General) Krymov, an unusually capable officer, is endowed with a measure of fictive individuality. During his interactions with the itinerant Vorontsov, this gruff and unkempt personality comes alive as a character in ways that most of the other high-ranking military presences do not: "He was in no hurry to get dressed and hide behind his epaulets but went on sitting on the edge of his bath in his undervest, emitting puffs of smoke."682

Like *War and Peace*, which shows a stunned and uncomprehending Pierre Bezukhov wandering the field of Borodino during that terrible battle, *August 1914* introduces into the combat environment a character with a wholly civilian identity. This is the revolutionary lawyer Lenartovich, newly drafted into the army as an ensign. By failing to make sense of this world of violence, he helps the reader do so. As the "red sphere"683 of the sun rises over the battlefield on a damp summer morning, evoking the Napoleonic/Tolstoyan *soleil d'Austerlitz*, Lenartovich's unmartial eye picks up a (parenthetic) detail: "You could see the big beads of moisture on rifle butts and bayonets (some of them bloodied)."684 In another nod to Tolstoy, "the military situation depicted in *August 1914* seems like a parody of the one described on the patriotic pages of *War and Peace*. In both cases we see an empty land, with enemy troops ... encountering abandoned towns and villages."685 At the same time, the Tannenberg sections, like the epic as whole, contain relatively few defamiliarizing passages, though one example is the description of Vorotyntsev's operational sense: "A beautiful woman can feel a man's eyes on her without turning around and Vorotyntsev's flesh felt the ravening enemy tide racing toward the 2nd Army from the silent area of the map"686 (*Kak krasotka chutkim telom dazhe so spiny, ne ogliadyvaias', oshchushchaet muzhskie vzgliady,—tak telom chuvstvoval Vorotyntsev eti zhadnye volny vraga, tekushchie na Vtoruiu armiiu c nemoi chasti karty*).687

Instead, we encounter an abundance of minutely detailed depictions of the savagery of war. Dr. Fedonin explains to Lenartovich the effect of modern ordnance on human flesh:

Shrapnel wound in the belly with prolapsed stomach, intestines and caul hanging out, man's fully conscious, lives for several hours, keeps begging us to put some ointment on his belly, inside. ... Bullet right through the skull, part of the brain coming out."[688]

The war chapters in *November 1916* expand this list of horrors, as when Sanya tells Kotya:

> Say what you like, there is something demoniac, diabolical about asphyxiating gases. Earth is no place for this form of warfare. Those who kill with poison gas are no longer human. They don't even look human, especially at night, lit by shell bursts—those white rubber skulls, with square goggles and green proboscises.[689]

Inside the fog of war surprising convergences and intersections occur, of which the most intriguing is Vorotyntsev's chance encounter with the flamboyant François during the climactic phase of the German counteroffensive. The German general is traveling in his staff car accompanied by three aides, while Vorotyntsev and his Cossack escort plus Blagodev are on horseback: evidence of the technological gulf separating the two armies. Single combat on the valorial field of battle is a mythological rite, but here instead of a trial of strength we get a duel of wits, Germanic/Gallic sarcasm vs. a salty Russian earthiness: "Herr Colonel, I ought to take you prisoner!"[690]—"Wasn't it your car we nearly knocked out yesterday?"[691] Once again we perceive a link to the Schöngraben truce scene in *War and Peace* with its bantering Russian and French soldiers who at the end of their encounter emit "peals of such healthy and good-humored laughter ... that the only thing left to do seemed to be to unload the muskets, explode the ammunition, and all return home as quickly as possible."[692] In *August 1914* the same notion is expressed in less *homely* terms: "The German with the light machine gun still had time to shoot the lot of them. But that was impossible after their exchange of courtesies."[693]

Yet these residual timocratic norms of combat are fated to disappear, a development consequent to the accelerating process of coarsening and brutalization that would overcome Germany and Russia in subsequent years and decades. The experience of trench warfare makes Kotya lose his religion, and his Hegel:

> Where is it, then, this place for the departed soul when the bullet has finished off the body? Am I supposed to believe in those fairy stories about

the Second Coming, believe in the resurrection of the body, with Scipio Africanus, Louis XVI, and I myself, Konstantin Gulai, one of these days individually resurrected?"[694]

This is strong stuff, with Kotya's atheistic despair contrastively complementing the many passages that assert or imply the Christian ideal. As one commentator notes, Solzhenitsyn "transforms characters from believers to the not-so-devout and from atheists to converts."[695] And then there is Chernega, the bellicose peasant officer who "learned to enjoy his war"[696] and became really good at making it, so that he pursues the path of violence as to the manner born in a fabulatory trajectory that eventually brings him over to the Bolshevik side, the most violent faction in a land infected with violence.

The commander of Sanya's battery, Lieutenant Colonel Boyer, is one of several exemplary field officers depicted in the epic. Indeed, he is more exemplary than most: "He believed that an enthusiasm for war was a natural masculine characteristic and that it could be awakened and developed in any man."[697] Boyer's name is a unit of secret code, for his character is an affectionate tribute to Solzhenitsyn's own CO in World War II, Major Pavel *Boyev*, whom he would go on to depict in the binary story "Zhelyabuga Village" and the novella "Adlig Schwenkitten."

15

So who is Georgi Vorotyntsev, the epic's almost-protagonist? He is, above all, a *warrior*, a character type that is surprisingly uncommon in the stories and novels that made Solzhenitsyn famous. These earlier works feature plenty of war veterans like Ivan Denisovich, Kostoglotov or Nerzhin, but their military experiences do not define them, leaving their core sense of self largely unaffected. Such is not the case with Vorotyntsev, who always wanted to be a soldier: "I never had any doubts, I knew what I wanted from my childhood on."[698] To that boyhood ambition he soon added another: "From his youth on, Vorotyntsev had craved one thing above all else: to influence his country's history for good, to drag or hustle uncouth Russia along the road to better things."[699]

When we first meet him, the hero's identity is entirely vested in his calling as an officer and patriot, at the expense of his relationship with his unhappy wife, Alina, and his understanding of non-military subjects such as politics or literature except where they bear on the profession of arms. One scholar suggests that he "would have made an excellent Roman legionnaire."[700] Yet like

Solzhenitsyn's other truth-seekers, Vorotyntsev is a "born rebel,"[701] as his friend General Svechin informs him: a designation not often applied to career soldiers, though it is one that is entirely appropriate for this self-sovereign personality who insists on going against the grain of history. As we find out in the play *Prisoners*, the colonel will fight with the Whites against the Bolsheviks, serve under Franco in the Spanish civil war, join Vlasov's Russian Liberation Army during World War II, and meet his death on a Soviet gallows in the year 1945.

In Solzhenitsyn, dragons do allegorical duty as scaly stand-ins for communism and its acolytes. Appropriately therefore, the epic's chief fictional counterrevolutionary is named after the most famous dragon slayer of them all, St. George, whom Vorotyntsev holds in sacred regard. The surname "Vorotyntsev," which Alina dislikes because she finds it "ponderous,"[702] is a cognate to *povorachivat'* (to turn) and *vozvrashchat'sia* (to return) and hints at the political and romantic tergiversations experienced by the hero in the course of the saga. It also carries a proleptic intimation of *vorot* (neck). By gallicizing Georgi to *Georges*, his genteel life's companion lightens that bothersome onomastic weight. In contrast, the colonel's lover, Olda, opts for the German *Georg*, in amorous acknowledgment of his martial vocation and masculine strength. Clearly, she has picked up on Vorotyntsev's "German" sense of self. (Vera Vorotyntseva's given name means "faith," and so she correspondingly keeps faith with her brother as well as the object of her unspoken love, the self-effacing Dmitriev.)

Vorotyntsev is of a pleasingly rugged appearance, "about forty years old"[703] with "even teeth"[704] and "light gray eyes" that "flash fire" when he is excited.[705] The observant Kovynev adds to these generic details: "His face was framed by a vigorous, close-clipped, bristly, auburn beard. He seemed very sure of himself (once his wife had gone)."[706] Indeed, the hero has a commanding presence, as a resentful Lenartovich reluctantly recognizes: "A lieutenant colonel mounted on a restive horse suddenly rode onto the square, bellowing—as was *his* right: 'Who's in charge here?'"[707] By way of contrast, Georgi intermittently displays a rather charming propensity to blush, as when Olda interrogates him about the state of his marriage.[708]

The colonel's martial masculinity carries a metallic tinge. His body possesses an "iron heaviness,"[709] and in a rare moment of insight, Alina senses that her husband had "let his spirit get weighted down with chunks of iron and was drowning with them."[710] As Georgi falls in love with Olda, he imagines himself "as having mass, as a thing of burnished metal."[711] By the same order of ferrous description, the two women in his life see him as a chivalric figure, with all the armorial associations that this implies. Looking back on their courtship, Alina feels that the "frank and simple delight" he once took in her was reminiscent of "a knight,"[712] and Olda tells Georgi, "You are a Russian knight-errant."[713] There is a textual connection here to Stolypin, "a *preux chevalier* ... 'with visor raised.'"[714] With his little beard and knightly bearing, Vorotyntsev also recalls the cinematic Sologdin in *The First Circle*, though unlike the snobbish engineer, the colonel is scripted as an authentic version of a Russian gentleman-warrior.

A graduate of the elite General Staff academy where he networked with other "Young Turks,"[715] forward-thinking officers of his generation like Svechin, Vorotyntsev "had cherished for years the dream of strategic perfection"[716]—"the Russian Schlieffen manqué,"[717] Alina sneers—and he hopes to employ his gifts on the field of battle. Also for years, he subscribed to the Social Darwinist notion that war was "a trial of strength" between nations and that "it was the same with all living things on earth."[718] (Herbert Spencer has a lot to answer for.) The colonel does not share Generalissimo Suvorov and Count Tolstoy's conviction that "morale decides everything"[719] and advocates the scientific application of the principles of war over the traditional Russian reliance on élan and force of numbers. There is something in this character of Andrei Bolkonsky in *War and Peace*, another military high-flyer with a prosaic personality and a problematic marriage who dreamed of winning glory at the start of an earlier, and equally disastrous, foreign campaign. Twentieth-century warfare, however, precludes meteoric displays of Napoleonic genius even by ambitious officers of exemplary education, as Georgi himself recognizes. The best he can hope for is to transmit his insights to the tragic commander of Second Army, but the latter is too sluggish of body and mind to act, although he recognizes the colonel's professional worth. Vorotyntsev obtains Samsonov's permission to go on an inspection tour of the theater of operations, his martial peregrinations and observations framing the account of the Tannenberg campaign. In the end, Vorotyntsev's presence in the field yields minimal results. As the invading Russian forces crumble before the German onslaught, he directs the defence of Usdau, a village that lies directly in the path of François's counteroffensive, and after the enemy is victorious guides a few stragglers back to the Russian lines. In a moving scene, the group inters the body of Colonel Kabanov, CO of the Dorogobuzh Regiment, after an impromptu service conducted by Blagodarev "in the manner of a church deacon,"[720] which serves as a sacramental coda for the tragedy of Tannenberg.

Vorotyntsev is a born leader of men to whom others naturally gravitate:

> Under the command of this experienced colonel ... it is as if the whole of Russia escapes encirclement: walking together are the leftwing Lenartovich and Kharitonov, who chose to enter the tsar's service contrary to family tradition, Blagodarev, who embodies the best traits of the peasant, and the wily, strong, situationally clever ... but also equivocal and rather frightening Kachkin."[721]

Later in the epic, the two unsympathetic members of the group, Lenartovich and Kachkin, will separately look back on that episode with something like pride.[722]

Nonetheless, as Svechin points out, Vorotyntsev would have done more good if instead of tarrying at Tannenberg he had returned to Supreme Command headquarters in keeping with his original instructions. And when the hero finally gets there after that long and perilous trek he (somewhat unbelievably) confronts the generals who had presided over the catastrophe, telling General Zhilinsky, the ex-chief of the General Staff, "It was you who signed Russia's suicide note, Your Excellency!"[723] It comes as no surprise that the colonel's career is scuppered by this outburst and he is banished to a "far-off southwestern shoulder of the front,"[724] to assume command of an infantry regiment. As a token of this change in fortune, he takes up smoking in early middle age,[725] having given it up three years earlier.[726]

At his new posting in the Carpathian mountains, the hero is beloved by his men, and for the best of reasons: "Vorotyntsev had no equal when it came to keeping his subordinates alive."[727] He suffers two wounds and is transformed into the complete man of war, tempered to a metallic hardness, like the veterans in Ernst Jünger's autobiographical novel *Storm of Steel* (1920). Vorotyntsev: "And the more sordid and offensive stories about the rear filtered in ... the cleaner he felt in the atmosphere in the trenches, with men of pure heart around him, men ready to die from one hour to the next."[728] Yet unlike Jünger's ravaged characters, the colonel does not abjure the world beyond the trenches and retract into a heroic, existential emptiness, but broadens his horizons, historically. He decides that "this particular war [is] all wrong,"[729] as were Russia's earlier wars all the way back to the Crimean, which, however, "had to be fought."[730] The hero's retrospective pacifism is bolstered by the belief that Germany lacks "the muscle and the weight to conquer Russia."[731] The colonel is now determined "to save Russia, to save our roots, our race, our seed, so that it will not perish,"⁷³² and concludes that a separate peace is preferable to a continuation of hostilities: "The Germans will be only too glad of a respite. What little of our land they have, they'll evacuate.... We have to liberate Poland anyway—let the Germans sort it out."⁷³³ Once again, Vorotyntsev's lack of knowledge beyond his ken is telling. As well as the notion of a victorious Second Reich "sorting out" Poland, his defeatist counterfactual entails Germany's political dominion over Europe and economic dominion over Russia for decades to come. Yet even so, this alternative scenario has something to recommend it when matched against what actually happened in Russia in 1917–18 and thereafter, which is why the hero must articulate it, in obedience to the author's sovereign will. At the same time, the colonel shows a commendable reluctance to engage in the kind of conspirological thinking that was as prevalent in Russian society then as it is now: "He suspected that this was an example of ordinary human readiness to make farfetched accusations against remote and enigmatic personages."⁷³⁴

Warrior, patriot, and fighter against chaos, Vorotyntsev is the epic's necessary man. In *November 1916*, his support is solicited by two historical figures, the former speaker of the Duma, Aleksandr Guchkov, and the rightwing general, Aleksandr Nechvolodov, who are separately plotting against the imperial government to stave off a national collapse. Where military matters are concerned, this thoughtful officer is usually the epic's most knowledgeable voice, even when other uniformed and non-uniformed experts such as Svechin and Obodovsky are in possession of facts or insights that complement his own. On the other hand, Vorotyntsev is singularly lacking in intellectual curiosity, unlike the truth-seekers Sanya and Zinaida. Once the colonel decides to become politically engaged and gets to know Shingarev, Guchkov, and Olda, he finds their differing political outlooks and preferred courses of action confusing no end. As a public actor, Vorotyntsev can be ingenuous or worse: his virtues lie outside the home and the extramarital bed, and beyond the world of books. In fact, Georgi holds no-nonsense literary views: Dostoevsky, he opines, populates his novels with "too many epileptics"⁷³⁵ and Tolstoy's heroes just need to pull themselves together: "Take Pierre and Bolkonsky—you keep ... wondering what they stand for."⁷³⁶ Instead, the "born rebel" prefers characters that are "strong-minded,"⁷³⁷ that is, like himself. There is no subtlety here, but then, Vorotyntsev is not a subtle man.

A revealing moment occurs just after the hero confesses his affair to Alina. Seeking comfort in the magic of literature, she asks him to read to her from *Jane Eyre*, one of her favorite books, and sustained by a guilty conscience, the errant Georgi does so for three straight hours:

> It was a story about the loftiest of sentiments, written by a woman of noble sentiments, for other women of noble sentiments about yet another such woman, eager to do justice to the lofty sentiments of others and exhibit her own noble nature ... a sentimental story.[738]

This Vorotyntsev-centric passage with its epistrophes à la Tolstoy is wrong on every textological point. Granted, it is Alina's treacly take on Charlotte Brontë's novel that prompts Georgi's manful rejection of that classic work. Yet the colonel's inadequacy as a reader has no bearing on his status as the epic's guardian of order, functioning instead as a counter-indicator of his supreme adequacy as a soldier. In any case, some of Georgi's cultural gaps are filled by Olda, who assesses her lover's virtues and flaws in an amorously pedagogical manner:

> He was like a clever peasant lad who had never attended his village school because he was busy working in the fields, and so couldn't read or write. He thinks the letter J looks like a scythe and the letter C looks like a sickle, but had he been properly instructed, he'd be completing the final grade by now.[739]

To sum up Vorotyntsev's report card: Shows promise. Must try harder.

Like many a hero in many a novel, Vorotyntsev married the wrong woman. A provincial Russian belle, Alina filters her attitude to her husband through a mawkish schoolgirl sensibility:

> Georgi did not much resemble the ideal man whose image Alina had carried in her heart since her school days: there was nothing of Pechorin in him, none of that cruel and lofty contempt for the world and for women which makes the Pechorins irresistible.[740]

Alina's notions about Pechorin and the male sex, jejune that they are, are identical to those of Nadya Nerzhin in *Love the Revolution*, even if Vorotyntsev's unhappy partner in marriage happens to be a good decade older. Like Nadya, she is modeled on Natalya Reshetovskaya, though not the loving wife of the 1940s but the clinging spouse of the 1960s, and she is an accomplished pianist, again like Reshetovskaya. Alina is a domestic builder of nests in the style of Kitty Shcherbatsky, but with a cloying, *Gemütlichkeit* sensibility that she expects Georgi to share: in the Vorotyntsev household, the table mat is known as "the little spider" and the chest of drawers as "tubby."⁷⁴¹ The reader cringes in unison with the manly colonel. Alina also has an annoying line in baby talk: "Nice little housikins? Whose little hands did it all, then?"⁷⁴² With her husband away at the front, she sees herself as a "grass widow"⁷⁴³ and is oblivious to the dangers that he must face every day on the field of battle. Still, like most people who are in the habit of declaring, "I am an exceptional person,"⁷⁴⁴ Mrs. Vorotyntseva is in fact perfectly ordinary. After faithless Georgi spills the beans about his affair, she oscillates between threats of suicide and sudden flights from the marital home while a world war rages and revolution stalks the land: "She will burn with the brightest of flames! Her head was filled with ideas for rearranging the furniture in the apartment, and plans for insanity were taking shape."⁷⁴⁵

The Vorotyntsev siblings' wise old nanny thinks she knows where the problem lies: "So why is it, truly, that the two of you have no children? Your lives would have been very different," she tells Georgi and Vera,⁷⁴⁶ who is quietly in love with the quiet, but taken, Dmitriev. This childlessness motif recalls Kostoglotov in *Cancer Ward* and Nerzhin in *The First Circle*. Unlike Alina, whose unfulfilled longing to be a mother lies at the root of her unhappiness, iron-souled Vorotyntsev is not, deep down, truly family minded: "He knew that children were supposed to be life's greatest joy ... but it was a tie he did not need himself."⁷⁴⁷ The Russian text reads: *Obiazatel'nym obriadom znal, chto deti—tsvety zhizni* ("He accepted the established view that children were the flowers of life").⁷⁴⁸ The colonel's reliance on this botanical bromide, which is derived from Gorky's story "Creatures That Were Once Men" ("Byvshie liudi"; 1899), is an effective instance of characterization by cliché. After all, Vorotyntsev is no book lover. In fact, as we saw, his literary tastes are downright embarrassing—in their own way, as unformed and uninformed as Alina's, who in a characteristically clueless moment decides that her stolid spouse is an incarnation of the demonic gambler Hermann from "Queen of Spades": "Maybe Georgi was like Pushkin's hero, except that his passion was not cards—but what? Maps, perhaps"⁷⁴⁹ (*Mozhet byt', Zhorzh i est'—pushkinskii Germann, tol'ko karty u nego—topograficheskie?*).⁷⁵⁰

Vorotyntsev's marriage to Alina and romance with Olda generate much of the epic's novelistic content. The colonel's connection to his lover begins before it begins, as it were. After a hard day's riding and worrying about the progress of Samsonov's offensive, he retires for the night in an abandoned house and has a dream about a beautiful stranger, "the inexpressible dear one, who was all women to him."⁷⁵¹ In the midst of war, Georgi's eternal feminine pays him a visit. Or is this his Jungian anima, acting true to archetype? In any case, Vorotyntsev's erotic dream is one of a number of private premonitions that punctuate the narrative to adumbrate a character's destiny while confirming the epic's mystic orientation. The hero's vision comes true, as we know it must, when two years later stalwart Georgi and brainy Olda meet at a gathering in Shingarev's apartment and are instantly attracted to each other. There follow eight days of secret trysts that reveal the lovers' erotic compatibility and intellectual complementarity. Alone together in the professor's book-lined flat, Olda of the "featherlike touch"[752] and Vorotyntsev of the "shaggy, battle-hardened breast" metaphorize into a "spirited rider"[753] spurring her "faithful steed" on a passion-filled "gallop"[754] that carries them away from the realities of the moment, if only for a moment. Actually, the lovers are not quite alone: the "Author's Note" in *November 1916* warns that "Andozerskaya is ... a vehicle for the views on monarchy of Professor Ivan Aleksandrovich Ilyin."[755] The pundit's goateed visage pops up on the extramarital pillow whenever the lovers' "languid" talk[756] turns to the big questions and Olda starts holding forth: "That's all these people have—their religion and the Tsar."[757] And: "Monarchy is a reproduction in miniature of the universal order."[758] And: "Lay one finger on the throne—and you'll start a landslide."[759] Still, though the professor's ventriloquizations of Ilyin make this *affaire de coeur* occasionally crowded, the week that Georgi spends with his lover becomes his first holiday from history.

Within a few weeks Olda finds herself falling in love and begins to acquire, by a process of erotic osmosis, a metallic quality herself, "turning from a kitten into a wedge-shaped iron [*utiug klinovidnyi*],"[760] though the domestic trope carries no housewifely associations. At the same time, she pictures the colonel as a "warm, silly log,"[761] an image that conjoins the fond with the phallic. As for Vorotyntsev, after eight years of unexciting matrimony he is enthralled by this alluring woman, though as the relationship evolves he finds her pedagogical ways increasingly vexing: Ilyin is not the best kind of aphrodisiac.

After he begins the affair, Vorotyntsev feels he is "vibrating"[762] in unison with the *metal* gong that hangs on Olda's wall. His once dormant erotic self is now awake and alert: "The world seemed new—especially the women in it."[763] Minutes after Georgi thinks this exciting thought he finds himself staring at a young girl, her "exquisitely molded form clad in a golden ankle-length dress, with long luxuriant hair falling in two cascades down her back."[764] This is Likonya, scripted as a dark-tressed version of Blok's Stranger as she enters Cubat's restaurant, a fashionable Petrograd establishment. Vorotyntsev even gives this exquisite creature the eye—"he did not find it improper to let his gaze linger just a little longer"[765]—though the manly hero recoils at the sight of Likonya's escort "with his neat tiers of gray ringlets [and] a hint ... of lipstick."[766] The coiffure and the makeup prompt this snappish comment to Svechin, inspired, no doubt, by unacknowledged male envy: "Imagine it—a milksop like that—when we're at war. I'd like to double him through the communication trenches with his head between his knees."[767]

Meanwhile in Moscow, Alina suspects, seethes, and broods. The recipient of her melodramatic confidences, the emotionally clever Susanna Korzner, offers Mrs. Vorotyntseva some sage advice: "There is a contradiction between his air of a man unpolished, a soldier on leave, that confident demeanor and penetrating gaze, and his hesitant conduct in this entire matter. Perhaps his feelings for his new object of affection are not as strong as they seem."[768] Indeed, the danger may lie entirely elsewhere. In his youth, Georgi was once overcome by a wild passion for the serene, amiable, and married Kalisa, but his advances were unamiably rejected. Vorotyntsev meets up with his old flame, who is now conveniently widowed, during the days and nights of the revolution, when he finds himself torn between his desire for Olda and his spousal obligation to Alina. There follows a sensual encounter, which once again takes the colonel out of public circulation, though this time just for a couple of days. Georgi's second erotic sabbatical is a psychologically believable, if not particularly admirable, act. The text, however, elevates this rather inglorious interlude to a metaphorical national plane via his indirectly rendered thoughts. The embodiment of voluptuous blonde beauty in the merchant style, Kalisa and her soothing ways become a carnal substitute for the hero's "native redeeming soil, but softer, warmer, more hospitable than ordinary soil. Only by keeping this woman close, clinging to her and pouring himself into her could he overcome his sickness and recover his health, from inside her body."[769] One is reminded of another widow with a nurturing disposition, Agafia Pshenitsyna in *Oblomov*, who gifted that novel's ill-starred protagonist a measure of final happiness. I am inclined to agree with Andrei Nemzer that earthy Kalisa may be the one true love of Georgi's life,[770] a novelistic situation par excellence. The epic leaves it unresolved, as it does all its others romantic subplots.

One of them involves the unspoken love between the colonel's sister, Vera, and the diffident engineer Dmitriev, who lives in a common law marriage with a "half-crazed ether-sniffer"[771] and her young, timorous daughter from a previous liaison: Dostoevsky updated for the early twentieth century. Then there is Likonya's self-abnegating devotion to lusty Polshchikov, whose child she longs to carry. Over in Moscow, Yarik Kharitonov tries to rid himself of a sudden, semi-incestuous attraction to Ksenia by spending the night with Wilma, a dark-haired Latvian wanton whom his fervid imagination transforms into a "firebird" in a crimson shawl[772] even as he rents her body for a few rubles, hours before catching the train that will carry him back to the front. By daybreak he has fallen in love with his Baltic siren, but the saga ends before we find out if the relationship has a future, or indeed if it was a relationship at all.

Though Vorotyntsev remains skeptical of Olda's Ilyinesque attachment to the throne, the lovers are of one mind where their indifference to children is concerned. Characteristically, Olda communicates her views on the subject in the form of a little lecture: "A child turns its mother into an exclusively custodian figure, which freezes all creativity and precludes the development of one's personality."[773] (Yet Olda obviously, and Solzhenitsyn certainly, had never read Simone de Beauvoir.) Despite her habit of channeling Ilyin, that patriarch of neo-feudalism, the professor believes as much as Kollontai that women ought to have equal rights with men within and outside marriage, even if she does not share the Bolshevist virago's opinion that prostitutes are "the most magnificent specimens of womanhood."[774] As Vorotyntsev gets to know his lover better, he learns that she is as manipulative as she is clever. And she does tend to go on like a professor at the lectern: "True, Olda knew a great deal, but in a very pedagogical way, turning what could be interesting into something slightly boring."[775] More to the point, she starts to nag and pout, like a clinging wife, but Georgi already has one of those.

At this point in the proceedings, the colonel can still be occasionally expansive in speech and thought, and during that encounter with his first love, Kalisa, he pours out his heart in a way that he never did with Alina or even Olda, but as the saga moves toward its conclusion his voice grows increasingly terse. Here is the hero in *April 1917* after another of his tiffs with Mrs. Vorotyntseva, which has left him bewildered in that classically clueless, male-matrimonial manner:

> Shagal v shtab, na khodu pytaias' umerit'sia.
> Chto zh on mog bol'she?
> On potushil—vsë. On—vernulsia. Chto eshchë?
> Sebia samogo. Zhivogo. Neuzheli malo?[776]
> He walked to HQ, trying to calm himself down.
> What else could he have done?
> He had put an end to it all. He had gone back. What else was there?
> His own self. Alive. Wasn't that enough?

The last of these micro-paragraphs is a stark instance of parataxis, that is, *On vernul ei* Sebia samogo, *prichëm* Zhivogo. Neuzheli *ei etogo* malo?—"He had given back to her *His own self*, and he was still *Alive*. Why *Wasn't that enough*?" It is as if the colonel is still at his regimental command post sending out telegraph messages. As for the question itself, the answer, alas, is *nyet*. Though he has broken off the affair with Olda for the sake of his marriage, or Russia, or peace of mind, Alina remains as unhappy and clamorous as ever.

16

Among the epic's many instances where public events or persons are fabulously refracted by the vox populi, there is one that occurs in *March 1917*. A housemaid reports her impressions of a political rally she had attended, her words carrying an ineffably sinister ring: "There's talk about *the old red-haired one*. ... And peregrines of the world, flocking together" [*O kakom-to* starom ryzhem *govoriat ... I—pereletaite vsekh stran, sobiraites'*]."⁷⁷⁷ The mysterious ancient is Vladimir Ilyich Ulyanov-Lenin, who heads a small Marxist faction colloquially known as the Bolsheviks, and two revolutions plus two decades ago he was the owner of a distinctive ginger mop. Though absent from Russia since 1908, during which period his influence on the situation there was minimal, the Bolshevik leader's image and words are now percolating down the strata of popular culture. He returns first as an occult phantom of street rumor, before his physical arrival at Petrograd's Finland Station in *April 1917*.

The Lenin of *The Red Wheel* would have been instantly recognizable to the epic's pre-scripted audience of Soviet-era readers, for whom he was a ubiquitous fact or fiction of life, in forms that were either visual (sculptures, portraits, posters, films) or printed (mandatory Marxism-Leninism lectures, mandatory Mayakovsky poems). The saga appropriates this multimedia Lenin Text and fictively edits and re-contextualizes it while employing the Leader's oh-so-familiar writing style as the governing diegetic mode in the chapters where he is the central presence. Solzhenitsyn's treatment of Lenin represents a creative extrapolation of extant cultural productions, but it is equally informed by the author's archival and ambulant researches: during his two-year sojourn in Zurich, he spent many days exploring the urban and nature locales associated with Lenin's Swiss domicile in 1914–17.

The Red Wheel turns the figure of political myth into a historicized literary character. Driven by a nihilistic loathing of imperial Russia, or even Russia itself, *this* Lenin, the author once commented, is "diabolically clever, boundlessly evil, and a condemned criminal."⁷⁷⁸ He will say anything and do anything to advance his goal: the revolution. As a fervent anti-patriot and global agent of chaos, the Bolshevik boss is a vocal contributor to the discourse of hate articulated by lesser revolutionary personages, for example, the Lenartovich aunties and nephew, or the thumping tinsmith Zhora:

> The press ... often gave figures of Russian casualties. Lenin always looked for these figures and made a mark by them—with surprise and satisfaction. The bigger the figures, the happier they made him: all those soldiers killed, wounded, or taken prisoner were stakes falling out of absolutism's fence and leaving the monarchy weaker.[779]

The Leader's violent thoughts echo Lenartovich's fulminations to Dr. Fedonin in *August 1914*, but where Sasha's rants are an expression of a generalized hatred of tsarist Russia, Lenin's enmity toward his homeland is disciplined and doctrinaire.

In a procedure that recalls the treatment of Stalin in *The First Circle*, the future successor to the tsars is ethnically othered. We learn about his "Mongol eyes"[780] and the "Kalmyk saber"[781] of his rhetoric; Lenin's native Russian is, to his own ears, a "semi-Tartar tongue,"[782] while Willi Münzenberg, a young German acolyte, thinks of him (approvingly) as "that Asiatic with wild ideas."[783] The ideas in question are of a homicidal cast. Like many a bookish intellectual, Lenin is intoxicated by the notion of violence in a good cause: "Knuckle-dusters! Clubs! Gasoline-soaked rags! Spades! Guncotton! Barbed wire! Nails (for use against mounted police)! ... Climb to the upper stories of buildings and rain stones down on the troops! Pour boiling water on them! Keep acid up there to pour on the police!"[784]

The Bolshevik boss is not the charismatic of legend: "Almost completely bald, in his shabby suit, with his sharp features, his habit of looking uneasily over his shoulder, and his neglected beard, he really did look rather like a spy."[785] The epic's deconstruction of Lenin is a multipronged affair that extends beyond the political and ideological to the anatomical. His corporeal self always looms large, much more so than that of Stolypin, the saga's other preeminent historical actor, whose body becomes fully textualized only when he is resting on his deathbed. The socialist sachem's most distinctive physical feature is his ball-like head (*shar golovy*).[786] Its preternaturally large size and kitchen-pot shape constitute one of the saga's Leninist motifs, a cranial signature shared by his revolutionary ally and rival Parvus as well as by his soon-to-be follower Chernega. The high-brow, high-strung émigré rues his lack of exercise: "Walking and scrambling about in the mountains or trampling the streets of Zurich were the only ways Lenin had of dissipating and soothing the ache of unused muscles."[787] Those walks and scrambles were meticulously reenacted by the empirical author, as noted above.

Most important, Solzhenitsyn's antihero is all talk, all the time. Nowhere else in the oeuvre does the author employ his skills as a pasticheur to better effect than in this multi-chapter riff on the Leader's pleonastic, juddering, lurching idiolect, which is signposted by a forest of exclamation points. Lenin's "Marxist vernacular"[788] is an oscillating vociferation of quotes from *The Communist Manifesto*, fluctuant dogmas of his own device, Bolshevik bluster, and points of order addressed to the workers of the world, united. Often it takes the form of "slogans ready to use"[789] with a political shelf life of a few weeks or days, for example, "Don't you realize that Switzerland is the most revolutionary country in the world??!"[790] or later, "We should have tried to bring about a revolution not in Switzerland, but in Sweden! Start it all from there!"[791] Such dictums are part of the Leninist rhetoric of repetition: "Keep hitting the same spot, over and over again, varying the words only slightly—that's the first rule of propagandists and preachers."[792] The statement reads like a paraphrase of *Mein Kampf*: "The most brilliant propagandist technique will yield no success unless one fundamental principle is borne in mind constantly and with unflagging attention. It must confine itself to a few points and repeat them over and over."[793]

Lenin's febrile intellect zooms in on the revolutionary politics of the moment or goes off on world-historical or homely what's-for-dinner tangents, with his occasional impressions of Switzerland and occasional impressions of his wife thrown in for good biographical measure. Once in a while the narration elides, via hybrid utterances and heteroglossic sleights of text, into an implied-authorial polemic with the wordy antihero that reverberates with mordant sarcasm, as in: "… The compelling power which manifested itself through him, and of which he was only the infallible interpreter, who always knew precisely what was right just for today, and indeed by the evening was not always quite what it had been in the morning."[794] We also learn that all this talk, talk, talk and hate, hate, hate is transmitted in a voice that "is tense, but lacking in resonance—it seems always to get lost in his chest, his larynx, or his mouth, and it slurs the r's."[795] Alexander Zholkovsky identifies a connection between Lenin's logorrhea as recorded in *The Red Wheel*, and other "maniacal discourses" such as Napoleon's in *War and Peace*, Pozdnyshev's in *The Kreutzer Sonata*, and the anonymous protagonist's in *Notes from the Underground*.[796]

Inside this human "whirlwind"[797] or vortex all personal relations are subsumed, including Lenin's marriage to the docile Nadezhda Krupskaya, a socialist drudge who can neither cook nor coo but is the world's most faithful Bolshevik. Nature or art or literature leave him unmoved except as a means to relax in the midst of the struggle. Even the death of his mother is but a regrettable development to be registered and acknowledged, nothing more. An ascetic of the proletarian Cause, Lenin masochistically mortifies his manuscripts, finding it "much pleasanter to handle the cheapest of envelopes, to write on the cheapest of paper."[798] As depicted, he comes close to the fanatical ideal set forth in Sergei Nechaev's "Cathechism of a Revolutionist" (1869), fragments of which were recalled by Varya as she ogled the infernal Zhora in *August 1914*. Close, that is, but not entirely: such a Nechaevian exemplar would never have made for an interesting literary character, as many a SocRealist novel has shown.

This is Lenin pondering his political moves as he consumes a meal of cold chicken and eggs in sight of his constant companion, Krupskaya:

> ... Kuba [Yakov Hanecki] had insisted that he should pay courtesy calls on Adler and Diamand, thank them all over again in person for obtaining his release.... Volodya smiled wryly, with specks of egg white and yolk around his mouth. It was certainly a tricky corner for him—having to go and make himself agreeable to moldy old revisionists, petit-bourgeois scum.[799]

The narration switches from its controlling Leninist register to a Krupskaya point of view, signaled by the diminutive "Volodya" and confirmed by the wifely descrying of the food particles that have attached themselves to the iconic visage, and then reverts back to Lenin's malevolent, Marxian perspective. In a marriage of long duration the spousal partners may attain a perfect congruence of thought, and the last sentence, which conveys the perceptions of Vladimir, or Nadezhda, or both, is a case in point.

The portrait is given texture by Lenin's foibles and eccentricities, his shabby domestic situation with ever-present shabby wife, but above all his passion for Inessa Armand, a revolutionary widow with five children and a red feather in her hat.[800] She is "the one person whose feelings he could not afford to hurt."[801] Thinking back on a performance of *La Dame aux camélias*, he deems it "unforgettable"[802] because he associates that classic tearjerker with the fragrant Inessa: perhaps the red camellia worn by the play's heroine reminds him of his lover's plume.

> Everything he had ever had in life—food, drink, clothes, house and home—had been not for *him*, indeed he had wanted nothing of all this

except as a means of keeping himself going for the sake of the Cause. ... Only Inessa, although she had entered his life through the Cause ... existed as if for him alone, complementing his existence with her own.[803]

Yet even so, "He could not, he had no right to let himself be slowed down and taken out of his way by those children,"[804] that is, the quintet of junior Armands, contrary to the Soviet notion of a twinkling Grandpa Lenin surrounded by a troop of tots and tykes, as depicted in sundry paintings by sundry SocRealist artists.

Alone among the swarm of followers, fellow travelers, and foes that inhabit Lenin's twilight world, the Russian-Jewish-German millionaire and conspirator Alexander Parvus remains to him a puzzle: "With this man alone he felt unsure of himself. He did not know whether he could stand up to Parvus as an enemy."[805] A puppet master pulling the strings of chaos on a global scale, he is the epic's Stavro Blofeld, whom he also resembles in his cosmopolitan background ("mother Odessa" and "stepmother Germany"),[806] high IQ, and gigantic girth, though not in his "dissipated ways."[807] For Parvus is a flamboyant sensualist whose "unwieldy body ... loved its bottle of champagne before breakfast, its leisurely bath, its little suppers with the ladies."[808] To the compendium of terrorist types described in Dostoevsky's *Devils*, *The Red Wheel* adds a new category, the sybaritic nihilist: "Parvus ... in possession of the riches he had so desired, and with them every imaginable carnal delight."[809]

The epic's most striking instance of indiciality, or experimental historiography, occurs in *November 1916*, chapters forty-seven to fifty, where a documented encounter between Lenin and Parvus is moved by authorial legerdemain from 1915 to 1916, and from Bern to Zurich, and is reconfigured as a "diabolical duet"[810] complete with occult transformations, transfusions, and levitations. In his memoir *Between Two Millstones*, Solzhenitsyn comments on this scene in carefully weighed terms:

> In 1916 there was no personal meeting in Zurich, just an exchange of letters. Therefore I had to set aside my usual realism and employ a fantastic device, allowing the correspondence to metamorphose, as it were, into a dialogue by means of a piece of devilry [*chertovshchina*]: a messenger brings with him not just a letter but a miniaturized Parvus inside a case. The fantasy lies solely in the device of his distension, manifestation, and, following the conversation, disappearance, whereas the entire Lenin-Parvus dialogue and the clash of their thoughts and plans are presented as real and are in full conformity with the historical truth.[811]

The author actually deprecates the imaginative scintillations of his own text, preferring to stress its factual accuracy and pragmatic function. Yet the scene is much more interesting than Solzhenitsyn suggests. For example, here is Lenin assailed by a sense of déjà vu even as he finds himself in the midst of this hallucinatory—surreal—experience: "It was just like the last time. Perhaps it *was* the last time? ... In Bern, in the room he rented from a housewife? Or was he in his room in the Zurich cobbler's house? Or not in a room at all? He seemed to be hearing it all for a second time."[812] We sense the bafflement felt by the militantly matter-of-fact antihero at this prima facie violation of the laws of physics. The Lenin-centered passage I quoted is also a diegetically actualized expression of the uchronic shift that is occurring in the fictive present.

The red magic begins when an elegantly dressed Vladimir Sklarz, one of Parvus's familiars, arrives in the Ulyanovs' Zurich apartment carrying a "light traveling salesman's case made of crocodile skin or maybe hippopotamus hide"[813] as well as the aforementioned letter, which is spelled out in block capitals on "thick vellum, crested."[814] As the weary host sits there reading this screed, "Parvus's hippopotamus blood spurted from the letter into Lenin's feverish hands, poured into his veins, swirled threateningly in his bloodstream."[815] The Parvus-to-Lenin body fluid transfer has commenced. More red magic: a kerosene lamp lights up seemingly by itself, the diminutive Sklarz shrinks to the size of a "little bird,"[816] and the case becomes "as big as a pig."[817] Next, Parvus materializes out of the now voluminous valise and assumes his full, sartorially splendid, corporeally revolting form: "There he stood, life-sized, in the flesh, with his ungovernable belly, the elongated dome of his head, the fleshy bulldog features, the little imperial, looking at Lenin with pale watchful eyes."[818] The room and everything inside it recedes from the Leader's fevered imaginings, and he finds himself in his old digs in Bern. Parvus "with all his pudgy immensity"[819] crowds Lenin's personal space on a "massive Swiss iron bed, with the two of them upon it, great men both, floating above a world pregnant with revolution."[820] Homoerotic?—perhaps. Phantasmagorical?—certainly. The floating conspirators, one brittle and slight, the other secretory and obese, and both of them grotesquely macrocephalic, touch heads across time and space to plot and to plan, but also to quarrel about strategy, tactics, and points of Marxist doctrine (as laid down in their respective writings). Parvus *presses* Lenin to accept his offer of German gold: "With money in your hands, power will be yours!"[821] Enraptured by his vision of a fallen empire, the elephant man cries out, "I AM SETTING THE DATE OF THE RUSSIAN REVOLUTION FOR JANUARY 22 NEXT YEAR!,"[822] his orgasmic howl set in all caps, like his letter. The "master plan"[823] for the destruction of the Russian Empire by a triple alliance of "the Central Powers, the Russian Revolutionaries, and the border peoples"[824] is taking form. But first Lenin must accept his designated place in this Machiavellian scheme as the German government's agent of choice. Meanwhile Parvus recalls biographical details of a private nature including a romance with Rosa Luxemburg, who however "had been ashamed of him—because of his appearance perhaps."[825] As the occult congress continues, the two eggheads disparage each other's street fighting man credentials: "Why did you lose heart so quickly in the Peter-Paul Fortress—was it the solitary confinement, the dampness?" sneers Lenin.[826] "Anybody would think you had fought on the barricades!" jibes Parvus.[827] Before long he is directly "pumping ... his hippopotamus blood"[828] into the Bolshevik chieftain who, though impressed by the "soundness and desirability" of "this grandiose program,"[829] is reluctant to play his assigned subordinate part. Later in the scene the bed lands back on the floor and Lenin's otherworldly caller is "catapulted upright on his fat columnar feet,"[830] but the revolutionary fracas goes on as visitor and host, or incubus and succubus, continue to squabble. Finally, the greenish Parvus transforms into a "streak of bluish mist" and "[seeps] through the window."[831] He is followed by Sklarz with case and a few moments later Sklarz's hat, which "whisked itself off the table and flung itself after them."[832] The Bolshevik boss "had preserved his greatest treasure—his honor as a Socialist,"[833] that is, his independence of action. The offer of German assistance, however, will be accepted, though on Lenin's, not Parvus's, terms: "In this alliance he would be the coy bride, not the eager bridegroom."[834]

Lenin's secret visitor, we are repeatedly told, is a figurative hippopotamus or, in Russian, *begemot*. In *Faust*, Mephistopheles materializes in the form of a black canine who accompanies the hero to his study (see Parvus's "bullgog features"), where he briefly assumes the aspect of a "hippo"[835] (*Welch ein Gespenst bracht ich ins Haus! / Schon sieht er wie ein Nilpferd aus*).[836] Solzhenitsyn certainly knew his Goethe! The revolutionary "moneybags"[837] Parvus is a shape-shifting, Mephistophelean tempter, his bank as bad as his bite, whose Boschian associates include the specter of communism *and* the gnomes of Zurich. See also the beast Behemoth: "Lo now, his strength *is* in his loins and his force *is* in the navel of his belly" (Job 40:16). This biblical verse fits Parvus to a B. Perhaps, then, Solzhenitsyn's Lenin can be read as Behemoth's counterpart, the beast Leviathan (Job 40:15–41:26), with additional Hobbesian interconnections. Either way, the episode of the floating bed directs one's thoughts to *The Master and Margarita*, in which the devil visits early Soviet Moscow in the guise of Woland, a glamorous foreign gentleman, who is accompanied by a colorful retinue of demons that includes the gigantic black cat Begemot. The hippo-Parvus of *The Red Wheel* may well be infernally related to Faust's Satanic corruptor or Woland's feline familiar, but beyond these cross-textual links one discerns a commonality of authorial agendas, or even visions: "Mephistopheles [with] his cowardly legions of fat devils."[838] And: "Bulgakov identified strongly with Woland and his unlimited satirical possibilities."[839] And: "Mockery of materialism in all its forms."[840]

Beast or not, the Bolshevik leader is the epic's most dynamically scripted character: one gets a sense of a passionate engagement of author with subject, even when Lenin is levitating. Zholkovsky notes "the thematic echoes and textual coincidences between the portraits of the two lone wolves of the underground."[841] In fact, the notion that Solzhenitsyn was in some crypto-autobiographical sense depicting himself in Leninist disguise has always enjoyed wide currency. Schmemann comments about *Lenin in Zurich*: "This book was written by a 'twin,' and written with a kind of tragic admiration [for Lenin]."[842] Dmitry Bykov confidently asserts, "*Lenin in Zurich* is less a pamphlet than a self-portrait."[843] Boris Paramonov, however, reminds us that "people who say this forget or do not even know that in art, every portrait is a self-portrait. Such are the mechanisms of art."[844] Mark Lipovetsky adds to this spectrum of scholarly responses: "Lenin is undoubtedly Solzhenitsyn's antihero (his hero is always the author's alter ego), therefore the similarity between the writer and the image of Lenin he creates becomes an effective instrument for the deconstruction of the cultural myth of Solzhenitsyn."[845]

As for the author's own position, over the years he made statements that agreed, in whole or in part, with every one of these interpretations. In 1974, that is, long before the entirety of the sequence of Lenin chapters was completed, the writer told Schmemann:

> He [Lenin] and I have a great deal in common. It's just that our principles are different. In moments of pride I truly feel I am the anti-Lenin. So I say to myself, let me blow up his cause so not a stone of it remains. ... But to do this, you need to be like him: a taut string, an arrow. ... After all, isn't it symbolic that he traveled from Zurich to Moscow, and I from Moscow to Zurich.[846]

Even more strikingly, a year or so later Solzhenitsyn confided to the same source, "I am Lenin ...,"[847] his version of *Madame Bovary, c'est moi*. Elsewhere the novelist claimed that his Lenin was just as much, or as little, a textualization of the authorial self as the sympathetic Shukhov ("Ivan Denisovich"), unsympathetic Rusanov (*Cancer Ward*) and Yakonov (*The First Circle*), or semi-sympathetic Podduev (*Cancer Ward*).[848]

The full truth of the matter is even more interesting. In *The Journal of "R-17,"* his chronicle of the writing of *The Red Wheel*, Solzhenitsyn explains (entry for February 27, 1975):

> On the wooden wall of my chalet in Sternenberg [an environ of Zurich] I have pinned several portraits of Ilyich, so that as I write I might have a better sense of it all and can pick out the traits I need, but the result made me think of a village reading room inside a log cabin, it was that ridiculous. Yet for three days now a single photograph looms larger than the rest: so much malevolence, perspicacity, and strength. He *sees* my conception and cannot (can he?) thwart it. A posthumous torment for him, an earthly contest for me.[849]

And in a subsequent entry, he adds: "For three weeks there he was, hanging on my wall in the mountains, watching me with hatred and fear as I was working."[850] Hints of "The Portrait" ("Portait"; 1833), Gogol's tale of demonic possession, Spivakovsky suggests,[851] though *The Picture of Dorian Grey* also comes to mind. In any case, far from being hexed by that diabolical photo, Solzhenitsyn used it as a mystical prop and a counter-source of artistic inspiration. His writerly magic turned out to be stronger than Lenin's revolutionary kind.

17

The scenes of revolutionary anarchy in *March 1917* and *April 1917* counterpoise the war chapters in the first two Knots, though the scale and intensity of the violence that erupts across the country does not begin to compare with those "versts of humiliation, sweat and death"[852] suffered by the imperial Russian army in East Prussia, Poland, and the Carpathians. One commentator, Yakov Lurié, discerns a contradiction in Solzhenitsyn's historiographical stance:

> Why and how did this revolution occur? If, when relating the events that lead up to it, Solzhenitsyn goes out of his way to emphasize the role of individual personalities such as, on the one hand, Stolypin and on the other, the talentless generals who were inspired by Tolstoy's ideas, when the author moves on to the outbreak of the revolution itself he depicts these [later] events, in contradiction of his predicated position, as being entirely spontaneous and shows that no one was capable of giving them direction. … The novelist, instead of confuting Tolstoy, confirms his views.[853]

So let us examine the epic's representation of the revolution of February 1917.

In Solzhenitsyn's telling, the February Revolution was a series of bloody street riots which the imperial authorities were too inept or craven to crush while the equally ineffectual opposition elites plotted to remove the tsar from his throne and tried to coopt the marching masses. The loss of authority by those in authority, and the discrete stages by which this happened, is depicted time and again, first of all in the case of Nicholas II, but also his ministers and generals as well as pro-government members of the Duma. Special emphasis is laid on the sudden collapse of discipline in the ranks, with concomitant massacres and looting, particularly among the men of the Petrograd garrison. With Nicholas going, going, gone, the parliamentary leaders assumed the mantle of power, though only *provisionally* and incompletely, and in competition with the newly constituted Petrograd Soviet. The proximate cause of the revolution was not hunger or military defeat, but a countrywide breakdown in the people's respect for the government and the very notion of political authority as such. The ultimate cause, however, was the national memory lapse described in that authorial formula, "Men have forgotten God." A medical orderly's drunken rant illustrates this programmatic point: "I'm not afraid even of God Himself! And all conscientious soldiers are on my side."[854] Here, as elsewhere, *The Red*

Wheel records how the violent rhetoric of the revolutionary parties was readily absorbed by the proletarian and soldierly masses, who enthusiastically regurgitated it as half-baked bluster and bombast.

The epic describes the crowds' behavior as well as the actions of Russia's rulers and politicians with the same degree of historiographical precision and the same careful balance between the individual character presences and the grand sweep of events with which it earlier depicted the imperial army in battle. Landmarks such as the palaces of Petrograd and Moscow's Kremlin serve as topographical points of reference. The chaos of revolution exhibits a surreal aspect, for example, "The entire crowd pulsated like a liquid lump" (*Vsia tolpa kolykhalas', kak zhidkaia glyba*)."[855] In a phantasmagorical moment, the tsar's brother, Grand Duke Mikhail Aleksandrovich, flees the Winter Palace in the dead of night, passing through

> hall after hall hung with paintings. As he hurried along with only a lantern to light the way, he was unable to see them properly or even to recognize any of them, and besides, Mikhail found himself confused by these halls with their gigantic, dimly visible still lifes and canvasses showing a variety of beasts or arrangements of dead game, fish and fruit, an extravagant, monumentally shrill abundance that brought no joy to his aching soul.[856]

A novelistic investigation of how assorted misfits and mavericks, brought together and guided by a malevolent intelligence, can turn into terroristic fiends was carried out by Dostoevsky in *Devils* half a century earlier, with appropriately proleptic relevance. *The Red Wheel*, however, does not dwell on the *operative* connection between the collective loss of religious faith and the Grand Guignol of the revolution: the sadistic outrages committed by the mobs, the nihilism of the professional extremists, the fecklessness of politicians across the ideological spectrum, or the false-Paschal street celebrations accompanied by frenetic bell-ringing and the exchange of the traditional Easter kiss, which begin concurrently with the violence and spread together with it across the land. All we have is a passage in which Father Severyan ponders the pernicious effects of the globalizing Age of Reason on his homeland:

> For almost two centuries now a fashionable, worldwide atheism, after first entering Russia via the intellects of Catherine's grandees, has been seeping all the way down to the sons of the village priests, flowing into every institution of educated society and washing away its religious faith.[857]

He goes on to observe that the Church had fallen "under the hand of the state" and had "majestically ossified,"[858] while more recently "a young generation" of "cruel and godless louts"[859] had arisen in the countryside, but the cerebral padre declines to pursue this line of inquiry any further. On the same note of ultimate incomprehension, Yarik Kharitonov, a rooted son of the south, thinks this dark thought: "It was as if someone had recited a pernicious anti-prayer over the whole of Russia ... a prayer not against sin but for sin."[860] The young officer is left with a single feeble hope: "If only they would come to their senses and rid themselves of this drunken haze!"[861] That's two ifs for the price of one. Meanwhile, "The dead bodies gave off a strong smell of alcohol."[862]

Corpses and chimes. The epic's campanological theme may be the only element it shares with the novels of Dorothy Sayers and her bell-ringing detective Lord Peter Wimsey, who doubtless would have been offended by "the guffaws of the bells of revolution,"[863] that is, the gongs of Hell. Here is Varsonofiev hearkening to their cacophony, the soundtrack of a nation's collapse:

> During the sixty years he had lived in Moscow, all of them in the same place, Varsonofiev had heard his share of pealing and tolling bells. This ringing, however, was not only unexpected and in contravention of the church calendar—this was the Friday of the third week of Lent—but made one think of a debauchee in the company of decent folk or a drunk surrounded by teetotalers. The clanging was prolonged, sometimes insistent, sometimes hollow, but always discordant, untidy, and crude. Those were not ringers who were working the bells. ... It was as if a horde of Tatars had climbed every steeple in Russia and had started pulling at the bell ropes.[864]

The passage is saturated with similes, which drive home the historiographical point. The latter is reiterated on multiple textual occasions, as when Ksenia Tomchak, who by now has recovered her faith, forms the impression that "the ringing was somehow counterfeit,"[865] a token or tocsin of the Great Lie that is descending upon the land. To quote Robert Walpole apropos the War of Jenkins' Ear, whose picayune beginnings were as grotesque as Russia's false dawn of liberty, "They may ring their bells now, before long they will be wringing their hands."

Unlike Ksenia, many of the epic's rooted, national personalities have definitively seceded from the Church or at least from its liturgical practices and rituals. In *November 1916*, as Vorotyntsev drives through the Kremlin, he imagines prostrating himself before the Cathedral of the Annunciation, yet he is too embarrassed to even make the sign of the cross in public.[866] In the same novel, Blagodarev's village neighbors call on him after he comes home on leave, but "only old Ilyukha ... crossed himself before the icons as they entered."[867] Yet only in the case of a few characters with mayhem on their mind such as Sasha Lenartovich, the anarchist Zhora, the revolutionary groupie Varya Matveeva, and the assassin Bogrov are we shown the intellectual and psychological mechanisms that induced them to become the agents of chaos, at their respective levels of ideological engagement.

The dynamics of mass psychology, however, receive extensive treatment. The text critically examines the Ilyin-Andozerskaya argument that the autocracy was the mystic glue that held the nation together and endowed it with its sense of self: therefore, the fall of the sovereign—the fall of Russia. A soldier with the Tatar name of Zanigatdinov dolefully comments, "There's no life without a tsar" (*Nel'zia bez tsaria*).[868] His words are echoed by a peasant woman in Kamenka: "We shan't survive without a tsar" (*Bez tsaria nam ne prozhit'*).[869] The residual popular attachment to the throne is ethnic- and gender-neutral.

On the other hand, the Hegelian Kotya Gulai "did not discern a causal relationship between the imperial abdication and the fall of Russia,"[870] perhaps out of an adherence to Hegel's notion that "cause not only has an effect but in the effect it stands, as cause, in relation to itself,"[871] that is, cause and effect, by being a part of the same objectivity, are ontologically congruent. A couple of pages later we learn that for Kotya, "this Russian Revolution is just another stage in the self-development of the *Weltgeist*."[872] In the end, the epopee treats the national collapse as a theodicean mystery which ipso facto lies beyond the scope of the author's, the characters', or the readers' understanding.

Instead, Solzhenitsyn gives us a guidebook to mob politics. Angry crowds coalesce, rampage, and interact, murderously or otherwise, with the forces of law and order as well as members of the public. Homicidal civilians acquire weapons which they use with *unpracticed* ease, and military units turn into armed gangs, both categories of villains lynching opponents with homicidal enthusiasm or incidental indifference, within four walls or in plain view. "By evening attitudes toward officers hardened and some had their shoulder boards ripped off. On Nevsky Prospect an officer who was missing a leg and walked on crutches refused to submit and was killed with a bayonet thrust,"[873] and in a quasi-cannibalistic moment, the multitude butchers a policeman, carefully wraps his body in official documents in the manner of a cocoon, and throws it into the fire.[874] Another policeman is tied to a pair of cars and torn apart.[875] The barbarian horde glimpsed by Irina Tomchak from her balcony a few months back has entered the city gates.

We are shown how a riotous assembly may accept or reject a claim to leadership advanced by this or that street orator or agitator. A speaker that looks and sounds suspiciously like Mayakovsky—he is described as "a person in a leather jacket" from the Military Driving School,[876] where the Futurist poet was posted at the time—climbs onto a table to harangue a group of soldiers, but to no effect. General Markov confronts a mob of mutineeers: "I was spared by a bullet in battle, so let one of my men do the deed."[877] He is greeted by a hurrah.[878] By then we have learned that

> The crowd seems to obey no one, but it will readily follow a chief. Yet the chief himself may be in a frenzied state and not even realize he is a chief, for what keeps him on top is élan, which can dissipate in a couple of minutes, and then he is nothing. Only a criminal, a born killer, or a man thirsting for revenge can retain power over the crowd, for now he is in his element."[879]

So goes the mob, and so goes Russia. *The Red Wheel* covers the events in Moscow, which follow a mostly peaceful course, in relatively sparing detail, chiefly via the perspective of Vorotyntsev, Sanya, and Ksenia, who are hostile to the revolution. The text makes plain that the rest of the country remained calm until the new authorities telegraphed the provinces to announce the change in government. As a site of political upheaval, Rostov, the home of the Kharitonov family, receives almost as much attention as Moscow. There are revolutionary vignettes set in other towns such as Mogilev, Tambov, and Novocherkassk, as well as Blagodarev's village of Kamenka. The impressions of Vorotyntsev and Kharitonov, who separately journey by train back to the front, turn into travelogues of an entropic land.

The epic treats the branches of the imperial army—infantry, cavalry, Cossacks, the navy—as test environments wherein the agents of chaos are shown undermining, assailing, and finally destroying a rigidly hierarchical institutional structure that relies on the traditional codes of honor, duty, and discipline. A good deal of discourse time is devoted to the mutinies on the naval vessels anchored in port, where the descent into mob rule lends itself particularly well to such fictive quantification. Here is a passage that describes Admiral Kolchak's concerns about the Black Sea Fleet, which he commands:

> He wondered what this [revolutionary propaganda] would mean for the fleet's exceedingly complex structure which rested on the mathematical formulae of insubmersibility, floodability, stability, hull shape, speed, and

buoyancy, as well as the rules of navigation and deviation, as the mob of barbarians and revolutionary imbeciles prepared to descend upon it.[880]

One senses that Kolchak, whom the saga treats as a courageous and farseeing historical actor second only to Stolypin himself, is thinking the author's own thoughts, so that we observe Solzhenitsyn's numerical sensibilities melding with those of the admiral's naval kind.

The epopee shows the ochlos as wicked and witless, and repulsive to behold by those that are neither:

> The mob is a strange, remarkable creature, one that is a law unto itself, human and non-human at the same time, but always ambulant, and many-headed with it. Each of its members is freed from his usual responsibility, while its strength is multiplied by the number of people present, yet their collective will is proportionately weakened.[881]

This fairly *pedestrian* observation reads like a paraphrase from *The Crowd* (*Psychologie des foules*; 1895), a treatise by Gustave Le Bon that is the foundational text of rabble studies (to coin a term). The epic's treatment of the insurgent masses hews to his programmatic notion that "the substitution of the unconscious actions of crowds for the conscious activity of individuals is one of the principal characteristics of the present age."[882] At one point, the socialist Vladimir Stankevich recalls Le Bon's dictum that "the majority of the people always seeks order rather than revolution."[883] In keeping with this principle, Stankevich's old friend Kerensky, now meteorically streaking across the political firmament, and numerous other figures of the left, are shown trying to appease or control or manipulate the mob, usually in vain. And how could it be otherwise when "the mood of the crowd changes by the minute, from rapture to fear and hatred"?[884] In the end, clever, maleficent Lenin, the epic's chief ochlocrat, will succeed in bending the masses to his will, and we watch him set about this task after he returns to Russia from his Swiss exile.

Two of Le Bon's rules of mob psychology are seen in operation, namely, "contagion [which is] a phenomenon of a hypnotic order [where] every sentiment and act is contagious ... to such a degree that an individual readily sacrifices his personal interest to the collective interest"[885] and "excessive suggestibility ... which much resembles the state of fascination in which the hypnotized individual ... becomes the slave of all the subconscious activities of his spinal cord."[886] But unlike the French anthropologist, who considered the multitude "anonymous,"[887] Solzhenitsyn periodically de-anonymizes it by depicting, often with a vibrantly descriptive stroke or two, individual members of the horde as they march, murder, or ululate. Some of these bit players are ideologically motivated, others are driven by an infectious kind of rage, others happen to be passive followers who are, to use Le Bon's phrase, the slaves of their spinal cords. Or in the words of General Svechin, "People, that is, highly intelligent beings, are suddenly transformed into a herd of bestial apes."[888]

The army's floundering attempts to restore order are treated with the same degree of discrimination: a face or a body is diegetically plucked out from those uniformed ranks and scrutinized for an instant of discourse time as the character in question obeys, evades, or violates the call of duty. Sergeant Timofei Kirpichnikov of the Volynsky regiment conspires to bring it to mutiny, thereby setting in motion the entire revolution, as he half-regretfully tells himself days later.[889] Meanwhile Private Klim Orlov, a Bolshevik sympathizer in the same unit, acquires the rudiments of a class consciousness: "'Mars himself advocated a war of aggression against Russian tsarism.' But who's Mars? Another delegate, thanks be to him, explained that Mars is the god of war and that Kaiser Wilhelm intends to put up a monument to him."[890] Two youthful ensigns, Vadim Andrusov and Kostya Grimm of the Preobrazhensky Guards, "[wake] up in the morning, [check] their mood—oh yes!—and [get] out of bed as revolutionaries."[891] As for the Bolsheviks, Shlyapnikov and Molotov do their damnedest to give the mobs some Marxist direction, but their leaflets and manifestos make little difference: every political party, however extreme, reveals its irrelevance as the street riots and rejoices.

Bystanders and curiosity seekers such as Gika Krivoshein, a student who is out of sympathy with the mob, contribute their impressions of what they see and hear, enhancing the spectrum of narrative angles and perspectives. On one occasion, Gika looks out of the fourth floor window of the family apartment, the high vantage point giving him a *detached* view of the scene below:

> He noticed some civilians, but most of them were soldiers. Strangely enough, they were not marching in formation and there were no officers to be seen, and even more strangely, the soldiers carried their rifles every which way: some rested them on their shoulders, some held them atilt, some underarm, so that the bayonets were pointing upward, sideways, or down. After two hours of freedom the men had already lost the habits they had been taught. These were fresh conscripts who had just been issued their greatcoats.[892]

The marchers carry crimson banners and chant revolutionary slogans, but are impelled by the secret workings of the collective unconscious, in Le Bon's sense of the term: "Crowds ... appear to be guided by those mysterious forces which the ancients denominated destiny, nature, or providence."[893] As set pieces, Solzhenitsyn's mass scenes evoke both *War and Peace*, where a patriotic mob lynches a suspected traitor hours before Napoleon's entry into Moscow, and *Devils*, which culminates in a provincial riot cum pogrom instigated by Pyotr Verkhovensky's terrorist cell.

Amidst the brutality occasional acts of compassion occur. A group of armed workers is about to execute three officers, one of whom is Captain Nekrasov, in the middle of the street, when it is surprised by a gaggle of deserters from the same regiment.

> One of them cried out, "You're hurting a cripple, rear-echelon heroes!"
>
> The circle wavered.
>
> "Who's the cripple?"
>
> "That's him." The soldiers gestured at Vsevolod Nekrasov. "See?" and pointed at his leg.
>
> A worker handed his rifle to one of his fellows and began fingering Vsevolod's leg through his trousers, going lower and lower. Presently he exclaimed, as if referring to a mannequin, "It's true. The leg is made of wood."
>
> The motionless, severely black semi-circle shifted, stirred, fell apart.
>
> "A cri-pple ..."
>
> "Lost his leg, he did ..."
>
> "Now that was a close call ..."[894]

The firing squad turns solicitous, asking the officers if they are cold and advising them to have a smoke: a *first*, rather than a *last*, cigarette. The "circle," a tiny analogue of the Wheel, has its own quality of mercy.

There are memorable images aplenty, metonymically or, more often, metaphorically rendered. As the riots begin, a bourgeois is filled with bourgeois fear: "The beaver hat informed [Kovynev], 'Four regiments have mutinied!'"[895] Soon vehicles packed with armed men are roaming the streets: "Giant hedgehogs of bayonets moved at speed, snorting and squealing, overtaking or narrowly missing each other, making screeching turns, heightening the tension. A bacchanal of hedgehogs!"[896] The revolutionary city is now populated by a motorized fauna with a Hobbesian complement of predators and prey, of which Obodovsky's slaughtered streetcar was just the first specimen described. Sometimes the narrative veers into whimsy as when it comments upon the facial features of the men in what was once an elite unit: "The noses were of a type, although most of the soldiers were nothing like the exemplary Pavlov Guards of old, but short, snub-nosed men, even if they still looked like Paul I."[897] By tradition, the regiment chose conscripts who bore a facial resemblance to that tsar, who "had hardly any nose."[898]

Mutinous noses are not the half of it. Nietzsche's "gruesome farce" is painted in garish colors, as when "the famous monarchist Shulgin inadvertently drove off to storm the Peter and Paul fortress under a red flag"[899] or in a Dostoevskian moment—think Nikolai Stavrogin—a deserter equipped with three officer's sabers plus rifle bites General Ivanov, the portly "dictator" tasked with putting down the riots, on the hand.[900] Elsewhere we learn that the Popular Socialist Party "was now so small that these days it consisted almost entirely of its leaders."[901] Among their number is one of Solzhenitsyn's historical walk-ons, Aleksei Peshekhonov. This longtime opponent of the tsarist regime exhorts a group of demonstrators to march against a row of government troops, who are entirely non-hostile, but the crowd is signally lacking in courage. So Peshekhonov gets hold of a red flag, approaches the soldiers with a firm and easy step and "walk[s] through the line of grenadiers, alone, almost wishing for a martyr's death ... and [goes] on walking and walking."[902] In the evening the veteran socialist sips tea in his snug apartment and looks back on that revolutionary amble as a "feat of courage."[903] With this comment, a prefigurative connection is completed, the bathos of Peshekhonov's adventure grotesquely complementing the "glorious episode" of the regimental colors in *August 1914*. As for the Popular Socialist himself, he joins the Provisional Government as minister for food supplies in May (*April 1917*), only to resign in August ("The Narrative Beyond the Point of Suspension)," but makes no impression in the halls of power. And in an instant of analeptic patterning, we are shown the arrival and brief presence on Petrograd's Palace Square of two companies of the Preobrazhensky Guards, which is depicted as a miniature and ridiculous reenactment of the Decembrist revolt.[904]

The excitement in the square may have been an unintended parody of that famous insurrection, but roughly at the same point in story time Veronika Lenartovich and her friend Fanechka, who are out to enjoy the sights and sounds of the insurgent capital, come across a *staged* piece of revolutionary theater, which happens to be motorized:

> Another automobile, this one a lorry with a large cargo platform, crawled down Zabalkansky Prospect with a grinding of gears, surrounded by a

shrieking mass of people. Some two dozen men and women stood on the platform, but they acted differently from the passengers in the first two vehicles, for they had the motionless appearance of statues. They did not acknowledge the homage of the crowd but instead displayed themselves in the manner of a sculptural group. Those in the front row leaned over the drivers' backs holding their rifles at the ready. Behind them was a man with a red flag, another one held aloft a rifle with no bayonet, which he would occasionally shake, and a third clutched a bayonet but no rifle, while the rest waved red kerchiefs and scarves. And so they slowly moved forward, statue-like, hailed on all sides by the throng.[905]

These motor-borne performance artists form one of several tableaux vivants mounted by actual or *acting* insurgents. When they vogue, they are the stars *and* the audience. "All revolutions love a spectacle, but they also love to watch themselves,"[906] notes the analytical Andozerskaya. A *divertimento* at the Mariinsky Theater attended by members of the Petrograd Soviet executive illustrates this truth. A dozen thespians costumed and made up (bearded up?) to represent a variety of famous writers and radicals appear on stage in a carefully arranged ensemble against the backdrop of an azure sky with painted sun. The cynosure of all eyes, however, is a "well-built woman with broken fetters on her wrists, who appeared to symbolize Liberated Russia (occasionally she would lift both arms to display the chains)."[907] We recall the famous passage in *War and Peace* that describes Natasha Rostova's defamiliarizing impressions during a visit to the opera. Or to employ an entirely anachronistic analogy, the Mariinsky pageant presages the album cover of *Sgt. Pepper's Lonely Hearts Club Band*.

As always happens during a violent struggle for power, communication is the key. Both sides rely on the telegraph, telegrams, but especially the telephone: the tsar's interior minister, Protopopov, even speaks, or rather thinks, of "the temptation of the phone."[908] Armored cars and motorcyclists patrol the city. The latter have the appearance of "men from the future": "They wear special clothing, long leather gloves, their leather cap straps tucked under the chin. They are self-confident and mighty!"[909] (oddly, their most futuristic aspect, the goggles, remains unmentioned). A hardline faction in the State Council proposes bombing the Duma from the air[910] and General Voeykov, commandant of the imperial palace, advises his sovereign "to rescue the [imperial] family from Tsarskoe Selo by using automobiles or even aeroplanes."[911] On a less elevated technological level, Lenartovich, the empress, and several officers of the Preobrazhensky Guards separately wonder that the phones are still working even as chaos consumes the capital. On the morning of February 28/March 13, however, the lines are cut: the operators at the Petrograd telephone exchange abandon their switches and headpieces, perhaps discomfited by the sight of a corpse left lying inside the building.

As a baying mob surrounds the Tauride Palace, the chairman of the Duma, the orotund Mikhail Rodzianko, endeavors to ingratiate himself with the throng by reading out his telegrams to the tsar: "If the insurgence transmits itself to the army, the fall of Russia, and the dynasty, will be inevitable."[912] Rodzianko is out of tune, out of time, and lucky to escape with his life. Subsequently he learns that Kerensky, hitherto an obscure socialist deputy, is now enjoying success as a street orator, and then observes his colleague greet a group of belligerent armed men who have brought in Ivan Shcheglovitov, Rodzianko's counterpart in the State Council, for a spot of revolutionary justice. Nothing in Kerensky's hitherto lackluster political career, which was distinguished only by the occasional meandering speech, suggests that he is the man of the hour. But the loquacious parliamentarian has grasped the Le Bonian truth that "the hero acclaimed by a crowd is a veritable god of that crowd"[913] and rouses the rabble in a "ringing" voice: "In the name of revolution's law."[914] Henceforth Kerensky will carry the charisma of a "people's tribune and a fearless revolutionary."[915] In a matter of days his presentational gifts will procure him a seat in the cabinet and by the time summer comes around, the premiership, though that development remains outside the scope of the narrative. *The Red Wheel* shows that Kerensky has the ambition, but not the ruthlessness and organizing intelligence, to make himself the country's new ruler, a lack for which he eventually paid the political price.

To repeat, the epic scripts the events of February as a Nietzschean "farce." The capture of Petrograd's House of Preliminary Detention by the mob becomes a bathetic parody of the storming of the Bastille,[916] while Karabchevsky, a famous defence lawyer, advises an uncomprehending Kerensky, "Forget about the French Revolution, it's for the best.... It would be shameful to follow in its bloody traces. We live in the twentieth century."[917] Karabchevsky is wise. In revolutionary France, ideological abstractions and constitutional theorizations led to "the disaggregation of society, its shattering into irreducibly hostile parties under the impact of political passions and principles that were all the less open to negotiation or concession the more absolute and universal they were."[918] The epic treats the Russian version of this discursive phenomenon as the true functional parallel between the upheavals of 1917 and 1789.

The revolution may be both brutal and exciting, a "hoyden" (*khuliganka*),[919] as that political delinquent Sasha Lenartovich affectionately puts it, but it is also a thing of flukes and accidents. We observe the haphazard manner in which the Petrograd Soviet constitutes itself as an organ of the popular will in competition with the Provisional Committee of the Duma, soon to become the Provisional Government. Socialist leaders, a mixture of up-and-coming men and revolutionary relics, appoint each other to the Soviet's executive committee, coopting a few persons who happen to have wandered into the Tauride Palace at the right moment in history. One such accidental people's representative is Private Vakhov, who was only looking for a place to snooze after a hard day's riot. Instead he finds himself installed as a delegate and must give a speech: "Comrades and brothers, it's like this. ... If we have to, we'll sort of take a stand."[920] Whereupon Vakhov departs the palace and the text, hoping he won't get nabbed as a deserter after he returns to the barracks.

One should add that although Eros is present at multiple points in the narrative, throughout the last two Knots a certain sexual decorum prevails. There are no scenes of carnal savagery, which historically have accompanied such epochal breakdowns in the public order. Marina Tsvetaeva's violently erotic poems of the revolutionary period, with which the epopee engages on multiple levels of obliquely formatted citation, do not seem to have inluenced the author in this regard. The younger contingent of male revolutionaries may be driven by ideological passion, but they are deadly chaste. None of them compares on the sexual aggression scale to rampant Zhora in *August 1914*, and their female co-extremists are correspondingly demure. Veronika and Fenichka climb onto a lorry crammed full of armed men, who take them on an exciting daytime, nighttime joy ride across the city, yet this motorized "dance of happiness"[921] entails no flirtation, no sexy banter, no kisses, whether stolen or freely given, just a socialist (realist?) "touching and gripping of hands, which transmitted the awesome power of the risen masses."[922] On a less salubrious note, "The brothels are so busy that they are unable to service all the soldiers, who make lawful payment in the form of loot collected over the last few days such as jewelry, bagatelles or even table silverware."[923] The warriors of the revolution must have their revolutionary fun, but what fun they have occurs entirely off-text.

Enthusiasm for what is perceived as the "universal brotherhood that was once an impossible dream but had now arrived and gladdened the heart"[924] prompts liberal members of the propertied elite to extend a welcoming hand, and meal, to the risen masses. Stankevich's third cousin Kolya, a reflective schoolboy who is disgusted by the "sordid riot"[925] sweeping Petrograd, is present at a celebratory repast organized by one of the city's wealthy families for a party of belching and expectorating soldiers, who are served a revolutionary menu of "caviar, salmon, the best kinds of sausage, not to mention kulebyakas, meat pies, and salads."[926] Later Kolya overhears a couple of the men commenting on the hospitality they received: "Lookit how the bastards live! But now they're afraid. Still, you can't buy us off with caviar. We'll effin' take care of these hoity-toity misses. ... And their college bookworms too."[927] The sexual subjugation of upper-class girls by their new Bolshevik masters is a familiar topos in Solzhenitsyn's fictions.

18

The main narrative leaves off with Vorotyntsev in a mood of melancholy contemplation, which metamorphoses into a chain of waking dreams that hint at the dark future that awaits Russia, and himself. Yet there are no purple passages, no grandiloquent monologues. We behold a tired middle-aged officer readying himself for what he already knows may be an unwinnable struggle. The absence of a denouement is itself a device: many classic Russian novels display the same "lack of a final curtain."[928] In Tolstoy, for instance, this statutory trope is a function of the shifting, evolving, or devolving dynamics of family and community life that underpin his great novels; and in Dostoevsky, a function of all those conversations across the nations, discursive tunes in his famous polyphony which resonate in the reader's own current-affairs here and now, where there are also bodies that suffer and minds that brood or rage or crack. Both considerations are applicable to the *The Red Wheel* and the manner of its ending or, rather, its succession of deferred endings, which extends into "The Narrative Beyond the Point of Suspension."

On the afternoon of May 5/18, 1917, the colonel makes his way to the parapet of the Mogilev citadel, a medieval castle that once towered over the Dnieper but had since fallen into ruin. As he *sits* on a bench in an utterly unmartial pose—Vorotyntsev's body language is as matter-of-fact now as it was at the start of the saga—he is preoccupied by thoughts of the "Circular Lie" (*Krugovoi Obman*),[929] the "enemy"[930] he must face, but the sight of the great river draws him out of this abstracted mental state. There follows a series of narrative *changements d'optique*. Instead of "elevation, beauty, a vista,"[931] the hero's "practiced"[932] military eye sees "folds in the terrain,"[933] and he muses: "How would you mount an attack here? ... How would you conduct a defence?"[934] A moment of prolepsis that points to the terrible battles that would be fought over the Dnieper crossings in the war against Hitler. Next: "What happiness it is to have such a broad view from a hill. To see the river, the flooded plain, and the spaces beyond. It's as if you are ascending above your own life."[935] Also, above your own literature, as in Gogol's tale "A Terrible Vengeance" ("Strashnaia mest'"; 1832), which includes a famous paean to the great river: "Wondrous is the Dnieper in calm weather, when freely and smoothly he races his full waters through forests and hills. ... Rare is the bird that flies to the middle of the Dnieper!"[936] Next: Vorotyntsev is visited by a "supra-real vision" (Nemzer):[937] "You see so much of Russia all at once, as never normally happens."[938] The colonel's mental gaze is directed in a cartographically precise "east-north-east" direction "beyond the forests and into the distance,"[939] to the core Russian provinces of Smolensk, Moscow, Vladimir, and Kostroma. Vorotyntsev was born in those latter parts and now senses that "he will never return there again."[940] Next: in the same key of mystical reverie, Georgi sees or imagines that Russia's "celebrated troika has drunkenly rolled into a ravine where it found itself stuck up to its shafts in the clay."[941] The reference here is to another much anthologized passage by Gogol, this time from his novel *Dead Souls*: "Art not thou too, O Rus, rushing onwards like a spirited troika that none can overtake? ... And on rushes the troika, all-inspired by God!"[942] Yet now that divine inspiration is missing and Russia is turning into a continental *terra nullius*, and the hero is there to watch it happen in his mind's eye as he "straightens his shoulders" and braces himself for the "inevitable" battle.[943] Vorotyntsev never once thinks of Alina as he peers into the future[944] and nor does he recall Olda or even Kalisa: his thoughts and visions are of Russia, his first and last love.

The "unbelievable mountain range" that Lazhenitsyn observed as he began his journey to war delineated the southern perimeter of Solzhenitsyn's imagined Russia, just as the trenches in Poland where Sanya spent long months fighting the Germans marked its westernmost limits. To the north and east, however, the homeland's expanse remains undefined and extends into a geographical incertitude, although he knows that "the real Russia, the forest Russia ... begins only at Voronezh,"[945] the town from which the Lazhenitsyns'—that is, the Solzhenitsyns'—ancestors once hailed. The passages of nature writing that begin and end the epic, like the classical works of Russian literature which they invoke, "mediate between place and written word in order to represent Russia and its provincial and Oriental peripheries";[946] and *beyond* that, nationalize the two characters, Sanya Lazhenitsyn and Georgi Vorotyntsev, with whom the two meta-framing stretches of text are respectively associated. The "700 or so versts"[947] of plain and forest that Vorotyntsev visualizes from the Mogilev parapet may be the nation's heartland, but over the mystical horizon, to the north, lie regions unexplored or untextualized. This is the space that farseeing

Obodovsky, who speaks with the voice of the author himself, saw as the seat of Russia's future prosperity, the locus of its manifest destiny.

That destiny is yet to play itself out, if play itself out it ever will, but the upturned Gogolian carriage is a powerful symbol of national hubris: in Russia, literature proposes, but history disposes. That storied conveyance makes its appearance long after the depiction of the "ruinous revolution" was textually completed in *March 1917*, although the troika was catastrophically prefigured on several earlier occasions, for example, as the teetering "chariot" of state that was rescued by Stolypin[948] or a "frenzied cart rear[ing] up on its hind wheels" on an abandoned East Prussian battlefield.[949]

If *August 1914* is the epic's "preview," *November 1916* its novelistic nub, and *March 1917* its historiographical heart, then *April 1917* amounts to an extended postscript. Rather than tying up history's loose ends, the concluding Knot adumbrates the manner of their continued unravelling as it traces the principal characters' fortunes and misfortunes in the weeks that follow the fall of the tsar. At the close of the dramatic proceedings most of the plot lines are left suspended in (historical) time and (national) space. The fates of the fictional personalities remain unresolved, while the empire of the tsars is set to perish at the hands of internal and external enemies. Some Russians, like Vorotyntsev, are determined to make a stand, even as they recognize that the surging tide of entropy may be too strong to staunch, but others rejoice at the loss of familiar values and structures, and others still try to lead private lives outside or despite the rush of events, in a life-affirming endeavor that will inevitably be impacted by death-affirming reality. In the end, one thing is made abundantly, achingly clear: the leveling forces of historical chaos are about to vanquish the national values of justice, kindness, and truth. The Wheel of Satan is also the Wheel of History. And so, darkness descends.

CHAPTER EIGHT

Return: The Shorter Fictions of the 1990s

Everything becomes and recurs eternally—escape is impossible!
—Friedrich Nietzsche, *The Will to Power*

The thinker or artist whose better self has fled into his works feels an almost malicious joy when he sees his body and spirit slowly broken into and destroyed by time; it is as if he were in a corner, watching a thief at work on his safe, all the while knowing that it is empty and that all his treasures have been rescued.
—Friedrich Nietzsche, *Human, All Too Human*

1

As he prepared to leave leafy Vermont for the turbulence of post-communist Russia, the writer considered his plans:

> I am very interested in the short form and I am beginning to work in it again now. It's not just a question of age. I began with short stories, but the task ahead was always first my novels, then *Gulag*, and then *The Red Wheel*, and I had to fulfill those tasks. Finally, I have the chance. Now I will replenish my impressions of life in Russia, of today's Russia, and I will definitely write short stories. For the moment, while I am still in Vermont, I am working on stories using materials from the twenties and thirties, because I cannot write about today's Russia without personal impressions of it. I remember well these things from my youth. And then having finished *The Red Wheel*—this huge beast now felled—there are many loose ends left over and it is unclear what to do with them. I have a mountain of leftover material that has to be sorted out.[1]

This notion of making his oeuvre in some formal sense complete was vintage Solzhenitsyn. He always favored symmetry and balance, not just as an artist but a public figure, as evidenced by the geographical trajectory of his return. His creative activities after he arrived in his country of birth conformed precisely to the pattern he laid down in Cavendish. In addition to publishing eight stories which, as he had promised, were historical or topical or both, he found himself undertaking a couple of unplanned projects, a second cycle of "Miniatures" and the final revision of *The Red Wheel*. Then there was "Adlig Schwenkitten," a long story or short novel that dramatizes the author's experiences as a frontline officer during the last months of World War II. He also brought out, in installments, *Between Two Millstones*, a memoir of his life in Switzerland and the United States, as well as several reviews and essays that form part of the *Literary Collection*. And he did a fair amount of polemical and historical writing, notably *Russia in Collapse* and *Two Hundred Years Together*, his last bestselling book.

Despite a willingness to comment publicly on matters of current import, Solzhenitsyn continued to hold the men of power at arm's length, although he met with President Yeltsin (once, in 1994) and President Putin (twice, in 2000 and 2007). He was frank about his priorities in this regard. "I have no intention of becoming a politician. As a type of human creativity, politics stands lower than philosophical or artistic endeavors. I shall act only through the use of language."[2] Here was a writer who was certain that printed words—*his* words— still mattered, even as the nation's cultural practices were being reshaped by a new post-logocentric paradigm which refused to privilege books over images, performances, or artistic artifacts but treated them all as intrinsically coequal in their semiotic contingency. By and large, Solzhenitsyn disdained to comment on these unwelcome developments, with the exception of "The Relentless Cult of Novelty," an ill-tempered denunciation of Postmodernism, or rather the author's version thereof, composed shortly before his departure from the United States.

Like the stories of the 1950s and 1960s, those of the post-exilic period constitute a kind of series, except more so. To begin with, they belong to a genre that Solzhenitsyn, an enthusiastic inventor of new literary forms, named the "bipartite tale" (*dvuchastnyi rasskaz*). His son Ignat reports that this binary pattern was a "serendipitous discovery" that emerged spontaneously during the process of composition.[3] Each tale comprises two parts of approximately equal length, which are linked thematically rather than fabulaically. The paired sections feature recurring plot elements and, in some cases, shared characters. "The binary method, as Solzhenitsyn handles it, is essentially a satirical device, designed to capture the doubleness—the double-facedness—of Russian life under communism,"[4] although "Fracture Points," "No Matter What," and "Zhelyabuga Village" are in part (two) set in the post-communist 1990s. The events described always take place at the nodalities of history as listed in "The Narrative Beyond the Point of Suspension" addendum to *The Red Wheel*, or as experienced by the Russian people in the decades after 1945. Story time in the two sections may overlap ("Nastenka," "Fracture Points"), or be separated by weeks, months, years ("Ego," "The New Generation") or even decades ("No Matter What," "Zhelyabuga Village"). The effect is of a provocative juxtaposition of social situations and ethical choices, with the gap between the coupled segments acting as a diegetic hinge as well as a formal confirmation that "all the stories center upon absence."[5]

The eight pieces are a chronicle of a nation's tragedies. Solzhenitsyn gives voice to victims and perpetrators but also characters that are both: the narrative, as ever, takes the form of indirect free discourse. And as he had promised, two of the stories deal with the early Soviet period when terror of the revolutionary rather than the bureaucratic variety was the engine of radical social change.

The binary tales are products of the author's writerly imagination, rather than writerly recollection, with exceptions. Parts One of "No Matter What" and "Zhelyabuga Village" are based on Solzhenitsyn's memories of his wartime service. Part two of the latter story, which describes the author's visit to the eponymous hamlet half a century later, is formatted as a piece of topical journalism, though most traveling reporters would not expect to be accompanied by "the heads of the regional and local administrations, carrying out their duty of hospitality."[6] At the same time, the tales exhibit a synoptic quality: every hero is an illustration, every personal experience an example. Metonyms are here, there, and everywhere. At times the style is terse to the point of stenographic: Solzhenitsyn squeezes a lot of history or current events into just a few pages, mostly to good effect. His favored enclosed/open space oppositions, which give the categories of good and evil a chronotopic expression, are present in "Ego," "The New Generation," "No Matter What," and "Zhelyabuga Village."

The stories make that undergraduate solecism, "the two protagonists," licit, since in most cases each story section features a different main character. When the same hero or heroine appears in both Parts One and Two, there is a radical difference between these paired iterations: "Times of Crisis," for instance, shows Marshal Zhukov as a young Red Army cavalryman and a retired military celebrity. None of the tales is didactic in the overt, extradiegetic manner of "Matryona's Home" or "Zakhar-the-Pouch," though as an exposé of rural poverty and injustice the second half of "Zhelyabuga Village" comes close. The interactions between the fictional characters and the major and minor historical figures they encounter follow the same fabulatory logic as in *The Red Wheel*.

Indeed, when writing "Ego" and "Times of Crisis" Solzhenitsyn relied on the research he had conducted for his magnum opus. These two stories are the closest to the saga in subject and style and may be read as its informal sequels. In "Ego" especially, the narration approaches the fractured, elliptic quality of *March 1917* and *April 1917*.

Taken as a whole, the cycle privileges public events over fictive individuation. The characters, even the victorious Marshal Zhukov, are objects of politics or history. They either lack agency, except in the narrow realm of personal choice, as when Zhukov rescues General Rokossovsky from the gulag; or if they possess it, are shown losing it as they bow to the fierce pressure of societal change, which happens to the anti-Bolshevik insurgent Ektov. Descriptions of people and places are brief to the point of perfunctory, though on occasion bodies are nicely textured. A hotshot businessman nervously negotiating his way through the chaotic 1990s is afflicted by a manual tic: "Tolkovyanov had a particular habit: he would rest his elbows on the table and put his ten fingers together, moving them slightly to create various shapes."[7] And Solzhenitsyn demonstrates his customary ear for the way his countrymen speak, from a professor's urbane accents to the folksy cadences of a Siberian peasant, and every sociolect in between.

If these works share a theme, it is that of betrayal: of one's comrades-in-arms ("Ego"), military honor ("Times of Crisis"), colleagues ("The New Generation"), employees ("Fracture Points"), culture ("Apricot Jam"), natural environment ("No Matter What"), voters ("Zhelyabuga Village"), or faith in God ("Nastenka"). One scholar describes the cycle as "an anthology of compromises" that depicts the "fateful" consequences for each protagonist of making a forced accommodation with metaphysical evil.[8] The accuracy of Solzhenitsyn's authorial memory never fails to impress, as in this description of the back alleys of Rostov, the city of his youth:

> You could reach the library by taking the narrow Nikolaevsky Lane that dropped down through the ravine that was there in those days, or you could go more directly through the city park. The park had many things to offer. There was a straight and level central pathway from which the ground sloped downward on both sides to little squares with flowerbeds and fountains. A band shell where there were free classical music concerts in summer stood on the hills on one side, and on the other side was a summer restaurant where a tiny variety band played irritating music.[9]

As is the rule in Solzhenitsyn, male characters dominate the proceedings, with the important exception of "Nastenka," which tells the story of two young women who suffer a spiritual downfall as they give in to the totalizing demands of the state. Tensions and conflicts between generations, which often include a political dimension, are a frequent theme. Members of the former middle classes react with baffled horror to the revolutionary transformation of society, though some of these çi-devants try to convince themselves that "an entirely new epoch was unfolding in a process that was evidently irreversible,"[10] and that this is a good thing. The familiar anti-SocRealist stance is still there ("Nastenka," part two), even though by 1994 this Soviet *mode of literary production* had long expired, like its industrial analogues which had been expropriated by robber capitalism ("Fracture Points"). In this regard, "Apricot Jam," where an establishment novelist glibly pontificates about art and history, is less an attack on the Soviet classics than a study of cultural cynicism and the anti-morality that sustains it.

The stories employ a multitude of historical markers to fix the fictive proceedings in time and place. 1925: village children are given politically correct names such as Vladlen and Marxina ("Nastenka"; 1928); a teenage girl grows a curly mane, defying "the fashion for keeping hair short"[11] ("The New Generation"); 1944: the student bread ration is 550 grams ("Fracture Points"); 1993: one of Yeltsin's reformist officials explores the byways of corruption, his tie liberally loose and collar democratically undone ("No Matter What"). Solzhenitsyn's metonymical shorthand produces an economy of vivid results. So does this instance of post-Tolstoyan estrangement, when a village girl fleeing the collectivized countryside encounters her first fridge: "A small electrical apparatus that cooled the things inside. You could keep your fresh food in it—sausage, ham, butter."[12] Elsewhere the same kitchen gadget hums its way into the text as an indicator of inconspicuous consumption in the homes of the Soviet elite: "The Writer [boasted] artlessly about a remarkable new appliance—an electric refrigerator he had brought from Paris."[13] Such are the poetics of white goods, Stalin-style.

2

The subject of the first binary tale, "Ego," is the Tambov peasant rebellion of 1920–21, which was provoked by the Bolsheviks' confiscations and depredations in the local villages under the policy of war communism. A recent cultural history of Russia notes that the communists' cruel treatment of the countryside during the civil war was ignored by the writers and poets of the period: "Sadly, there were not many works written about those horrible years, despite the fact that Russia was predominantly a peasant country with a powerful tradition of idolizing the peasantry in literature."[14] So once again, Solzhenitsyn fills a historiographical lacuna with a meticulously researched, densely structured text.

"Ego" is a concise history of the Tambov revolt, lightly fictionalized to provide a measure of human interest and narratively structured to a coiled tightness. The main character, Pavel Ektov, is modeled on an actual participant in the insurrection and there are walk-on parts for other historical actors such as its leaders Pyotr Tokmakov and Aleksandr Antonov, as well as Grigory Kotovsky, a flamboyant Red Army commander. The rebel ranks include two characters from *The Red Wheel*, rooted Arseny Blagodaryov [sic], here identified as "one of the people who had begun the revolt," and "wild, combative" Terenty [sic] Chernega, who "had joined the Bolsheviks in 1917 and served with them for two years ... but after he had seen the things that were happening ... went back to the side of the peasants."[15]

Ektov enters the story with a minimum of exposition. A pacifist and "staunch democrat,"[16] he was active in the pre-revolutionary cooperative movement, like the quiet Zyablitsky in *November 1916*, whom he resembles in manner and speech. A committed proponent of the middle way, during the civil war the protagonist shunned both Red and White. He has a much-loved wife and baby daughter. Also like Zyablitsky, Ektov strongly identifies with the Russian people. He is drawn to these rural folk in part because of "their well-reasoned thrift (boots for going to church, bast shoes for the village, and bare feet for plowing)."[17] Ektov's admiration for the peasants' provident ways mirrors Solzhenitsyn's own oft-expressed views.

This gentle soul joins the insurgents out of an irresistible moral impulse: "As a Russian populist and lover of the people, Ektov saw no alternative."[18] He acquires his odd pseudonym, Ego, by accident. The protagonist is about to introduce himself to Antonov but hesitates: "What came from his throat was only, 'a ... ga ...'"[19] The rebel chief hears these sounds as "Egov," and so the nom de guerre "Ego" is born: the word made fiction. Later it becomes clear that the hero's vocal spasm was an augury/aurality of things to come.[20]

Although Ego never loses his civilian ways, he rises to the position of "assistant to the regimental commander of the special forces regiment attached to the staff of the first army."[21] As his elaborate title indicates, the rebels have a sophisticated command structure. One of Solzhenitsyn's metapoints is that the insurrection was not a chaotic jacquerie but a well-organized movement with clear political goals. The peasants refer to the insurgents as "partisants" (*partizanty*),[22] but the Soviet authorities call them "bandits," which twentieth-century oppressors were wont to do when referring to the irregular forces that fought against them.

Always privileging the hero's participatory perspective, the story does a neat job of summarizing the complicated course of this guerrilla war. It saw few pitched battles but constant hit-and-run attacks against the Red Army, which responded with punitive sweeps and terror tactics. Villages are razed, hostages shot, families sent to concentration camps: the term is put in quotation marks to signify Ektov's gentlemanly perplexity at this horrible innovation. The Reds employ sexual violence as an instrument of counterinsurgency: "There were instances when they ordered a certain number of women be sent to them for the night, and the village would comply—what else could they do?"[23] In the camps, "the guards... amused themselves with the women and girls sent there or simply raped them."[24] Although he is committed to the rebel cause, Ektov keeps an open mind. He recognizes that barbaric acts are committed by his own side: an insurgent murders a child "so that the boy would not later give him up," "communist wives" are massacred along with their menfolk,[25] and like the Reds, the rebels gouge out the eyes of their prisoners. Sometimes the quality of rebel mercy depends on the victim's race, as when two foreign members of a food requisitioning unit seek shelter in a village. "The Chinaman was found and executed, but the old peasant felt sorry for the Finn and, risking his own neck, hid him in a haystack."[26] Still, the balance of terror definitely lies with the Bolsheviks.

A student of history, the hero wonders if the Tambov rebellion is "a new Vendée," but decides that it is not: "Our Orthodox clergy, living in some other world, did not join forces with the rebels; they did nothing to inspire them, as the militant Catholic clergy of France had done."[27] In another analytical moment, he expands on a famous apothegm from Pushkin's novel *The Captain's Daughter* (*Kapitanskaia dochka*; 1836), "God save us from seeing a Russian revolt, senseless and merciless!"[28] Ektov's wordier version reads: "It's a long and difficult task to get the Russian peasant to move, but once the pressure from the people's ferment bursts forth, it cannot be contained by the limits of reason."[29] Like many a Russian intellectual, he would rather use a dozen words where one or two will do.

If part one is a potted history of the rebellion, with Ektov's textual role that of a participant/witness, in part two his character assumes central prominence. After six months in the field he is captured and taken to the Lubyanka. Once again Sozhenitsyn shows us the jail cell and interrogation room, walled-in loci where strong bodies and precious identities are destroyed under unbearable pressure from the terror state. Three interrogators, each in his own way representative of the Cheka in its earliest revolutionary phase, take turns trying to make the prisoner crack.

> One, Maragaev, looked Caucasian and worked only at night and so gave Ektov no chance to sleep. His interrogation technique had little subtlety: he shouted and raged, striking Ektov's face and body and leaving blue bruises.
> Another, Oboyanovsky, had a gentle manner that betrayed his blue blood. He did not interrogate as much as try to instill a feeling of hopelessness in the prisoner, even seeming to sympathize with him.
> The third, the fat-cheeked, black-haired Libin, cheerful and lively, never laid a finger on the prisoner and never shouted. … He tried to awaken the prisoner's democratic conscience.[30]

But when Ektov eventually succumbs, as we know he must, it is not because of these forensic mind games but for a simpler, more brutal reason. The Cheka track down his family and cheerful Libin threatens to have his wife violated and his daughter put in an orphanage. This is Ektov's Room 101, the topos of "depravity, suffering, or horror"[31] when a prisoner goes through his most extreme carceral experience. While fighting the Reds the hero learned that sexual violence is civil war by other means; now its threat looms over his family and even, on some macabre level, his identity as a man:

> How he hated that swarthy face of Libin with its insolent, triumphant expression and those eyes with their predatory gleam! Giving up would bring a kind of relief. It was probably the same feeling a woman has when she ceases to struggle. All right, you're stronger than I am. I'll throw myself on your mercy. It's a way to make dying a little easier.[32]

Pavel—*Paul*—Ektov is forced into a reverse Damascene moment, veering from the path of righteousness to the path of betrayal. Veering away, we suspect, from his beloved wife as well. Her name, Polina, is a feminine version of "Paul." Before, Pavel and Polina were as one. The damage to his core sense of self suggests that such closeness between them might no longer be possible, even if the Cheka keep their word and let him go.

Presently, Ektov receives his assignment. He must guide a Red Army task force to a meeting with rebel commanders, where they will be ambushed. The prisoner tries to convince himself that helping the Bolsheviks is a historical necessity: "They were a powerful generation! The new Huns, but armed with a socialist ideology. A strange mixture..."[33]

As he rides to the ambush site, Ektov's pistol is empty and his horse is a "puny nag."[34] He is in costume and these are the props. In his unwilling progress through the countryside the hero is repeating behaviors from times past when he roamed the same forests and fields as a mounted officer in the rebels' "special forces regiment." This time, though, his martial demeanor is a scripted performance conducted at the direction of others.

> Gender ought not to be construed as a stable identity or locus of agency from which various acts follow; rather, gender is an identity tenuously constituted in time, instituted in an exterior space through a *stylized repetition of acts*.[35]

Now that he is a double agent, Ektov has no agency. Still, *pace* Judith Butler, gender in Solzhenitsyn's worlds is a stable, social given rather than a contingent cultural construct sanctioned by the powers that be via a hegemonic typology of norms and transgressions. This writer does not grade gender on a curve. After all, it took a vile threat inside a vile space to un-man Ektov, the onetime freedom fighter. He gave up one masculine identity, that of a soldier, to preserve another, that of a paterfamilias, but ended up as neither.

The Red Army commander tasked with the operation is Grigory Kotovsky (1881–1925). The name would have rung a bell with the story's Russian readers. Together with Vasily Chapaev and Nikolai Shchors, he belonged to a trinity of civil war commanders heroicized by Soviet propaganda, which turned them into mythical Red knights, humble-born yet glamorous warriors for the revolution. In the case of Kotovsky, a onetime rural brigand, the myth was a fib with a twist. After he was murdered by a former pimp his body was embalmed and put on public display in a mausoleum near Odessa. Other than Lenin, he was the only Soviet figure so honored. Victor Pelevin's novel *Buddha's Little Finger* (*Chapaev i pustota*; 1996), a cult work of Russian Postmodernism, shows this bullet-headed, Slavic mother's son as a sinister occultist and cocaine addict (Chapaev is a hard-drinking Bodhisattva). In Solzhenitsyn's tale, however, Kotovsky is just another revolutionary cutthroat, who looks like an incarnation of one of Lombroso's criminal types. Genteel Ektov shudders at the sight of this "huge, powerful man with a shaven head and the savage face of a convict."[36] By now the rebel army is on the run and things go off without a hitch. Dozens of insurgents are massacred, though some escape into the woods, to be hunted down later.

The ambush scene is built around this writer's customary stress on his characters' movements (or lack thereof) inside a confined, ethically delineated space. Discourse time slows down as Ektov's guilty eye registers faces, weapons, and deaths. These violent happenings are *effectively* under-narrated:

> The dashing, sharp-eyed fellow in the corner managed to fire back twice and drop two Kotovsky men. Then a saber cut off that head with the twisted mustache, and it tumbled onto the floor; a crimson stream of blood spurted from the neck to the floor, forming a pool around the body.[37]

Here narrative restraint, which elsewhere in the text ensures a balance between the personal and the historical, confirms the story's historiographically schematic register (see the latter volumes of *The Red Wheel*).

A few hours earlier the protagonist had been about to warn the rebels, "but at the same moment, his throat seized as if it had been scalded."[38] A fateful laryngeal spasm, just like the one that inspired his strange moniker. Yet the cause of Ektov's recurring dysphonia—some hidden psychological quirk? an excessive love of self?—is left unexplained. This minor secret makes the bookish insurgent a bit more intriguing as a personality.

Still, Ektov is not really a flesh-and-blood character, despite his throat problem. As a textual presence, he is layered culturally, rather than physiologically or psychologically. Throughout the story, his body and face remain a fictive blank, although we learn that those six months in the field had given him a rugged appearance: "He now looked severe and tough; his skin had darkened from sun and wind."[39] The description is nominal, signifying the statutory topos of a civilian transformed into a veteran by the rigors of combat. Yet, the ellipses in which parts of Ektov are lost from readerly sight are themselves a device. They enable the hero to discharge his diegetic function as an informed eyewitness and source of indirect free discourse without distracting the reader from the historical facts that are the story's real subject.

3

"Times of Crisis" deconstructs a famous military legend, that of Marshal Georgy Zhukov. The story's publication coincided with the fiftieth anniversary of the Soviet victory over Nazi Germany, which saw the marshal's full elevation to the status of a national hero. As part of this procedure, he received municipal recognition with the unveiling of an equestrian statue at the entrance to Red Square, an unclassical replica of the monument to Bartolomeo Colleoni in Venice's Campo Santi Giovanni e Paolo.

The story shows Zhukov at four stages of his life: the young trooper fighting the enemies of the revolution; the middle-aged general losing and winning epic battles against the Wehrmacht; the Khrushchev-era minister of defense; and the old soldier fading away during the stagnant Brezhnev years. Part one covers the same historical ground as "Ego," for most of it is devoted to the Tambov rebellion as seen through the eyes of the protagonist, then a junior Red Army officer, while part two deals with the events of World War II and beyond.

Solzhenitsyn wrote the story with his mind made up. His first published comment on the famous wartime leader, which dates back to *The Oak and the Calf*, was brutal: "Our de Gaulle manqué ... a lackey like all our marshals and generals. How low our nation has sunk: even among the military command there is not a single real personality."[40] "Times of Crisis" expands on this contrarian judgment, which nonetheless rings historically true. Consider. In the case of revolutionary and Napoleonic France, "the war completed the expropriation of the old society by incorporating its values, particularly its military values, into the heritage of the Revolution" and "the men of war ... realized the dream of a whole generation, which consisted, not in wiping out aristocratic culture altogether, but in providing a democratic version of it by replacing the criterion of birth by that of merit."[41] This was not the case in the Soviet Union. From the moment of its founding, the Workers' and Peasants' Red Army was characterized by a Leninist proscription of such "aristocratic" norms of conduct, with obvious consequences for its institutional culture, which privileged loyalty to the Party over the warrior's timocratic code. Accordingly, Solzhenitsyn's Zhukov is an ideological drone, sedulously subservient to his communist bosses, and those famous victories at Moscow, Stalingrad, and Berlin come at a horrendous cost in Russian blood, to which the marshal is callously indifferent. In retirement, he doctors his memoirs with a trembling hand, anxious to please the men in the Politburo lest they take his opulent villa away. He retains an admiration for his nemesis Stalin even though he knows about the dictator's blunders and crimes and, moreover, was repeatedly insulted by the latter in the vilest and most personal terms. *This* Zhukov is neither a man of respect, nor a man of honor.

Solzhenitsyn's point of departure is the marshal's memoirs, that is, their unexpurgated version, which was published just before the collapse of the Soviet

Union.⁴² As is the case with the imperial family chapters in *The Red Wheel*, the informed reader discerns the outline of a hypotextual autobiographical narrative from which the fictional account derives. This, then, is a palimpsest. Zhukov's wooden prose is magically transformed by Solzhenitsyn's pen. He makes clever use of facts and details provided by the marshal, from the "raspberry red" breeches⁴³ young Georgy wore as a newly minted squadron commander to his variable impressions of Stalin as tyrant and warlord.

Unlike the fictively disembodied Ektov, Solzhenitsyn's Zhukov boasts a solid textual build: "Though he wasn't that tall, he was strong and broadshouldered."⁴⁴ We learn about his injuries ("concussed by an Austrian shell,"⁴⁵ "wounded by a hand grenade"),⁴⁶ bouts of typhus ("that plague was just jumping from one person to the next"),⁴⁷ horsemanship ("you are the complete master of your body, the sweep of your saber"),⁴⁸ facial features ("a granite chin, and a jaw to match!")⁴⁹ and even the timbre of his voice ("rings like steel!").⁵⁰ And as the aging marshal broods in his riverside dacha, his heart attacks, headaches, and insomnia assume increasing textual prominence.

The protagonist is defined in the succinctest of fashions: "Zhukov loved soldiering more than anything else,"⁵¹ a formula which calls to mind the opening sentence in Napoleon's youthful novel (*Clisson et Eugénie*; 1795), "From birth Clisson was strongly attracted to war."⁵² Not that there is much of Napoleon about this general, who is very much a son of rural Russia: "Yorka Zhukov, born into a peasant family, could handle a rake at hay cutting when he was seven and helped around the family farm as he got older."⁵³ Still, the private man is left largely undescribed: the marshal's first wife and daughters from that marriage are barely mentioned, while his second marriage to a woman thirty years his junior, an event full of potential narrative value, is dealt with in four lines of text. Nor is there any attempt to show Zhukov's motivation for joining the Bolsheviks: Solzhenitsyn's main source is always the marshal's memoirs, which are supremely uninformative on every personal point.

Part one is a portrait of young Yorka (Georgy-boy) as a hard-fighting Red cavalryman: Zhukov before he was Zhukov. An ill-educated soul who believes every word of Bolshevik agitprop, he hacks down a succession of class enemies: Ural Cossacks, counterrevolutionary Kalmyks, Kuban Cossacks and finally the "bandits" of Tambov. Yet he is much more than a simple roughrider. The tough trooper displays leadership qualities ("everyone could see he was made to command"),⁵⁴ a trait that is given a boost by an encounter with Mikhail Tukhachevsky, the celebrated Red Army general, during the Tambov campaign. Known for his scientific conduct of military operations, he employed airplanes, armored cars, and poison gas against poorly armed farmers to win a crushing victory.

The impact of the Red warlord's charisma on the young officer is stunning:

> Tukhachevsky was rather short, but he carried himself proudly, as stately as a peacock.
>
> ...
>
> Zhukov could not take his eyes off the army commander. This was probably the first time in his life he was seeing a genuine military leader, someone completely different from us simple cut-and-thrust commanders.... How self-confident he was!... There was nothing of the peasant in his face; it was aristocratic and well-groomed. He had a long, slender white neck and large, velvet eyes. He'd kept his side whiskers long, but they were carefully trimmed. And he didn't speak at all the way we did.
>
> ...
>
> ... His white hand...[55]

The adulatory male-on-male gaze first maps Tukhachevsky's body shape and posture ("rather short," "carried himself proudly"), then scans the upper torso and limbs: face—neck—face—hand. Yorka's vision and hearing, sharpened by three years of class warfare, pick out the markers of noble birth: the etiolated features, pale skin, upper-class accent. Tukhachevsky is a patrician of the revolution, a communist Catiline commanding an army of plebeians.

Tukhachevsky's martial masculinity appeals and seduces. This is the eroticism of disciplined power. The great captains from Alexander the Great to George Patton have always had this effect on their men. Zhukov's idolizing contemplation of the Red general recalls *War and Peace*, where Nikolai Rostov gazes longingly, adoringly at Tsar Alexander I as he reviews the Russian troops before Austerlitz. Yet the intriguing narrative moment of hero worship and masculine desire quickly passes: "And, with the same proud bearing, he left and drove off in his armored trolley."[56]

This brief encounter is the genesis of Zhukov's thirst for glory, his non-ideological desire to command and to win. The moment in time when man of destiny first glimpses his destiny is another familiar topos. To quote Napoleon again, "It was only on the evening of Lodi that I believed myself to be a superior man, and that the ambition came to me of executing the great things which so far had been occupying my thoughts only as a fantastic dream."[57] The future emperor was twenty-six when he led his soldiers across the bridge at

Lodi; Zhukov is a year younger when he has that inspirational meeting with Tukhachevsky.

Meanwhile the campaign against the Tambov rebels moves to its bloody conclusion, the hero excusing the shooting of hostages and the use of poison gas with soldierly nonchalance: "No great commander can manage without harsh measures."[58] An early indication of the ruthlessness Zhukov would display commanding the Red Army on the Eastern Front. Part one is full of such proleptic pointers, inviting the reader to discern in the rough-hewn trooper the canonical military figure of later wars.

Part two shows the marshal as he reminisces about the past in retirement, so now the diegetic orientation is analeptic, and in places faintly self-referential where the empirical author is concerned: "It's the last freedom left to old age: to spend your time thinking, gazing at the river, and writing a few more lines."[59] Zhukov's reimagined reminiscences lay bare their signature quality of chronological discontinuity, skipping over or compressing months and years: "The most boring part is writing about times long past. ... The real interest begins from the time the Soviet system got well and truly established."[60] The narrative pace is more sedate, reflecting the aging warrior's reflective mood. Solzhenitsyn grants Zhukov a couple of nature-loving lines that would not have been out of place in the "Miniatures," such as a description of the view from his villa: "It's on a high bank, right among the pine trees—real beauties, with trunks rising toward the sky."[61] Occasionally the steady listing of facts and names and places is effectively disrupted by instances of parataxis: *Stal i nedoslyshivat'. Ne vsiakuiu ptitsu, ne vsiakii shorokh*[62] ("My hearing's not what it used to be, either. I don't pick up the sound of each bird and every rustle in the forest").[63]

Having been twice disgraced, first by Stalin and then by Khrushchev, the marshal is a wary memoirist: "Of course, I ... have to weigh my words carefully: there are things that *can't* be brought up at all. The things that can be brought up have to be said with great caution."[64] An old man with a young family, he is concerned about what will happen to his wife and daughter after he is gone. He is painfully aware of the contingent nature of the Soviet good life: "The dacha itself is wonderful, though it belongs to the state, and every stick of furniture has an inventory number tacked onto it. I have possession *for life*."[65] Such are the fictive preliminaries to the account of Zhukov's glory years.

Solzhenitsyn briskly walks us through the details of Zhukov's service at the divisional and corps level and his experiences during the Great Terror: he was denounced but escaped arrest. Half a dozen lines are devoted to his first victory, when in the summer of 1939 he smashed the Japanese Imperial Army at Khalkhin-Gol in Outer Mongolia: "Without waiting for artillery and infantry, he threw a whole tank division directly at them. Two-thirds of them never made it back."[66] This version of events errs on the side of denigration. The episode in question occurred in early July during the initial phase of the operation, when the Japanese were threatening to break through and Zhukov, who was short of infantry, improvised an effective counterblow. Most military historians are impressed with his handling of the troops at this stage but especially subsequently. On August 24 the Soviet commander launched a general offensive, using armor to execute a double envelopment of the Japanese forces, which presaged his tactics at Stalingrad. Within a week the enemy was destroyed. But there is nothing about any of this in the story.

As the newly appointed Chief of Staff, the general must soon contend with Hitler's invasion and the Red Army's catastrophic retreat into the depths of Russia. A succession of field commands ("Zhukov was like Stalin's personal fire department")[67] leads to the great victories that break the Wehrmacht's back, won at immeasurable cost: "The Supreme Commander was always interested to hear about enemy casualties, but he never asked about our own."[68] Let us recall that in *November 1916*, Vorotyntsev "had no equal when it came to keeping his subordinates alive." Zhukov remembers Stalin as a malevolent, graceless character and is fully aware of the dictator's blunders, from his blind trust in Hitler's word before the war to his incompetent generalship during its initial stages. On balance, however, the marshal accords him respect: "A few dimwits were trying to stain his reputation by telling cock-and-bull stories"[69] (a jab at Khrushchev). In retirement Zhukov remains in thrall to the man he served, even adopting Stalin's catechistic style and pedestrian reasoning: "Yet why did our GHQ emerge stronger that Hitler's? Precisely because it was based on Marxism-Leninism."[70]

The hero's indirectly rendered interior monologue features an admiring (parenthetic) reference to General Andrei Vlasov's military skills.[71] In *The Gulag Archipelago* and other nonfictional works Solzhenitsyn tried to restore the reputation of this Soviet commander who in 1942 went over to the Germans and formed the anti-communist Russian Liberation Army, and here the author coopts his fictional Zhukov to this revisionist cause. A less controversial point concerns the crudities of Soviet military historiography: "The Germans, though, had a first-class army. We never write about that or, if we do, it's done with contempt. Yet an attitude like that only cheapens our victory."[72] In another passage, the protagonist criticizes the Soviet high command's performance in the last two years of the war: "All Stalin wanted was to clear [the Germans] off Soviet territory as quickly as possible, even if they left fully intact."[73] In fact,

Operation Bagration, the 1944 summer offensive that annihilated army group Center in Byelorussia, proves the reverse. The lengthy feud between Marshals Zhukov and Konev, which humanizes these otherwise crassly martial figures, is mentioned *en passant*. Solzhenitsyn or his narrator concedes that in the course of the war, "Zhukov turned into a *strategist* [who] acquired a real insight into the mind of the enemy, along with a constant sense, both intellectual and instinctive, of all *our* forces simultaneously."[74] He also allows his protagonist some attractive personal qualities, such as Zhukov's friendship with two other marshals, Konstantin Rokossovsky, whom he rescues from the gulag, and Aleksandr Vasilevsky, who loyally defends him after he is forcibly retired by Khrushchev. A reference to the 150,000 people "burned to death" in the "unnecessary bombing of Dresden"[75] is derived from David Irving's discredited book *The Destruction of Dresden* (1963).

Victory over the Nazis is followed by official disfavor and consequent demotions, first to a posting in Odessa and then banishment to the boondocks as the commander of the Ural District. The supine Zhukov readies a suitcase with a change of underwear, in case he is arrested. Still, he refuses to accept that Stalin is behind this change of fortune, blaming Beria instead. He gets his own back after the Generalissimo dies and the new Party leaders task the marshal with placing the secret police chief in custody. Some of the colorful details are here: "He took him by the elbows and with the strength of a bear jerked him away from the table …,"[76] although the account of the arrest in Khrushchev's memoirs is superior in raw narrative verve if not, perhaps, in historical accuracy.[77] Zhukov becomes defense minister, the de-Stalinizing Twentieth Party Congress comes and goes ("The crimes of Stalin they had uncovered! So many! Absolutely unthinkable!"),[78] and he contemplates taking power himself, but as a "real communist"[79] decides against it. The following year he rescues Khrushchev from an intra-Party coup. His reward? Removal from all his posts by that "little speck of cornmeal"[80] and early retirement, where he plays the accordion and potters in his garden. He starts writing his book after a second heart attack, though without that old rancor toward the generals who now claim credit for his victories. Then Khrushchev himself is sacked and the old soldier is restored to pubic prominence, while his memoirs are accepted for publication, but at a textual price: once again, he must cut and trim, but this time to satisfy the new Party bosses' priorities and even vanities. And so he obediently inserts a reference to a certain Red Army colonel whom "he had never met … during the war, not even on that tiny bridgehead near Novorossiysk."[81] The colonel's name is Leonid Brezhnev. The story concludes on a wistful note, with Zhukov wondering whether he should have laid claim to supreme power after all.

Writerly hatred of the subject may produce happy narrative outcomes, as we saw with the treatment of Lenin in *The Red Wheel*. Here, however, the authorial position is different. It is one of contempt. The marshal's military talents are deprecated and he is portrayed as an ethical nullity. Still, the controlling diegetic voice, a cleverly realized extrapolation of the stodgy narrative accents in Zhukov's memoirs, more than sustains this palpable bias. In effect, the story seconds an earlier literary verdict by Joseph Brodsky, whose poem "On the Death of Zhukov" ("Na smert' Zhukova"; 1974) commemorated

> the exploits of those who, though bold,
> marching triumphant through foreign cities,
> trembled in terror when they came home.[82]

Solzhenitsyn, normally not a big fan of his fellow Nobel laureate, described the last two lines as "brilliantly put."[83] It is a curious fact that the late marshal provided the occasion for these two very different artists to find themselves in artistic agreement: an indication that for all his flaws, Zhukov remains a pivotal figure in Russian history.

4

Like "The Right Hand," "The New Generation" depicts two characters of contrasting ages, backgrounds, and outlooks. The scene is Rostov. In Part one, set in 1926, Anatoly Vozdvizhensky (Builder), a professor of civil engineering, takes pity on a failing student, working class Lyoshka Konoplyov, and gives him an undeserved pass. "I'll never forget this …," sighs Lyoshka after he gets his reprieve,[84] and indeed he does not. Part two, in which the action takes place five years later, sees Konoplyov, now a member of the secret police, pressure the professor into becoming an informer. The story includes a portrait of Lyolka, fifteen, Vozdvizhensky's headstrong daughter, who hates everything Soviet. The near-homonymy of the names Lyoshka and Lyolka is an onomastic cue pointing to the moral and intellectual *difference* between the two young people. In fact, "The New Generation" relies on stark oppositions: highbrow Vozdvizhensky vs. doltish Konoplyov, or the purity of science vs. the crudity of ideology. There is a connection to Mikhail Bulgakov's tale "Heart of a Dog" (*Sobach'e serdtse*; 1925), whose hero, Professor Preobrazhensky (Transformer), transplants a human pituitary gland and testicles into a stray mutt to create a crassly proletarian New Soviet Man.

The academic hero is almost a parody of that staple of Russian literature, the diffident, self-doubting intellectual: "The way he had stretched the truth in Konoplyov's record book today continued to weigh heavily on his conscience."[85] Punctilious in dress and manner, the professor sports a white collar and tie while his faculty colleagues, anxious to display their proletarian cred, are seen abroad in "a simple shirt, belted and worn outside their trousers."[86] Vozdvizhensky observes the political changes taking place around him with a worried eye even as he clings to the middle-class values that defined his life under the tsar. Reluctantly, he "makes allowances"[87] for the dullards from the Worker's Faculty and urges obstreperous Lyolka to join the Komsomol: "You know, … this new generation of young people really does have something, some truth that we can't fully understand."[88] A gentle soul, the professor is technologically accomplished, thoroughly decent and, as we soon learn, terrified of physical pain. A vulnerable kind of identity to have in this country, at this moment in history. Political developments intrude into Lyolka's life as well: her school is about to lose its popular principal who has been there since before the revolution and a fellow pupil is driven to suicide by Komsomol bullies. As for Konoplyov, his last name is a cognate to *konoplia*, the Russian word for "hemp." As we all know, the plant in question is used in the manufacture of marijuana, a narcotic that slows down the thought process and affects short-term memory. Appropriately therefore, Konoplyov is slow on the uptake, just like a pothead with a roach: "This stuff's so complicated it's buggered up my whole brain."[89]

Lyoshka's transformation from dunce to detective is given context by a political meeting held at a local House of Culture, which he attends immediately following the exam. At this festival of cod ideology, a scampering speaker denounces "rubbish like theorems in geometry"[90] and calls on "our new generation"[91] to reject "the sense of humanity in general."[92] In the USSR circa 1926, math and universal human values are out. Instead, the hopping hack proclaims a revolution in the bedroom: "We switch our bioenergy onto socially creative rails."[93] This radical idea sends the youthful audience into transports of erotic delight: "Most of the questions were about sexual liberation."[94]

In part two, where the action takes place in 1931, the campaign against "traitor" engineers is in full swing and people Vozdvizhensky knows start vanishing into "oblivion."[95] The hero finally recognizes "the stupidity and shoddy practices of the party bosses":[96] definitely, a thought crime. And so the reader is not surprised to learn that "one night … they *came* for Vozdvizhensky."[97]

Following his arrest the professor spends a month in an overcrowded cell surrounded by prisoners who must endure beatings or worse. Terrified, he awaits his first interrogation. When the dread hour arrives, the officer assigned to his case theatrically reveals himself as that former academic underachiever, Lyoshka Konoplyov: "The interrogator switched on his desk lamp, rose, switched on the overhead light, and moved to the middle of the room."[98] The onetime knucklehead has learned the tricks of his new trade.

The pair of encounters between Vozdvizhensky and Konoplyov constitute an emblematic power switch that takes place at two different moments of historical time: the tail end of the NEP period (part one) and the conclusion of the collectivization campaign in the countryside (part two). At the exam Konoplyov is "almost in tears,"[99] and the professor breaks into sobs when he at last agrees to become an informer: a lachrymal role reversal, though Vozdvizhensky's predicament is by far the more tragic. Still, we get a sense that by his own dim lights, the Chekist is doing his old teacher a good turn.

The characters are defined through their respective sociolects: Vozdvizhensky pontificates like the professor he is, Lyoshka splutters and grunts, and adolescent Lyolka is adolescently forthright, as in, "The Komsomol is disgusting."[100] As she makes this declaration, she tosses her curly locks: an American teenager would have rolled her eyes. The New Soviet Man, Konoplyov, is given a couple of physiognomic markers to raise his textual profile: he is the owner of a "large and broad" nose and "thick lips."[101] The very picture of Chichikov's malodorous manservant Petrushka in *Dead Souls*, minus the beard: "A fellow of thirty or so ... with very thick lips and nose."[102] There are several linkages to Solzhenitsyn's other works. Before he enrolled in the Worker's Faculty, Lyoshka was a tinsmith, like the infernal Zhora in *August 1914*. The comical lecture on sex and socialism recalls Shamsetdinov's Stalinist sermon in *The First Circle*. After his arrest Vozdvizhensky undergoes the same prison processing as Volodin in that novel, though here the chilling details are compressed into a single sentence: "Stripped naked, having all the buttons of your clothes cut and the soles of your shoes pierced with an awl."[103] One of Investigator Konoplyov's throwaway lines is, "The GPU doesn't make mistakes"[104] (*u GPU oshibok ne byvaet*);[105] in "Incident at Kochetovska Station," we recall, an NKVD officer gives the same message to Zotov (*u nas braka ne byvaet*). And like the tragic Ektov, Vozdvizhensky breaks down when confronted with the ultimate choice: "So—is it the camps? Just keep in mind: your daughter will also get kicked out of her last year as a class alien."[106]

5

"Nastenka" is a diminutive form of Anastasia, a name that means "resurrection" in Greek but which here counteractively denotes a class of *fallen* women with a membership of two. In part one, the orphaned granddaughter of a village priest suffers poverty and sexual violence during the postrevolutionary transformation of the countryside, until she meets a civil war hero who whisks her to Moscow and the Soviet good life: a pilgrim's regress. Her namesake in part two is also her coeval, the daughter of a middle-class Moscow family who grows up to be a high school teacher, only to abandon her cultural values as she becomes integrated into the Soviet educational system. The urban and linguistic realities of Rostov, the city where the author grew up, inform part two of "Nastenka," as they did "The New Generation."

The first Nastenka has a life out of Dickens crossed with Dostoevsky. At school the "red-haired, freckled" waif is taunted as "the priest's granddaughter" and must fend off the boys' wandering hands.[107] This she accomplishes by laying into her tormentors with a branch of acacia: orphan Nastya has spunk. After her seven years of schooling are up, an aunt offers counsel: "You've got to understand that the Komsomol's your only choice. Otherwise, you might as well hang yourself."[108] A piece of family advice that echoes, if crudely, the words spoken by Vozdvizhensky to Lyolka.

Before she swears the Komsomol oath, the young heroine performs a secret rite:

> Late one evening when no one was watching, Nastya took out the little icon of Christ and gave it one final and penitent kiss. Then she tore it into tiny pieces so that no one could tell what it had been.[109]

She is now Anastasia the Apostate.

Put in charge of a village reading room, Nastya is ostracized by the peasants as "a dyed-in-the-wool part of Soviet power."[110] Other librarian positions come and go, in the Russian and Ukrainian sticks. Meanwhile her life follows a descending sexual spiral as her rural bosses exact a carnal fee for their patronage: *le droit du camarade*. At sixteen, Nastya suffers serial rapes, first by the chairman of the village soviet ("Korzun was masterful and insatiable"),[111] then by his regional superior ("Arandarenko had compliments for her: 'You're turning into a proper young tart. Your eyes sparkle, you're lovely'").[112] In the way of the sexually abused, she develops feelings for the latter, but in vain. A handsome

Ukrainian gets her pregnant, then deserts her. After an attempt to miscarry and a failed suicide, her Komsomol cell arranges a shotgun wedding. Nastya gives birth on top of a Russian stove, an addendum to its list of domestic functions as recorded in "Matryona's Home." Her no-good husband leaves her for good; she gets a divorce. From now on Nastya feels "constant cravings" for sex.[113] Affairs and abortions follow, again and again. Nastya's grandfather is deported to the Solovki concentration camp, where he dies. Her aunt, who is now employed in a GPU brothel, recruits her for the same line of work, which the by now thoroughly debauched Nastya considers "carefree fun"[114] even as she studies for her teaching certificate. The text periodically reminds us that this promiscuous young woman has a daughter, little Yulka, but the child is merely a fictive attribute of corrupted motherhood. Except for a scar on her foot, she remains a tiny cipher. Nastya's two happy years as a GPU prostitute end when the aunt is arrested, and soon thereafter she meets her civil war veteran, a one-armed true believer who bears the power name of Viktor and attends the prestigious Industrial Academy in Moscow (Nadezhda Alliluyeva, Stalin's second wife, is a fellow student). He whisks mother and daughter to the capital, a cornucopia where "you could eat whenever you felt like it."[115] It is now 1932, and in the collectivized countryside there is terror and famine, but the heroine's misadventures are at an end, at least in formal, fabulatory terms. This working girl has entered the workers' paradise.

The story of Nastya the prodigal orphan reads like a schema for a full-length novel. This is not a criticism. Solzhenitsyn squeezes a large amount of history into a dozen pages, integrating it with the particulars of individual lives and some vivid details such as the heroine's macabre sleeping arrangements: inside a former church, Nastya and Yulka "made a bed on the table where they had once laid the shroud or rested the coffin at funerals."[116] The heroine is one of the writer's most tragic creations, a subaltern figure through and through who always remains a passive victim of horrible circumstances, without voice or agency, a furtive, freckled presence controlled by the predatory men in her life. Although a victim of sexual trauma may resort to promiscuity as a way of seizing agency, the story's treatment of Nastya's personality and behavior implicitly disavows such an interpretation. The narrative always reflects her perspective, but she never utters a single word in the form of direct speech: a diegetic indicator of her status as a fictive object, rather than subject. Nastya's chaotic sex life makes her different from any other female character in Solzhenitsyn, although the hurried listing of her lovers and agitprop appointments leaves no room for a fuller treatment of adolescent sexual trauma, the experience that shapes her identity and determines the bad choices she makes. Silenced by the author, Nastya is not allowed to tell us the *why* of her transformation from rape victim to nymphomaniac, a change that can only be explained in psychological terms, but which the story historicizes, to the exclusion of every other factor.

If the first Nastenka is a career librarian, the second Nastenka is a lifelong reader. Several of Solzhenitsyn's works feature characters that are actual or would-be writers, but part two is his only text in which the protagonist is a *consumer* of literature. As in part one, the narration takes the form of free indirect discourse, though *this* Nastya is the daughter of an educated Moscow family and her language and attitudes express a refined, almost exaggerated sensibility. There are interesting moments of diegetic discontinuity when the narrative departs from the heroine's genteel perspective and makes programmatic cultural points in the recognizable accents of the author himself, as in the framing passages about Moscow and Rostov, the city where he grew up. The difference between the right and the wrong way of reading literature is a central theme and famous writers serve as cultural referents for both Nastya and her father, an epidemiologist who is "a great lover of Chekhov":[117] one medical man admiring the extra-medical productions of another.

Little Nastya grows up in a leafy part of Moscow, surrounded by beauty and art and taking private lessons even as World War I is followed by revolution and years of nationwide violence. These catastrophic events, however, do not intrude into the cozy apartment with its rows of books whose spines are "like a flower garden."[118] From early on, Nastenka possesses a vivid, even hallucinatory imagination: the heroes and heroines of Turgenev and Pushkin "stood before her as if alive, right next to her; she could see them in the flesh and hear their voices."[119] How's that for suspension of disbelief! At her elite high school, which "by some miracle" remains open after the Bolsheviks take over, she meets a charismatic teacher, "ashen-haired"[120] Maria Feofanovna, a name saturated with sacral meanings: Maria—the mother of Jesus, Theophanes—"manifestation of God." Thanks to this celestial figure, the young girl comes to understand that literature ought to be read analytically:

> She learned to look at books in a new way—not just to live with the characters but to live constantly with the author: What was he feeling when he wrote that? How did he regard his characters? Was he the sole master of their lives, or were they independent of him? How did he organize this scene or that one, and what words and phrases did he choose in doing so?[121]

From a childish absorption in the text to a critical examination of it, even if the premise—"to live constantly with the author"—may strike a twentieth century lit. major as jejune. Nastenka decides she wants to be a teacher, like her favorite schoolmistress, but the "ideologically outmoded"[122] Maria Feofanovna is swept away by the tempest of revolution. The same ill wind blows over Nastenka's father, who is posted to Rostov, and so they must leave for those southern and, in Solzhenitsyn's book, insalubrious parts. Nastenka is a reading heroine and thus inevitably oriented toward the first, and paradigmatic, female reader in Russian literature, Tatyana Larina in Pushkin's verse novel *Eugene Onegin*, a book that undoubtedly formed part of the bibliographical orchard on her shelf.

Nastenka is now sixteen: the same age as her namesake in part one when *her* life took a tragic turn. Sorrowfully, she contemplates her departure from the city she loves:

> Moscow! There could be no city more beautiful than Moscow, a place that had been formed not by the lifeless plan of some architect but by the active lives of many thousands over the course of centuries. Its boulevards and its two ring roads, its noisy, colorful streets, and its crookedly wandering lanes and grassy courtyards in which people lived their separate lives, its sky filled with the many voices of bells ringing in every pitch and timbre. Moscow, with its Kremlin, its Rumiantsev Library, its famous university, and its Conservatory.[123]

This paean to the Russian capital has a distinctly Tolstoyan feel ("the active lives of many thousands") spliced with a touch of Tsvetaeva ("loved the whole of Moscow by heart"), even if its campanological ring is pure Solzhenitsyn. There are echoes of much-anthologized encomiums from *Eugene Onegin*, Lermontov's long poem *Sashka* (c. 1835–6), and his essay "A Panorama of Moscow" ("Panorama Moskvy"; c. 1833–4). Like the Agnia chapter in *The First Circle* or the episode of Lazhenitsyn's Moscow excursion in *August 1914*, the passage records the author's nostalgia for the city as he had never known it, with its historically asymmetrical aspect and colorful street life.

As Nastya discovers, Rostov cannot compete with Moscow's poetic appeal. While her Chekhovian father goes about his medical duties, she struggles to adjust to her new surroundings: "... The city ... seemed utterly foreign, not Russian, because of its multiracial population and, in particular, because of its corrupted language: the sounds of the local speech were distorted, and the stresses on words were not right."[124] It is no wonder that with attitudes like these Nastya makes no friends at her new school. To add political insult to phonetic injury, she must join the Komsomol if she is to go to college (a familiar predicament). By way of cultural self-protection, the right-speaking heroine decorates her new home with portraits of the Russian classics, among them a deathbed likeness of the poet Nikolai Nekrasov, a lugubrious populist: "She loved him fiercely for his unfailing response to the tribulations of the people."[125] As this affirmation suggests, Nastya has grown into an earnest young woman who lives and breathes literature. When her father falls ill with tuberculosis, she sees a connection to her favorite poet as well as the paternal literary totem: "Was there some sinister resemblance to Nekrasov here? ... how many lives had it already carried away? Even Chekhov's."[126]

Nastya enrolls in the local pedagogical institute, hoping to follow in the footsteps of the supernal Maria Feofanovna, but her college experience is a dreary one, for the curriculum relies on cod Marxist interpretations of the classics. Pushkin, she learns, "expressed the mindset and ideology of the mid-level landowners during the incipient crisis of Russian feudalism."[127] By way of compensation, she acquires a boyfriend, darkly handsome Shura Gen, who soon wants to sleep with her. Though as middle-class as Nastya, Shura is a fiery Komsomol and spends much of his time ranting, as in, "After the revolution we need not just new words but even new letters for them! Even the periods and commas of the past become repulsive."[128] This is funny. And if we bear in mind that "Shura" is a diminutive of "Aleksandr" and "Gen" just begs to be expanded into an aptronym of distinction, we get Solzhenitsyn's other little joke: Shura Gen—Alexander the Genius. In any case, romantic Nastya is enthralled by Shura's fulminations, though even his grammatical ardor cannot induce her to go all the way.

At this point things start to sag. The story turns into a polemical commentary on the devolution of Russian literature into its terminal SocRealist stage. Nastya, Shura, and their friends read and debate lots of bad novels and poems, passionately and at length. There are a dozen pages of this, and they seldom work. The stream of references to books, movements, and writers' groups, most of them deservedly forgotten, overshadows important events in the heroine's life such as her breakup with Shura and the death of her father. Nastya's unhappy circumstances become props for Solzhenitsyn's literary interpretations and annotations.

Things pick up in the last couple of pages. At the high school where she gets a job after graduation, our heroine is transformed into Anastasia Dmitrievna, a pedagogical matron. She tries and fails to steer a middle course between her love of the classics and the curricular demands for "Demyanizing literature,"[129] after the revolutionary versifier Demyan Bedny (a Stalinist Maya Angelou, with mustache). The socialist reconstruction of reality, with its never-ending workweek and worsening food shortages, intrudes into Nastya's schoolmarmish existence. She tells her mother, a religious believer, that "Communism ... is based on the same ideals as Christianity; it just takes a different path to reach them,"[130] and is able to convince herself, if not the latter. Soon thereafter the empirical author discreetly enters the story when he depicts his schoolboy self in the guise of Anastasia Dmitrievna's favorite pupil, "a skinny boy with disheveled hair that would never stay in place."[131] Eventually the heroine gives in and embraces the ideological strictures of the day and the decade: "She herself could no longer even express what she had once felt."[132] The story ends on this unhappy note. The implied conclusion is that Nastya's secular humanist worldview, a trait she shares with her sympathetic father, was not enough to sustain her integrity as a teacher or reader. Like the Nastya of part one, she is an apostate.

Much of part two amounts to a less-than-gripping account of how the various schools of Soviet literature adjusted, or failed to adjust, to the Party line, replete with a glossary of obscure names and titles: Solzhenitsyn's Parthian shot at SocRealism. Nastya's mother is first mentioned two-thirds of the way into the story, long after the move to Rostov has taken place. This reader initially assumed that the heroine lost her at birth and that the empyrean Maria Feofanovna had, on some psychodynamic level, taken her place in Nastya's affections. Again, we learn what the heroine looks like very late in the proceedings. Her face, we are told, "was rather broad, and her figure was nothing special, but her eyes were filled with an amazing radiance and she had a smile that simply captured people's hearts"[133] (*shirokovatoe litso, da i figura tozhe nekhorosha, no zamechatel'no blesteli glaza, i ulybka takaia, chto razbirala serdtsa*),[134] which may be the flattest passage in the whole of Solzhenitsyn. That said, the resonant authorial accents, which periodically obtrude into the point-of-view narration that always privileges Nastya's perceptual stance, more than redeem these stylistic flubs and longueurs.

6

"Apricot Jam" marks a return to earlier themes, the realities of life and death in the gulag and the moral cost of being an establishment artist in a carceral state. The story showcases Solzhenitsyn's customary strengths such as the skillful construction of historically framed idiolects and an eye for the revealing trait, traitor, or quirk. The two sections are radically different in their subject matter and diegetic registers. Part one takes the form of a letter from a dying forced laborer, the teenage son of an expropriated kulak, to a famous novelist. This is a maximal narrator text that particularizes the terminal horror of the teller's camp experience by foregrounding his malformed, distorted speech patterns, which have a terrible descriptive power: a "condensed version of 'Ivan Denisovich.'"[135] In part two, the prisoner's celebrity addressee, identified only as The Writer, is visited at his well-appointed dacha by an observant academic who is variously charmed and appalled by this charismatic, larger-than-literature figure. Here Solzhenitsyn employs the mimetic techniques of imitation, representation, and portrayal to very considerable effect.

The prisoner in part one, whose name is Fedya (that is, Fyodor or Theodore—"the gift of God"), relates the savagery he suffered as a Soviet work slave in a matter-of-fact, matter-of-death manner: Arctic temperatures, impossible production quotas, shoes of sacking and wire. With its "living conveyor belt" of workers[136] digging a giant hole for some unnamed industrial purpose, the text calls to mind Andrei Platonov's novel *The Foundation Pit* (*Kotlovan*; 1929–30). Still, Solzhenitsyn's factual, historical focus is very different from the dystopian thrust of that anti-totalitarian classic. These six pages are a stylistic tour de force, with the author displaying his old mastery of "superbly reproduced popular speech with an admixture of camp slang"[137] (see the highlighting of early Soviet sociolects in Platonov).

> When you came back from working the cold and into the barracks, the lice would all come right lively and we'd spend some time squashing them. And there was not a scrap of industriosity left in our lives.[138]
>
> [*A v barak c morozu vernësh'sia—tut vshi ozhivliaiutsia, davim ikh. I ne ostavalos' v nashei zhizni uzhe nikakoi prilezhnosti.*][139]

Years earlier Shalamov had remarked on the unlikely absence of vermin in Ivan Denisovich's camp,[140] so here the author corrects that tiny omission, which actually was not an omission.[141] Another connection to Solzhenitsyn's first published work is Fedya's memories of village life. Like the grizzled hero of that earlier tale, the teenager fondly recalls the pre-collectivized village as a place of good eats: "Apricots were our most favorite fruit, and I never ever tasted any as good as ours. In the summer kitchen in the yard my mother would make us apricot jam, and my brothers and I just couldn't get enough of that sweet foam."[142]

Young Fedya's misfortunes begin when his family is deported for owning four horses, three cows, and a house with a metal roof. Only in a country as wretchedly poor as Russia would such modest chattels be considered proof of living large. He does time in a GPU prison and eventually is drafted into the Logistical Support Forces, a militarized structure designed to extract an industrial corvée from political undesirables (the original idea was Trotsky's). Thieves, members of the former middle classes, and ex-kulaks toil in conditions that are no different from those in the gulag. Winter comes. After months of laboring half-dressed and half-fed, Fedya is *in extremis*. A doctor gives him two weeks to live, hence that desperate plea for help: "Would it cost too much for you to send me a food parcel? Please take pity on me."[143]

The protagonist in part two is a notionally disguised Aleksei Tolstoy (a relation of sorts), the author of *Peter the First* (*Pëtr Pervyi*; 1929–45), perhaps the finest historical novel in Russian literature. Known as the Red Count, Tolstoy provided important cultural services to the Stalin regime while injecting a note of aristocratic glamor into the dictator's entourage of lowborn hoodlums and hacks. He was also the recipient of a famous slap in the face, delivered by the hand of Osip Mandelshtam in 1934. Many contemporaries ascribed the poet's tragic death in the gulag to the Red Count's ensuing malevolence. One of them was Anna Akhmatova, who shared her impressions of the SocRealist panjandrum with Isaiah Berlin:

> He was a very gifted and interesting writer, a scoundrel, full of charm, and a man of stormy temperament; he is dead now; he was capable of anything, anything; he was abominably anti-Semitic; he was a wild adventurer, a bad friend, he only liked youth, power, vitality, he didn't finish his *Peter the First* because he said that he could only deal with Peter as a young man; what was he to do with all those people when they were old? He was a kind of Dolokhov, he called me Annushka—that made me wince—but I liked him, even though he was the cause of the death of the best poet of our time, whom I loved and who loved me.[144]

(Fyodor Dolokhov is the coldly charismatic roué in *War and Peace*.)

Solzhenitsyn's portrait of this lesser Tolstoy complements Akhmatova's colorful character sketch. The narrative angle shifts between the point of view of Vasily Kiprianovich, a professor of cinema studies who has been summoned to brief the Red Count on screenwriting techniques, and a more detached diegetic perspective that indicates a measure of historical distance from the events described: the author speaketh, or rather implieth. A second visitor to this cultural tea party, the dwarfish critic Efim Martynovich, is modeled on Osip Beskin, a rabid ideologue mentioned in part two of "Nastenka."

The professor, a decent if timorous soul, arrives at the villa knowing what his host is about: "Vasily Kiprianovich had little respect for this Writer; he had a huge talent, to be sure, and weighty, meaty turns of phrase, but what a cynic he was!"[145] The visitor's cinematic eye picks out details of the decor: reproductions of Monet, white-tiled stoves, a French-made refrigerator. He sequentially registers the Writer's physical traits: the "fleshy, broad body,"[146] pendulous jowls, and a substantial bald spot that seems to wax and wane in keeping with his flights of rhetoric: the host has a pronounced fondness for the sound of his own voice. Surprisingly in one so double-chinned and triple-dimpled, this is a "reedy tenor."[147] Not that the orotund novelist uses his squeaky vocals to spout nonsense. In fact, he has some clever things to say: "I believe that *every* sentence has a gesture to go with it, and sometimes even every word. A person is constantly gesturing—if not physically, then always emotionally"[148] (the notion is derived from Nietzsche).[149] Solzhenitsyn takes his subject at his word and in a literalizing twist, lays fictive stress on the Writer's body language: "His arms, not powerful and even a bit plump but still flexible and free of rheumatism in the hands and fingers, extended to show the scale on which he was prepared to work."[150] Proud of his entrée into the corridors of power, the novelist casually drops Stalin's name over tea and pastries, shocking timorous Vasily Kiprianovich with the mensal mention of that totemic signifier: "Was this last little phrase appropriate for a tea table? But no, it had now become the fashion to speak this way in private gatherings. And the Writer, as everyone could see, was in Stalin's personal favor."[151] Later the host declares that "the *language* of a work of art is simply *everything*!"[152] To illustrate this ideologically dicey notion, he mentions his use of certain archival materials:

> "And do you know what set me on the right path? Studying legal documents from the seventeenth century and earlier. When an accused was being questioned and tortured, the scribes would record precisely and concisely what he said. While someone was being flogged, stretched on the rack, or burned with a hot iron, the most unadorned speech, coming from his very bowels, would burst forth from him. And this is something absolutely new! It's the language Russians have been speaking for a thousand years, but none of our writers have used it. Now this," he said, dripping some of the thick apricot jam from a teaspoon onto a small glass dish, "this very amber transparency, this surprising color and light should be present in the literary language as well."[153]

The reference to "the language Russians have been speaking for a thousand years" (*eto iazyk, na kotorom russkie govoriat uzhe tysiachu let*)[154] is a nicely crafted slip of the tongue that suggests a millennium of enhanced interrogations. Yet the statements by the ample-bodied wordsmith are derived from Tolstoy's articles or public remarks, which Solzhenitsyn combed through, doubtless holding his nose, as he worked on the story, a procedure similar to the one he undertook when designing his fictional Lenin for *The Red Wheel*.

The talents and flaws that Akhmatova listed are all here. The Writer not only speaks the Lie and writes the Lie, but revels in his authorship of it. He derives a Goebbels-like thrill from a well-turned demagogic sally: "American novelists are no better than the pickpockets of an obsolescent culture."[155] He struts his socialist stuff while wallowing in pre-revolutionary luxury, his manor guarded by a magnificently bearded watchman "who might have stepped from some nineteenth-century painting."[156] Still, the protagonist is much more than a self-satisfied purveyor of clever falsehoods. In some ways he is a charming, even attractive personality (as Akhmatova noted). With his stout build and "a particular Russian, expansive cordiality without the least affectation,"[157] he resembles old Count Rostov in *War and Peace*, though without the sprawling family.

Honest Vasily Kiprianovich is puzzled by this SocRealist sybarite: "How could a man with such talent keep pounding with his sledgehammer and doing it in such inspired language, as if carried away in a rush of sincerity."[158] Naturally, the diffident academic does not question his host along such lines, but we are given to understand that *this* Tolstoy is a voluptuary who derives an equal pleasure from the conspicuous exercise of his oh-so-flexible literary skills and the inconspicuous enjoyment of the material goods they earn him. In general, hedonistic personalities à la the Red Count rarely feature in Solzhenitsyn's fictions. Perhaps only sensuous, cowardly Yakonov (*The First Circle*) and sensuous, power-hungry Parvus (*The Red Wheel*) belong in the same category. Mounted in Solzhenitsyn's display cabinet like some fleshy moth, Aleksei Tolstoy represents a late addition to the collection of Stalinist notables depicted in *The First Circle*.

Having identified torture records as his primary source, the novelist mentions a letter he recently received from "a workman building a factory in Kharkov," written in a language so "compelling" that he intends to borrow it for his fictions: "Things like that you can't invent, even if you swallow your pen."[159] The kindhearted professor asks if he will write back to the man who sent him that amber-worded missive, but the Writer dismisses the notion: "The point isn't in the answer. The point is in discovering a language."[160] The inflections, or infections, of Modernism . . .

Tolstoyan in more ways than one, "Apricot Jam" joins narrative laconicism (part one) with expansive story-telling (part two). Fedya's letter, with its wrenchingly naïve epistolary voice that lists the hideous stages in the teenager's journey to death, is as memorable as anything Solzhenitsyn has written, while the portrait of the Writer is novelistic in its multi-layeredness and meticulousness of always relevant detail. There are descriptive moments of real power: "The Critic shrank like a mushroom near a flame"[161] (*Kritika poëzhilo kak grib ot blizkogo ognia*).[162] The recurring references to apricots—hints, perhaps, of the fabulous uriuk in *Cancer Ward*—constitute a symbolical link between the Fedya and Tolstoy sections. As a child, Fedya loved apricot jam and the Writer has an identical preference, which he freely indulges as he holds forth to his tiny audience. To venture a metaphor, fruit preserve is the sticky stuff that glues the two segments together. One final point. The brutal Mamaev,[163] a pistol-waving commissar at Fedya's work camp, and the urbane novelist are both members of the All-Union Executive Committee, the USSR's collective presidency. Picture some Kremlin ceremony, with the leather-clad jailer seated on a dais next to the tweedy author, and you have the two faces of Soviet despotism.

7

The thematic continuity between Parts One and Two of the next binary tale, "No Matter What," consists of life's truth, institutionally framed, that rank hath its privileges. There is always a gulf between those who make decisions and those who make do, whether in the Red Army during World War II or in the Siberian sticks half a century later. Like the formula "For the Good of the Cause," the titular phrase generates an ironic motif: "no matter what" (*vsë ravno*) can mean either "at any price" or "who cares!" It all depends on the moment in time, the moment in history.

November 1942. The battle of Stalingrad is nearing its terrible climax, but the military men that populate part one are not doing any fighting. Officers and conscripts in a reserve regiment, they await their turn to be sent to the front. The main character is newly minted Lieutenant Pozushan, "a straight arrow not so much from service … but from his internal sense of duty,"[164] that is, a second Vasya Zotov. Like the zealous hero of "Incident at Kochetovka Station," the lieutenant finds himself having to match the realities of wartime against an assimilated set of political rules. In Pozushan's case, his inner conflict hinges on this less-than-fateful quandary: what should he do about the pilferage of potatoes from the mess by soldiers in his company? Complicating the situation is the protagonist's painful awareness that the latter regard him as a military novice (which he is) and that he has yet to prove himself either as an officer or, indeed, a *man*. The lieutenant reports the theft to the battalion commissar, Major Fatyukov, though he hopes this will not result in the kind of outcome that is typical of Stalinist justice: "The episode is directly suited for court-martial, but how can we go that far? (Not only out of pity for them, the fools, but heading for the front, it is also unwise to thin one's own ranks.)"[165] To Pozushan's surprise, the commissar invites his vigilant subordinate to partake of a pot of potatoes, likewise removed from the regiment's food supply, though this time for the benefit of its senior officers. When the lieutenant, rigid with shock, refuses to chow down, Fatyukov tells him that the men should be allowed to consume the stolen victuals.

The economy of description is stark. Callow Pozushan is a voice and a set of inhibitions. He is always hungry (the only physiological element in the portrayal) and youthfully self-conscious: "He crisply brought his hand to his temple (he was getting good at saluting)."[166] In Solzhenitsyn, we recall, the crispness or otherwise of a young officer's salute serves as an indicator of his martial identity, or lack thereof. The men in Pozushan's company are outlines of an outline: Private Timonov has a family who are "being hounded for something"[167] back on their collective farm, and Sergeant Guskov, a go-getter with "little mobile eyes,"[168] is a bit of a crook. The commissar is a more substantial presence: he has "wide clear eyes"[169] (his physical marker, twice mentioned in the text) and a relaxed awareness that the agitprop he dispenses has little to do with the way things really are. A combat veteran, he watches over Pozushan with an almost fatherly indulgence. Most important, he possesses a life's wisdom that the lieutenant has yet to acquire: "You cannot change human nature even under socialism."[170] A truth still not universally acknowledged in AD 2019.

Part two is set half a century later and half a continent away. The focus is on the environmental threat posed to Siberia's Angara River by the economic reforms of the early 1990s, made worse by the residual impact of Soviet-era central planning. Once again Solzhenitsyn records the depredations of modernity, now not of the communist, but post-communist, kind. Like "For the Good of the Cause," this is a piece of topical realism, conscientiously fictionalized.

A powerful official, to whom the other characters refer as "the minister" (he's that important!), is sailing down the Angara on a fact-finding visit in connection with the planned construction of a huge hydroelectric station. During this excursion, which features picturesque riverside views and a champagne luncheon, the VIP conducts a meet-and-greet with regional notables. As he does so, he learns that the proposed power plant, a Soviet-style white elephant of obsolete design, will flood vast tracts of land, displace rural communities, and destroy the surrounding taiga, already ravaged by decades of ruthless exploitation. Solzhenitsyn had traveled to the Angara region in 1994 and the writing conveys the immediacy of personal impression[171] while calling up Valentin Rasputin's novel *Farewell to Matyora* (*Proshchanie s Matëroi*; 1976): with its almost identical plot, set in the same parts, that earlier work becomes a hypotext for part two.

Although the man from Moscow remains nameless throughout, his sculpted hair and relaxed body language are presentational markers that identify him as one of Yeltsin's Young Reformers, even if in politics youth is an elastic concept. As a matter of fact, the visitor is "in middle age, naturally vibrant, alert. His tie, according to some new fashion, was lowered; and the collar was unbuttoned at the top. Leg over leg, even swinging back and forth at times."[172]

The story's grim ecological message is delivered by Valentina Filippovna, the "chairman of the regional committee for environmental protection and rational use of natural resources"[173] (yes, her full title is given), who briefs the minister on these matters of concern. "An applied chemist, a graduate of the Forestry Academy and with work experience at her back,"[174] Valentina knows her stuff. Her "open face" and "head-on look without any flirting mannerism"[175] make her a cross-generational sister to Lydia Georgievna, the earnest teacher in "For the Good of the Cause." As the well-briefed ecologist recites her facts and figures—"phenols and turpentine, ... waters ... degraded down to Class V, now even Class VI"[176]—she never "stumbles" or "tires,"[177] for which the implied author gives her implied credit. As for the official, he listens closely and his assistant takes notes. This affable bigwig is nothing like the wooden Party bosses of yesteryear, so the intense ecologist begins to hope she might be getting through. For his part, as the minister watches Valentina Filippovna rushing to put her points across, he thinks a sexist thought: "She is so hot and bothered about all this! Must be she's not married."[178] Reformer, reform thyself!

Part two's appeal, however, lies not in Valentina's erudite disquisition but in the other characters we encounter on board the cutter or, in one case, on dry land. The captain, mild-mannered Anatoly, "love[s] the Angara like his wife"[179] and knows every bend and shoal: a one-river man. Despite his professional expertise, he is a touch intimidated by the presence of all these VIPs. The ship's mechanic, gruff Semyon Khripkin, is not so easily impressed: "I don't believe any of those bosses, whether the old ones or the new ones."[180] Eventually the bulbous engine room jockey—"head like a ball, body like a ball"[181]—gives the visiting dignitary a piece of his mind: "How about the timber complex, why did they rip it into forty enterprises? Now they have all stopped. For every man there are three foremen, and all are out of work. Meanwhile, those who broke it up lined their pockets with millions."[182]

Next, a regional administrator, Zdeshnev (Man from Here), relates that in Old Keul, a village flooded by Moscow's edict, the residents had tried to defend their homes with pitchforks and axes: a scene out of a medieval chronicle. All were forcibly resettled on land unsuitable for habitation. An unassuming sort in mismatched jacket and trousers, Zdeshnev peppers his speech with imported words like *imidzh*[183] and *pressing*,[184] but for all that talks a lot of sense. The events planner, paunchy Scepura, could not be more different from pugnacious Khripkin or homespun Zdeshnev. A "round-headed little man, energetic despite being on the wrong side of fifty, and quick with words,"[185] he is a juiced-in hustler tasked with taking care of the minister's travel needs, a fleshier version of the enterprising Sergeant Glushkov in part one. Scepura has put together a lavish spread in the salon: principled Valentina initially refuses to partake, just like principled Pozushan all those years ago. One imagines that should the minister request it, the frisky fixer could arrange for more private forms of diversion as well.

During the cruise the party visits a village slated for flooding. It stands intact but eerily empty. This is a different kind of sinister rural locus from the one explored by Volodin and Klara in *The First Circle*. Here it is not the presence of evil but the absence of life that is affecting. "No one. No chickens to peck at the ground here, no cat to sneak by."[186] Zdeshnev, who is cleverer than he looks, arranges a seemingly chance encounter with a peasant, Zabolotnov (Beyond the Marsh), a smallholder who insisted on staying put. He explains the challenges of being a farmer in these post-Soviet times—"scoundrel speculators," "the meat plant cheats you"[187]—and talks about his father, a prosperous peasant who lost everything under the communists. One of Zabolotnov's sons drowned in the Angara, but the old man refuses to despair: "I do love God."[188] His profession of faith makes everyone in the group, whatever their individual human worth, feel "uncomfortable and awkward."[189] For these secularists, the devout farmer is a very strange bird indeed. Zabolotnov's Siberian-inflected Russian is a discursive high point, while his life's philosophy comes straight out of the author's compendium of proverbs: "What course has been set—for river or for man—is the one to follow."[190] The story's moral is made abundantly clear. That said, the folksy agriculturalist is its most memorable personality, a figure out of Tolstoy or Bunin who by some quirk of history has found himself on the wrong side of the Urals in the last decade of the twentieth century.

The vessel, a water-borne site of corruption which stands, or floats, in opposition to the pristine wilderness stretching out on either side, is turned into an allegorical ship of state circa 1993. As part two unfolds we realize that the minister is a well-meaning sort who is not unmoved by the chorus of voices pleading for the suspension of the project. However, upon his return to Moscow he learns that the cabinet's mind is made up and so decides to leave well enough alone, like Major Fatyukov in part one. Granted, when a powerful functionary ignores the human cost of his government's policies at a time of economic collapse, that abnegation is by an immoral order of magnitude worse than a wartime officer's habit of peculating potatoes. As the acerbic Khripkin puts it, "They steal in a big way, not like us—and they know how to hide it and not get caught."[191] But it is the minister who has the last word, or thought: "If a decision is adopted, and even reconfirmed, there is no changing it anyway, no matter what."[192]

8

"Fracture Points" was Solzhenitsyn's second fictional take on Russia's Turbulent Nineties. Other than *Lenin in Zurich*, this is his only work of prose that features, in part one, a protagonist that is truly and irredeemably evil. Dmitry Yemtsov is the tough, ambitious sixty-five-year-old head of a defense conglomerate who has successfully negotiated the transition from communism to capitalism. A can-do Stalinist, he has reconfigured himself as a Yeltsin-era tycoon: "My view is that making money is an interesting occupation. No less interesting than being the beating pulse of the military-industrial complex or, say, understanding cybernetics."[193] This section of the story is, in essence, a summary of the antihero's work record, rendered via Sozhenitsyn's favorite technique of free indirect speech and copiously illustrated with facts and stats. Part two, in which Yemtsov is also present, albeit briefly, depicts the murderous goings-on in the world of post-Soviet banking: too brutal to fail.

Yemtsov's parentage is historically representative. He is the son of a shop foreman and a noblewoman, a revolutionary mésalliance that recalls the marriage of Volodin's parents in *The First Circle*.[194] As a student, the protagonist must choose between atomic energy and automated aircraft systems as his field of specialization, and opts for the latter, on impulse rather than by informed choice. He is lucky, for had he gone nuclear, "he would have been locked away in secret laboratories for years on end."[195] In fact, Yemtsov is a bit of a gambler with a "devil-may-care boldness"[196] that repeatedly boosts his career. Prominent figures take a hand in giving its trajectory an upward slant, among them a "lively and generous" Khrushchev[197] and a stolid Dmitry Ustinov, the head of the Soviet arms industry. Like all successful men, Yemtsov has a knack for meeting the right people at the right time.

The antihero's association with the military-industrial complex begins in the late 1940s when he decides, again on the spur of the moment, to exchange a promising position as an up-and-coming Moscow Party activist for a posting in the provinces. At this point the white goods motif of the earlier binary tales reemerges. Yemtsov's first managerial assignment is to retro-engineer a British-made fridge with a view to commencing domestic production. Initially things do not go well: "Buyers would return the refrigerators with complaints and curses: 'The damned thing won't stay cold!'"[198] A couple of pages later, however, the problem is fixed and the "damned things" start selling like hot cakes or frosted donuts. The can-do Yemtsov graduates from fridges to radar systems to ICBMs. Years pass, Five Year Plans are fulfilled and over-fulfilled, the protagonist climbs to the very top of the managerial ladder and glories in his leadership of Tezar, as the conglomerate comes to be known. Not all in his life is radars and rockets, however. Solzhenitsyn does a nice job of depicting the poetics of corporate masculinity, Soviet-style. Unlike the "grim faces with their flabby cheeks, double chins, expressionless eyes" populating the *nomenklatura*, Yemtsov is energetic and trim and possesses an "aristocratic forehead,"[199] a genetic gift from his aristocratic mother. He has two sons by the same wife, the youngest having been born after the mogul turned sixty, a procreational achievement that fills him with pride.

Meanwhile, history marches on. Yemtsov watches in disgust as Gorbachev's bungled economic reforms collapse but is impressed with those of Yeltsin's shockingly therapeutic variety. He jumps ahead of the post-communist curve by taking ownership of the gigantic industrial organization he controls: the sleek tycoon has connections at the highest levels of government. After the neo-liberal academic Yegor Gaidar assumes charge of the sinking economy, "Yemtsov squeezed into an airplane with the vice premier, and while they were en route to a conference, he obtained permission to privatize Tezar and break it up."[200] The Red Director in airborne conclave with the Young Reformer: a scene that everts a common topos of the SocRealist production novel, the *productive meeting* between the labor-intensive hero and a supportive official.

Tezar is duly carved into sixty separate pieces, workers are sacked by the thousands, and those that remain go without pay, but Yemtsov still sees a profit, now turning out gas meters and hats and renting out properties. He becomes a pioneer of the new leisure industry, opening a casino and a "regular brothel," even if the goings-on inside are an affront to his Stalinist tastes: "I'd be happy to pay those half-baked impotents not to listen to their music."[201] Who said that disco is dead?

Yemtsov is an entirely historicized character, his personality traits and managerial record always correlated with the signature events of postwar Soviet history. He is as much a product of the System as one of his radar installations. His admiration for Stalin is not ideological but power-related, for as he sees it, the late dictator had put in train a "great Impetus"[202] that sustained the Soviet project, and Yemtsov's career, for decades thereafter. With his adventurous streak and senior citizen virility, the protagonist has a vivid textual presence, but it is his generic traits that are most important: the take-charge Red Director is metonymically representative of a class and a generation. One nostalgic commentator, enthralled by the power of the portrayal, even suggested that "Fracture Points" "justifies the grandeur of Stalin's leap into the future."[203] But that is a different story.

The second half of "Fracture Points" is served by a lurid plot that features bankers, gangsters, and a cynical detective: Solzhenitsyn's venture into post-Soviet prose noir. Alyosha Tolkovyanov (Wilted Sense), a twenty-eight-year-old financier with a science background, narrowly survives an assassination attempt ordered by business rivals. The policeman in charge of the case, fortyish Colonel Kosargin, is a former KGB officer and proud of it, but finds the anarchy of the 1990s abhorrent. The two men have a history: in his Chekist incarnation, Kosargin had once questioned Tolkovyanov, who as a perestroika-era student dabbled in democratic politics.

The hero of part two is a very different personality from the communist cum corporate Yemtsov. With "a face that seemed a bit simple," he reminds the professionally observant Kosargin of a "village cowherd dressed in city clothes."[204] In fact, the banker is a decent sort, like the equally Russian-visaged Grachikov in "For the Good of the Cause." Tolkovyanov's aura of rooted authenticity is validated by cherished memories of a childhood spent in a "district of little single-story houses with their gray, decrepit, carved gables" on the Volga.[205] Growing up, Alyosha and his friends pretended they were partisans fighting the invading Chinese on the banks of the great river. In the Soviet Sixties, Cowboys and Indians—Leninists and Maoists. A teenage fascination with "Black Holes that swallowed up matter utterly and without a trace"[206] prompts the hero to choose physics as his university major (Stephen Hawking, thank you). His studies are interrupted when he is drafted into the army, but after he returns to civvy street he finds that he has lost his scientific vocation. Like Yemtsov all those years ago, Tolkovyanov makes a spur-of-the-moment, life-changing decision and opts for finance over science. The implosion of the planned economy has opened up opportunities for college boys with capitalism on the brain. Alyosha's banking business takes off. Although the ex-physicist is "disgusted with himself" because his clients are shysters and criminals, he is hopeful that at some future point he will "put the bank on solid, honest money,"[207] a strategy adopted by the oligarch Mikhail Khodorkovsky a few years later, with mixed results.

In the course of the investigation the cop and the moneyman form a bond. Both are pragmatists with a patriotic streak who want to make good in a country gone bad. They discuss the destiny of Russia, their speculations fueled by a bottle of booze the colonel pulls out of a filing cabinet. Meanwhile, the would-be killer is arrested and given a ridiculously light sentence, and the sinister businessmen who hired him escape justice altogether. Tolkovyanov must now go about town wearing a bulletproof vest, but he refuses to pack up and leave: "Should he flee somewhere abroad? This would be a way to save his wife, his son, and himself, of course. But Alyosha could not run away."[208] And so the hero is trapped, even as his pretty wife seeks comfort in religion: "Don't you realize that we were doomed? That we were saved by some Higher Power?"[209] Yemtsov makes a brief and final appearance, and promises to help. He is as tough as ever, like one of those missiles he used to manufacture: "We've charted our course and off we go, no room for the gutless!"[210] Wilted Sense, however, goes on wilting. "Yet a faint light persisted":[211] somehow, somewhere, perhaps through his love of family, he might find a solution.

Tanya Tolkovyanova, the hero's wife, is a shadowy presence. As a young mother, she is understandably concerned by the banker's stubborn refusal to give up and get out. There are hints of a feline sexiness ("Tanya ... placed her cheek against his")[212] and, as already noted, an inchoate religious sensibility. On the whole, however, she remains confined to the realm of nature or folklore, as when she offers Alyosha this piece of homely advice: "My grandmother used to say, 'A needle will serve when it's got an eye, a person will serve when he's got a soul.'"[213]

As for Kosargin, he has an appropriately anonymous appearance, "fit and neat with a distinct military bearing."[214] His identity is entirely institutional, as shown by the colonel's warm recollections of his service under Yuri Andropov, the onetime chairman of the KGB. Kosargin does not have much of a past, at least in narrative terms, but he worries about the future: "If only, through some miracle, the Organs could regain their former power, their significance. But could that ever happen?"[215] As we now know, it could and it did. Vladimir Putin's rise to power in 2000 and the subsequent penetration of every level of government and business by former or actual Chekists, often with Kosargin-like personalities and patterns of thought, gives this secondary character a wider meaning. The ex-spook is associated with Solzhenitsyn's favored allegorical formula, Communism—the Dragon. As the colonel contemplates the local landmark, a monument that depicts the heads of a worker, a soldier, and a peasant sprouting from a rock in cross-class solidarity, he recalls that the townspeople had nicknamed it Zmei-Gorynich, after the three-headed fire-breathing monster of Russian folklore. Solzhenitsyn also gives us a toponymical joke: banker Tolkovyanov's high-end apartment happens to be located on Karl Marx Street.

Marx or Mammon, "Fracture Points" favors neither. Despite his undeniable talents, the ruthless Yemtsov is a thoroughly bad egg; as morally putrid, in fact, as the plodding Stalinists in *The First Circle*, to whom he is superior only in the cut of his suits. The Red Director's preternatural youthfulness has demonic undertones: "He was now almost seventy, yet he still had the same vitality, the same eye for the ladies, and the same agile body and mind. And how had he been able to survive all this?"[216] In other words, what Faustian contract had he signed? There is no hope for him, unlike Tolkovyanov, whose wrong choices have yet to define him completely, though it is entirely possible that they might, in which case, the text implies, he will devolve from a fledgling of robber capitalism into a fresh-faced Yemtsovian clone. Indeed, the oligarch's attitude toward Alyosha is a mixture of affection and contempt, like that of a bad father figure: "So, the greenhorn's here. Tell me, how's your little half-assed moneymaker doing?"[217]

At the end of the story, the scientific concepts and theories that so enthralled the teenage Tolkovyanov acquire a cosmic darkness of meaning:

There was, however, a different kind of explosion, the Big Bang.

There were also Black Holes.

And there was the incomprehensible foresight of the DNA molecule.[218]

Compared with the narrative tightness and vivid historicism of part one, part two lacks fictive verve, despite its complement of cops and wise guys. As often happens with less-than-inspired prose, even when it is composed by a great writer, here and there clichés creep in. After the banker and his partners have that violent falling out, the Tolkovyanov-inflected narrative voice intones: "When money is involved, there's no limit to the passion and the thirst for vengeance"[219] (*Gde kasaetsia deneg—net predela ni strastiam, ni mesti*).[220]

Nonetheless, the story paints a true picture of early onset Russian capitalism. The details are all there: the transformation of Tezar into a haberdashery cum cathouse, Tolkovyanov's bank with its "vast expanse of glass and one of the enigmatic names they were now inventing,"[221] the bodyguards with brutal haircuts. Solzhenitsyn displays a Balzacian grasp of the social and moral discontinuities that characterized Russia's transition to a mafia market economy. In *La Comédie humaine*, "Balzac metonymically connects his contemporary fictional universe to the historical past" and "reminds us of society's historical porousness in that Napoleon's narrative presence serves as a political commentary magnifying the absence of a strong ruling power in postrevolutionary France."²²² Yemtsov and Tolkovyanov have different backgrounds and outlooks, but both are decentered figures operating in an emergent, money-obsessed society which lives in the shadow of an epic and sanguinary national experience that is now receding from sight. In particular, the portrait of Kosargin, the nostalgic secret policeman, hits all the right notes. Yet the national landscape depicted here is far more diseased than that of Restoration or July Monarchy France, while the myths of the Soviet past will never compare in aesthetic grandeur to those of the Napoleonic era. In the end, "Fracture Points" is a colorful snapshot of extreme banking, Russian-style. As Cyril Connolly so memorably put it, "Destroy him as you will, the bourgeois always bounces up—execute him, expropriate him, starve him out *en masse*, and he reappears in your children."²²³

9

In formal terms, "Zhelyabuga Village" is the most heterogeneous of the post-exilic stories. Part one offers a dramatized, maximal narrator account of Solzhenitsyn's wartime experiences in and around the eponymous hamlet in the summer of 1943, part two is a factual memoir of his visit to the same place fifty years later. The work is one part Modernist, part two realist. The element of structural binarism is stark, for the story relies on a double fictive shift. Real-life people, including the author of record, appear first as literary characters, but subsequently, after half an hour of discourse time and half a century of story time, acquire a new status as de-fictionalized material witnesses in a journalistic here and now. The narration is in the first person, which generates a degree of diegetic continuity across these two generically dissimilar, thematically conjoined units of prose. The conjunction in question turns on a patriotic homily delivered at the end of part one by a political officer to a group of peasants: "And all our things that the Germans destroyed, we'll rebuild. Our land will sparkle even more than before. There'll be a *fine* life for us after the war, comrades, the like of which we've never seen."²²⁴ Alas, it is not to be, for in part two we find a few ragged villagers who have survived the intervening decades engaged in dolorous conversation with the historical Aleksandr Solzhenitsyn, seventy-six, amid the accumulated poverty of Soviet and post-Soviet misrule.

The (c)overtly autobiographical hero of part one, Sasha, is a lieutenant with a sound-ranging unit who after four days of hard fighting finds himself in a state of "joyous exhaustion,"²²⁵ thrilled to be a part of the Red Army's victorious advance following the battle of Kursk. For much of the text, however, the narrative focus lies elsewhere, on the manner in which the officers and men in this specialized branch of the artillery go about their frontline business. There are numbers of how-it-is-done passages in which the military details, some of them highly technical, are carefully correlated with the mental and physical demands the reconnaissance gunners must face. "Each listening post has four or five men, and they have a lot of heavy equipment to carry. A single storage battery is enough to throw out your entire shoulder."[226] Moreover, this is a Russian army with a "Russian way"[227] of fighting familiar to us from *War and Peace* and *The Red Wheel*. A truck drives at speed over a minefield, with Sasha holding on for dear life, because "switching to any of the side roads meant a long detour."[228]

We are told little about the hero's past and nothing of his appearance, though we learn that he is a chain smoker. Nevertheless, Sasha's personality and physical self occupy an important place in the fictive proceedings: unlike, say, the equally autobiographical Ignatich in "Matryona's Home," he is a true protagonist. War may be 99% boredom and 1% terror, but Sasha's day is 99% hard slog, yet he also experiences his share of bone-chilling dread. He witnesses one of his men suffer a death wound and twice feels the (undeserved) wrath of senior officers who respectively threaten him with a stint in a punishment battalion and summary execution: "I can do whatever I like with you."[229]

Young Sasha is a mixture of things. Already a veteran soldier, in other ways he is still very callow. He is a committed communist, though apparently not a card-carrying one. His bookish politics recall Nerzhin's Marxist conceits in *Love the Revolution*, as we discover when the hero informs his best friend, Ovsyannikov, in appropriately fervent tones, "We'll keep on blasting them, and then—into Europe like a spring uncoiling. After a war like this, there's bound to be a revolution, don't you think? It's straight out of Lenin."[230] And yet, Sasha's love of country is unmediated by the dialectic: "You could die without regrets for this Russian heartland."[231] A mathematician in civilian life, he does not always go by the numbers when directing his guns: "It's best not to make corrections, just give it a volley and scare the shit out of them!"[232] There's that "Russian way" again.

As for Sasha's unit, it is a collection of lightly sketched bodies, personalities, and relationships. In army friendships, rank tells: the two men he is closest to are also officers, "open hearted" Lieutenant Ovsyannikov, who is "like a brother,"[233] and Lieutenant Kuklin (Doll-like), "a sweet-tempered young fellow with the face and the stature of a boy,"[234] whom he mentors. Major Boyev, the much-decorated battalion commander, and Lieutenant Proshchenkov, Sasha's counterpart in Four Battery, possess an "unyielding solidity" of jaw and shoulder that conveys "a masculine strength."[235] These indicators of martial physiology complement the protagonist's own body-centric sensations that day.

The rank-and-file soldiers in Sasha's sixty-man unit include "stocky little Burlov,"[236] "the imperturbable Siberian, Yermolaev," "Shukhov, a quick and capable fellow,"[237] "dark, sullen Volkov," "gloomy, freckle-faced Yemelyanov,"[238] "thin, agile Dygin,"[239] "saucy Yenko,"[240] "tall, stolid" Lyakhov, "plump little Pashanin,"[241] "bright-eyed"[242] Ptashinsky, "sharp-eyed Konchits."[243] The laconic descriptions are the diegetic equivalent of name, rank, and serial number. Here and there the narrative, which constantly shifts between the modes of descriptiveness and discontinuity, includes snippets of dialogue and glimpses of living body parts such as Pashanin's "hairy chest and back"[244] or Lipsky's "soft white hands ... on the ribbon of paper spread out across the table."[245]

As the plot unfolds, some of these secondary characters come into focus, among them "short and swarthy" Andreyashin,[246] a recent conscript with family in still-occupied Oryol a few miles away, whom he plans to look up after the city is liberated. Another soldier, Shmakov, is a deserter from an anti-tank unit who "couldn't take the close combat"[247] but has performed well since joining Sasha's command: a micro-biography that throws an unexpected light on wartime practices in the Red Army. The battery's political officer, Kochegarov (Stoker), who is destined to deliver that uplifting lecture to the Zhelyabuga peasants, once worked as a driver for a regional Party committee. As this detail suggests, the ex-automotive commissar is surplus to military requirements. Then there are those staples of war fiction, the tough sergeant who is "a capable manager"[248] and the "regimental mascot" Mitka Petrykin, a fourteen-year-old who was adopted by the battery when it passed through the town of Novosil, which is now a ruin. Another figure, familiar from countless novels and movies, is Private Pugach. A lawyer in civilian life, he "can always find some loophole to get him the easier jobs."[249]

The disconnect between the men doing the fighting and the generals in their headquarters is nicely delineated, as when Sasha observes that nighttime offers the optimal conditions for sound reconnaissance. "The people higher up have never taken this rule into account, though. If they had any sense, they'd have us move by day, not by night."[250] Another effective element is the attention paid not just to what veteran troops do, but what they don't do. When sighting a FW-189 reconnaissance plane, nicknamed "the picture frame" for its distinctive twin-boom design, the Russian flak holds its fire because "they always manage to dodge the shrapnel," and Sasha's gunners have "long since stopped wearing gas masks and just toss them all in the back of the truck."[251]

Unlike the World War I campaigns in East Prussia (*August 1914*) or eastern Poland (*November 1916*), this is fully mechanized warfare that is fought in all three dimensions. Iconic Russian and German war machines such as the IL-2 Sturmovik, the Katyusha rocket launcher, and the Ju-87 Stuka sow death all day long. The latter is vividly animated: "As always, you can see his front wheels that seem to be reaching out for you like talons; he lets loose the bomb that falls like a droplet from his beak."[252] A second Stuka dives on the hero ("a huge crash," "scorching heat," "a terrible noise in my head"),[253] and then the two aircraft fly away: "They have their own lives to lead, up there in the sky, one racing after the other, and the sky now is no longer concerned with the earth below it"[254] (*Tam, naverkhu, svoia razygryvaetsia zhizn', goniaiutsia drug za drugom, nebu stanovitsia ne do zemli*).[255] The notion, though not the phrasing, is recognizably Tolstoyan.

Soon after Sasha has that near-death, surface-to-air encounter, Andreyashin is mortally wounded by a German shell:

> Cherneykin ... is carrying something. ... He's holding it well away from himself so as not to soil his clothes.
> Is that a leg he's carrying?
> It is a leg, from the knee down, still in a boot, with a tattered puttee flapping.[256]

The stress of combat compounded by a lack of sleep puts the protagonist into a fugue state:

> The hours flow by, and from all the racket, the confusion, and the trying to do three things at once, the extreme strain under which you've been working begins to sink you into torpor. Your whole being seems to be in fog; your head feels swollen, both from the lack of sleep and the effects of the shell bursts that haven't yet passed; your head droops, your eyes are red. It's as if the various parts of your brain and your soul have been torn to pieces and will simply not move back to their proper places.[257]

(In *November 1916*, Kotya Gulai had the same experience hours before he visited Sanya's dugout and went off on his nihilistic rant.)

Place names and topographic references occur throughout the text: the hero is a gunner with a gunner's eye for the lie of the land. The Soviet side of the front line has been cleared of local inhabitants "out of fear of treachery" and is "without a living soul, no crops planted, and the fields overgrown with weeds as in the time of the

Polovtsians [Cumans]"[258] (an oblique expansion of the text into the historical past), but the fields around Zhelyabuga, which until recently was occupied by the Germans, are cultivated and a few villagers have stayed put. This gladdens Sasha's patriotic heart: "It's very odd and very cheering for us to see living Russian peasants."[259]

Part one includes an open space/enclosed space dichotomy, that is, the field of battle vs. a cellar in Zhelyabuga, where some of the villagers have taken shelter. Sasha establishes his forward post in this subterranean locus. Here the vectors of military operations and civilian survival intersect. Clustered in the dark, dank cavity are half a dozen women, an old man, a couple of children. Such are the wartime demographics of the Russian countryside. Sasha meets a peasant girl with an unusual name, Iskiteya, whom the other villagers call Iskorka (Little Sparkle). This rustic beauty is pretty, blonde, and voluptuous: "Her dress is tightly belted at the waist but is quite full above and below."[260] Pert and saucy, Iskorka fends off a soldier's gruff advances as well as Sasha's decorous officer-and-gentleman attentions. Also hiding in the cellar is a ten-year-old boy who buried his schoolbooks because he refused to study while the Germans were occupying his village: a child's act of sacrifice that stands in cross-textual contrast to little Nastenka's destruction of the paper icon in the eponymous story.

Sasha's day of "madness and stupefaction"[261] ends with a few rounds of drinks in the battalion staff truck. The occasion is Major Boyev's twenty-ninth birthday. A toast is offered: "For you, war is existence itself, as if you have no existence outside of war. So, may you live through all this."[262] Boyev is taken aback by this unconventional tribute, the author of which is, of course, Sasha, who sees the major as the embodiment of martial valor, down to his last name. It means, serendipitously, "fighting man."[263] As in the case of that other birthday party in *The First Circle*, the festive details are a function of the celebrants' life situation: a pair of towels in lieu of a tablecloth, cans of American sausage and Russian fish, a mixture of glasses and tin mugs. The set piece in the back of the truck includes one of those beautifully modulated dialogues at which Solzhenitsyn excels. After the toasts, the tired officers talk about the enemy "with passion, though not with hatred. That's just for the newspapers."[264] They discuss the likelihood of a Second Front and go over the day's fighting. But soon the party is over and Sasha repairs to the cellar, where he overhears the commissar, Kochegarov, issue that promise of a radiant future to the Zhelyabuga residents.

As a factual rather than fictional production, part two somewhat resists a philological *analyse de texte*. That said, it is a discrete component of a literary whole, a piece of topical quasi-journalism that explores the themes of war memory, poverty and environmental degradation, and is pervaded by a sense of entropy.

Solzhenitsyn's military muse cedes place to her social counterpart, though the events of 1943 still figure prominently in this section, which is built around the familiar topos of a return visit by a veteran to the battlefields of his youth.

The opening lines connect the documentary prose of part two to the literary prose of part one on the plane of authorial and character identity, and national history:

> And so fifty-two years later, in May 1995, I was invited to Oryol for the commemoration of the fiftieth anniversary of Victory Day. Vitya Ovsyannikov and I (Vitya was now a retired lieutenant colonel) were fortunate enough to drive and walk over the routes of the 1943 offensive, from the Neruch, from Novosil, and from our station at elevation 259.0 to Oryol.[265]

Solzhenitsyn's memory circuit begins when he meets Mitka, the youngster who was adopted by the battery during the war. He is now Dmitry Fyodorovich Petrykin, a grizzled paterfamilias who brings his children and grandchildren to pose for pictures with the famous author. After that photo op, Solzhenitsyn and Ovsyannikov travel by jeep, another iconic machine—"jeeps hadn't changed much over the last fifty years"[266]—to Zhelyabuga. They are accompanied by a pair of officials whose clothes convey the subtleties of bureaucratic rank. "The local one was more plainly dressed, with a rain jacket over his suit. The man from the region wore a blue tie and a good gray pinstripe suit with nothing over it."[267]

The intra-textual relationship between the story's paired sections is complex. In the opening pages of part two as well as some later passages, the author revisits the events of July 1943, adding to the fictionalized war record in part one and confirming its basis in fact. We learn that one of Solzhenitsyn's men was killed in the service area at Hill 259.0; that the German trenches contained veritable rooms of earth and logs with windows and planted flowers, though these underground chambers gave off "a doggy smell"[268] from insect powder (smells rarely feature in the fictions); that a dugout where Solzhenitsyn had been just ten minutes earlier suffered a direct hit, which killed the three men inside. On occasion these excursuses into the authorial past extend to the months and years *after* the combat of Zhelyabuga, an instance of a diegetic past pluperfect. Q.v. the passage where Ovsyannikov recalls a "Prussian night"[269] in 1945, when Major Boyev and Private Shmakov, the semi-deserter mentioned in part one, lost their lives.

When the two friends reach the village, they discover it is a ruin, the unrepaired devastation of war compounded by the effects of time: "The street was no longer a street but merely a few islands of houses [*izbianye ostrovki*[270]]."[271] A tiny *archipelago* of misery that calls to mind the title of Solzhenitsyn's most tragic work.

Zhelyabuga is a rural slum very much like the ones depicted in *The First Circle* and "Matryona's Home," and another confirmation of the pre-modern poverty of the Russian countryside, damned to desuetude by the vagaries of history. Seeking out familiar landmarks, the author's gaze moves over the misshapen dwellings and broken agricultural equipment, but Solzhenitsyn can find no trace of the cellar: the chronotopic binary of part one is canceled. The two veterans pick up a cluster of lilies of the valley,[272] walk past "Andreyashin's spot"[273] where that soldier suffered his death wound (although we are not told this, the wildflowers are meant for him), and next encounter a couple of shabby old women basking in the spring sun. One of the "grannies"[274] is dressed in a workman's padded jacket and shoes of felt and rags, the other wears an odd garment of black velour. Solzhenitsyn inquires about her age: she is seventy-two. When the author, awkwardly making conversation, remarks that he is five years older, she replies, "Somehow you don't look it.... Our folks don't walk about much after seventy, they have to crawl.'"[275] In the degraded environment of Zhelyabuga, a septuagenarian's ability to ambulate is a marker of social class. The exchange situates Solzhenitsyn and his interlocutor relative to the post-communist hierarchies of power, a procedure that is potentially problematic since it points to the author's privileged status not just *inside* but *outside* the text.

A recent review of documentary books that examined the impact of the 2008 economic crisis in the United States includes this observation:

> The documentaries about the new depression all betray uneasiness in the relation of journalist to subject. The writers keep returning to their own class background and financial standing... their reportorial methods, how they met the people they're writing about, their hesitations in making an approach, their moral ambivalence about whether and how to help.[276]

Each one of these writerly anxieties is present here, even if the plight of American families hurt by the Great Recession pales in comparison with the Zhelyabugians' medieval poverty:

> "A bit of bread and we could get by and we wouldn't squawk..."
> "We'd have some hope left..."
> "Rye bread, now, that's solid stuff."[277]

A few moments earlier, when Solzhenitsyn made the mild comment that more could be done for the villagers, the senior of the two officials offered a bristling response: "Some of them have televisions."[278] As is to be expected, this local bigwig seeks to put the best PR spin on the worst possible situation, though even his presentational efforts cannot transform Zhelyabuga Village into one of the Potemkin kind.

It turns out that the woman in black is Iskiteya, but when the author excitedly recalls their meeting in the cellar all those years ago, she is unmoved: "Well, I forget what I need to forget."[279] There are no hugs and kisses, no shared remembrances. But if on this occasion Solzhenitsyn's onetime acquaintance displays indifference, a few minutes later things change. On their way back the author and his companion once again come across Iskiteya and her friend, as well as several other women and a senile old man. The villagers launch into a litany of complaints about food supplies and government benefits. Although the two officials make soothing noises and promise to help, one is left with the impression that nothing will get done, just as nothing was done for the Zhelyabuga residents in the five decades after the war. As the "man from the region" puts it, Moscow should not be bothered "with things like this, absolutely not."[280] The reader is left to wonder what constitutes the baser act: a wartime propagandist's canned promise of future happiness or the post-communist state's neglect of the most helpless and poor among its subjects.

Beyond its generic function as a current affairs exposé, part two is a meta-meditation on the ethics and efficacy of polemical reportage. Solzhenitsyn had always made a point of speaking truth to power, yet the visit to Zhelyabuga carried official sanction, and the narrative/journalistic *I* acknowledges this tricky truth: "We looked to the left and saw our two jeeps coming toward us. ... They must have worried when we disappeared."[281] The pair of suits who follow him everywhere are Solzhenitsyn's minders and lictors, and their presence bestows upon him the unwanted status of a VIP. Such are the ambiguities that result from the truth speaker's proximity to those who rule, even if in this case the authority they wield extends to only a dozen decrepit hamlets.

10

In *Human, All Too Human* Nietzsche makes this observation:

> Against war one can say: It makes the victor stupid, the vanquished malignant. In favor of war: Through both of these effects it barbarizes and thereby makes more natural; it is a sleep or a winter for culture, and man emerges from it stronger for good and evil.[282]

All great war narratives from the *Iliad* to *The Naked and the Dead* exemplify these uncomfortable truths, and "Adlig Schwenkitten," Solzhenitsyn's final work of fiction, is no exception.

In the last days of January 1945, as the armored hosts of the Second Byelorussian Front rolled across northern Germany toward the Baltic Sea, Captain Aleksandr Solzhenitsyn, twenty-six, found himself marching and fighting in the same Prussian locations as Samsonov's tragic army thirty years before, a coincidence the normally down-to-earth writer would later ascribe to the action of some mysterious "force."[283] "Adlig Schwenkitten," which carries the subtitle "A Tale of Twenty-Four Hours," is a dramatized memoir of an episode from that campaign as well as a paean to a generation of young Russians who fought and died on the Eastern Front. This is Solzhenitsyn's *Chanson de Roland*, and to an extent that we encounter nowhere else in the oeuvre, the narration adopts what Julia Kristeva calls "the systematic mode of language": "Epic logic pursues the general through the specific; it thus assumes a hierarchy within the structure of substance. Epic logic is therefore causal, that is, theological; it is a *belief* in the literal sense of the word."[284]

"Adlig"'s heroes are soldiers whose virtue is valor, and the work is replete with mythic codes and topoi which evoke some of the oldest texts in the canon, while the narrative relies on a set of diegetically modulated tropes that are typical of this writer's later, innovative prose. A dedication to his wartime comrades, Major Pavel Boyev and Major Vladimir Baluev, who are also the principal characters, confirms the tale's status as an act of remembrance. In the continuum of Solzhenitsyn's autobiographical works these fifty or so pages of episodic prose, divided into twenty-four mini-chapters to symbolize each hour of the day and night, occupy a place between "Zhelyabuga Village" and the play *Victory Celebrations*, while covering some of the same factual ground as chapter eleven ("Prussian Nights"; "Prusskie nochi") of the long poem *The Road*.

The events described can be summarized thus. After the Red Army breaks through the German defenses, it enters "an undamaged land of abundance"[285] largely emptied of its civilian population (see *August 1914*), while the remnants of the Wehrmacht are variously scattering to the four winds or making a desperate last stand. In this fluid military environment, a Soviet artillery unit finds itself cut off by the enemy; or rather, the German lines, tattered though they are, now happen to lie athwart its flanks and rear owing to the speed of the Russian advance. Within a day the gunners have fought their way out of encirclement, with heavy losses. In the larger scheme of things these developments are a minor setback, the result of a mistake by a general at army HQ who had allowed "a completely undefended brigade of heavy artillery to deploy so early in a place that was an operational void."[286]

"Adlig," which was published in tandem with "Zhelyabuga," shares that story's emphasis on the brutally mundane side of war. Men lose their lives to bullets and shells but also perish when the guns are silent. The first casualties come in before the day's fighting erupts. "On the morning of January 26, seven of the brigade's tractor and truck drivers died in convulsions after drinking methyl alcohol. There were also some victims from the gun crews, and others who went blind."[287] The final chapter concludes with another dark incident, when a German deserter who had crossed over to give warning of the impending attack is shot by the brigade SMERSH officer. As one of those responsible for the disaster, he is anxious to hide the truth, and does so in standard Lubyanka fashion.

Sourced by authorial memory, "Adlig" depicts an exclusively masculine universe: there are few women and fewer love scenes in the *chansons de geste*. As an account of a day and a night in its characters' lives, the tale comprises the same length of story time as "Ivan Denisovich," an equally androcentric production, thereby providing a fitting symmetry of form between Solzhenitsyn's first and last published works of fiction. In another parallel, the characters are *ranked*, in this text, literally. Majors Boyev and Baluev are in the thick of the action as the brigade battles its way out of encirclement, but perish during the desperate fighting. The rest of the officers shown (all the principals hold commissioned rank) include a pair of lieutenants, one a conscientious youth striving to please his father, a Red Army general, the other a middle-aged ex-agronomist set in his civilian ways; a boyish captain with a brittle attitude; a loud-voiced, weak-willed colonel; a sybaritic commissar; and that man from SMERSH.

The murderous spook may be the tale's chief villain, but he is just one figure among many: the reader encounters a range of human types and situations, with characters that are in the right, the wrong, or somewhere in between. Whatever their individual moral worth, all are subject to the strictures of military discipline and the generals' orders or whims. As happens in every army that is engaged in combat, these are sometimes ignored or circumvented. And then there is the deadly play of chance: "Solid shot didn't cause any wounds from shrapnel, though a direct hit was fatal, of course."[288] Grand strategy and frontline tactics provide another frame of reference which situates the text as an occasionally critical commentary on the Red Army's military doctrine and battlefield performance. Once again we see war machines in action, among them the King Tiger panzer and the Soviet IS-3 heavy tank with armor so thick that "enemy shells would bounce off it like sunflower seeds,"[289] and there are telling details that convey the nature of the fighting during these last months of the war: "The bodies of the gun crews, a few dozen of them, still lay unburied among the guns and back toward Adlig. A few had been stabbed to death: the Germans were saving their bullets."[290]

The tale is told in a mixture of the first person plural (the controlling register) and the third person singular (a subsidiary register, but textually the more prevalent one). That soldierly "we" stands for the men of the heavy artillery brigade, or the Second Shock Army, or the Second Byelorussian Front, while giving voice to the companionship of arms the novella describes and honors. In the Epilog, which sums up the events that take place in the days and weeks that follow, the same pronoun diegetically contracts to denote the men who survived the fighting: "On February 2 we again captured Liebstadt and the area to the west of it, and reconnaissance troops from our artillery brigade entered Adlig Schwenkitten.... We searched for the bodies of Major Boyev and his battery commanders."[291]

The authorial alter ego, Sasha, an older version of the hero of "Zhelyabuga Village," is only a minor presence. In the words of a reviewer, "Following the principle of his longer prose, [Solzhenitsyn] crowds out his autobiographical hero."[292] Throughout the tale, Sasha remains half-hidden amid the interstices of the text as "the commander of the instrument reconnaissance battalion in [a] long overcoat"[293] or "a man in a neat officer's overcoat ... a mathematician."[294] Solzhenitsyn's last prose work was also the last time he sent out his fictionalized self to visit a narrative in secret costume, in this case, a brown *shinel*.

Despite its abundance of carefully recorded detail, this is a maximal narrator text that tends toward the paratactic, elliptic, and impressionistic: "Oleg bent over the wounded man. A major. Hair the color of flax. He wasn't moving"[295] (*Oleg naklonilsia nad ranenym. Maior. Volosa kak lën. Nedvizhen*).[296] The incidence of such staccato passages increases with each successive chapter, until the "requiem-like"[297] Epilog, which in its concluding paragraphs attains a "compactness and power reminiscent of Pushkin's prose,"[298] a comment that hits close to the truth. The narration rhythmically shifts between the diegetic present and the unhappy decades of the 1920s and 1930s, via discrete, framed accounts of a given dramatis persona's family background or prewar experiences, notably Boyev's lonely childhood and Kandalintsev's employment as an agricultural expert in the Soviet countryside. These biographical divagations slow down the narrative pace but do not increase the narrative tension. In this regard, the tale follows the Homeric model of epic storytelling as defined by Auerbach:

> With their indications of the earlier and as it were absolute existence of the persons described, [the digressions] prevent the reader from concentrating exclusively on a present crisis; even when the most terrible things are occurring, they prevent the establishment of an overwhelming suspense.[299]

Each excursus is rendered in the form of free indirect speech, as are the characters' perceptions of their life situations and, occasionally, of each other: "Boyev looked at Veresovoy out of the corner of his eye. There was no negotiating with your commanders, even those closest to you."[300]

The soldiers in "Adlig" sometimes wonder what the future holds. With victory almost in sight, the general mood is hopeful, though wiser, older heads beg to differ. In a bleak moment of prolepsis, the middle-aged officer, Kandalintsev, who witnessed some terrible things during the collectivization drive, warns the youthful lieutenant with the general for a father, "No, Oleg, nothing is going to change at home. We'll be lucky if it doesn't get worse."[301] The violent actualities of combat do not exhaust the text's historical meanings.

Like the war chapters in *August 1914*, this is the story of a violent encounter between the Russian Self and the German Other. The practices and values of a conquering army impose themselves, often cruelly, upon the spaces of an alien land. "Clusters of stone houses with tall, steep roofs"[302] worry the Russian eye with their unfamiliar shapes, and the civilians who have stayed behind are shadowy figures who fearfully serve their new masters: "Both the double doors to the dining room to one side were opened wide, and supper would soon be served there. Two or three women passed back and forth, one wearing a bright dress, evidently a German."[303] This makeshift seraglio caters to a quartet of senior officers (including the man from SMERSH), whose decision to enjoy "supper and other delights"[304] instead of staying in touch with the troops contributes to the brigade's near-destruction.

The officers' exercise of the right of conquest belongs to a pattern of misdeeds that extends up and down the chain of command:

> Gravestones of German soldiers had been standing in Poland since 1915. When they were on the Narew, the signals officer Ishchukov had dug up the German graves and scattered the bones—he was "taking revenge."[305] No one said anything to him: Larin, the SMERSH officer, had been standing right beside him.[306]

(This is a different SMERSH-man from the one who murders the German deserter.)

The phrase "taking revenge" (*mstil*) is an assimilated slogan or quote. The ghoulish Ishchukov could have picked it up from any of a thousand authorized sources, most probably one of Ehrenburg's newspaper rants. The fighting soldiers, however, have little time for agitprop. Such crude attempts at cognitive manipulation may have an alienating effect on those that remain outside their target audience of the credulous and uninformed, and these veterans are neither. They consider the alcoholic party organizer, Gubaydulin, a walking, wobbling ideological cliché, a "laughingstock."[307] Solzhenitsyn's Red Army men are driven not by the canned hate of propaganda but the eternal soldierly imperatives of loyalty, honor, and pride. Still, Ishchukov is not the only despoiler of the dead we encounter, for he has a German counterpart, as we learn in the Epilog. This writer never forgets to show the balance of good and evil across political and national divides.

The main characters are Boyev, Baluev, and Kandalintsev, who because of his relatively advanced years—he is thirty-nine—is known in the brigade as

"Dad."[308] These battle-hardened officers have a darkness about them, for they are travelers "between two seas, wandering like a heavy cloud between past and future," to quote Nietzsche's Zarathustra.[309]

Pavel Boyev, still CO of Second Battalion, is the standout personality. Like that other complete warrior, Colonel Vorotyntsev of the Imperial Russian Army, he is "a born soldier"[310] who can "read a topographical map faster than he could read a book,"[311] but where the hero of *The Red Wheel* has a complicated personal life and political concerns and commitments outside the trenches, this Red Army commander belongs wholly to the realm of war: a Soviet samurai. Even the major's quirks are martial—Spartan. In the dead of night, he chooses to get some shut-eye on a sofa rather than one of those downy German four-posters, because "it wasn't proper to lie in a bed with your boots on, and with your boots off, what kind of soldier are you?"[312] Such asceticism is the hallmark of a certain warrior type: the celebrated Suvorov made it a habit to sleep on the bare floor, both on campaign and in peacetime.

Solzhenitsyn is not one to glamorize his subjects, but he makes an exception for this commemorative portrait of his wartime commander, whom he obviously admired. Whenever the major makes an appearance, the narration acquires an ascendant, even eulogistic tone. These stretches of idealized prose possess a stark grandeur. There is little or no psychological detail, though the portrait is succinctly historicized, as also holds true for Baluev and Kandalintsev. An extended analeptic excursus that takes up the whole of chapter six shows scenes from the major's past. As a hungry, shoeless youth from the steppes of southern Siberia, he was enchanted by the army's codes of order and discipline: "Life was organized on a precise schedule of drills, forming up, saluting, and marching, and your whole life had a purpose."[313] Yet to a different personality type, the same regimentation might appear repugnant, as we know from *All Quiet on the Western Front*. If "Adlig" contains a polemical strand, it is its insistence, *pace* Remarque and other antiwar writers, on the value and even beauty of the military way of life.

The description of Boyev centers on just one or two physical traits. The major's angular head, which in "Zhelyabuga" was identified as the seat of his heroic masculinity,[314] is again depicted as a sculpted thing of angles and lines:

> His long head with closely trimmed hair stood out like a rectangle whose corners were formed by his temple and jaw. His eyebrows were not quite level and his nose twisted just slightly toward a deep crease in his cheek, as if he were in a constant state of tension.[315]

Boyev is a hard man, but a good one. "The battalion was his family, the officers his brothers, the soldiers his sons, and each one of them was a treasure."[316] A veteran of three wars, he has the decorations to prove it:

> His tunic was covered with an amazing array of orders and medals: two Orders of the Red Banner, an Alexander Nevsky, an Order of the Fatherland War, and two Orders of the Red Star (one came from as far back as the battle with the Japanese at Lake Khasan, the other from the Finnish War; and there was a third Red Star, the most recent, but it had been lost or stolen after he'd been wounded). And so his whole chest was covered in metal, since he wore the orders themselves, not just the ribbons, and it was a soldier's pleasure to feel the weight of them.[317]

This passage of phaleristic prose is richly coded. The steady listing of Boyev's battle honors, each one awarded for gallantry or outstanding leadership in the field, constitutes mensurable evidence of the length and meritoriousness of his military service and confirms his trans-textual status as the ultimate warrior in Solzhenitsyn's oeuvre. Like all Soviet awards, the medals on the major's chest are large and colorful. The shining metallic mass of these signifiers of courage, which feature a variety of human and heraldic images, forms a kind of breastplate that invites associations with an armored knight or, on a classical literary plane, with the famous description of the shield of Achilles in the *Iliad*. Wrought for the hero by the god Hephaestus out of bronze, tin, silver, and gold, this wondrous object was decorated with intricately wrought scenes of the sky and earth, and peace and war, the enumeration and depiction of which occupies dozens of lines of hexameter: "Blazoning well-wrought emblems all across its surface."[318]

Gérard Genette refers to this extended digression in book eighteen of Homer's poem as "a pause and an amusement during the narrative [which has] a purely aesthetic role similar to that of a piece of sculpture in a classical building."[319] Genette's point that the description of the Shield possesses a self-sufficient, decorative quality is entirely valid, though surely the passage has other functions such as diegetic retardation and mythological illustration. By the same Homeric token, the ekphrasis of Boyev's badges of valor fictionalizes this Soviet officer along overtly epic lines, beyond its biographical and historical meanings. He is a hero; an Achillean or Rolandian figure in history's most terrible war.

Joseph L. Henderson, a disciple of Carl Jung, writes that

> in wartime, for instance, one finds increased interest in the works of Homer, Shakespeare, or Tolstoy, and we read with a new understanding those passages that give war its enduring (or "archetypal") meaning. ... The battles on the plains of Troy were utterly unlike the fighting at Agincourt or Borodino, yet the great writers are able to transcend the differences of time and place and express themes that are universal. We respond because these themes are fundamentally symbolic.[320]

"Adlig Schwenkitten" invokes this tradition of symbolic storytelling. On one or two occasions, the narration leaves the realm of war and history and ascends to the empyrean, allowing us a direct glimpse of Boyev's connection to those celestial archetypes of myth:

> The moon had had some special power over Pavel Boyev since he had been a child. In his youth, it would make him stop or sit or lie down simply to gaze at it. He would think about the kind of life that lay ahead of him and about the kind of girl he would meet.[321]

That life, however, did not happen: the major is a bachelor who has never had a sweetheart. Perhaps on some Jungian level, his masculine self is betrothed to the Moon, which in ancient times was symbolically linked to "the dominating power of the feminine."[322] Whatever the cause, a strange inhibition had always prevented Boyev from finding a lady love of his own: "Pavel would be simply paralyzed before a woman; he was in awe of her tenderness, her fragility, and he not only feared he might break her but even that he might scorch her with his very breath."[323] This is the hero scripted as a brave, benign dragon, an eversion of the imaginative practice in *The First Circle*, where dragons are demons. The manly major sees members of the opposite sex as almost a different species: "Beauty is an entirely feminine quality, even in the least attractive women"[324] (there is a parallel here with Vorotyntsev, who is forever baffled by women and their patterns of perception and behavior). As we watch the major muse along these emphatically gendered lines, we learn that "the moon was shining over his shoulder. He turned to look at it. Then a cloud obscured it again."[325] Selene's mortal lover, protégé, or ward—Boyev grew up an orphan—takes leave of her before going into battle, and she, of him.

Homer does not show Achilles's death. By the same epic token, the major's heroic last moments occur off-text. The portrait of Boyev's body as found by his comrades on the battlefield is the imaginative climax of the tale:

> He had been shot through the head and through the jaw; he lay on his back. His fur jacket had been taken from him, along with his felt boots, and his cap was missing. As well, one of the Germans had taken a liking to his medals and wanted them to prove the success of their attack. He had used his knife to cut out the large piece of the tunic on which Boyev wore all his medals, and the congealed blood of the knife wounds could still be seen on his chest.[326]

The postmortem wound, the reader surmises, may be in the shape of a *red circle* or *wheel*.

The sepulture of a fallen warrior is another heroic topos. Almost the entirety of Book XXIII of the *Iliad* is devoted to the obsequies of Patroclus, and in the *Chanson de Roland* Charlemagne brings the bodies of the hero and his comrades-in-arms Olivier and Archbishop Turpin back to France:

> Beneath
> White monuments he hath the lords entombed
> At Saint-Romain. Here those three Barons lie.[327]

The military rites that take place as Major Boyev's body is lowered into the ground do not receive the same textual prominence. The Epilog covers them in a single sentence: "He was buried in the central square in Liebstadt, where a monument to Hindenburg stood."[328] We recall that in "Matryona's Home" the heroine's funerary service is mentioned only in passing and her burial is not described at all. A thoughtful reader, should he so wish, may fill in the narrative gaps that leave unmentioned the presence of Boyev's fellow warriors, the honor guard, the final salute. In fact, earlier in the tale we are shown, at some length, the burial of two soldiers whose deaths by alcohol poisoning were a different kind of wartime tragedy: "Gusev could only ask in a choked voice: 'Why, boys? Why'd you have to end that way?'"[329] In the Epilog, however, the extreme narrative laconicism makes manifest, rather than masks, the mythical meaning of Boyev's death and interment. The town square is a chronotope. The municipal association with the field marshal of hollow memory is ceremonially displaced by a new Soviet (or Russian) symbology, set in a new historical frame: World War II has superseded World War I.

In a few months, when the Allies redraw the borders of these bloodlands, Liebstadt will become Milakowo, a Polish town. The effigy of Hindenburg will be taken down, by the Soviets or the Poles, in an act of national vengeance. All these events, however, lie beyond the confines of the text. Instead, in the last few paragraphs the narrative threads are tidied up. We learn of the commanding general's private regrets over the brigade's fate, for which he blames himself. He reviews the list of those recommended for a decoration, angrily crossing out the names of the officers who (*we* know) had enjoyed that leisurely meal with its postprandial pleasures while the Germans pounded the exposed and scattered unit. Boyev is posthumously awarded the Order of the Patriotic War, First Class, "but no one ever saw this golden medal, and his sister Praskovya never received it."[330] That amazing breastplate, looted by the enemy, is never recovered, reassembled, restored. Lastly, we learn that Major Baluev, the tale's second dedicatee, went altogether unmentioned in the division commander's memoirs. "He simply disappeared, as if he had never existed":[331] the theme of absence, restated. As Auerbach remarks of the *Chanson de Roland*, "The things that happen are stated with paratactic bluntness which says that everything must happen as it does happen, it could not be otherwise, and there is no need for explanatory connectives."[332]

Vladimir Baluev is a bearer of the same military virtues as Boyev. He has seen a good deal of action but a wound suffered in 1943 and a subsequent year of study at the general staff academy kept him away from the front until now.

Appointed to a regimental command just three days before the German attack, he orders his forward troops to screen Boyev's battalion after the latter briefs him on the tactical situation. When the two men meet, they recognize each other's martial worth: "Baluev thought that he had a firm handshake, but Boyev had a grip of iron."[333]

Baluev too is an orphan:

> Whether it was from the dreams themselves, from something he'd read, or from the stories of others, Baluev had formed the idea that when his time came to die, Mama would draw near and embrace him.
>
> That was what he dreamed last night: he felt Mama's breath on his face and her very firm embrace—where did she get such strength?
>
> Everything in the dream was so warm and so joyous. But when he woke up he recalled the omen.[334]

This premonition will come true, as premonitions always do in epics: a dream foretoken that extends the tale's mythic compass to this character as well.

In a text more Homeric than Tolstoyan, Kandalintsev is the only character that is psychologically layered. A "quiet, well-educated man"[335] who once worked at a plant breeding station in the southern Russian province of Voronezh, he was present during the "maliciously calculated plague" of collectivization:

> The impressions of those months and years had caused Pavel Kandalintsev to become desensitized to the life around him, which now seemed somehow inauthentic. It was as if his nerve endings had grown numb, as if his vision, his sense of smell, and his sense of touch had become less acute and would never be fully restored. ... He had been at war for more than three years now, still unable to feel anything with his whole being, as if alien even to himself and his own body.[336]

These symptoms—numbing, derealization (the sense that the external world is unreal), and depersonalization (the sense that one's own self is unreal)—allow for a readerly diagnosis of post-traumatic stress disorder. As a piece of psychologically informed prose, the passage connects "Adlig" to "Zhelyabuga," with its fugue episode experienced by Sasha, though *his* condition was combat-related and transitory: by the end of the day the effects were gone and Solzhenitsyn's young alter ego was having a good time at that soldierly birthday party. Still, despite the dark burden he carries, Kandalintsev remains a high-functioning personality and is an excellent platoon leader. He looks out for Gusev, the young officer who is forever trying to please his father, the general, and calmly faces down an enraged colonel when the latter wrongly demands that he deploy his howitzers in an anti-tank ambush.

It is instructive to compare "Adlig" with one of the defining epistemologies of combat in twentieth-century literature, Ernst Jünger's war chronicle "Storm of Steel," that paean to *Soldatentreue* (soldierly comradeship). The two texts describe two different world wars, from two different national perspectives, but share the same austere diction and diegetic alternations to show the savagery of the fighting and its disfiguring impact on bodies and minds. The soldiers that these works depict have identities which are subsumed by the terrible reality of battle, so that peacetime is but a strange memory and the future holds little promise or meaning. Both works are eulogies to the fallen as well as a tribute those who had lived through it all, even if Jünger's novelistic account of his four years on the Western Front encompasses a far greater length of story time than the miniaturized epic that is "Adlig Schwenkitten." Boyev in particular epitomizes the Jüngerian values of noble abnegation and calm in the midst of carnage, though he never attains that mystical state of being which the German writer considered war's sublime gift to the fighting man. Instead this tough officer remains down-to-earth, down-in-the-trenches, even as he apprehends the ghastly contingency of the world of mechanized violence that he inhabits. Myths are his halo, but history is his context. Thus, Solzhenitsyn follows the storytelling practice identified by T. S. Eliot in his review of *Ulysses*:

> In using the myth [of the *Odyssey*], in manipulating a continuous parallel between contemporaneity and antiquity, Mr. Joyce is pursuing a method which others must pursue after him. ... It is simply a way of controlling, of ordering, of giving a shape and a significance to the immense panorama of futility and chaos which is modern history. ... Instead of narrative method, we may now use the mythical method. It is ... a step toward making the modern word possible for art.[337]

In an echo of the subtitle's temporal reference, Baluev thinks to himself: "An army on the move is an ever-changing structure. Sometimes it can form a wall as hard as marble in twenty-four hours; sometimes it can dissolve like an apparition in two hours."[338] Which is what would have happened to Second Battalion, indeed the entire brigade, had it not been for his own sacrifice and that of men like him.

11

In 1996 the author sent the editors of *Novy Mir* some newly written "Miniatures," accompanied by a brief annotation: "Only after my return to Russia was I able to compose them again, for I could not do it *there*..."[339] This blended form was always dear to Solzhenitsyn's heart, but to employ it he needed to breathe Russian air, see Russian sights: he needed to be *in situ*.

Whenever a writer resumes work in a particular genre after a period of years, let alone decades, the question arises, are there any structural changes? stylistic innovations?

In comparison with the earlier "Miniatures," the differences are tonal as much as thematic. The mood is darker yet the diction is more restrained, even as the poetic/prose subject laments Russia's travails of the 1990s or reflects on the advent of old age. As in the first cycle, some of the vignettes are "miniature parables"[340] that trace an allegorical connection between aspects of nature and the human condition. "The Larch" is built around an extended simile that compares this deciduous conifer with its soft, needle-like foliage and rock-hard wood "to people who share those same qualities."[341] Perhaps Solzhenitsyn was thinking of some trait in himself.[342] "Lightning" ("Molniia") likens the workings of the human conscience to the eponymous fire from the sky: "And after such a blow there is no telling who of us will remain standing, and who will not."[343] The voltage of sin is death!.. Once again, the writer's movements across geographical space serve as a textual point of departure or arrival, notably in "The Bell at Uglich" ("Kolokol Uglicha"), which resumes the campanological motif of *The Red Wheel*. The poetic/prose persona is no longer a cultural pilgrim viewing Russia's churches from outside and from afar: fame and status have made him an honored guest where earlier he would have been denied entry. In consequence, his impressions of Uglich are not just visual, but tactile. The authorial alter ego rings the ancient bell that was once *whipped* and *exiled* to Siberia for sounding the tocsin when the Tsarevich Dmitry, Ivan the Terrible's young son, died a mysterious death in that town. "Shame" ("Pozor") ponders "the implacable truth—that nations of the earth have sometimes perished utterly,"[344] a fate that might yet befall Solzhenitsyn's own people, though the patriotic/lyrical subject's wanderings through "the Russian heartland"[345] give him reason to hope.

The most interesting pieces, however, are those that explore the effect of advancing years and failing health on the human body—the author's body. Nowhere else in Solzhenitsyn do we encounter a franker and more direct textualization of his physical self, not even in "The Right Hand." There are wrenchingly intimate depictions of the changes taking place inside his aging organism, so that the distinction between author and his self-presentation is almost erased or, rather, relegated to a narrowly diegetic plane. In "Growing Old" ("Starenie"), the writerly *I* looks back on his near-mortal bout with cancer—"my readiness and resignation outstripped that of my own body"[346]—and lists the private blessings of old age: "You can no longer get through a whole day's work at a stretch, but how good it is to slip into the brief oblivion of sleep, and what a gift to wake once more to the clarity of your second or third morning of the day."[347] There is no raging against the dying of the light. Instead the authorial voice finds comfort in the manner in which a senescent metabolism suppresses the appetites of the flesh: "And your spirit can find delight in limiting your intake of food, in abandoning the pursuit of novel flavors"[348] (not that Solzhenitsyn was ever anything but abstemious). "Nocturnal Thoughts" ("Nochnye mysli") compares a healing thought that visits the writer on a sleepless night to "control rods inserted into a nuclear reactor to impede a meltdown":[349] perhaps, a simile too far.

The standout piece is "The Curtain" ("Zavesa"), a medically informed meditation on the different ways that cancer and heart disease affect the sufferer's state of mind. Susan Sontag reminds us that in the Western cultural consensus, "cardiac disease implies a weakness, trouble, failure that is mechanical; there is no disgrace, nothing of the taboo that … surrounds those who have cancer."[350] "The Curtain" questions these valuations of morbidity:

> When a tumor swells ominously within you, at least you can face the implacable truth and work out how long there is to go. But heart disease plays cunning tricks: At times you seem quite healthy—so you're not doomed after all! Why, it's as if you'd never been ill!
> Blissful ignorance. What a merciful gift![351]

The cycle ends with a "Prayer for Russia" ("Molitva o Rossii") in which the writer begs the Lord to rescue his country from the "Calamity,"[352] the effects of its post-Soviet collapse. If the first "Prayer" was released into circulation in spite of Solzhenitsyn's wishes, the decision to publish the second one was entirely his own. Here the impulse is one of profound patriotic anxiety, to which the author gave voice in "Shame." Now, however, he speaks not as a man of letters or even a moralist, but simply and purely as a Christian believer who loves his country and fears for its future:

Don't let, don't let her be cut short
To no longer be.³⁵³

The meaningfulness (let alone the efficacy) of a believer's devotions is unrelated to their aesthetic form—unrelated, that is, unless they are reconfigured as a published literary production. It is possible to argue that the language, with its controlling diminutive *Rossiiushka*³⁵⁴ ("gentle Russia"), comes perilously close to affectation. At the same time, one must acknowledge the continuity between the literary sensibility that informs the other thirteen pieces in the cycle, and its concluding orison. The "Prayer for Russia" is a touching coda to this second collection of prose poems, but also to the vast, profoundly patriotic, and compassion-filled corpus of Solzhenitsyn's writings.

CHAPTER NINE

Modernist?

No artist tolerates reality, but no artist can live without it either.
—Friedrich Nietzsche, *The Will to Power*

However extreme the chaos to which the modern world succumbs in its evolving complexity, human creativity will, nonetheless, always be able to preserve itself on some yet more exalted level.
—Aleksandr Solzhenitsyn, Review of Brodsky's *Selected Poems*

1

Forty-five years ago the editors of *The Sunday New York Times* commissioned Gore Vidal to write a survey of the top ten fiction bestsellers for the week of January 7, 1973. Residing at No. 4 that day among a clutch of middlebrow novels—historical, adventure or gothic—was *August 1914* (the earlier version). Perhaps America's premier wit and cultural commentator, Vidal had the polemical gifts to tackle Solzhenitsyn, then at the height of his fame. He did so with patrician, polyglot confidence. This was *le grand Vidal des années passées*, the essayist in his prime, and his article remains the wittiest review Solzhenitsyn has ever received. Its author may have been writing for the Mr. and Mrs. Upper East/West Side crowd, but in these three or four pages he was able to engage with the novel comprehensively and on a variety of levels. He did not find it pleasing. As a veteran Hollywood screenwriter, he dismisses the Screens as "inept"[1] but readily identifies the influence of Dos Passos in the Glance at the Newspapers sections (which he likes), all the while scattering apothegms such as "Tolstoi hangs over the work like a mushroom cloud"[2] and "I fear that the best one can say of Solzhenitsyn is *goré vidal* (a Russian phrase meaning 'he has seen grief')."[3] Still, the review is not all bite and persiflage, for example, "As for the movies, the best Russian product is recalled, particularly *Battleship Potemkin*."[4]

Of course, the novel that Vidal tackled was a version of a version, mistranslated by Michael Glenny and subsequently much expanded by its creator. Besides, reviewer and author were separated by a vast distance of culture and life experience. As we read the essay, we behold the clash of two incompatible discourses. One self-confident, *readerly* voice, Vidal's, confronts another self-confident, *writerly* voice, Solzhenitsyn's. Still, the reviewer begins his review by conceding his subject's greatness: "I daresay as an expression of one man's indomitable spirit in a tyrannous society we must honor if not the art the author."[5]

Here is a judgment that is far from universally shared, and least of all in Solzhenitsyn's own country. As one scholar puts it, "It is hard to think of another prominent writer whose thought and character have been subjected to as many willful distortions and vilifications over the past thirty years,"[6] even by academic authorities who should know or read better. All too often, the belittlers and faultfinders miss the fictive point. This is especially true of rancorous Russian critics such as the neo-Stalinist publicist Vladimir Bushin or the anti-Stalinist satirist Vladimir Voinovich, who not surprisingly lack the aristocratic Vidal's cultural nous and polemical polish. The title of Bushin's diatribe, *Genius of the First Gob*,[7] speaks volumes, or rather gallons, about the man who wrote it, while Voinovich's *A Portrait Against the Backdrop of Myth*,[8] though a less secretory production, is notable for its bilious tone and ad hominem jibes. Both authors exhibit an aggressive parochialism, willfully ignoring Solzhenitsyn's dialogic connection to the Russian and Western literary tradition, and do not even try to account for the empirical fact that his readership around the world numbers in the millions. What escapes these detractors in their baleful cross-ideological solidarity is the layered subtlety, the semiotic richness—the sheer artistry—of Solzhenitsyn's fictions. Reject his politics, if you must; deny his reading of Russian or Soviet history; refute his membership in the canon; but try to acknowledge those imaginative, intricate textures! Still, as Joseph Conrad tells us, "You shall judge of a man by his foes as well as by his friends,"[9] and the brace of voluble Vladimirs, I submit, would be an adornment to any writer's enemies list.

As a cultural fact, the greatness of which Vidal spoke is both consensual and problematic. Consensual, because a body of opinion must assign a given novelist, poet, playwright, composer, painter, sculptor, architect high status within the culture, in terms of that culture, sometimes belatedly, sometimes posthumously. Problematic, because a great artist will always break cultural norms, thereby confronting contemporaries with the problem of evaluating his creations by reference to familiar, extant concepts and formats. To quote Claude Debussy, "Works of art make rules; rules do not make works of art."[10]

Nietzsche solved this conundrum by positing that great music is the product of a larger, nurturing decadence. The music of Richard Wagner "developed out of a culture whose soil is rapidly sinking," he explained.[11] This is a point that may be extended to literature, indeed all the arts, as was done by Solzhenitsyn himself: "Significant works, not to mention great works, have nearly always and everywhere been created in periods of stability, be it a good or bad stability"[12] (Nietzsche would have said, bad!). A society in decline produces a last, concluding genius who is simultaneously of it and transcends it—overwrites it. Even at the time of their creation his masterpieces already refer back to the dying culture wherein they were born while anticipating an as yet unwritten, unsung, unpainted, unsculpted, unvisualized future that will bestow upon them canonical status. A *chef d'oeuvre* is always analeptic *and* proleptic. Or in the words of a poet whom Nietzsche never met but greatly admired,

> Tu m'as donné ta boue et j'en ai fait de l'or.[13]
> [You gave me your mud and I turned it into gold.]

In Solzhenitsyn's case, it was Soviet culture whose soil was subsiding. He composed his works as the USSR was succumbing to the entropic processes of history; indeed, his novels and stories were historical events in themselves, hastening the collapse of a transcontinental empire and its secular religion and signposting the stages of that great unravelling. For like all important artists, Solzhenitsyn was a destroyer. In a larger sense, of the universalizing Lie. In a narrower one, of the plots, genres, and tropes generated by its cultural practices. He was the assassin of SocRealism. Still, the author was less concerned with showing the exemplars of the "vainglorious literature of the establishment"[14] how (not) to write than with freeing the minds of his Soviet readers. To that end, he bent the methods and productions of official literature to his own creative purposes by coopting, recontextualizing, and even rewriting bits and pieces of its narratives. And so SocRealism, that textual detritus of a base civilization, was put to service as the growing medium for Solzhenitsyn's fictions of truth.

"What is Socialist Realism? Ask five specialists and you will get five different answers."[15] Like kitsch or porn, SocRealism is one of those subpar phenomena that forever escape definition. The scholarly consensus, such as it is, holds that "among the various canonical accounts of it there is not *one* that is incontrovertible or in any sense comprehensive"[16] and that the term itself is "meaningless."[17] Solzhenitsyn is blunter. SocRealism, he writes, was a "solemn pledge to abstain from truth."[18] He denies ever having had any interest in this muddy tissue of falsehoods: "I did not waste my time or exasperate myself by trying to keep up with it."[19]

The forms of his fictions confirm, however, that this was not realistically the case. Solzhenitsyn's antagonistic interactions with SocRealism were a source of creative friction. *The First Circle* and *Cancer Ward* abound in references to important Soviet writers and their books. The former actually features a SocRealist novelist (Galakhov) and a SocRealist critic (Golovanov), and the latter, a SocRealist hero (Zatsirko) and SocRealist reader (Rusanov). Both novels wickedly mock the idioms of the illiberal Soviet arts. Indeed, when "lightening" *The First Circle* to get it past the censors Solzhenitsyn set out to subvert certain SocRealist conventions, as he cheerfully admitted himself:

> And so I openly substituted a well-known Soviet plot from 1949, the period in which the novel is set. In that year a film was shown in my country, the Soviet Union, in which a doctor who has given French doctors an anti-cancer drug is denounced, in all seriousness, as a traitor.[20]

Exasperated or not, the writer made a point of keeping abreast of establishment literature, the better to lampoon and confute it. Much of Solzhenitsyn's prose, poetic, and dramatic output is oriented *against* the practices of Soviet literature, in the same way that Tolstoy's fictions before 1881 are consistently anti-Romantic in their aesthetics, ethics, and formal values (though after his terrible existential crisis of that year he began writing works which were, in a sense, anti-Tolstoyan). "The whole point about realism—*real* realism—is that it needs no identifying prefix. Solzhenitsyn's work demonstrates this for all time."[21] One might say more. In his engagement with the Soviet canon, the author displays an absolute command of its tropes, manipulating them with inspired ease and, often, coruscating wit, the better to demonstrate their artistic and ethical nullity. Hans Robert Jauss identifies a category of literary texts which, "using the artistic standards of the reader, have been formed by conventions of genre, style, or form. These purposely evoke responses so that they can frustrate them. This can serve not only a critical purpose but can even have a poetic effect."[22] Indeed, Solzhenitsyn shows himself to be an excellent pasticheur who can do SocRealism as well as any SocRealist. His parodic manipulations anticipate the "strategy for the transformation of Socialist Realism" invented by Vladimir Sorokin, whereby this Postmodernist writer "elucidates the implicit mythologism of Socialist Realist discourse, gives it a 'plot,' and makes it 'graphically visible' by translating the hidden mechanisms forming the text into a direct depiction of ritual action,"[23] which gives his prose its "intensely stylized and intertextual" character.²⁴ No wonder some of Solzhenitsyn's more earnest readers missed the joke. Georg Lukács once suggested that his "novellas²⁵ represent a significant step in the renewal of the socialist realism of the nineteen-twenties,"²⁶ an analysis which prompted Octavio Paz to remark that "Lukács tried to turn their author into a dissident *within* the Church."²⁷ Yet the Hungarian Marxist was not alone. A similar reading was proposed by Solzhenitsyn's friend Heinrich Böll, who imagined that he had metamorphosed into a Modernist by first learning to write like a good Soviet writer: "Along with the magnificent epic tradition of the Russian 19th century he used methods of socialist realism and found—you cannot call it a combination, but a unity and also a transition to very, very modern forms of the novel in the West."²⁸ And Joseph Brodsky even described Solzhenitsyn as "the genius of Socialist Realism,"²⁹ a comment that must have rankled.

Still, Lukács and Böll were on to something. After all, numbers of Solzhenitsyn's fictions show mensurable characteristics they share with the productions of SocRealism, which extend well beyond the author's parodic practices. His earliest (published) piece of fiction, *Love the Revolution*, stylistically echoes the Soviet novels of the prewar period he had read as a young man, though its discourse is decidedly anti-Stalinist, if not anti-communist. "Ivan Denisovich" had such a shattering impact on Russian readers in part because its formats were so very familiar to them, leading even an informed judge like Lev Kopelev to deprecate it upon a first lecture as "typical socialist realism"³⁰ (how he must have rued that comment!). On the other hand, the story "For the Good of the Cause," a mildly critical look at provincial Soviet life, does not break any of the precepts of the official doctrine of literature, which is why the author later said that it left "a nasty taste" in his mouth.³¹ Mark Lipovetsky offers this formula: SocRealism was a literary model to which Solzhenitsyn "belonged aesthetically although he opposed it ideologically."³² His magic turned propagandistic dross into literary gold dust.

SocRealism and its deconstruction, however, is just half the story. Solzhenitsyn was a remarkably thoughtful reader and as the essays in his *Literary Collection* show, would spend hours poring over the books that fascinated or exasperated him, pencil in hand. Throughout this study I tried to show the connections between his works and those of other writers, major and minor, Russian and foreign, with the shadow of Tolstoy looming larger than any other across his fictive spaces, even if in a totally non-nuclear sense. Some of the linkages in question the author was prepared to acknowledge, although he was very uncomfortable with—in fact, positively hostile to—the academic focus on intertextuality, as he told me in no uncertain terms: "I consider the persistent search for literary influences and borrowings to be a serious fallacy and even disease of contemporary literary studies."³³

Still, the citational adduction of characters, scenes, and tropes from anterior texts, whether canonical or otherwise, has been a distinctive feature of the Russian literary tradition and happens to be a practice that is highly characteristic of Solzhenitsyn's own prose. He relocates and rescripts passages from the Russian classics to adumbrate the patterns of entropy in the national culture in its twentieth-century devolution; or, in a post-representational twist, to push the boundaries of realist verisimilitude, thereby reifying the new conventions of his own literature of truth. In either case, Solzhenitsyn's dialogues with his writerly *others* generate ambivalence, as defined by Julia Kristeva:

> The writer can use another's word [Bakhtin's *slovo*], giving it a new meaning while retaining the meaning it already had. The result is a word with two significations: it becomes *ambivalent*. This ambivalent word is therefore the result of a joining of two sign-systems. ... The forming of two sign-systems relativizes the text. Stylizing effects establish a distance with regard to the words of another—contrary to *imitation* ... which takes what is imitated (repeated) seriously, claiming and appropriating it without relativizing it. This category of ambivalent words is characterized by the writer's exploitation of another's speech—without running counter to its thought—for his own purposes; he follows its direction while relativizing it.[34]

Solzhenitsyn fictions feature both categories of ambivalence, the relativizing and the appropriative, but his purpose is always pragmatic: the cross-textual dialogues are a fictive means to an ethical end. Yet there was also the special writerly pleasure of competing with an illustrious predecessor on his own territory, as Tolstoy was wont to do with Turgenev and Dostoevsky, and Solzhenitsyn did with all three, and a good many *others* besides.

Carlo Ginzburg notes that Tolstoyan defamiliarization is a "means by which we overcome appearances and arrive at a deeper understanding of reality,"[35] and thus an instrument of "social and moral critique,"[36] and traces its origin to a literary tradition that includes Marcus Aurelius, La Bruyère, and Voltaire. But he also identifies a different type of defamiliarization, which is found in Dostoevsky's novels such as *Devils* but was fully developed by Proust, who "seems in some ways to have the opposite end in view—to be trying to preserve the freshness of appearances against the intrusion of ideas, by presenting things 'in the order of perception' and uncontaminated by causal explanations," thereby generating "an impressionistic immediacy."[37] Solzhenitsyn's fictions employ both tropes, with the works of the 1950s and 1960s favoring Tolstoyan estrangement, and *The Red Wheel* and the bipartite stories offering examples of its Proustian counterpart, as in rustic Arseni Blagodarev's first sight of a piano, inside a looted German house: "That was a funny sort of billiard table, with no cloth or cushions, smooth and black."[38] See the description of the same musical instrument as observed by a puzzled D-503 in *We*: "This black box... was called 'a grand piano.'"[39] In Zamyatin, however, the defamiliarized image discharges the function of "social and moral critique" by confirming the hero's status as the subject of a Neoplatonic state in which art as *we* know it is not allowed to exist.

On at least one occasion, we encounter an instance of estrangement that operates as a quantum of coded historiographical commentary. In *March 1917*, foreign minister Milyukov watches a restless Kerensky "fidgeting" on his chair and "stealing glances" at their cabinet colleagues: "He looked like a schoolboy [*on byl kak by gimnazist*] who has been awarded a medal upon finishing school and suddenly finds himself appointed as its headmaster."[40] So far, so defamiliarizing, in a recognizably satirical sense. Yet beyond *Professor* Milyukov's jaundiced view of his jittery, "boyish" rival lurks a pair of extratextual references: to the biographical fact that Kerensky graduated from the Tashkent Boys' Gymnasium in the year 1899 with a gold medal, and to the historical one that years earlier his father had served as the principal of the Simbirsk Boys' Gymnasium, from which institution a certain Vladimir Ulyanov emerged into the adult world, also with a gold medal, in the year 1887.

An argument can be made that each of the stories and novels ascends from one or more canonical productions, interrogating them in ways that may be exegetic, satirical, polemical, or approbatory, but never mechanically imitative. In this genealogical sense, a work by Solzhenitsyn is always a creative derivation or, to employ Gérard Genette's term, a hypertext. Let us recall the common critical judgment that *August 1914* is this writer's *War and Peace* and *November 1916* is his *Anna Karenina*. Without going into hypertechnical detail, suffice it to say that Genette's five "transtextual relations"[41] and six "hypertextual practices"[42] are abundantly present, singly or in combination, across the oeuvre. I hasten to add that the status of Solzhenitsyn's fictions as second- or even third-order cross-literary analogues does not begin to exhaust the meanings they contain, or their cultural import. Nonetheless, I found the search for such connections to be one of the most intellectually rewarding aspects of this project, not least because it gave me the chance to address the author's habits as a reader and to examine his skills as a cultural commentator; and to work out what books he had placed on reserve in the library of his mind, and sometimes even why.

2

Having delineated the writer's relation to the cultural tradition within which he lived and worked, we must next ask the question: What is artistically problematic—analytically intriguing—about Solzhenitsyn's novels and stories?

My answer: his recognition that all imaginative writing, including his own literature of truth, is "not innocent," to use Bataille's phrase; and his consequent reconfiguring of the fictive and the real, and the operative relationship between the two. Throughout this book, I have tried to show that the writer's fictions communicate a Bataillean "hypermorality" that resolves and transcends the ethical difficulties engendered by the aestheticizing function of the text, particularly in those instances where it mimetically engages with human suffering that is brought about by metaphysical evil. I also examined the manner in which Solzhenitsyn developed, over the course of half a century of sustained creative work, a set of original narrative strategies as well as a rich arsenal of tropes in order to depict the dark events of the Russian twentieth century and the state of the human condition in those times of national tragedy.

Now, numerous commentators have remarked on the historical and autobiographical precision of Solzhenitsyn's productions. George Steiner speaks of his "genius for exact memory."[43] As for the writer himself, he defiantly stated:

> I really cannot envisage any higher task than to serve reality—that is to recreate a reality that has been crushed, trampled and maligned. And I do not consider imagination to be my task or goal. I have not the slightest desire to dazzle the reader with my imaginative powers. Imagination is simply a means by which the artist can concentrate reality.[44]

This is a view Solzhenitsyn rephrased with aphoristic succinctness in the "Author's Note" to *November 1916*: "Art demands distillation of actuality." An authorial profession of faith that covers both the representational and the storytelling angles.

Yet dazzle Solzhenitsyn most assuredly does even as he transmits the harsh lessons of history. In his works real-life, verifiable content, and lofty ethical messages coexist with a gossamer-like intricacy of structure and expression. Through his command of the literary arts he fuses the factual and the imagined into a syncretic fictive whole. On at least one occasion, he does so by means of an externalized compositional procedure: "Zhelyabuga Village" is an autobiographical war story conjoined with a journalistic sketch, though here the seams show through the fabric of the text, and not necessarily to its disadvantage. As for Solzhenitsyn's notion of concentrating reality, this truly is a defining feature of his prose. It is saturated with detail, and it is time- and space-condensed. Even *The Red Wheel*, which runs to ten hefty volumes, is no exception. Those "discrete stretches of time" really are discrete: *August 1914* describes the twenty-one days of the Battle of Tannenberg, while *November 1916*, *March 1917*, and *April 1917* respectively cover twenty-two, twenty-four, and thirty-eight days of history. As for the individual chapters in the individual Knots, many of them chronicle just a few hours or even minutes in the life of the characters, or the nation, or both.

Frames and forms. … Let us go back to Vidal's review. One of his critical comments concerns what he calls "mirror scenes," that is, episodes that are usually found at the beginning of a novel, in which the hero or heroine is shown inspecting his or her reflection and which are "used by all pop-writers to tell us what the characters look like."[45] Next, Vidal discusses the passage that describes Irina Tomchak, Ksenia's sister-in-law, performing her toilette on a salubrious summer morning in the privacy of her boudoir:

> As she sat looking into the mirror of her dressing-table she was not even comforted by the sight of her naturally rosy skin, her round shoulders, the hair which fell down to her hips and took four buckets of rain-water to wash.[46]

Perhaps one might agree with the reviewer that Irina's mirror paragraph bares the device (and Irina herself) too much: a young female body displayed, a lingering male gaze adduced. That said, the description of the heroine letting her hair down like a Rapunzel of the steppes and the precise reference to the quantity of sky water habitually, even ritually used by this beautiful nude woman for her matinal ablutions, inside her secret feminine space, possess a fairy-tale quality. The passage represents a discrete instance of functionality in what is a programmatically indicial text. In this regard, it recalls fugitive Anna's fabulous encounter with her larger-than-life policeman in "What a Pity."

In fact, this writer's fictions are full of material mirrors (as well as verbal mirrorings), which so often reflect some asymmetrical trait in his imagined men and women while symbolically or metonymically substantiating the distorted or chaotic aspect of the worlds they inhabit. At the same time, Solzhenitsyn's looking glass episodes exhibit a consistent, gendered logic. In the case of a female character, a mirror will confirm or affirm or even *expand* her identity, whatever the heroine's ethical status. This notion of female self-empowerment via optical reflectivity may not be all that original, but Solzhenitsyn's textual execution usually is. Just before Anna Modestovna—Modest Anna—meets her magical cop, this gentle soul turns a single raindrop into a tiny "convex mirror" cum loupe as she takes delight in the promise of spring. The daughter of a political prisoner, she lives a life that is contingent on male sanction and approval, but for a minute or two she becomes an alchemist or sorceress, and the city boulevard assumes the aspect of an enchanted garden. Here is a mirror scene—a *micro*-mirror scene—that even the acidulous Vidal might have found pleasing. And what about the vamp Lyuda in *The First Circle*? As the Komsomol cocotte primps in front of the mirror, her blond curls eerily mutate into a crypto-Freudian *Medusenhaupt*, with all kinds of mythological ribbons and erotic extensions woven into her coiffure. Even before she goes on the hunt, this maneater is already feeling the thrill, as she revels in the cephalic, sexual "snares" sprouting out of her head.

With Solzhenitsyn's male personae, things are different. When they find themselves standing in front of a mirror, they confront a challenge to their identity, or even experience its visual cancellation or dematerialization. As Kostoglotov contemplates his gaunt reflection inside Tashkent's Central Department Store, much more is going on here than just a tired novelistic trick meant to give us an idea of the hero's appearance following his painful recovery from a near-terminal illness. We encounter a dynamic psycho-optics of contested identity. Kostoglotov and his laterally inverted two-dimensional double undergo a succession of sinister cognitive recodings in ways that are assertively indicial, unlike Irina's boudoir scene. I discussed these subtleties in chapter six, where I invoked the mirror theories of James Frazer and Jacques Lacan in a manner which, I trust, was suitably reflective. Elsewhere, Pryanchikov inspects himself "*en face*, at an angle, and in profile" in a full-length mirror, trying to discover how his prison experiences have marked him, but oblivious of the presence across the room of the monstrous Abakumov (*The First Circle*);[47] the anti-Bolshevik rebel Ektov, much changed after six months of combat, "scarcely recogniz[es]" himself in the "shoddy" mirror of "some peasant hut" ("Ego");[48] and the hermitlike Ignatich (Solzhenitsyn's most fugitive narrator) is *unable* to see his reflection in the opaque, "tarnished mirror" hanging on Matryona's wall ("Matryona's Home").[49] On the other hand, the Red Guards searching for Kutepov are "enthralled" by their "terrifying" mirror images (*March 1917*), but then, they are already likenesses or clones or reflections of each other ("of similar height and appearance and wearing the same black clothes"), and are therefore exempt from the general rule. But the most unusual instant of fictive reflectivity occurs in the early comedy *Victory Celebrations*, where "an enormous wall mirror several meters high"[50] is placed horizontally, as such objects never are, to serve as a festive table for the Red Army men and women who want to make merry at war's end. They eat, drink, flirt, and dance, in a world—or that portion of it which is vanquished Germany—turned upside down. Almost inevitably, the sight of this gigantic, reflective party prop induces one of the characters to come up with a mythological reference: "King Arthur used to entertain at a round table, but who had a meal on a mirror?"[51]

And so, on to Shlyapnikov in *November 1916*. The sympathetic Leninist, being of two minds whether to have a studio portrait taken by his photographer brother-in-law, examines himself in a cracked looking glass:

> He looked every day of his thirty-two years, and could have been taken for forty. His face was Russian, but not strikingly Russian: looking at the group photograph taken in a French factory, when he had trimmed his mustache differently and parted his hair, you would have been hard put to single out the one Russian from his French fellow workers. In a decent suit he could pass, say, for a French traveling salesman.
>
> He himself would have liked to look a bit more heroic, to have more of the revolutionary about him. ... Modest mustache, modestly close-cropped hair. But what made the man in the mirror a stranger, a mystery to himself, was something different: he looked like someone who *knew*, rather than someone who did things. ... The eyes were wrong, not those of a fighter, and so was the smile—a sad one. Why, whatever pose he struck for the camera, did he always end up looking so strange? Not a bit like a real revolutionary.[52]

(The husband of Shlyapnikov's sister is a seedy type with a sideline in political pornography, the house cum studio is correspondingly shabby, and the mirror is as tired and tainted as the hero himself.)

Shlyapnikov is an important presence, and the passage allows us to see what he looks like by means of that looking glass trope which Vidal so deprecated. But again, something else is happening here as well. The brooding Bolshevik is estranged from his reflection. He takes pride in his shop floor origins, yet he is anxious to better himself so that he might fit in with the intellectuals in charge of his party and prove deserving of the glamorous Alexandra Kollontai, a member of that leadership group. In fact, amorous Alexandra is drawn to Shlyapnikov—or rather, *was* drawn to him—*because* of his air of calloused masculinity. For her, the affair was a form of erotic slumming which had the charitable bonus of "putting some polish" on an "undomesticated working-class youth from an Old Believer background."⁵³ The text hints at these inner and outer tensions. The hero's physiognomic Russianness, which in Solzhenitsyn so often serves as a marker of a character's rootedness, is multiculturally reframed ("French fellow workers") in keeping with the Bolshevik spirit of international solidarity, while Shlyapnikov's introspective nature is very remote from the kind of proletarian machismo Kollontai finds exciting. Actually, brawny Zhora from *August 1914* would have been more her style. In the end, the sad-eyed revolutionary declines to have his picture taken, the sight of his reflected image precluding the creation of a photographic one. The melancholy hero is yet to learn that chic Kollontai has decided to break off the relationship because Shlyapnikov, "with his unremarkable, vulgar face [*so svoim neznachitel'nym meshchanskim litsom*] is unworthy of being her companion."⁵⁴ For this daughter of a tsarist general, classism outclasses the class struggle.

3

Ezra Pound surprisingly believed that "all good art is realism of one sort or another."⁵⁵ No doubt the author of *The Red Wheel* would have concurred. A self-proclaimed "traditionalist by inclination,"⁵⁶ he was something of a Victorian, seemingly immune to the joys and conceits of the art of the Modern. His unapologetic writerly embrace of heroic values and characters is a case in point: Kostoglotov, Vorotyntsev, and Boyev are modern knights valiant writ unskeptically, unironically large. For if, in Paul Ricœur's formulation, "the modern novel abounds in situations where one usually speaks of a character's loss of identity in exact opposition to the fixity of the hero which characterizes folklore, fairy-tales, and so forth,"⁵⁷ then Solzhenitsyn's prose is a revalidation of these ancient storytelling practices, even when he reconfigures them indicially. His heroes are heroes—*tout court*.

Solzhenitsyn rejected "the quasi-eschatological mythologeme of the End which became entrenched in Western culture starting in the late nineteenth century, as in the death of God (Nietzsche), the inevitable and imminent decline of Europe (Spengler), or the disappearance of the novel (Mandelshtam)."⁵⁸ Generally appalled by the stridently iconoclastic character of the Russian and European avant-garde, he particularly disliked the claims of its practitioners, or the more experimental among them, to have superseded 2000 years of cultural tradition. In one acerbic comment, he writes, "It was suggested that literature should start anew 'on a blank sheet of paper.' (Indeed, some never went much beyond this stage.)"[59] He makes the same sarcastic point fictively. Star-crossed Likonya enters *The Red Wheel* as a mannered Silver Age groupie, a "citizen of the universe"[60] given to batting her eyelashes as she declaims Gumilev's apocalyptic verses (the cosmic reference is from Ibsen's play *Peer Gynt*; 1876). At least initially, this bohemian maiden belongs in the same category of literary lampoons as Aviette Rusanova, the aspirant poetess in *Cancer Ward*. Later in the saga, however, Likonya falls hard for her Volga merchant, shedding all archness as she bears the torments of a difficult love affair, and swaps Gumilev for Tsvetaeva, whose lovelorn lyrical voice she adopts as her own. She transforms herself into an informed reader. In other words, she grows up.

Solzhenitsyn treats his reading characters like Likonya as exemplars, whatever their academic qualifications or receptor stance. In *The First Circle*, books are either "friends" or "enemies" for Nerzhin, study aids to be employed for his reconceptualization of Russia's present and past; for Volodin, the poetry of the Silver Age is a window into the history of his family, and the nation; for Klara Makarygina, the masterworks of SocRealism are terminally insipid; for Uncle Avenir, the Party newspaper *Pravda* serves as a lying repository of the historical truth. For Kostoglotov, Tolstoy's story "What Men Live By" is strong medicine (*Cancer Ward*); for Vera Vorotyntseva, Dmitry Grigorovich and Nikolai Leskov are "living companions"[61] (*The Red Wheel*); for Nastenka Mark II, the Russian classics act as a shield against the encroachments of a vulgarizing environment, though eventually she succumbs to her surroundings and the bad literature she must read and teach ("Nastenka").

To repeat, among Solzhenitsyn's artistic negations, Socialist Realism looms much larger than any other cultural phenomenon or school. If SocRealist novels were propaganda delivery systems, then this writer inserted a gigantic textual spanner into the works. His fictions are dynamic confutations of the Soviet "mode of literary production," to use Terry Eagleton's term, as well as case-specific confutations of the subgenres of SocRealist prose, for example, the revolutionary novel, war novel, factory novel, kolkhoz novel, spy novel, science novel. Or even SocRealist erotica, if there ever was such a thing. By contrast, programmatic anti-Modernist representations or themes in Solzhenitsyn's prose are relatively few in number: in addition to pouting Likonya and the ecstatic Zinaida Gippius (*The Red Wheel*), we have Tsezar Markovich, the Eisenstein acolyte who believes that "art isn't what you do, it's how you do it" ("Ivan Denisovich"), and the unprovoked attack on Cubism in "The Easter Procession." Of course, some of the writer's works are far removed from the

Modernist aesthetic, indeed implicitly hostile to it, and none more so than the two cycles of "Miniatures."

"It has become a commonplace to say that Solzhenitsyn's poetics belong to the nineteenth century and that it was because of this circumstance that he acquired a readership—in the first place, abroad, but also in our own country," writes Mikhail Novikov.[62] He reiterates the widespread assumption that the artist was a stylistic conservative: see Czeslaw Milosz's comment, "The Western reader is living at the end of the twentieth century, Solzhenitsyn in a writer of the nineteenth century."[63] The hostile comments in the writer's *Tendenzenschriften* concerning the new trends in literature offer plenty of evidence to support this view. (Yet he was aware, and approved of, the post-Brechtian reconfiguration of the formats of "modern drama.")[64] There are parallels here with an earlier and equally outspoken traditionalist, Ivan Bunin, his predecessor as "the leading figure of the Russian literary diaspora,"[65] and the first Russian writer to receive the Nobel Prize in Literature (1933). Notable for his "self-chosen role as the heir to the great tradition of nineteenth-century Russian realism and his hostility toward Modernist experimentation,"[66] Bunin was a passionate opponent of the Bolsheviks and everything they stood for. He felt a political revulsion from the Symbolists "because they glossed over and persisted in giving a religious apologia of the revolution."[67] Moreover, "his polemics with political movements and Modernist art ... often spill[ed] into his fiction"[68] and were repaid in kind by those whom he criticized. In 1943 the tragic Shalamov was given a ten-year sentence, his third prison term, for calling Bunin "a great Russian author."[69] Yet recent scholarship has identified important "Modernist and aestheticizing tendencies"[70] in Bunin's poetry and prose, which connect him to the very same experimental and avant-garde practices he so loudly decried. Or as Solzhenitsyn told the Austrian novelist Daniel Kehlmann, "The realist tradition comprises not only the realist manner of narration but also other forms and devices, as long as they assist the reader in apprehending reality as it exists."[71] This definition comes very close to a cooptation of Modernism, which, after all, recognizes the reality of the real even as it imaginatively alters and fractures it. Here let me quote a comment by Arkady Belinkov, the dissident Russian literary scholar:

> The apparently traditional nature of his style is akin to the art of the Renaissance, which seemed close to the art of the ancient world, but only at a distance and upon a casual view. Solzhenitsyn's writing is not only similar to the Renaissance, in fact it is the Renaissance of Russian spiritual life.[72]

So what about *this* writer's (dis)engagement from Modernism, "the embittered art of the 20th century," as he called it?[73] To begin with, he associated its practitioners with the radical left, rather than the radical right, D'Annunzio, Marinetti, Hamsun, Nolde, Dali, Brasillach, Céline, Eliade, Wyndham Lewis, and Pound himself notwithstanding. And let us not forget Russia's own Merezhkovsky and Gippius, that fellow-traveling democratic/fascist duo, whom *The Red Wheel* lampoons as hammy revolutionary enablers. In the words of one scholar, "Common denominators uniting Modernist aesthetics and fascism include concepts of cultural, political, and biological regeneration; the use of avant-garde techniques, such as montage; notions of 'secular religion'; primitivism; and anti-capitalist theories of space and time."[74] Solzhenitsyn's focus, though, is, as ever, on his homeland. Modernism or "avant-gardism" carried with it an aesthetic of "destruction" and played a nefarious role, especially in Russia, where it "preceded and foretold the most physically destructive revolution of the twentieth century."[75] The discourses and tropes of Modernism were catastrophic from the start: "Before erupting on the streets of Petrograd, this cataclysmic revolution erupted on the pages of the artistic and literary journals of the capital's bohemian circles."[76] The guilt, even the ethical crime, is one of proleptic association. In effect, Modernism stands accused of being teleologically complicit in the nation's collapse, if not of actually causing it. After all, Solzhenitsyn believed that literature has the power to heal and to enlighten, but also to kill: *The Red Wheel* presents the Russian defeat at Tannenberg as a material consequence of *War and Peace*. Across the epic, the treatment of avant-garde figures from Severyanin to Meyerhold is broadly satirical and Petrograd's Stray Dog café, the famous Acmeist/Futurist hangout, is panned as a "refuge of disheveled theatricality,"[77] though the phrase belongs to Sasha Lenartovich, ever-resentful of Likonya's boho ways. Other artistic innovators, however, such as the poets Tsvetaeva and Gumilev and the artist Mikhail Vrubel, are cast, and cited, in a positive textual light.

The writer singles out the Futurists for special censure as the artistic enablers and collaborators of the new Bolshevik regime, which in turn entrusted them with the "power to administrate over culture," until culture and country, and the Futurists themselves, were engulfed by "a 70-year-long ice age."[78] He may have been thinking of Zamyatin's story "The Cave" with its depiction of revolutionary Petrograd as a land of glaciers and snow drifts and mammoths where terrified members of the former middle classes revert to their inner and outer caveman. Solzhenitsyn had a particular disdain for Mayakovsky, the most famous Futurist of them all. In *The First Circle*, Klara Makarygina, whose views on literature are the author's own, thinks of Mayakovsky not as cutting-edge and shocking, but boring, boring, boring! It seems there was something about his strident poetic style and strutting masculinity that grated on Solzhenitsyn, for nowhere in the fictions or nonfictions does he acknowledge Mayakovsky's outsized talent or address his tragic death by suicide. Instead, *March 1917* contains a tiny documentary stab at the Futurist poet in the form of a directive signed by the revolutionary commandant of Petrograd: "Volunteer Dmitry Tairov and Private Vladimir Mayakovsky are hereby ordered to conduct the election of unit representatives in the Military Driving School and to organize the repair of vehicles."[79] As for that other literary progressive, the lavishly whiskered Gorky, Klara finds him "so very right but so very unalluring."[80] She may have a point. Yet if she does, *The Red Wheel* renders it moot, or at least to some extent, when we realize that Likonya's lover, the charismatic merchant Gordey, is surrounded by references to Gorky's novel *Foma Gordeyev* (admittedly, one of his better works of fiction), beginning with Gordey's given name. Granted, the epic invariably shows the *empirical* Gorky to his disadvantage, chiefly via the impressions of Shlyapnikov, who in his working-class way is alert to the signals of revolutionary hypocrisy emitted by the great proletarian writer.

On the other hand, in *The First Circle* the truth-seeking Volodin is culturally uplifted when he stumbles across a treasure trove of letters and journals from the Russian Silver Age. Those years of Symbolist decadence and Futurist scandal-mongering were also, it turns out, a time of artistic vitality and achievement: "Early twentieth-century Russia, with its ideological battles, its dizzy proliferation of trends and movements, its unbridled imagination, and its anxious forebodings, looked out at Innokenty from these yellowing pages."[81] Lines which suggest that at times Solzhenitsyn found himself reluctantly admiring some of the artistic practices of the Modern. Moreover, as a professional man of letters he was interested in how these practices changed the relationship between text and "reality", however defined (or denied). Here is his evaluation of Boris Pilnyak's novel of the Russian Revolution, *The Naked Year* (*Golyi god*; 1921), which on the whole he had found displeasing:

> In spite of the fragmentary, discontinuous quality of the narration, it undoubtedly retains a breadth of meaning as well as a marked richness of content, so as an experiment it is certainly a success. (One almost gasps at how far our prose had moved away from Chekhov in the space of just twenty years! ... Yet surely, this can be remedied?)[82]

In fact, *The Naked Year* "anticipates many of the features of the work of both Dos Passos and Solzhenitsyn in its use of montage as well as its treatment of the Bolsheviks as heartless automatons who are indifferent to the values and mores of the heartland."[83] And the "Letter to the Congress of Writers," Solzhenitsyn's most powerful public endorsement of the principle of artistic autonomy, refers to "the brilliance of the experiments" that distinguished Soviet literature in the 1920s[84] and even puts in a kind word or two about Mayakovsky. Things, it seems, are not that simple where the author's attitude to Modernism is concerned.

In the Struve interview, Solzhenitsyn was asked to list his most important literary influences. Predictably, he named Pushkin as well as Dostoevsky and the later Tolstoy (whom, he implied, he liked better than the creator of *War and Peace*),[85] but also Dos Passos, Tsvetaeva, and Zamyatin. Now, the last three are all luminaries of Modernism. Even the Tolstoy of the post-*Karenina* period was not only a (skeptical) witness to the early stages of that literary model, but directly anticipated some of its treatments of the written word.

Solzhenitsyn's take on Tsvetaeva and Zamyatin is revealing. Tsvetaeva's prose, which has "a verbal compactness with such dynamic twists and turns, and explosions," is "a prose for writers, not readers, and it would have to be diluted ten times over in order for ordinary people to be able to read it."[86] Now, how's that for an exclusionary statement! In effect, he adopts the early Modernist position that some Modernists are just not for everyone, and that this is a good thing.[87] As for Zamyatin, Solzhenitsyn admires his descriptive laconicism: "Sometimes with a single word, he catches a portrait as expressive as one done by a painter."[88] In the *Literary Collection*, he adds:

> I made him one of my teachers in matters of syntax.... Once a scene or a character has been sketched, he avoids adding a single superfluous word, with so much remaining implicit that some readers may be left none the wiser.... But most of all I liked the tightness of his syntax.[89]

These comments function on the plane of writerly pragmatics, but Solzhenitsyn's fondness for the author of *We* has a broader, axiological frame. In the Nobel Lecture he mentions Zamyatin (along with Akhmatova) as an artist whose persecution by the Soviet authorities was "a calamity for the whole nation."[90] Both men were scientists by education who were concerned with the modern cultural opposition between the sciences and the arts; both mined mathematics as a source of symbols and referents; both reversed the Jakobsonian rule that prose tends toward metonymy, by metaphorizing their narratives (though they also liked synecdoches); above all, both were satirists of the first water who employed their comedic gifts to deconstruct the significant myth of communism as well as its sub-myths and constituent mythemes.

Another favorite writer—perhaps *the* favorite—was Mikhail Bulgakov, whom Solzhenitsyn considered a "brother." His published comments about *The Master and Margarita*, a novel in which the historical Jesus, a very literary Devil, and 1920s Moscow coexist in the same composite phantasmagorical world, hint at an impression so powerful that one suspects Solzhenitsyn felt it would be safer if he kept it unrecorded. He refers to the novel's "pirouettes of fantasy," "bursts of wild laughter," the "gallop" of "Woland's cavalcade," "the affinity with Gogol," but also its "perverse obsession with the forces of evil."[91] And then there is this remark, fascinating in its conceptual implications: "And how do we explain the extraordinary interpretation of the gospel story, presented so as to degrade Christ, as though it were all seen through the eyes of Satan?"[92] In fact, Bulgakov's portrait of Yeshua-Jesus conforms exactly to Nietzsche's reading of the "psychological type of the Redeemer" as set forth in *The Antichrist*.[93] In a non-Nietzschean, non-Christological key, Ilya Kukulin discerns an underlying commonality of styles between the two novelists, suggesting that in a "typological" sense Solzhenitsyn, like Bulgakov, displays "intentionally supported anachronism" even as he "vividly responds to so many events of the modern world."[94] In this interpretation, an ostentatious traditionalism of form functions as an experimental device, a kind of meta-pastiche or "travesty" (see Genette) that remedies the excesses of Modernism.

Finally, there was Nabokov, of whom Solzhenitsyn said, "I always considered him a writer of genius."[95] Solzhenitsyn's letter to the Swedish Academy, in which he nominated the émigré novelist for the Nobel Prize, commends him as a master of "psychological observation," "elaborate word play," and "scintillating" formal compositions.[96] Nabokov, he avers, is one of those writers who are "identifiable from a single paragraph":[97] a point that applies equally well to Solzhenitsyn himself. Elsewhere, the author observes of his elder confrère: "He wrote absolutely brilliant novels in Russian—the early Émigré novels."[98] Still, these encomiums tell us little about which of Nabokov's fictions he liked or even what it was that he liked about them. In a 1993 interview, Solzhenitsyn was much more forthcoming:

> I am grieved that Nabokov, who came from a family which so avidly participated in the affairs of Russia,[99] who could have written so much and compiled even more material on the Russian Revolution a long time before

me, well, I am grieved that he washed his hands of it and busied himself only with literary successes. I am pained by this. I do not understand it. I do not understand how this is possible.

As it happens, I do not like *Lolita* at all. It seems to me in bad taste. But he has some fine novels like *Invitation to a Beheading* and many others; I rate him very highly. But I don't like *Lolita* because it is an unworthy play on sexuality, in my opinion.[100]

Putting the (perfectly reasonable) objections to *Lolita* aside, Solzhenitsyn's chief criticism of Nabokov is that he is not Solzhenitsyn. At the same time, this and other statements hint at an irreducible readerly response, one of keen, sensuous pleasure. It would be fair to conclude that our author *relished* Nabokov: writers do read other writers for enjoyment, after all. Especially, perhaps, when the enjoyment stems from the consumption of aesthetic meanings enfolding and beautifying things that are foreign, perhaps even wrong in one's own book. "The pleasure of the text does not prefer one ideology to another,"[101] explains Barthes. Or to return to Bataille's formula, as a medium of communication, imaginative literature, in and of itself, will always remain ethically problematic. For Solzhenitsyn, there was also the disappointment that the man who wrote *Pale Fire* had not employed his literary gifts to change the world, or at least Russia. On one occasion, the author remarked to Alexander Schmemann, apropos Nabokov, "If only, with that talent of his!..."[102] Finally, in *The Red Wheel* we encounter a touching mini-tribute to the latter when Solzhenitsyn has Vladimir Nabokov père, a leading liberal politician of the period, think an affectionate thought about his "excellent children,"[103] one of whom is the seventeen-year-old future novelist.

As for Vladimir Nabokov fils, he refused to see the artistic merit in Solzhenitsyn's prose ("he has nothing to tell but his story of illness and imprisonment"),[104] including *The Gulag Archipelago*, which he sniffily dismissed as "juicy journalese."[105] This may be classified as one of Nabokov's crasser remarks, redolent of that peculiar streak of refined bad taste that occasionally surfaces even in his fictions. But then, in the Age of the Modern, great writers have been known to commit such lapses of judgment, the reason perhaps being that, as Barthes also observes, "Around 1850 ... classical writing ... disintegrated, and the whole of Literature, from Flaubert to the present day, became the problematics of language."[106] After that date, consensus across the cultures was no longer possible. One writer's paragon could be another reader's bugbear, and vice versa. Take, for instance, Solzhenitsyn's own preference for Nekrasov and Yesenin, or his aversion to Gorky and Mayakovsky. Experience shows that there are as many predicates of personal taste as there are literature professors. Arguably, the only post-1850 commentator who invariably showed impeccable judgment in his evaluations of cultural figures and texts was Nietzsche, but then, he was one of the inventors of the Modern and, as such, the author of a discourse that had first defined those very problematics of language. And anyway, I said, arguably.

Solzhenitsyn's writings readily reveal their textual and structural congruences with the prose of authors whom he admired such as Dostoevsky, Tolstoy, or Zamyatin. Nabokov's novels are a less obvious referent, although as we saw, the (very) short story "What a Pity" contains descriptive elements that might qualify as Nabokovian. The more important connection, however, is that Nabokov and Solzhenitsyn are creators of enigmatic texts. As Kristeva notes apropos the former, "The polyphonic mastery of writing consists in ceaselessly doing and undoing a jigsaw puzzle piece by piece—not the puzzle of a 'world' considered by this or that metaphysical artist to be inaccessible … but that of an *essential enigma*."[107] An enigma, I submit, that is actualized in the form of a diegetic meta-topos, which invokes one or several hypotextual narratives or events within a designated cultural continuum by means of a bespoke code. It simultaneously invites and resists readerly engagement while reaffirming the text's status as a dialogically contingent production. In other words, both writers enjoy conducting literary games and inserting into their narratives elaborately camouflaged and sometimes humorous clues, even if in Solzhenitsyn's case such artistic play is mostly pragmatic, designed as it is to support an overarching historiographical or ethical message. In *August 1914*, the "stargazer" Varsonofiev, a wise reader and writer of books, informs a baffled Sanya and a scoffing Kotya that "the best poetry is found in riddles."[108] His formula applies as much to the four linked novels in which they are characters as to the astral realm that the white-haired augur visits in his dreams. Nevertheless, Varsonofiev's statement comes with a small word, or morpheme, of warning: the pattern of thought in a riddle, he tells his young friends, is "lacy," *kruzhevnoi*.[109] The qualifier is a cognate to *krug* ("circle") and therefore an indicator of ethical darkness or danger: the same adjective performs the same function in the opening sentence of *The First Circle*, as shown in chapter five of this study.

Sometimes, a secret hint may hold a reminder of the contingency of all literature and all literary characters, even those that are fictionalizations of real-life people: at the end of *The Red Wheel*, the deposed tsar is shown wondering if at some future time "a few interested souls will read about the details of what happened in Russia in March 1917 and how it happened."[110] And sometimes the *sub rosa* message may be of an entirely private nature, readable by no one except the author himself and half a dozen people in the know, as in the case of Colonel Boyer in *The Red Circle*, whose name is a coded homage to Solzhenitsyn's commanding officer in World War II, Major Boyev. Boyer's appearance and manner confirm the connection, for he has a "narrow head"[111] and a voice that holds "a peculiarly icy politeness,"[112] just like the Red Army major. Only after the publication of "Zhelyabuga Village" and "Adlig Schwenkitten," where Boyev appears heroically undisguised, was the (meticulous) reader handed the key to the secret clue.

Next, Nabokov's fictions feature "a special type of intertextual reference ... which comprises 'meaningful names' of characters (usually minor)."[113] This onomastic trope operates in Solzhenitsyn's fictions as well, where it is employed much more broadly. We saw that in *The First Circle*, Yakonov—*ya*—"I" or "ego." Other character names are straight aptronyms—Vorotyntsev—The One Who Returns—or function as coded parodies or ploys, for example, the prison poet Vdovushkin—Little Widower, whose muse or "wife" is as dead as the dodo. Such names are masks that give off a whiff of the carnival or the fancy dress party and once again remind us that all storytelling is a thing of artifice.

In the same key of intertextual allusion and eversion, Solzhenitsyn's prose employs variations on scenes from canonical works, as I have shown throughout this study. In *The First Circle*, the partocratic soirée at the Makarygins' evokes Madame Schérer's salon in *War and Peace*, and during his disputation with Dr. Fedonin in *August 1914*, the embryonic revolutionary Lenartovich speaks, or rants, in the voice of Dostoevsky's Smerdyakov. So when we read in one of Solzhenitsyn's interviews the claim that he follows the example of his nineteenth-century predecessors, who "wrote very responsibly. They did not play games,"[114] we should take this declaration with a grain of salt. Extraordinary as it may seem, this writer had his playful side. It's just that he kept it under textual wraps.

Both Nabokov and Solzhenitsyn display a predilection for historical counterfactuality, whether explicit (*Ada*) or implied (*The Red Wheel*). There is also their personal connection to the sciences and their fondness for scientific characters and themes. Nabokov believed that "in a work of art there is a kind of merging between ... the precision of poetry and the excitement of pure science,"[115] a view that Solzhenitsyn would have found to his liking. Nabokov's biographer draws this illuminating comparison:

> At about the time that Nabokov was most deeply engaged in lepideptorological research, Alexander Solzhenitsyn was carrying out experiments in

acoustics at the Marfino prison research camp described in *The First Circle*. Solzhenitsyn undertook the work with passion, drawing on his training in mathematics and physics, but for him this kind of research was an accident, and tangential to the obsession [with] the historical importance of the First World War and the revolution that it brought into being. For Nabokov, on the other hand, lepidoptera were at once a field of research and a passion that ... shaped all his art.[116]

(When he was working on *The Red Wheel*, Solzhenitsyn developed an elaborate cataloguing system of folders and envelopes, for example, "Children" and "Birds and Animals,"[117] not unlike Nabokov's famous index cards.)

Where Solzhenitsyn's writing is concerned, one might go further. In his fictions, physics, mathematics, or medicine enjoy a strong presence metonymically, that is, in a fabulatory or thematic sense; metaphorically, that is, as a source for his imaginaries; and dialogically, that is, as referents for his diegetic strategies, in a manner that brings us back to Zamyatin and his anti-utopia *We*. Far more than most scientifically inspired novelists, all three authors employed their knowledge of the quantifiable disciplines to enhance their artistic methodologies. And like Nabokov with his looking glass doublings or triplings, when a character may act as "a controller of the mirror image" or become "a victim to it,"[118] Solzhenitsyn explores the confusions and dangers consequent to an encounter between the physical self and its optical reflection or refraction.

Just as intriguing as the textual relationship between Nabokov and Solzhenitsyn was their real-life one. On the day that the author of *The Gulag Archipelago* was banished from the Soviet Union, Nabokov penned a warmly worded letter to welcome his "passage to the free world from our dreadful homeland" and to thank him for nominating him for the Nobel Prize.[119] A meeting was subsequently agreed to, but owing to a strange and inevitably symbolic misunderstanding it never happened: when the Solzhenitsyns' car pulled up at the entrance to the Montreux Palace Hotel where the Nabokovs resided, no one was there to greet them, so they slowly and regretfully drove away. In fact, the hosts were waiting inside the hotel restaurant at a table laid for four, and remained in this preprandial attitude for a full hour, no less baffled than their missing guests. Thus, the shores of Lake Léman became the site of one of those legendary non-encounters between two Russian literary masters, a sequence that includes Pushkin and Lermontov, Tolstoy and Dostoevsky, as well as Solzhenitsyn and Brodsky.

4

Solzhenitsyn certainly knew how to weave the threads of fiction. Yet in spite of his uncommon ability to invent places and characters and give them aesthetic form, he was opposed to the notion of the artist as a demiurge or a self-sovereign purveyor of beauty for a discriminating audience. After all, this was a writer who liked to remind others, and sometimes even himself, that invention was not his goal but his method. "I am not an innovator, I even dislike being innovative," he wrote in *The Journal of "R-17"* as he was composing the innovative Lenin-Parvus heads-on-the-bed sequence.[120] When the Swedish Academy awarded Solzhenitsyn the Nobel Prize "for the ethical force with which he has pursued the indispensable tradition of Russian literature,"[121] it was referring to works such as "Ivan Denisovich," *The First Circle*, and *Cancer Ward*, which display connections to the nineteenth-century cannon that are immediately and obviously identifiable. As for *The Red Wheel*, that mega-saga challenges the receptor, even one with a thorough knowledge of Solzhenitsyn's earlier productions, to learn an entirely new way of relating to the text. "What does it mean to show the entire Revolution in a large work? There are some 200 characters, hundreds of scenes. Certainly, new devices are necessary to fit all this material together," Solzhenitsyn confided to an American reporter.[122] In fact, many—perhaps most—of the epic's characters ought not to be received as fictive simulacra, but as archetypal or discursive or documentary representations that actualize its historiographical purpose. The alternate history strands, mimetic refractions, and diegetic disjunctions grow ever more conspicuous with each successive Knot and generate numerous points of contact with Modernism. They also anticipate Magical Historicism, as Alexander Etkind calls the "bizarre but instructive imagery that has evolved out of post-catastrophic, post-Soviet culture"[123] found in a variety of speculative novels by a younger generation of Russian writers, among them Tatyana Tolstaya and Vladimir Sorokin. The epopee *looks* experimental, with a variety of fonts, indents, and other polygraphic devices that denote its constituent complexities materially, on the printed page. Even the most casual reader will know that this is a work in which forms are important.

Here is a definition of the Modernist model proposed by Brian McHale, which hinges on the concept of the dominant as formulated by Yuri Tynianov and Roman Jakobson:

> The dominant of Modernist fiction is *epistemological*. That is, Modernist fiction deploys strategies which engage and foreground questions such as

... "How can I interpret this world of which I am a part? And what am I in it?" Other typical Modernist questions might be added: What is there to be known?; Who knows it?; How do they know it, and with what degree of certainty?; How is knowledge transmitted from one knower to another, and with what degree of reliability?; How does the object of knowledge change as it passes from knower to knower?; What are the limits of the knowable?[124]

McHale's epistemological imperative operates across all four Knots of *The Red Wheel* and reifies the special in-text status of a select group of personae who possess intellectual agency while conforming to Russian literature's truth-seeking, justice-affirming norm for its best heroes and heroines. Solzhenitsyn's questers include Vorotyntsev, Lazhenitsyn, Varsonofiev, Altanskaya, and even Likonya. These characters face the urgent task of apprehending the causes that brought about the collapse of the national and cultural environments they inhabited, while defending (Vorotyntsev, Varsonofiev) or constructing (Lazhenitsyn, Altanskaya, Likonya) their own identities as sovereign public or private actors.

Forms are just as important in the post-exilic prose works, whose fictive tenor, if not their themes, was largely incompatible with the literary fashions of the day, especially the various strands of Postmodernism, which Solzhenitsyn contemptuously dismissed as "a forced playing upon the strings of emptiness."[125] After his return to Russia he encountered a cultural scene that was being transformed by these avant-garde practices, whether empty or fraught. Visual and performance artists now enjoyed greater prominence than novelists, in a flamboyantly hedonistic and commercialized national space, which as the century turned became suffused with what Etkind calls "petromachismo," that is, "the synergy between the oil and gas trade and security services [that] create[d] a hypermasculine, cynical, and misogynistic culture."[126] In this perplexing new environment, "the old Russian logocentrism, with its idolization of the word and its magic properties, was waning."[127] Twenty-first-century Russia may still be a country where a poetry-loving schoolteacher can murder a friend over his preference for prose,[128] but influential voices there are now heard saying things like "Dostoevsky's hysterical search for God is as relevant to today's world as the clay tablets of Sumer."[129]

Now, where Solzhenitsyn's reception of modern literature is concerned, his attitude to Joseph Brodsky, arguably the leading exponent of the Modernist sensibility in late twentieth-century Russian literature, is very revealing. The two Nobel Laureates were contemporaries, not friends, and their comments about each other's works were addressed to a public audience rather than to each other. There was, however, an exception. In 1977 Solzhenitsyn penned his only letter to Brodsky: "I never omit to read your poems, whichever Russian journal they appear in, and I never cease to admire your brilliant artistry [*ne perestaiu voskhishchat'sia Vashim blistatel'nym masterstvom*]. At times I fear that in some sense you are destroying poetry [*razrushaete stikh*], although even this you accomplish with incomparable skill."[130] This is damning with strong praise! Discussing Solzhenitsyn's letter, Brodsky's friend Lev Loseff, a very fine poet himself, makes a shrewd point: "The elders do not understand their juniors and apprehend their poetic speech not as text, but in large part as semiotic noise, philosophical chaos."[131] He also offers this insight: "Solzhenitsyn, who hopes to be read by the masses, creates a literary language that in its artificiality bears comparison to that of the Futurists. Brodsky, who imagines his reader as, at best, his own alter ego, employs as his point of departure the demotic speech of his contemporaries."[132] In consequence, the two authors' respective appeal is very different. As another commentator, Alexander Genis, observes, Solzhenitsyn is read "by one kind of audience, whereas Brodsky's poems are read ... by an entirely different kind of audience, and these two audiences are not connected, but instead ignore the other side's author."[133]

Loseff was right. There is a long-standing dichotomy within the Modernist tradition between productions that are arcane, demand a sophisticated viewer- or readership, and thereby preclude mass consumption, for example, James Joyce or Ezra Pound; and those that, though they may be no less experimental, are democratically or fascistically or communistically accessible, for example, Camus or Dali or Picasso, or the Italian and Russian Futurists. At the same time, Solzhenitsyn's quasi-dramaturgical preference for character dialogue democratizes his texts while chiming with Céline's principle that the best kind of writing relies on the forms and patterns of oral speech. Or, to quote the French novelist himself, "Me, I've slipped the spoken word into print."[134]

Brodsky found much to disagree with in Solzhenitsyn's artistic and political opinions.[135] His attitude to the writer's literary system combined respect with more than a hint of censure as well as an appreciation of its creatively destructive function—a mirror image of the views expressed by Solzhenitsyn about Brodsky's poetry. The latter's most interesting remarks concerning his senior compatriot were delivered in 1978, following a poetry reading at the University of Iowa. Addressing the student audience in idiosyncratic, slangy English, Brodsky called him "one of the greatest and most courageous men" of the twentieth century.¹³⁶ He dismissed the notion that Solzhenitsyn was somehow just a Victorian writer out on a stylistic limb in the Age of the Modern and then discussed his art from an axiological perspective:

> He has been reproached quite a bit by various critics, by various men of letters, for being a second-rate writer, or a bad writer. I don't think it's just ... because the people who are judging the work of literature are sort of building their judgment on the basis of systems of aesthetics which we inherited from the Nineteenth Century. What Solzhenitsyn is doing in literature cannot be judged by this aesthetic standard just as his subject-matter cannot be judged by this aesthetic standard just as his subject-matter cannot be judged by our ethical standards. Because when the man is talking about the annihilation or liquidation of sixty million men, there is no room, in my opinion, left to talk about literature and whether it's a good type of literature or not. In his case, literature is absorbed in the story.¹³⁷

Therefore, it is not Solzhenitsyn but his disparagers who are behind the times, a judgment that continues to hold true in the second decade of the twenty-first century. Brodsky goes on to evaluate the oeuvre as a whole. He intuitively grasps the logic of Solzhenitsyn's artistic evolution, even though the true chronology of his most important works was not yet publicly known, while the integral text of *The Red Wheel* had not even been completed, let alone published. Solzhenitsyn's purpose, the poet suggests, is to construct high narrative value, while his method entails formal experimentation, sometimes on the grandest of scales:

> He *uses* literature, and not in order to create a new aesthetics but for its ancient, original purpose: to tell the story. And, in doing that, he's unwittingly, in my opinion, expanding the framework of literature. From the beginning of his career, as far as we can trace it on the basis of his successive publications, you see quite an obvious erosion of the genres.
>
> What we start with, historically, is a normal novella, *One Day*, yes? Then he goes to something bigger, *Cancer Ward*, yes? And then he went to something which is really neither a novel nor a chronicle but somewhere in between, *The First Circle*. And then we've got this *Gulag* which is, I think, a new kind of epic. It's a very dark epic, if you wish, but it's an epic.
>
> I think that the Soviet rule has its Homer in the case of Solzhenitsyn. I don't know what else to say. And forget about legends, that is real crap... about every writer.¹³⁸

What Solzhenitsyn would have made of this analysis must remain a mystery, though he once conceded that "*forms* become obsolete, that tastes in the twentieth century change abruptly and cannot be ignored by any author."[139] In his comments on his own works he seemed at times to agree that they contain Modernist elements, for example, the meta-tropes of ellipsis and discontinuity. On one occasion, whilst in the midst of writing *The Red Wheel*, he stated: "These days, I try to throw out every superfluous word. If there's any way I can do without a word, I throw it out."[140] Remarks such as this call to mind his appreciation of Zamyatin. Granted, Solzhenitsyn's traditionalist statements substantially outnumber his endorsements of some representatives or some elements of the Modernist paradigm. For instance, he mentions an international literary conference that took place in Leningrad in 1963 at which the death of the novel was proclaimed, to the horror of all reading Russia or at least of the author himself: "And I had *The First Circle* already written and was working on *Cancer Ward*."[141] Mind you, Solzhenitsyn always disliked the term "novel": "Odious word! surely we could find a better one? …," he exclaims with heartfelt philological indignation.[142] In a conversation I had with him in 2005, he elaborated: "We are talking about a love story, a love intrigue. When we apply this term [the novel] to a given prose genre, to large-scale [works] with a different content and different orientations, this narrows our understanding of it."[143]

Note that Solzhenitsyn refers to a *readerly* "understanding" of longer literary productions such as *The Red Wheel*: he privileges the receptor's epistemological position over the academic emphasis on typological precision or nomenclatural correctitude. A position that is very much in keeping with the Modernist one, notwithstanding the writer's strictures against the word "novel." Still, even Solzhenitsyn was unable to describe *The First Circle* as anything but such a thing.

Now, Mikhail Bakhtin identifies a category of writers "who produce a specific novel and then declare *it* the only correct, necessary and authentic form of the novel."[144] Of course, Solzhenitsyn never made any such claims for *The First Circle*, yet as his only prose work that is so designated it carries a unique *generic* significance. In the words of Heinrich Böll, "There is little that is novelistic in this novel."[145] The conclusion offers itself that in some implied authorial sense, *The First Circle* was the one "correct, necessary and authentic" novel among the half dozen or so long or longish productions Solzhenitsyn created (though he once suggested that *August 1914* is, in some sense, a novel[146]).

Bakhtin also says that novelists who insist on the paradigmatic status of their works tend to live in times when the literary tradition within which they operate is experiencing cross-textual or cross-generic stress:

> Often they ["normative definitions of the novel"] deeply and faithfully reflect the novel's struggle with other genres and with itself (with other dominant and fashionable variants of the novel) at a particular point in its development. They come closer to an understanding of the peculiar position of the novel in literature, a position that is not commensurate with that of other genres.[147]

In fact, Solzhenitsyn carefully disassociates himself from standard taxonomical practices of genre description. His choice of genre specifiers is idiosyncratic. He called "Ivan Denisovich" a "short story" and *Cancer Ward*, a "tale" (*povest'*), despite all formal evidence to the contrary. Still, if this is how their creator chose to describe them, we ought to take him at his word. To borrow Tzvetan Todorov's formula, both texts "disobey their genre":[148] the narrative sweep of "Ivan Denisovich" suggests a short novel or a novella whereas *Cancer Ward*, with its multiple plot lines and sprawling social content is as recognizably a novel as any production by Dostoevsky or Dickens. More interesting is Solzhenitsyn's invention of entirely new forms which, in Brodsky's formulation, "erode" the old genres: *The Red Wheel* is "A Narrative in Discrete Periods of Time"; *The Gulag Archipelago*, "An Essay in Literary Investigation"; *The Oak and the Calf*, "Sketches of Literary Life." The critic Boris Paramonov even proposes that this last work is Solzhenitsyn's "best novel" because "its center is legitimately occupied by a heroic personality, the most novelistic of inspirations."[149] After all, as Paramonov's colleague Dmitry Bykov would have it, "Russian literature is always, in essence, not about the adventures of the hero, but the adventures of the genre."[150]

All this goes to show that Solzhenitsyn's archaizing impulse coexisted with a commitment to experimentation that actually grew stronger and more pronounced in his middle and later years, after he emerged from the literary underground and became an established, though never *establishment*, writer.

5

Any analysis of Solzhenitsyn's poetics ought to account for where he stands in relation to his nineteenth-century "teachers," Dostoevsky and Tolstoy, which I have tried to do throughout this book. The author of "Ivan Denisovich" offered his own explanation, and a pretty thoughtful one it is:

> I have a very great feeling of respect and kinship to both of them, although in different ways. I am closer to Tolstoy in the form of the narrative, of the

delivery of material, the variety of characters and circumstances. But I am closer to Dostoyevsky in my understanding of the spiritual interpretation of history.[151]

With regard to the exact degree of Solzhenitsyn's connection to Tolstoy, opinions vary. Georges Nivat and other scholars, myself included, have identified direct and specific "borrowings" from *War and Peace* in *August 1914*,[152] and from this and other works by Tolstoy across the oeuvre. On the other hand, Oleg Pavlov, the Russian Booker-winning novelist, prefers to stress the differences between the laird of Yasnaya Polyana and the sage of Vermont. His focus is on their respective writerly temperaments and the manner in which these found expression in their texts:

> Tolstoy believed in the World Will and embodied this belief in *War and Peace*, whereas in *The Red Wheel* Solzhenitsyn fractionalizes the World Will into individual fates and shards, and dissolves it in his almost hourly chronicle of the events of history. Tolstoy assumed that he brought some kind of suffering to his people. Solzhenitsyn believes that he is freeing his people from suffering. In other words, one of them felt himself alienated and alone in his convictions, whereas the other wrote on behalf of millions.[153]

Clearly, however, several of Solzhenitsyn's works have a pronounced Tolstoyan "feel," most prominently "Ivan Denisovich," *Cancer Ward*, and Knots I–II of *The Red Wheel*. Both novelists are concerned with the dynamics of private and family life, socially framed, and share an awareness of its fragile, contingent nature, which may at any moment be disrupted or destroyed by some personal calamity or historical cataclysm. Both relate the individual to the organic life of the nation. There is also the curious fact that late in their writing careers, Tolstoy and Solzhenitsyn grew more experimental, more "modern." To illustrate this last point, let me compare two passages, from *Anna Karenina* and *August 1914*.

Toward the end of Tolstoy's novel there is a scene in which Anna enters the nursery of her infant daughter, Annie. The little girl's textual markers are her swarthy complexion and dark hair, which she inherited from her father, Vronsky. "The baby, sitting at the table, kept persistently banging it with the stopper of a decanter, looking blankly at her mother with her two black currants—her black eyes"[154] (*gliadela na mat' dvumia smorodinami—chernymi glazami*).[155]

In *August 1914*, Sanya Lazhenitsyn and his friend Kotya find themselves engrossed in a conversation with Varsonofiev: this is when the mystic makes his comment about the poetic nature of riddles. His eyes, we recall, are deep-set and "cavernous," that is, Platonic. When Sanya asks him whether justice is a sufficient foundation on which to build a society (see Plato's just city, Kallipolis), Varsonofiev "turn[s] the two brilliantly lit caverns toward him [*povernul k nemu Varsonof'ev svetiashchikhsia dve peshchery*[156]],"[157] before affirming that it is. Here the ocular or occult metaphor lacks an appended *elucidation*. Instead, it stands alone as the controlling trope, formatted via a diegetic contraction or blank. Compared with Tolstoy's proto-experimental description of little Annie's eyes, its analogue in *August 1914* is in full conformity with the practices of the modern novel.

The writer's relationship to his other "teacher," Dostoevsky, is more ambiguous. Solzhenitsyn claimed that his own fictional works possess the quality of "polyphonism," which in an interview he gave me in 2007 he defined in these broadly Bakhtinian terms: "In my case, polyphonism means that I give an approximately equal opportunity to all the characters to put forward *their* interpretation of events and their point of view. While one is reading a chapter, the character it depicts becomes, as it were, the protagonist."[158] The terms "polyphonism" and "polyphony," however, are themselves polysemic, while their application to Solzhenitsyn's fictions, even though it carries the author's own sanction, has been contested in recent scholarship.

So let us examine this issue more closely.

In "Word, Dialogue and Novel," Julia Kristeva discusses the evolution of the polyphonic discourse from the genesis of the European novel to the practices of early Modernism:

> A break occurred at the end of the nineteenth century: while dialogue in Rabelais, Swift and Dostoevsky remains at a representative, fictitious level, our century's polyphonic novel becomes "unreadable" (Joyce) and interior to language (Proust, Kafka). Beginning with this break—not only literary but also social, political and philosophical in nature—the problem of intertextuality (intertextual dialogue) appears as such.[159]

Now, if Solzhenitsyn is a polyphonist in the second sense employed by Kristeva ("interior to language"), then he is ipso facto a Modernist. Of course, even on the most creatively deconstructionist reading, it is unlikely that the author of *The First Circle* would qualify as a practitioner of *l'écriture féminine*, which for Kristeva is the essential polyphonic medium, though she adduces some male writers such as Sade, Joyce, Céline, and Khlebnikov as authorially self-transgendered purveyors of these sorts of womanly texts: "There are men, enthralled by archaic mothers, who dream of being women."[160] True, occasionally in Solzhenitsyn, we also encounter *characters* thus enthralled, even if their dreams are *never* gender-transformative. Such a one is Pavel Boyev, with his astral connection to the Moon, that mythical emblem of femininity ("Adlig Schwenkitten"). Like the Red Army officer—or Tatyana Larina in *Eugene Onegin*, Russian literature's original moon child—Sanya Lazhenitsyn occasionally appears in *his* text bathed in the same unfiltered lunar radiance: "These solitary walks by moonlight made him feel younger, cleared his thoughts, raised them to higher things."[161]

Here let me add that Solzhenitsyn happens to be one of the most masculine authors in Russian literature, like his poetic bête noire, Mayakovsky, whose hyper-manly "poetic 'I' thrusts at the sun" (Kristeva),[162] or the guitar bard Vladimir Vysotsky, whom the writer originally disliked but learned to appreciate after he settled in Vermont, thanks to his young sons' enthusiasm for the gravel-voiced singer:[163] an unusual instance of a children-to-parent cultural transfer.[164] The theme of masculine self-construction and self-assertion is central to Solzhenitsyn's prose, where the female characters are so often depicted from the perspective of a young or youngish hero, their femininity refracted by filial longing or male desire. Only the stories "What a Pity" and "Nastenka" feature women protagonists *and* a sustained female-point-of-view narrative stance, though *The First Circle, Cancer Ward*, and *The Red Wheel* contain substantial sections that are wholly devoted to a particular female presence and the gynocentric world she creates and inhabits. In addition to exploring the dimensions of the heroine's private self these framed units of prose always show her uneasy or antagonistic relationship with a severely gendered social environment where jackbooted or tie-wearing male authority rules the roost.

Of course, Solzhenitsyn never read Kristeva (nor would he have wanted to!) and, as I noted, he uses the term "polyphonism" in a loosely Bakhtinian sense. In *his* reading or writing, the word is merely an indicator of the coequal presence of multiple articulated character standpoints in the text. Here we can certainly agree that the longer fictions feature a plurality of distinct voices and consciousnesses, some of which are antagonistic to each other and to those of the (implied) author: in one of the essays in the *Literary Collection*, we encounter the term "polyphony of ideas."[165]

Like the author of *Crime and Punishment*, Solzhenitsyn not only allows his characters to speak their piece but makes sure they put forward their best philosophical, ideological, or personal case: a multivocality constructed around what he calls "coequally powerful arguments" (*oboestoronne sil'nye argumenty*).[166]

Take, for instance, his representation of Lenin who, in a manner of *speaking*, is an extended stretch of interior/exterior monologue, his fierce rants revealing a powerful mind married to an almost poetic lust for destruction (*The Red Wheel*); or the "brilliant engineer" Obodovsky, a patriotic socialist dedicated to building a strong, but not necessarily democratic, Russia (ibid.); or the "ethical socialist" Shulubin, a veteran Bolshevik who invents a quasi-Fabian philosophy of political altruism (*Cancer Ward*); or the "technological elitist" Gerasimovich, a passionate believer in government by those fit to govern, who puts Ayn Rand to shame (*The First Circle*). The novelist Galakhov, a portrait of the empirical Konstantin Simonov, earnestly explains what makes an honest SocRealist tick (ibid.) and a nominally disguised Aleksei Tolstoy gives sinuous justification to his artistic subservience before a despotic government ("Apricot Jam"). And the list goes on.

Again like Dostoevsky, Solzhenitsyn even arranges for characters that are generally or particularly in the wrong to articulate the (authorial) truth. The Bolshevik Shlyapnikov is scathing about Molotov and Stalin's personal and political flaws, while Lenin deprecates Trotsky's charismatic conceits (*The Red Wheel*); cynical Yakonov privately mocks the scientific ignorance of his Stalinist colleagues (*The First Circle*); snobbish Sologdin devises a critique of Marxism-Leninism that shows surprising similarities to Karl Popper's refutation of same (ibid.); and the crook Chaly subjects Soviet central planning to informed, if crooked, criticism (*Cancer Ward*).

There are, however, crucial differences between Solzhenitsyn's and Dostoevsky's polyphonic techniques. Solzhenitsynian prose tends toward monologism and is therefore more like Tolstoy's; in fact, occasionally more so than Tolstoy's. By way of explanation, here is Bakhtin's definition of the monologic novel:

> Whatever discourse types are introduced by the author-monologist, whatever their compositional distribution, the author's intentions and evaluations must dominate over all the others and must form a compact and unambiguous whole. Any intensification of others' intonations in a certain discourse or a certain section of the work is only a game, which the author permits so that his own direct or refracted word might ring out all the more energetically.[167]

A monologic text does not preclude the suspension of belief by a receptor who finds the ideological *content* of the authorial discourse alien or objectionable, provided he can accept its *stylistics* as palatable, or better still, aesthetically pleasing. It is possible, even advisable, to immerse oneself in the sexually paranoid world of the *Kreutzer Sonata* without sharing Tolstoy's views about the correct relationship between the sexes (that is, no relationship), indeed whilst actively disagreeing with them.

Dostoevsky's receptors, however, possess much greater sovereignty than Tolstoy's. They are able to pick and choose among the characters and their existential/ethical/philosophical positions or even individual statements and acts: when reading *Devils*, the young Joseph Goebbels, a fanatic in the making, was enthralled by Shatov's declaration that far from obeying the rules of reason, all nations are consumed by "an insatiable desire to go on until the end, while at the same time denying that there is an end."[168] It is just as easy to imagine the future Nazi propagandist identifying with Kirillov's man-god project or grimly grooving to Stavrogin's various pranks and crimes. In Solzhenitsyn, things are different. The authorial discourse performs a continuous framing function that assigns the character voices their "correct" ideological and historical contexts and axiologically evaluates each individual utterance, usually via the technique of free indirect speech, for accuracy, honesty, and ethical value. In consequence, Solzhenitsyn's works resist the same degree of proactive intrusion into the text by the receptor, however mentally acrobatic or emotionally adrenalized. Just try reading *The First Circle* as a panegyric to high Stalinism or *The Red Wheel* as a heroic depiction of Lenin's march to revolution.

A closer parallel with Dostoevsky, as well as Andrei Bely and Joseph Conrad, is Solzhenitsyn's fascination with revolutionists as cultural types. This is most evident in *The Red Wheel*, with its textured portrait of Stolypin's assassin, Bogrov; the two terrorist aunties raving about the bombers and regicides that made their youth such bliss; Sasha Lenartovich, a hero of the people in his own mind; and the saturnine anarchist Zhora, whose homicidal drives are complemented by his sexual debauchery. In addition to the extended character study of Lenin, the saga includes sketches of other revolutionary leaders such as Kerensky, Trotsky, and Stalin. Lesser figures like Shlyapnikov, Gimmer, and Peshekhonov have multiple chapters devoted to them. Subaltern ideologues, for example, fellow-traveling Sonya Arkhangorodskaya and her friend Naum Galperin, receive attention throughout the saga, as does a gallery of soapbox orators and extremist agitators who are as verbally incontinent as they are vocally shrill. Elsewhere we encounter *would-be* revolutionaries, for example, the fanatical grammarian Sasha Gen who wants to fight those reactionary commas almost as much as the forces of world imperialism ("Nastenka," part two), and the young Gleb Nerzhin with his violent fantasies of a Europe liberated from capitalist exploitation by Red Army bayonets (*Love the Revolution*).

So how does Solzhenitsynian multi-voicedness differ from true Dostoevskian polyphony?

Part of the answer is that this writer's framing narrators, whether first- or third-person, enjoy a great deal more authority than Dostoevsky's. Their voices are privileged; assertive; and often resonate with those instantly recognizable Solzhenitsynian inflections. The voices lay down the diegetic law and act as agents of an integrating, unitary message that is present, on some narrational plane or other, at many given points in the text. A good example of this is the first person plural narrator in *Adlig Schwenkitten*, where the storytelling, omniscient "we" actualizes the novella's Homeric quality yet precludes readerly identification with the heroic warriors Boyev and Baluev, by erecting a perceptual barrier between text and reader.

To quote Bakhtin once again, "An absolute epic distance separates the epic world from contemporary reality, that is, from the time in which the singer (the author and his audience) lives."[169] Or as an American scholar explains, epic distance "requires an inviolable boundary between the distant past and whoever narrates it, and it is the space that lies between this 'absolute past' and the present of the narrator that renders the distance epic."[170] This boundary extends beyond the borders of the text into the readerly here and now, so that the receptor, even as he suspends his disbelief, remains confined to his personal present, which may or may not be congruent with that of the narrator.

Next, in those frequently occurring stretches of text that take the form of free indirect speech, which is a Tolstoyan rather than a Dostoevskian device, the narrative often ironizes a particular character's stance; spins it, again in a manner of *speaking*. In this way, the individual personalities to whom the authorial presence is opposed constantly undergo in-text subversion, and sometimes sabotage, even if their voices are articulate, cogent, and ideologically on message. In *The Red Wheel* this happens to Lenin and General François, to name just two of the dozens of figures subjected to such skeptical or hostile treatment. In Solzhenitsyn, the implied author is all over and under the text! Dostoevsky, on the other hand, adopts a very different storytelling procedure, for

> while objectifying the thought, the idea, the experience, [he] never has anything up his sleeve, never attacks from behind. From the first to the final pages of his artistic work he was guided by the principle: never use for objectifying or finalizing another's consciousness anything that might be inaccessible to that consciousness, that might lie outside its field of vision.[171]

The issue of Solzhenitsyn's multivocality has preoccupied a number of scholars, who tried to square his self-description as a polyphonist with the requirements of Bakhtinian theory. Pavel Spivakovsky suggests that the author of *The Red Wheel* invented a new type of polyphony that is of a different order from Dostoevsky's:

> Solzhenitsynian polyphony is the *polyphony of perceptual worlds* (in other words, *the polyphony of individual perceptions*), with the polyphonic conflict largely occurring not on the plane of ideology, but on the plane of confrontation among the incompatible subjective and individual worlds of the characters, who inhabit the same living reality.[172]

This analysis, which is based on a close examination of the epic's diegetic matrices, is insightful, but stretches the concept of polyphony to a post-Bakhtinian breaking point. For his part, Aleksandr Urmanov argues that the epic's "fictive world is volumetric [ob"ëmen], but not at all polyphonic in the strict sense of the word."[173] Accordingly, he proposes that

> in order to describe the narrative structure of *The Red Wheel* as well as the fictive picture of the world created by the author-demiurge, instead of the term "polyphony" ... one might use the word "stereophony," which is preferable precisely because it does not carry a sense that the voices heard in the work are co-equal among themselves. ... In this semantic context, stereophony is a narrational principle that allows the author, by means of a "nodal" combination of a multitude of contiguously presented voices ... to create a volumetric model of the historical period he is describing.[174]

In the end, it may perhaps be more productive to acknowledge that Solzhenitsyn's narratives are multivocal and heteroglossic and that his characters happen to be talkative, opinionated, and in active or passive disagreement with each other and, quite often, the author of record, and leave it at that.

As for Bakhtin himself, though he never subjected any of the writer's works to a formal analysis, his opinion was clear: "I imagine him as a figure of Dostoevskian stature!" (*Ia ... predstavliaiu ego velichinoi formata Dostoevskogo!!*).[175]

6

The uses of Solzhenitsyn's monologic dialogism (to coin a term) are best understood with reference to the dynamics of reader response. Umberto Eco proposes that the discourse of the text and the practices of the receptor are distinct and autonomous things: "Every act of reading is a difficult transaction between the competence of the reader (the reader's world knowledge) and the kind of competence that a given text postulates in order to be read in an economic way."[176] The operative words here are "difficult" and "economic." The competent reader's reward for his sometimes onerous task of interpretation is the right to generate new textual values—fictive, aesthetic, even political—subject to certain conceptual and interpretative constraints. Eco calls this procedure "'moderate' deconstructionism."[177] Solzhenitsyn's post-1968 fictions, with their high diegetic quotient, offer more opportunities for a non-radical reconfigurative reading than the novels and stories that first brought him fame.

In those earlier works, the relationship between text and reader is hierarchical; the transactions between them perforce "economic," to use Eco's term. The text imposes itself on the receptor, who as well as consuming it, is consumed by it. Many empirical readers of "Ivan Denisovich" were shattered when they read the tale in November 1962, with some Stalinist receptors experiencing an intellectual or discursive breakdown—deconstructed by the text, as it were, like the gorgonian Comrade Zakharova of the Ministry for the Protection of Public Order. Others, to the contrary, underwent a positive process of self-construction, among them the late dissident Valeria Novodvorskaya, a thorn in the besuited sides of Russian leaders from Brezhnev to Putin: "This short book made my decision for me [*knizhka reshila za menia vsë*]. ... I now knew what I should live by, and how and why I should live."[178]

Or consider *The First Circle*. What we have here is an isochronous text, where story time equals discourse time. This aspect of the novel has interesting implications. Paul Ricœur reasons that "temporality [is] that structure of existence that reaches language in narrativity and narrativity [is] the language structure that has temporality as its ultimate reference. Their relationship is therefore reciprocal."[179] In the case of Solzhenitsyn's only "official" novel, this relationship actually transcends reciprocity, for as refracted in the text, temporality and narrativity converge into an ontological congruity or even sameness. One can readily imagine some alert, sleepless soul taking three days and nights to plough through this ninety-six-chapter story of the seventy-two hours in the life of Volodin, Nerzhin, and their families, friends, and enemies. Indeed, Tvardovsky spent almost exactly this length of time poring over *The First Circle*, in its expurgated "medical" version, when he visited Solzhenitsyn in Ryazan on May 25, 1964, an event chronicled in *The Oak and the Calf*. The editor of *Novy Mir* found the novel so devastating that he required repeated shots of cognac, reluctantly supplied by the host, to sustain himself during this traumatic reading experience. If waded through (almost) without a pause, as was done by Tvardovsky chez Solzhenitsyn, the text imposes ever-growing cognitive burdens on the ever more tired and sleepless reader. Receptor-fatigue will *productively* distort his perceptions and render the fictive world more and more disturbing and phantasmagorical as Volodin arrives at the moment of maximum danger and Nerzhin departs for a Siberian labor camp. This is suspension of disbelief with a vengeance!

A feature of all the prose works from *Love the Revolution* to the binary tales is their postulation of a receptor who is careful, thoughtful, and ethical: they require of those who wish to enter the narrated world a certain measure of decency. Continually variable on the lexical, syntactic and diegetic level, these texts will always slow such a conscientious reader down; and sometimes bring him to a swift and helpful halt. This feature of Solzhenitsyn's writing was noted by the author of an early and effusive review of "Ivan Denisovich":

> From the very first pages of his tale Solzhenitsyn posits a different, long-forgotten, sacral, and humble manner of putting letters together, syllable by syllable. Solzhenitsyn showed that all those arguments about physics vs. lyrics are pointless if one is to accept that a literary text may be read one sigh, one pause, one tiny, iron-cast and oh-so-courageous paragraph at a time.[180]

The Oak and the Calf is, among other things, the story of Tvardovsky the Reader, the establishment poet and Party grandee who finds himself stunned, distressed and eventually reconfigured by his encounter with Solzhenitsyn's literature of truth. The memoir presents the Solzhenitsyn-Tvardovsky connection as one not between writer and editor, but subject and object of a world-historical literary process. In Solzhenitsyn's telling, Tvardovsky's readerly torments loom far larger that the poetry he writes or the journal he directs. He is depicted, often movingly, as a study in contradictions, worldly but ingenuous, wise but blinkered. The "portrayal … is overharsh; yet somehow that seems almost deliberate, as if the author wishes us to take sides with the erring Tvardovsky against his too censorious judge."[181] Perhaps what we have here is a doubling of the author, who stands in continuous dialogue with his own self, in his own text. Yet if fans of the poet and family members found the book's treatment of Tvardovsky unfair and upsetting, then the depiction of General Samsonov in *August 1914* as a national *homme-type*, which was directly inspired by Solzhenitsyn's impressions of his onetime sponsor, is a tribute that honors this conflicted figure and thereby goes a long way toward redressing the balance. To quote the author, "I found it easier to understand Tvardovsky through Samsonov, and Samsonov through Tvardovsky, the two of them simply became joined together in my head and in my heart."[182] Solzhenitsyn also appreciated Tvardovsky's traditionalist stance in matters of literary style and form. In an interview with Barry Holland of the BBC, the writer conceded that the editor of *Novy Mir* had "sensed better than I did the future destiny of Russian literature" and had been anxious to protect it against "avant-garde trickery" (*avangardistskaia ekvilibristika*)[183] and "outlandish experiments" (*shal'nye eksperimenty*).[184] Looking forward to a time when Russia would be free of censorship, Solzhenitsyn foresaw "terrible dangers" for those writers who were hoping to embrace "the freedom to be completely irresponsible."[185] By responsibility he meant a duty of loyalty, not to one's art, but to the nation.

7

Czeslaw Milosz offered this evaluation of Solzhenitsyn's achievement, which emphasized the historiographical and restorative meaning of his art:

> On page after page he deplores the terrible loss brought about by the Revolution, not only in terms of millions of human victims, but also in terms of the destruction of so many precious things: community ties, kindness, respect, piety, architectural beauty—and the sound of bells without which Russia is not Russia.[186]

Milosz was seconded by another Nobel Prize-winning exile, Joseph Brodsky: "You have the millions of dead behind him. The force of the individual who is alive grows proportionately—it's not him essentially, but them."[187]

Yes, there was praise, but there was also dispraise, and not only from ill-intentioned parochialists like Voinovich or Bushin. A common criticism is that there is an appreciable difference in quality between the works where Solzhenitsyn writes from personal experience and those stretches of narrative, such as the Makarygin chapters (*The First Circle*) or the Lenartovich-Likonya story line (*The Red Wheel*), where he invents plots, characters, and situations more or less from scratch. Such critics find support for their view in the author's frequent declarations that his literary methodology was mnemonic and reconstructive, rather than imaginative. The unspoken—sometimes spoken—notion is that this is a narrowly autobiographical writer whose literary skills are inadequate to the demands of his literary agenda: a second Fadeyev or Fedin. To this objection I can only reiterate that time and again Solzhenitsyn follows the Tolstoyan practice of constructing his heroes and heroines as fictive simulacra, artfully designed thinking, walking, talking, emoting human approximations. If, as one scholar observes, *Anna Karenina* is "the novel as a truly representational art form, one that attempts to create the illusion for readers that they are not reading words describing a character but instead actually 'seeing' a 'living, lovely woman,'"[188] then the same principle of hallucinatory suspension of disbelief holds true for Solzhenitsyn's novels and stories. The characters' relationships make sense, too: we can understand why Kostoglotov is so powerfully attracted to blonde, vivacious Zoya but falls in love with darkly beautiful, clever Vera; or how gawky Varya Matveeva finds leather-clad Zhora's aura of proletarian aggression so seductive; or why Vorotyntsev, torn between his love for Olda and his spousal obligation to Alina, ends up going to bed with Kalisa, a woman he had desired years before as a very young man.

One difference, however, is that as a rule, Solzhenitsyn's fictional personalities and their behaviors and worldviews are primarily or ultimately shaped by outside factors rather than the operation of internal psychological mechanisms, as happens for example in *Anna Karenina*. And starting with *The Red Wheel* or even some sections of *The First Circle*, the narratives become terse, paratactic, sometimes creatively schematic. The writer uses fewer and fewer words to drape his characters' bones in fictive flesh, even as the fictions grow in length and sweep. "I dream of the greatest possible laconicism."[189] Often his heroes and villains are now more voice than body, like those hircine revolutionists who spend their time disputing and conspiring in the last two novels of *The Red Wheel*. In fact, that saga features an entire class of personae, many of them real-life cultural or social actors, who are mostly (sometimes entirely) units of historical meaning in a quasi-fictionalized record of a war and a revolution, even as they interact with the more textured, more "Tolstoyan" presences. Similarly, in several of the binary tales the personalities depicted are but cogitating and emoting contours showing white or black against the shifting backcloth of public events, for example, Professor Vozdvizhensky or Nastenka Mark II. At the same (discourse) time, the character voices grow more dramatic and distinctive, the incidence of lexical and figurative tropes rises, and textual stylistics come to the fore—ironically, as per Tsezar's dictum, "Art isn't what you do, it's how you do it." Finally, from *Love the Revolution* to *The Red Wheel*, the frequency of citational elements steadily increases, with the epic morphing into an anthology of Russian literature replete with overt and subtextual glosses and annotations.

We thus observe an overall shift from predominantly mimetic (minimal narrator) texts, such as "Ivan Denisovich," *The First Circle*, and *Cancer Ward*, to predominantly diegetic (maximal narrator) texts, of which *The Red Wheel* is by far the most important example. That discontinuous, fissiparous epic marked the end of Solzhenitsyn's decades-long antagonistic engagement with "the loathsome ceremonial forms of so-called 'Socialist Realism'"[190] and ushered in his formal reorientation toward the practices of Russian and European Modernism. To quote Auerbach,

> At the time of the first World War and after—in a Europe unsure of itself, overflowing with unsettled ideologies and ways of life, and pregnant with disaster—certain writers distinguished by instinct and insight find a method which dissolves reality into multiple and multivalent reflections of consciousness.[191]

The German philologist was referring to James Joyce, Virginia Woolf, and other members of that first generation of experimental novelists, but Solzhenitsyn's magnum opus relies on the same fictive practice. Yet even when the tetralogy "dissolves reality" in this Auerbachian sense, its author brings his customary ethical focus to bear on the representation of societies and individuals.

The Red Wheel is a sprawling saga comprising a plethora of fictional or fictionalized personalities, lives and voices, literary experimentations, indented folk sayings, newspaper clippings, official documents, private letters and memoirs, and analytical essays on a variety of historical topics. Or to put it differently, it is a gigantic collage of texts and topoi in which the Tomchak/Lazhenitsyn/Vorotyntsev/Andozerskaya/Lenartovich/Likonya/Polshchikov/Kovynev/Altanskaya/Blagodarev/Katyona chapters are the human interest stickum that holds all these disparate pieces of historiography and documentation together. In *March 1917* and *April 1917*, which treat the revolution as a world-historical *dégringolade*, the text acquires a starkness of expression that is unlike anything else in Solzhenitsyn. There is a terrible and tragic a story to be told and the telling of it is as dark as its subject, so that the text effects a formal rapprochement of literary style and historical fact: "An artist must not concoct a form, unless the material dictates it to him."[192] Like *The Gulag Archipelago*, for which Solzhenitsyn designed a new figurative language appropriate for the depiction of extreme human suffering and rampant human evil in a redemptive but factologically oriented narrative, *The Red Wheel* is a diegetic text that employs a metaphor-centered discourse to evaluate a national catastrophe and its associated traumas while proposing ethical and political strategies for overcoming them in the reader's own time and place. He must work harder, but the rewards are commensurate, for he acquires new rights over the text, even if not complete receptor sovereignty. Throughout the saga, the reader finds himself in dialogue with an encyclopedic, often engaging, occasionally partisan, sometimes mystical, broadly Menippean, narrowly topical, elaborately textured novelistic chronicle, which poses the same "cursed questions" that have haunted Russia since the nineteenth century. Eco's dictum, "A text is a machine conceived for eliciting interpretations,"[193] is eminently applicable here. *March 1917* is an amalgam of fluctuating, collapsing narratives that show the revolution rampant and triumphant, a garish gala of murderous joy and joyful murder, while *April 1917* depicts its aftermath in similarly dynamic fashion as a nationwide, mock-Paschal, true-demonic celebration of evil by a people and a generation who know not what they have done, or what awaits them.

So let us consider the oeuvre as a fluctuant system of mutable parts. Solzhenitsyn would "restore," rewrite, rearrange, shuffle, and reshuffle the component parts of his published or unpublished or semi-published works with conspicuous writerly impetuosity, as required by his authorial preferences or the exigencies of the authorial situation. This is true of *The First Circle*, of which there are two extant versions, the "medical" and the "atomic"; but most prominently, *The Red Wheel*, which exists in three published redactions. As we have seen, this writer was a textual perfectionist who expanded, or contracted, or corrected his fictions even after they had appeared in print, even after they had entered the canon. But whether he was being creative or just finicky, with every such postscriptive intervention Solzhenitsyn asserted his ontological status as the omnipotent, omniscient Author, *pace* Barthes and Foucault and Derrida. A stance that is at variance with—militantly opposed to—the Modernist ideology of the text, which posits that "the author will be invisible and unobtrusive, above or behind but not *in* his creation."[194] Actually, the strongly autobiographical content of so many of the fictions, and the way their creator employed them as vehicles for his public quest to expose the Lie, make him anything but a redundant or liminal author. But then, his identity as a practising artist, an artificer of worlds, had a very personal physiological meaning. "When in 1954, as he was dying of cancer, he began writing and the disease unexpectedly retreated, Solzhenitsyn all of a sudden realized that he would live only for as long as he was writing."[195]

Scribo, ergo sum.

So is it surprising that this author declined to adopt the Modernists and Postmodernists' reconfiguring of the notion of authorship and their skepticism about the ontological status of the text? He observes disapprovingly: "We know that after the First World War, Western intellectuals increasingly succumbed to irony as a way of looking at the world. ... In the twentieth century, a writer 'finds it impossible to take [even] himself absolutely seriously.'"[196] He is thus in formal agreement with Paul Fussell, who calls irony "the dominating form of modern understanding [which] originates largely in the application of mind and memory to the events of the Great War."[197] Despite his own writerly preoccupation with that terrible conflict, Solzhenitsyn's heroic authorial stance was predicated on very different principles, one of which was that he took himself very seriously as an artist. A lifelong optimist who always felt an almost physical connection to his land and his people, he found the cultural despair that infused so much of modern art incomprehensible: in a 1993 lecture he blames the "howl" of Existentialism on the "piercing loneliness" (*svistiashchee odinochestvo*) of modern life.[198] Beyond this, the refusal of many twentieth-century artists to defer to religious or ethical certainty was entirely alien to him. Taken singly or together, Solzhenitsyn's literary and non-literary productions stand in majestic opposition to Jean-François Lyotard's programmatic announcement about "the decline of the unifying and legitimating power of the grand narratives of speculation and emancipation."[199]

And so he invented or in places borrowed, from Dos Passos, Zamyatin, Tsvetaeva, perhaps even Nabokov, a set of fictive instrumentalities that may be described as Modernist, in the sense that Modernism "is our art [because] it is the one art that responds to the scenario of our chaos."[200] Yet if Solzhenitsyn is a Modernist, or at least a stylist of the Modern, then he is one that *overwrites chaos*—even though chaos is his subject and, perhaps, his darker inspiration—by consistently restoring fallen, distorted, shattered meanings as he proclaims a nationally based, conceptually absolute system of ethical and aesthetic values.

As I have tried to show, Solzhenitsyn is a remarkably sophisticated, subtle, and aware artist whose literary achievement should in no way be underestimated or overlooked because of the controversies surrounding some of his political or cultural views. His later fictions are, to a degree, as "readerly" as they are "writerly," to use those Barthian terms. But all his works possess a formal elegance that was sometimes missed even by sophisticated receptors like Nabokov or Vidal, who were culturally primed to apprehend them as political docudramas or quasi-Tolstoyan exercises in the realist representation of life. Yet, if one approaches a Solzhenitsynian novel or story as a dynamic, variable object of knowledge, rather than just an empirical textual artifact triggering the reader's passive suspension of disbelief, one may arrive at some interesting, even provocative conclusions. And mine is this: a self-proclaimed and outspoken anti-Modernist, this writer learned to employ Modernist means in order to pursue anti-Modernist ends.

As a world-historical commemorator of a nation's tragedy, Solzhenitsyn presented the life stories and death stories—some imagined, some recollected, some reconstructed from the documentary record—of the heroes, victims, and perpetrators of the Soviet experience. He accomplished this somber task sustained by a belief in "the very irrationality of art, its dazzling convolutions, its unforeseeable discoveries, its powerful impact."[201] The narrative splicing of fact and fiction, auto-referentiality and auto-representativity, semiotic manipulations, geometrical structuring and image-making, even cultural gamesmanship were just some of the tricks and tropes he employed as he composed his literature of truth. As I conclude my examination of this thoughtful creator of beauty and nuance, I fancy that he might have agreed with Nietzsche, who once upon a time proclaimed, "Are we not … adorers of forms, of tones, of words? And therefore—*artists*?"[202]

APPENDIX

Three Interviews with Aleksandr Solzhenitsyn (2003–7)

Aleksandr Solzhenitsyn: Answers for Richard Tempest

Aleksandr Isaevich, in your 1976 TV interview with the BBC you were asked about Western writers with whom you felt an affinity, and you mentioned Dickens, adding that in your youth you had read his novels several times over.[1] Which of his works and which of their aspects do you most appreciate?

Dickens enthralled me with his always optimistic, life-affirming view of reality and the human potential. His warmhearted attitude toward people. The vibrant composition of his works.

During your recent meeting with readers at the Russian State Library,[2] you mentioned that as a child you had read all of Jack London[3] (news of whose death receives momentary mention à la Dos Passos in one of the newspaper fragments in chapter ten of November 1916*).[4] What is your attitude toward him now?*

I have not read Jack London since childhood.

In November 1916 *you introduce the character of Olda Andozerskaya, a Petersburg intellectual. The personality of this intelligent and passionate woman reminded me of Ibsen's heroines. Would you agree that there is something Ibsenian about Olda?*

There is no connection to Ibsen's heroines. The historical terrain is different and so are this character's life goals.[5]

Both in Russia and abroad, the profusion of books and articles devoted to your writings includes only a small proportion of studies that are purely philological in nature. How do you account for this fact?

Scholars were fascinated by the inescapable political situation in which I found myself owing to harsh circumstances. Yet this state of affairs is now changing, and is certain to change even more after my death.

There are few children in your works. Why is that?

Where this is appropriate, there are children, of different ages.

From a close reading of your works, a scholar might infer that they include the occasional sideways intertextual nod or gesture by the author. In August 1914, chapter ten, we meet General Samsonov, one of the central characters in this Knot. The chapter suggests a rhyming and semantic association, Samsonov—Oblomov: the general has "lain down," and the object on which he is recumbent is a sofa (see "samoson").[6] Would you care to comment?

There is *no* association between Samsonov and Oblomov. The former is a different type.

The subtextual historisophical debate with Tolstoy is one of The Red Wheel's *main components. In this connection, I have another question about Samsonov, who begins to sense, and I quote, that he is "no longer a man of action but only the mouthpiece of events."[7] To what extent is this character a polemical construct by means of which you engage with Tolstoy's mythologization of Kutuzov as a wisely fatalistic commander? I note that in August 1914, General François, the true victor of Tannenberg, displays a Napoleonic orientation.*

If *August 1914* includes a polemic with Tolstoy, this involves the character of General Blagoveshchensky, not Samsonov.

A number of passages in your literary and polemical works indicate an interest in the figure of Napoleon. How do you account for the high status accorded to this historical personality in Russian culture? As a writer and scholar of Russia's past, do you feel a measure of sympathy for Napoleon? How would you describe your attitude toward him?

I have never felt any sympathy toward Napoleon.

Every writer needs a sympathetic first reader, and then a stern editor. Who discharges these functions in your creative process, and how do they do this?

My constant, invaluable editor and assistant is my wife, Natalia Dmitrievna.

I find that Thomas Mann's novel The Magic Mountain *and your tale* Cancer Ward *share certain features (Tolstoyan allusions and motifs, a narrow, clearly defined space that is institutionally or topographically delineated within the narrative, which it both symbolizes and constricts, a group of sufferers who may be described as the patients of their era). How legitimate are these parallels?*

I have not read *The Magic Mountain*. If you find there are parallels, these lie in the morbid sense of oppression (*v samoi boleznennoi ugnetënnosti*).

In your opinion, which of your works most clearly show the influence of Russian or Western Modernism?

I have never hearkened to any kind of "Modernism" [*ni na kakoi "modernizm" ia ne ogliadyvalsia*]. For the enormous concretion that is *The Red Wheel*, I tried to find fresh genre devices that would complement a traditional narrative.

In aesthetic terms, the most brutal journalistic or governmental opponents of the great Russian writers were much inferior to them. Let us recall the persecutors of Pushkin and Tolstoy, or in the twentieth century, Akhmatova and Pasternak. Do you feel a sense of affinity with your literary predecessors on this point?

This affinity resides on the surface of my texts.

Is the title of your book Bodalsia telënok s dubom [The Oak and the Calf] *a homonymical allusion to* Byloe i dumy [My Past and Thoughts] *by Alexander Herzen? What is your opinion of Herzen's memoirs?*

There is no allusion. The epochs are different and the circumstances are incommensurate.

*Like certain other modern writes, for example John Fowles, you have released new versions of books that were already published (*August 1914, *The First Circle,* and even "One Day in the Life of Ivan Denisovich"). Fowles says that most literary texts emerge from under a writer's pen "at some stage of imperfection,"[8] and that consequently the latter feels a need to revise them. What are your thoughts about this?

"Ivan Denisovich" and *The First Circle* existed in variants that were designed *solely* to circumvent the censorship. *August* was *never revised*, but only expanded through the addition of extra material.[9] What I subsequently published were not "new" texts, but the original, restored ones.

My General Concluding Comment

I consider the dedicated search for literary influences and borrowings to be a grave fallacy and even disease of modern literary studies. *Any* author can *only* be explained with reference to his personality, life experience, and unique artistic style.

June 23, 2003. A. Solzhenitsyn

Phone Interview with Aleksandr Solzhenitsyn
June 13, 2005

(questions submitted prior to interview)

1. *In one of the footnotes to* The Oak and the Calf *you describe the word "novel" as "odious" and ask, "Surely we can find a better one?" Could you elaborate on this statement?*
2. *What is your opinion of the canon of works about World War I in English, German, and French literature? I refer to Wilfred Owen, Thomas Hardy, Siegfried Sassoon, Richard Aldington, Ernst Jünger, Erich Maria Remarque, and Henri Barbusse.*
3. *Why was the story "What a Pity" published twenty years after it was written? Was it inspired by an actual person or incident?*
4. *Does the story "The Buddha's Smile"[10] express your view of Eleanor Roosevelt?*
5. *Other than Kulikovo Field and Yasnaya Polyana, what other places sacral to the Russian national consciousness could you mention?*
6. *Is St. Petersburg or some part thereof one of these places?*

7. *In your view, was Stalin a truly remarkable personality, that is, a historical figure of the same stature and importance as Lenin? And where would you place Parvus in relation to these two?*
8. *In your opinion, who were the leading commanders of World War I?*
9. *At the time you were writing August 1914, were you familiar with* The World Crisis, *Churchill's memoirs of World War I? And how would you describe his role in history?*
10. *What would you say if one were to compare* The Red Wheel *to Wagner's* Ring of the Nibelung? *How do you feel about Wagner's music?*
11. *Would you agree that the structure of the last chapters in* The Red Wheel, *which display an increasingly fragmentary, discontinuous, and sporadic quality, is expressive of the precipitously expanding processes of entropy in the society, culture, and human consciousness of those times?*
12. *You have made a number of critical statements directed at Modernism and Postmodernism. Do you discern the influence of Nietzsche on these two aesthetic models, which many consider defining? And how would you evaluate this philosopher?*
13. *What is your view of the current state of Russian literature?*

So, Richard, with regard to your first question. We are talking about a love story, a love intrigue. When we apply this term to a given prose genre, to large-scale [works] with a different content and different orientations, this narrows our understanding of it.

Understood.

The word "novel" [*roman*] has its own derivation. But with us, it is taken to mean that the topic is, shall we say, love, a love story. This explains my objection.

I understand.

Good. Now, to question two. Or, by way of a single answer to five of your questions. Concerning the circumstances of my life in the department of physics and math, the mathematics department.[11] I tried to study at two universities simultaneously.[12] This was a heavy burden in itself [*eto bylo uzhe dostatochno peregruzki*]. Then the war started. I went to war. Then after the war, there was prison. Then exile to the boondocks, banishment, to a remote location, where there wasn't a single book to be found. Then, when I returned to Central

Russia, and having already formulated my plans for *The Gulag Archipelago* and a history of the Russian Revolution,[13] I had to develop them and search for sources, which were completely inaccessible; to operate, as it were, in the underground, that is, never giving my name, never revealing why I was looking for these materials, even what exactly I was looking for, while at the same time working as a schoolteacher. I never had the leisure for unfettered serious reading [*svobodnoe dobrotnoe chtenie*], reading just for pleasure, reading to broaden my outlook—I never had any of that. Always, I had to work hard and look for the resources I needed for my secret conception. This is by way of a preamble to your questions. To questions nine and twelve. As for question two, of the English, French [and German] authors you listed I have read only Remarque. I could give you my opinion of Remarque separately. Or would you like me to do so now?

As you wish. Everything you say is very interesting, Aleksandr Isaevich. Now would be fine.

I read Remarque before I acquired my own military experience.[14] Then I was not in a position to judge. The impression I got was spooky [*proizvodilo zhutkovatoe vpechatlenie*]. But after I gained military experience of my own, I realized that his view is very narrow and tendentious. All the other authors you listed I have never read.

I understand.

Now for the story "What a Pity." In fact, the plot involves Professor Vladimir Aleksandrovich Vasilyev, with whom I had crossed paths in prison.[15] I had already written about this incident and then, much later, I decided to write it down in different form, as the short story "What a Pity." It was published, though not twenty years after I had written it, but thirteen.[16] Still, this is of secondary importance. From the substance of my works, one can't infer any intention on my part about when I would have liked to see them published. Circumstances dictated this to me. You see? I couldn't publish it for many years. Generally speaking, this has been known to happen in my case. Back to the question about "What a Pity." You ask if the character is a real person. This was a real incident, which I describe in *The Gulag*.[17] Next you asked if this is my most Nabokovian work.

It contains vivid images that are memorable in a Nabokovian kind of way. Especially the dactyloscopy and the raindrops on Anna Modestovna's fingers, they stuck in my memory.

This was entirely my own observation. As for Nabokov... Neither in our choice of material, nor in our choice of artistic forms do we have anything in common, rather, instead of connecting, we are antipodes. But the drop on her fingers, it happened, I inspected this drop and remembered it.

It's a wonderful image. Still, I know of your regard for Nabokov as a writer.

I nominated him for the Nobel Prize. I consider him extremely talented. But as writers, we don't connect.

Your fictive worlds stand completely apart.

Question four, the one about Eleanor Roosevelt, which I have already answered in part. I never spent any time studying this figure, I know nothing about her. I used her as an example of Western myopia, when one doesn't see what's right there in front of you. That's all. Next you ask—in question five—about places that are sacral to the Russian national consciousness. I can tell you there are many such places that Russians consider sacral. Scores of monasteries, starting with the Trinity Lavra of St. Sergius, which constituted the historical center of Russia when it endured a brutal siege.[18] The Solovetsky Monastery or Solovki.[19] There are so many monasteries, it's impossible to name them all. The places associated with Sergius of Radonezh[20] and Seraphim of Sarov.[21] Then there are the kremlins. A multiplicity of kremlins, because the one in Moscow is not unique. There are a number of towns, including some that are very small and even decaying [*zakhirevshie*], which have a kremlin.[22] Each one is connected to that locality. It is always sacral and is heavily saturated with spiritual meaning. Still, one cannot list them all in the expanse of Russia.

What about the camps, in which hundreds of thousands or millions of people perished? In your view, when will they become the same kind of place in the Russian consciousness?

This is impossible to foretell. The memory of those who suffered... Few physical and material possibilities remain for creating memorials of some kind, for giving them some sort of shape. There are people who simply have an impulse of the soul [to do this], but it's very hard to realize.

Further to the matter of sacral spaces. In the "Miniatures" you wrote very powerfully about Petersburg and its beauty, but you also said that it was built on the bones of peasants, who were driven there to work on its construction. And yet this is an amazingly beautiful city, with its own history and its own place in Russian literature.

What you read in the "Miniatures," about the way that construction in Russia is founded on violence, on the use of a [coerced] labor force, that many died, and that initially it [Petersburg] was the bearer of a Western consciousness, prevented it, of course, from becoming a center of the Russian national spirit. Yet the Petersburg period witnessed many cultural events. First, the lives of individual writers and artists. You know what I mean, the sites associated with Pushkin, Dostoevsky and others. Museums were established, such as the Russian Museum.²³ The architectural monuments, which formed part of our heritage. So, in general terms, it did enter the Russian national consciousness and Russian history. Now, for question seven. You know, Richard, I never considered him [Stalin] an exceptional personality. He was exceptional only in his cruelty. Truly exceptional. Millions of people, the extermination of millions, meant nothing to him. I know about the manner in which that war was fought, about his orders demanding—and the generals had to pass those orders on—that a given location be captured by a given day, at a given moment, whatever the cost. We lost so many people. I don't see any sign of strategic ability here. Look at how he missed the bus on the outbreak of war [*prokhlopal nachalo voiny*], at how bewildered he was in 1942, and of course in 1941 as well. I refuse to recognize his genius. He sacrificed thirty million people, which is the price he paid for victory. I believe he was a mediocre man, but as a mediocrity, one that was also balanced. A mediocre but balanced individual, who had a good understanding of how to behave toward the masses. This is what enabled him to continue Lenin's cause. And so he continued it. But Lenin was politically imaginative, resourceful, audacious, an entirely exceptional figure, though also a frightening one [*zhutkii*]. Now, Parvus had a lot in common with Lenin, because he too was a schemer of genius, that is, a revolutionary schemer. No, Stalin bears no comparison. Yet when Stalin received Lenin's legacy, he proved to be enough of a schemer to knock down his rivals. And then, having taken possession of Lenin's legacy, he carried out a policy that was entirely Leninist. That is, he did what Lenin would have wanted, though much later and in a much less skilled fashion, that's all.

What about Trotsky, who is present in The Red Wheel, *where would you place him?*

I would place him next to Lenin and Parvus as well.

You mean, as an able but depraved personality, as well as an undoubtedly cruel one?

They are very resourceful, very sharp in their perceptions. Trotsky was just as cruel. He never bothered to keep count of how many people he wanted shot. Question eight. Here is my preamble. I never studied the course of World War I in the west in any detail. I was only able to apprehend the course of our own war, that is, the one that was fought on our front. Which is why I abstain from passing judgment on those prominent commanders. For the same reason, I denied myself the pleasure of reading Churchill's memoirs of World War I, simply because, as I said, my life was such that I didn't have enough time for everything. There was too much going on [*slishkom nervnaia byla zhizn'*]. How would I evaluate Churchill's role in history, even if in a very general way? Clearly, Churchill was an outstanding political actor, simply outstanding. It was no accident he was able to rescue England from such a grave predicament.²⁴ A figure on the grandest of scales [*masshtabneishii on*]. Shall I continue?

Please do, Aleksandr Isaevich.

You ask about and compare *The Ring of the Nibelung* and *The Red Wheel*. You know, I find this comparison insightful. For me it is unexpected, but it's insightful. I never thought along these lines, but when I read your comments... Here's where I will agree with you. The scope, the tension inherent in both conception and action, the magnitude, the general tonality—yes, there is a similarity. This is your idea, and I accept it.

In this connection, I would like to add another question. There is an entire set of epic, even hyper-epic narratives, for instance Balzac's Human Comedy *as a sequence of novels, or* Eugene Onegin, *or* Anna Karenina, *which it took their authors years or even decades to write. In a sense, these works amount to a journal of their artistic experiments and intellectual evolution. It seems to me the same is true of Wagner. I wonder what you think. In any case, just as a reader, when I'm reading* The Red Wheel—*and I have done so several times—I see in it a progression, not only with regard to the characters and the representation of historical events, but also where your artistic inventions or innovations, which appear in successive volumes, are concerned. Could you comment about this?*

It's true, it took me a long time to compose. Not only did I spend half a century thinking about it, I spent twenty-one years uninterruptedly writing it. Clearly, over the course of twenty-one years you learn many new things, you come up with many additional peripheral conceptions. Which, of course, helped me in the creation of such a majestic canvas [*kartina velichestvennogo razmakha*]. In this sense, I also agree.

Then could you tell me about some of the new insights you had when you were writing the later volumes?

It's not that I discovered them, but [they came to me] over the entire course my life, constantly ... I can tell you privately that at present, in these last years of my life, I have found the energy to undertake one more redaction of *The Red Wheel*, which is yet to be published—well, I don't know exactly when, perhaps in a couple of years, but no sooner than that.

What is the nature of this redaction?

I took another look at it [*The Red Wheel*] after the passage of ten years. I wanted to see what's less important, what could be sacrificed, what could be removed in order to lighten the overall structure. Here, by the way, we are touching on one of your questions—number eleven—the one about the fragmentary nature of the last chapters in *The Red Wheel*. You were right to notice this. Indeed, *April 1917* is characterized by a profusion of fragments, a fissiparousness, a multiplicity of heterogeneous events happening in a variety of places. Nevertheless, in this latest redaction, which will be the last one of my life, I'm removing some of them, I'm trimming here and there, because the same effect can be achieved with less of an effort, with fewer examples. I'm certain that the abridgement I'm carrying out will be limited in scope. These cuts are minor, but they will substantially and qualitatively facilitate the reception of *The Red Wheel*. The general structure will manifest itself more clearly.

So this version will be the final one?

For the very serious reason that this is the end. I'm at the end of my life.

It will coexist with the earlier versions?

No, I hope that the second redaction will simply exist. That my second redaction will be the final word [*tol'ko moia vtoraia redaktsiia i budet*].

That is, you want it to be the definitive one?

I simply want it to be *The Red Wheel*. Since God has granted me these extra years, I have decided to put them to use. Before, I didn't know and I didn't expect that I would still be working. You know what my life was like. Shall we proceed?

Please.

About Nietzsche. Nietzsche is one of the figures I referred to in my preamble. I didn't have the luxury ... As for his impact on Western thought, on world thought, I appreciate it in general terms, but I wouldn't go so far as to say I have full knowledge of it. What do I think about the condition of Russian literature today? I can tell you I think about it a great deal. The state of our literature is a consequence of the general spiritual crisis we experienced both under the Bolshevik dictatorship and during the chaotic, unchecked convulsions of the last fifteen or twenty years. All this shook us up to such an extent that it was bound to have an effect across the rest of our spiritual life, including literature. Besides, from the beginning of the twentieth century there has been this notion in literature—here I'm referring to the twentieth century as a whole—that art is supposedly subject to progress. Just as it is with science, where undoubtedly there is progress, so it must be with art, where we have the right to perfect or invent, just for novelty's sake. No, there's no progress in art. It is impossible. There are downswings followed by unexpected upswings, but there is no ascendant line, no clambering up to some invented new pinnacle. The pinnacles may be repeated, or they may for a long time remain unrepeated. You see? What else can I say? There are many writers in my country. There is an unprecedentedly large number of writers. Many rushed to write solely in the hope of finding some way to dazzle us with form, style, or even nonsense [*nesusvetitsa*], even absurdity [*nesuraznost'*], even trickery [*khitrost'*]. They try to do this every which way they can. I consider it a very harmful, hollow tendency, which they themselves call Postmodernism, or rather, the name was just assigned to them. In my view, it's all ugliness of some sort or other. So. But in the midst of this chaos there are some honest, questing, truly talented young people, who are looking for the right true path, who want to keep faith with life's truth, with truth in literature. I don't know that we have paid them enough attention. We shall continue to pay attention. Generally speaking, it's hard to evaluate all of literature through a single lens, when it is so variegated and there's no common criterion ...

And yet you have retained a measure of optimism about Russian literature, which lived through the most terrible periods in its history and not only survived, but continued to exist because of its best tendencies.

It's better to conform to the optimistic view that Russian literature has always endured. Yet it has never experienced the kinds of challenges it faces now. So. Of course, there is hope, but this hope depends on what will happen to Russia in the larger scheme of things. Because with the process of extinction that we are experiencing, this terrible decline, how many of us will be left on the planet, what does the future hold, how many will continue to read Russian, and to what extent will the Russian language survive beyond our borders? I've been told that some Russian language departments over there have closed.

Some have closed, but on the other hand, among our students, including my own, and also among non-native speakers both here[25] and in Britain—I know this from experience—interest in Russian literature has remained stable.

God grant that this continues to be so.

I was referring to non-Russian speakers, non-Russian readers, who use translations. I don't think their interest will ever disappear.

But it's translations they are reading.

Nonetheless, they are still interested, which makes them engage with Russia. And since we are now talking about English language matters, Aleksandr Isaevich, I have a couple of questions relating to English literature. They will help me to picture more clearly, to adumbrate, if you like, your profile as a writer, in relation to certain classical works of English literature. I know that in Russia, female authors such as Jane Austen or the Brontë sisters—I refer you to Jane Eyre—*are seen as sentimental writers, as writers for women,[26] while in Britain and the United States this attitude is far less common. So what is your view?*

Indeed, I did read *Jane Eyre*, the book you mention, but prefer to withhold judgment.

I understand. I asked about Jane Eyre *because this was one of the first works in English and world literature to depict the psychological evolution of a child, a young girl.*

I shall withhold judgment. This is not my field.

And one last question, Aleksandr Isaevich. I have just finished reading Love the Revolution, *your early work, which you wrote at Marfino, but never completed.*

I tried to add some finishing touches later, but didn't have the time.

As a reader familiar with The First Circle, *would I be within my rights to consider* Love the Revolution *a kind of prologue to that novel?*

Certainly, it shows the same Nerzhin.

The same Nerzhin and the same Nadya?

At different stages in their lives… but they are entirely the same characters. From the story "Zhelyabuga Village," where I'm writing directly in the first person, you can see that this state of mind stayed with me for a long time [*eto dolgo vo mne delo ne vylezalo*]. When I was young, my sense of the world was highly convoluted. Its elements clashed and conflicted with each other: my views were very different from what they are now. Indeed, as a young man I was interested in dialectical and historical materialism, which was the cause of all this.

Also in Love the Revolution, *there is an intriguing moment when Gleb Nerzhin, who is serving with the baggage train, thinks to himself that he has landed in some sort of male assemblage, which he sees as alien and strange. He doesn't understand the system of relationships, the hierarchy, because as a young married man, he has never encountered people like this before. It has always seemed to me, Aleksandr Isaevich, that you are particularly accurate and inventive when you write about the kinds of environments, the army or prison, where men live together and coexist and form a small community of males.*

I wouldn't describe it as a small community but a distinctive, wholly psychological environment, which a man who's living an ordinary life, where there are women and children, can't even begin to imagine or comprehend. A purely male milieu. It is very distinctive. There are many examples in history. Look at the military academies, the camps in our country. I certainly considered it worth depicting, this separate current of existence, which in real life, the ordinary lives of ordinary people, doesn't make itself felt.

As a writer, you find it of interest?

Very much so. It can greatly strengthen a man [*eto ochen' sil'noe muzhskoe ukreplenie*]. It tempers the spirit.

Answers to Richard Tempest's Questions
(May 2007)

One of the characters in the comedy Victory Celebrations *is Sergei Nerzhin, who is a Red Army captain and the commander of a sound reconnaissance battery. Where does this Nerzhin stand in relation to Gleb Nerzhin, the hero of the novel* Love the Revolution *(in which he appears as a student and army conscript), the drama* Republic of Labor *(a prisoner and "recently a frontline officer")[27], and the novel* The First Circle *(a prisoner who has spent "five years in harness")?[28] Would it be appropriate to regard these works as a tetralogy, in so far as Gleb/Sergei Nerzhin has a central part in all of them?*

Sergei and Gleb Nerzhin are the same character. But I don't consider these works a tetralogy, because their genres are too different.

In The First Circle, *Nerzhin declares: "The seventeenth century had Rembrandt, and Rembrandt's still here—just try and go one better today! Whereas seventeenth-century technology seems primitive to us now. Or think of the great inventions of the eighteen seventies. To us they look like children's toys. Yet those were the years in which* Anna Karenina *was written. If you know of anything finer, I would like to hear about it!"[29] Are there any contemporary artistic productions, that is, any dating from the late twentieth or early twenty-first century, of which we could say the same thing?*

From such a short distance in time, I would rather not say.

In the final chapter of The First Circle, *the correspondent of the newspaper* Libération *sees an orange and blue van bearing the legend "Meat," which is carrying Nerzhin and the other zeks to the transit prison. The reporter, who is shown as the bearer of an uncomprehending Western, "progressive" view of the realities of Stalinism, takes the van as proof of the excellence of Moscow's food supply. Now, his pen and automobile are the same "dark red" color, which I read as an indicator of the stylistic excesses in the culture to which he belongs. Am I right? I also wanted to know why you chose the name* Libération. *Jean Paul Sartre founded his eponymous broadsheet in 1973, years after the novel was completed.*

The pen color represents a thematic echo [*pereklichka tem*]. As for the name *Libération*, well, I needed a generic title for a leftwing newspaper. But I was not aware of their publishing history.

In an interview you gave to Nikita Struve to mark the publication of November 1916, *you referred to your works as polyphonic.*[30] *The term "polyphony" was first applied to literary texts by Bakhtin, who employed it to describe the coequal status of all the voices that are present in Dostoevsky's novels, including the voice of the author. Bakhtin writes: "Dostoevsky, like Goethe's Prometheus, creates not voiceless slaves ... but* free *people, capable of standing alongside their creator, capable of not agreeing with him and even of rebelling against him."*[31] *What meaning do you attach to the term "polyphony"? To what extent does the polyphonism of your works differ from that found in Dostoevsky's novels?*

In my case, polyphonism means that I give an approximately equal opportunity to all the characters to put forward *their* interpretation of events and their point of view. While one is reading a chapter, the character it depicts becomes, as it were, the protagonist.

Pavel Varsonofiev, who is a character in The Red Wheel, *has an identity as a mystic and seer that makes him a unique presence in the epopee as well as across your other works. His dreams made a particularly strong impression on me. Could you provide any details about how you thought up these vivid, strange, and apocalyptic visions, which make one think of Rozanov and Bely?*

Some of his dreams such as "Christ at the Stock Exchange"[32] and "The Sealing of the Church"[33] were actually dreamt by me, so I wrote them down.

Varsonofiev's eyes are described as "brilliantly lit caverns."[34] *When you designed this metaphor were you thinking of Plato and his parable of the cave and the fire burning inside it?*

Yes, I had in mind, in a parallel sense, these Platonic images.

According to your authorial definition, Cancer Ward *and "Adlig Schwenkitten" are "tales" [*povesti*], though in the West the former is considered a novel, owing to its multiplicity of characters and plots. What meaning do you ascribe to the term "tale"?*

A *tale* differs from a *story* by containing a sufficiently large number of characters or events. And it differs from the *novel* by the more limited range of its plot.

Where "Adlig" is concerned, I used this definition by design (twenty-four chapters, twenty-four hours in a day, the small size, the larger significance).

George Bush Sr. once let slip these words: "I don't know that atheists should be regarded as citizens, nor should they be regarded as patriotic."[35] *Do you agree with the opinion expressed by the forty-first President of the United States? After all, several of your best-known and most beloved characters such as Ivan Shukhov, Gleb Nerzhin, or Oleg Kostoglotov stand far apart from religion (in one hospital debate, Kostoglotov even proclaims himself an atheist), yet they are all pure, honorable personalities, while Nerzhin and Kostoglotov are also spiritual questers after the truth.*

You have actually answered your own question.

In 1983, you stated: "Evil appears in beautiful form. But this is always a mask."[36] *Could you provide examples of such aesthetically appealing masks that hide the face of evil, whether in art or in other spheres of human endeavor?*

I can think of all too many examples, but I have not developed this theme in detail.

May 27, 2007. A. Solzhenitsyn

Notes

Preface

1. Dmitrii Aziattsev, Nadezhda G. Levitskaia, and Mariia Benina, *Aleksandr Isaevich Solzhenitsyn. Materialy k biobibliografii* (St. Petersburg: Rossiiskaia natsional'naia biblioteka, 2007).
2. Friedrich Nietzsche, *Reevaluation of All Values*, in Walter Kaufmann, trans., *The Portable Nietzsche* (New York: Penguin Books, 1976), 568.
3. Virginia Woolf, "The Russian Point of View," in *The Common Reader* (New York: Harcourt Brace Jovanovich, 1925), 174.
4. On one occasion, when we were discussing her husband's reading habits as a young man, Natalia Dmitrievna commented that for a Russian lover of literature, Balzac and Dickens are as "Russian" as Turgenev or Tolstoy.
5. Tzvetan Todorov, *Genres in Discourse*, trans. Catherine Porter (New York: Cambridge University Press, 1990), 39.
6. Aleksandr Solzhenitsyn, *Cancer Ward*, trans. Nicholas Bethell and David Burg (New York: Farrar, Straus and Giroux, 1991), 536.
7. Andrei Zorin, "Vrach ili bol'?", *Neprikosnovennyi zapas* 1 (1999), http://magazines.russ.ru/nz/1999/1/zorin.html.
8. Solzhenitsyn admired Latin for its clarity and vigor, and during his Vermont years read many works from the Golden Age of Latin literature (Ignat Solzhenitsyn, private communication).
9. Quoted in Joseph Pearce, *Solzhenitsyn: A Soul in Exile* (Grand Rapids: Baker Books, 2001), 309.
10. Bertrand Russell, *A History of Western Philosophy* (New York: Simon & Schuster, 1967), 762.
11. Friedrich Nietzsche, *Ecce Homo*, in Walter Kaufmann, ed. and trans., *Basic Writings of Nietzsche* (New York: The Modern Library, 1992), 687.
12. Pavel Spivakovskii, "Akademik Aleksandr Isaevich Solzhenitsyn (k 85-letiiu so dnia rozhdeniia)," *Izvestiia Rossiiskoi Akademii Nauk. Seriia literatury i iazyka* 63 (Moscow: Nauka, 2003), 6:67.
13. Solzhenitsyn, *Cancer Ward*, 62.
14. Almost a century earlier, Vermont had hosted another Nobel Prize-winning writer, Rudyard Kipling, who spent the years 1892–6 in Dummerston, a town

some forty-five miles south of Cavendish, where he wrote *The Jungle Book* and *Captains Courageous*.
15. Solomon Volkov and Aleksandr Genis, "Vekhi novoi Rossii. Solzhenitsyn-Brodskii, Sviridov-Shnitke," *Radio Svoboda*, April 19, 2011, http://www.svoboda.org/content/transcript/9498105.html.
16. Donald Michael Thomas, *Alexander Solzhenitsyn: A Century in His Life* (New York: St. Martin's Press, 1998), 515.

Chapter One

1. Vladimir Nabokov, *Lectures on Literature* (New York: Harcourt Brace Jovanovich, 1980), 146.
2. Aleksandr Solzhenitsyn, Nobel Lecture, in Edward E. Ericson Jr. and Daniel J. Mahoney, eds., *The Solzhenitsyn Reader: New and Essential Writings, 1947–2005* (Wilmington: ISI Books, 2006), 513.
3. Solzhenitsyn, Nobel Lecture, 514–15.
4. "Fragmenty stenogrammy fil'ma Aleksandra Sokurova 'Besedy s Solzhenitsynym,'" http://www.rhga.ru/science/conferences/rusm/russian_thought/sokurov&solzh.php.
5. Harold Bloom, *The Western Canon: The Books and School of the Ages* (New York: Harcourt Brace, 1993), 335.
6. "'Chashche vsego v zhizni ia rukovodstvuius' niukhom, slukhom i zreniem ... ' Beseda A. Mikhnika s I. Brodskim," trans. B. Gorobets, *Staroe literaturnoe obozrenie* 2 (2001), http://magazines.russ.ru/slo/2001/2/mihn.html.
7. Aleksandr Solzhenitsyn, "Ugodilo zërnyshko promezh dvukh zhernovov. Ocherki izgnaniia," Chast' pervaia (1974–8), Glava 1, *Novyi mir* 9 (1998), http://magazines.russ.ru:81/novyi_mi/1998/9/sol.html.
8. Christopher Hitchens, "The Man Who Kept on Writing," *Slate*, August 4, 2008, http://www.slate.com/id/2196606/.
9. Clive James, "Solzhenitsyn Warns the West," CliveJames.com, July 25, 2012, http://www.clivejames.com/books/visions/warns.
10. Aleksandr Solzhenitsyn, "The City on the Neva," in Ericson and Mahoney, *The Solzhenitsyn Reader*, 619.
11. Aleksandr Solzhenitsyn, *In the First Circle: A Novel. The Restored Text*, trans. Harry Willetts (New York: Harper Perennial, 2009), 292–3.
12. Aristotle, Horace, and Longinus, *Classical Literary Criticism* (London: Penguin Books, 1965), 115.
13. Ibid., 147.
14. Solzhenitsyn, Nobel Lecture, 521.
15. Theodor Adorno, "Cultural Criticism and Society," in Rolf Tiedeman, ed., *Can One Live After Auschwitz? A Philosophical* Reader (Stanford: Stanford University Press, 2003), 162.

16. James Berger, "Trauma and Literary Theory," review of *Unclaimed Experience: Trauma, Narrative and History*, by Cathy Caruth, *Representing the Holocaust: History, Theory, Trauma*, by Dominick LaCapra, and *Worlds of Hurt: Reading the Literatures of Trauma*, by Kalí Tal, *Contemporary Literature* 38, no. 3 (1997): 573.
17. Georges Bataille, *Literature and Evil* (London: Marion Boyars, 2001), x.
18. Friedrich Nietzsche, *Beyond Good and Evil: Prelude to a Philosophy of the Future*, in Kaufmann, *Basic Writings of Nietzsche*, 348.
19. Solzhenitsyn, *Cancer Ward*, 481.
20. Iosif Brodskii, "Geografiia zla," *Literaturnoe obozrenie* 1 (1999), http://solzhenitsyn.ru/o_tvorchestve/articles/works/index.php?ELEMENT_ID=667.
21. Leona Toker, *Return from the Archipelago: Narratives of Gulag Survivors* (Bloomington: Indiana University Press, 2000), 3.
22. Solzhenitsyn, Nobel Lecture, 515.
23. Stanislav Iarzhembovskii, "Prorok i ego otechestvo," *Zvezda* 12 (2008), http://magazines.russ.ru/zvezda/2008/12/ia12.html.
24. Thomas, *Solzhenitsyn*, 266.
25. Hilton Kramer, "A Talk with Solzhenitsyn," *The New York Times*, May 11, 1980.
26. Nataliia Solzhenitsyna, "Solzhenitsyn ne chital 'Arkhipelag' svoim detiam," *Russkii pioner*, September, http://ruspioner.ru/honest/m/single/5146.
27. Vasily Rozanov, *Dostoevsky and the Legend of the Grand Inquisitor* (Ithaca: Cornell University Press, 1972), 76.
28. Ibid., 208.
29. Ibid., 209.
30. Clive Staples Lewis, "Bluspels and Flalansferes: A Semantic Nightmare," in *Selected Literary Essays* (Cambridge: Cambridge University Press, 1969), 265.
31. Aleksandr Solzhenitsyn, "Interv'iu s Devidom Eikmanom dlia zhurnala 'Taim' (Kavendish, 23 maia 1989)," in *Publitsistika v trëkh tomakh. Tom 3. Stat'i, pis'ma, interv'iu, predisloviia* (Yaroslavl: Verkhniaia Volga, 1997), 3:325.
32. Paul Gray, David Aikman, and John Kohan, "Russia's Prophet in Exile," *Time*, July 24, 1989, http://www.time.com/time/magazine/article/0,9171,958205-1,00.html.
33. Aleksandr Solzhenitsyn, *Sobranie sochinenii*, 30 vols. (Moscow: Vremia, 2006–), 8:199.
34. Aleksandr Solzhenitsyn, *August 1914. The Red Wheel: A Narrative in Discrete Stretches of Time. Knot I*, trans. H. T. Willetts (New York, NY: Farrar, Straus and Giroux, 1989), 582.
35. Aleksandr Solzhenitsyn, "Moi Bulgakov. Iz 'Literaturnoi kollektsii,'" in *Solzhenitsynskie tetradi. Materialy i issledovaniia*, vol. 2 (Moscow: Russkii put', 2013), 13.
36. See Yevgeny Zamyatin's story "The Dragon" ("Drakon"; 1918) and Yevgeny Shvarts's identically titled play (1944).
37. Solzhenitsyn, *The First Circle*, 295.

38. Solzhenitsyn, *Sobranie sochinenii*, 16:257.
39. Leo Tolstoy, *War and Peace*, ed. George Gibian, trans. Aylmer Maude and Louise Maude, 2nd ed. (New York: W. W. Norton, 1995), 536.
40. Aleksandr Solzhenitsyn, "Interv'iu s Rudol'fom Augshtainom dlia zhurnala 'Shpigel'" (Kavendish, 9 oktiabria 1987)," in *Publitsistika*, 3:317.
41. "Fragmenty stenogrammy fil'ma Sokurova 'Besedy s Solzhenitsynym.'"
42. José Ortega y Gasset, *The Revolt of the Masses* (New York: W. W. Norton, 1957), 63.
43. In "The Narrative Beyond the Point of Suspension" appendix to *The Red Wheel*, the list of outrages perpetrated by revolutionary activists includes this item: "In the military hospitals the junior clinical staff humiliate the doctors and nurses" (Solzhenitsyn, *Sobranie sochinenii*, 16:616).
44. Gray, Aikman, and Kohan, "Russia's Prophet in Exile."
45. Aleksandr Solzhenitsyn, "An Interview on Literary Themes with Nikita Struve, March 1976," in John B. Dunlop, Richard S. Haugh, and Michael Nicholson, eds., *Solzhenitsyn in Exile: Critical Essays and Documentary Materials* (Stanford: Hoover Institution Press, 1985), 301.
46. Fyodor Dostoevsky, *Devils*, trans. Michael R. Katz (New York: Oxford University Press, 1992), 245.
47. Solzhenitsyn interview with Pavel Licko (March 1967), quoted in Keith Armes, introduction to *Candle in the Wind*, by Alexander Solzhenitsyn (London: The Bodley Head/Oxford University Press, 1973), 8.
48. Aleksandr Solzhenitsyn, Letter to Komoto Sedze, November 15, 1966, in *The Oak and the Calf: Sketches of Literary Life in the Soviet Union*, trans. Harry Willetts (New York: Harper & Row, 1980), 457.
49. Solzhenitsyn. *Sobranie sochinenii*, 12:46.
50. Aleksandr Solzhenitsyn, "Pis'mo Prezidentu El'tsinu," in *Publitsistika*, 3:353.
51. Ibid., 5.
52. Ibid., 682.
53. Ibid., 679.
54. Solzhenitsyn, *Sobranie sochinenii*, 18:283.
55. Aleksandr Solzhenitsyn, "The Easter Procession," in Ericson and Mahoney, *The Solzhenitsyn Reader*, 60.
56. Solzhenitsyn, *Sobranie* sochinenii, 12:697.
57. Aleksandr Solzhenitsyn, *November 1916. The Red Wheel: A Narrative in Discrete Stretches of Time. Knot II*, trans. H. T. Willetts (New York: Farrar, Straus and Giroux, 2000), 347.
58. Solzhenitsyn, *Sobranie sochinenii*, 14:254.
59. Ibid., 14:255.
60. Roland Barthes, "Introduction to the Structural Analysis of Narratives," in Susan Sontag, ed., *A Barthes Reader* (New York: Hill and Wang, 1982), 265.

61. Barthes, "The Structural Analysis of Narratives," 265.
62. Kornei Chukovskii, *Dnevnik. 1930–1969* (Moskva: Sovremennyi pisatel', 1995), 466.
63. Samuel Coleridge, *Biographia Literaria*, in *Poetry and Prose* (New York: Bantam Books, 1965), 215.
64. Nikita Struve, "Spor ob 'Avguste Chetyrnadtsatogo,'" in *Pravoslavie i kul'tura* (Moscow: Russkii put', 2000), 484.
65. Solzhenitsyn, *The First Circle*, 374.
66. In one version of *The Love-Girl and the Innocent*, the Nerzhin character's name is Rodion Nemov (Alexander Solzhenitsyn, *Three Plays. Victory Celebrations. Prisoners. The Love-Girl and the Innocent*, trans. Helen Rapp et al. [New York: Farrar, Straus and Giroux, 1986]).
67. A prisoner in a Soviet camp or jail.
68. Solzhenitsyn, *The First Circle*, 180.
69. Thomas, *Solzhenitsyn*, 439.
70. Natalia Solzhenitsyna, private communication.
71. Ibid.
72. Ibid.
73. Aleksandr Solzhenitsyn, "'Peterburg' Andreia Belogo. Iz 'Literaturnoi kollektsii,'" *Novyi mir* 7 (1997), http://magazines.russ.ru/novyi_mi/1997/7/solgen.html.
74. Volumes one to five of the almanac *Solzhenitsynskie tetradi* (2012–16) contain newly published essays on Nikolai Leskov, Mikhail Bulgakov, Ivan Goncharov, Aleksandr Ostrovsky, and Anna Akhmatova.
75. Friedrich Nietzsche, *Twilight of the Idols or, How One Philosophizes with a Hammer*, in Kaufmann, *The Portable Nietzsche*, 467.
76. Toker, *Return from the Archipelago*, 99.
77. Ibid., 118.
78. Erich Auerbach, *Mimesis: The Representation of Reality in Western Literature*, trans. Willard R. Trask (Princeton: Princeton University Press, 1968), 521.
79. Czeslaw Milosz, *Unattainable Earth* (New York: Ecco Press, 1986), 78.
80. Although science fiction and fantasy writers, who enjoy a greater freedom to fabulate than other authors, continue to depict Hell as a physical locale inhabited by demonic and human characters. See Piers Anthony's cycle of novels *Incarnations of Immortality* (1983–2007).
81. Aleksandr Solzhenitsyn, "Nashi pliuralisty," in *Publitsistika v trëkh tomakh. Tom 1. Stat'i i rechi* (Yaroslavl: Verkhne-Volzhskoe knizhnoe izdatel'stvo, 1995), 1:411.
82. Aleksandr Solzhenitsyn, "Matryona's Home," in Ericson and Mahoney, *The Solzhenitsyn Reader*, 38.
83. Solzhenitsyn, *The First Circle*, 505.
84. Solzhenitsyn, *Sobranie sochinenii*, 13:537.
85. Solzhenitsyn, *The First Circle*, 48.

86. Ibid., 146.
87. Alexander Pope, "Essay on Man," in *Selected Poems* (New York: F. S. Croft, 1933), 70–71.
88. Svetlana Sheshunova, *Natsional'nyi obraz mira v epopee A. I. Solzhenitsyna "Krasnoe Koleso"* (Dubna: Mezhdunarodnyi universitet prirody, obshchestva i cheloveka, 2005).
89. At the Aleksandr Solzhenitsyn as Writer, Myth-Maker and Public Figure conference (University of Illinois, June 14 2007), Ignat Solzhenitsyn provoked a lively discussion by making this very point.
90. Solzhenitsyn, *August 1914*, 530.
91. Solzhenitsyn, "An Interview with Struve," 302.
92. The head of the Soviet secret police, Lavrenty Beria, liked to jibe, "Let me have one night with him and I'll have him confessing he's the King of England" (Simon Sebag Montefiore, *Stalin: The Court of the Red Tsar* [New York: Vintage Books, 2003], 277).
93. Solzhenitsyn, *The First Circle*, 321.
94. Solzhenitsyn, "Matryona's Home," 46.
95. Viktor Bukhanov, "U Solzhenitsyna v Riazani," in Vladimir Glotser and Elena Chukovskaia, eds., *Slovo probivaet sebe dorogu. Sbornik statei i dokumentov ob A. I. Solzhenitsyne. 1962–1974* (Moscow: Russkii put', 1998), 50.
96. Galina Vishnevskaya, *Galina: A Russian Story*, trans. Guy Daniels (London: Sceptre, 1986), 400.
97. "Soljénitsyne, le courage d'écrire" [color insert], *Solzhenitsynskie tetradi. Materialy i issledovaniia*, vol. 1 (Moscow: Russkii put', 2012).
98. Galina Tiurina, "Pervaia prezentatsiia solzhenitsynskogo arkhiva v Moskve. Biografiia v rukopisiakh," *Solzhenitsynskie tetradi. Materialy i issledovaniia*, vol. 3 (Moscow: Russkii put', 2014), 205.
99. "Vystavka 'Dostoevskii i Solzhenitsyn.' Literaturno-memorial'nyi muzei F. M. Dostoevskogo. Sankt-Peterburg. 7 oktiabria-25 noiabria 2014" [color insert], *Solzhenitsynskie tetradi. Materialy i issledovaniia*, vol. 4 (Moscow: Russkii put', 2015).
100. Friedrich Nietzsche, *Thus Spoke Zarathustra: A Book for All and None*, in Kaufmann, *The Portable Nietzsche*, 250.
101. Solzhenitsyn, *Sobranie sochinenii*, 2:163.
102. Solzhenitsyn, *November 1916*, 642.
103. Alexander Parvus, the enigmatic Bolshevik-Menshevik-Trotskyist-Leninist, as the Jabba the Hutt of the Russian Revolution. Now, isn't that something!
104. Anna Arkatova, "The Feminine Eros As the Motive Force of Russian History: Aleksandr Solzhenitsyn's Intertextual Dialogue with Marina Tsvetaeva" (PhD diss., University of Illinois, 2015), 25.
105. Solzhenitsyn, *The First Circle*, 250.

106. Tatiana Smykovskaia, "Zhenskie obrazy A. Solzhenitsyna v kontekste paskhal'noi traditsii (na primere epopei 'Krasnoe Koleso')," *Vestnik Riazanskogo gosudarstvennogo universiteta* 40, no. 3 (2013): 99.
107. Solzhenitsyn, *Sobranie sochinenii*, 11:588.
108. Ibid., 15:170.
109. Niall Ferguson, *The War of the World: Twentieth-Century Conflict and the Descent of the West* (New York: Penguin Books, 2006), li.
110. Solzhenitsyn, *The First Circle*, 456.
111. Ibid.
112. Aleksandr Solzhenitsyn, "Fracture Points," in *Apricot Jam and Other Stories*, trans. Kenneth Lantz and Stephan Solzhenitsyn (Berkeley: Counterpoint, 2011), 289.
113. Ibid., 324.
114. Gérard Genette, *Palimpsests: Literature in the Second Degree*, trans. Channa Newman and Claude Doubinsky, 8th ed. (Lincoln: University of Nebraska Press, 1997), 7.
115. Janet G. Tucker, "Introduction: Parody, Satire, and Intertextuality in Russian Literature," in Janet G. Tucker, ed., *Against the Grain: Parody, Satire, and Intertextuality in Russian Literature* (Bloomington: Slavica, 2002), 1.
116. Ivan Turgenev, *Home of the Gentry*, trans. Richard Freeborn (Harmondsworth: Penguin Books, 1970), 73.
117. Tolstoy, *War and Peace*, 278.
118. Solzhenitsyn, *November 1916*, 690.
119. Ibid., 689.
120. Ibid., 691.
121. Ibid., 695.
122. Ibid., 691.
123. Solzhenitsyn, *August 1914*, 16–17.
124. "Interv'iu s Bernarom Pivo dlia frantsuzskogo televideniia. Kavendish, 31 oktiabia 1983," in *Publitsistika*, 3:193.
125. Nietzsche, *Thus Spoke Zarathustra*, 174.
126. Aleksandr Solzhenitsyn, Interview with Daniel Kehlmann ("My tvorim svoiu istoriiu sami, sami zagoniaem sebia v iamy" [2006]), *Izvestiia*, December 11, 2008.
127. Gore Vidal, "The Top Ten Best Sellers According to *The Sunday New York Times* As of January 7, 1973," in *United States: Essays 1952–1992* (New York: Broadway Books, 2001), 83.
128. Anne Lounsbery, "'To Moscow, I Beg You!': Chekhov's Vision of the Russian Provinces," *Toronto Slavic Quarterly* 9 (2004), http://www.utoronto.ca/tsq/09/lounsbery09.shtml.
129. Aleksandr Solzhenitsyn, "No Matter What," in *Apricot Jam*, 362.
130. Solzhenitsyn, *November 1916*, 130.
131. Solzhenitsyn, *Sobranie sochinenii*, 11:65, 109, 538, 539; 12:28.

132. Ibid., 11:9.
133. David Remnick, *Lenin's Tomb: The Last Days of the Soviet Empire* (New York: Random House, 1993), 271.
134. Solzhenitsyn, *August 1914*, 4.
135. Ibid., 6.
136. Ibid., 5.
137. Solzhenitsyn, *November 1916*, 457.
138. Aleksandr Shmeman, *Dnevniki. Tetrad' II (noiabr' 1974-avgust 1975)*, November 22, 1974, azbuka.ru, https://azbyka.ru/otechnik/Aleksandr_Shmeman/dnevniki/2.
139. Natalia Solzhenitsyna, private communication.
140. Mrs. Solzhenitsyna, a native-born Muscovite who loves her city with a passion, recalls explaining to her husband, "Moscow is my Ryazan," private communication.
141. Solzhenitsyn, *Sobranie sochinenii*, 12:697.
142. Ibid., 12:702.
143. Ibid., 7:203.
144. Solzhenitsyn, "Moi Bulgakov," 16. The title, *Moi Bulgakov*, was meant to recall "Moi Pushkin" ("My Pushkin" [1937]), a famous essay by Marina Tsvetaeva.
145. Shmeman, *Dnevniki. Tetrad' II*, May 12, 1975.
146. Solzhenitsyn, *The First Circle*, 162.
147. Natalia Solzhenitsyna, private communication.
148. Solzhenitsyn, *Sobranie* sochinenii, 14:560.
149. Quoted in David Remnick, *Resurrection: The Struggle for a New Russia* (New York: Vintage Books, 1998), 128.
150. Bloom, *The Western Canon*, 312.
151. As a young man, Solzhenitsyn read Dickens "several times from beginning to end" (Aleksandr Solzhenitsyn, "Teleinterv'iu kompanii Bi-bi-si v sviazi s vykhodom knigi 'Lenin v Tsiurikhe' [25 fevralia 1976]," in *Publitsistika v trëkh tomakh. Tom 2. Obshchestvennye zaiavleniia, pis'ma, interv'iu* [Yaroslav: Verkhne-Volzhskoe knizhnoe izdatel'stvo, 1996], 2:352).
152. Auerbach, *Mimesis*, 63.
153. Solzhenitsyn, *November 1916*, 776.
154. Solzhenitsyn, *Sobranie sochinenii*, 18:289.
155. Isabelle Hervouet-Farrar and Max Vega-Ritter, *The Grotesque in the Fiction of Charles Dickens and Other 19th-century European Novelists* (Newcastle upon Tyne: Cambridge Scholars Publishing, 2014), 7.
156. Solzhenitsyn, *November 1916*, 486.
157. Solzhenitsyn, "An Interview with Struve," 323.
158. Solzhenitsyn, *Sobranie sochinenii*, 11:424.
159. Aleksandr Balk, *Gibel' tsarskogo Petrograda: Fevral'skaia revoliutsiia glazami gradonachal'nika A. P. Balka*, 27 fevralia [1917], http://statehistory.ru/5571/Gibel-tsarskogo-Petrograda/.

160. Solzhenitsyn, *Sobranie sochinenii*, 11:413.
161. Ibid., 12:245.
162. Jean-Paul Sartre, *Nausea* (New York: Penguin, 2000), 204.
163. Natalia Solzhenitsyna, private communication.
164. Ibid.
165. Ibid.
166. Vladimir Lakshin, *Solzhenitsyn i koleso istorii*, https://www.e-reading.club/chapter.php/1041962/62/Kaydash-Lakshina_-_Solzhenicyn_i_koleso_istorii.html.
167. Solomon Volkov, "'Muzykal'naia polka.' Solzhenitsyn i muzyka: k 90-letiiu pisatelia," *Radio Svoboda*, December 8, 2008, https://www.svoboda.org/a/476431.html.
168. Solzhenitsyn, *Cancer Ward*, 154.
169. Ibid., 210.
170. Ignat Solzhenitsyn, private communication.
171. Ibid.
172. Volkov, "Solzhenitsyn i muzyka."
173. Mira Petrova, "Sud'ba avtora i sud'ba romana," in Aleksandr Solzhenitsyn, *V kruge pervom, Roman* (Moscow: Nauka, 2006), 664.
174. Natalia Solzhenitsyna, private communication.
175. Volkov, "Solzhenitsyn i muzyka."
176. Gray, Aikman, and Kohan, "Russia's Prophet in Exile."
177. Liudmila Saraskina, *Aleksandr Solzhenitsyn*, 2nd ed. (Moscow: Molodaia Gvardiia, 2009), 123–4.
178. Aleksandr Solzhenitsyn, "Tri otryvka is 'Dnevnika R-17,'" in Nikita Struve and Viktor Moskvin, eds., *Mezhdu dvumia iubileiami: pisateli, kritiki, literaturovedy o tvorchestve A. I. Solzhenitsyna*, (Moscow: Russkii put', 2005), 9.
179. Kramer, "A Talk with Solzhenitsyn."
180. Solzhenitsyn, "An Interview with Struve," 299.
181. The Soviet secret police was successively known as the Cheka (*Chrezvychainaia komissiia*, Extraordinary Commission), 1917–22; GPU (*Gosudarstvennoe politicheskoe upravlenie*, State Political Directorate), 1922–34; NKVD (*Narodnyi Komissariat Vnutrennikh Del*, People's Commissariat of Internal Affairs), 1934–46; MGB (*Ministerstvo gosudarstvennoi bezopasnosti*, Ministry of State Security), 1946–54; and KGB (*Komitet gosudarstvennoi bezopasnosti*, Committee for State Security), 1954–91. Each of these institutional iterations is present in Solzhenitsyn's writings, although the author himself preferred "The Cheka-GB": "A resonant, convenient, and concise name for this organization and one which also preserves its continuity in time" (Aleksandr Solzhenitsyn, *The Gulag Archipelago 1918–1956: An Experiment in Literary Investigation III–IV*, vol. 2, trans. Thomas P. Whitney [New York: Westview Press, 1992], 353).

182. The narrative poem *The Road*, most of which Solzhenitsyn composed in the Ekibastuz camp, comprises 7,000 lines.
183. At the time Solzhenitsyn very much looked the part: a witness recalls that in 1963 he had the appearance of "an ordinary, very typical schoolteacher" (Anatolii Krasnov-Levitin, *Dva pisatelia* [Paris: Poiski, 1983], 6).
184. Solzhenitsyn, *The Oak and the Calf*, 5.
185. Ibid., 7.
186. Aleksandr Solzhenitsyn, "The Writer's Retrospect," in Alexis Klimoff, ed., *"One Day in the Life of Ivan Denisovich." A Critical Companion* (Evanston: Northwestern University Press, 1997), 103.
187. Lidiia Chukovskaia, *Zapiski ob Anne Akhmatovoi v trëkh tomakh. Tom 2. 1952–1962*, 3rd ed. (Moscow: Soglasie, 1997), 2:533.
188. Vasilii Rozanov, "Vekovaia godovshchina (30 maia 1811—30 maia 1911)," in *O pisatel'stve i pisateliakh* (Moscow: Respublika, 1995), 533.
189. Solzhenitsyn, *The Oak and the Calf*, 52.
190. Quoted in Saraskina, *Solzhenitsyn*, 497.
191. Cyril Connolly, *Enemies of Promise* (Chicago: University of Chicago Press, 2008), 109.
192. Mikhail Golubkov, "'V kruge pervom.' Opyt monograficheskogo analiza: zhanr, problematika, siuzhet i kompozitsiia, sistema personazhei," *Aleksandr Isaevich Solzhenitsyn* [official site], http://www.solzhenitsyn.ru/o_tvorchestve/articles/works/index.php?ELEMENT_ID=672.
193. Tvardovsky's editorial input was limited to "Ivan Denisovich" and "Matryona's Home."
194. Aleksandr Solzhenitsyn, "Ugodilo zërnyshko promezh dvukh zhernovov. Ocherki izgnaniia," Chast' chetvërtaia" (1987–1994), Glavy 14–16, *Novyi mir* 11 (2003), http://magazines.russ.ru/novyi_mi/2003/11/solzhenicyn.html.
195. Gray, Aikman, and Kohan, "Russia's Prophet in Exile."
196. Thomas, *Solzhenitsyn*, 478.
197. Solzhenitsyn, "Nashi pliuralisty," 443.
198. Stephen King, *Firestarter* (New York: Signet, 1980–1981), 180.
199. Solzhenitsyn, "Zërnyshko. Chast' chetvërtaia."
200. Ibid.
201. "Pi'smo Predsedatelia Soveta Ministrov RSFSR I. Silaeva pisateliu A. Solzhenitsynu," *Sovetskaia Rossiia*, August 18, 1990.
202. Solzhenitsyn, "Tri otryvka," 25.
203. Quoted in Thomas, *Solzhenitsyn*, 514.
204. Thomas, *Solzhenitsyn*, 514.
205. Nietzsche, *Ecce Homo*, 701.
206. Nikolai Bukharin, "Bukharin's Testament," in Anna Larina, *This I Cannot Forget: The Memoirs of Nikolai Bukharin's Widow*, trans. Gary Kern (New York: W. W. Norton, 1994), 344.

207. Aleksandr Solzhenitsyn, *The Gulag Archipelago 1918–1956: An Experiment in Literary Investigation I–II*, vol. 1, trans. Thomas P. Whitney (New York: Harper Perennial, 1991), 417.
208. Toker, *Return from the Archipelago*, 103–104.
209. Ignat Solzhenitsyn, "Aleksandr Solzhenitsyn was my father," *The Times*, January 5, 2010.
210. Remnick, *Resurrection*, 137.
211. Nietzsche, *Twilight of the Idols*, 488.
212. By means of a ricin injection authorized by KGB chairman Yuri Andropov (the future Soviet leader) and surreptitiously administered during Solzhenitsyn's visit to Rostov in August, with the certain knowledge of KGB generals Filipp Bobkov (still living as of 2018) and Ivan Abramov. For an account of the abortive assassination by one of its participants, see Boris Ivanov, "Moskva—Rostov ili KGB protiv Solzhenitsyna. Vospominaniia chekista," in Aleksandr Solzhenitsyn, *Bodalsia telënok s dubom. Ocherki literaturnoi zhizni*, 2nd ed. (Moscow: Soglasie, 1996), 675–84; also, Dmitrii Likhanov, "Smertel'naia zhara," *Sovershenno sekretno*, July 30, 2009, http://www.sovsekretno.ru/articles/id/2240/.
213. Aleksandr Solzhenitsyn, *"The Russian Question" at the End of the Twentieth Century*, trans. Yermolai Solzhenitsyn (New York: Farrar, Straus and Giroux, 1995), 78.
214. Solzhenitsyn, Nobel Lecture, 526.
215. See the dedication "in swollen, blood-red letters ... TO THE MEMORY OF THOSE WHO FIRST ROSE UP FROM BONDAGE: VORKUTA, EKIBASTUZ, KENGIR, BUDAPEST, NOVOCHERKASSK" (Aleksandr Solzhenitsyn, "Tanks Know the Truth! Film Scenario for Variable-Sized Screen," trans. Michael Nicholson, *Studies in Russian & Soviet Cinema* 7, no. 1 [2013]: 156).
216. Solzhenitsyn, *November 1916*, 54.
217. Aleksandr Solzhenitsyn, "Live Not By Lies!", in Ericson and Mahoney, *The Solzhenitsyn Reader*, 559.
218. Friedrich Nietzsche, *On the Genealogy of Morals: A Polemic*, in Kaufmann, *Basic Writings of Nietzsche*, 495.
219. Nietzsche, *The Genealogy of Morals*, 496.
220. Solzhenitsyn, *The Oak and the Calf*, 11.
221. Solzhenitsyn, *The First Circle*, 511.
222. Aleksandr Solzhenitsyn, *The Gulag Archipelago: 1918–1956. An Experiment in Literary Investigation V–VII*, vol. 3, trans. Harry Willetts (Boulder: Westview Press, 1998), 49.
223. Vladimir Vasilik, "Razgovor o Solzhenitsyne. Chast' 2. 'V kruge pervom,'" *DeloRus*, August 28, 2011, http://www.delorus.com/good/index.php?ELEMENT_ID=5151.
224. Quoted in Neal Ascherson, "Law v. Order," review of *Inside Putin's Russia*, by Andrew Jack, *Putin's Progress*, by Peter Truscott, and *Putin, Russia's Choice*, by

Richard Sakwa, *London Review of Books* 26, no. 10 (2004), https://www.lrb.co.uk/v26/n10/neal-ascherson/law-v-order.

225. Pavel Basinskii, "Dnevnik pisatelia. Kak Dmitrii Bykov Solzhenitsyna otygral," *Topos. Literaturno-filosofskii zhurnal*, May 29, 2002, http://www.topos.ru/article/328.
226. Solzhenitsyn, Nobel Lecture, 525.
227. Andozerskaya describes the monarch as "the one binding force" (Solzhenitsyn, *November 1916*, 341); *monarkh—edinstvennaia skrepa* (Solzhenitsyn, *Sobranie sochinenii*, 9:337); and the Socialist Revolutionary Sergei Maslov observes that "the revolution has broken the ancient trusses [*skrepy*] of the state" (ibid., 16:435).
228. Vladimir Putin, Address to the Federal Assembly (Moscow, December 12, 2012), President of Russia [official site], http://en.kremlin.ru/events/president/news/17118.
229. The subtitle of Solzhenitsyn's essay "Rebuilding Russia."
230. Nikolai Ul'ianov, "Zagadka Solzhenitsyna," *Novoe russkoe slovo*, August 1, 1971.
231. A bizarre cultural topos of the Cold War. In 1974, the science fiction writer Philip K. Dick wrote to the FBI to denounce his Polish colleague Stanislaw Lem as "probably a composite committee rather than an individual, since he writes in several styles and sometimes reads foreign, to him, languages and sometimes does not" ("Philip K. Dick to the FBI, September 2, 1974," Stanislaw Lem—The Official Site, http://english.lem.pl/faq#P. K.Dick).
232. Aleksandr Solzhenitsyn, Templeton Lecture, in Ericson and Mahoney, *The Solzhenitsyn Reader*, 583.
233. Aleksandr Solzhenitsyn, "Repentance and Self-Limitation in the Life of Nations," in Ericson and Mahoney, *The Solzhenitsyn Reader*, 532.
234. Solzhenitsyn, "Repentance and Self-Limitation," 534.
235. Ibid., 549.
236. Solzhenitsyn, "Nashi pluralisty," 439.
237. Ibid., 549.
238. Solzhenitsyn, *Cancer Ward*, 27.
239. Ibid., 27.
240. Solzhenitsyn, "Interv'iu s Augshtainom," 302.
241. Pearce, *Solzhenitsyn*, 292.
242. Solzhenitsyn, Interview with Kehlmann.
243. Dmitrii Bykov, "Dvesti let vmeste," review of *Dvesti let vmeste*, by Aleksandr Solzhenitsyn, October 21, 2009, http://berkovich-zametki.com/Nomer24/Bykov1.htm.
244. Its use of plot, character, and dialogue qualifies it as a verse novel.
245. Aleksandr Solzhenitsyn, *Sobranie sochinenii*, 18:86–7.

246. Solzhenitsyn, *The First Circle*, 598.
247. Solzhenitsyn, "An Interview with Struve," 309.
248. Aleksandr Solzhenitsyn, "On the Fragments by Boris Souvarine," in Dunlop, Haugh, and Nicholson, *Solzhenitsyn in Exile*, 337.
249. Gray, Aikman, and Kohan, "Russia's Prophet in Exile."
250. Aleksandr Solzhenitsyn, "'Ia ne propustil ni odnogo istochnika ...,'" *Rodina* 6 (2002), 16–17.
251. Aleksandr Solzhenitsyn and Igor Shafarevich, "Ne stalinskie vremena", in *Publitsistika*, 2:73.
252. Solzhenitsyn, *The First Circle*, 141.
253. Ibid., 98.
254. Aleksandr Solzhenitsyn, "Kruglyi stol v gazete 'Iomuri' (13 oktiabria 1982)," in *Publitsistika*, 3:94.
255. Aleksandr Solzhenitsyn, "Interv'iu shveitsarskomu ezhenedel'niku 'Wel'tvokhe' (13 sentiabria 1993)," in *Publitsistika*, 3:393.
256. Natalia Solzhenitsyna, private communication,
257. *Der Spiegel* interview with Alexander Solzhenitsyn: "I Am Not Afraid of Death," August 30, 2007, http://www.spiegel.de/international/world/spiegel-interview-with-alexander-solzhenitsyn-i-am-not-afraid-of-death-a-496003.html.
258. Aleksandr Solzhenitsyn, "Press-konferentsiia v Londone (11 maia 1983)," in *Publitsistika*, 3:109.
259. Solzhenitsyn, *The Oak and the Calf*, 438.
260. Solzhenitsyn, "Press-konferentsiia v Londone," 109.
261. Solzhenitsyn, *The Russian Question*, 90.
262. Aleksandr Solzhenitsyn, "'Russkii vopros' k kontsu XX veka," in *Publitsistika*, 1:687.
263. Solzhenitsyn, *The Russian Question*, 96.
264. Solzhenitsyn, "'Russkii vopros,'" 692.
265. Solzhenitsyn, "Press-konferentsiia v Londone," 109.
266. Milovan Djilas, *Conversations with Stalin*, trans. Michael B. Petrovich (New York: Harcourt Brace Jovanovich, 1962), 120–21.
267. Solzhenitsyn, *The Oak and the Calf*, 90.
268. Ibid., 42n3.
269. Victor Erofeyev, "How Russia Lost World War II," *The New York Times*, May 10, 2005. The term "unenlightened" covers all manner of crassness. In a speech he gave on November 4, 2015, Patriarch Kirill of the Russian Orthodox Church offered his assessment of Joseph Stalin: "The achievements of this or that state leader who was at the forefront of the country's restoration and modernization ought not to be put in doubt, even if the statesman in question was a notorious villain [*dazhe esli etot rukovoditel' otlichilsia zlodeistvami*]." Kirill went on to refer

to Stalin's "power of will, strength, intellect, and political decisiveness" as allegedly manifested in World War II ("Glava gosudarstva i Predstoiatel' Russkoi Pravoslavnoi Tserkvi otkryli vystavku 'Pravoslavnaia Rus'' v Moskve," http://www.patriarchia.ru/db/text/4263139.html).
270. Solzhenitsyn, *The Oak and the Calf*, 42.
271. Quoted in Roy Medvedev, *Solzhenitsyn i Sakharov* (Moscow: Prava cheloveka, 2002), 125.
272. Natalia Solzhenitsyna, private communication.
273. Alexander Rahr, "Die meisten Russen sind noch autoritärer als Putin," *Die Welt*, January 2, 2014.
274. "Ukaz Prezidenta Rossiiskoi Federatsii ot 5 iiunia 2007 g. 'O prisuzhdenii Gosudarstvennoi premii Rossiiskoi Federatsii za vydaiushchiesia dostizheniia v oblasti gumanitarnoi deiatel'nosti 2006 goda,'" *Rossiiskaia Gazeta*, June 7, 2007.
275. Vladimir Kuz'min, "Iz pervykh ruk. Vchera president Putin vruchil Gosudarstvennye premii luchshim predstaviteliam tvorcheskoi intelligentsii," *Rossiiskaia gazeta—Stolichnyi vypusk*, June 6, 2007.
276. Robert Horvath, "Apologist of Putinism? Solzhenitsyn, the Oligarchs, and the Specter of Orange Revolution," *The Russian Review* 70, no. 2 (2011): 301–2. The "Reflections" (written 1980–83) were originally slated for inclusion in *The Red Wheel*. On his wife's advice, Solzhenitsyn put them aside as being surplus to the epic's historiographical requirements (Natalia Solzhenitsyna, private communication).
277. Horvath, "Apologist of Putinism?", 315.
278. "Aleksandr Solzhenitsyn schitaet seichas neumestnym priniatie gossimvoliki Rossii," *news.ru*, December 13, 2000, http://www.newsru.com/russia/13dec2000/mneniya.html.
279. *Spiegel* interview with Solzhenitsyn. This policy that was reversed in 2013.
280. Ibid.
281. Ibid.
282. "Washington's Farewell Address 1796," http://avalon.law.yale.edu/18th_century/washing.asp.
283. Kuz'min, "Iz pervhykh ruk."
284. Minor Planet 4915.
285. Mikhail Metzel, "Putin Calls Nelson Mandela 'Greatest Humanist of Our Time,'" *The Moscow Times*, December 11, 2013, https://themoscowtimes.com/articles/putin-calls-nelson-mandela-greatest-humanist-of-our-time-30346.
286. Natalia Solzhenitsyna, private communication.
287. "'Arkhipelag GULAG' Aleksandra Solzhenitsyna teper' budut izuchat' v shkole," Pervyi kanal, October 26, 2010, http://www.1tv.ru/news/social/163789.
288. Nataliia Solzhenitsyna, "Esli by ne Putin, 'Arkhipelagu' ne byvat' by v shkol'noi programme," *Aleksandr Isaevich Solzhenitsyn* [official site], http://solzhenitsyn.ru/v_shkole/articles/index.php?ELEMENT_ID=1071&PAGEN_1=6.

289. Natalia Solzhenitsyna interviewed by Vladimir Pozner, December 15, 2014, *Pozner Online. Ofitsial'nyi sait Vladimira Poznera*, http://pozneronline.ru/2014/12/9904/.
290. Thomas, *Solzhenitsyn*, 530.
291. Iarzhembovskii, "Prorok i ego otechestvo."
292. Pearce, *Solzhenitsyn*, 311.

Chapter Two

1. George Steiner, "In Exile Wherever He Goes," review of *Alexander Solzhenitsyn: A Century in His Life*, by D. M. Thomas, *The New York Times*, March 1, 1998.
2. Solzhenitsyn, "The Writer's Retrospect," 103.
3. Saraskina, *Solzhenitsyn*, 464.
4. Tatiana Vinokur, "O iazyke i stile povesti A. I. Solzhenitsyna 'Odin den' Ivana Denisovicha,'" *Voprosy kul'tury rechi. Institut russkogo iazyka AN SSSR*, no. 6 (1965). *Aleksandr Isaevich Solzhenitsyn* [official site], http://www.solzhenitsyn.ru/o_tvorchestve/articles/general/index.php?ELEMENT_ID=1143.
5. Aleksandr Solzhenitsyn, *One Day in the Life of Ivan Denisovich*, trans. Harry T. Willetts (New York: Farrar, Straus and Giroux, 1991), 141–2.
6. Ibid., 82.
7. Solzhenitsyn, *Sobranie sochinenii*, 1:59.
8. Solzhenitsyn, *Ivan Denisovich*, 164.
9. Ibid., 3.
10. Ibid., 9.
11. Ibid., 20.
12. Solzhenitsyn, *Sobranie Sochinenii*, 1:24.
13. Ibid., 21.
14. Solzhenitsyn, *Sobranie Sochinenii*, 1:25.
15. "Shoulder boards" in the English translation (Solzhenitsyn, *Ivan Denisovich*, 9).
16. Solzhenitsyn, *Ivan Denisovich*, 9.
17. Solzhenitsyn, *Sobranie sochinenii*, 1:18.
18. Solzhenitsyn, *Ivan Denisovich*, 48.
19. Solzhenitsyn, *Sobranie sochinenii*, 1:39.
20. Solzhenitsyn, *Ivan Denisovich*, 160.
21. Ibid., 163.
22. Ibid., 75.
23. Ibid., 40.
24. Ibid., 57.
25. Fyodor Dostoevsky, *The House of the Dead*, trans. David McDuff (New York: Viking Penguin, 1985), 130.
26. Solzhenitsyn, *Ivan Denisovich*, 39.

27. Ibid., 39.
28. Ibid., 39.
29. Ibid., 36.
30. Ibid., 167.
31. Ibid., 40.
32. Ibid., 45.
33. Nietzsche, *Twilight of the Idols*, 471.
34. Solzhenitsyn, "An Interview with Struve," 305–6.
35. Ibid., 305.
36. Solzhenitsyn, *The Gulag Archipelago*, 1:x.
37. Solzhenitsyn, *Ivan Denisovich*, 126.
38. Toker, *Return from the Archipelago*, 84.
39. Ibid., 86.
40. Ibid., 87.
41. Ibid., 89.
42. Ibid., 91.
43. Ibid., 93.
44. Oleg Pavlov, "Russkii chelovek v XX veke. Aleksandr Solzhenitsyn v zazerkal'e karataevshchiny," in Pavel Spivakovskii and Tamara Esina, eds., *"Ivanu Denisovichu" polveka. Iubileinyi sbornik 1962–2012* (Moscow: Russkii put', 2012), 593.
45. A character's sequential double imprisonment, first by the Nazis and then by the Soviets, is one of Solzhenitsyn's gulag topoi: see Bondarenko (*The Road*), and Bobynin, Pryanchikov, Lyubimichev, the engraver, and a nameless zek who had been a prisoner in Auschwitz (*The First Circle*).
46. Mihajlo Mihajlov, *Russian Themes*, trans. Marija Mihajlov (New York: Farrar, Straus and Giroux, 1968), 80.
47. Solzhenitsyn, *Ivan Denisovich*, 45.
48. Ibid., 154.
49. Krasnov-Levitin, *Dva pisatelia*, 12.
50. Solzhenitsyn, *Ivan Denisovich*, 168.
51. After Khrushchev's Secret Speech, the commandant of Solzhenitsyn's camp found employment as a guard in a food store: "[He] complains that he is mistreated and visits his former zeks with a quarter bottle of vodka to talk about life" (Vladimir Lakshin, *"Novyi mir" vo vremena Khrushcheva: dnevnik i poputnoe [1953–1964]* [Moscow: Knizhnaia palata, 1991], 91).
52. Solzhenitsyn, *The Love-Girl and the Innocent*, 243.
53. Solzhenitsyn, *Ivan Denisovich*, 30.
54. Ibid., 19.
55. Ibid., 19.
56. Ibid., 171.
57. In his subtle gloss of "Ivan Denisovich," Oleg Pavlov suggests that the protagonist,

like his hypotextual referent Platon Karataev (*War and Peace*), is "womanlike" (*zhenopodobnyi*): they both "speak with a sugary softness" and their personalities contain an element of "the feminine," which finds expression in these characters' status as captive "servants" (*sluzhki*) (Pavlov, "Russkii chelovek v XX veke," 594). One might add that many of the things that Shukhov does inside the camp fall under the category of traditional feminine chores, for example, sewing, washing floors, and waiting on others.

58. Solzhenitsyn, *Ivan Denisovich*, 14.
59. Vladimir Radzishevskii, "Kommentarii," in *Sobranie sochinenii*, 1:584.
60. Solzhenitsyn, *Ivan Denisovich*, 75.
61. Michael Scammell, "Solzhenitsyn the Stylist," *The New York Times Sunday Book Review*, August 29, 2008.
62. Solzhenitsyn, "An Interview with Struve," 307.
63. Vladimir Dal', *Tolkovyi slovar' zhivogo velikorusskogo iazyka*, vol. 4 (Moscow: Russkii iazyk, 1980), 651.
64. Solzhenitsyn, *The Gulag Archipelago*, 1:ix.
65. Solzhenitsyn, *The First Circle*, xxvii.
66. John Keegan, *A History of Warfare* (New York: Knopf, 1993), 164.
67. Solzhenitsyn, *Ivan Denisovich*, 24.
68. Ibid., 22.
69. Ibid., 38.
70. Ibid., 132.
71. Ibid., 69.
72. Ibid., 21–22.
73. In *Cancer Ward*, Kostoglotov, a member of the same zek tribe, knows "by the positions of Cygnus and Pegasus what time it is" (Solzhenitsyn, *Cancer Ward*, 299). But unlike Shukhov, the college-educated Kostoglotov identifies the stars by their correct astronomical names.
74. Solzhenitsyn, *Ivan Denisovich*, 3.
75. Ibid., 123.
76. Auerbach, *Mimesis*, 521.
77. Solzhenitsyn, *Ivan Denisovich*, 83: another gulag topos. In *The First Circle*, Nerzhin uses not one but two faith-based similes to describe the transcendent pleasure to be derived from eating prison porridge: "It's Holy Communion! You receive it with awed reverence, as though it were the life's breath of the yogis!" (Solzhenitsyn, *The First Circle*, 39).
78. Benjamin Jowett, trans., *The Republic of Plato*, 3rd ed. (Oxford: The Clarendon Press, 1908), 2:585 D.
79. Tolstoy, *War and Peace*, 859.
80. Ibid., 860.
81. Krasnov-Levitin, *Dva pisatelia*, 11.
82. Solzhenitsyn, *Ivan Denisovich*, 46.

83. Ibid., 88.
84. Ibid., 46.
85. Ibid., 47.
86. Ibid., 104.
87. Ibid., 16.
88. Ibid., 119.
89. Ibid., 63.
90. Ibid., 73.
91. Ibid., 76.
92. Ibid., 83.
93. Ibid., 39.
94. Victor Pelevin's story "A Short History of Paintball in Moscow" [Kratkaia istoriia peintbola v Moskve (1997)] twists the last of these aphorisms around: "Jean-Paul Sartre is also hell." Solzhenitsyn would have nodded yes (Viktor Pelevin, "Kratkaia istoriia peintbola v Moskve," *Sait tvorchestva Viktora Pelevina*, http://pelevin.nov.ru/rass/pe-paint/1.html).
95. Vladimir Nabokov, *Nikolai Gogol* (New York: New Directions Books, 1961), 73.
96. Lev Tolstoi, *Polnoe sobranie sochinenii*, vol. 34 (Moscow: Khudozhestvennaia literatura, 1952), 101.
97. Tolstoi, *Sobranie sochinenii*, 34:103.
98. Solzhenitsyn, *The Gulag Archipelago*, 3:414.
99. Alice K. Turner, *A History of Hell* (New York: Harcourt Brace, 1993), 98.
100. *Kaliki perekhozhie. Sbornik stikhov. Izsledovanie P[etra] Bezsonova* (St. Petersburg: Tipografiia Bakhmeteva, 1863), 5:195.
101. Georgii Fedotov, *Stikhi dukhovnye (russkaia narodnaia vera po dukhovnym stikham)* (Moscow: Progress/Gnozis, 1991), 133.
102. Sheshunova, *Natsional'nyi obraz mira*, 17.
103. *The Complete Prose and Poetry of John Milton* (New York: Modern Library, 1950), 131.
104. Milton, *Prose and Poetry*, 131.
105. Solzhenitsyn, *Ivan Denisovich*, 167–8.
106. Milton, *Prose and Poetry*, 131.
107. Solzhenitsyn, *Ivan Denisovich*, 35.
108. In the original version of the tale, Buynovsky was a comic figure, an earnest naval person ridiculously unable to understand the kind of place he had found himself in. But Khrushchev's advisor Vladimir Lebedev asked for the satire be toned down, so the author agreed not to play the captain for laughs (Solzhenitsyn, *The Oak and the Calf*, 39–40). In the end, this probably worked to the novella's advantage.
109. V. Pallon, "Zdravstvuite, kavtorang!", in Spivakovskii and Esina, *"Ivanu Denisovichu" polveka*, 159.

110. Ibid.
111. Ibid., 159.
112. Solzhenitsyn, *Ivan Denisovich*, 126.
113. Ibid., 37–8.
114. Ibid., 37.
115. Ibid., 62.
116. Ibid., 14.
117. Solzhenitsyn, *The Gulag Archipelago*, 3:59.
118. Gary Saul Morson, "Sideshadowing and Tempics," *New Literary History* 29, no. 4 (1998): 601.
119. Dostoyevsky, *House of the Dead*, 355; Mihajlov, *Russian Themes*, 81.
120. Solzhenitsyn, *Ivan Denisovich*, 89.
121. Aleksandr Tvardovskii, "Vmesto predisloviia," in Glotser and Chukovskaia, *Slovo*, 15.
122. Solzhenitsyn, *The Oak and the Calf*, 20.
123. Ibid., 21.
124. Ibid., 21. One of those literary persons was Aleksandr Maryamov, a member of the *Novy Mir* editorial board, who reports that during their phone conversation Tvardovsky told him: "I'm not simply reading. I got out of bed, put on a black suit and tie, and I am sitting at my desk" (Arkadii Belinkov, "Pochemu byl napechatan 'Odin den' Ivana Denisovicha,'" in Spivakovskii and Esina, *"Ivanu Denisovichu" polveka*, 465).
125. Roy A. Medvedev and Zhores A. Medvedev, *Khrushchev: The Years in Power* (New York: W. W. Norton, 1978), 138.
126. Aleksei Adzhubei, "Te desiat' let: fragmenty vospominanii," in Iurii Aksiutin, ed., *Nikita Sergeevich Khrushchev: materialy k biografii* (Moscow: Politizdat, 1989), 315.
127. William Taubman, *Khrushchev: The Man and His Era* (New York: W. W. Norton, 2003), 527.
128. Quoted in Saraskina, *Solzhenitsyn*, 493.
129. Michael Scammell, *Solzhenitsyn: A Biography* (New York: W. W. Norton, 1984), 433–4.
130. Solzhenitsyn, *The Oak and the Calf*, 40.
131. Ibid., 40.
132. Taubman, *Khrushchev*, 527.
133. Solzhenitsyn, *Bodalsia telënok s dubom*, 66.
134. Ol'ga Kuchkina, "Eto byla bol'shaia istoriia, i on byl ee tvorets. Svetloi pamiati Igoria Vinogradova," *Novaia gazeta*, June 3, 2015.
135. Ibid.
136. Solzhenitsyn, *The Oak and the Calf*, 437.
137. Djilas, *Conversations with Stalin*, 120.

138. Nikita Khrushchev, *Khrushchev Remembers: The Glasnost Tapes*, trans. and ed. Jerrold L. Schecter and Vyacheslav V. Luchkov (Boston: Little, Brown, 1990), 197.
139. Djilas, *Conversations with Stalin*, 120.
140. Hans Robert Jauss, "Literary History as a Challenge to Literary Theory," *New Literary History* 2, no. 1 (1970): 14.
141. Aleksandr Tvardovskii, "Rabochie tetradi 60-kh godov," *Znamia* 7 (2000): 135.
142. Edward Crankshaw, *Khrushchev: A Career* (New York: The Viking Press, 1966), 3.
143. Solzhenitsyn, *The Oak and the Calf*, 46.
144. Sergei Khrushchev, *Khrushchev on Khrushchev: An Inside Account of the Man and His Era, by His Son, Sergei Khrushchev*, ed. and trans. William Taubman (Boston: Little, Brown: 1990), 208.
145. Saraskina, *Solzhenitsyn*, 621. "Ivan Denisovich" has always been Solzhenitsyn's most-read, best-read work. With its inclusion in the Russian high school syllabus (1991), its canonical status became institutionalized, an outcome he scarcely could have imagined on that day in *his* life at the camp in Ekibastuz.
146. Solzhenitsyn, *The Oak and the Calf*, 104.
147. Aleksandr Solzhenitsyn, *Invisible Allies*, trans. Alexis Klimoff and Michael Nicholson (Washington, DC: Counterpoint, 1995), 66.
148. Il'ia Zil'berberg, *Neobkhodimyi razgovor s Solzhenitsynym* (England: No Publisher, 1976), 51–2.
149. Coleridge, *Biographia Literaria*, 176.
150. Letter from Varlam Shalamov to Solzhenitsyn, November 1962, in Galina Tiurina, ed., *"Dorogoi Ivan Denisovich!..." Pis'ma chitatelei 1962–4* (Moscow: Russkii put', 2012), 136.
151. Alexander Etkind, *Warped Mourning: Stories of the Undead in the Land of the Unburied* (Stanford: Stanford University Press, 2013), 642.
152. Krasnov-Levitin, *Dva pisatelia*, 8.
153. Viktor Erofeev, "Russkie tsvety zla," http://royallib.com/read/erofeev_viktor/russkie_tsveti_zla.html#0.
154. Letter from Shalamov to Solzhenitsyn, November 1962, 133.
155. See: "There isn't a single extraneous, unnecessary, or non-functional word in 'Ivan Denisovich.' It is a verbal construction that is absolute, that is, essentially a phenomenon of poetry rather than prose" (Boris Paramonov, "Ves' ad russkoi istorii," *Radio Svoboda*, July 19, 2015, http://www.svoboda.org/content/transcript/27140921.html).
156. Solzhenitsyn, *The Gulag Archipelago*, 3:473.
157. Letter by Anna Zakharova to the *Izvestia* newspaper, October 1, 1964, in Glotser and Chukovskaia, *Slovo*, 113–17.
158. Solzhenitsyn, *Ivan Denisovich*, 20.

159. The Vdovushkin character was based on Nikolai Borovkov, a prisoner in Solzhenitsyn's camp, who was not offended by the portrait (Radzishevskii, "Kommentarii," in Solzhenitsyn, *Sobranie sochinenii*, 1:587).
160. Solzhenitsyn, *Ivan Denisovich*, 23.
161. Ibid., 20.
162. Ibid., 85.
163. Ibid., 86.
164. Ibid., 85.
165. Ibid., 85–6.
166. Tsezar was based on the film director Lev Grossman, who was "proud that Tsezar Markovich was modeled on him" (Lakshin, *Solzhenitsyn i koleso istorii*).
167. Solzhenitsyn, *Ivan Denisovich*, 31.
168. Ibid., 158.
169. Solzhenitsyn, *Sobranie sochinenii*, 1:101.
170. Aleksandr Urmanov, *Tvorchestvo Solzhenitsyna. Uchebnoe posobie*, 2nd ed. (Moscow: Flinta/Nauka, 2003), 12.
171. John Jones, *Dostoevsky* (Oxford: Oxford University Press, 1983), 15.
172. Solzhenitsyn, *Ivan Denisovich*, 23.
173. Solzhenitsyn, *Sobranie sochinenii*, 1:26.
174. Solzhenitsyn, *Ivan Denisovich*, 135.
175. Ibid., 116.
176. Ibid.
177. Ibid., 115.
178. Ibid.
179. Ibid., 175.
180. Ibid., 16.
181. Letter from Shalamov to Solzhenitsyn, 1966, "Perepiska s Solzhenitsynym A. I.," *Varlam Shalamov*, http://shalamov.ru/library/24/21.html.
182. Solzhenitsyn, *The Oak and the Calf*, 9.
183. Nietzsche, *Beyond Good and Evil*, 278.
184. Terence des Pres, "The Heroism of Survival," in John B. Dunlop, Richard Haugh, and Alexis Klimoff, eds., *Aleksandr Solzhenitsyn: Critical Essays and Documentary Materials*, 2nd ed. (New York: Collier Books, 1975), 46.
185. Solzhenitsyn, *Ivan Denisovich*, 89.
186. Ibid., 176.
187. Solzhenitsyn, *The Oak and the Calf*, 43–4.
188. Toker, *Return from the Archipelago*, 112–14.
189. Solzhenitsyn, *Ivan Denisovich*, 177.
190. Ibid., 4.
191. Chukovskii, *Dnevnik*, 329.
192. Ibid.

193. Dmitry Bykov interviewed by Marina Koroliova, "Osoboe mnenie," *Ekho Moskvy*, June 5, 2015, http://echo.msk.ru/programs/personalno/1559918-echo/.
194. Zakharova, Letter to *Izvestiia*, 117.

Chapter Three

1. Pavlov, "Russkii chelovek v XX veke," 592–3.
2. John B. Dunlop, "Solzhenitsyn's 'Sketches,'" in Dunlop, Haugh, and Klimoff, *Solzhenitsyn: Essays and Materials*, 319.
3. Daniel J. Mahoney, *Aleksandr Solzhenitsyn: The Ascent from Ideology* (Lanham: Rowman and Littlefield, 2001), 161.
4. I am grateful to Anna Arkatova, who prompted me to make this connection.
5. Adrian Wanner, *Russian Minimalism: From the Prose Poem to the Anti-Story* (Evanston: Northwestern University Press, 2003), 18.
6. Ibid.
7. Friedrich Schiller, *On Simple and Sentimental Poetry*, in *The Complete Works of Friedrich Schiller*, vol. 8 (New York, P. F. Collier & Son, 1911), 296.
8. Solzhenitsyn, *The Oak and the Calf*, 26. Cf.: The "Miniatures" "read like excerpts from a private notebook of random sketches" (Richard Locke, "Solzhenitsyn's Short Fiction," review of *Stories and Prose Poems*, by Aleksandr I. Solzhenitsyn, *The New York Times*, July 16, 1971).
9. Solzhenitsyn, *The Oak and the Calf*, 87.
10. Aleksandr Solzenitsyn, "A Storm in the Mountains," in Ericson and Mahoney, *The Solzhenitsyn Reader*, 618.
11. Solzhenitsyn, "The City on the Neva," 619.
12. Aleksandr Solzhenitsyn, "Along the Oka," in Ericson and Mahoney, *The Solzhenitsyn Reader*, 624.
13. Ibid.
14. Solzhenitsyn, "Means of Locomotion," in ibid., 619.
15. Solzhenitsyn, "The Fire and the Ants," in ibid., 622.
16. Solzhenitsyn, "Reflection in Water," in ibid., 618.
17. Solzhenitsyn, "The Old Bucket," in ibid., 620.
18. Solzhenitsyn, "A Poet's Ashes," in ibid., 617.
19. Solzhenitsyn, "Approaching the Day," in ibid., 623.
20. Ibid..
21. Solzhenitsyn, "A Prayer," in ibid., 625.
22. Solzhenitsyn, *Sobranie sochinenii*, 1:554.
23. Anna Akmatova, "Prayer," https://sites.google.com/site/poetryandtranslations/anna-akhmatova/prayer.
24. Anna Akhmatova, *Stikhotvoreniia i poemy* (Leningrad: Sovetskii pisatel', 1979), 109.

25. The "Prayer" "slipped out" into samizdat and, eventually, "worldwide publication" after Solzhenitsyn's copyist shared it with her contacts (Solzhenitsyn, *Invisible Allies*, 68).
26. Todorov, *Genres in Discourse*, 21.
27. Virginia Woolf, From *To the Lighthouse*, in Mitchell A. Leaska, ed., *The Virginia Woolf Reader: An Anthology of Her Best Short Stories, Essays, Fiction, and Nonfiction* (Wilmington: Mariner Books, 1984), 69.
28. Aleksandr Solzhenitsyn, "Ugodilo zërnyshko promezh dvukh zhernovov. Ocherki izgnaniia," Chast' pervaia (1974–8), Glavy 2–3, *Novyi mir* 11 (1998), http://magazines.russ.ru/novyi_mi/1998/11/solg.html.
29. Solzhenitsyn, *The Oak and the Calf*, 114.
30. Alexander Solzhenitsyn, "The Right Hand," in *Stories and Prose Poems*, trans. Michael Glenny (New York: Farrar, Straus and Giroux, 1971), 164 (amended translation).
31. Solzhenitsyn, *Sobranie sochinenii*, 1:157.
32. Thirty years after writing "The Right Hand" Solzhenitsyn would give the Tambov rebellion its literary due in the bipartite tales "Ego" and "Times of Crisis."
33. Solzhenitsyn, "The Right Hand," 162.
34. Ibid., 153.
35. Ibid., 154.
36. Ibid., 151–2.
37. Ibid., 155 (amended translation).
38. Ibid., 154.
39. Ibid., 151.
40. Ibid., 155.
41. Ibid.
42. Ibid., 156; *polosataia shutovskaia kurtochka* (Solzhenitsyn, *Sobranie sochinenii*, 1:152). A sartorial connection to Kostoglotov, who "looked extremely odd [*prekomichno vygliadel*] … in the badly made woman's dressing gown" (Solzhenitsyn, *Cancer Ward*, 225; *Sobranie sochinenii*, 3:199).
43. Solzhenitsyn, "The Right Hand," 156.
44. Ibid., 159.
45. Tolstoy, *War and Peace*, 124.
46. Solzhenitsyn, "The Right Hand," 164.
47. Iurii Lotman, *Semiosfera. Vnutri mysliashchikh mirov*. Chast' vtoraia, http://www.uic.unn.ru/pustyn/lib/lotman.ru.html.
48. In *August 1914*, the mortally wounded Stolypin makes the sign of the cross over Tsar Nicholas II with his left hand: a sinistral—sinister portent (Solzhenitsyn, *August 1914*, 606).
49. Solzhenitsyn, "The Right Hand," 156.
50. Solzhenitsyn, *Sobranie sochinenii*, 1:152.

51. Solzhenitsyn, "The Right Hand," 160.
52. Ibid., 156.
53. Ibid.
54. Ibid.
55. Margaret Ziolkowski, "Dostoevsky and the Kenotic Tradition," in George Pattison and Diane Oenning Thompson, eds., *Dostoevsky and the Christian Tradition* (Cambridge: Cambridge University Press, 2001), 33.
56. Ibid.
57. Ibid.
58. Lakshin, *Solzhenitsyn i koleso istorii*.
59. Solzhenitsyn, *The Oak and the Calf*, 29.
60. Solzhenitsyn, "Matryona's Home," 25.
61. Ibid.
62. Ibid.
63. Ibid., 26.
64. Ibid., 27.
65. Ibid., 31.
66. Ibid., 28.
67. Ibid., 37.
68. Thomas, *Solzhenitsyn*, 263.
69. Solzhenitsyn, "Matryona's Home," 41.
70. Ibid., 29.
71. Ibid.
72. Solzhenitsyn, *Sobranie sochinenii*, 1:121.
73. Solzhenitsyn, "Matryona's Home," 30.
74. Ibid., 39.
75. Ibid.
76. Wislawa Szymborska, "Our Ancestors' Short Lives," *Poems New and Collected, 1957–1997*, trans. Stanislaw Baranszak and Clare Cavanagh (New York: Harcourt, 1998), 194.
77. Solzhenitsyn, "Matryona's Home," 42.
78. Ibid.
79. Ibid., 43.
80. Ibid., 37.
81. Ibid., 33.
82. Ibid., 45.
83. Ibid., 28.
84. Ibid., 31.
85. Ibid., 25.
86. Mircea Eliade, *The Sacred and the Profane. The Nature of Religion* (New York: Harcourt Brace Jovanovic, 1987), 44.

87. Ibid., 42.
88. Ibid., 52.
89. Solzhenitsyn, "Matryona's Home," 41.
90. Aleksandr Pushkin, "Stikhi, sochinennye noch'iu vo vremia bessonitsy," in *Polnoe sobranie sochinenii v desiati tomakh*, vol. 3 (Moscow/Leningrad: izdatel'stvo Akademii Nauk SSSR, 1950), 198.
91. Solzhenitsyn, "Matryona's Home," 38.
92. Ibid.
93. Plinio Apuleyo Mendoza and Gabriel García Márquez, *The Fragrance of Guava* (London: Verso, 1983), 59–60.
94. Christopher Warnes, "Magical Realism and the Legacy of German Idealism," *The Modern Language Review* 101, no. 2 (2006): 490.
95. Bloom, *The Western Canon*, 317.
96. Solzhenitsyn, "Matryona's Home," 30.
97. M. Keith Booker, *The Post-Utopian Imagination: American Culture in the Long 1950s* (Westport: Greenwood Press, 2002), 55.
98. Nicholas Nekrassov, "Who Can Be Happy and Free in Russia?", http://www.fullbooks.com/Who-Can-Be-Happy-And-Free-In-Russia-1.html.
99. Vladimir Nabokov, *Lectures on Russian Literature*, trans. Juliet M. Soskice (New York: Harcourt Brace Jovanovich, 1981), 313.
100. Solzhenitsyn, "Matryona's Home," 38.
101. Ibid., 39.
102. Ibid., 29.
103. Solzhenitsyn, *Sobranie sochinenii*, 1:121.
104. Solzhenitsyn, "Matryona's Home," 41.
105. For example, *Gathering the Harvest* (*Uborka khleba*; 1910) and *Harvest* (*Zhatva*; 1915).
106. Solzhenitsyn, "Matryona's Home," 40.
107. Ibid., 43.
108. Ibid., 55.
109. Ibid., 47.
110. Ibid., 50.
111. Ibid., 54.
112. Ibid., 51.
113. Ibid., 52.
114. Ibid.
115. See Tolstoy's article "Progress and the Definition of Education" ("Progress i opredelenie obrazovaniia"; 1862), in which he averred that "the spirit of the people was always hostile to … the railways" and that their introduction had harmed the rural population (Lev Tolstoi, *Polnoe sobranie sochinenii*, vol. 8 [Moscow: Khudozhestvennaia literatura, 1936], 344). See also Nikolai Nekrasov's poem "The

Railway" ("Zheleznaia doroga"; 1865), a lament for the peasant laborers who suffered and died during the construction of the St. Petersburg-Moscow railroad.
116. Solzhenitsyn, "Matryona's Home," 36.
117. David M. Bethea, *The Shape of Apocalypse in Modern Russian Fiction* (Princeton: Princeton University Press, 1989), 96.
118. Solzhenitsyn, *Sobranie sochinenii*, 1:129.
119. Solzhenitsyn, "Matryona's Home," 38.
120. Ibid.
121. Ibid., 56.
122. The Eastern Orthodox tradition recognizes nine Beatitudes (Mathew 5:3–11), while the Western tradition usually lists eight (Mathew 5:3–10).
123. "The name Jesus and also the name Christ were known from the beginning and were honored by the Inspired Prophets" (Eusebius Pamphilius, *The Church History*, in *Church History. Life of Constantine. Oration in Praise of Constantine*, ed. Philip Schaff, trans. Arthur Cushman [New York: Christian Literature Publishing Co., 1890], 93); "What is now called the Christian religion existed even among the ancients and was not lacking from the beginning of the human race until 'Christ came in the flesh.' From that time, true religion, which already existed, began to be called Christian" (St. Augustine, *The Retractions*, trans. M. Inez Borgan [Washington: Catholic University of America Press, 1968], 52).
124. Vasilii Rozanov, "Tolstoy i Dostoevskii ob iskusstve," in *O pisatel'stve i pisateliakh*, 214.
125. Ziolkowski, "Dostoevsky and the Kenotic Tradition," 33.
126. Margaret Ziolkowski, *Hagiography and Modern Russian Literature* (Princeton: Princeton University Press, 1988), 188.
127. Friedrich Nietzsche, *The Antichrist: Attempt at a Critique of Christianity*, in Kaufmann, *The Portable Nietzsche*, 612–13.
128. Solzhenitsyn, *Bodalsia telënok s dubom*, 47.
129. Kochetovka (built 1876) is a station on the South-East Railway in Tambov Province. As for Kochetov, he is now a footnote to a footnote.
130. Aleksandr Solzhenitsyn, "An Incident at Krechetovka Station," in *Stories*, 172.
131. Ibid., 184.
132. Ibid., 222.
133. Solzhenitsyn, *Sobranie sochinenii*, 1:196.
134. Solzhenitsyn, "An Incident at Krechetovka Station," 180.
135. Ibid., 175.
136. Ibid., 189.
137. Ibid., 193.
138. Ibid., 196.
139. Ibid., 173.
140. Ibid.
141. Ibid., 177.

142. Ibid.
143. Ibid., 182.
144. Ibid., 200.
145. Ibid., 201.
146. Ibid., 203.
147. Ibid., 210.
148. Ibid., 222–3.
149. Ibid., 224.
150. The People's Militia comprised sixteen divisions of poorly armed volunteers, many of them members of the free professions. It suffered exceptionally heavy casualties in the fighting near Moscow.
151. Ibid., 225.
152. Ibid., 227.
153. Ibid., 230.
154. Ibid., 231.
155. Ibid., 238.
156. Ibid., 240.
157. Solzhenitsyn, *Sobranie sochinenii*, 1:209.
158. Solzhenitsyn, "An Incident at Krechetovka Station," 171.
159. The available English translation is based on the *Novy Mir* text. Solzhenitsyn subsequently removed the entire first section, which consisted of dialogue among the teachers reminiscent of the opening of "Kochetovka."
160. Solzhenitsyn, *The Oak and the Calf*, 66–7.
161. Boris Eikhenbaum, "Pushkin i Tolstoi," in *O proze. O poezii. Sbornik statei* (Leningrad: Khudozhestvennaia literatura, 1986), 83.
162. Solzhenitsyn, "For the Good of the Cause," in *Stories*, 87.
163. Ibid., 116.
164. The story was based on an incident involving a vocational school in Solzhenitsyn's home town of Ryazan. Fifty years on, this institution, now known as the Ryazan College of Electronics, is still hoping to get custody of the building in question, a situation which the college website patriotically compares to imperial Russia's cession of Alaska to the United States (I. A. Blinkov, "Istoriia sozdaniia i etapy razvitiia Riazanskogo kolledzha elektroniki," http://ркэ.рф/index.php/2015-03-27-07-16-00/stranitsy-istorii).
165. Solzhenitsyn, "For the Good of the Cause", 114. Amended translation.
166. Katerina Clark, *The Soviet Novel: History as Ritual*, 3rd ed. (Bloomington: Indiana University Press, 2000), 115.
167. Georg Lukács, *Solzhenitsyn* (London: The Merlin Press, 1969), 25.
168. Solzhenitsyn, *The Gulag Archipelago*, 3:440.
169. Natalia Solzhenitsyna, private communication.
170. Solzhenitsyn, "For the Good of the Cause," 63.
171. Ibid., 68.

172. Ibid., 67.
173. Solzhenitsyn, *Sobranie sochinenii*, 1:229–30.
174. Solzhenitsyn, "For the Good of the Cause" 113–14.
175. Ibid., 80.
176. Ibid., 84.
177. Ibid., 84–5.
178. Solzhenitsyn, "For the Good of the Cause," 123. When revising the story, Solzhenitsyn changed the ending by deleting the penultimate paragraph in the *Novy Mir* version, which shows Fyodor Mikheevich railing helplessly in the face of triumphant injustice like one of those "little people" in Pushkin or Gogol: "Just you wait, just you wait, you swine!" (ibid., 123).
179. Solzhenitsyn, *Sobranie sochinenii*, 1:247.
180. Solzhenitsyn, "Zakhar-the-Pouch," in *Stories*, 133.
181. Ibid., 135.
182. Ibid., 136.
183. Ibid., 134.
184. Ibid., 136.
185. Solzhenitsyn, *Sobranie sochinenii*, 1:250.
186. Solzhenitsyn prefers to reference this source rather than the better-known but aesthetically inferior *Battle Beyond the Don* [Zadonshchina; c. 1389].
187. Aleksandr Blok, "Na pole Kulikovom," in *Polnoe sobranie sochinenii v 20 tomakh*, vol. 3 (Moscow: Nauka, 1997), 911.
188. Solzhenitsyn, "Zakhar-the-Pouch," 137.
189. Solzhenitsyn, *The Oak and the Calf*, 125. At the time of writing, fears of a war with China were growing across all strata of Soviet society. In his critical appreciation of Boris Pilnyak's novel *Naked Year* (*Golyi god*; 1922), Solzhenitsyn comments approvingly on its "intriguingly" cryptic theme of a future Chinese conquest or absorption of Russia (Aleksandr Solzhenitsyn, "'Golyi God' Borisa Pil'niaka. Iz 'Literaturnoi kollektsii.'" *Novyi mir* 1 (1997), http://magazines.russ.ru/novyi_mi/1997/1/solgen.html). In *Between Two Millstones*, however, he acknowledges that he had "inflated" the Chinese threat (Solzhenitsyn, *Zërnyshko*. Chast' pervaia, Glava 1).
190. Alexander Solzhenitsyn, *Letter to Soviet Leaders*, trans. Hilary Sternberg (London: Index on Censorship, 1974), 8.
191. Solzhenitsyn, "Zakhar-the-Pouch," 134.
192. Ibid., 148–9.
193. Solzhenitsyn, "Zakhar-the-Pouch," 139–40.
194. Solzhenitsyn, *Sobranie sochinenii*, 1:252.
195. Solzhenitsyn, "Zakhar-the-Pouch," 147.
196. Ibid., 144.
197. Feodor Dostoevsky, *Crime and Punishment*, trans. Jessie Coulson, ed. George Gibian, 3rd ed. (New York: W. W. Norton, 1989), 58.

198. Solzhenitsyn, "Zakhar-the-Pouch," 144. Ekaterina Furtseva, Soviet Minister of Culture in 1960–74. In the second edition of *The Oak and the Calf*, Solzhenitsyn describes Zakhar's extra-literary fate: "It was said that, discomfited by this character, Furtseva ordered that the Custodian of the Field be sacked. Such are the ways of the world: while political battles are fought in the gloomy capital, peasants faraway get their heads chopped off" (Solzhenitsyn, *Bodalsia telënok s dubom*, 137).
199. James George Frazer, *The New Golden Bough. A New Abridgment of the Classic Work by Sir James George Frazer*, ed. Theodor H. Gaster (New York: Criterion Books, 1959), 160.
200. Solzhenitsyn, *The Oak and the Calf*, 25.
201. Solzhenitsyn, "Zakhar-the-Pouch," 146. Amended translation.
202. Ibid., 148.
203. Solzhenitsyn, *Sobranie sochinenii*, 1:257.
204. Solzhenitsyn, "Zakhar-the-Pouch," 143.
205. The English translation uses the *Novy Mir* text; this includes two subsequently deleted paragraphs in which the narrator calls Zakhar the Field's "red-haired tutelary spirit" (Solzhenitsyn, "Zakhar-the-Pouch," 150) and refers to the historical importance of the site.
206. Solzhenitsyn, *The Gulag Archipelago*, 3:410.
207. Ibid.
208. Solzhenitsyn was never fond of Soviet-era Moscow, but he liked its boulevards, even though they had been part-destroyed by the "crazed, unfilial hand" of communist city planners (Solzhenitsyn, *Letter to Soviet Leaders*, 25).
209. Queuing for a *spravka* was a universal, and universally unpleasant, experience. It is a frequent topos in Soviet-era literature.
210. Aleksandr Solzhenitsyn, "What a Pity," in Ericson and Mahoney, *The Solzhenitsyn Reader*, 63.
211. Ibid., 65.
212. Ibid.
213. Ibid.
214. Ibid., 66.
215. Ibid., 64.
216. In the Russian text, the narrator's use of the diminutive "Anya" and the heroine's habit of referring to her parents as "mummy" and "daddy" (*mama i papa*) underscore this motif.
217. Ibid., 66.
218. Ibid.
219. Ibid.
220. Ibid.
221. Ibid., 63.
222. Ibid.

223. Vladimir Nabokov, *The Gift* (London: Weidenfeld and Nicholson, 1963), 12–13.
224. Letter from Kornei Chukovskii to Solzhenitsyn of December 2, 1965, in Elena Chukovskaia, ed., "Perepiska Aleksandra Solzhenitsyna s Korneem Chukovskim (1963–9)," *Novyi mir* 10 (2011), http://magazines.russ.ru/novyi_mi/2011/10/ch11-pr.html.
225. Solzhenitsyn, *Sobranie sochinenii*, 1:259. I am grateful to Pavel Spivakovsky for directing my attention to these details.
226. The writers' settlement near Moscow.
227. Aleksandr Solzhenitsyn, "The Easter Procession," in Ericson and Mahoney, *The Solzhenitsyn Reader*, 57.
228. Ibid., 58.
229. Solzhenitsyn, *Sobranie sochinenii*, 1:265.
230. Solzhenitsyn, "The Easter Procession," 58. In Solzhenitsyn, this style of smoking is a marker of vulgar masculinity (for women, the equivalent is the munching of sunflower seeds. See the prison guard's wife in "A Poet's Ashes," who is "cracking sunflower seeds on the porch" [Solzhenitsyn, "A Poet's Ashes," 617]). In *August 1914*, the assassin Bogrov preens in the dock "cigarette in mouth, arms Napoleonically folded" (Solzhenitsyn, *August 1914*, 633).
231. Solzhenitsyn, *Sobranie sochinenii*, 1:264.
232. Solzhenitsyn, "The Easter Procession," 58.
233. Ibid., 59.
234. Ibid. For Solzhenitsyn's reception/rejection of popular music from the Roaring Twenties to the Swinging Sixties and beyond, see Richard Tempest, "Tainye iazyki iskusstva v proizvedeniiakh A. I. Solzhenitsyna," in Liudmila Saraskina, ed., *Lichnost' i tvorchestvo A. I. Solzhenitsyna v sovremennom iskusstve i literature* (Moscow: Russkii put', 2018).
235. Solzhenitsyn, "The Easter Procession," 60.
236. Ibid., 59.
237. Ibid., 58.
238. Ibid., 59.
239. Ibid., 60.
240. Solzhenitsyn, *Sobranie sochinenii*, 12:403.
241. Solzhenitsyn, "The Easter Procession," 61.
242. "Uail'd snova ne daet pokoia. Aktivisty pytalis' sorvat' spektakl' v MKhT im. Chekhova," *Argumenty i fakty*, November 29, 2013; "Russian Orthodox Activists Throw Pig's Head at Prestigious Moscow Theater," *The Moscow Times*, April 1, 2015.
243. Auerbach, *Mimesis*, 60.
244. Ibid., 52.
245. Ibid., 53.
246. Ibid.
247. Ibid., 60.

Chapter Four

1. Aleksandr Solzhenitsyn, *Dorozhen'ka* (Moscow: Nash dom, 1999).
2. Thomas, *Solzhenitsyn*, xiv.
3. Edward E. Ericson, Jr. and Alexis Klimoff, *The Soul and Barbed Wire. An Introduction to Solzhenitsyn* (Wilmington: ISI Books, 2008), 74.
4. Iurii Tynianov, "O kompozitsii *Evgeniia Onegina*," in *Poetika. Istoriia Literatury. Kino* (Moscow: Nauka, 1977), 60.
5. Aleksandr Solzhenitsyn, Solzhenitsyn, *Sobranie sochinenii*, 18:389.
6. Ericson and Klimoff, *The Soul and Barbed Wire*, 74.
7. Gérard Genette, *Paratexts: Thresholds of Interpretation*, trans. Jane E. Lewin (Cambridge: Cambridge University Press, 1997), 10.
8. Ibid., 2.
9. Ibid.
10. Saraskina, *Solzhenitsyn*, 169.
11. Genette, *Paratexts*, 91.
12. Solzhenitsyn, *Sobranie sochinenii*, 18:252.
13. Ibid., 18:261. Timeless indeed: an almost identical passage occurs in *August 1914*, where drunken recruits dance at rural train stations to the strains of the balalaika as families weep and make the sign of the cross (Solzhenitsyn, *August 1914*, 10).
14. Clark, *The Soviet Novel*, 199.
15. Solzhenitsyn, *Sobranie sochinenii*, 18:267.
16. Clark, *The Soviet Novel*, p. 199.
17. Solzhenitsyn, *Sobranie sochinenii*, 18:257.
18. Solzhenitsyn, *The First Circle*, 347.
19. Solzhenitsyn, *Sobranie sochinenii*, 18:280.
20. Ibid., 18:300.
21. Ibid., 18:260.
22. Ibid., 18:255.
23. Ibid., 18:258.
24. Ibid., 18:261.
25. Ibid., 18:287.
26. Ibid., 18:282.
27. Ibid., 18:283.
28. Ibid., 18:331.
29. Ibid., 18:330.
30. Ibid., 18:323.
31. Ibid., 18:322.
32. Ibid., 12:106.
33. Ibid., 18:267.

34. Ibid., 18:334.
35. Ibid., 18:272.
36. Ibid., 18:330.
37. Ibid., 18:260.
38. Ibid., 18:264.
39. Ibid.
40. Jowett, *The Republic of Plato*, 2:488 C.
41. Ibid., 2:490 B.
42. Ibid., 2:491 D.
43. Solzhenitsyn, *Sobranie sochinenii*, 18:274.
44. Ibid., 18:253.
45. Ibid., 18:257.
46. Ibid., 18:324.
47. Ibid., 18:281.
48. Ibid., 18:329.
49. Ibid., 18:338.
50. Ibid., 18:288.
51. Ibid., 18:266.
52. Ibid., 18:289.
53. Ibid., 18:30.
54. Ibid., 18:283.
55. Ibid., 18:325.
56. Ibid.
57. Ericson and Klimoff, *The Soul and Barbed Wire*, 9.
58. Solzhenitsyn, *Sobranie sochinenii*, 18:340.
59. Ibid., 18:303.
60. Perhaps, had the novel been completed, this unmartial accessory would have traveled with Gleb during the next stage in his military career: in a letter home from the Third Leningrad Artillery School (relocated to Kostroma), Cadet Solzhenitsyn complained: "The political officer referred to the fact that I keep a special briefcase for my books as 'student disorderliness' [*studencheskaia raspushchennost'*] and ordered me to get rid of it" (Saraskina, *Solzhenitsyn*, 197).
61. Solzhenitsyn, *Sobranie sochinenii*, 18:305.
62. Erich Maria Remarque, *All Quiet on the Western Front*, trans. A. W. Wheen (New York: Random House, 2013), 19.
63. Richard Tempest, "Phone Interview with Aleksandr Solzhenitsyn. June 13, 2005," Appendix.
64. Solzhenitsyn, *Sobranie sochinenii*, 18:335.
65. Ibid., 18:319.
66. Ibid., 18:311.
67. Ibid., 18:312.

68. Ibid., 18:313.
69. Ibid., 18:322.
70. Ibid., 18:313.
71. Ibid., 18:325.
72. Ibid., 18:320.
73. Ibid., 18:320–21.
74. Jane Austen, *Pride and Prejudice*, in *The Oxford Illustrated Jane Austen* (Oxford: Oxford University Press, 1988), 2:5.
75. Solzhenitsyn, *Sobranie sochinenii*, 18:380.
76. Ibid., 18:381.
77. Ibid., 18:384.
78. Ibid., 18:385.
79. Ibid., 18:388.
80. Ibid.

Chapter Five

1. Stalin had doctored the record: he was born on December 18, 1878.
2. Lev Losev, "Poeziia i pravda u Solzhenitsyna," *In memoriam. Solzhenitsyn i Losev*, http://kulle.livejournal.com/90176.html.
3. Aleksandr Solzhenitsyn, "Answers for Richard Tempest," Appendix.
4. Solzhenitsyn, *The First Circle*, 81.
5. Ibid., "Author's Note," xxxi.
6. Aleksandr Solzhenitsyn, *Sobranie sochinenii* (Vermont/Paris: YMCA-Press, 1978), vol. 1–2.
7. Solzhenitsyn, *V kruge pervom*.
8. Aleksandr Solzhenitsyn, *V pervom krugu* [sic] (London: Flegon Press, 1968).
9. Solzhenitsyn, *The First Circle*, 5. During his visit to Tver, Volodin tells Uncle Avenir that "the first bomb will be tested very shortly" (ibid., 452), and in fact that test took place on August 29, 1949, that is, four months before Volodin phones the US embassy. These discrepancies reflect Solzhenitsyn's "severe lack of knowledge" about the Soviet atomic project at the time of writing (Aleksei Klimov [Alexis Klimoff], "Roman 'V kruge pervom' i 'shpionskii siuzhet,'" *Novyi mir* 11 (2006): 202–3).
10. Solzhenitsyn, "An Interview with Struve," 305.
11. Petrova, "Sud'ba avtora," 664.
12. Zhorzh Niva (Georges Nivat), *Solzhenitsyn*, trans. Simon Markish (Moscow: Khudozhestvennaia literatura, 1992), 61.
13. Lev Losev, "Poeziia i pravda u Solzhenitsyna," *In memoriam. Solzhenitsyn & Losev continued*, http://kulle.livejournal.com/90505.html.
14. Viktor Chalmaev, *Aleksandr Solzhenitsyn. Zhizn' i tvorchestvo* (Moscow: Prosveshchenie, 1994), 98–9.

15. Vladimir Berezin, "Pred"iavite dostoinstva!", http://www.book-review.ru/news/news3260.html.
16. Alla Latynina, "Istinnoe proisshestvie' i 'raskhozhii sovetskii siuzhet,'" *Novyi mir* 6 (2006), http://magazines.russ.ru/novyi_mi/2006/6/la11.html.
17. Tatjana Aleksic, "National Definition Through Post-Modern Fragmentation: Milorad Pavic's *Dictionary of the Khazars*," *Slavic and East European Journal* 53, no. 1 (2009): 88.
18. Solzhenitsyn, *The First Circle*, 40.
19. Rembrandt was Solzhenitsyn's favorite artist (Tiurina, "Pervaia prezentatsiia solzhenitsynskogo arkhiva," 204).
20. Solzhenitsyn, *The First Circle*, 418.
21. Ibid. Rubin brings up engineering because, as an applied discipline that directly shapes people's environments and lives, it has undeniable social implications (thank you, Katerina Polychronopoulos).
22. Solzhenitsyn, *The First Circle*, 418.
23. Ibid.
24. C. P. Snow, *The Two Cultures: And a Second Look* (Cambridge: Cambridge University Press, 1964), 14–15.
25. Natalya Reshetovskaya, *Sanya: My Husband Aleksandr Solzhenitsyn* (London: Hart-Davis, MacGibbon, 1977), 109.
26. Solzhenitsyn, *The First Circle*, 19.
27. Ibid., 22.
28. Ibid., 218.
29. Plutarch, *Lives*, trans. Bernadotte Perrin (New York: G. P. Putnam's Sons, 1917), 5:479.
30. Solzhenitsyn, *The First Circle*, 64.
31. Ibid., 217.
32. "Ia—academik Vavilov," http://amnesia.pavelbers.com/Zabitie%20imena%20147.htm.
33. Martin Malia, *The Soviet Tragedy: A History of Socialism in Russia, 1917–1991* (New York: The Free Press, 1994), 295.
34. Solzhenitsyn, *The First Circle*, 149.
35. Ibid., 150–51.
36. Vladimir Sorokin, *Goluboe Salo*, Vldmr Srkn. Ofitsial'nyi sait Vladimira Sorokina, http://www.libros.am/book/read/id/53564/slug/goluboe-salo.
37. Solzhenitsyn, *Cancer Ward*, 122.
38. Clark, *The Soviet Novel*, 255.
39. Solzhenitsyn, *The First Circle*, 96–7. Lest the reader lose sight of the System's inherent cruelty and stupidity, Solzhenitsyn inserts into the last chapter the story of Romashov, an engineer who during his nineteen years in prison compiled "a fat file containing clippings, notes, and calculations ... on the con-

struction of hydroelectric power stations" (ibid., 729). The file is impounded, to be destroyed.
40. Clark, *The Soviet Novel*, 255.
41. Ibid.
42. Ibid.
43. Solzhenitsyn, *The First Circle*, 19.
44. Ibid., 384.
45. Zhores Medvedev and Roi Medvedev, *Neizvestnyi Stalin*, 4th ed., 2015, http://www.litmir.co/br/?b=169925&p=1.
46. Goryainov-Shakhovskoy is a presence in chapter four of *The Road* and under his real name, Dmitry Mordukhai-Boltovskoi, in *The Red Wheel*.
47. Solzhenitsyn, *The First Circle*, 363.
48. As did another Marfino inmate, the American Morris Hershman, in his memoir *The Adventures of an American in Russia (1931–90)* (New York: Effect Publishing, 1995).
49. Solzhenitsyn, *The First Circle*, 471.
50. Ibid., 432.
51. Ibid., 398.
52. Ibid., 509.
53. Solzhenitsyn, *Sobranie sochinenii*, 2:497.
54. Solzhenitsyn, *The First Circle*, 125.
55. Ibid., 2.
56. Ibid., 406.
57. Ibid., 240–41.
58. Ibid, 241. Solzhenitsyn describes his own handwriting as "naturally minute 'onion seed'" (Solzhenitsyn, *The Oak and the Calf*, 5).
59. Solzhenitsyn, *The First Circle*, 407.
60. Ibid., 213.
61. Solzhenitsyn, *Sobranie sochinenii*, 2:216.
62. Solzhenitsyn, *The First Circle*, 404.
63. Upon reading *The First Circle*, Simonov realized that Galakhov was a lampoon of himself and so conceived an honest dislike of both author and novel. In 1967, he declared, "I cannot accept *The First Circle* and I oppose its publication," though he added that he was in favor of seeing *Cancer Ward* in print (Solzhenitsyn, *The Oak and the Calf*, 470).
64. Solzhenitsyn, *The First Circle*, 465.
65. Ibid., 214.
66. A diminutive of Erzsebet, the Hungarian form of Elizabeth. The English translation uses the Russian form, *Erzhika*, as rendered in the original text.
67. Solzhenitsyn, *The First Circle*, 351.
68. Ibid., 476.
69. Ibid., 319.

70. Ibid., 321.
71. Nikolai Bukharin, *Problemy teorii i praktiki sotsializma* (Moscow: Politizdat, 1989), 168.
72. Solzhenitsyn, *The First Circle*, 493.
73. John B. Dunlop, "The Odyssey of a Skeptic: Gleb Nerzhin," in Dunlop, Haugh, and Klimoff, *Solzhenitsyn: Essays and Materials*, 241.
74. Georges Nivat, "Solzhenitsyn's Different *Circles*: An Interpretive Essay," in Dunlop, Haugh, and Nicholson, *Solzhenitsyn in Exile*, 219.
75. Solzhenitsyn, *The First Circle*, 41.
76. Ibid., 459.
77. Ibid., 382.
78. Ibid., 539.
79. Ibid., 325.
80. Ibid.
81. The actual painting by Ivashev-Musatov (1966) was shown at the Fine Arts Museum of Moscow in 2013–14 as part of the "From Under the Rubble" Solzhenitsyn exhibit (*Aleksandr Solzhenitsyn: Iz-pod glyb: Rukopisi, dokumenty, fotografii: K 95-letiiu so dnia rozhdeniia* [Moscow: Russkii put', 2013]).
82. Solzhenitsyn, *The First Circle*, 78.
83. Ibid., 411.
84. Ibid.
85. Ibid., 412.
86. Ibid., 447.
87. Ibid., 585.
88. Ibid., 665.
89. Ibid., 666.
90. Ibid., 664.
91. Ibid., 282.
92. Ibid., 601.
93. Ibid., 605–6.
94. Ibid., 184.
95. Ibid., 208.
96. Ibid.
97. Ibid., 195.
98. Solzhenitsyn, *The Gulag Archipelago*, 2:248.
99. Solzhenitsyn, *The First Circle*, 192.
100. Ibid., 703.
101. Private communication, Natalia Solzhenitsyna.
102. Alexander Solzhenitsyn, *Victory Celebrations*, in *Three Plays*, 33.
103. Aleksandr Solzhenitsyn, *Respublika Truda*, in Solzhenitsyn, *Sobranie sochinenii*, 19:307.

104. Solzhenitsyn, *Three Plays*, 323.
105. Solzhenitsyn, *The First Circle*, 23.
106. Ibid.
107. Ibid., 32.
108. Ibid.
109. Ibid., 276.
110. Ibid., 253.
111. Ibid., 66.
112. Ibid., 660.
113. Solzhenitsyn, *Sobranie sochinenii*, 2:643.
114. Solzhenitsyn, *The First Circle*, 40.
115. Ibid.
116. Ibid., 402.
117. Ibid., 495.
118. Nivat, "Solzhenitsyn's *Circles*," 212.
119. Solzhenitsyn agreed with Mirra Petrova that Nerzhin is "light blue" (Petrova, "Sud'ba avtora," 674), an imaginative definition which escapes me.
120. Andrei Nemzer, "Rozhdestvo i Voskresenie. O romane Aleksandra Solzhenitsyna 'V kruge pervom,'" in *Pri svete Zhukovskogo. Ocherki istorii russkoi literatury*, https://lit.wikireading.ru/30645.
121. Aleksandr Solzhenitsyn, "Po povodu retsenzii M. A. Lifshitsa na roman 'V kruge pervom,'" in Solzhenitsyn, *V kruge pervom*, 619.
122. Solzhenitsyn, *Sobranie sochinenii*, 2:400.
123. Solzhenitsyn, *The First Circle*, 407.
124. Ibid., 222.
125. Ibid., 518.
126. Ibid., 547.
127. There may be a hint of authorial self-irony here. Solzhenitsyn abominated the indiscriminate importation into Russian of foreign words. In later life he campaigned against "the contemporary tide of the international English wave. ... If we heedlessly admit into the Russian language such insupportable words as *uik-end*, *brifing*, *isteblishment* and even *isteblishmentskii* ... we must perforce say goodbye to our native tongue" (Aleksandr Solzhenitsyn, "Ob"iasnenie," in *Russkii slovar' iazykovogo rasshireniia* [Moscow: Russkii put', 2000], 3).
128. Solzhenitsyn read him later: Popper is quoted in "Rebuilding Russia."
129. Karl Popper, *The Open Society and Its Enemies*, revised 5th ed. (London: Routledge, 1993), 2:198.
130. Solzhenitsyn, *The First Circle*, 483.
131. Karl Popper, *The Poverty of Historicism* (London: Routledge, 1991), 131.
132. Solzhenitsyn, *The First Circle*, 483.
133. Popper, *The Open Society*, 2:243.

134. Solzhenitsyn, *The First Circle*, 483.
135. Karl Popper, *The Poverty of Historicism*, 134.
136. Solzhenitsyn, *The First Circle*, 484.
137. Popper, *The Open Society*, 2:138.
138. Solzhenitsyn, *The First Circle*, 513.
139. Popper, *The Open Society*, 2:138.
140. Solzhenitsyn, *The First Circle*, 513.
141. Popper, *The Open Society*, 2:138.
142. Solzhenitsyn, *The First Circle*, 490.
143. Ibid., 533.
144. Ibid., 519
145. Ibid., 517.
146. Solzhenitsyn, *Sobranie sochinenii*, 2:504.
147. Solzhenitsyn, *The First Circle*, 401.
148. Ibid., 248.
149. Ibid., 597.
150. Ibid., 599.
151. Solzhenitsyn, *Sobranie sochinenii*, 2:584.
152. Solzhenitsyn, *The First Circle*, 267.
153. Solzhenitsyn, *Sobranie sochinenii*, 2:268.
154. The description of the church service attended by Agnia and Yakonov contains another overused image, *lavinoi lilis' khvaly i epitety Deve Marii* (Solzhenitsyn, *Sobranie sochinenii*, 2:173)—"an inexhaustibly eloquent outpouring of praise for the Virgin" (Solzhenitsyn, *The First Circle*, 169). But to repeat, the definitive version of the novel contains hardly any stylistic lapses.
155. Solzhenitsyn, *The First Circle*, 282.
156. Solzhenitsyn, *Sobranie sochinenii*, 2:617.
157. Solzhenitsyn, *The First Circle*, 633.
158. Ibid., 278.
159. Ibid., 665.
160. Ibid., 667.
161. Ortega y Gasset, *The Revolt of the Masses*, 115.
162. Solzhenitsyn, *The First Circle*, 672.
163. Ibid.
164. Dmitry Mirsky, *A History of Russian Literature from Its Beginnings to 1900* (New York: Vintage Books, 1958), 9.
165. Clark, *The Soviet Novel*, 201.
166. Toker, *Return from the Archipelago*, 109.
167. One of the supernumerary characters; an ethnic Tatar.
168. Solzhenitsyn, *The First Circle*, 396.
169. Dostoevsky, *The House of the Dead*, 190.

170. Solzhenitsyn, *The First Circle*, 562.
171. Vladimir Mayakovsky, *Sochineniia v trekh tomakh* (Moscow: Khudozhestvennaia literatura, 1965), 3:276.
172. Petrova, "Sud'ba avtora," 664.
173. Ibid., 679.
174. Solzhenitsyn, *The First Circle*, 428.
175. Ibid., 431.
176. Yevgeny Zamyatin, *We*, trans. Clarence Brown (New York: Penguin Books, 1993), 73.
177. Solzhenitsyn, *The First Circle*, 349.
178. Ibid., 355.
179. Ibid., 347–8.
180. Ibid., 352.
181. Sigmund Freud, "Medusa's Head," trans. John Strachey, in Sigmund Freud, *Sexuality and the Psychology of Love* (New York: Touchstone, 1997), 212–13.
182. Craig Owens, "The Medusa Effect or, the Specular Ruse," in Marjorie Garber and Nancy J. Vickers, eds., *The Medusa Reader* (New York: Routledge, 2003), 205.
183. Solzhenitsyn, *The First Circle*, 349.
184. Ibid., 354.
185. Vera Dunham, *In Stalin's Time: Middle-Class Values in Soviet Fiction* (Cambridge: Cambridge University Press, 1976), 42.
186. Solzhenitsyn, *The First Circle*, 378. The reader is meta-referred to Dostoevsky's prison novel *The House of the Dead*.
187. Veniamin Kaverin, Epilog, https://www.e-reading.club/bookreader.php/1031601/Kaverin_-_Epilog.html.
188. Solzhenitsyn, *The First Circle*, 504.
189. Ibid., 507.
190. Ibid., 173.
191. Ibid., 511.
192. Scammell, *Solzhenitsyn*, 497.
193. Aleksandr Solzhenitsyn, "Beseda so studentami-slavistami v Tsiurikhskom universitete (20 fevralia 1975)," in *Publitsistika*, 2:220.
194. Solzhenitsyn, *The First Circle*, 186.
195. Solzhenitsyn, *Victory Celebrations*, 11.
196. Solzhenitsyn, *The First Circle*, 349.
197. Petrova, "Sud'ba avtora," 706.
198. Pavel Spivakovsky, thank you!
199. Solzhenitsyn, *The First Circle*, 7.
200. Ibid., 486.
201. Petrova, "Sud'ba avtora," 680.
202. Solzhenitsyn, *The First Circle*, 645.

203. See the midnight presentation of the Russian edition of *The Fright of Real Tears* (2001) in the Krasnodar city cemetery, September 5–6, 2016, conducted by the local chapter of the Behemoth heavy metal band fan club, in which Zizek participated via Skype.
204. Vladimir Radzishevskii, "Kommentarii," in Solzhenitsyn, *Sobranie sochinenii*, 2:722.
205. Solzhenitsyn, *Sobranie sochinenii*, 2:13.
206. Solzhenitsyn, *The First Circle*, 1.
207. Ibid., 314.
208. Ibid., 51.
209. Solzhenitsyn, *Sobranie sochinenii*, 2:51.
210. Solzhenitsyn, *The First Circle*, 41.
211. Ibid., 25.
212. Solzhenitsyn, *Sobranie sochinenii*, 2:36.
213. Solzhenitsyn, *The First Circle*, 74.
214. Ibid., 270.
215. Ibid., 274.
216. Ibid., 245.
217. Ibid., 637.
218. Ibid., 641.
219. Johann Wolfgang von Goethe, *Faust—Parts I & II*, trans. A. S. Kline (Poetry in Translation: 2015), 46, https://www.poetryintranslation.com/PITBR/German/FaustIScenesItoIII.php.
220. Solzhenitsyn, *The First Circle*, 598–9.
221. Ibid., 295.
222. Dante Alighieri, *The Divine Comedy. I. Inferno*, trans. John D. Sinclair (New York: Oxford University Press, 1961), 23.
223. The date carries no *Russian* Christological associations: according to the Julian calendar, in the twentieth century the Eastern Orthodox Christmas fell on January 7.
224. Solzhenitsyn, *The First Circle*, 378.
225. Solzhenitsyn, *Sobranie sochinenii*, 2:373.
226. Solzhenitsyn, *The First Circle*, 47.
227. Ibid., 249.
228. Ibid., 740.
229. Ibid., 95.
230. Ibid., 248.
231. Ibid., 741. The legend "Meat" spelled out on the van "is the only fragment in the text of the novel that is graphically highlighted: it is printed in 'ladder' form and references the poetics of the avant-garde of the 1920's," notes Ilya Kukulin, who goes on to identify Andrei Bely and Boris Pilnyak plus "one of the intertitles in Eisenstein's film *October*" as additional referents (Ilya Kukulin, *Mashiny*

zashumevshego vremeni. Kak sovetskii montazh stal metodom neofitsial'noi kul'tury [Moscow: Novoe literaturnoe obozrenie, 2015], 329–30). See also Mayakovsky, a famous practitioner of "ladder" verse. The correspondent's car is "dark red" (Solzhenitsyn, *The First Circle*, 740), and so is the ink he uses (ibid., 741): Solzhenitsyn intended for the color to be "a thematic echo" or symbol (Aleksandr Solzhenitsyn, "Answers to Richard Tempest's Questions" [May 2007], Appendix). The (unmentioned) red traffic light (Solzhenitsyn, *The First Circle*, 740) is another clue.

232. Solzhenitsyn, *The Oak and the Calf*, 119n4.
233. Solzhenitsyn, "Answers to Tempest's Questions."
234. Solzhenitsyn, *The First Circle*, 337.
235. Ibid., 687.
236. Ibid., 62.
237. Ibid., 125.
238. Umberto Eco, "Overinterpreting Texts," in Umberto Eco et al., *Interpretation and Overinterpretation*, ed. Stefan Collini (Cambridge: Cambridge University Press, 1992), 47.
239. Solzhenitsyn, *The First Circle*, 441.
240. Solzhenitsyn, *Bodalsia telënok s dubom*, 239.
241. Solzhenitsyn, *The Gulag Archipelago*, 1:154; amended translation.
242. Solzhenitsyn, *The First Circle*, 104.
243. Ibid., 7–8.
244. Ibid., 614.
245. Ibid., 175.
246. Ibid., 617.
247. Ibid., 223.
248. Ibid., 149.
249. Ibid., 33.
250. Dante, *Inferno*, 299.
251. Solzhenitsyn, *The First Circle*, 130.
252. Ibid., 52.
253. Ibid., 630.
254. Ibid., 27.
255. Ibid., 275.
256. Solzhenitsyn, *Sobranie sochinenii*, 2:275.
257. Solzhenitsyn, *The First Circle*, 186.
258. Solzhenitsyn, *Sobranie sochinenii*, 2:189.
259. Solzhenitsyn, *The First Circle*, 31.
260. Ibid., 90.
261. Ibid., 79.
262. Ibid., 43.

263. Solzhenitsyn, *Sobranie sochinenii*, 2:54.
264. Solzhenitsyn, *The First Circle*, 712.
265. Ibid., 244.
266. Solzhenitsyn, *Sobranie sochinenii*, 2:246.
267. Solzhenitsyn, *The First Circle*, 244.
268. Ibid., 55.
269. Ibid.
270. Ibid.
271. Ibid.
272. Ibid., 56.
273. Ibid., 55–6.
274. Ibid., 29.
275. Solzhenitsyn, *Sobranie sochinenii*, 2:39.
276. Solzhenitsyn, *The First Circle*, 66.
277. Ibid., 656.
278. Solzhenitsyn, *Sobranie sochinenii*, 2:638.
279. Solzhenitsyn, *The First Circle*, 162.
280. Ibid., 165.
281. Ibid., 167.
282. Ibid., 162.
283. Ibid., 169.
284. Chalmaev, *Solzhenitsyn*, 91.
285. Solzhenitsyn, *The First Circle*, 165.
286. Ibid., 163, 168.
287. Ibid., 163.
288. Solzhenitsyn, *The First Circle*, 167.
289. H. G. Wells, *The Wonderful Visit* (London/New York: Macmillan, 1895), 16.
290. Ibid., 21.
291. Solzhenitsyn, *The First Circle*, 438.
292. Ibid., 625.
293. Ibid., 711.
294. Ibid., 597.
295. Solzhenitsyn, *Sobranie sochinenii*, 2:582.
296. Vladimir Dal', *Tolkovyi slovar' zhivogo velikorusskogo iazyka*, vol. 1 (Moscow: Russkii iazyk, 1978), 242.
297. Solzhenitsyn, *The First Circle*, 52.
298. Ibid., 83.
299. Ibid., 618.
300. Ibid., 618.
301. Heinrich Böll, "The Imprisoned World of Solzhenitsyn's *The First Circle*," in Dunlop, Haugh, and Klimoff, *Solzhenitsyn: Essays and Materials*, 220.

302. Solzhenitsyn, *Sobranie sochinenii*, 2:53.
303. Solzhenitsyn, *The First Circle*, 42.
304. Solzhenitsyn, *The Oak and the Calf*, 32.
305. Galina Zalomkina, "Polumir, rozenkreitsery i gosuzhas: goticheskaia interpretatsiia sovetskoi deistvitel'nosti v romane Solzhenitsyna 'V kruge pervom,'" *Vestnik Samarskogo Gosudarstvennogo Universiteta* 38, no. 4 (2005): 108.
306. Quoted in Charles Esdaile, *Napoleon's Wars: An International History, 1803–1815* (New York: Viking Penguin, 2008), 68.
307. Solzhenitsyn, *The First Circle*, 97.
308. Ibid., 98.
309. Solzhenitsyn, *The Oak and the Calf*, 78.
310. Solzhenitsyn, *The First Circle*, 129.
311. Ibid., 146.
312. Ibid., 145.
313. Eusebius, *The Life of Constantine*, 764.
314. "Solzhenitsyn v dnevnikakh Aleksandra Gladkova. Unikal'nyi arkhivnyi material—ko dniu rozhdeniia pisatelia," *Colta* (December 11, 2015), http://www.colta.ru/articles/literature/9538.
315. Solzhenitsyn, *The Oak and the Calf*, 78.
316. Solzhenitsyn, *The First Circle*, 98.
317. Ibid., 104.
318. The mangled Russian in which the American attaché converses with Volodin has the same farcical quality.
319. Solzhenitsyn, *The First Circle*, 100.
320. Ibid., 43.
321. Ibid., 101
322. Ibid., 114.
323. Ibid., 116.
324. Ibid., 135.
325. Ferguson, *The War of the World*, 437.
326. Quoted in Leonid Bezymenskii, *Operatsiia Mif, ili skol'ko raz khoronili Gitlera*, "Pisal li Stalin Gitleru?", http://militera.lib.ru/research/bezymensky2/01.html.
327. Victor Davis Hanson, *The Second World Wars: How the First Global Conflict Was Fought and Won* (New York: Basic Books, 2017), 249.
328. Alan Bullock, *Hitler and Stalin: Parallel Lives* (New York: Alfred A. Knopf, 1992), 351.
329. Carlos Rangel, *Third World Ideology and Western Reality* (New York: Routledge, 1986), 15.
330. A. James Gregor, *The Fascist Persuasion in Radical Politics* (Princeton: Princeton University Press, 1974), 132.
331. Adolf Hitler, *Hitler's Table Talk* (Oxford University Press: Oxford, 1988), 8.

332. Ibid., 587.
333. Ferguson, *The War of the World*, 424.
334. Solzhenitsyn, *The First Circle*, 450.
335. Quoted in Montefiore, *Stalin*, 491.
336. Perry Anderson, *Spectrum: From Right to Left in the World of Ideas* (London/New York: Verso, 2005), 76.
337. Solzhenitsyn, *The Gulag Archipelago*, 1:411.
338. Solzhenitsyn, *Sobranie sochinenii*, 18:240.
339. Solzhenitsyn, "Moi Bulgakov," 10.
340. Solzhenitsyn, *The First Circle*, 289.
341. Ibid., 472.
342. Andrei Belyi, *Peterburg* (Moscow: Nauka, 1981), 422.
343. Zamyatin, *We*, 116.
344. Solzhenitsyn, *August 1914*, 705.
345. Nietzsche, *Thus Spoke Zarathustra*, 250.
346. Solzhenitsyn, *The First Circle*, 130.
347. Ibid., 456.
348. Ibid.
349. Böll, "The Imprisoned World," 225.
350. A point made preemptively and obliquely earlier in the novel when Ruska tells Klara he had once offered a market seller 18,000 roubles for the medal in question (Solzhenitsyn, *The First Circle*, 284).
351. Solzhenitsyn, *The First Circle*, 457–8.
352. Ibid., 458.
353. Ibid., 463.
354. Leo Tolstoy, *War and Peace*, 7.
355. Solzhenitsyn, *The First Circle*, 458
356. Tolstoy, *War and Peace*, 9.
357. Solzhenitsyn, *The First Circle*, 476.
358. Ibid., 477.
359. Ibid., 458.
360. Ibid., 466.
361. Ibid., 473.
362. Bulat Okudzhava, "Sentimental'nyi marsh," http://www.ruthenia.ru/60s/okudzhava/sent_vals.htm.
363. Aleksandr Solzhenitsyn, "Slovo pri poluchenii Templtonovskoii premii," in *Publitsistika*, 1:445.
364. Solzhenitsyn, *Sobranie sochinenii*, 18:49–50.
365. Vladimir Radzishevskii, "Kommentarii," in Solzhenitsyn, *Sobranie sochinenii*, 18:415.
366. Solzhenitsyn, *The First Circle*, 466.
367. Solzhenitsyn, "Apricot Jam," in *Apricot Jam*, 12.
368. Solzhenitsyn, *The First Circle*, 473.

369. Ibid.
370. Ibid., 466.
371. Losev, "Poeziia i pravda," part 1.
372. Solzhenitsyn, *The First Circle*, 1.
373. Ibid., 2.
374. Ibid., 433.
375. Ibid.
376. Ibid., 436–7.
377. Ibid., 290.
378. Ibid., 291.
379. Ibid., 292.
380. Ibid., 296.
381. Ibid.
382. Ibid.
383. Ibid., 435.
384. Ibid., 441.
385. Ibid., 440.
386. Ibid., 699.
387. Solzhenitsyn, "Matryona's Home," 25.
388. Petrova, "Sud'ba avtora," 691.
389. Solzhenitsyn, *The First Circle*, 302.
390. Ibid., 306.
391. Ibid., 307.
392. Ibid.
393. Michel Foucault, "The Body of the Condemned," in Paul Rabinow, ed., *The Foucault Reader* (New York: Pantheon Books, 1984), 173.
394. Solzhenitsyn, *The First Circle*, 308.
395. Ibid., 683–4.
396. Ibid., 309.
397. Ibid., 310.
398. Ibid.
399. Ibid., 450.
400. Robert M. Adams, "Nabokov's Game," review of *The Defense*, by Vladimir Nabokov, *The New York Review of Books*, January 14, 1965, http://www.nybooks.com/articles/archives/1965/jan/14/nabokovs-game/.
401. Solzhenitsyn, *The First Circle*, 67.
402. Ibid., 28.
403. Nietzsche, *Beyond Good and Evil*, 279.
404. Solzhenitsyn, *The First Circle*, 66.
405. Constantine P. Cavafy, "Che Fece … Il Gran Rifiuto," in Constantine P. Cavafy, *Collected Poems. Revised Edition*, trans. Edmund Keeley and Philip Sherrard (Princeton: Princeton University Press, 1992), 12.

Chapter Six

1. Alain Corbin, "Le peril vénérien au début du siècle: prophylaxie sanitaire et prophylaxie morale," *Recherches* 11, no. 29 (1977): 246.
2. Susan Sontag, *Illness As Metaphor* (New York: Farrar, Straus & Giroux, 1978), 17.
3. Solzhenitsyn, *Cancer Ward*, 110.
4. Scammell, *Solzhenitsyn*, 481.
5. Solzhenitsyn, *The Oak and the Calf*, 470. The novelist Aleksandr Borshchagovsky, though sympathetic to Solzhenitsyn, felt that the "small mountain of breasts" image "went beyond the limits of the necessary" ("Stenogramma rasshirennogo zasedaniia biuro tvorcheskogo ob"edineniia prozy Moskovskoi pisatel'skoi organizatsii SP RSFSR," in Glotser and Chukovskaia, *Slovo*, 248), that is, the limits of nineteenth-century realism.
6. Michel Foucault, *Madness and Civilization: A History of Insanity in the Age of Reason*, trans. Richard Howard (Vintage Books: New York, 1988), 6. For the novel's hero, cancer survivor Oleg Kostoglotov, that terror still holds: asked to name the worst disease he can think of, he answers, leprosy (Solzhenitsyn, *Cancer Ward*, 150).
7. Solzhenitsyn, *The Oak and the Calf*, 477.
8. Quoted in Ronald Hingley, *Chekhov: A Biographical and Critical Study* (London: George Allen & Unwin, 1950), 151.
9. Anton Chekhov, "Ward Number Six," in *Ward Number Six and Other Stories*, trans. Ronald Hingley (Oxford: Oxford University Press, 1988), 25.
10. "[Ragin's] entire philosophy is that of a layabout relaxing next to a cesspit [*Vsia ego filosofiia—filosofiia lezheboka na kraiu pomoinoi iamy*]," comments Solzhenitsyn, who had mixed feelings about this tale. He criticizes Chekhov for joining Gogol, Bunin, and Gorky in depicting the Russian provinces as an "undifferentiated animal snout" (*slitnoe rylo*), but praises the descriptions of mental illness and of the hospital itself (Aleksandr Solzhenitsyn, "Okunaias' v Chekhova. Iz 'Literaturnoi kollektsii,'" *Novyi mir* 10 (1998), http://magazines.russ.ru/novyi_mi/1998/10/solg.html).
11. Quoted in "Kommentarii," in Anton Chekhov, *Polnoe sobranie sochinenii i pisem v tridtsati tomakh*, 30 vols. (Moscow: Nauka, 1985), 8:458.
12. Scammell, *Solzhenitsyn*, 481.
13. Aleksandr Solzhenitsyn, "Beseda v Tsiurikhskom universitete," 226.
14. Mirra Petrova, "Pervyi opyt raboty tekstologa s avtorom," in Struve and Moskvin, *Mezhdu dvumia iubileiami*, 427.
15. *The Oak and the Calf*, 25. See *Patients and Doctors* [*Bol'nye i vrachi*], another of Tvardovsky's suggestions (Scammell, *Solzhenitsyn*, 481; Saraskina, *Solzhenitsyn*, 520).
16. Caryl Emerson, "The Word of Aleksandr Solzhenitsyn," in Harold Bloom, ed., *Aleksandr Solzhenitsyn* (Chelsea House; Philadelphia, 2001), 176.
17. Solzhenitsyn, *The Oak and the Calf*, 477.

18. Solzhenitsyn, *Cancer Ward*, 523.
19. In *The Gulag Archipelago*, Solzhenitsyn recalls the "tumor the size of a large man's fist" he developed in the Ekibastuz camp (Rusanov's malignancy is described in exactly the same terms; Solzhenitsyn, *Cancer Ward*, 19), adding: "What was most terrifying about it was that it exuded poisons and infected the whole body. And in this same way our whole country was infected by the poisons of the Archipelago" (Solzhenitsyn, *The Gulag Archipelago*, 2:632).
20. Solzhenitsyn, *Cancer Ward*, 497.
21. Ibid., 498.
22. Georges Nivat, "On Solzhenitsyn's Symbolism," in Kathryn Feuer, ed., *Solzhenitsyn: A Collection of Critical Essays* (Englewood Cliffs: Prentice-Hall, 1976), 50.
23. Solzhenitsyn, *Cancer Ward*, 341.
24. Nivat, "Solzhenitsyn's Symbolism," 50.
25. Chalmaev, *Solzhenitsyn*, 125.
26. Aleksandr Solzhenitsyn, "Tri otryvka," 26.
27. Solzhenitsyn, *The Oak and the Calf*, 237.
28. Solzhenitsyn, "Answers for Tempest."
29. Solzhenitsyn, *Cancer Ward*, 32–3.
30. Ibid., 486.
31. Irina Meike, "Vospominaniia ob A. I. Solzhenitsyne," *Transactions of the Association of Russian-American Scholars in the United States*, vol. XXXVI, 2010.
32. *The Oak and the Calf*, 477.
33. Krasnov-Levitin, *Dva pisatelia*, 36.
34. Solzhenitsyn, *Cancer Ward*, 305.
35. Thomas Mann, *The Magic Mountain*, trans. John E. Woods (New York: Vintage International, 1995), 604.
36. Solzhenitsyn, *Cancer Ward*, 152.
37. Ibid., 153.
38. Ibid., 299. The first iteration of this image occurs in the poem "Return to the Stars" ("Vozvrashchenie k zvëzdam"; 1953) in *Sobranie sochinenii*, 18:241.
39. Solzhenitsyn, *Cancer Ward*, 123.
40. Ibid., 26.
41. Sontag, *Illness As Metaphor*, 14.
42. She is a cross-textual sister to the female prisoner with the face of "a sensitive and educated person" who is washing the stairs as Alevtina Makarygina sweeps by (*The First Circle*).
43. Thompson Bradley, "Aleksandr Solzhenitsyn's *Cancer Ward*: The Failure of Defiant Stoicism," in Dunlop, Haugh, and Klimoff, *Solzhenitsyn: Essays and Materials*, 299.
44. Robert Service, *A History of Modern Russia* (Cambridge: Harvard University Press, 2005), 320.
45. Solzhenitsyn, *Cancer Ward*, 194.

46. Ibid., 104.
47. Ibid., 106.
48. Ibid., 107.
49. Ibid., 48.
50. Ibid., 320.
51. Ibid., 192.
52. Jorge Luis Borges, "Isaac Babel," in *Selected Non-Fictions* (New York: Penguin Books, 1999), 163.
53. Solzhenitsyn, *Cancer Ward*, 190.
54. Ibid., 191.
55. Ibid., 193. See: "Stalin started observing himself, discerned the latent menace in his gestures and glances, and began consciously cultivating them" (Solzhenitsyn, *The First Circle*, 134).
56. Solzhenitsyn, *Cancer Ward*, 11.
57. Chekhov, "Ward Number Six," 32.
58. Solzhenitsyn, *Cancer Ward*, 19.
59. Ibid., 20.
60. Nietzsche, *Beyond Good and Evil*, 301.
61. Solzhenitsyn, *Cancer Ward*, 44.
62. Ibid., 106.
63. Nabokov, *Gogol*, 74.
64. Ibid., 63.
65. Ibid., 67.
66. Ibid., 70.
67. Nabokov, *Lectures on Literature*, 126.
68. Nabokov, *Gogol*, 73.
69. Ibid., 70.
70. See *Between Two Millstones*: "Over the years I endured poverty and persecution as a child, war, prison, mortal illness, life in the underground, fame, persecution on an all-Union scale, homelessness, banishment from my native country: surely, a lengthy sequence. Yet, the sequence had lacked vulgarity [*poshlost'*]. Gradually, but oh so gradually, its turn came too" (Aleksandr Solzhenitsyn, "Ugodilo zërnyshko promezh dvukh zhernovov," Chast' tret'ia [1982–7], Glavy 11–13, *Novyi mir* 4 (2001), http://magazines.russ.ru/novyi_mi/2001/4/sol.html).
71. Solzhenitsyn, *The First Circle*, 213.
72. Aleksandr Solzhenitsyn, "Ischerpanie kul'tury?", in Aleksandr Solzhenitsyn, *Na vozvrate dykhaniia. Izbrannaia publitsistika* (Moscow: Vagrius, 2004), 618.
73. Regarding Rusanov, Solzhenitsyn notes: "He ascribes every famous quotation only to Gorky" (quoted in Vladimir Radzishevskii, "Kommentarii," in Solzhenitsyn, *Sobranie sochinenii*, 3:477).
74. Solzhenitsyn, *Cancer Ward*, 149.

75. Ibid., 182.
76. Ibid., 147.
77. Ibid., 4.
78. Ibid., 181.
79. Kathryn B. Feuer, "Solzhenitsyn and the Legacy of Tolstoy," in Dunlop, Haugh, and Klimoff, *Solzhenitsyn: Essays and Materials*, 133.
80. Nabokov, *Lectures on Russian Literature*, 146.
81. James M. Curtis, "Solzhenitsyn's Traditional Imagination: Tolstoy," in Bloom, *Aleksandr Solzhenitsyn*, 47.
82. Curtis, "Solzhenitsyn's Traditional Imagination," 48.
83. Ibid., 44.
84. Solzhenitsyn, *Cancer Ward*, 108.
85. Ibid., 188.
86. Ibid., 191.
87. Ibid., 188.
88. A scatological reading of the dream is also possible, with the pipe a metaphorical colon and Rusanov a lump of waste.
89. Solzhenitsyn, *The Oak and the Calf*, 475–6.
90. Ibid., 476.
91. Solzhenitsyn, *Cancer Ward*, 178.
92. Ibid.
93. Ibid., 179.
94. Ibid., 183.
95. Ibid., 290.
96. Ibid., 281.
97. Ibid., 285.
98. Ibid., 289.
99. "Stenogramma rasshirennogo zasedaniia," 294.
100. Solzhenitsyn, *Cancer Ward*, 464.
101. Ibid., 62.
102. Ibid., 62.
103. Solzhenitsyn, *Sobranie sochinenii*, 3:59.
104. Solzhenitsyn, *Cancer Ward*, 62.
105. Ibid., 224.
106. Ibid., 12.
107. Ibid., 13.
108. Ibid., 29.
109. Petrova, "Sud'ba avtora," 689.
110. Solzhenitsyn, *Cancer Ward*, 70.
111. Solzhenitsyn, *Sobranie sochinenii*, 3:209. "Warm curving little shelves" in the English translation (Solzhenitsyn, *Cancer Ward*, 243).

112. Ibid., 228.
113. Ibid., 338.
114. Ibid., 299.
115. Solzhenitsyn, *Sobranie sochinenii*, 3:253.
116. Solzhenitsyn, *Cancer Ward*, 58.
117. Solzhenitsyn, *Sobranie sochinenii*, 3:55.
118. Solzhenitsyn, *Cancer Ward*, 465.
119. Solzhenitsyn, *Sobranie sochinenii*, 3:386.
120. Solzhenitsyn, *Cancer Ward*, 64.
121. Allen Thorndike Rice, introduction to *Reminiscences of Abraham Lincoln by Distinguished Men of His Time* (Charleston: BiblioBazaar, 2009), xxi.
122. Solzhenitsyn, *Cancer Ward*, 232.
123. Solzhenitsyn, *The First Circle*, 217.
124. Ibid., 218.
125. Solzhenitsyn, *Cancer Ward*, 29.
126. Ibid., 65.
127. Ibid., 221.
128. Dostoevsky, *Crime and Punishment*, 2–3.
129. Dostoevsky, *Crime and Punishment*, 96.
130. Solzhenitsyn, *Cancer Ward*, 508.
131. Andrew Sullivan, "America Learns to Live with Human Frailty," *The Sunday Times*, April 1, 2007.
132. Solzhenitsyn, *Cancer Ward*, 222.
133. Ibid., 409.
134. Ibid., 139.
135. Nietzsche, *Thus Spoke Zarathustra*, 307.
136. Solzhenitsyn, *Cancer Ward*, 33.
137. Nietzsche, *Ecce Homo*, 680.
138. Nietzsche, *Beyond Good and Evil*, 281.
139. Solzhenitsyn, *Cancer Ward*, 77.
140. Ibid., 138.
141. Ibid., 411.
142. Ibid., 410.
143. Ibid., 118.
144. Ibid., 120.
145. Ibid., 88.
146. Mann, *The Magic Mountain*, 3.
147. Solzhenitsyn, *Cancer Ward*, 470.
148. Ibid., 411.
149. Ibid., 71.
150. Solzhenitsyn, *Sobranie sochinenii*, 3:324.

151. Solzhenitsyn, *Cancer Ward*, 385.
152. Ibid., 534.
153. Ibid., 21.
154. Ibid., 410.
155. Ibid., 411.
156. Solzhenitsyn, *The Oak and the Calf*, 146.
157. Solzhenitsyn, *Cancer Ward*, 461.
158. Solzhenitsyn, *Ivan Denisovich*, 14.
159. Solzhenitsyn, *Cancer Ward*, 462.
160. Ibid., 462.
161. Solzhenitsyn, *Sobranie sochinenii*, 3:384.
162. Solzhenitsyn, *Cancer Ward*, 462. "Above the domino-playing level" (*ne razvityi vyshe igry v domino*) in the Russian text (Solzhenitsyn, *Sobranie sochinenii*, 3:384).
163. Mann, *The Magic Mountain*, 273.
164. Stephen Greenblatt, *Learning to Curse: Essays in Early Modern Culture* (London: Routledge, 1990), 88.
165. Leo Tolstoy, *Anna Karenina*, trans. David Magarshack (New York: Signet Classic, 1961), 133.
166. Leo Tolstoy, *The Death of Ivan Ilyich and Other Stories*, trans. Rosemary Edmonds (London: Penguin Books, 1960), 127.
167. Tolstoy, *Anna Karenina*, 130.
168. Solzhenitsyn, *August 1914*, 122.
169. Solzhenitsyn, *Cancer Ward*, 73.
170. Ibid.
171. Ibid., 33.
172. Ibid., 76.
173. Ibid., 80.
174. Ibid., 76.
175. Arthur Gordon, "Six Hours with Rudyard Kipling," *The Kipling Journal*, June 1967, 7.
176. Solzhenitsyn, *Cancer Ward*, 69.
177. Solzhenitsyn, *Sobranie sochinenii*, 3:35.
178. Solzhenitsyn, *Cancer Ward*, 32.
179. Ibid., 138.
180. Ibid.
181. Ibid., 78.
182. Ibid.
183. Sontag, *Illness As Metaphor*, 64.
184. Georges Bataille, *Death and Sensuality. A Study of Eroticism and the Taboo* (New York: Walker and Company, 1962), 11.
185. Feuer, "Solzhenitsyn and Tolstoy," 133.

186. Solzhenitsyn, *Cancer Ward*, 300.
187. Mann, *The Magic Mountain*, 696.
188. Solzhenitsyn, *Cancer Ward*, 332.
189. Ibid., 375.
190. Solzhenitsyn, *Invisible Allies*, 104.
191. Ibid., 105.
192. Ibid., 104–5. Solzhenitsyn and Petrova "put in many hours" going over his manuscripts at "an elaborate old secretary that, according to legend, had come from an estate along the Smolensk highway where Napoleon had spent a night and where he was alleged to have worked at this very writing table" (ibid., 105).
193. Solzhenitsyn, *Cancer Ward*, 36.
194. Ibid., 244.
195. Solzhenitsyn, *Sobranie sochinenii*, 3:209.
196. Solzhenitsyn, *Cancer Ward*, 351.
197. Ibid.
198. Ibid., 346.
199. Solzhenitsyn, *Sobranie sochinenii*, 3:80.
200. Solzhenitsyn, *Cancer Ward*, 86. Amended translation.
201. Solzhenitsyn, *Sobranie sochinenii*, 1:263.
202. Zamyatin, *We*, 6.
203. Ibid., 52.
204. Solzhenitsyn, *Cancer Ward*, 228. In the English translation, the same image is rendered via a simile, "resembled two triangles."
205. R. E. Allen, ed. and trans., *The Dialogues of Plato* (New Haven: Yale University Press, 1991), 2:132.
206. Zamyatin, *We*, 9.
207. Ibid., 51.
208. Ibid., 59.
209. Ibid., 70.
210. Aleksandr Urmanov, "Kontseptsiia Erosa v tvorchestve A. Solzenitsyna," in Struve and Moskvin, *Mezhdu dvumia iubileiami*, 378.
211. Solzhenitsyn, *Cancer Ward*, 245.
212. Solzhenitsyn, *Sobranie sochinenii*, 3:210.
213. Solzhenitsyn, *Cancer Ward*, 69.
214. Ibid., 219.
215. Zamyatin, *We*, 70.
216. Pavel Florenskii, *Stolp i utverzhdenie istiny. Opyt pravoslavnoi teoditsei v dvenadtsati pis'makh* (Moscow: Put', 1914), 174.
217. Solzhenitsyn, *Cancer Ward*, 226.
218. Ibid., 27.

219. Solzhenitsyn, *Sobranie sochinenii*, 3:39. "Teddy-bear with the golden hair" in the English translation (Solzhenitsyn, *Cancer Ward*, 37).
220. Ibid., 164.
221. Ibid., 164.
222. Ibid., 17.
223. Ibid., 18.
224. Ibid., 30.
225. Ibid., 159.
226. Ibid., 159.
227. Ibid., 174.
228. Manly Kostoglotov approves of this traditional feminine occupation, which gives him "a comfortable feeling" (ibid., 37).
229. Ibid., 33.
230. Ibid., 36.
231. Ibid., 236.
232. In *We*, when D-503 and I-330 have their first romantic encounter, I-330 sheds her "yuny" and puts on "a light dress of an old-fashioned cut, saffron-yellow" (Zamyatin, *We*, 54).
233. Solzhenitsyn, *Cancer Ward*, 165.
234. Ibid., 241.
235. Ibid., 242.
236. Ibid., 245.
237. Ibid., 245.
238. Ibid., 246.
239. Though mostly the man's, this being Bataille.
240. Bataille, *Death and Sensuality*, 104.
241. Ibid., 105.
242. Solzhenitsyn, *Cancer Ward*, 243.
243. Solzhenitsyn, *Sobranie sochinenii*, 3:208.
244. Solzhenitsyn, *Cancer Ward*, 246.
245. Ibid., 354
246. Ibid., 237.
247. Ibid., 473.
248. Ibid., 474.
249. Ibid., 298.
250. Ibid., 234.
251. Ibid., 351.
252. Ibid., 344.
253. Solzhenitsyn, *Sobranie sochinenii*, 18:241.
254. Solzhenitsyn, *Cancer Ward*, 347.
255. Ibid., 345.

256. Ibid., 346.
257. Ibid., 347.
258. Ibid.
259. Ibid., 349.
260. Ibid., 231.
261. Ibid., 329.
262. Ibid., 330.
263. Ibid., 333.
264. Ibid., 336.
265. Ibid.
266. Ibid., 337.
267. Ibid.
268. Ibid., 339.
269. Ibid., 340.
270. *Sobranie sochinenii*, 3:286. "The mysterious flash" in the English translation.
271. Solzhenitsyn, *Cancer Ward*, 339.
272. Jowett, *The Republic of Plato*, 2:509.
273. Ibid., 2:509 D.
274. Viktor Loshak, "Raskalennyi vopros (beseda s A. I. Solzhenitsynym)," *Moskovskie novosti*, June 19–25, 2001, http://newcanada.com/raskalennyy-vopros.
275. Solzhenitsyn, *Cancer Ward*, 352.
276. Ibid., 305.
277. Ibid., 388.
278. Ibid., 387.
279. Ibid., 390. Amended translation.
280. Ibid., 127.
281. Ibid., 126.
282. For Kostoglotov, Vera Gangart is Vega, after the star in the heavens; for Dyoma, Asya is like a star of the earthly, celluloid variety.
283. Solzhenitsyn, *Cancer Ward*, 131.
284. Ibid., 133.
285. An anachronism: Bill Haley & His Comets recorded "Rock around the Clock" in April 1954. The following year, the song became a number one hit when it was featured in the film *Blackboard Jungle*, which received its opening on March 19, 1955. It is beyond the realm of possibility that kids in Moscow would have been grooving to Haley (or Elvis Presley, or Chuck Berry) at this early date. So when later in the novel Aviette Rusanov complains, "That rock'-n'-roll dance, it's absolutely debauched" (ibid., 284), she, too, is musically jumping the gun.
286. Solzhenitsyn, *Cancer Ward*, 134.
287. Ibid., 398.
288. Ibid.

289. Chalmaev, *Solzhenitsyn*, 134.
290. Michel Foucault, "The Politics of Health in the Eighteenth Century," in Rabinow, *The Foucault Reader*, 284.
291. Ibid., 284.
292. In *Fathers and Sons*, Bazarov, a student of medicine, dies following a carelessly performed autopsy. Arthur Hailey's medical melodrama *The Final Diagnosis* (1959) includes a subplot about a student nurse who loses her leg to cancer, and the film *The Doctor* (1991) starring William Hurt tells the story of an arrogant surgeon who develops throat cancer.
293. Sontag, *Illness As Metaphor*, 41.
294. Solzhenitsyn, *Cancer Ward*, 449.
295. Ibid., 392.
296. Ibid., 125.
297. Ibid.
298. Ibid., 289. Yet Vadim possesses some critical sense, for he realized, even when Stalin was still alive, that the Leader's speeches were pleonastic and mediocre: see Nerzhin in *Love the Revolution*.
299. Solzhenitsyn, *Cancer Ward*, 250. "[These are] my traits, as I was before the war…," Solzhenitsyn told Mirra Petrova (Petrova, "Sud'ba avtora," 642).
300. Solzhenitsyn, *Cancer Ward*, 253.
301. Clark, *The Soviet Novel*, 255.
302. Solzhenitsyn, *Cancer Ward*, 207.
303. Ibid., 309.
304. Ibid.
305. Nabokov, *Gogol*, 161.
306. Solzhenitsyn, *Cancer Ward*, 310.
307. Ibid., 320.
308. Ibid., 321.
309. Ibid., 306.
310. Ibid., 438.
311. Ibid.
312. Ibid., 439.
313. Friedrich Nietzsche, *Notes*, in Kaufmann, *The Portable Nietzsche*, 456.
314. Solzhenitsyn, *Cancer Ward*, 447.
315. Ibid., 446.
316. Ibid., 447.
317. Adam Ferguson, *An Essay on the History of Civil Society* (Cambridge: Cambridge University Press, 1995), 56.
318. Solzhenitsyn, "Live Not By Lies!", 565.
319. Ibid., 559.
320. Ibid., 558.

321. Auerbach, *Mimesis*, 522.
322. Solzhenitsyn, *Cancer Ward*, 189.
323. Ibid., 110.
324. Ibid., 109.
325. Ibid.
326. Russell, *A History of Western Philosophy*, 679.
327. Nancy Harstock, "The Feminist Standpoint: Developing the Ground for a Specifically Feminist Historical Materialism," in Sandra Kemp and Judith Squires, eds., *Feminisms* (New York: Oxford University Press, 1997), 154.
328. Solzhenitsyn, *Cancer Ward*, 84.
329. Ibid., 94. A counter-allusion to Lenin's article "A Great Beginning" ("Velikii pochin"; 1919): "Notwithstanding all the laws emancipating woman, she continues to be a domestic slave, because petty housework crushes, strangles, stultifies and degrades her, chains her to the kitchen and the nursery, and she wastes her labour on barbarously unproductive, petty, nerve-racking, stultifying and crushing drudgery. The real emancipation of women, real communism, will begin only where and when an all-out struggle begins ... against this petty housekeeping" (Vladimir Lenin's "A Great Beginning," *marxists.org*, https://www.marxists.org/archive/lenin/works/1919/jun/19.htm).
330. Solzhenitsyn, *Cancer Ward*, 93.
331. Joseph Brodsky, "Catastrophes in the Air," in *Less Than One: Selected Essays* (New York: Farrar, Straus and Giroux, 1986), 297.
332. Solzhenitsyn, *Cancer Ward*, 94.
333. Ibid., 42.
334. Ibid.
335. Ibid.
336. Ibid., 47.
337. Ibid., 103.
338. The reference is to the film *Heroes of Shipka* (*Geroi Shipki*; 1954).
339. Solzhenitsyn, *Cancer Ward*, 316.
340. Ibid., 60.
341. Solzhenitsyn, *Cancer Ward*, 358.
342. Ibid.
343. Solzhenitsyn, *Cancer Ward*, 112.
344. Ibid.
345. Ibid., 34.
346. Ibid., 10.
347. Ibid., 11.
348. "Two Asians" in the English translation (Solzhenitsyn, *Cancer Ward*, 12).
349. Solzhenitsyn, *Sobranie sochinenii*, 3:17.
350. Solzhenitsyn, *Cancer Ward*, 20.

351. Ibid., 521.
352. Ibid., 410.
353. Ibid., 329.
354. Ibid., 489.
355. Ibid., 222.
356. Ibid., 473.
357. Ibid., 470.
358. Ibid., 473–4.
359. Mann, *The Magic Mountain*, 3.
360. Solzhenitsyn, *Cancer Ward*, 492.
361. On April 26, 1966, Tashkent was destroyed by a 5.1 earthquake, after which the city, including the Old Town, was rebuilt along utilitarian Soviet lines. *Cancer Ward* became a commemoration of Tashkent as it once was, and would never be again.
362. Solzhenitsyn, *Cancer Ward*, 492.
363. Ibid., 341.
364. Ibid., 492–3.
365. Ibid., 492.
366. Solzhenitsyn, *Sobranie sochinenii*, 3:410.
367. Solzhenitsyn, *Cancer Ward*, 493. Amended translation.
368. Ibid., 494.
369. Ibid., 492.
370. Ibid., 503.
371. Frazer, *The Golden Bough*, 159.
372. Solzhenitsyn, *Cancer Ward*, 504.
373. Ibid.
374. Jacques Lacan, "The Mirror Stage as Formative of the *I* Function as Revealed in Psychoanalytical Experience," in Jacques Lacan, *Écrits*, trans. Bruce Fink (New York: W. W. Norton, 2006), 75.
375. Ibid., 79.
376. Ibid., 75–6.
377. Nietzsche, *Thus Spoke Zarathustra*, 195.
378. Solzhenitsyn, *Cancer Ward*, 505.
379. L. A. J. R. Houwen, "Animal Parallelism in Medieval Literature and the Bestiaries: A Preliminary Investigation," *Neophilologus* 78, no. 3 (1994): 483.
380. Solzhenitsyn, *Cancer Ward*, 508.
381. Ibid., 505.
382. Ibid., 506.
383. Ibid., 325.
384. Ibid., 507.
385. Ibid., 508.

386. "An old bum's clothes" in the English translation (ibid., 507).
387. Ibid., 509.
388. Ibid.
389. Solzhenitsyn, *The Oak and the Calf*, 478.
390. Solzhenitsyn, *Cancer Ward*, 510.
391. Ibid.
392. Ibid.
393. Ibid.
394. Ibid., 510–11.
395. Ibid., 511.
396. Bataille, *Death and Sensuality*, 143.
397. Francesco Petrarca, *The Sonnets, Triumphs and Other Poems of Petrarch* (London: George Bell and Sons, 1890), 173.
398. Solzhenitsyn, *Cancer Ward*, 515.
399. Ibid., 516.
400. Ibid., 517.
401. Ibid. We recall the picture of the Peter and Paul fortress on Vera's wall.
402. Solzhenitsyn, *Cancer Ward*, 532.
403. Ibid.
404. The definitive Russian text omits two further concluding sentences, which occur in the version of the novel used for the English translation: "An evil man threw tobacco in the Macaque Rhesus's eyes. / Just like that" (ibid., 536).

Chapter Seven

1. Hisham Matar, "The Return. Letter from Libya," *The New Yorker*, April 8, 2013, 46.
2. Ortega y Gasset, *The Revolt of the Masses*, 91.
3. Quoted in Ericson and Klimoff, *The Soul and Barbed Wire*, 174.
4. Solzhenitsyn, Templeton Lecture, 577.
5. Solzhenitsyn, *August 1914*, 578.
6. Walter Besant and Henry James, *The Art of Fiction* (Boston: Cupples and Hurd, 1884), 84.
7. Carl Eric Scott, "Daniel Mahoney and the Truth About Solzhenitsyn," *National Review*, September 18, 2014, http://www.nationalreview.com/Post-Modern-conservative/388303/daniel-mahoney-and-truth-about-solzhenitsyn-carl-eric-scott.
8. Aleksandr Solzhenitsyn, "Interv'iu s Danielem Rondo dlia parizhskoi gazety 'Liberas'on' (Kavendish, 1 noiabria 1983)," in *Publitsistika*, 3:202.
9. Lev Losev, "Velikolepnoe budushchee Rossii. Zametki pri chtenii 'Avgusta Chetyrnadtsatogo' A. Solzhenitsyna," *Kontinent* 42 (1984): 292.

10. Daniel J. Mahoney, *The Other Solzhenitsyn: Telling the Truth About a Misunderstood Writer and Thinker* (South Bend: St. Augustine's Press, 2014), 28.
11. Solzhenitsyn, *August 1914*, 559.
12. By equivalence with *samoupravstvo* or "arbitrary rule." General Nechvolodov characterizes *narodopravstvo* (mistranslated as "the people's rights") as a way for the opposition parties to claim "power for themselves" (Solzhenitsyn, *November 1916*, 904): *Oni govoriat "narodopravstvo," a eto znachit*—*ikh vlast'* (Solzhenitsyn, *Sobranie Sochinenii*, 10:433). A more conventional calque of "democracy" is *narodovlastie*, used, for example, by Kotya Gulai (ibid., 7:372).
13. Ibid., 16:29.
14. Ibid., 9:186.
15. Ibid., 13:101.
16. Ibid., 11:32; 13:101.
17. Ibid., 12:31.
18. Kramer, "A Talk with Solzhenitsyn."
19. Pavel Bogdanovich, *Vtorzhenie v Vostochnuiu Prussiiu v avguste 1914 goda: vospominaniia ofitsera general'nogo shtaba armii generala Samsonova* (Buenos Aires: No Publisher, 1964).
20. Niva (Nivat), *Solzhenitsyn*, 75.
21. Solzhenitsyn, *Invisible Allies*, 67.
22. Solzhenitsyn, *Sobranie sochinenii*, 16:557.
23. Aleksandr Solzhenitsyn, *Stolypin i tsar'; Lenin. Tsiurikh–Petrograd; Nakonets-to revoliutsiia. Glavy iz knigi "Krasnoe Koleso,"* 4 vols. (Ekaterinburg: U-Faktoriia, 2001).
24. Natalia Solzhenitsyna, private communication.
25. Konstantin Dushenko, *Muzy i gratsii. Aforizmy o teatre, muzyke, zhivopisi, kino i prochikh iskusstvakh* (Moscow: Eksmo, 2005), 405.
26. Gray, Aikman, and Kohan, "Russia's Prophet in Exile."
27. Solzhenitsyn, *August 1914*, 223.
28. Losev, "Velikolepnoe budushchee," 296.
29. Solzhenitsyn, *August 1914*, 531.
30. Genette, *Paratexts*, 4.
31. Gray, Aikman, and Kohan, "Russia's Prophet in Exile."
32. Solzhenitsyn, *Sobranie sochinenii*, 14:502.
33. Solzhenitsyn, *August 1914*, 258.
34. Aleksandr Solzhenitsyn, *Lenin v Tsiurikhe. Glavy* (Paris: YMCA-PRESS, 1975).
35. Simon Karlinsky, "'Like Taking the Napoleon Chapters Out of *War and Peace*,'" review of *Lenin in Zurich*, by Aleksandr Solzhenitsyn, *The New York Times*, April 25, 1976.
36. "[Stolypin] was Russia's greatest statesman of the entire twentieth century" (*samyi velikii deiatel' Rossii za ves' XX vek*), Solzhenitsyn told Vladimir Putin in

2000 (Dmitrii Kaistro, "Aleksandr Solzhenitsyn: ushedshie ne ischezaiut," *vesti.ru*, August 4, 2008, https://www.vesti.ru/doc.html?id=198681).
37. The current high school history standards (2013) refer to the Great Russian Revolution (*Velikaiia rossiiskaia revoliutsiia*) of 1917–23 ("Avtory novoi kontseptsii uchebnika istorii ob"edinili Oktiabr'skuiu i Fevral'skuiu revoliutsii v Velikuiu rossiiskuiu," *newsru.com*, October 31, 2013, http://www.newsru.com/russia/31oct2013/uchebnik.html).
38. Solzhenitsyn, "An Interview with Struve," 316.
39. Solzhenitsyn, *Sobranie sochinenii*, 14:469.
40. Solzhenitsyn, *August 1914*, 46.
41. Solzhenitsyn, *November 1916*, 98.
42. Solzhenitsyn, *Sobranie sochinenii*, 14:266.
43. Ibid., 14:286.
44. Solzhenitsyn, *November 1916*, 975.
45. Nataliia Solzhenitsyna, "Kratkie poiasneniia," in Solzhenitsyn, *Sobranie sochinenii*, 14:658; 16:708.
46. Natalia Solzhenitsyna, private communication.
47. Solzhenitsyn, "An Interview with Struve," 315.
48. Solzhenitsyn, *November 1916*, 365.
49. Other than the film script *Tanks Know the Truth!*
50. Ilya Kukulin, "A Prolonged Revanche: Solzhenitsyn and Eisenstein," *Studies in Russian and Soviet Cinema* 5, no. 1 (2011): 88.
51. Kukulin, *Mashiny zashumevshego vremeni*, 314.
52. Kukulin, "A Prolonged Revanche," 74.
53. Solzhenitsyn, *Sobranie sochinenii*, 13:256.
54. Solzhenitsyn, "An Interview with Struve," 316.
55. Solzhenitsyn, *August 1914*, 221.
56. Solzhenitsyn, *Sobranie sochinenii*, 12:535–6.
57. Ibid., 13:409.
58. "Vystavka 'Pravoslavnaia Rus': Romanovy' b'et rekordy po chislu posetitelei," *ntv.ru*, October 11, 2013, http://www.ntv.ru/novosti/721496/.
59. Solzhenitsyn, *The First Circle*, 735.
60. Solzhenitsyn, *August 1914*, 551.
61. Solzhenitsyn, *Sobranie sochinenii*, 11:374.
62. Ibid., 15:603.
63. Solzhenitsyn, *November 1916*, 334.
64. Ibid., 894.
65. Ibid., 20.
66. Ibid., 81.
67. Solzhenitsyn, *August 1914*, 374.
68. Solzhenitsyn, *Sobranie Sochinenii*, 11:556.

69. Tolstoy, *War and Peace*, 860.
70. Solzhenitsyn, "An Interview with Struve," 317.
71. Solzhenitsyn, *August 1914*, 783.
72. Solzhenitsyn, *November 1916*, 137.
73. Solzhenitsyn, *Sobranie sochinenii*, 12:687.
74. Solzhenitsyn, *August 1914*, 650.
75. Remnick, *Resurrection*, 149.
76. Solzhenitsyn, "An Interview with Struve," 325.
77. Aleksandr Shmeman, *Dnevniki. Tetrad' I (ianvar' 1973-noiabr' 1974)*, May 30, 1974, azbuka.ru, https://azbyka.ru/otechnik/Aleksandr_Shmeman/dnevniki/1_1.
78. Solzhenitsyn, *November 1916*, 133.
79. Ibid., 609.
80. Ibid., 627.
81. Ibid., 626.
82. Ibid., 613.
83. Ibid., 633.
84. Ibid.
85. Solzhenitsyn, *Sobranie sochinenii*, 16:93.
86. Solzhenitsyn, *November 1916*, 796.
87. Solzhenitsyn, *Sobranie sochinenii*, 14:512.
88. Ibid., 15:343.
89. Solzhenitsyn, *November 1916*, 121.
90. Solzhenitsyn, *August 1914*, 602.
91. Solzhenitsyn, *Sobranie sochinenii*, 8:220.
92. Solzhenitsyn, *August 1914*, 515.
93. Ibid., 606.
94. Solzhenitsyn, *Sobranie sochinenii*, 8:343.
95. Solzhenitsyn, *August 1914*, 716.
96. Lev Tolstoi, *Polnoe sobranie sochinenii*, vol. 11 (Moscow: Khudozhestvennaia literatura, 1940), 6.
97. Tolstoy, *War and Peace*, 537.
98. Solzhenitsyn, *August 1914*, 716.
99. Ibid.
100. Solzhenitsyn, *Sobranie sochinenii*, 11:644.
101. Aleksandr Solzhenitsyn, "Interv'iu s N. A. Struve ob 'Oktiabre Shestnadtsatogo' dlia zhurnala 'Ekspress' (Kavendish, 30 sentiabria 1984)," in Solzhenitsyn, *Publitsistika*, 3: 279.
102. Solzhenitsyn, *Sobranie sochinenii*, 13:602.
103. Ibid., 11:681.
104. Ibid., 14:529.
105. Ibid., 12:295.

106. Ibid., 11:622.
107. Ibid., 14:337.
108. Ibid., 12:295.
109. Ibid., 11:32.
110. Ibid., 11:147.
111. Ibid.
112. Ibid., 11:191.
113. Ibid., 12:116.
114. Ibid., 13:358.
115. Ibid., 15:316.
116. Ibid., 13:140.
117. Ibid., 14:101.
118. Ibid., 14:528.
119. Ibid., 14:434.
120. Ibid., 11:443.
121. Ibid., 13:87.
122. Ibid., 13:514.
123. Ibid., 12:133.
124. Ibid., 13:359.
125. Ibid., 11:508.
126. Ibid., 12:139.
127. Ibid., 12:705.
128. Ibid., 14:437.
129. Ibid., 13:663.
130. Ibid., 13:127.
131. Ibid., 13:461.
132. Zinaida Gippius, *Siniaia Kniga. Peterburgskii dnevnik. 1914–18* (Belgrade: Russkaia biblioteka, 1929), 119.
133. Nietzsche, *Beyond Good and Evil*, 239.
134. On the down-market side, Valentin Pikul, a jingoistic writer popular with Soviet and post-Soviet audiences, produced a brace of novels that are in stuttering dialogue with the saga: *Demonic Forces* (*Nechistaia sila*; 1979; 1989), in which a priapic Rasputin casts an evil spell on the imperial couple, and *I Have the Honor…* (*Chest' imeiiu*; 1986), in which a Russian staff officer with a passing resemblance to Vorotyntsev joins the Bolsheviks and becomes an international spy. See also *General Samsonov* (a.k.a. *Zhertva. Roman o generale Samsonove*; 1990), a pulp novel by Sviatoslav Rybas.
135. Solzhenitsyn, *Sobranie sochinenii*, 12:138–9.
136. Nietzsche, *The Antichrist*, 639.
137. Philip Norman, *Paul McCartney: The Life* (New York: Little, Brown, 2016), 570.
138. Solzhenitsyn, *August 1914*, 486.
139. Ibid.

140. Ibid., 485.
141. Ibid., 486.
142. Daniel J. Mahoney, "The Wheel Turns," review of *November 1916/Knot II*, by Aleksandr Solzhenitsyn, *The New Criterion* 36, no. 6 (1999), http://www.newcriterion.com/articles.cfm/wheelturns-mahoney-2929.
143. Solzhenitsyn, *August 1914*, 6.
144. Ibid., 4.
145. Ibid., 338.
146. Modeled on Solzhenitsyn's fellow writer and friend Boris Mozhaev: Aleksandr Solzhenitsyn, "S Borisom Mozhaevym," in Boris Mozhaev, *Zemlia zhdet khoziaina: Starye i novye istorii* (Moscow: Russkii put', 2003).
147. Solzhenitsyn, *August 1914*, 339. Like Volodin in *The First Circle* or, for that matter, the author himself.
148. Solzhenitsyn, *November 1916*, 340.
149. Ibid., 113.
150. Ibid., 686.
151. Ibid., 21.
152. Ibid., 23.
153. Solzhenitsyn, *Sobranie sochinenii*, 13:588.
154. Solzhenitsyn, *November 1916*, 35.
155. Ibid., 23.
156. Solzhenitsyn, *August 1914*, 31.
157. Solzhenitsyn, *Sobranie sochinenii*, 12:698.
158. Ibid., 12:697.
159. Ibid., 15:79.
160. Ibid., 16:237.
161. Ibid., 12:141.
162. Solzhenitsyn, *November 1916*, 615.
163. Solzhenitsyn, *Sobranie sochinenii*, 16:96.
164. Solzhenitsyn, *November 1916*, 87.
165. Ibid., 189.
166. Solzhenitsyn, *Sobranie sochinenii*, 11:544.
167. Solzhenitsyn, *November 1916*, 334.
168. Thomas, *Solzhenitsyn*, 487.
169. Solzhenitsyn, *November 1916*, 185.
170. Solzhenitsyn, *Sobranie sochinenii*, 11:173.
171. Ibid., 14:605.
172. Nietzsche, *Thus Spoke Zarathustra*, 300.
173. Solzhenitsyn, *Sobranie sochinenii*, 14:608.
174. Solzhenitsyn, *November 1916*, 617.
175. Ibid., 476–7.

176. Ibid., 23.
177. Ibid.
178. Thomas, *Solzhenitsyn*, 479.
179. Solzhenitsyn, "Interv'iu s Rondo," 197.
180. Solzhenitsyn, *Sobranie Sochinenii*, 16:27.
181. Ibid.
182. Ibid.
183. Solzhenitsyn, *November 1916*, 735–6.
184. Ibid., 162.
185. Ibid., 186.
186. Ibid., 190.
187. Ibid., 186.
188. Ibid., 985.
189. Solzhenitsyn, *August 1914*, 294.
190. Ibid., 814.
191. Solzhenitsyn, *November 1916*, 892.
192. Ibid., 592.
193. Ibid.
194. Solzhenitsyn, *Sobranie Sochinenii*, 12:701.
195. Solzhenitsyn, *November 1916*, 976.
196. Ibid., 294.
197. Ibid., 705.
198. Ibid., 156.
199. Ibid., 130.
200. Solzhenitsyn, *Sobranie Sochinenii*, 11:612.
201. Ibid.
202. Solzhenitsyn, *Sobranie Sochinenii*, 11:544.
203. Solzhenitsyn, "Interv'iu s Eikmanom," 326.
204. Solzhenitsyn, *Sobranie sochinenii*, 11:186.
205. Ibid., 11:237.
206. Ibid., 11:590.
207. Ibid., 11:622.
208. Ibid.
209. Ibid., 12:208.
210. Ibid., 12:766.
211. Ibid.
212. Ibid., 13:168.
213. Ibid., 13:179.
214. Ibid., 13:641.
215. Ibid., 14:304.
216. Ibid., 15:29.

217. Ibid., 15:450.
218. Ibid., 15:517.
219. Ibid., 16:143.
220. Ibid., 15:287.
221. Ibid., 15:482.
222. Ibid., 14:190.
223. Ibid., 12:434.
224. Vladimir Nabokov, *Vremennoe pravitel'stvo i bol'shevistskii perevorot*, http://www.sakharov-center.ru/asfcd/auth/?t=page&num=11161.
225. Mikhail Bulgakov, *The Master and Margarita* (New York: Penguin Books, 1997), 89.
226. Solzhenitsyn, *November 1916*, 642.
227. Solzhenitsyn, *Sobranie Sochinenii*, 10:161.
228. Solzhenitsyn, November 1916, 677.
229. Ibid.
230. Solzhenitsyn, *August 1914*, 577.
231. Ibid., 602.
232. Solzhenitsyn, *Sobranie Sochinenii*, 8:224.
233. Solzhenitsyn, *August 1914*, 606.
234. Ibid., 506.
235. Solzhenitsyn, *Sobranie Sochinenii*, 7:260.
236. Solzhenitsyn, *August 1914*, 217.
237. Ibid., 278.
238. Ibid., 354.
239. Solzhenitsyn, *November 1916*, 564.
240. Ibid., 626.
241. Ibid., 780; *Sobranie sochinenii*, 11:302, 684.
242. Solzhenitsyn, *November 1916*, 147.
243. Ibid., 481.
244. Publisher's Note, Solzhenitsyn, *August 1914*.
245. Julia Kristeva, *Desire in Language: A Semiotic Approach to Literature and Art*, ed. Leon S. Roudiez, trans. Thomas Gora, Alice Jardine, and Léon S. Roudiez (New York: Columbia University Press, 1980), 82.
246. Solzhenitsyn, *November 1916*, 986.
247. Svetlana Sheshunova, "Koleso i Krest," *Posev* 12 (2003), http://www.solzhenitsyn.ru/o_tvorchestve/articles/works/index.php?ELEMENT_ID=1149.
248. Solzhenitsyn, *August 1914*, 10.
249. Solzhenitsyn, *Sobranie sochinenii*, 8:428.
250. Solzhenitsyn, *August 1914*, 796.
251. Ibid., 790.
252. Iurii Lotman, "'Pikovaia dama' i tema kart i kartochnoi igry v russkoi literature nachala XIX veka," in *Izbrannye stat'i* (Tallinn: Aleksandra, 1992), 2:392.

253. René Descartes, *The Philosophical Works* (Cambridge: Cambridge University Press, 1911), 24.
254. Solzhenitsyn, *November 1916*, 986.
255. Ibid., 984.
256. Ibid., 991.
257. Ibid., 993.
258. Ibid.
259. Ibid., 994.
260. Ibid., 994–5.
261. Ibid., 988.
262. Ibid.
263. Ibid., 995.
264. Ibid., 996–9.
265. Ibid., 999.
266. Ibid.
267. Ibid., 1000.
268. I am grateful to Pavel Spivakovsky, who directed my attention to this passage.
269. Solzhenitsyn, *Sobranie sochinenii*, 13:302.
270. Ibid.
271. Tolstoy, *War and Peace*, 588.
272. Ibid., 590.
273. Gray, Aikman, and Kohan, "Russia's Prophet in Exile."
274. Solzhenitsyn, *Sobranie sochinenii*, 16:100.
275. Solzhenitsyn, *August 1914*, 503.
276. Ibid., 175.
277. Solzhenitsyn, *November 1916*, 643.
278. In an interview he gave to Joseph Pearce, Solzhenitsyn agreed that his fictions contain the same "far-off gleam or echo of the *evangelium* in the real world" found in Tolkien's "supposedly 'escapist' fantasies" (Pearce, *A Soul in Exile*, 308).
279. Sheshunova, "Koleso i Krest."
280. Solzhenitsyn, *November 1916*, 360.
281. Solzhenitsyn, *Sobranie sochinenii*, 12:653.
282. Ibid., 12:705.
283. Leonid Dobrokhotov, ed., *Ot Yel'tsina… k Yel'tsinu. Prezidentskaia gonka-96* (Moscow: Terra, 1996), 93.
284. Aleksandr Solzhenitsyn, "Nauka v piratskom gosudarstve," in *Na vozvrate dykhaniia*, 628.
285. Liudmila Gerasimova, "O pravoslavnom prochtenii proizvedenii A. I. Solzhenitsyna," https://eparhia-saratov.ru/Articles/article_old_5830.
286. Arkatova, "The Feminine Eros," 49.
287. Ibid.
288. Solzhenitsyn, *Sobranie sochinenii*, 11:101.
289. Ibid., 11:315.

290. Solzhenitsyn, *November 1916*, 472.
291. Solzhenitsyn, *August 1914*, 447.
292. Ibid.
293. Ibid., 484.
294. I am grateful to Pavel Spivakovsky, who set me thinking along these lines.
295. Solzhenitsyn, *August 1914*, 13.
296. Solzhenitsyn, *November 1916*, 24.
297. Ibid., 280.
298. Ibid., 272.
299. The grandfather of Nikita Struve, Solzhenitsyn's publisher and interviewer.
300. Solzhenitsyn, *Sobranie sochinenii*, 11:245.
301. Solzhenitsyn, *November 1916*, 272.
302. Ibid., 273.
303. Solzhenitsyn, *August 1914*, 111.
304. Ibid., 113.
305. Solzhenitsyn, *November 1916*, 431.
306. Solzhenitsyn, *Sobranie sochinenii*, 11:356.
307. Solzhenitsyn, *November 1916*, 685.
308. Ibid.
309. Ibid., 688.
310. Ibid., 393.
311. Solzhenitsyn, *Sobranie sochinenii*, 12:269.
312. Max Horkheimer and Theodor W. Adorno, "Excursus I: Odysseus or Myth and Enlightenment," in Max Horkheimer and Theodor W. Adorno, *Dialectic of Enlightenment: Philosophical Fragments*, ed. Gunzein Schmid Noerr, trans. Edmund Jephcott (Stanford: Stanford University Press, 2002), 61.
313. Solzhenitsyn, *Sobranie sochinenii*, 11:562.
314. Solzhenitsyn, *August 1914*, 336.
315. Vladimir Solov'ev, *Sochineniia v dvukh tomakh* (Moscow: Mysl', 1988), 2:672.
316. Sanya is impressed by Evgeny Troubetskoi's article "The Debate between Tolstoy and Soloviev Concerning the State" ("Spor Tolstogo i Solov'eva o gosudarstve"; 1912), which discusses this work in highly favorable terms (Solzhenitsyn, *November 1916*, 715).
317. Solzhenitsyn, *August 1914*, 340.
318. Varsonofiev is a fictionalization of the philosopher and jurist Pavel Novgorodtsev (1866–1924).
319. Solzhenitsyn, *November 1916*, 972.
320. Solzhenitsyn, *August 1914*, 340.
321. Ibid., 341.
322. Ibid., 342.
323. Solzhenitsyn, *November 1916*, 714.
324. Ibid., 292.

325. Solzhenitsyn, *August 1914*, 788–9.
326. Ibid., 789.
327. Ibid., 166.
328. Ibid., 167.
329. Ibid., 209.
330. Ibid., 537.
331. Ibid., 732.
332. Solzhenitsyn, *November 1916*, 427.
333. Ibid., 442.
334. Solzhenitsyn, *August 1914*, 426.
335. Ibid., 515.
336. Ibid., 570.
337. Solzhenitsyn, *November 1916*, 890.
338. Solzhenitsyn, *Sobranie sochinenii*, 12:703.
339. Ibid., 14:387.
340. Solzhenitsyn, *August 1914*, 614.
341. Ibid., 660.
342. Solzhenitsyn, *Sobranie sochinenii*, 11:479.
343. Ibid., 16:536.
344. Ibid., 14:434.
345. More specifically, the volumes containing Lenin's correspondence (Natalia Solzhenitsyna, private communication).
346. Solzhenitsyn, *August 1914*, 689.
347. Solzhenitsyn, "Interv'iu s Pivo," 181.
348. Pavel Spivakovskii, *Fenomen A. I. Solzhenitsyna: novyi vzgliad* (Moscow: INION RAN, 1998), 54.
349. Solzhenitsyn, *August 1914*, 227.
350. Solzhenitsyn, *November 1916*, 281.
351. Solzhenitsyn, *Sobranie sochinenii*, 16:235.
352. Solzhenitsyn, *August 1914*, 461–81.
353. Solzhenitsyn, *Sobranie sochinenii*, 14:121.
354. Solzhenitsyn, *August 1914*, 714.
355. Ibid., 175.
356. Solzhenitsyn, *November 1916*, 401.
357. Ibid., 53.
358. Solzhenitsyn, *Sobranie sochinenii*, 13:231.
359. Ibid., 14:124.
360. Ibid., 14:210. In real life, Natalya Anichkova (1896–1975), who was later imprisoned in the gulag but always retained "her lively—even capricious—disposition" (Solzhenitsyn, *Invisible Allies*, 90). She became one of Solzhenitsyn's trusted secret helpers during his struggle with the authorities in the 1960s and 1970s.

361. Solzhenitsyn, *Sobranie sochinenii*, 14:211–12.
362. Solzhenitsyn, *August 1914*, 114.
363. Ibid., 441.
364. Solzhenitsyn, *November 1916*, 204.
365. Ibid., 372.
366. Ibid.
367. Ibid., 142.
368. Ibid., 145.
369. Ibid., 130.
370. Ibid., 131.
371. Solzhenitsyn, *Sobranie sochinenii*, 11:561.
372. Solzhenitsyn, *November 1916*, 408.
373. Ibid.
374. Solzhenitsyn, *August 1914*, 585.
375. Solzhenitsyn, *Sobranie sochinenii*, 11:620.
376. Ibid., 12:167.
377. Sorokin's novel reproduces the diurnal structure of "Ivan Denisovich."
378. Vladimir Sorokin, "Pisatel' Vladimir Sorokin: Moi 'Den' oprichnika'—eto kupanie avtorskogo krasnogo konia," in *Izvestiia*, August 25, 2006.
379. Solzhenitsyn, *August 1914*, 247.
380. Ibid., 807.
381. Ibid., 808.
382. Ibid.
383. Solzhenitsyn, *November 1916*, 335.
384. Solzhenitsyn, *August 1914*, 601.
385. Letter from Friedrich Nietzsche to Franz Overbeck, October 18, 1888, in *Selected Letters of Friedrich Nietzsche*, ed. and trans. Christopher Middleton (Indianapolis: Hackett Publishing Company, 1996), 315.
386. Solzhenitsyn, *Sobranie sochinenii*, 13:602.
387. Solzhenitsyn, *August 1914*, 530.
388. Ibid., 544.
389. Ibid., 565.
390. Ibid., 564.
391. Ibid., 563.
392. Ibid., 576.
393. Ibid., 591.
394. Ibid., 580.
395. Ibid., 581.
396. Ibid., 580.
397. Ibid., 581.
398. Ibid.
399. Ibid., 585.

400. Ibid., 581.
401. Ibid., 559.
402. Ibid., 560.
403. Ibid., 582.
404. Solzhenitsyn, *August 1914*, 644.
405. Solzhenitsyn, *Sobranie sochinenii*, 16:531.
406. Solzhenitsyn, *August 1914*, 815.
407. Ibid., 816.
408. Ibid., 5.
409. Solzhenitsyn, *Sobranie sochinenii*, 16:31.
410. Solzhenitsyn, *August 1914*, 534.
411. Solzhenitsyn, *Sobranie sochinenii*, 12:634.
412. Solzhenitsyn, Nobel Lecture, 520.
413. Solzhenitsyn, *August 1914*, 328–9.
414. The same device is present in *The Road* (see Zakhar Tomchak), "Ivan Denisovich" (see Pavlo), *Cancer Ward* (see Proshka), and *Tanks Know the Truth!* (see the Ukrainian zeks).
415. Solzhenitsyn, *August 1914*, 34.
416. Solzhenitsyn, *November 1916*, 182.
417. Solzhenitsyn, "An Interview with Struve," 312.
418. Solzhenitsyn, *Sobranie sochinenii*, 13:85.
419. Solzhenitsyn, *November 1916*, 18.
420. Solzhenitsyn, *August 1914*, 134.
421. Solzhenitsyn, *November 1916*, 148.
422. Solzhenitsyn, *August 1914*, 60.
423. Solzhenitsyn, *November 1916*, 529.
424. Ibid., 529–30.
425. Ibid., 95.
426. Solzhenitsyn, *August 1914*, 118.
427. Solzhenitsyn, *November 1916*, 30–31.
428. Fedor Tiutchev, *Polnoe sobranie stikhotvorenii* (Leningrad: Sovetskii pisatel', 1987), 191.
429. Solzhenitsyn, *November 1916*, 606.
430. Ibid., 421.
431. Solzhenitsyn, *August 1914*, 198.
432. Solzhenitsyn, *Sobranie sochinenii*, 7:218.
433. Solzhenitsyn, *August 1914*, 197.
434. Solzhenitsyn, *November 1916*, 596.
435. Solzhenitsyn, *August 1914*, 136.
436. Solzhenitsyn, *November 1916*, 386.
437. Solzhenitsyn, *Sobranie sochinenii*, 7:155.

438. Solzhenitsyn, *August 1914*, 141.
439. Tolstoy, *War and Peace*, 151.
440. Solzhenitsyn, *November 1916*, 151.
441. Solzhenitsyn, *Sobranie sochinenii*, 12:92.
442. Ibid.
443. Balk, "Gibel' tsarskogo Petrograda."
444. Solzhenitsyn, "An Interview with Struve," 311.
445. Andrei Nemzer, *"Krasnoe Koleso" Aleksandra Solzhenitsyna. Opyt prochteniia* (Moscow: Vremia, 2011), 92.
446. Ibid., 102.
447. Solzhenitsyn, *November 1916*, 395.
448. Ibid., 749.
449. Solzhenitsyn, *Sobranie sochinenii*, 11:195.
450. Solzhenitsyn, *November 1916*, 48.
451. Solzhenitsyn, *August 1914*, 324.
452. Solzhenitsyn, *November 1916*, 214–15.
453. Solzhenitsyn, *Sobranie sochinenii*, 13:316.
454. Ibid., 11:290.
455. Solzhenitsyn, *November 1916*, 321.
456. Solzhenitsyn, *Sobranie sochinenii*, 13:124.
457. Ibid., 13:586.
458. Ibid., 12:373.
459. Ibid., 14:118.
460. Solzhenitsyn, *November 1916*, 382.
461. Solzhenitsyn, *August 1914*, 99.
462. Ibid., 808.
463. Ibid., 665.
464. Solzhenitsyn, *November 1916*, 906.
465. Ibid., 757.
466. Solzhenitsyn, *August 1914*, 1.
467. Solzhenitsyn, *Sobranie sochinenii*, 16:467.
468. Ibid., 16:468.
469. Alexander Herzen, *My Past and Thoughts* (Berkeley: University of California Press, 1982), 62.
470. Solzhenitsyn, *November 1916*, 162.
471. Natal'ia Reshetovskaia, *Aleksandr Solzhenitsyn i chitaiushchaia Rossiia* (Moscow: Sovetskaia Rossiia, 1990), 16.
472. Solzhenitsyn, *August 1914*, 42.
473. Ibid.
474. Solzhenitsyn, *Sobranie sochinenii*, 14:560.
475. Andrei Bely, *Petersburg* (Bloomington: Indiana University Press, 1978), 163.

476. Arkatova, "The Feminine Eros," 28, 43–44.
477. Liudmila Saraskina, "Aktivisty khaosa v rezhime Action," in *Literaturnaia gazeta*, February 27–March 5, 2002.
478. Solzhenitsyn, *August 1914*, 339.
479. Ibid.
480. Solzhenitsyn, *November 1916*, 295.
481. Solzhenitsyn, *Sobranie sochinenii*, 15:172.
482. Vasilii Rozanov, *Apokalipsis nashego vremeni*, in *Sochineniia* (Leningrad: Vasil'evskii ostrov, 1990), 473.
483. Solzhenitsyn, *November 1916*, 393.
484. Ibid., 501.
485. Ibid., 504.
486. Ibid.
487. Solzhenitsyn, *Sobranie sochinenii*, 11:97.
488. Solzhenitsyn, *August 1914*, 446.
489. Solzhenitsyn, *November 1916*, 445.
490. Ibid.
491. Ibid.
492. Solzhenitsyn, *Sobranie sochinenii*, 14:453–4.
493. Ibid., 16:390.
494. Ibid., 11:106–7.
495. Vladimir Mayakovsky and Boris Pasternak, *The Golden-Mouthed: Selected Poetry*, trans. Andrey Kneller (Otsego: PageFree Publishing, 2004), 31–2.
496. Roman Timenchik, "K simvolike tramvaia v russkoi poezii," in *Trudy po znakovym sistemam. Simvol v sisteme kul'tury*, vol. 21 (Tartu: Tartuskii gosudarstvennyi universitet, 1987), 141
497. Liliia Bel'skaia, "Kak 'zabludivshiisia tramvai' prevratilsia v 'tramvai-ubiitsu,'" *Russkaia rech'* 2 (1998): 20.
498. Vladimir Nabokov, "A Guide to Berlin," *The New Yorker*, March 1, 1976, 27.
499. Solzhenitsyn, *Sobranie sochinenii*, 14:523.
500. Ibid., 14:529.
501. Ibid., 12:11–12.
502. Solzhenitsyn, *November 1916*, 382.
503. Solzhenitsyn, *Sobranie sochinenii*, 14:128.
504. Alexander Kurpin, *The Garnet Bracelet*, in Carl R. Proffer, ed., *An Anthology of Russian Short Stories* (Bloomington: Indiana University Press, 1969), 444.
505. Solzhenitsyn, *Sobranie sochinenii*, 7:39.
506. Solzhenitsyn, *August 1914*, 31–2.
507. Solzhenitsyn, *Sobranie sochinenii*, 12:604.
508. Solzhenitsyn, *August 1914*, 65.
509. Solzhenitsyn, *Sobranie sochinenii*, 12:679.
510. Ibid., 11:9.

511. Solzhenitsyn, *August 1914*, 530.
512. Solzhenitsyn, *Sobranie sochinenii*, 11:483.
513. Solzhenitsyn, *November 1916*, 190.
514. Solzhenitsyn, *August 1914*, 77.
515. Ibid., 83.
516. Ibid., 122.
517. Vsevolod Garshin, *Razskazy*, 10th ed. (St. Petersburg: Literaturnyi Fond, 1905), 433.
518. Solzhenitsyn, *August 1914*, 121.
519. Ibid., 122.
520. Ibid., 124.
521. Fyodor Dostoyevsky, *The Brothers Karamazov. A Novel in Four Parts and an Epilogue*, trans. David McDuff (New York: Penguin Books, 1993), 258.
522. Solzhenitsyn, *August 1914*, 125.
523. Ibid., 794.
524. Solzhenitsyn, *November 1916*, 502.
525. Solzhenitsyn, *August 1914*, 287.
526. Ibid., 364.
527. Solzhenitsyn, *Sobranie sochinenii*, 11:48.
528. Solzhenitsyn, *August 1914*, 11.
529. Ibid., 3.
530. Solzhenitsyn, *November 1916*, 397.
531. Solzhenitsyn, *August 1914*, 3.
532. Leo Tolstoy, *The Cossacks and Other Stories*, trans. David McDuff and Paul Foote (New York: Penguin Books, 2006), 15–16. See also Pushkin's travelogue *A Journey to Arzrum* (*Puteshestvie v Arzrum*; 1830; 1836). Intriguingly, there are also echoes of Sergei Bulgakov's treatise *Unfading Light* (1917): "O mountains of the Caucasus, how well I remember you! As I gazed upon the sparkling glaciers that stretched from sea to sea, the snows that showed crimson in the light of dawn, the peaks thrusting up into the sky, my soul was filled with bliss. . . . I saw rise up before me, like a flame, the first day of Creation" (Sergei Bulgakov, *Svet nevechernii. Sozertsaniia i umozreniia*, http://az.lib.ru/b/bulgakow_s_n/text_1917_svet_nevecherny.shtml).
533. Solzhenitsyn, *August 1914*, 539.
534. Ibid., 4.
535. Tolstoy, *The Death of Ivan Ilyich*, 159.
536. Solzhenitsyn, *August 1914*, 10.
537. Ibid., 6.
538. Ibid., 5.
539. Ibid.
540. Lev Tolstoi, *Polnoe sobranie sochinenii*, vol. 58 (Moscow: Khudozhestvennaia literatura, 1934), 86.

541. Ibid., 58:87.
542. "Dom Tolstogo v Iasnoi Poliane stoit kak-to koso," a chapter title in Viktor Shklovsky's study *Energy of Delusion: A Book on Plot* (*Energiia zabluzhdeniia. Kniga o siuzhete*; 1981).
543. Maxim Gorky, *Reminiscences of Leo Nikolaevich Tolstoy*, trans. S. S. Koteliansky and Leonard Woolf (New York: B. W. Huebsch, 1920), 2.
544. Gorky, *Reminiscences of Tolstoy*, 15.
545. Ibid., 11.
546. Heinz Guderian, *Panzer Leader* (Cambridge: De Capo Press, 2002), 256–7.
547. Solzhenitsyn, *August 1914*, 14–15.
548. The English translation misidentifies *lipy*—lindens as limes.
549. Solzhenitsyn, *August 1914*, 15.
550. Ibid.
551. Ibid.
552. Ibid.
553. Ibid., 16.
554. Ibid., 15
555. Ibid., 16.
556. Ibid.
557. Ibid.
558. Ibid., 17.
559. Solzhenitsyn, Nobel Lecture, 521.
560. Ibid., 522.
561. Solzhenitsyn, *August 1914*, 17.
562. Ibid., 16.
563. Ibid., 334.
564. Ibid.
565. Ibid.
566. Ibid., 339.
567. Ibid., 344.
568. Ibid.
569. Solzhenitsyn, *November 1916*, 93.
570. Solzhenitsyn, *August 1914*, 345.
571. Ibid.
572. Ibid.
573. Ibid., 346
574. Ibid., 347.
575. Ibid.
576. Mikhail Epstein, "The Phoenix of Philosophy: On the Meaning and Significance of Contemporary Russian Thought," *Symposion. A Journal of Russian Thought* 1 (1996): 48.

577. Georgii Gachev, "Natsional'nye obrazy mira," http://www.polit.ru/article/2007/05/24/kulturosob/.
578. Gachev, "Natsional'nye obrazy mira."
579. Georgii Gachev, *Natsional'nye obrazy mira. Amerika v sravnenii s Rossiei i Slavianstvom* (Moscow: Raritet, 1997), 434.
580. Solzhenitsyn, *August 1914*, 348
581. Solzhenitsyn, *November 1916*, 47.
582. Ibid.
583. Dostoyevsky, *The Brothers Karamazov*, 41.
584. Solzhenitsyn, *November 1916*, 9.
585. Solzhenitsyn, *August 1914*, 125, 370.
586. Solzhenitsyn, *Sobranie sochinenii*, 11:102.
587. Solzhenitsyn, *November 1916*, 41.
588. Ibid., 40.
589. Ibid.
590. Ibid., 55.
591. Ibid., 45.
592. Ibid., 43.
593. Ibid., 45.
594. Ibid., 46.
595. Ibid.
596. Ibid.
597. Ibid., 47.
598. Ibid., 49.
599. Ibid., 53.
600. Ibid., 55.
601. Ibid., 55.
602. Nietzsche, *The Antichrist*, 612.
603. Solzhenitsyn, *November 1916*, 46.
604. Valentin Sventsitskii, *Dialogi o vere i neverii*, "Dialog chetvërtyi. O Tserkvi," http://azbyka.ru/otechnik/Valentin_Sventsitskij/dialogi/4.
605. Shmeman, *Dnevniki, Tetrad' II*, May 12, 1975.
606. Solzhenitsyn, *August 1914*, 9.
607. Ibid., 13.
608. Ibid., 64.
609. Ibid., 38–9.
610. Ibid., 39.
611. Solzhenitsyn, *Sobranie sochinenii*, 13:249.
612. Ibid., 16:367.
613. Solzhenitsyn, *November 1916*, 394.
614. Solzhenitsyn, *Sobranie sochinenii*, 13:587.

615. Ibid., 15:606.
616. Solzhenitsyn, *August 1914*, 7.
617. Ibid., 11.
618. Ibid., 48.
619. Ibid., 50.
620. Ibid.
621. Ibid., 49.
622. Ibid., 52.
623. Ibid., 53.
624. Ibid.
625. Dostoyevsky, *The Brothers Karamazov*, 274.
626. Solzhenitsyn, *August 1914*, 53.
627. Solzhenitsyn, *November 1916*, 21.
628. Solzhenitsyn, *August 1914*, 54.
629. Ibid., 55.
630. Ibid., 56.
631. Ibid., 57.
632. Ibid., 55.
633. Solzhenitsyn, *November 1916*, 190.
634. Solzhenitsyn, *August 1914*, 57.
635. Ibid., 58
636. Solzhenitsyn, *Sobranie sochinenii*, 7:69.
637. Solzhenitsyn, *August 1914*, 59.
638. Solzhenitsyn, *November 1916*, 997.
639. Solzhenitsyn, *August 1914*, 57.
640. Ibid., 58.
641. Lev Tolstoi, *Polnoe sobranie sochinenii*, vol. 19 (Moscow: Khudozhestvennaia literatura, 1935), 348.
642. Leo Tolstoy, *Anna Karenina*, 760.
643. Solzhenitsyn, *August 1914*, 58.
644. Solzhenitsyn, *November 1916*, 380.
645. Solzhenitsyn, *August 1914*, 786–90.
646. Solzhenitsyn, *Sobranie sochinenii*, 13:173.
647. Arkatova, "The Feminine Eros," 54.
648. Solzhenitsyn, *Sobranie sochinenii*, 13:602.
649. Solzhenitsyn, "Answers for Tempest."
650. Solzhenitsyn, *August 1914*, 85.
651. Ibid., 361.
652. Ibid., 369.
653. Saraskina, *Solzhenitsyn*, 726.
654. Solzhenitsyn, *August 1914*, 69.

655. Ibid., 272.
656. Ibid., 320.
657. Ibid., 361.
658. Ibid.
659. Ibid., 360.
660. Ibid., 361.
661. Ibid., 388.
662. Ibid., 384.
663. Ibid., 387.
664. Ibid., 390.
665. Ibid., 278.
666. Ibid., 333.
667. Solzhenitsyn, *Sobranie sochinenii*, 7:359.
668. Solzhenitsyn, *August 1914*, 198.
669. Nikita Eliseev, "'Avgust Chetyrnadtsatogo' Aleksandra Solzhenitsyna—skvoz' raznye stekla," *Zvezda* no. 6 (1994): 146.
670. Tolstoy, *War and Peace*, 255.
671. Solzhenitsyn, "Interv'iu s Augshtainom," 287.
672. Solzhenitsyn, *August 1914*, Table of Contents.
673. Ibid., 417.
674. Ibid.
675. Ibid.
676. Ibid., 77.
677. Solzhenitsyn, *Sobranie sochinenii*, 11:702.
678. Solzhenitsyn, *August 1914*, 85.
679. Ibid., 90.
680. Solzhenitsyn, *Sobranie sochinenii*, 11:366.
681. Solzhenitsyn, *August 1914*, 413.
682. Ibid., 130.
683. Ibid., 290.
684. Ibid.
685. Eliseev, "'Avgust Chetyrnadtsatogo' Solzhenitsyna," 146.
686. Solzhenitsyn, *August 1914*, 87.
687. Solzhenitsyn, *Sobranie sochinenii*, 7:99–100.
688. Solzhenitsyn, *August 1914*, 121.
689. Solzhenitsyn, *November 1916*, 706.
690. Solzhenitsyn, *August 1914*, 310.
691. Ibid., 311.
692. Tolstoy, *War and Peace*, 152.
693. Solzhenitsyn, *August 1914*, 12.
694. Solzhenitsyn, *November 1916*, 711.

695. James E. Pontuso, "Why We Need God: Solzhenitsyn's *The Red Wheel*," review of *The Red Wheel*, by Aleksandr Solzhenitsyn, *Modern Age* 56, no. 3 (2014): 26.
696. Solzhenitsyn, *November 1916*, 711.
697. Ibid., 12.
698. Ibid., 288.
699. Solzhenitsyn, *August 1914*, 210.
700. Pontuso, "Why We Need God," 28.
701. Solzhenitsyn, *November 1916*, 891.
702. Ibid., 82.
703. Solzhenitsyn, *August 1914*, 79.
704. Ibid., 310.
705. Ibid., 829.
706. Solzhenitsyn, *November 1916*, 177.
707. Solzhenitsyn, *August 1914*, 127.
708. Solzhenitsyn, *November 1916*, 394.
709. Ibid., 110.
710. Ibid., 85.
711. Ibid., 497.
712. Ibid., 83.
713. Ibid., 383.
714. Solzhenitsyn, *August 1914*, 569.
715. Ibid., 99.
716. Ibid., 92.
717. Solzhenitsyn, *November 1916*, 115.
718. Ibid., 117.
719. Solzhenitsyn, *August 1914*, 133.
720. Ibid., 407.
721. Nemzer, *"Krasnoe Koleso" Solzhenitsyna*, 77.
722. Solzhenitsyn, *Sobranie sochinenii*, 12:166; ibid., 14:295.
723. Solzhenitsyn, *August 1914*, 845.
724. Solzhenitsyn, *November 1916*, 367.
725. Ibid., 113.
726. Solzhenitsyn, *August 1914*, 128.
727. Solzhenitsyn, *November 1916*, 118.
728. Ibid., 116.
729. Ibid., 117.
730. Ibid., 118.
731. Ibid., 119.
732. Ibid., 120.
733. Ibid., 892.
734. Ibid., 122.

735. Ibid., 382.
736. Ibid.
737. Ibid., 382.
738. Ibid., 697.
739. Solzhenitsyn, *Sobranie sochinenii*, 13:67.
740. Solzhenitsyn, *November 1916*, 83.
741. Ibid., 110.
742. Ibid.
743. Ibid., 114.
744. Solzhenitsyn, *Sobranie sochinenii*, 11:267.
745. Ibid., 11:267.
746. Ibid., 11:200.
747. Solzhenitsyn, *November 1916*, 286.
748. Solzhenitsyn, *Sobranie sochinenii*, 9:280.
749. Solzhenitsyn, *November 1916*, 685.
750. Solzhenitsyn, *Sobranie sochinenii*, 10:206.
751. Solzhenitsyn, *August 1914*, 211.
752. Solzhenitsyn, *November 1916*, 389.
753. Ibid.
754. Ibid., 390.
755. Solzhenitsyn, "Author's Note," in *November 1916*.
756. Solzhenitsyn, *November 1916*, 383.
757. Ibid., 385.
758. Ibid., 385–6.
759. Ibid., 388.
760. Solzhenitsyn, *Sobranie sochinenii*, 11:69.
761. Ibid.
762. Solzhenitsyn, *November 1916*, 497.
763. Ibid.
764. Ibid., 501.
765. Ibid.
766. Ibid.
767. Ibid.
768. Solzhenitsyn, *Sobranie sochinenii*, 11:544.
769. Ibid., 12:192.
770. Nemzer, *"Krasnoe Koleso" Solzhenitsyna*, 236–7.
771. Solzhenitsyn, *November 1916*, 202.
772. Solzhenitsyn, *Sobranie sochinenii*, 14:150.
773. Ibid., 12:71.
774. Ibid., 14:508.
775. Ibid., 11:07.

776. Ibid., 16:258.
777. Ibid., 13:177.
778. Solzhenitsyn, "Tri otryvka," 21.
779. Solzhenitsyn, *November 1916*, 594.
780. Ibid., 491.
781. Ibid.
782. Ibid., 596.
783. Ibid., 484.
784. Ibid., 640–41.
785. Solzhenitsyn, *August 1914*, 179–80.
786. Solzhenitsyn, *Sobranie sochinenii*, 10:198.
787. Solzhenitsyn, *November 1916*, 578.
788. Solzhenitsyn, *August 1914*, 182.
789. Ibid.
790. Solzhenitsyn, *November 1916*, 491.
791. Solzhenitsyn, *Sobranie sochinenii*, 12:691.
792. Solzhenitsyn, *November 1916*, 489.
793. Adolf Hitler, *Mein Kampf* (London: Pimlico, 1992), 168.
794. Solzhenitsyn, *August 1914*, 180.
795. Solzhenitsyn, *November 1916*, 489.
796. Aleksandr Zholkovskii, "Bender v Tsiurikhe," *Zvezda*, no. 10, 2011, http://magazines.russ.ru/zvezda/2011/10/zh15.html.
797. Solzhenitsyn, *August 1914*, 180.
798. Solzhenitsyn, *November 1916*, 636.
799. Solzhenitsyn, *August 1914*, 187–8.
800. Ibid., 186.
801. Solzhenitsyn, *November 1916*, 583.
802. Ibid., 580.
803. Ibid., 581.
804. Ibid., 583.
805. Ibid., 637.
806. Ibid., 647.
807. Ibid., 646.
808. Ibid., 657.
809. Ibid., 646.
810. Solzhenitsyn, "Tri otryvka," 20.
811. Aleksandr Solzhenitsyn, "Zërnyshko," Chast' pervaia, Glava 1.
812. Solzhenitsyn, *November 1916*, 645.
813. Ibid., 635.
814. Ibid., 637.
815. Ibid.

816. Ibid., 641.
817. Ibid., 639.
818. Ibid., 643.
819. Ibid., 645.
820. Ibid.
821. Ibid.
822. Ibid., 646.
823. Ibid.
824. Ibid., 648–9.
825. Ibid., 651.
826. Ibid., 658.
827. Ibid.
828. Ibid., 660.
829. Ibid., 661.
830. Ibid., 674.
831. Ibid., 678.
832. Ibid.
833. Ibid.
834. Ibid., 662.
835. Goethe, *Faust*, 52.
836. Johann Wolfgang von Goethe, *Faust: Eine Tragödie, Projekt Gutenberg – DE*, Kapitel 6, http://gutenberg.spiegel.de/buch/-3664/6.
837. Solzhenitsyn, *November 1916*, 805.
838. Bloom, *The Western Canon*, 210–11.
839. Lesley Milne, *The Master and Margarita—A Comedy of Victory* (Birmingham: The Department of Russian Language & Literature, University of Birmingham, 1977), 21.
840. Milne, *The Master and Margarita—A Comedy of Victory*, 7.
841. Zholkovskii, "Bender v Tsiurikhe."
842. Aleksandr Shmeman, *Dnevniki. Tetrad' III (avgust 1975-mai 1976)*, October 17, 1975, azbuka.ru, https://azbyka.ru/otechnik/Aleksandr_Shmeman/dnevniki/3.
843. "Dmitrii Bykov o Solzhenitsyne i russkom natsionalizme," *Otkrytaia Rossiia*, https://openrussia.org/post/view/329/.
844. Ivan Tolstoi and Boris Paramonov, "Ves' ad russkoi istorii," *Radio Svoboda*, July 19, 2015, https://www.svoboda.org/a/27140921.html.
845. Mark Lipovetskii, "Ardis' i sovremennaia russkaia literatura: tridtsat' let spustia," *Novoe literaturnoe obozrenie* 1 (2014), http://www.nlobooks.ru/node/4521.
846. Shmeman, *Dnevniki. Tetrad' I*, May 30, 1974.
847. Shmeman, *Dnevniki. Tetrad' II*, February 16, 1975.
848. Solzhenitsyn, "An Interview with Struve," 309.
849. Solzhenitsyn, "Tri otryvka," 19.

850. Ibid., 21.
851. *Transactions of the Association of Russian-American Scholars in the United States*, vol. XXXVI, 201.0, 128
852. Solzhenitsyn, *November 1916*, 4.
853. Iakov Lur'e, *Posle L'va Tolstogo. Istoricheskie vozzreniia Tolstogo i problemy XX veka*, http://az.lib.ru/t/tolstoj_lew_nikolaewich/text_0360.shtml.
854. Solzhenitsyn, *Sobranie sochinenii*, 14:551.
855. Ibid., 11:529.
856. Ibid., 11:727.
857. Ibid., 14:231.
858. Ibid., 14:233.
859. Ibid., 14:235.
860. Ibid., 14:244.
861. Ibid., 14:291.
862. Ibid., 11:487.
863. Ibid., 13:52.
864. Ibid.
865. Solzhenitsyn, *Sobranie sochinenii*, 13:245.
866. Solzhenitsyn, *November 1916*, 133.
867. Ibid., 470.
868. Solzhenitsyn, *Sobranie sochinenii*, 13:327.
869. Ibid., 14:165.
870. Ibid., 13:697.
871. Georg Hegel, *Science of Logic* (Blackmask Online, 2001), 76.
872. Solzhenitsyn, *Sobranie sochinenii*, 14:86.
873. Ibid., 11:660.
874. Ibid.
875. Ibid., 12:209.
876. Ibid., 12:134.
877. Ibid.
878. Ibid., 14:539.
879. Ibid., 12:57.
880. Ibid., 13:577.
881. Ibid., 11:107.
882. Gustave Le Bon, *The Crowd: A Study of the Popular Mind* (Kitchener: Batoche Books, 2001), 6.
883. Solzhenitsyn, *Sobranie sochinenii*, 13:118.
884. Ibid., 12:57.
885. Le Bon, *The Crowd*, 17–18.
886. Ibid., 18.
887. Ibid., 17.

888. Solzhenitsyn, *Sobranie sochinenii*, 14:578.
889. Ibid., 14:652.
890. Ibid., 15:255.
891. Ibid., 12:28.
892. Ibid., 11:395.
893. Le Bon, *The Crowd*, 6.
894. Solzhenitsyn, *Sobranie sochinenii*, 12:20–21.
895. Ibid., 11:378.
896. Ibid., 12:56–7.
897. Ibid., 11:290.
898. Anonymous, *The Russian Diary of an Englishman. Petrograd, 1915–17* (New York: Robert M. McBride, 1919), 64.
899. Solzhenitsyn, *Sobranie sochinenii*, 12:33.
900. Ibid., 12:379.
901. Ibid., 11:500.
902. Ibid., 11:501.
903. Ibid., 11:577.
904. Ibid., 11:472–5.
905. Ibid., 11:529.
906. Ibid., 15:343.
907. Ibid., 14:215.
908. Ibid., 11:650.
909. Ibid., 11:144.
910. Ibid., 11:513.
911. Ibid., 11:648.
912. Ibid., 11:505.
913. Le Bon, *The Crowd*, 44.
914. Solzhenitsyn, *Sobranie sochinenii*, 11:507.
915. Ibid., 11:209.
916. Ibid., 11:383–4.
917. Ibid., 13:144.
918. Patrice Gueniffey, *Bonaparte: 1769–1802* (Cambridge: The Belknap Press, 2015), 97.
919. Solzhenitsyn, *Sobranie sochinenii*, 11:632.
920. Ibid., 11:627.
921. Ibid., 11:532.
922. Ibid., 11:530.
923. Ibid., 13:176.
924. Ibid., 13:173.
925. Ibid., 13:120.
926. Ibid., 13:121.
927. Ibid., 13:122.

928. George Steiner, *Tolstoy or Dostoevsky: An Essay in Contrast* (London: Faber and Faber, 1989), 105.
929. Solzhenitsyn, *Sobranie sochinenii*, 16:557.
930. Ibid.
931. Ibid., 16:558.
932. Ibid.
933. Ibid.
934. Ibid.
935. Ibid.
936. Nikolai Gogol, *The Collected Tales of Nikolai Gogol*, trans. and annot. Richard Pevear and Larissa Volokhonsky (New York: Vintage, 1999), 50.
937. Nemzer, *"Krasnoe Koleso" Solzhenitsyna*, 326.
938. Solzhenitsyn, *Sobranie sochinenii*, 16:558.
939. Ibid.
940. Ibid., 16:559.
941. Ibid.
942. Nikolay Gogol, *Dead Souls. A Poem*, trans. Robert A. Maguire (New York: Penguin Books, 2004), 282–3.
943. Solzhenitsyn, *Sobranie sochinenii*, 16:559.
944. Nemzer, *"Krasnoe Koleso" Solzhenitsyna*, 124n.
945. Solzhenitsyn, *August 1914*, 14.
946. Katya Hokanson, *Writing at Russia's Border* (Toronto: University of Toronto Press, 2008), 225.
947. Solzhenitsyn, *Sobranie sochinenii*, 16:558.
948. Solzhenitsyn, *August 1914*, 543.
949. Ibid., 438.

Chapter Eight

1. Remnick, *Resurrection*, 155–6.
2. Zhores Medvedev, *Solzhenitsyn i Sakharov* (Moscow: Prava cheloveka, 2002), 99.
3. Dalya Alberge, "Alexander Solzhenitsyn's 'Last Stories' Will Appear in English at Last," *The Observer*, June 11, 2011, http://www.guardian.co.uk/books/2011/jul/24/alexander-solzhenitsyn-short-stories.
4. Adam Kirsch, "The Harsh Taste of Apricots," review of *Apricot Jam and Other Stories*, by Aleksandr Solzhenitsyn, *The New Statesman*, October 31, 2011, http://www.newstatesman.com/books/2011/10/apricot-jam-solzhenitsyn-ivan.
5. Lisa Ryoko Wakamiya, *Locating Exiled Writers in Contemporary Russian Literature* (New York: Palgrave Macmillan, 2009), 94.
6. Aleksandr Solzhenitsyn, "Zhelyabuga Village," in *Apricot Jam*, 216.
7. Solzhenitsyn, "Fracture Points," 334.

8. Mikhail Golubkov, "Na izlomakh. Russkii natsional'nyi kharakter v tvorchestve A. I. Solzhenitsyna," http://www.philol.msu.ru/~xxcentury/st_golubkov2.htm.
9. Aleksandr Solzhenitsyn, "Nastenka," in Solzhenitsyn, *Apricot Jam*, 101.
10. Aleksandr Solzhenitsyn, "Ego," in Solzhenitsyn, *Apricot Jam*, 16.
11. Aleksandr Solzhenitsyn, "The New Generation," in *Apricot Jam*, 63.
12. Solzhenitsyn, "Nastenka," 91. One almost wishes that Solzhenitsyn had employed the word "box" (*iashchik*) instead of "appliance" (*pribor*—see Solzhenitsyn, *Sobranie sochinenii*, 1:356), which would have nailed down the defamiliarizing effect.
13. Solzhenitsyn, "Apricot Jam," in *Apricot Jam*, 13.
14. Volkov, *The Magical Chorus*, 80.
15. Solzhenitsyn, "Ego," 30.
16. Ibid., 23.
17. Ibid., 25.
18. Ibid., 29.
19. Ibid., 31.
20. In medical terms, Ektov experiences an attack of adductor spasmodic dysphonia, or the involuntary tightening of the vocal cords. The miniature misunderstanding that ensues recalls the organizing plot twist in Yuri Tynianov's novella "Lieutenant Kijé" ("Podporuchik Kizhe"; 1927), set in the reign of Emperor Paul I, in which a clerk's slip of the pen results in the eponymous officer's bureaucratic materialization.
21. Solzhenitsyn, "Ego," 41.
22. Solzhenitsyn, *Sobranie sochinenii*, 1:279.
23. Solzhenitsyn, "Ego," 27.
24. Ibid., 40.
25. Ibid., 27.
26. Ibid., 35. The English translation reads "the Chinese," which is an anachronism.
27. Ibid., 34. Though in "A Reflection on the Vendée Uprising" ("Slovo o Vandeiskom vosstanii"; 1993), Solzhenitsyn refers to the Tambov rebellion and other peasant revolts of the civil war period as "our Vendée" (Aleksandr Solzhenitsyn, "A Reflection on the Vendée Uprising," in Ericson and Mahoney, *The Solzhenitsyn Reader*, 604).
28. Alexander Pushkin, *The Captain's Daughter*, in *The Captain's Daughter and Other Stories*, trans. Natalie Duddington and T. Keane (New York: Vintage, 2012), 139.
29. Solzhenitsyn, "Ego," 27.
30. Ibid., 43–4. The order for Solzhenitsyn's arrest in 1945 was signed by a Captain Libin of Department No. 4, Second Directorate of the NKGB (Vladimir Radzishevskii, "Kommentarii," in Solzhenitsyn, *Sobranie sochinenii*, 1:631).
31. See chapter two.
32. Solzhenitsyn, "Ego," 49.
33. Ibid.
34. Ibid., 51.

35. Judith Butler, *Gender Trouble: Feminism and the Subversion of Identity* (New York: Routledge, 1999), 179.
36. Solzhenitsyn, "Ego," 50.
37. Ibid., 56–7.
38. Ibid., 53.
39. Ibid., 44.
40. Solzhenitsyn, *The Oak and the Calf*, 115n.1. A comment occasioned by Zhukov's 1965 visit to the Central Writers' Club in Moscow, which was witnessed by Solzhenitsyn. The same event is mentioned in "Times of Crisis," but from the marshal's perspective: "The Moscow intelligentsia ... applauded furiously. ... That was something to remember!" (Aleksandr Solzhenitsyn, "Times of Crisis," in Solzhenitsyn, *Apricot Jam*, 280). One imagines the author kept his arms resolutely folded.
41. Gueniffey, *Bonaparte*, 295.
42. Georgii Zhukov, *Vospominaniia i razmyshleniia. V 3 tomakh*, 10-e izdanie, dopolnennoe po rukopisi avtora (Moscow: Novosti, 1990). To assist him in his writing, Solzhenitsyn's Zhukov requests access to documents from the KGB archives, but is told that they have been destroyed "as being without any historical significance" (Solzhenitsyn, "Times of Crisis," 281). The KGB used the same justification when in 1990 it incinerated the 105 volumes of Solzhenitsyn's case file as lacking "historical or operational significance": somebody inside the Lubyanka must have been getting worried! (Martin Ebon, *KGB: Death and Rebirth* [Westport: Praeger Publishers, 1994], 88).
43. Solzhenitsyn, "Times of Crisis," 233.
44. Ibid., 231.
45. Ibid.
46. Ibid., 232.
47. Ibid.
48. Ibid., 247.
49. See: ... *Odin podborodok chego stoit, cheliust'!* ..., in Solzhenitsyn, *Sobranie sochinenii*, 1:314. The English text reads: "Give him your hand and he'll want your whole arm!" (Solzhenitsyn, "Times of Crisis," 256).
50. Solzhenitsyn, "Times of Crisis," 256.
51. Ibid., 241.
52. Napoleon Bonaparte, *Clisson and Eugénie* (London: Gallic Books, 2009), 13.
53. Solzhenitsyn, "Times of Crisis," 231. Though there *is* a connection to Napoleon's marshals Jean Lannes (also a peasant's son), Joachim Murat (son of an innkeeper), and Michel Ney (son of a cooper).
54. Solzhenitsyn, "Times of Crisis," 232.
55. Ibid., 239–41.
56. Ibid., 241.
57. Philip Dwyer, *Napoleon: The Path to Power* (New Haven: Yale University Press, 2007), 215.

58. Solzhenitsyn, "Times of Crisis," 245.
59. Ibid., 246.
60. Ibid., 246–7.
61. Ibid., 246.
62. Solzhenitsyn, *Sobranie sochinenii*, 1:307.
63. Solzhenitsyn, "Times of Crisis," 246.
64. Ibid., 245.
65. Ibid., 246.
66. Ibid., 249.
67. Ibid., 252.
68. Ibid., 255. The text passes over in silence Operation Mars, the offensive against the Rzhev salient west of Moscow carried out by the Western and Kalinin Fronts and coordinated by the marshal simultaneously with the double envelopment at Stalingrad. David Glantz describes this operation as "Zhukov's greatest defeat." However, Glantz's eponymous study appeared in 1999, four years after the story was published; a Russian edition came out in 2006. David L. Glantz, *Zhukov's Greatest Defeat: The Red Army's Epic Disaster in Operation Mars, 1942* (Lawrence: The University Press of Kansas, 1999). Other historians maintain that Operation Mars was merely an "ancillary operation"—see Antony Beevor, *The Second World War* (New York: Little, Brown and Company, 2012), 370.
69. Solzhenitsyn, "Times of Crisis," 250.
70. Ibid., 259.
71. Ibid., 253.
72. Ibid., 259.
73. Ibid., 266.
74. Ibid., 264.
75. Ibid., 267.
76. Ibid., 272.
77. Nikita Khrushchev, *Khrushchev Remembers*, trans. and ed. Strobe Talbot (Boston: Little, Brown, 1970), 337–8.
78. Solzhenitsyn, "Times of Crisis," 274.
79. Ibid.
80. Solzhenitsyn, "Times of Crisis," 276.
81. Ibid., 284.
82. Joseph Brodsky, "On the Death of Zhukov," in *Collected Poems in English*, trans. Jonathan Aaron et al. (New York: Farrar, Straus and Giroux, 2002), 85.
83. Aleksandr Solzhenitsyn, "Iosif Brodskii—izbrannye stikhi. Iz 'Literaturnoi kollektsii,'" *Novyi mir* 12 (1999), http://magazines.russ.ru/novyi_mi/1999/12/solgen.html.
84. Solzhenitsyn, "The New Generation," 62.
85. Ibid., 63.

86. Ibid., 62.
87. Ibid., 61.
88. Ibid., 64. See Ektov's forced epiphany that the "Hunnish" Bolsheviks are "a powerful generation" (Solzhenitsyn, "Ego").
89. Ibid., 60.
90. Ibid., 66.
91. Ibid.
92. Ibid., 67.
93. Ibid.
94. Ibid., 68.
95. Ibid.
96. Ibid., 69.
97. Ibid.
98. Ibid., 71.
99. Ibid., 61.
100. Ibid., 64.
101. Ibid., 60.
102. Gogol, *Dead Souls*, 6.
103. Solzhenitsyn, "The New Generation," 69.
104. Ibid., 72.
105. Solzhenitsyn, *Sobranie sochinenii*, 1:344.
106. Solzhenitsyn, "The New Generation," 73.
107. Solzhenitsyn, "Nastenka," 76.
108. Ibid., 78.
109. Ibid.
110. Ibid., 79.
111. Ibid., 81.
112. Ibid., 83.
113. Ibid., 86.
114. Ibid., 88.
115. Ibid., 91.
116. Ibid., 86.
117. Ibid., 92.
118. Ibid., 91.
119. Ibid.
120. Ibid., 92.
121. Ibid.
122. Ibid.
123. Ibid.
124. Ibid. Solzhenitsyn made a similar point about the Rostovians' "horrible" Russian to his biographer Michael Scammell: "Rostov, of course, delayed my linguistic

development. ... It was impossible to acquire proper Russian there. It was by a miracle and thanks to my own hard work that I eventually learned it" (Scammell, *Solzhenitsyn*, 109).

125. Solzhenitsyn, "Nastenka," 93.
126. Solzhenitsyn, "Nastenka," 94.
127. Ibid.
128. Ibid., 97.
129. Ibid., 104.
130. Ibid., 105. Anastasia Dmitrievna is modelled on Anastasia Grunau, Solzhenitsyn's Russian literature teacher in fifth–seventh grade.
131. Ibid., 109–10.
132. Ibid., 111.
133. Ibid., 101.
134. Solzhenitsyn, *Sobranie sochinenii*, 1:364.
135. Kirsch, "The Harsh Taste of Apricots."
136. Solzhenitsyn, "Apricot Jam," 6.
137. Kornei Chukovsky, "Literaturnoe chudo," in Chukovskaia, *Zapiski*, 2:768.
138. Solzhenitsyn, "Apricot Jam," 6.
139. Solzhenitsyn, *Sobranie sochinenii*, 1:375.
140. Letter from Varlam Shalamov to Solzhenitsyn, November 1962, 135.
141. In Ivan Denisovich's barrack, "two hundred men slept on fifty bug-ridden bunks" (Solzhenitsyn, *Ivan Denisovich*, 7).
142. Solzhenitsyn, "Apricot Jam," 2.
143. Ibid., 9.
144. Isaiah Berlin, *Personal Impressions* (Harmondsworth: Penguin Books, 1982), 194.
145. Solzhenitsyn, "Apricot Jam," 10.
146. Ibid., 12.
147. Ibid.
148. Ibid., 13.
149. See Friedrich Nietzsche in "Toward the Teaching of Style" (1882): "The richness of life reveals itself through a *richness of gestures*. One must *learn* to feel everything—the length and retarding of sentences, interpunctuations, the choice of words, the pausing, the sequence of arguments—like gestures" (Lou Salomé, *Nietzsche*, trans. and ed. Siegfried Mandel [Urbana: University of Illinois Press, 2001], 77).
150. Solzhenitsyn, "Apricot Jam," 15–16.
151. Ibid., 15.
152. Ibid., 19.
153. Ibid.
154. Solzhenitsyn, *Sobranie sochinenii*, 1:385.

155. Solzhenitsyn, "Apricot Jam," 11.
156. Ibid., 12.
157. Ibid.
158. Ibid., 11.
159. Ibid., 20.
160. Ibid.
161. Ibid., 17.
162. Solzhenitsyn, *Sobranie sochinenii*, 1:383.
163. See Khan Mamai, the Mongol potentate who was defeated at Kulikovo.
164. Solzhenitsyn, "No Matter What," 341.
165. Ibid., 346.
166. Ibid.
167. Ibid., 344.
168. Ibid., 345.
169. Ibid.
170. Ibid., 348.
171. *Russia in Collapse* offers up the surreal image of "a metal-and-glass mountain of trash" towering above a village next to one of the Angara dams (Ericson and Mahoney, *The Solzhenitsyn Reader*, 469).
172. Ibid., 353.
173. Ibid., 352.
174. Ibid., 353.
175. Ibid., 352.
176. Ibid., 353.
177. Ibid.
178. Ibid., 356.
179. Ibid., 350.
180. Ibid., 351.
181. Ibid., 350.
182. Ibid., 362.
183. Ibid., 355. One of the English borrowings selected by the writer for special censure in his *Russian Dictionary for the Expansion of the Language* (Solzhenitsyn, *Russkii slovar' iazykovogo rasshireniia*, 3).
184. Solzhenitsyn, "No Matter What," 354.
185. Ibid., 356.
186. Ibid., 358.
187. Ibid.
188. Ibid.
189. Ibid.
190. Ibid., 362.
191. Ibid.

192. Ibid., 365.
193. Solzhenitsyn, "Fracture Points, 312–13.
194. Dmitry's blue-collar dad, a low information communist, "would get very angry" when the noble-born Mrs. Yemtsov spoke French to her mother (ibid., 288), whereas in *The First Circle*, the widowed Mrs. Volodin is able to teach her son that language. Granted, her revolutionary husband is heroically dead.
195. Ibid., 287.
196. Ibid., 310.
197. Ibid., 291.
198. Ibid., 293.
199. Ibid., 301.
200. Ibid., 309.
201. Ibid., 312.
202. Ibid., 296.
203. Vladimir Bondarenko, "Smert' proroka," *Zavtra*, August 20, 2008.
204. Solzhenitsyn, "Fracture Points, 316.
205. Ibid., 318.
206. Ibid., 320.
207. Ibid., 326.
208. Ibid., 338.
209. Ibid., 337.
210. Ibid., 340.
211. Ibid.
212. Ibid., 337.
213. Ibid., 328.
214. Ibid., 314.
215. Ibid., 331.
216. Ibid., 340.
217. Ibid.
218. Ibid., 337.
219. Ibid., 339.
220. Solzhenitsyn, *Sobranie sochinenii*, 1:441.
221. Solzhenitsyn, "Fracture Points, 315.
222. Alana Eldridge, "Writing Visual History into *La Comédie humaine*: Balzac and the Napoleonic Myth," in *European Studies Conference Selected Proceedings* (University of Nebraska at Omaha, 2007), http://www.unomaha.edu/esc/2007Proceedings/Eldrige_Balzac.pdf. Balzac was one of the authors Solzhenitsyn had read as a young man (Natalia Solzhenitsyna, private communication).
223. Cyril Connolly, *The Observer*, March 7, 1937.
224. Solzhenitsyn, "Zhelyabuga Village," 213.
225. Ibid., 172.

226. Ibid., 177.
227. Ibid., 190, 199.
228. Ibid., 190.
229. Ibid., 200.
230. Ibid., 188.
231. Ibid., 174.
232. Ibid., 199.
233. Ibid., 186.
234. Ibid., 179.
235. Ibid., 208.
236. Ibid., 177.
237. The real-life Private Shukhov, who inspired some of the hero's traits in "Ivan Denisovich" (Solzhenitsyn, "An Interview with Struve," 307–8).
238. Solzhenitsyn, "Zhelyabuga Village," 178.
239. Ibid., 180.
240. Ibid., 181.
241. Ibid., 182.
242. Ibid., 186.
243. Ibid., 198.
244. Ibid., 182.
245. Ibid., 198.
246. Ibid., 184.
247. Ibid., 178.
248. Ibid., 175.
249. Ibid., 181.
250. Ibid., 180.
251. Ibid., 177. Before the battle of Kursk, "all soldiers had to practice chemical defense, wearing uncomfortable gas masks for up to eight hours at a time in the increasingly warm weather of early summer" (David M. Glantz and Jonathan M. House, *The Battle of Kursk* [Lawrence: University Press of Kansas, 1999], 77).
252. Solzhenitsyn, "Zhelyabuga Village," 196.
253. Ibid.
254. Ibid., 197.
255. Solzhenitsyn, *Sobranie sochinenii*, 1:460.
256. Solzhenitsyn, "Zhelyabuga Village," 201–2.
257. Ibid., 205.
258. Ibid., 174. On October 15, 1942 the Soviet high command ordered the creation of a twenty-five kilometer zone behind the front line from which the civilian population was to be removed. The order was confirmed on April 21, 1943 in the run-up to the battle of Kursk (Glantz and House, *The Battle of Kursk*, 31).

259. Solzhenitsyn, "Zhelyabuga Village," 174.
260. Ibid., 194.
261. Ibid., 209.
262. Ibid., 210.
263. Ibid., 208.
264. Ibid., 210.
265. Ibid., 213.
266. Ibid., 216.
267. Ibid., 223.
268. Ibid., 215.
269. Ibid., 222.
270. Solzhenitsyn, *Sobranie sochinenii*, 1:475.
271. Solzhenitsyn, "Zhelyabuga Village," 216.
272. *Convallaria majalis* ("lily of May"). See May 9, V-Day in Russia).
273. Solzhenitsyn, "Zhelyabuga Village," 217.
274. Ibid., 219.
275. Ibid., 220.
276. George Packer, "Don't Look Down: The New Depression Journalism," *The New Yorker*, April 29, 2013, 74.
277. Solzhenitsyn, "Zhelyabuga Village," 227.
278. Ibid., 223.
279. Ibid., 220.
280. Ibid., 230.
281. Ibid., 222.
282. Friedrich Nietzsche, *Human, All-Too-Human*, in Kaufmann, *The Portable Nietzsche*, 60–61.
283. Solzhenitsyn, "Interv'iu s Pivo," 176. As in *August 1914*, the East Prussian toponyms in "Adlig Schwenkitten" have a military resonance that predates both world wars: in the spring and summer of 1807 Napoleon completed the destruction of the armies of the Fourth Coalition after a series of hard-fought battles in the area south of Königsberg.
284. Julia Kristeva, "Word, Dialogue and Novel," in Toril Moi, ed., Léon S. Roudiez and Sean Hand, trans., *The Kristeva Reader* (New York: Columbia University Press, 1986), 48.
285. Aleksandr Solzhenitsyn, "Adlig Schwenkitten," in Solzhenitsyn, *Apricot Jam*, 114.
286. Ibid., 170.
287. Ibid., 114.
288. Ibid., 165.
289. Ibid., 166.
290. Ibid., 169.
291. Ibid.

292. Michael Nicholson, "*Apricot Jam and Other Stories* by Aleksandr Solzhenitsyn—Review," *The Guardian*, November 4, 2011.
293. Solzhenitsyn, "Adlig Schwenkitten," in Solzhenitsyn, *Apricot Jam*, 119.
294. Ibid., 126.
295. Ibid., 161.
296. Solzhenitsyn, *Sobranie sochinenii*, 1:521.
297. Iurii Kublanovskii, "Proza zrimaia, slyshimaia, oboniaemaia... Opyt prochteniia voennykh rasskazov Aleksandra Solzhenitsyna," in Struve and Moskvin, *Mezhdu dvumia iubileiami*, 516.
298. Kublanovskii, "Proza zrimaia," 517.
299. Auerbach, *Mimesis*, 11.
300. Solzhenitsyn, "Adlig Schwenkitten," 121.
301. Ibid., 132.
302. Ibid., 114.
303. Ibid., 122.
304. Ibid.
305. A mistranslation: Ishchukov had despoiled the *gravestones*. See: *V Pol'she nemetskie voennye nadgrob'ia s Piatnadtsatogo goda stoiali Ishchukov, nachal'nik sviazi, na Nareve vyvorachival ikh, valial,*—mstil (Solzhenitsyn, *Sobranie sochinenii*, 1:490).
306. Solzhenitsyn, "Adlig Schwenkitten," 117.
307. Ibid., 116.
308. Ibid., 130.
309. Nietzsche, *Thus Spoke Zarathustra*, 340.
310. Solzhenitsyn, "Adlig Schwenkitten," 128.
311. Ibid., 126.
312. Ibid. In this regard, the major is even more austere that the austere Vorotyntsev, who during the battle of Tannenberg, "with his last remaining strength ... took off his belt, tugged off his boots, tucked his revolver under the feather pillow, put matches handy, blew out the lamp, and finally sank into the luxurious softness" (*August 1914*, 210).
313. Solzhenitsyn, "Adlig Schwenkitten," 127.
314. Solzhenitsyn, "Zhelyabuga Village," 208.
315. Solzhenitsyn, "Adlig Schwenkitten," 115.
316. Ibid., 128.
317. Ibid., 114–15.
318. Homer, *The Iliad*, trans. Robert Fagles (New York: Penguin Books, 1991), 483.
319. Gérard Genette, "Boundaries of Narrative," *New Literary History* 8, no. 1 (1976): 6.
320. Joseph L. Henderson, "Ancient Myths and Modern Man," in Carl G. Jung, ed., *Man and His Symbols* (New York: Dell Publishing, 1964), 99.
321. Solzhenitsyn, "Adlig Schwenkitten," 141.
322. Jolande Jacobi, "Symbols in Individual Analysis," in Jung, *Man and His Symbols*, 328.

323. Solzhenitsyn, "Adlig Schwenkitten," 141.
324. Ibid.
325. Ibid.
326. Ibid., 169.
327. *La Chanson de Roland*, trans. Léon Gautier (New York: Henry Holt, 1885), 189.
328. Solzhenitsyn, "Adlig Schwenkitten," 169.
329. Ibid., 117.
330. Ibid., 170.
331. Ibid.
332. Auerbach, *Mimesis*, 101.
333. Solzhenitsyn, "Adlig Schwenkitten," 146.
334. Ibid., 150.
335. Ibid., 132.
336. Ibid., 133.
337. T. S. Eliot, "*Ulysses*, Order and Myth," *The Dial* 75, no. 3 (1923): 483.
338. Solzhenitsyn, "Adlig Schwenkitten," 140.
339. Aleksandr Solzhenitsyn, "Krokhotki," *Novyi mir* 1 (1997), http://magazines.russ.ru/novyi_mi/1997/1/solg.html.
340. Saraskina, *Solzhenitsyn*, 851.
341. Aleksandr Solzhenitsyn, "The Larch," in Ericson and Mahoney, *The Solzhenitsyn Reader*, 626. See Varlam Shalamov's prose poem "The Resurrection of the Larch" ("Voskreshenie listvennitsy"; 1966), in which the conifer is described as "a tree of the Kolyma, a tree of the concentration camps." Varlam Shalamov, *Kolymskie rasskazy* (Moscow: Sovetskaia Rossia, 1992), 2:260.
342. I am grateful to Pavel Spivakovsky for this insight.
343. Aleksandr Solzhenitsyn, "Lightning," in Ericson and Mahoney, *The Solzhenitsyn Reader*, 626.
344. Aleksandr Solzhenitsyn, "Shame," in Ericson and Mahoney, *The Solzhenitsyn Reader*, 630.
345. Solzhenitsyn, "Shame," 630.
346. Aleksandr Solzhenitsyn, "Growing Old," in Ericson and Mahoney, *The Solzhenitsyn Reader*, 629.
347. Ibid.
348. Ibid.
349. Aleksandr Solzhenitsyn, "Nocturnal Thoughts," in Ericson and Mahoney, *The Solzhenitsyn Reader*, 633.
350. Sontag, *Illness As Metaphor*, 9.
351. Aleksandr Solzhenitsyn, "The Curtain," in Ericson and Mahoney, *The Solzhenitsyn Reader*, 631.
352. Aleksandr Solzhenitsyn, "A Prayer for Russia," in Ericson and Mahoney, *The Solzhenitsyn Reader*, 634.

353. Solzhenitsyn, "A Prayer for Russia," 634.
354. Solzhenitsyn, *Sobranie sochinenii*, 1:571.

Chapter Nine

1. Vidal, "The Top Ten Best Sellers," 83.
2. Ibid., 82.
3. Ibid., 83.
4. Ibid.
5. Ibid., 82.
6. Daniel J. Mahoney, "Traducing Solzhenitsyn," *First Things*, August/September 2004, http://www.firstthings.com/article/2007/01/traducing-solzhenitsyn-36.
7. Vladimir Bushin, *Genii pervogo plevka* (Moscow: Algoritm, 2005).
8. Vladimir Voinovich, *Portret na fone mifa* (Moscow: EKSMO-Press, 2002).
9. Joseph Conrad, *Lord Jim. A Tale* (Edinburgh/London: William Blackwood, 1900), 349.
10. Quoted in Jean-Claude Risset, "Composing Sounds with Computers," in John Paynter et al., *Companion to Contemporary Musical Thought* (London: Routledge, 1992), 1:590.
11. Friedrich Nietzsche, *Nietzsche Contra Wagner: Out of the Files of a Psychologist*, in Kaufmann, *The Portable Nietzsche*, 668.
12. Solzhenitsyn, *Spiegel* interview.
13. Charles Baudelaire, *Les Fleurs du mal* (Paris: Éditions Garnier Frères, 1961), 220.
14. Solzhenitsyn, *The Oak and the Calf*, 7.
15. Solomon Volkov, *The Magical Chorus: A History of Russian Culture from Tolstoy to Solzhenitsyn* (New York: Alfred A. Knopf, 2008), 125.
16. Clark, *The Soviet Novel*, 3.
17. Edward J. Brown, *Russian Literature Since the Revolution*, rev. ed. (Cambridge: Harvard University Press, 1982), 15.
18. Solzhenitsyn, *The Oak and the Calf*, 8.
19. Ibid., 7.
20. Aleksandr Solzhenitsyn, "Press-konferentsiia v Parizhe (10 aprelia 1975)," in *Publitsistika*, 2:239–240.
21. Christopher Hitchens, "The Man Who Kept on Writing."
22. Jauss, "Literary History," 13.
23. Mark Lipovetsky, *Russian Post-Modernist Fiction: Dialogue with Chaos* (New York: M. E. Sharp, 1999), 205.
24. Evgenii Bershtein and Jesse Hadden, "The Sorokin Affair Five Years Later On Cultural Policy in Today's Russia" [sic], *ArtMargins* [Online], June 26, 2007,

http://www.artmargins.com/index.php/featured-articles-sp-829273831/121-the-sorokin-affair-five-years-later-on-cultural-policy-in-todays-russia.
25. That is, the stories published in *Novy Mir* in 1962–6.
26. Georg Lukács, *Solzhenitsyn* (London: The Merlin Press, 1970), 33.
27. Octavio Paz, "Gulag: Between Isaiah and Job," in *On Poets and Others* (London: Paladin, 1992), 129.
28. "Heinrich Böll on Solzhenitsyn," in Dunlop, Haugh and Klimoff, *Solzhenitsyn: Critical Essays and Documentary Materials*, 13.
29. Joseph Brodsky, "Geography of Evil," *Partisan Review*, no. 4 (1977): 639.
30. Solzhenitsyn, *Invisible Allies*, 34.
31. He also deprecated *Candle in the Wind* ("the least successful thing I ever wrote"; *The Oak and the Calf*, 12), even though Tvardovsky had deemed it "very stageable" (ibid., 113).
32. Mark Lipovetskii, "'Novyi realism'—eto rannii simptom zatiazhnoi bolezni," *Colta*, April 23, 2014, http://www.colta.ru/articles/literature/3003.
33. Solzhenitsyn, "Answers for Tempest."
34. Kristeva, "Word, Dialogue and Novel," 43–4.
35. Carlo Ginzburg, *Wooden Eyes: Nine Reflections on Distance* (New York: Columbia University Press, 2001), 18.
36. Ibid., 19.
37. Ibid.
38. Solzhenitsyn, *August 1914*, 231.
39. Zamyatin, *We*, 18.
40. Solzhenitsyn, *Sobranie sochinenii*, 12:744.
41. Genette, *Palimpsests*, 1.
42. Ibid., 28.
43. Steiner, "In Exile Wherever He Goes."
44. Solzhenitsyn, "An Interview with Struve," 307.
45. Vidal, "Top Ten Best Sellers," 77. Though Vidal was happy to employ the same device in his novel *Washington, D. C.* (1967).
46. Alexander Solzhenitsyn, *August 1914* (London: Book Club Associates, 1973), 27.
47. Solzhenitsyn, *The First Circle*, 91.
48. Solzhenitsyn, "Ego," 44.
49. Solzhenitsyn, "Matryona's Home," 28.
50. Solzhenitsyn, *Victory Celebrations*, 13.
51. Ibid., 44.
52. Solzhenitsyn, *November 1916*, 828–9.
53. Solzhenitsyn, *Sobranie sochinenii*, 14:511.
54. Ibid.

55. Ezra Pound, *Literary Essays* (New York: New Directions, 1968), 420.
56. Kramer, "A Talk with Solzhenitsyn."
57. Paul Ricœur, "Narrative identity," in *Philosophy Today* 35, no. 1 (1991): 78.
58. Pavel Spivakovskii, "Khudozhestvennaia funktsiia obrazov Vavilonskoi bashni i mirovogo kolodtsa v epopee A. I. Solzhenitsyna 'Krasnoe Koleso,'" http://www.portal-slovo.ru/philology/37238.php.
59. Aleksandr Solzhenitsyn, "The Relentless Cult of Novelty and How It Wrecked the Century," http://www.catholiceducation.org/en/culture/art/the-relentless-cult-of-novelty.html.
60. Solzhenitsyn, *August 1914*, 446.
61. Solzhenitsyn, *Sobranie sochinenii*, 14:128.
62. Mikhail Novikov, "Poslednii prorok russkoi literatury," *Kommersant*, December 15, 1998.
63. Czeslaw Milosz, "Questions," in Dunlop, Haugh, and Klimoff, *Solzhenitsyn: Essays and Materials*, 449.
64. Solzhenitsyn, *The Oak and the Calf*, 113.
65. Volkov, *The Magical Chorus*, 109.
66. Wanner, *Russian Minimalism*, 44.
67. Mary Petrusewicz, *Into the Heart of Darkness: Ivan Bunin and the Modernist Poetics of Memory* (Madison: University of Wisconsin Press, 1996), 7.
68. Robert Bowie, afterword to *Night of Denial: Stories and Novellas*, by Ivan Bunin (Evanston: Northwestern University Press, 2006), 657.
69. Volkov, *The Magical Chorus*, 112.
70. Alexander Zholkovsky, *Text Counter Text: Rereadings in Russian Literary History* (Stanford: Stanford University Press, 1996), 110.
71. Solzhenitsyn, Interview with Kehlmann.
72. "Obsuzhdenie rukopisi A. Solzhenitsyna 'Rakovyi korpus' na zasedanii biuro sektsii prozy s aktivom 17 noiabria 1966 goda," in *Delo Solzhenitsyna*, 2nd ed. (Paris: Éditions de la Seine, 1970), 1:38.
73. Solzhenitsyn, Templeton Lecture, 582.
74. Mark Antliff, "Fascism, Modernism, and Modernity," *The Art Bulletin* 84, no. 1 (2002): 149.
75. Solzhenitsyn, "The Relentless Cult of Novelty."
76. Ibid.
77. Solzhenitsyn, *Sobranie sochinenii*, 14:454.
78. Solzhenitsyn, "The Relentless Cult of Novelty."
79. Solzhenitsyn, *Sobranie sochinenii*, 12:30.
80. Solzhenitsyn, *The First Circle*, 291.
81. Ibid., 439.
82. Solzhenitsyn, "'Golyi god' Pil'niaka."
83. James M. Curtis, *Solzhenitsyn's Traditional Imagination* (Athens: University of Georgia Press: 2008), 146.

84. Aleksandr Solzhenitsyn, "Pis'mo IV Vsesoiuznomu s"ezdu Soiuza sovetskikh pisatelei (16 maia 1967)," in *Publitstika*, 2:29.
85. Solzhenitsyn, "An Interview with Struve," 328.
86. Ibid., 326.
87. See Mayakovsky's verdict on his fellow Futurist Velimir Khlebnikov (1922): "Khlebnikov is not a poet for consumers [*ne poet dlia potrebitelei*]. He is impossible to read. Khlebnikov is a poet for producers [*poet dlia proizvoditelei*]" (Vladimir Maiakovskii, "V. V. Khlebnikov," in *Polnoe sobranie sochinenii v trinadtsati tomakh*, vol. 12 [Moscow: Khudozhestvennaia literatura, 1959], 23). See also Boris Eikhenbaum's comment apropos Andrei Bely (1926): "Why can't we finally say it: there is a literature for readers, and there is a literature for literature?" (Boris Eikhenbaum, "'Moskva' Andreia Belogo," in *O literature. Raboty raznykh let* [Moscow: Sovetskii pisatel', 1987], 425).
88. Solzhenitsyn, "An Interview with Struve," 326.
89. Aleksandr Solzhenitsyn, "Iz Evgeniia Zamiatina. 'Literaturnaia kollektsiia,'" *Novyi mir* 10 (1997) http://magazines.russ.ru/novyi_mi/1997/10/solgen.html.
90. Solzhenitsyn, Nobel Lecture, 520.
91. Solzhenitsyn, *The Oak and the Calf*, 237–8.
92. Ibid., 238.
93. Nietzsche, *The Antichrist*, 600.
94. Ilya Kukulin, "A Prolonged Revanche," 97.
95. Solzhenitsyn, *Zërnyshko, Chast' pervaia*, Glava 1.
96. Aleksandr Solzhenitsyn, "Shvedskoi korolevskoi akademii (12 aprelia 1972)," in Solzhenitsyn, *Publitsistika*, 2:44.
97. Ibid.
98. Kramer, "A Talk with Solzhenitsyn."
99. Nabokov's father, Vladimir Nabokov *père*, was a leading member of the Constitutional Democratic Party, or Kadets.
100. Remnick, *Resurrection*, 148. We also know that he enjoyed *The Defense* [*Zashchita Luzhina*; 1930), which he praised in a letter to Mirra Petrova of June 3, 1969 (Petrova, "Sud'ba avtora," 713). He had also read *The Gift* [*Dar*; 1937–8; 1952; Liudmila Saraskina, "V. V. Nabokov i A. I. Solzhenitsyn: v prostranstve bol'shikh Idei," in Liudmila Saraskina, ed., *Zhizn' i tvorchestvo Aleksandra Solzhenitsyna: na puti k "Krasnomu Kolesu." Sbornik statei* [Moscow: Russkii put', 2013], 282).
101. Roland Barthes, *The Pleasure of the Text*, trans. Richard Miller (New York: The Noonday Press, 1989), 31.
102. Shmeman, *Dnevniki. Tetrad' I*, May 30, 1974.
103. Solzhenitsyn, *Sobranie sochinenii*, 13:662.
104. Simon Karlinsky, ed., *The Nabokov-Wilson Letters: Correspondence between Vladimir Nabokov and Edmund Wilson 1940–1971* (New York: Harper Colophon Books, 1980), 332.

105. Brian Boyd, *Vladimir Nabokov: The American Years* (Princeton: Princeton University Press, 1991), 648. Although there are parallels between Solzhenitsyn's masterpiece and the New Journalism of Tom Wolfe, Norman Mailer, and co., Nabokov meant something else.
106. Roland Barthes, *Writing Degree Zero*, trans. Annette Lavers and Colin Smith (London: Jonathan Cape, 1967), 3.
107. Julia Kristeva, *Strangers to Ourselves*, trans. Léon S. Roudiez (New York: Columbia University Press, 1991), 34.
108. Solzhenitsyn, *August 1914*, 342.
109. Solzhenitsyn, *Sobranie sochinenii*, 7:370.
110. Ibid., 16:245.
111. Ibid., 13:321.
112. Solzhenitsyn, *November 1916*, 14.
113. Omry Ronen, "Emulation, Anti-Parody, Intertextuality, and Annotation," *Facta Universitatis. Series: Linguistics and Literature* 3, no. 2 (2005), http://facta.junis.ni.ac.rs/lal/lal2005/lal2005-02.pdf.
114. Gray, Aikman, and Kohan, "Russia's Prophet in Exile."
115. Vladimir Nabokov, *Strong Opinions* (New York: Vintage Books, 1990), 10.
116. Boyd, *Nabokov: The American Years*, 114.
117. Nataliia Solzhenitsyna, "Kartoteka 'Krasnogo Kolesa': zamysel i osushchestvlenie," in Saraskina, *Zhizn' i tvorchestvo Solzhenitsyna*, 445.
118. Rodney Madocks, "The Incomplete Text and the Ardent Core: The Role of Unfulfilment in the Work of Vladimir Nabokov" (PhD diss., University of Nottingham, 1980), 94.
119. Vladimir Nabokov, *Selected Letters 1940–77*, ed. Dmitri Nabokov and Mathew J. Bruccoli (London: Vintage, 1977), 527–8.
120. Solzhenitsyn, "Tri otryvka," 19.
121. Quoted in Thomas, *Solzhenitsyn*, 357.
122. Kramer, "A Talk with Solzhenitsyn."
123. Alexander Etkind, "Post-Soviet Russia: The Land of the Oil Curse, Pussy Riot, and Magical Historicism," *boundary2. An International Journal of Literature and Culture* 41, no. 1 (2014): 161.
124. Brian McHale, Brian McHale, *Postmodernist Fiction* (New York: Routledge, 1991), 9.
125. Solzhenitsyn, "The Relentless Cult of Novelty."
126. Etkind, "Post-Soviet Russia," 162.
127. Volkov, *The Magical Chorus*, 289. The current decade, in which the timbre of the times has changed yet again, is seeing a retreat from Postmodernist shock and sneer in favor of more traditional literary practices. Still, the petrol-heads and petromachistas have not lost their high-octane strut.
128. Maria Tadeo, "Russian Teacher 'Kills Friend in Heated Poetry Versus Prose Argument,'" *The Independent*, January 30, 2014.

129. Aleksandr Nevzorov, "U russkoi literatury konchilsia srok godnosti," *Snob*, May 29, 2014, https://snob.ru/profile/20736/blog/76791.
130. Aleksandr Solzhenitsyn, letter to Joseph Brodsky of May 14, 1977, in Lev Losev, *Solzhenitsyn i Brodskii kak sosedi* (St. Petersburg: izd-vo Ivana Limbakha, 2010), 365.
131. Ibid., 364.
132. Ibid., 375.
133. Volkov and Genis, "Solzhenitsyn-Brodskii."
134. Louis-Ferdinand Céline, "The Art of Fiction No. 33," *The Paris Review* 31 (1964), http://www.theparisreview.org/interviews/4502/louis-ferdinand-celine-the-art-of-fiction-no-33-louis-ferdinand-celine.
135. See Brodsky's article "Geography of Evil," in which he discusses *From Under the Rubble* (*Iz-pod glyb*; 1977), a collection of essays by Solzhenitsyn and other like-minded figures, and the interview he gave Adam Michnik, "'Chashche vsego v zhizni.'" Yet there were points of congruence, as evidenced by Brodsky's open letter to Vaclav Havel of 1994: "Cowboys believe in law, and reduce democracy to people's equality before it: that is, to the well-policed prairie" (Joseph Brodsky, "'The Post-Communist Nightmare': An Exchange," *The New York Review of Books*, February 17, 1994, http://www.nybooks.com/articles/1994/02/17/the-post-communist-nightmare-an-exchange/). Solzhenitsyn: "I am simply suffocating in the West, I find it poisonous and insufferable, I loathe this kind of existence, in which everything is reduced to justice in the legal sense [*suchshestvovaniie, vsë svodimoe k iuridicheskoi pravote*]" (letter to Lydia Chukovskaia of March 27, 1979, in "'… Rabotaiu radostno i mnogo.' Iz perepiski Aleksandra Solzhenitsyna i Lidii Chukovskoi [1977–9]," *Solzhenitsynskie tetradi*, vol. 3, 24).
136. "Questions and Answers after Brodsky's Reading, 21 February 1978," *The Iowa Review* 4 (1978): 7.
137. Ibid., 7–8.
138. Ibid., 8. Still, Brodsky never warmed to Solzhenitsyn's stylistic practices: "He began using Dahl's dictionary. Worse than that, while he was working on *The Red Wheel* he learned about another writer, whom he resembled, Dos Passos" ("'Chashche vsego v zhizni'"). Also, Brodsky was annoyed by the barbs directed at the Russian Conceptualists in "The Relentless Cult of Novelty": "Sad though it is, Solzhenitsyn is nothing but an obscurantist" (Bozhena Shellkross [Bozena Shallcross], "Morton-strit, 44," in Iosif Brodskii, *Bol'shaia kniga interv'iu* [Moscow: Zakharov, 2000], 262).
139. Solzhenitsyn, *The Oak and the Calf*, 11.
140. Solzhenitsyn, "An Interview with Struve," 304.
141. Ibid., 301.
142. Solzhenitsyn, *The Oak and the Calf*, 24n2.
143. Tempest, Phone Interview with Solzhenitsyn.

144. Mikhail Bakhtin, "Epic and Novel: Toward a Methodology for the Study of the Novel," in *The Dialogic Imagination: Four Essays* (Austin: University of Texas Press, 1981), 9.
145. Böll, "The Imprisoned World," 225.
146. Solzhenitsyn, *August 1914*, 531.
147. Bakhtin, "Epic and Novel," 9.
148. Todorov, *Genres in Discourse*, 14.
149. Boris Paramonov and Ivan Tolstoy, "Ves' ad russkoi istorii," *Radio Svoboda*, July 19, 2015, https://www.svoboda.org/a/27140921.html.
150. "Otkrytyi urok s Dmitriem Bykovym. Urok 12. Solzhenitsyn. Kuda prikatilos' 'Krasnoe Koleso,'" December 8, 2014, http://www.rtvi.com/video/21455.
151. Gray, Aikman, and Kohan, "Russia's Prophet in Exile."
152. Georges Nivat, *Soljénitsyne* (Paris: Seuil, 1980), 146.
153. Pavlov, "Russkii chelovek v XX veke," 587.
154. Tolstoy, *Anna Karenina*, 746.
155. Lev Tolstoi, *Polnoe sobranie sochinenii*, 19:334.
156. Solzhenitsyn, *Sobranie sochinenii*, 7:375.
157. Solzhenitsyn, *August 1914*, 348.
158. Solzhenitsyn, "Answers to Tempest's Questions."
159. Kristeva, "Word, Dialogue and Novel," 42.
160. Kristeva, *Desire in Language*, 166.
161. *November 1916*, 713.
162. Kristeva, *Desire in Language*, 29.
163. Natalia Solzhenitsyna, private communication.
164. On this occasion, the primary agent of transmission was the writer's eldest son, Yermolai (Ignat Solzhenitsyn, private communication). While Solzhenitsyn enjoyed Vysotsky's later songs, with their epic and folkloric motifs, he disliked the satirical ones (Natalia Solzhenitsyna, private communication), as he did those in which the singer adopted an outlaw persona: "He utterly rejected Vysotsky's criminalized songs [*priblatnënnye pesni*], saying that ... this criminalized lyricism just misleads people" (Solzhenitsyna, "Solzhenitsyn ne chital 'Arkhipelag' svoim detiam"). Solzhenitsyn especially liked "Wolf Hunt" ("Okhota na volkov"; 1968) (Natalia Solzhenitsyna, private communication) and "The Apples of Paradise" ("Raiskie iabloki"; 1978) (Ignat Solzhenitsyn, private communication). Mrs. Solzhenitsyna also reports that her husband was "completely overwhelmed" by the bard's songs about World War II (Solzhenitsyna, private communication).
165. Aleksandr Solzhenitsyn, "Feliks Svetlov—'Otverzi mi dveri.' Iz 'Literaturnoi kollektsii,'" *Novyi mir* 1 (1999), http://magazines.russ.ru/novyi_mi/1999/1/solge.html.
166. Solzhenitsyn, "Feliks Svetlov."
167. Mikhail Bakhtin, *Problems of Dostoevsky's Poetics* (Minneapolis: University of Minnesota Press, 1984), 203–4.

168. Ralf Georg Reuth, *Goebbels* (New York: Harper Brace, 1993), 37; Fyodor Dostoevsky, *Devils* (Oxford: Oxford University Press, 1992), 264.
169. Bakhtin, "Epic and Novel," 13.
170. Simone Oettli-van Delden, *Surfaces of Strangeness: Janet Frame and the Rhetoric of Madness* (Wellington, Victoria University Press, 2003), 24.
171. Bakhtin, *Problems of Dostoevsky's Poetics*, 278.
172. Spivakovskii, *Fenomen Solzhenitsyna*, 64.
173. Aleksandr Urmanov, *Khudozhestvennoe mirozdanie Aleksandra Solzhenitsyna* (Moscow: Russkii put', 2014), 412.
174. Urmanov, *Khudozhestvennoe mirozdanie*, 413.
175. Quoted in Saraskina, *Solzhenitsyn*, 917n.
176. Umberto Eco, "Between Author and Text," in Eco et al., *Interpretation and Overinterpretation*, 68.
177. Eco, "Between Author and Text," 68.
178. Valeriia Novodvorskaia, "Tovarishch po Gulagu," *The New Times/Novoe vremia*, November 12, 2012, *Aleksandr Isaevich Solzhenitsyn* [official site], http://www.solzhenitsyn.ru/o_tvorchestve/articles/works/index.php?ELEMENT_ID=1533&sphrase_id=229.
179. Paul Ricœur, "Narrative Time," in *Critical Inquiry* 7, no. 1 (1980): 169.
180. Ion Drutse, "O muzhestve i dostoinstve cheloveka" (excerpts), in Glotser and Chukovskaia, *Slovo*, 32–3.
181. Thomas, *Solzhenitsyn*, 366.
182. Aleksandr Solzhenitsyn, "Teleinterv'iu v Parizhe (11 aprelia 1975)," in *Publitsistika*, 2:270.
183. Aleksandr Solzhenitsyn, "Radiointerv'iu k 20-letiiu vykhoda 'Odnogo dnia Ivana Denisovicha' dlia Bi-bi-si (Kavendish, 8 iunia 1982)," in *Publitsistika*, 3:27.
184. Ibid., 3:29.
185. Ibid.
186. Milosz, "Questions," 451.
187. Joseph Brodsky, "The Art of Poetry XXVIII" (with Sven Birkerts, 1979), in *Conversations*, ed. Cynthia L. Haven (Jackson: University Press of Mississippi, 2002), 81
188. Mack Smith, *Literary Realism and the Ekphrastic Tradition* (University Park: Pennsylvania State University Press, 1995), 153.
189. Solzhenitsyn, "An Interview with Struve," 328.
190. Solzhenitsyn, "The Relentless Cult of Novelty."
191. Auerbach, *Mimesis*, 551.
192. Solzhenitsyn, "An Interview with Struve," 314.
193. Umberto Eco, "An Author and His Interpreters," in Rocco Capozzi, ed., *Reading Eco: An Anthology* (Bloomington: Indiana University Press, 1997), 59.
194. McHale, *Pöstmödernist Fictiön*, 199.

195. Spivakovskii, *Fenomen Solzhenitsyna*, 9.
196. Aleksandr Solzhenitsyn, "Iosif Brodskii."
197. Paul Fussell, *The Great War and Modern Memory* (New York: Oxford University Press, 1975), 35.
198. Aleksandr Solzhenitsyn, Address to the International Academy of Philosophy, in *The "Russian Question"*, 120. The translation reads, "overwhelming loneliness."
199. Jean-François Lyotard, *The Post-Modern Condition: A Report on Knowledge* (Manchester: Manchester University Press, 1984), 38.
200. Malcolm Bradbury and James McFarlane, "The Name and Nature of Modernism," in Malcolm Bradbury and James McFarlane, eds., *Modernism: A Guide to European Literature 1890–1930* (New York, Penguin Books, 1991), 27.
201. Solzhenitsyn, Nobel Lecture, 514.
202. Nietzsche, "Nietzsche Contra Wagner," 683.

Appendix

1. Solzhenitsyn, "Teleinterv'iu kompanii Bi-bi-si," 352.
2. May 16, 2000.
3. Aleksandr Solzhenitsyn, "Vstrecha s chitateliami v RGB," in Aleksandr Solzhenitsyn, *"Priamaia liniia": nado dumat' ob obshchei bede* (Moscow: AST, 2016), 175.
4. Solzhenitsyn, *November 1916*, 107.
5. Solzhenitsyn once recalled that as a child, "I read the whole of Ibsen, imprinting him on my mind" (Solzhenitsyn, "Vstrecha s chitateliami," 175).
6. Solzhenitsyn, *August 1914*, 76.
7. Ibid., 77.
8. John Fowles and Diane Vipond, "An Unholy Inquisition," in John Fowles, *Wormholes: Essays and Occasional Writings* (New York: Henry Holt, 1998), 372.
9. Yet the definitive "atomic" version of *The First Circle* included three new chapters, in addition to numerous rewrites and stylistic emendations, while the final redaction of *The Red Wheel* features a number of deletions, particularly in Knots III and IV, as well as some textual changes.
10. *The First Circle*, chapter fifty-nine. See chapter five of this study.
11. The physics and math department of the University of Rostov, where Solzhenitsyn was a student in 1936–41.
12. In 1939 Solzhenitsyn enrolled in the correspondence department of the Moscow Institute of Philosophy, Literature and Art.
13. *The Red Wheel*.
14. That is, before October 18, 1941, when Solzhenitsyn was conscripted into the Red Army.
15. Vladimir Vasilyev (1880–?), identified in the Glossary to *The Gulag Archipelago* as a professor at the Moscow Higher Technical Academy and a "railway engineer,

hydrotechnician, prisoner, and exile" (Solzhenitsyn, *Sobranie sochinenii*, 6:525). See also chapter three of this study.

16. The story first appeared in volume three of the Vermont *Collected Works* (1978).
17. Solzhenitsyn, *The Gulag Archipelago*, 3:410.
18. The Trinity Lavra (founded 1337), in the town of Sergiev Posad northeast of Moscow. In 1608–10 it was besieged by the army of False Dmitry II.
19. The monastery (founded 1436) stands on the Solovetsky Islands in the White Sea. It was disestablished by the Bolsheviks, who converted it into one of the country's first prison camps. Reconsecrated in 1990.
20. The Venerable Sergius of Radonezh (1314 or 1322–92), founder of the Trinity Lavra.
21. St. Seraphim of Sarov (1754 or 1759–1833), an elder (*starets*) of the Russian Orthodox Church.
22. For example, Nizhny Novgorod, Pskov, Ryazan, Tula, Kolomna, Vologda, and Zaraisk.
23. The Russian Museum (founded 1898) houses works by Russian artists.
24. In 1940.
25. The United States.
26. See Vorotyntsev's manful rejection of *Jane Eyre* as discussed in chapter seven of this study.
27. Solzhenitsyn, *Sobranie sochinenii*, 19:265.
28. See "The Fifth Year in Harness," the title of chapter nine, *The First Circle*.
29. See chapter five of this study.
30. Solzhenitsyn, "Interv'iu dlia zhurnala 'Ekspress,'" 264.
31. Bakhtin, *Dostoevsky's Poetics*, 6.
32. Solzhenitsyn, *Sobranie sochinenii*, 14:560.
33. Ibid., 14:562.
34. Solzhenitsyn, *August 1914*, 348.
35. Comment reportedly made by Vice President G. H. W. Bush to Rob Sherman at Chicago O'Hare Airport on August 27, 1988 about the American Atheists organization during that year's presidential campaign.
36. Solzhenitsyn, "Interv'iu s Rondo," 209.

Selected Bibliography

Works by Aleksandr Solzhenitsyn

In Russian

Solzhenitsyn, Aleksandr. *Bodalsia telënok s dubom. Ocherki literaturnoi zhizni*. 2nd ed. Moscow: Soglasie, 1996.
Solzhenitsyn, Aleksandr. *Literaturnaia kollektsiia. Novyi mir* 1, 4, 7, 10 (1997); 1, 4, 7, 10 (1998); 1, 7, 10, 12 (1999); 7 (2000); 4, 6, 8, 10, 12 (2003); 2, 6, 9, 12 (2004); *Chto chitat'* 1 (2008); *Solzhenitsynskie tetradi* 1 (2012), 2 (2013), 3 (2014), 4 (2015), 5 (2016).
Solzhenitsyn, Aleksandr. *Publitsistika*. 3 vols. Yaroslavl: Verkhne-Volzhskoe knizhnoe isdatel'stvo/Verkhniaia Volga, 1995–7.
Solzhenitsyn, Aleksandr. *Sobranie sochinenii*. 30 vols. Moscow: Vremia, 2006–.
Solzhenitsyn, Aleksandr. *Ugodilo zërnyshko promezh dvukh zhernovov. Ocherki izgnaniia. Novyi mir* 9, 11 (1998); 2 (1999); 9, 12 (2000; 4 (2001); 11 (2003).
Solzhenitsyn, Aleksandr. *V kruge pervom. Roman*. Moscow: Nauka, 2006.

In Translation

Solzhenitsyn, Aleksandr. *Apricot Jam and Other Stories*. Translated by Kenneth Lantz and Stephan Solzhenitsyn. Berkeley: Counterpoint, 2011.
Solzhenitsyn, Aleksandr. *August 1914. The Red Wheel: A Narrative in Discrete Stretches of Time. Knot I*. Translated by H. T. Willetts. New York, NY: Farrar, Straus and Giroux, 1989.
Solzhenitsyn, Aleksandr. *November 1916. The Red Wheel: A Narrative in Discrete Stretches of Time. Knot II*. Translated by H. T. Willetts. New York: Farrar, Straus and Giroux, 2000.
Solzhenitsyn, Aleksandr. *Cancer Ward*. Translated by Nicholas Bethell and David Burg. New York: Farrar, Straus and Giroux, 1991.
Solzhenitsyn, Aleksandr. *The First Circle*. Translated by Thomas P. Whitney. New York: Harper & Row, 1968.
Solzhenitsyn, Aleksandr. *In the First Circle: A Novel. The Restored Text*. Translated by Harry T. Willetts. New York: Harper Perennial, 2009.
Solzhenitsyn, Aleksandr. *The Gulag Archipelago 1918–1956. An Experiment in Literary Investigation*. 3 vols. Translated by Thomas P. Whitney (vols. 1–2) and Harry Willetts (vol. 3). New York: Harper Perennial (vol. 1), Westview Press (vols. 2–3), 1991–2.

Solzhenitsyn, Aleksandr. *Invisible Allies*. Translated by Alexis Klimoff and Michael Nicholson. Washington, DC: Counterpoint, 1995.

Solzhenitsyn, Aleksandr. *The Oak and the Calf: Sketches of Literary Life in the Soviet Union*. Translated by Harry Willetts. New York: Harper & Row, 1980.

Solzhenitsyn, Aleksandr. *One Day in the Life of Ivan Denisovich*. Translated by Harry T. Willetts. New York: Farrar, Straus and Giroux, 1991.

Solzhenitsyn, Aleksandr. *"The Russian Question" at the End of the Twentieth Century*. Translated by Yermolai Solzhenitsyn. New York: Farrar, Straus and Giroux, 1995.

Solzhenitsyn, Aleksandr. *The Solzhenitsyn Reader: New and Essential Writings, 1947–2005*. Edited by Edward E. Ericson, Jr. and Daniel J. Mahoney. Wilmington: ISI Books, 2006.

Solzhenitsyn, Aleksandr. *Three Plays. Victory Celebrations. Prisoners. The Love-Girl and the Innocent*. Translated by Helen Rapp, Nancy Thomas, Nicholas Bethell, and David Burg. New York: Farrar, Straus and Giroux, 1986.

Solzhenitsyn, Alexander. *Stories and Prose Poems*. Translated by Michael Glenny. New York: Farrar, Straus and Giroux, 1971.

Secondary Sources

In Russian

Aziattsev, Dmitrii, Nadezhda Levitskaia, and Mariia Benina. *Aleksandr Isaevich Solzhenitsyn. Materialy k biobibliografii*. St. Petersburg: Rossiiskaia natsional'naia biblioteka, 2007.

Glotser, Vladimir and Elena Chukovskaia, eds. *Slovo probivaet sebe dorogu. Sbornik statei i dokumentov ob A. I. Solzhenitsyne. 1962–1974*. Moscow: Russkii put', 1998.

Niva, Zhorzh (Georges Nivat). *Solzhenitsyn*. Translated by Simon Markish. Moscow: Khudozhestvennaia literatura, 1992.

Saraskina, Liudmila. *Aleksandr Solzhenitsyn*, 2nd ed. Moscow: Molodaia Gvardiia, 2009.

Saraskina, Liudmila, ed. *Lichost' i tvorchestvo A. I. Solzhenitsyna v sovremennom iskusstve i literature*. Moscow. Russkii put', 2018.

Saraskina, Liudmila, ed. *Zhizn' i tvorchestvo Aleksandra Solzhenitsyna: na puti k "Krasnomu Kolesu." Sbornik statei*. Moscow: Russkii put', 2013.

Shmeman, Aleksandr. *Dnevniki. Tetrad' I (ianvar' 1973-noiabr' 1974)*, https://azbyka.ru/otechnik/Aleksandr_Shmeman/dnevniki/1_1; *Tetrad' II (noiabr' 1974-avgust 1975)*, https://azbyka.ru/otechnik/Aleksandr_Shmeman/dnevniki/2; *Tetrad' III (avgust 1975-mai 1976)*, https://azbyka.ru/otechnik/Aleksandr_Shmeman/dnevniki/3.

Spivakovskii, Pavel. *Fenomen A. I. Solzhenitsyna: novyi vzgliad*. Moscow: INION RAN, 1998.

Struve, Nikita and Viktor Moskvin, eds. *Mezhdu dvumia iubileiami: pisateli, kritiki, literaturovedy o tvorchestve A. I. Solzhenitsyna*. Moscow: Russkii put', 2005.

Urmanov, Aleksandr. *Khudozhestvennoe mirozdanie Aleksandra Solzhenitsyna*. Moscow: Russkii put', 2014.

In English and French

Dunlop, John B., Richard Haugh, and Alexis Klimoff, eds. *Aleksandr Solzhenitsyn: Critical Essays and Documentary Materials*, 2nd edn. New York: Collier Books, 1975.

Dunlop, John B., Richard S. Haugh, and Michael Nicholson, eds., *Solzhenitsyn in Exile: Critical Essays and Documentary Materials*. Stanford: Hoover Institution Press, 1985.

Mahoney, Daniel J. *Aleksandr Solzhenitsyn: The Ascent from Ideology*. New York: Rowman & Littlefield, 2001.

Mahoney, Daniel J. *The Other Solzhenitsyn: Telling the Truth about a Misunderstood Writer and Thinker*. South Bend: St. Augustine's Press, 2014.

Nivat, Georges. *Soljénitsyne*. Paris: Seuil, 1980.

Pearce, Joseph. *Solzhenitsyn: A Soul in Exile*. Grand Rapids: Baker Books, 2001.

Remnick, David. *Resurrection: The Struggle for a New Russia*. New York: Vintage Books, 1998.

Scammell, Michael. *Solzhenitsyn: A Biography*. New York: W. W. Norton, 1984.

Thomas, Donald Michael. *Alexander Solzhenitsyn: A Century in His Life*. New York: St. Martin's Press, 1998.

Toker, Leona. *Return from the Archipelago: Narratives of Gulag Survivors*. Bloomington: Indiana University Press, 2000.

Vidal, Gore. "The Top Ten Best Sellers According to *The Sunday New York Times* As of January 7, 1973." In *United States: Essays 1952–1992*. New York: Broadway Books, 2001.

Index

Abakumov, Viktor, 31, 182, 190, 194, 212, 227, 232, 234, 236, 241, 245, 249, 539
Abe, Kobo, 290
Adorno, Theodor, 7, 378
Akhmatova, Anna, 49, 84, 11, 121, 136, 494, 496, 546, 576
Aksyonov, Vasily, 290
Aldanov, Mark, 400
  Cave, The, 400
  Escape, 400
  Key, The, 400
Aldington, Richard, 577
Alekseev, Mikhail, 409
Alexander I, Emperor of Russia, 64, 480
Alexander II, Emperor of Russia, 350, 387
Alexander III, Emperor of Russia, 142
Alexandra Fyodorovna, Empress, 46, 462
Alliluева, Nadezhda, 488
Alliluyeva, Svetlana, 242
Andropov, Yuri, 215, 233–234, 390, 505
Anichkova, Natalya, 658n360
  fictional portrayal of, 45, 386
Anthony, Piers, 595n80
Antonov, Aleksandr, 473
Apocalypse of Paul, The, 86–87
Archimedes, 187
Armand, Inessa, 381, 447–448
Artamonov, Leonid, 369, 429
Astafiev, Viktor, 21

Auerbach, Erich, xiv, 25, 45, 55, 83, 121, 160, 321, 518, 524, 569–570
Augustine, St., 138
Austen, Jane, 585
  Pride and Prejudice, 178
Azhaev, Vasily, 195
  Far from Moscow, 195

Babel, Isaak, 176
  Red Cavalry, 176
Bach, Johann Sebastian, 47
Bacon, Francis, 319
Bakhtin, Mikhail, xiv, 383, 535, 556, 559–561, 564–565, 588
Balk, Aleksandr, 46, 339
Baluev, Vladimir, 516, 524
  fictional portrayal of, 517, 519–520, 524–526, 563
Balzac, Honoré de, 134, 506, 582
  "*Comédie humaine, La*," 506, 582
Barbusse, Henri, 577
Barsanuphius, St., 379
Barthes, Roland, xiv, 20, 548, 571
Bataille, Georges, xiv, 3, 8, 100–101, 293, 302, 333, 337, 537, 548
  "Dead Man, The," 3
  Death and Sensuality, 302
Baudelaire, Charles, 107, 260
Baum, Lyman Frank, 409
  "Story of Little Boy Blue, The," 409
Bedny, Demyan, 492

702 | Index

Beethoven, Ludwig van, 47, 187
Belinkov, Arkady, 543
Belinsky, Vissarion, 25, 131–132, 137
   "Letter to Gogol," 131
Bely, Andrei, 24, 244, 404, 562, 588
   Petersburg, 24, 244, 404
Berezin, Vladimir, 184
Beria, Lavrenty, 182, 233, 276, 280, 483
Berlin, Isaiah, 494
Beskin, Osip, 495
Bierut, Boleslav, 239
Bizet, Georges, 305
   Carmen, 305
Blagoveshchensky, Aleksandr, 15, 431, 575
Blok, Aleksandr, 152, 375, 403–405
   On Kulikovo Field, 152
   Retribution, 404–405
   Scythians, 403
   Twelve, The, 405
Bloom, Harold, 5, 15, 44, 131
Bogdanovich, Pavel, 343
Bogrov, Dmitry, 31, 341, 355, 358, 366, 369, 374, 376, 381–383, 391, 395, 401–403, 456, 562
Böll, Heinrich, 183, 236–237, 245, 534, 556
Borges, Jorge Luis, xv, 257, 271
   "Library of Babel, The," 257
Borodin, Alexander, 212–213
   Prince Igor, 212
Borshchagovsky, Aleksandr, 636n5
Boyev, Pavel, 434, 512, 516, 550
   fictional portrayal of, 508–509, 511, 517–526, 541, 550, 560, 563
Brahms, Johannes, 47
Brasillach, Robert, 544
Brezhnev, Leonid, xxv–xxvi, 51, 62, 93, 115, 126, 152, 182, 215, 355, 388, 390, 478, 483, 566

Brodsky, Joseph, 5, 8, 24, 67, 323, 339, 484, 530, 534, 551, 553–555, 557, 568
   "On the Death of Zhukov," 484
Brontë, Charlotte, 438–439
   Jane Eyre, 438, 585
Brontë, Emily, 86, 105
   Wuthering Heights, 86
Buchanan, George, 398
Bukharin, Nikolai, 54–55, 197
Bulgakov, Mikhail, 12, 24, 34, 43, 87, 155, 243, 290, 365, 404, 451, 484, 547
   Days of the Turbins, The, 243
   "Heart of a Dog," 484
   Master and Margarita, The, 34, 43, 155, 365, 369, 450–451, 547
   Young Doctor's Notebook, A, 404
Bunin, Ivan, 107, 112, 364, 501, 543
   "Calf's Head, The," 107
   "Idol, The," 107
Burgess, Anthony
   Clockwork Orange, A, 159
Burke, Edmund, 7, 101
   Philosophical Inquiry into the Origin of Our Ideas of the Sublime and Beautiful, A, 7
Bush, George H. W., 589
Bushin, Vladimir, 531, 568
   Genius of the First Gob, 531
Butler, Judith, xiv, 476
Bykov, Dmitry, 61, 104–105, 451, 557

Caesar, Julius, 409
   Gallic War, 409
Campanella, Tommaso, 186
Camus, Albert, 554
Cavafy, Constantine Peter, 339
   "Waiting for the Barbarians," 339
Céline, Louis-Ferdinand, 290, 544, 554, 559

Cervantes, Miguel de
    Don Quixote, 349
Chaikovsky, Nikolai, 368
Chaliapin, Feodor, 47, 132
Chalmaev, Viktor, 184
Chamberlain, Neville, 394
Chanson de Roland, 515, 523–524
Chapaev, Vasily, 476
Chapman, Mark, 358
Chekhov, Anton, xiv, 24, 113, 116, 140, 195, 202, 261, 272, 290, 314, 364, 409, 489, 490–491, 545
    "Ward Number Six," 261, 314
Chernov, Viktor, 368
Chernyshevsky, Nikolai, 404
    What Is To Be Done? 404
Chesterton, G. K., 374
    Ball and the Cross, The, 374
Chkheidze, Nikolai, 368
Churchill, Winston, 194, 382, 578, 582
Clark, Katerina, 189, 316
Coleridge, Samuel, 20, 97
Colleoni, Bartolomeo, 478
Conrad, Joseph, 339, 531, 562,
Constantine, Roman Emperor, 240
Cooper, James Fenimore, 409
Crisp, Quentin, 231
Cromwell, Oliver, 46
Cronin, Archibald Joseph, 190
Cruikshank, George, 228

Dahl, Vladimir, 80, 89, 137
    Explanatory Dictionary of the Living Great Russian Language, 80, 89
Dali, Salvador, 544, 554
D'Annunzio, Gabriele, 544
Dante, Alighieri, 11, 25, 59, 87, 223, 225, 228, 231, 256
    Divine Comedy, The, 11, 224
    Inferno, 87, 225, 228, 231
    Paradiso, 256

Danton, Georges, 46, 357, 395, 408
Debussy, Claude, 531
Demidov, Igor, 368
Dennis, Eugene (Waldron, Francis Xavier), 232
Derrida, Jacques, 571
Descartes, René, 187, 371
Dick, Philip K., 602n231
Dickens, Charles, xv, 11–12, 21, 44–45, 80, 131, 202, 424, 487, 557, 574
    Dombey and Son, 44
Djilas, Milovan, 63, 93–94
Dmitry I, Grand Prince of Moscow, 154
Dos Passos, John, 347, 349, 530, 546, 572, 574
    USA, 347
Dostoevsky, Fyodor, xiv–xv, xvii, 5, 10–12, 15, 21, 24, 50, 70, 77, 86, 90–91, 101, 120, 136, 138, 213, 219, 222–223, 268, 283, 350, 359, 365, 403, 409–411, 438, 442, 448, 454, 465, 487, 535, 546, 549–551, 553, 557, 559, 560–564, 581, 588
    Brothers Karamazov, The, 10, 15, 77, 86, 123, 411, 420, 425, 550
    Crime and Punishment, 10, 37, 153, 283–284, 403, 560
    Devils, 15, 86, 136, 222, 234, 250, 302, 403, 448, 454, 460, 535, 562
    House of the Dead, The, 70, 74, 77, 90, 213
    Idiot, The, 120–121, 136
    Notes from the Underground, 302, 446
    "Peasant Marey, The," 219
    Poor Folk, 101
Dovlatov, Sergei, 344
Doyle, Arthur Conan, 290
Duma, Alexandre *fils*
    Dame aux camélias, La, 447
Dürrenmatt, Friedrich, 16
    Physicists, The, 16

Eagleton, Terry, 542
Eco, Umberto, xiv, 229, 565–566, 570
Ehrenburg, Ilya, 122, 168, 171, 196, 519
  "We Shall Pull Through," 168
Eikhenbaum, Boris, 146, 352
Eisenstein, Sergei, 54, 90, 100–101, 171, 207, 349, 542
  Alexander Nevsky, 207
  Ivan the Terrible, 100
Eliade, Mircea, 129–130, 544
Eliot, George, 223
Eliot, Thomas Stearns, 86, 526
Elucidarium, The, 87
Engels, Friedrich, 176–177, 189, 191, 412
  Revolution and Counter-Revolution in Germany, 176
Epicurus, 102, 198
Ericson, Edward, ix, xiv
Etkind, Alexander, 97, 552–553
Eusebius of Caesaria, 138, 240

Fadeyev, Aleksandr, 568
False Dmitry I, Russian pretender, 237
False Dmitry II, Russian pretender, 695n18
Fedin, Konstantin, 568
Fedorov, Nikolai 380, 420
Ferguson, Adam, 319
  Essay on the History of Civil Society, An, 319–320
Flaubert, Gustave, 548
  Madame Bovary, 451
Fleming, Alexander, 189–190
Fleming, Ian, 359
Florensky, Pavel, 298
Foster, William, 232
Foucault, Michel, xiv, 254, 261, 314, 571
Fowles, John, 576–577
Franco, Francisco, 239, 435

François, Hermann von, 19, 354, 369, 382, 398, 429–430, 433, 436, 564, 575
Frazer, James, 330, 539
Freud, Sigmund, 216–217, 268
Frisch, Max, 16
  Chinese Wall, The, 16
Furtseva, Ekaterina, 153
Fussell, Paul, 572

Gachev, Georgii, 420
Gaidar, Yegor, 503
Garshin, Vsevolod, 410
Genette, Gérard, xiv, 36, 163, 345, 383, 521, 536, 547
Genis, Alexander, 554
George, St., 12, 218, 404, 427, 435
Gimmer, Nikolai, 354, 368, 562
Ginzburg, Carlo, xiv, 535
Gippius, Zinaida, 357, 408, 542, 544
Gladkov, Aleksandr, 240
Glantz, David, 677n68
Glenny, Michael, 531
Glinka, Mikhail, 47, 133
Goebbels, Joseph, 496, 562
Goering, Hermann, 182
Goethe, Johann Wolfgang von, 103, 176, 191, 225, 228, 429, 450, 588
  "Erlkönig, Der," 429
  Faust, 225, 228, 450–451
Gogol, Nikolai, xvii, 14, 25, 27, 30, 39, 43, 45, 74, 86–87, 131–132, 224, 274, 387, 409, 452, 466, 547
  Dead Souls, 27, 86, 224, 274, 317, 466, 486
  "Overcoat, The," 30, 74
  "Portrait, The," 452
  "Terrible Vengeance, The," 466
Goncharov, Ivan, 343, 428
  Oblomov, 14, 409, 428, 442, 575

Gorbachev, Mikhail, xix, xxvii–xxviii, 53, 58, 62, 215, 234, 245, 503
Goremykin, Ivan, 45
Gorky, Maxim, 140, 195, 197, 219, 251, 260, 271, 362, 369, 400, 404, 408, 415–416, 440, 545, 549
  "Creatures That Were Once Men," 440
  Foma Gordeyev, 362, 545
  Life of Klim Samgin, The, 400
  Lower Depths, The, 219
  Mother, 271
  Petty Bourgeois, The, 404
  Reminiscences of Tolstoy, 415
  Vassa Zheleznova, 197, 404
Granin, Daniil, 190
  Those Who Seek, 190
Grass, Günter, 58
Greene, Graham, 11, 183
Grigorovich, Dmitry, 409, 542
  "Anton Goremyka," 409
Gromyko, Andrei, 156
Grunau, Anastasia, 679n130
Guchkov, Aleksandr, 342, 382, 393, 399, 438
Guderian, Heinz, 415
Gumilev, Nikolai, 406–408, 542, 544
  "Streetcar That Lost Its Way, The," 408
Gvozdev, Kozma, 389

Hamsun, Knut, 21, 409, 544
Hardy, Thomas, 577
Hegel, Georg, 64, 206, 318, 405, 419, 433, 456
Heine, Heinrich, 54
Hemingway, Ernest, 172, 191, 232, 305
  Death in the Afternoon, 232
Henderson, Joseph L., 522
Hershman, Morris, 625n48
Herwegh, Georg, 319
Herzen, Alexander, 403–404, 576
  My Past and Thoughts, 404, 576

Hindenburg, Paul von, 430, 523–524
Hitler, Adolf, 14, 39, 79, 100, 164, 167, 199, 228, 239, 241–242, 251, 268, 298, 388, 418, 465, 482
  Mein Kampf, 446
Hogarth, William, 228
Holland, Barry, 567
Homer, 426, 521–523, 555
  Iliad, 426, 521, 523
Horkheimer, Max, 378
Horvath, Robert, 65

Ibsen, Henrik, 140, 542, 574
  Peer Gynt, 542
Igor, Prince of Novgorod-Seversk, 212
Ilyin, Ivan, 59, 441, 443, 456
Irving, David, 483
  Destruction of Dresden, The, 483
Ivan I, Grand Prince of Moscow, 154
Ivanov, Nikolai, 368, 461
Ivashev-Musatov, Sergei, 199

Jakobson, Roman, 546, 552
James, Henry, 341
Jauss, Hans Robert, 94, 533
Joyce, James, 9, 163, 328, 526, 554, 559, 570
  Ulysses, 163, 274, 526
Jung, Carl, 378, 440, 522
Jünger, Ernst, 358, 437, 526, 577
  Storm of Steel, 437, 526
Justinian, Byzantine Emperor, 379

Kaganovich, Lazar, 139, 145
Karabchevsky, Nikolai, 463
Karamzin, Nikolai, 64
Kartsev, Viktor, 368
Kataev, Valentin, 104–105, 163
  Time, Forward!, 163
Kaverin, Veniamin
  Open Book, The, 174

Keats, John, 259
Kehlmann, Daniel, 543
Kerbabayev, Berdy, 277–279
Kerensky, Alexander, 15, 46, 214, 354, 356–359, 369, 374, 382, 389, 395, 408, 458, 463, 536, 562
Khabalov, Sergei, 431
Khlebnikov, Velimir, 345, 559
Khodorkovsky, Mikhail, 504
Khrushchev, Nikita, xvi–xvii, xxiv–xxv, 14, 39, 49, 62–64, 69, 91–96, 115, 122, 126, 146, 215, 236, 264, 276, 287, 360, 478, 481–483, 502
Khvat, Aleksei, 188–189
King, Stephen, 53
  Firestarter, 53
Kipling, Rudyard, 292
Kirill, Patriarch of the Russian Orthodox Church, 603n269
Kirov, Sergei, 119
Kirpichnikov, Timofei, 459
Kishkin, Nikolai, 368
Klimoff, Alexis, ix, 600n186, 610n147, 611n184, 612n2, 621n3, 622n57, 623n9, 626n73, 632n301, 637n43, 639n79, 648n3, 687n28, 688n63
Kluev, Nikolai, 432
Knox, Alfred, 398
Kochetov, Vsevolod, 138
Kolchak, Aleksandr, 247, 390, 457–458
Kollontai, Aleksandra, 32, 354, 364, 443, 540–541
Komissarzhevskaya, Vera, 399
Kopelev, Lev, 23, 192, 232, 534
Kornilov, Lavr, 390
Kotovsky, Grigory, 473, 476–477
Kramer, Hilton, 343
Krasnov, Pyotr, 400
  From Double Eagle to Red Flag, 400
Kristeva, Julia, xiv, 370, 515, 535, 549, 559–560

"Word, Dialogue and Novel," 559
Kropotkin, Peter, 319
Krupskaya, Nadezhda, 446–447
Kryukov, Fyodor, 342
Krymov, Aleksandr, 348, 432
Kukulin, Ilya, 349
Kulyabko, Nikolai, 369
Kuprin, Aleksandr, 93, 409
  "Garnet Bracelet, The," 409
Kurlov, Pavel, 369, 382
Kuskova, Ekaterina, 214
Kutepov, Aleksandr, 16–17, 366, 390, 539
Kutuzov, Mikhail, 428, 430–431, 575

La Bruyère, Jean de, 535
Lacan, Jacques, xiv, 223, 330–331, 539
Lagerlöf, Selma, 409
Lannes, Jean, 676n53
Larina, Anna, 55
Latynina, Alla, 184,
Lavater, Johann Kaspar, 30, 282
Lavrenyov, Boris, 163–164
  "Marina," 163
Lay of the Host of Igor, The, 212
Le Bon, Gustave, 458–460, 463
  Crowd, The, 458
Lem, Stanislaw, 290
Lenin, Vladimir, xv, xxvi, 12–13, 15, 17, 19, 23, 30–31, 39, 42–43, 45–46, 62–63, 153, 168, 172–173, 189, 218, 236–237, 240, 242, 249–250, 257, 260, 276, 287–288, 306, 342–343, 347, 352, 354–355, 360, 366–369, 374, 381–383, 386, 398, 412, 444–452, 458, 476, 484, 496, 502, 508, 552, 561–562, 564, 578, 581
Leontius, 160
Lermontov, Mikhail, 174, 399, 409, 425, 490, 551

Hero of Our Time, A, 14, 174, 409, 425, 439
Masquerade, 399
"Panorama of Moscow, A," 490
Sashka, 490
Leskov, Nikolai, 93, 138, 261, 542
Lewis, Clive Staples, 11
Lewis, Percy Wyndham, 544
Liber, Mikhail, 368
Licko, Pavel, 594n47
Life of St. Feodosy of Pechersk, 121
Lincoln, Abraham, 282
Lipovetsky, Mark, 451, 534
Lombroso, Cesare, 30, 476
London, Jack, 82, 295, 574
Longinus, 7, 101
Loseff, Lev, 184, 250, 341, 554
Lounsbery, Anne, ix, 39
Ludendorff, Erich, 430
Lukács, Georg, 147, 534, 617n167, 687n26
Lukyanov, Anatoly, 234
Lurié, Yakov, 453
Luxemburg, Rosa, 450,
Lvov, Georgi, 401–402
Lvov, Vladimir, 368
Lyotard, Jean-François, 572
Lysenko, Trofim, 189

McHale, Brian, xiv, 552–553
Mahoney, Daniel, ix, xiv
   Solzhenitsyn Reader, xiv
Mailer, Norman, 690n105
   Naked and the Dead, The, 515
Mamai, Khan, 150–151
Mann, Thomas, 21, 256, 264, 268, 286, 576
   Magic Mountain, The, 264–265, 268, 286, 289–290, 322, 328, 576
Mantel, Hilary, 354
Mao, Zedong, 194

Marcellinus, Ammianus, 160
   History of Rome, 160
Marcus Aurelius, Roman Emperor, 535
Marie Antoinette, Queen of France, 46
Marinetti, Filippo, 544
Markov, Sergei, 457
Marlowe, Christopher, 86
Márquez, Gabriel García, 131
   One Hundred Years of Solitude, 131
Martos, Nikolai, 391, 410
Martynov, Valentin, 23
Marx, Karl, 141, 174, 191, 287, 506
   Communist Manifesto, The, 446
   Kapital, Das, 141, 278
Maugham, Somerset, 290
Mayakovsky, Vladimir, 172, 196, 213–314, 407, 444, 457, 544–546, 549, 560
   150,000,000, 213
   "Kindness to Horses," 407
   Mystery-Bouffe, 213
   Very Good!, 214
Meredith, James, 223
Merezhkovsky, Dmitry, 408, 544
Meyerhold, Vsevolod, 399, 406, 544
Michnik, Adam, 5
Mikhail Aleksandrovich, Grand Duke, 454
Mikhalkov, Sergei, 157, 215
   I Want to Go Home, 215
   Uncle Steeple, 157
Milosz, Czeslaw, 25, 543, 568
Milton, John, 25, 86, 88
   Paradise Lost, 86
Milyukov, Pavel, 214, 374, 536
Molotov, Vyacheslav, 156, 165, 167, 459, 561
Mordukhai-Boltovskoi, Dmitry, 625n46
Morris, William, 186
Morson, Gary Saul, 90
Mozhaev, Boris, 653n146

Mugabe, Robert, 239
Münzenberg, Willi, 445
Murat, Joachim, 676n53
Mussolini, Benito, 242

Nabokov, Vladimir *fils*, xv, xxvi, 3, 9, 133, 157, 257, 274, 276, 339, 390, 408, 547–548–551, 572, 579–580
   Ada, 390, 550
   Gift, The, 157
   "Guide to Berlin, A," 408
   Invitation to a Beheading, 548
   Lolita, 548
   Pale Fire, 548
Nabokov, Vladimir *père*, 369, 548
Nadson, Semyon, 406
Nakhamkes-Steklov, Yuri, 368
Napoleon Bonaparte, Emperor of the French, 46, 59, 170, 194, 237–238, 241, 247, 357, 373, 382, 392, 409–411, 428–432, 436, 446, 460, 479–480, 506–507, 575–576
   Clisson et Eugénie, 479
Napoleon III, Emperor of the French, 411
Nechaev, Sergei, 447
   "Cathechism of a Revolutionist," 447
Nechvolodov, Aleksandr, 393, 403, 438
Nekrasov, Nikolai, 132, 491, 548
   Who is Happy in Russia?, 132
Nemzer, Andrei, 442
Nepenin, Adrian, 349
Nevsky, Alexander, Prince of Novgorod, 207
Ney, Michel, 676n53
Nicholas I, Russian Emperor, 64, 387
Nicholas II, Russian Emperor, 13, 15, 33, 62, 341, 342, 348, 351, 354–356, 366, 379, 383, 385, 389, 409, 453

Nietzsche, Friedrich, xiii, xvii, 3, 8, 24, 31, 38, 54–56, 69, 74–75, 103, 106, 138, 161, 181, 244, 257–261, 273, 284–285, 292, 319, 331, 339, 357–358, 362, 392, 422, 461, 468, 495, 514, 520, 530, 532, 541, 547, 549, 573, 578, 584
   Antichrist, The, 26, 422, 547
   Beyond Good and Evil, 8, 259, 339, 357
   Ecce Homo, 3
   Gay Science, The, 106
   Human, All Too Human, 161, 181, 468, 514
   On Truth and Lies in an Extra-Moral Sense, 259
   Thus Spoke Zarathustra, 31, 69, 244, 331, 362, 520
   Will to Power, The, 468, 530
Nivat, Georges, 184, 263, 558
Nobs, Ernst, 369
Nolde, Emil, 544
Novgorodtsev, Pavel, 657n318
Novikov, Mikhail, 543
Novodvorskaya, Valeria, 566

Ogarev, Nikolai, 403–404
Okudzhava, Bulat, 248
   "Sentimental March," 248
Ortega y Gasset, José, 14, 16, 111, 211, 339–340, 384
   Revolt of the Masses, The, 211
Orwell, George, 69, 96
   1984, 96
Ostrovsky, Aleksandr, 409
Ostrovsky, Nikolai, 163, 271, 316
   How Steel Was Tempered, 163, 271, 316
Owen, Robert, 353
Owen, Wilfred, 577

Panferov, Fyodor, 131–132
   Bruski, 131

Panin, Dmitry, 192
  Notebooks of Sologdin, The, 192
Paramonov, Boris, 451, 557
Parvus, Alexander, 31, 43, 342, 354, 366, 369, 374, 398, 445, 448–451, 496, 552, 578, 581
Pasternak, Boris, xxiv, 5, 335, 400, 576
  Doctor Zhivago, 284, 321, 400, 418
Patton, George, 480
Pavic, Milorad, 184
  Dictionary of the Khazars, 184
Pavlov, Oleg, 558
Paz, Octavio, 534
Pelevin, Victor, 161, 476
  Buddha's Little Finger, 161, 476
Peshekhonov, Aleksei, 461, 562
Peter the Great, Russian Emperor, 6, 40, 237, 346, 394, 419, 494
Petrarch, 334
Petrova, Mirra, 214, 221, 295
Philippe, Nizier Anthelme, 356, 377
Picasso, Pablo, 554
Pikul, Valentin, 652n134
Pilnyak, Boris, 545
  Naked Year, The, 545–546
Pinochet, Augusto, 239
Pivot, Bernard, 38
Plato, xvii, 30, 78, 83, 170, 176, 297, 311, 379, 421, 559, 588
  Republic, The, 78, 83, 170, 311
  Symposium, The, 297
Platonov, Andrey, 493
  Foundation Pit, The, 493
Plutarch, 187
Pope, Alexander, 596n87
Popper, Karl, 207–208, 561
  Open Society and Its Enemies, The, 207
  Poverty of Historicism, The, 207
Porta, Giambattista della, 30
Poskryobyshev, Aleksandr, 182, 230, 241

Pound, Ezra, 106, 541, 541, 544, 554
  Canto LXXIV, 106
  Canto CXV, 181
Powell, Enoch, 58
Prinzip, Gavrilo, 358
Protopopov, Aleksandr, 377, 379, 462
Proust, Marcel, 420, 535–536, 559
Przybyszewski, Stanislaw, 409
Pushkin, Aleksandr, xiii, 64, 130, 162, 178, 191, 194, 319, 335, 371, 376, 387, 402, 409, 440, 474, 489–491, 518, 546, 551, 576, 581
  Bronze Horseman, The, 402–403
  Captain's Daughter, The, 474
  Eugene Onegin, 14, 162, 214, 402, 422, 490, 560, 582
  "Lines Written at Night during Insomnia," 130
  "Queen of Spades, The," 371, 440
Putin, Vladimir, xxix–xxx, 30, 58, 60, 64–66, 215, 347, 469, 505, 566

Rabelais, François, 290, 316, 559
  Gargantua, 290
  Pantagruel, 290
Racine, Jean, 197
Rahr, Alexander, 65
Rasputin, Grigory, 351, 377–378
Rasputin, Valentin, 41, 499
  Farewell to Matyora, 499
Remarque, Erich Maria, 161, 176, 358, 520, 577, 579
  All Quiet on the Western Front, 161, 520
Rembrandt, Harmenszoon van Rijn, 185–186, 587
Remnick, David, 58, 351
Reshetovskaya, Natalya, xxii–xxiv, xxvi, xxix, 47, 51, 186, 192, 195, 216, 417, 439
Ribbentrop, Joachim von, 242
Ricœur, Paul, 541, 566

Robespierre, Maximilien, 46, 241, 357, 389
Rodzianko, Mikhail, 369, 463
Rokossovsky, Konstantin, 471, 483
Rondeau, Daniel, 341
Roosevelt, Eleanor, 214, 577, 580
Roosevelt, Franklin Delano, 194
Rostropovich, Mstislav, 28, 47
Rozanov, Vasily, 10–11, 50, 405, 420, 588
   Apocalypse of Our Time, The, 405
   Dostoevsky and the Legend of the Grand Inquisitor, 10
Rybakov, Anatoly, 236
   Children of the Arbat, The, 236
Rybas, Sviatoslav, 652n134

Sade, Donatien Alphonse François de, 358, 559
Samsonov, Aleksandr, 15, 19, 341, 343, 346, 354, 366, 369, 371, 398, 409–410, 428–431, 436, 515, 567, 575
Saraskina, Lyudmila, ix, 48, 405
Sartre, Jean-Paul, 46, 86, 184, 228, 587
   Nausea, 46
Sassoon, Siegfried, 577
Sayers, Dorothy, 455
Scammell, Michael, 220
Schelling, Friedrich von, 12
Schiller, Friedrich, 108, 290
Schlesinger, Arthur, 58, 346
Schmemann, Alexander, 43, 352, 422, 451, 548
Schnittke, Alfred, 344
Schoenberg, Arnold, 186
Schubert, Franz, 47
Schultz, Bruno, 210
Scott, Walter, 355
Scriabin, Alexander, 170
   Mysterium, 170

Serafimovich, Aleksandr, 163
   Iron Flood, The, 163
Seraphim of Sarov, St., 580
Serebriakova, Zinaida, 133
Sergius, St., 580
Severyanin, Igor, 406, 544
Shafarevich, Igor, viii, 59
Shakespeare, William, 59, 240, 522
   Hamlet, 191, 274
Shakhovskoi, Dmitry, 368
Shalamov, Varlam, 97–98, 100, 103, 493, 543
   Kolyma Tales, 97, 103
Sharipov, Adii, 277–278
Shcheglovitov, Ivan, 463
Shcherbak, Irina, 411
Shcherbak, Taissia, 35, *see also* Solzhenitsyna (Shcherbak), Taissia
Shcherbak, Zakhar, xxi, 249
Shcherbakov, Aleksandr, 229
Shchors, Nikolai, 476
Shelley, Percy Bysshe, 86
Sherman, Robert, 695n35
Sheshunova, Svetlana, 27, 371, 374
Shingarev, Andrei, 368, 376–377, 384, 393, 404, 438, 441
Shklovsky, Viktor, 664n542
Shlyapnikov, Aleksandr, 354, 389, 408, 459, 540–541, 545, 561–562
Sholokhov, Mikhail, 59, 171, 400
   Quiet Don, The, 59, 342, 400
Shostakovich, Dmitry, 47
Shulgin, Vasily, 342, 395, 461
Shvarts, Yevgeny, 593n36
Sibelius, Jean, 47
Silaev, Ivan, 53
Simonov, Konstantin, 195–196, 223, 561
Sklarz, Vladimir, 449–450
Smollett, Tobias, 290

Index | 711

Snow, Charles Percy, 16, 185
"The Two Cultures," 185
Sokolov, Nikolai, 368
Solovyov, Sergey, 151
 History of Russia, 151
Solovyov, Vladimir, 319, 378, 421
 Three Conversations on War, Progress, and the End of the World History, 378, 421
Solzhenitsyn Aleksandr
 "Adlig Schwenkitten," xxix, 22, 434, 469, 515–526, 550, 560, 563, 588
 "Age of Hatred, The," 34
 "Apricot Jam," xiv, xxviii, 11, 41, 249, 471–472, 492–497, 561
 Another Time, Another Burden, 24
 April 1917, xxviii, 23, 34, 51, 342–343, 345–346, 348, 361, 364, 373, 376–377, 384, 403, 411, 418, 422, 443–444, 453, 461, 467, 471, 538, 570, 583
 August 1914, vii, xiv, xviii, xxvi–xxvii, 12, 15, 22, 38, 42, 52, 244, 291, 341, 344–346, 349, 358, 363, 368–369, 383, 388, 390–393, 396, 400, 410–411, 413, 418, 420, 427–433, 445, 447, 461, 464, 467, 486, 490, 510, 516, 519, 530, 536, 538, 541, 549–550, 556, 558–559, 567, 575–576, 578
 Between Two Millstones, xiv, xxix, 24, 93, 108, 448, 469
 "Buddha's smile, The," 195, 212, 214–215, 577
 Cancer Ward, xv–xvi, xxv, 5, 7–8, 11, 14, 18, 20, 23, 26, 30–36, 39–40, 43, 47, 51, 56–57, 60, 75, 93, 96, 115–119, 150, 172, 189, 244, 259–335, 363, 366, 380, 432, 440, 452, 497, 533, 542, 552, 555–558, 560–561, 569, 576, 588
 Candle in the Wind, xxiv, 16, 22
 Dictionary for the Expansion of the Russian Language, 58
 "Easter Procession, The," xxv, 19, 45, 113–114, 158–160, 297, 542
 "Ego," xxviii, 28, 40, 470–478, 539
 First Circle, The, xiv–xv, xxiv–xxv, xxvii, xxx, 5, 7, 11–23, 26, 28, 30–36, 39, 41–45, 48–49, 51–52, 56–57, 62–63, 65, 74, 81, 87, 90, 93, 96, 107–108, 114–115, 150, 163, 166, 169–174, 181–258, 262–264, 270, 272, 274, 278, 282, 285, 288, 294, 314–315, 322, 344, 350–351, 363, 369, 373, 404, 419, 436, 440, 445, 452, 486, 490, 496, 501–502, 506, 511, 513, 522, 533, 539, 542, 544–545, 549–552, 555–556, 559–562, 566, 568–571, 576–577, 586–587
 "For the Good of the Cause," xxv, 27, 32–33, 39, 112, 114, 145–150, 497, 499–500, 504, 534
 "Fracture Points," xxix, 35, 39, 470–472, 502–507
 Gulag Archipelago, The viii, xv, xviii, xxiv, xxvi, xxviii, 5, 8–9, 11, 24–25, 43, 56–57, 67, 74–76, 81, 86, 90, 104, 155–156, 158, 203, 213, 230, 236, 243, 262, 287, 339, 341, 346, 389, 427, 468, 482, 548, 551, 555, 557, 570, 579
 "Incident at Kochetovka Station," xxv, 23, 52, 112–114, 138–145, 248, 497
 Invisible Allies, 25
 Journal of "R–17", The, xxviii, 24, 452, 552
 "Land of the Pyramids," 48
 Lenin in Zurich, xxvi, 347, 381, 451, 502

Literary Collection, xxix, 24, 243, 469, 534, 546, 560
"Live Not By Lies!," xxvi–xxvii, 56, 320
Love-Girl and the Innocent, The, xxiv, xxviii, 21, 72, 164, 204–205, *see also Republic of Labor*
Love the Revolution, xv, xxiii–xxiv, 11, 18, 21, 23, 33, 42, 45, 48, 51, 141, 161–180, 192, 194, 203, 205, 219, 235, 317, 380, 396, 412, 418, 439, 508, β534, 562, 566, 569, 585–587
March 1917, xxvii, 16, 26, 34, 43, 45–46, 168, 342, 346–350, 358, 366, 369, 373, 381–382, 384, 386, 398, 401–402, 407, 420, 429, 444, 453, 467, 471, 536, 538–539, 545, 570
"March the Fifth," 243
"Matryona's Home," x, xxiv–xxv, 18, 21–22, 25–26, 28, 30–33, 35, 39–44, 47, 51, 67, 107, 112–115, 121–138, 145, 153, 253, 274, 315, 376, 470, 488, 508, 513, 523, 539
"Miniatures," xxiv–xxv, xxix, 6, 26, 41, 43, 107–112, 151, 255–256, 349, 469, 481, 527–529, 543, 580–581
 "Along the Oka," 109, 159, 255
 "Approaching the Day," 111
 "Bell at Uglich," 527
 "City on Neva, The," 6, 109
 "Curtain," 528
 "Elm Log, The," 110
 "Fire and the Ants, The," 110
 "Growing Old," 528
 "Larch, The," 43, 527
 "Lightning,", 527
 "Nocturnal Thoughts," 528
 "Old Bucket, The," 110
 "Poet's Ashes, A," 110
 "Prayer," xxv, 107, 111–112, 528
 "Prayer for Russia," 528–529
 "Reflection in water," 107, 110
 "Shame," 527–528
 "Storm in the Mountains, A," 108
"Nastenka," xxviii, 11, 26, 33, 35, 41, 470–472, 487–492, 495, 511, 542, 560, 562, 569
"New Generation, The," xxviii, 470–472, 484–487
"No Matter What," xxviii, 22, 40–41, 45, 470–472, 497–502
November 1916, xiv, xxvii, 32–33, 36–37, 342, 346, 348, 371, 380, 397, 400, 402, 412, 427, 433, 438, 441, 448, 455, 473, 482, 510, 536–540, 574, 588
Oak and the Calf, The, xxvi, xxix, 24–28, 64, 154, 278, 288, 478, 557, 566–567, 576–577
"One Day in the Life of Ivan Denisovich," xiii, xv, xvii, xxiv–xxv, 5, 7, 14–15, 18, 20–21, 25–28, 30, 39, 49–52, 57, 59, 67, 69–105, 107, 111, 115, 121–122, 131, 181–182, 204, 219–220, 233, 267–268, 282, 287–288, 315–317, 434, 452, 493, 516, 534, 542, 552, 555, 557–558, 566–569, 577
"Our Pluralists," 3
Prisoners, xxiii, 23, 167, 170, 381, 435
"Rays, The," 48
"Rebuilding Russia," xxviii, 53, 65
Red Wheel, The, viii, xiv–xv, xviii–xix, xxii, xxvi, xxviii, xxx, 5, 11–15, 18–27, 30–36, 39–56, 58, 62–63, 75, 87, 90, 121, 151, 160, 164, 166, 181, 201, 210, 252, 257, 262–263, 276, 293, 323, 339–470, 473, 477, 479, 484, 496, 508, 520, 527, 536, 538, 541–542,

Index | 713

544–545, 548–565, 568–571, 575–576, 578, 581–584, 588
"Reflections on the February Revolution," 65
"Relentless Cult of Novelty, The," xxviii, 469
Republic of Labor, The, xxiv, 21, 587
"Right Hand, The," xxiv, 22, 34, 113–121, 131, 145, 177, 484, 528
Road, The, xxiii, 21, 23, 61, 72, 161–162, 164, 167, 170–172, 174, 203, 205, 248–249, 516
Russia in Collapse, xxix, 65, 469
"'The Russian Question' at the End of the Twentieth Century," xxviii, 24, 392
"Shch–854," 69, *see also* "One Day of Ivan Denisovich"
"Smatterers, The," 58
Tanks Know the Truth!, xxiv, 47
Templeton Lecture, xxvii, 340
"Times of Crisis," xxviii, 40, 42, 470–471, 477–484
Two Hundred Years Together, xiv, xxix, 469
Victory Celebrations, xxiii, xxviii, 21, 203, 221, 516, 540, 587
"Return to the Stars," 305
"What a Pity," xxv, 32, 113–114, 155–158, 296, 538, 549, 560, 577, 579
"Zakhar-the-Pouch," xxv, 22, 35, 39, 51, 112–115, 150–154, 413, 470,
"Zhelyabuga Village," xxix, 22, 41, 434, 470–471, 507–514, 516–517, 537, 550, 586
Solzhenitsyn, Ignat, viii, xxvi, 47, 55, 469
Solzhenitsyn, Isaaki, xxi, 22, 35, 359, 413, 417
Solzhenitsyn, Stephan, viii
Solzhenitsyn, Yermolai, xxvi

Solzhenitsyna (Svetlova), Natalia, vii–vii, xvi, xviii, xxvi, xxviii, 24, 44, 47, 67, 203, 348
Solzhenitsyna (Reshetovskaya), Natalya, *see* Reshetovskaya Natalya
Solzhenitsyna (Shcherbak), Taissia, xxi–xxii, *see also* Shcherbak, Taissia
Sontag, Susan, xiv, 259–260, 268, 293, 314, 528
Illness as Metaphor, 259
Sorokin, Vladimir, 106, 189, 391, 533, 552
Blue Lard, 189
Day of the Oprichnik, 391
"Month in Dachau, A," 106
Spencer, Herbert, 436
Spengler, Oswald, 420, 541
Spivakovsky, Pavel, ix, 452, 564
Staël, Germaine de, 238
Stalin, Joseph, xv, xxii–xxiii, 13–15, 26, 31, 33–35, 39–40, 43, 51, 57–58, 62–65, 69, 74, 77–78, 82, 83–84, 86, 91, 101, 104, 114, 116–117, 131, 139, 142, 144–146, 149, 155–156, 164–165, 172–174, 178, 181–183, 188–200, 211–213, 215, 222–223, 225, 228–234, 236–245, 248–249, 255–256, 260, 264, 266, 2680293, 278–280, 298, 304, 308, 317–321, 333, 354, 369, 388, 418, 445, 472, 478–483, 488, 492, 494–498, 502–504, 561–562, 578, 581
Marxism and Problems of Linguistics, 191
Stankevich, Vladimir, 458, 464
Steiner, George, 58, 537
Stolypin, Pyotr, 12, 15, 19, 27, 30, 276, 341, 347, 351, 354–355, 358–359, 366, 381, 383–384,

390–395, 409, 424, 436, 445, 453, 458, 467, 562
Strindberg, August, 409
Struve, Nikita, ix, 21, 189, 347, 349–350, 356, 400, 546, 588
Struve, Pyotr, 368, 377
Stürmer, Boris, 45, 368
Suvorov, Aleksandr, 398, 436, 520
Svechin, Aleksandr, 366, 369, 381, 406, 435–438, 442, 459
Sventsitsky, Valentin, 339, 421–422
   Antichrist (Notes of a Strange Man), The, 339
   Dialogues on Faith and Unbelief, 421
Swift, Jonathan, 559

Tale of the Battle against Mamai, The, 151
Tamerlane, Sultan, 323
Tchaikovsky, Pyotr, 47, 263, 294, 335
   Sleeping Beauty, 47, 263, 305, 311, 335
Thomas, Donald Michael, 23, 362, 364
Timenchik, Roman, 408
Todorov, Tzvetan, xiv–xvi, 111, 557
Toker, Leona, 9, 25, 76, 104
Tokmakov, Pyotr, 473
Tolkien, John Ronald Reuel, 374
   Lord of The Rings, The, 374
Tolstaya, Tatyana, 552
Tolstoy, Aleksei, 249, 400, 494, 496–497, 561
   Peter the First, 494
   Road to Calvary, The, 400
Tolstoy, Leo, xiv–xv, 5, 9–15, 22, 36–39, 51, 54, 58–59, 68–70, 80, 86, 93, 107, 110, 113, 126, 136, 146, 169, 175, 179, 193–194, 218–219, 223, 235, 237, 243–244, 246, 251, 260, 265, 272, 276, 291–294, 298, 307–308, 317, 322, 350–354, 364–366, 381–382, 400–402, 404, 408, 410, 412, 414–418, 421–422, 424, 430–432, 436, 438–439, 453, 465, 501, 522, 533–535, 542, 546, 549, 551, 557–559, 561–562, 568, 575–576
   "Albert," 146
   Anna Karenina, 14, 136, 185, 194, 223, 244–245, 251, 274, 276, 291, 307–308, 346, 359, 400–401, 414, 426, 536, 546, 558, 568–569, 582, 587
   Childhood, 110
   Cossacks, The, 322, 412
   Death of Ivan Ilyich, The, 14, 272, 276, 413
   "Destruction of Hell and the Restoration Thereof, The," 86
   "Devil, The" 68
   Hadji Murad, 68
   Kreutzer Sonata, The, 36–37, 446, 562
   Living Corps, The, 68
   Power of Darkness, The, 136
   War and Peace, 10, 13, 15, 22, 36–37, 48, 84, 119, 141, 169, 175, 193–194, 218–219, 223, 235, 237, 241, 246–247, 250, 263, 274, 294, 308, 348, 350–352, 355, 373, 382, 398, 400–401, 410, 414, 427, 429–433, 436, 438, 446, 460, 462, 480, 494, 496, 508, 536, 544, 546, 550, 558
   "What Men Live By," 39, 276, 317, 542
   "Woodfelling, The," 194
Trotsky, Leon, 242, 345, 354–355, 369, 494, 561–562, 581–582
Tsiolkovsky, Konstantin, 380, 420
Tsvetaeva, Marina, 406–407, 464, 490, 542, 544, 546, 572
Tukhachevsky, Mikhail, 116, 120, 479–481
Turgenev, Ivan, 36–37, 43, 93, 102, 106–107, 112, 123, 148, 158, 206, 219, 235, 285, 409, 489, 535

Fathers and Sons, 102, 148, 285
Home of the Gentry, 36–37, 235
Literary and Autobiographical Reminiscences, 158
"The Execution of Tropmann," 158
"Mumu," 409
Rudin, 206
Sketches from a Hunter's Album, 219
Tvardovsky, Aleksandr, 51, 80, 86, 88, 91–92, 94, 97, 108, 112, 115, 121–122, 137–138, 183, 214, 261–262, 566–567
Tyorkin in the Other World, 86, 88
Vasily Tyorkin, 80
Tynianov, Yuri, 45, 387, 552
Tyutchev, Fyodor, 397
"These poor villages …," 397

Ulyanov, Nikolai, 58–59
Ulyanov-Lenin, Vladimir, 449, 536, *see also* Lenin
Urmanov, Aleksandr, ix, 565
Ustinov, Dmitry, 502

Valéry, Paul, 3
Mauvaise pensées et autres, 3
Valuev, Fyodor, 368
Vasilyev, Vladimir, 155, 579
Vasilevsky, Aleksandr, 483
Vavilov, Nikolai, 188
Vertinsky, Aleksandr, 406–407
Vidal, Gore, 39, 129, 530–531, 538–540, 572
Vinaver, Maksim, 368
Vishnevskaya, Galina, 28–30
Vishnevsky, Vsevolod, 197
Vision of Tundale, The, 87
Vitkevich, Nikolai, xxiii, 23
Vlasov, Andrei, 59, 435, 482
Voeykov, Vladimir, 462
Voinovich, Vladimir, 531, 568

Portrait Against the Backdrop of Myth, A, 531
Volkov, Solomon, 47
Voltaire, François-Marie, 58, 535
Vrubel, Mikhail, 399, 544
Pan, 399
Vysotsky, Vladimir, 69, 560
"Gypsy Song," 69

Wagner, Richard, 47, 59, 340, 532, 578, 582
Ring des Nibelungen, Der, 47, 340, 578, 582
Walesa, Lech, 354
Walpole, Robert, 455
Waugh, Evelyn
Brideshead Revisited, 428
Webern, Anton, 186
Wells, Herbert George, 235, 380
Time Machine, 380
Wonderful Visit, The, 235
Wilde, Oscar, 233, 406
Ideal Husband, The, 160
Picture of Dorian Grey, The, 452
Wilhelm II, German Emperor, 377, 388, 394, 459
Willetts, Harry, xiv, 183, 346
Williams, William Carlos, 290
Woolf, Virginia, xiv, 112, 570
To the Lighthouse, 112

Yefremov, Ivan, 368
Yeltsin, Boris, xxviii–xix, 52–53, 60, 64–65, 93, 215, 374, 469, 472, 499, 502–503
Yermilov, Vladimir, 196
Yesenin, Sergei, 186, 205, 218, 253, 548
"The golden birch-tree grove has fallen silent …," 186
Yevtushenko, Yevgeny, 214, 279

Zakharova, Anna, 98–99, 105, 566
Zamyatin, Yevgeny, 24, 74, 88, 197, 215,
　　257, 281, 296–297, 536, 544, 546,
　　549, 551, 556, 572
　"Cave, The," 74, 88, 544
　"Dragon, The," 88
　We, 215, 244, 257, 281, 296–297, 536,
　　546, 551

Zhdanov, Andrei, 229
Zheleznyak, Grigory, 98
Zhilinsky, Yakov, 437
Zholkovsky, Alexander, 446, 451
Zhukov, Georgy, 42, 470–471,
　　477–484
Zizek, Slavoj, 223

www.ingramcontent.com/pod-product-compliance
Lightning Source LLC
Chambersburg PA
CBHW071351300426
44114CB00016B/2026